A BIOGRAPHICAL
DICTIONARY
OF IRISH WRITERS

TO ANTONY FARRELL
WHO MADE THIS EDITION POSSIBLE,
WITH DEEP APPRECIATION

A BIOGRAPHICAL DICTIONARY OF IRISH WRITERS

Anne M. Brady
and
Brian Cleeve

ST. MARTIN'S PRESS
New York

ISBN 0-312-07871-4

Library of Congress Cataloging in Publication Data
Main entry under title:

A Biographical Dictionary of Irish writers   .

   Rev. Ed. of: Dictionary of Irish Writers / Brian Cleeve. 1967-1971.
   Includes bibliographical references.
   Contents: Writers in English – Writers in Irish and Latin.
   1. Authors, Irish – Biography – Dictionaries.
   2. Ireland – Biography – Dictionaries.
   3. English literature – Irish authors – Bio-bibliography.
   4. Irish literature – Bio-bibliography.
   5. Latin literature, Medieval and modern – Ireland – Bio-bibliography.
   I. Brady, Anne   II. Cleeve, Brian Talbot, 1921–

   III. Cleeve, Brian Talbot, 1921–   . Dictionary of Irish writers.
PR8727.B5 1985   820'.9'9415 [B]   85-40074
ISBN 0-312-07871-4

CONTENTS

PREFACE

This new edition of the *Dictionary of Irish Writers*, renamed *A Biographical Dictionary of Irish Writers*, has been completely revised and considerably enlarged. Particular attention has been paid to present-day writers in both Irish and English, and here the editors have faced difficulties. Contemporaries are notoriously bad judges of literary merit, and it may well be that we have left out some young writers whose genius will be clear to all in a few years' time, and that we have included some others whose present reputations will by then have faded into deserved obscurity. For this we can only apologise in advance.

Another difficulty has been with writers of academic books. All professors and most university lecturers have published at least one book on their specialist subject, and often many. How should one decide which of these scholarly authors are of sufficient general interest to be included here? No rule of thumb could be satisfactory, and the editors do not pretend to have solved the problem to anyone's satisfaction but their own. In general, if a book of this kind has made some stir outside specialist circles, we have included its author, while if the author's reputation is purely academic, confined to his colleagues and students, we have left him out. But again we will inevitably have made mistakes, and again we can only apologise, and hope that a future edition will allow us to make amends.

There is a third apology we must make. This is not a Bibliographical Dictionary. It is not intended to be, and it is for that reason that the word *Biographical* has been added to the title. Excellent bibliographies exist, some of them noted in this Dictionary. Our intention has been to offer as much biographical and critical material as possible in the given space, about as many Irish writers as possible, from the time of St Patrick to the present day, and while we list an author's principal, and usually his secondary works as well, our purpose is to give the general reader and the non-specialist student an idea of the author's substance and interest, rather than a minutely detailed list of all his works with their various editions and publishers. The specialist can find such information elsewhere. The ideal might be to fulfil both requirements, bibliographical and biographical, but space and cost forbid. We have therefore in most cases given only the place and date of a book's first edition, and of a play's first performance or publication. Where we have broken this self-imposed rule it was because there seemed to us some reason for doing so.

Finally a word must be said about the spelling of Irish names and book titles in Part 2. Over the past three generations there has been a number of spelling reforms in the Irish language. This means that a modern author may have spelled his name in different ways during the course of his career, and the title of a book may change between one edition and another. For the most part these changes are so slight that the non-specialist might not notice them, but in a few cases they will even alter the alphabetical position a writer occupies and make two editions of the same book appear to be different works. Even the names of Irish language organisations such as Conradh na Gaeilge have altered slightly, and for events and publications prior to 1960 you will find *Conradh* spelled as *Connradh*. So far as is possible we have given the spellings in vogue at the time of a book's first publication, but this rule again has had to be broken at times for the sake of clarity or consistency within the one entry. Once more, if we have made mistakes to offend the purist, we apologise, and take shelter behind the authority of Sean Mac Mathuna of Conradh na Gaeilge who has given us more than patient help with such problems and saved us from many worse errors.

In an introductory essay to the Irish language and Latin section of the first edition of the *Dictionary of Irish Writers,* I suggested that the outlook for Irish as a living language was bleak. In the 15 years since then the vitality and quantity of Irish publishing may seem to have contradicted so pessimistic a view. New poets, new novelists and story-tellers and dramatists have appeared each season. Works of value have been reprinted in answer to a healthy and insistent demand.

Is it possible that membership of the European Common Market, friendly in many tangible ways to regional as opposed to national aspirations, has also favoured minority languages, among them Irish? One may hope so, and yet wonder how deep and lasting the effects may be. Every year since that essay was written the Gaeltachtaí, the areas where Irish is claimed as the natural, everyday language of the people, have shrunk in dimensions, and numbers of native speakers, while the claims on census forms that such and such a percentage of citizens speak Irish 'often' or 'well' are actually meaningless. The reality of such pipe dreams can be tested in any busy shopping centre or bus queue, where a word or two of Irish would cause heads to turn in surprise or bewilderment.

The facts of the revival are that the government, every government of the past 15 years, has abandoned the ambition of turning the Republic of Ireland into a bilingual State. The methods of compulsion previously used were ill-considered and counter-productive. The attitude of authority was more often than not hypocritical. And the results were too often a lively hatred of a language that represented for school children not the best and dearest of Irish secular traditions, but a source of misery and physical punishments.

Nevertheless, there was then a commitment to the language, no matter how ill-conceived. What has replaced it is not a better-conceived, wiser commitment, but no commitment at all; rather, a sly indifference and even hostility, masked by pious expressions of interest and laments about lack of funds. Irish speakers have gone to prison because authority refused to address them in Irish over some bureaucratic necessity – a licence for a television set, for example. Under the British administration, such acts of petty narrowmindedness were rightly regarded as an outrage. In the North of Ireland they still are. In the South they signal the government's true attitude to the language.

In the face of such an attitude, and general public indifference, is the dedication of a small minority of readers, writers and publishers enough? Common sense says 'no'. But occasionally common sense is wrong, and belied by irrational optimism. May it be so with the revival of Irish as a loved and spoken language. Evidence as to why it deserves to be loved and spoken, and widely read, exists in abundance in the following pages. In the necessarily close set and often far too brief entries lies the story of 1500 years of Irish literature, from the time of St Patrick to the young poets and story-tellers of today. It is a wonderful story, and the chance to make it better known even to a handful of new readers is enough justification for publishing it, and enough reward for writing it.

It only remains for us to thank all the other kindly people who have helped us in one way or another. It would be impossible to list everyone who has given us a name or a fact or a date that we could not find for ourselves, and perhaps it is unjust to mention some when we cannot mention all. But it would be even more unjust not to express our gratitude to the following. Again, and first of all, to Sean Mac Mathuna, who went out of his way to do far more for us than we could have dared to ask. Dr Andrew Carpenter, the authority on Swift's contemporaries, and his colleague, Dr Seamus Deane, both of UCD, helped us with a number of entries. Proinsias Ó Conluain sent us some valuable suggestions and corrections for the improvement of the first edition, all of which we have gratefully accepted. The library staffs of Trinity College and University College Dublin, of the National Library and the Royal Dublin Society, of the *Irish Times,* the *Irish Press* and the *Irish Independent,* have all given us their time and patience, as have the staff of the Arts Council. Dr Alan Eager of the RDS Library, Miss Margaret O'Rahilly of the Arts Council staff, and Mrs M. Woods of the Abbey Theatre Publicity Department have been particularly kind to us. Niall Ó Muilleóir, Diarmuid Ó Cathasaigh and Donncha Ó Súilleabháin went out of their way to clarify certain obscurities, as did Jeremy Addis of *Books Ireland.*

The following names to whom we owe much are at least some of those who contributed their time and knowledge to the first edition: Miss Anna Boylan and her father Henry; Cyril Ó Ceirin; Ronald Wilson of Hertfordshire; Miss Monica Dowling and Mrs Isobel Buckler; and of course the publishers of that edition, Mercier Press of Cork, and their Managing Director, Captain Sean Feehan, who suggested that the Dictionary should be written. Finally, when perhaps their names should have headed the list, we must thank the present publishers, Antony Farrell and his Lilliput Press, together with his American associates, St Martin's Press of New York. In

PREFACE

particular, Antony Farrell not only gave great encouragement but also contributed much information and a number of entries.

ANNE M. BRADY
BRIAN CLEEVE
August 1985

The publisher would like to thank Vincent Hurley, Jim Reynolds and Robert Towers for their interest and advice on entries, and to invite from readers suggestions and corrections for future editions of this work.

An Addendum is given at the end of Part 1 (p. 254).

NOTES ON METHOD USED FOR ENTRIES

Where the title of a book or play is followed immediately by a date, this means the first edition appeared in London that year. Where the name of a town or country occurs before the date, the first edition appeared in that place. Where two towns are listed without comment, the book appeared simultaneously in both. Where the date refers to the first performance of a play, the name of the theatre precedes the date, or the fact is stated.

If a writer has been known by a pseudonym and his own name, both appear in the appropriate places, but if a pseudonym has become by common practice the one normally used for all public purposes, the entry will appear under that one, with the writer's legal name after it.

For the purpose of alphabetical listing M', Mac and Mc are all treated as MAC. Thus M'Carthy follows MacCann, and is followed by M'Clure.

In Part 2 the spelling of the prefix as well as of the patronymic is taken into consideration. This presents no problem with the vast majority of prefixed names beginning MAC or O, but the reader should bear in mind that very occasionally these prefixes vary to MAG, and to UA or UI, which will considerably alter the placing of the name that follows. DE is also treated as a prefix. The earliest writers are entered under their Christian names; for example, ADAMNÁN, COLMÁN, TORNA EIGEAS, because these are the names by which they are generally known. Broadly speaking, patronymics are used for writers later than the 11th century. Thus the 12th century AED MAC CRIMTHAINN appears as MAC CRIMTHAINN, Aed.

Usually the writer's name appears in its Irish spelling. If the writer has been well known under the English form of his name as well, both spellings are entered in the appropriate places, with cross-references, the entry proper appearing under the form of his name by which he is best known. Thus the entries for such writers as Douglas Hyde and Patrick Pearse appear under the English versions of their names. Where a pseudonym is well known or even better known than the real name of the writer, this too is entered in its appropriate place with cross references. In other cases any pseudonym is given in parenthesis after the writer's real name. In all cases we have followed the spellings used in the Natonal Library Catalogues.

As far as possible abbreviations have been avoided in the entries. Even the few that follow have been used as sparingly as possible.

ABBREVIATIONS

b.	born
BA	Bachelor of Arts
BL	Bachelor of Law
Bar	called to Irish Bar
BBC	British Broadcasting Corporation
Bt	baronet
c.	*circa*
CBS	Christian Brothers School
d.	died
DD	Doctor of Divinity
Dept	Department
D.Lit.	Doctor of Literature
D.Litt.	Doctor of Letters
ed.	educated, editor, edited by, edition, accord. to context
facs.	facsimile
fl.	*floruit*
Fr	Father
FRS	Fellow of Royal Society
FRSL	Fellow of Royal Society of Literature
govt	government
Hon.	Honorary
Inst. for Adv. Studies	Institute for Advanced Studies
ITS	Irish Texts Society
Kt	knight
LL.D.	Doctor of Laws
MD	Doctor of Medicine
MIAL	Member of Irish Academy of Letters
MRIA	Member of Royal Irish Academy
MS	manuscript
MSS	manuscripts
NGI	National Gallery of Ireland
NMI	National Museum of Ireland
NUI	National University of Ireland
NUU	New University of Ulster
NY	New York
ODC	Order of Discalced Carmelites
OFM	Order of Friars Minor
OSA	Order of St Augustine
Ph.D.	Doctor of Philosophy
pseud.	pseudonym
pub.	published
QC	Queen's Counsel
QUB	Queen's University, Belfast
RAMC	Royal Army Medical Corps
RCSI	Royal College of Surgeons of Ireland
RDS	Royal Dublin Society
RE	Radio Éireann
rep.	reprinted
repub.	republished
rev.	revised
RHA	Royal Hibernian Academy
RIA	Royal Irish Academy
RIAM	Royal Irish Academy of Music
RTE	Radio Telefís Éireann
TCD	Trinity College, Dublin
trans.	translated into, translated by, translation, accord. to context
UCC	University College, Cork
UCD	University College, Dublin
UCG	University College, Galway
US	United States of America
V.H.	Vincent Hurley
vol.	volume
vols	volumes

Part 1

WRITERS IN ENGLISH

A

ABBOTT, Thomas Kingsmill, the Reverend, b. Dublin 1829, d. Dublin 1913. Ed. TCD; Fellow 1854. Professor of Greek 1875; Hebrew 1879. Also Librarian. Wrote *Elements of Logic,* Dublin 1885, and *Essays on Original Texts of Old and New Testaments,* 1891, both of which remained standard works for many years.

ADAMS, Michael William Atheridge, b. Dublin 1937. Ed. Enniskillen, QUB. Publisher: Sceptre Books 1963-68; managing director Irish Academic Press 1974–; Four Courts Press. *Censorship: The Irish Experience,* Dublin and Alabama 1968; *The Hard Life,* Dublin 1977, Illinois 1978; *Single-minded,* Dublin 1979. Translates various books of theological import.

ADRAIN, Robert, b. Carrickfergus 1775, d. New Brunswick, USA 1843. One of the few mathematicians to have led a body of revolutionary troops, which he did in the Rising of 1798. Escaping to America he became a school-teacher and finally Vice-Provost of University of Pennsylvania. Wrote on the *Exponential Law of Error,* published mathematical journals, *The Analyst,* Phil.1808 seq., and *The Mathematical Diary,* NY 1825-27. Pub. important calculations on the measurements of the earth in papers for *The Transactions of the American Philosophical Society,* vol.1, 1818.

AE see RUSSELL, George

ALEXANDER, Cecilia Frances, née Humphries, b. Wicklow 1818, d. Derry 1895. Married William Alexander. Popular and prolific writer of hymns, including 'There Is a Green Hill Far Away'. Published several volumes of sacred poetry.

ALEXANDER, William, b. Derry 1824, d. Torquay 1911. Bishop of Derry 1867, Archbishop of Armagh 1893. Husband of Cecilia. Last Irish bishop to sit in House of Lords. Theologian and poet. Books include *Logics of Life and Light,* 1878. *Primary Convictions,* NY 1893, contained his lectures on 'Evidences of Christianity'.

ALLEN, Alfred, b. Co. Cork, 1925. Poet and farmer. Lives and farms at Ovens. Poetry: *Clashenure Skyline,* Dublin 1970; *Interrogations,* Cork 1975; *Shades of a Rural Past* (collected poems), Cork 1978.

ALLEN, F. M., pseud. of Edmund Downey, b. Waterford 1856, d. Waterford 1937. Son of a ship-owner. Went into business in London 1878 and became well known as writer of sea stories. Also wrote on Irish life, for example, *Through Green Glasses.*

ALLINGHAM, William, b. Ballyshannon 1824, d. Hampstead 1889. Customs officer, editor of *Fraser's Magazine,* 1874-79. Close friend of Carlyle and the Pre-Raphaelite group in London. Published several volumes of poetry and one play, *Ashley Manor*. *Laurence Bloomfield*, 1864, was his most ambitious work and in the year it appeared he was granted a Civil List pension. Other volumes include *Day and Night Songs* illustrated by D. G. Rossetti and Millais, 1854, 2nd series 1855, and *Flower Pieces and Other Poems* illustrated by Rossetti, 1888. Also wrote *A Diary*, 1907, repub. 1967 and 1985.

AMBROSE, Joseph Gerard, b. Fethard, Co. Tipperary 1957. Ed. De La Salle Bros Waterford, UCD. Reviewer and critic. A biography, *The Dan Breen Story*, Cork 1981; a forthcoming work on Garrett Fitzgerald.

AMORY, Thomas, b. Bunratty 1691, although both place and date have been questioned, d. London 1788. Famous as the author of two extraordinary biographical works; *Memoirs containing the Lives of Several Ladies of Great Britain...etc.*, 1755, and *The Life of John Buncle, Esq.*, in 2 vols, 1756 and 1766. Both are extravaganzas, part fiction, part biography, part autobiography, part religious speculation and part near-pornography. A friend of Swift, his earlier works may have influenced Sterne.

ANDERSON, Paris, b. Kilkenny (?) *c.* 1790, d. Dublin *c.* 1860. Served in Kilkenny Militia 1815. Novelist and essayist. *Nooks and Corners of the Co. Kilkenny* appeared in the *Kilkenny Moderator*, 1848, repub. Kilkenny 1914. One novel *The Warden of the Marches*, Kilkenny 1884.

ANSTER, John Martin, b. Charleville 1793, d. Dublin 1867. Ed. TCD. Bar 1824, LL.D. 1825, Civil List pension 1841. Contributor to *Dublin University Magazine*. Made first English translation of Goethe's *Faust*, part I 1835, part II 1864. Several volumes of poetry.

ARBUCKLE, James, b. Down 1700, d. Dublin 1734. Ed. Glasgow. Schoolmaster in north of Ireland. Editor *Dublin Weekly Journal*. Essay on Swift, *Momus Mistaken*, pub. Dublin 1735. Published some mock-heroic poems in Glasgow, *Snuff* and *Glotta*, in 1717 and 1721.

ARCHDEACON, Matthew, b. Castlebar *c.* 1800, d. 1863. Schoolmaster locally. Wrote four novels about the Rising of 1798: *Legends of Connaught*, Dublin 1829; *Connaught, a Tale of 1798*, Dublin 1830; *Everard, an Irish Tale*; and *Shawn the Soggarth, the Priest Hunter*.

ARMSTRONG, Edmund John, b. Dublin 1841. Ed. TCD. Great promise as poet, but d. Kingstown, 1865. His work was collected and published after his death by his brother (see following) as *Poems by the late Edmund J. Armstrong*, 1865, rep. and revised, with *Essays and Sketches by E. J. Armstrong*, 1877.

ARMSTRONG, George Francis Savage, b. Co. Dublin 1846, d. Co Down 1906. Ed. TCD, Professor of History and Literature in Queen's College Cork. Biographer of his brother Edmund. Wrote much verse, and *Stories of Wicklow*, 1886. His satire *Mephistopheles in Broadcloth*, 1888, was admired.

ARCHDALL, Mervyn, b. Dublin 1723, d. Slane 1791. Ed. TCD. Antiquary and rector of Slane. Wrote *Monasticum Hibernicum,* 1786, after long gestation. Edited Lodge's *Peerage of Ireland,* 7 vols, 1789.

ARSDEKIN, Richard (known also as Archdekin and Mac Giolla Cuddy), b. Kilkenny 1618, d. Antwerp 1693. Ed. Louvain. Jesuit 1642. His most famous works are *A treatise of Miracles, together with New Miracles, and Benefits obtained by the sacred reliques of S. Francis Xaverius exposed in the Church of the Society of Jesus at Mechlin,* Louvain 1667, in English and Latin, supposed to be the first book printed in both languages in conjunction; and a *Life of St Patrick,* Louvain 1671, in Latin. These and other works had a wide circulation and influence. Spent many years as Professor of Philosophy and Moral Theology in Louvain and Antwerp.

ASHE, Thomas, b. Glasnevin 1770, d. Bath 1835. Served briefly in the British Army and then began travels in Europe and America. In France fought a duel with the outraged brother of a girl he had seduced, wounded his opponent and was imprisoned. Returned to Dublin after his release and was made Secretary of the Diocesan and Endowed Schools Commission. Getting into debt he resigned and went to Switzerland and later to America, his pattern of life continuing much as it had begun, 'free and unconstrained' in his own words. His travel books and memoirs include *Travels in America in 1806,* 1808; *Memoirs and Confessions,* 1815. Novels include *The Spirit of the Book,* 1811; *The Liberal Critic,* 1812; *The Soldier of Fortune,* 1816.

ASHTON, Robert, b. *c.* 1720. Author of immensely popular verse-tragedy *The Battle of Aughrim,* Dublin 1756. At least eight editions were produced in Ireland during next hundred years, and innumerable pirate and chapbook versions. Written from the Orange viewpoint, the poem's popularity with the Catholic peasantry astonished Thackeray among others. The reason is its portrayal of Sarsfield and his lieutenants as epic figures. Ashton's intention was to make the Orange victory the greater. The result, as in *Paradise Lost,* was for the villains to steal the story.

ATKINSON, Sarah, b. Athlone 1823, d. Dublin 1893. Her husband was part proprietor of the *Freeman's Journal.* Wrote *Life of Mary Aikenhead,* 1879. *Essays* published posthumously in 1895, repub. 1907.

B

BAGWELL, Richard, b. Clonmel 1840, d. Clonmel 1918. Ed. Harrow and Christ Church, Oxford, Bar. Remembered for two major historical works, *Ireland Under the Tudors,* 3 vols, 1885-90, and *Ireland Under the Stuarts,* 3 vols, 1909.

BANIM, John, b. Kilkenny 1798, d. 1842. Son of small Catholic shop-keeper. Family sacrifices allowed him attend Protestant St John's College, Kilkenny, where Congreve and Swift among other Irish writers had also been pupils. In 1813 went to Dublin to study art. In 1820 sent an unfinished poem to Sir Walter Scott, who praised it. Published in Dublin, 1821, as 'The Celt's Paradise'. In 1822 his verse-tragedy *Damon and Pythias* was put on with Macready and Kemble in the leads, and made money. He married and moved to London. Deeply influenced by Scott he set out to interpret Ireland to England and bridge the gulf between the countries in a series of *Tales* and historical novels, with his brother Michael for helper. Interrupted by much hack journalism the first result of the plan was *The Tales of the O'Hara Family,* 1825. A second series of *Tales* appeared 1826 as did his first historical novel, *The Boyne Water.* These three titles contain Banim's best work, including the stories *Crohoore of the Billhook* and *The Nowlans.* *The Boyne Water* has been compared to the best of Scott, although it is hamstrung by a wish to be fair to all sides, and to teach rather than to grip. This urge to teach ruined much of Banim's work and none of the remainder reaches the level of these stories. *The Croppy,* 1828, *The Last Baron of Crana,* and the *Conformists,* both pub. 1830, cover the period from the Treaty of Limerick to the Rising of 1798. Michael's share in all this has been much overrated. After publishing *The Smuggler,* 1831, John's health broke and he retired to Kilkenny on a small Civil List pension. In his last work *Father Connell* he attempted a different and much softer type of book.

BANIM, Michael, b. Kilkenny 1796, d. Booterstown 1874. Brother of John, ed. locally, and read for Bar, but family difficulties prevented his being called. Helped his brother with *Tales of the O'Hara Family,* and throughout his life with encouragement. Became postmaster Kilkenny, 1852. Own novels: *Clough Fionn,* 1852; *The Town of the Cascades,* 1864.

BANVILLE, John, b. Wexford 1945, ed. CBS Wexford. Sub-editor on *Irish Press* until 1984. Short stories: *Long Lankin,* 1970, revised ed. 1984. Novels: *Nightspawn,* 1971; *Birchwood,* 1973; *Doctor Copernicus,* 1976; *Kepler,* 1980, all repub. NY; and *The Newton Letter,* 1982 (adapted as film, *Reflections,* 1984). Winner of numerous literary awards and prizes. Acclaimed as one of major Irish novelists to appear in '70s.

BARBER, Mary, b. 1690, d. 1757. Married a tailor in Dublin. Swift admired her poetry and gave her introductions in England which enabled her to publish by subscription *Poems on Several Occasions,* 1734. This was well received but brought her little money, and in 1738 she again appealed to Swift who allowed her to publish his *Polite Conversations* that year. She did very well out of this and appears to have lived comfortably to the end of her life.

BARDWELL, Leland, née Hone, b. India 1928 of Irish parents. Raised

Co. Kildare. Ed. Dublin and London. Teacher in Scotland, among many jobs. Married 1948. Poems: *The Mad Cyclist*, Dublin 1970. Plays: *Thursday*, 1975. *The Edith Piaf Story* (musical), 1983, both produced Dublin. Novels: *Girl on a Bicycle*, 1977; *That London Winter*, 1981, pub. Dublin; and *The House*, Dingle 1984. Joint-ed. *Cyphers*, a Dublin literary magazine.

BARLOW, Jane, b. Clontarf 1857, d. Co. Wicklow 1917. Daughter of the Rev. James B., later Vice-Provost TCD. Extremely popular writer of poems and sketches of Irish life, including *Bogland Studies* (poetry), 1892; *A Creel of Irish Stories; Irish Idylls*, which went into at least eight editions; *Irish Neighbours; Strangers at Lisconnel*, and a novel, *Flaws*.

BARRETT, Eaton Stannard, b. Cork 1786, d. Glamorgan 1820. Ed. London, TCD and Middle Temple. Under pseud. 'Polypus' wrote and published a satirical poem on British political figures, *All the Talents*. It sold twenty editions in the same year, 1807. He wrote a number of other political satires, poetry and a comedy, *My Wife, What Wife?*, 1815.

BARRINGTON, Jonah, Kt, b. Abbeyleix 1760, d. Versailles 1834. Ed. TCD. Bar 1788. MP for Tuam, Clogher and Banagher in the Irish Parliament, where he voted against the Act of Union. He had been made an Admiralty Court Judge in 1798 and could have had the Solicitor-Generalship if he had agreed to vote for the Union. He gives himself and perhaps deserves great credit for this renunciation, but his political manoeuvres of the period 1801-2 were far from simple. Between 1805 and 1810 his debts led him to misappropriate court funds and he was finally brought to account for this in 1830. Deprived of office, he left Ireland and Britain for France, where he died. His works include *Historic Anecdotes and Secret Memoirs of the Legislative Union between Great Britain and Ireland*, 1809; *Personal Sketches of his own time*, 3 vols, 1827-32, the book by which he is now chiefly remembered; and *The Rise and Fall of the Irish Nation*, Paris 1833, a reworking of earlier memoirs. All of these books are valuable documents for the social and political life of 18th-century Ireland. Barrington has been much frowned on by puritan critics but he was simply a politician of his time whose chief fault was to be found out. It is absurd to condemn him for not sharing the high standards of modern Irish political life.

BARRINGTON, Margaret, b. Malin, Co. Donegal 1896, d. 1982. Ed. Dungannon, TCD. Married Edmund Curtis 1922, then Liam O'Flaherty 1926: separated 1932. Wrote many highly acclaimed short stories and in 1939 published a fine novel, *My Cousin Justin*. A selection of her short stories was published in 1982, *David's Daughter, Tamar*. During the 1930s she spent several years working and writing in England, where she was active in helping refugees from Nazi Germany.

BARRY, Lo (sometimes Lod, or Lodwick), b. Co. Cork 1591, supposedly 2nd son of Lord Barry, and probably christened James. Date of death unknown. 'Lo' on the title page of his book would then mean 'Lording' or 'the Honourable'. Reputed the first Irish dramatist for his comedy *Ram Alley, or Merry Tricks*, produced in London, 1610. He was at Oxford shortly before this.

BARRY, Michael Joseph, b. Cork 1817, d. 1889. Bar. Enthusiastic Young Irelander until 1848. Imprisoned for his share in the events of that year, but in comparative luxury. Afterwards changed his politics and ended his life as a police magistrate in Dublin. As well as being a poet and barrister he was a celebrated wit, contributing to *Punch* in its early days. He was undoubtedly the author of the famous couplet on the Scinde campaign of 1845, '*Peccavi! I've Scinde* cried Lord Ellen so proud. Dalhousie more modest said *Vovi I've Oudhe*'. Barry wrote several volumes of poetry including *A Waterloo Commemoration*, 1854, and *Heinrich and Leonore, an Alpine Story;* contributed many leaders to the London *Times*, and edited *The Songs of Ireland*, 1845.

BARRY, Sebastian, b. Dublin 1955. Son of actress Joan O'Hara; nephew of singer Mary O'Hara. Novel: *Macker's Garden*, 1982. Novellas: *Time Out of Mind* and *Strappado Square*, 1983. Poems: *The Water-Colourist*, 1983; *The Rhetorical Town*, 1985. Children's book: *Elsewhere*, 1984. All pub. Dublin.

BARRY, P., b. Cork *c*. 1825, d. London 1907. Wrote on sociology and economics. *Wealth and Poverty Considered*, 1869, and *The Workman's Wrongs and the Workman's Rights*, 1870, are his best-known books.

BARRY, Tom, b. Co. Cork 1898, d. 1980. Joined British Army 1915 and served in Mesopotamian campaign, 1916-17. Returned to Ireland after war and in 1919 joined W. Cork Brigade of Republican Army as military instructor. Became its commander and turned it into the most successful military formation on either side. At the battle of Crossbarry dispersed and defeated 5000 British troops with 104 men. At the outbreak of the Civil War was interned by Free State authorities. Escaped and fought on Republican side. Wrote an account of the War of Independence, *Guerilla Days in Ireland*, Dublin 1949.

BAX, Arnold Edward Trevor, Kt, b. London 1883, d. 1953. Inspired by Yeats's poetry, came to Ireland in 1902 and began writing stories and poetry under the pseud. 'Dermot O'Byrne'. Friend of Padraic Pearse and many other 1916 leaders: wrote the famous 'A Dublin Ballad – 1916' which was banned by the British military authorities as seditious and dangerous. Has been adopted as an 'honorary Irishman', and so considered himself. His main fame of course is as a composer, and Master of the King's Musick.

BEAUFORT, Francis, Kt, b. Navan 1774, d. London 1857. Creator of 'Beaufort Scale' of wind velocities. Son of the Rev. Daniel Augustus B., rector of Navan, who himself published a map and memoir of Ireland in 1792, he grew up in an atmosphere of geographical interest. He entered the navy in 1787 and served throughout the Napoleonic wars. Wounded off Malaga in 1803 he used his convalescence to establish a telegraph line from Dublin to Galway, working with his brother-in-law Richard Lovell Edgeworth, father of Maria. Wounded again off Turkey in 1812 he became interested in the Turkish coast and in 1817 published *Karamania, or A Brief Description of the South Coast of Asia Minor and the Remains of Antiquity.* Made Hydrographer to the Navy 1829. His scale of wind forces and alphabetical notation system for weather conditions both remain in general use among meteorologists. His son Francis Lestock (1815-79) wrote the *Digest of the Criminal Law Procedure in Bengal,* 1850.

BECKETT, James Camlin, b. 1912. Ed. Royal Belfast Academical Institution and QUB. Professor of Modern History QUB 1958-75. *A Short History of Ireland,* 1952, 3rd ed. 1966; *The Making of Modern Ireland, 1603-1923,* 1966; *Confrontations: Studies in Irish History,* 1972; *The Anglo-Irish Tradition,* 1976, paperback ed. Belfast 1982. Also ed. *Belfast, the Making of the City,* Belfast 1982.

BECKETT, Samuel, b. Dublin 1906. Ed. TCD. Lecturer in English, École Normale Superieure, Paris, 1928-30; lecturer in French, TCD, 1930-32. Returned to Paris 1932, friend and occasional secretary to Joyce. Has written mostly in French. His novels, beginning with *Murphy,* 1938, *Watt,* 1944 and *Molloy,* 1951, created his reputation among a small but devoted band of readers. *Malone Meurt,* 1952; *L'Innominable,* 1953, confirmed and enlarged this, but his popular reputation depends on his plays, beginning with *Waiting for Godot,* 1952, and continuing with a series of bleakly horrifying comedies: *Endgame, All That Fall* (for radio), *Krapp's Last Tape, Happy Days,* etc. Numerous shorter works ('dramaticules') are gathered in *Collected Shorter Plays,* 1984. Poetry includes *Whoroscope,* 1930; *Echo's Bones,* 1935; *Collected Poems in English and French,* Paris 1977; *Collected Poems 1930-78,* 1984, and he has published two volumes of short stories, *More Pricks than Kicks,* 1934, and *Nouvelles et Textes Pour Rien,* 1955. A further two novels have appeared: *Comment C'Est,* Paris 1961 (English trans. 1964); and *Mercier et Camier,* Paris 1970 (English trans. London 1974, NY 1975). Three novellas: *Company,* 1979; *Mal Vu Mal Dit,* Paris 1981 (English trans. 1982); *Worstward Ho,*1983. Short stories and texts published individually; many collected: *Têtes-Mortes,* Paris 1967; *No's Knife,* 1967; *First Love and Other Shorts,* NY 1974; *Disjecta,* 1983; and *Collected Shorter Prose,* 1984.

BEHAN, Brendan, b. Dublin 1923, d. Dublin 1964. Member of a family intimately connected with the national movement; nephew of Peadar Kearney, author of 'The Soldier's Song'. Joined the Fianna, Irish Republican Boy Scouts before he was 10, and the IRA before he was 15. In 1939 he was arrested in Liverpool for carrying explosives and sentenced to three years in Borstal, inspiration of his later autobiography, *Borstal Boy,* 1958, a world best seller. Deported in 1941 he was sentenced the following year in Ireland to 14 years for shooting a policeman with intent to kill. His prison experiences reappeared in his first major play *The Quare Fellow,* first performed at the Pike, Dublin, 1954, and subsequently everywhere. Released under amnesty in 1945, he worked as a housepainter and began writing for newspapers, achieving a reputation in a narrow but devoted circle. He went to France, and to England again, and in 1956 was recognised as a major playwright with the London production of *The Quare Fellow* by Joan Littlewood. She also produced his second play *The Hostage,* 1959. Just as *The Quare Fellow* owed something to Wilde's 'Ballad of Reading Gaol', so *The Hostage* – a translation of his play in Irish, *An Giall* – owed much to O'Connor's famous short story, 'Guests of the Nation', and both plays owed something to Joan Littlewood.

Many critics prefer Behan's prose work to his plays, in spite of their enormous present reputation, and regret that he did not devote himself to it entirely. Later books include *Brendan Behan's Island,* illustrated by Paul Hogarth, 1962; *Hold your Hour, and have Another,* 1963, illustrated by his wife Beatrice, daughter of the artist Cecil French Salkeld and herself well known in Dublin as a painter. In 1964 *Brendan Behan's New York,* illustrated by Paul Hogarth, appeared just after Behan's death. *The Confessions of an Irish Rebel* came out in 1965. These two last volumes consisted of tape recorded conversations collected and edited by Rae Jeffs. *The Scarperer,* a novel, pub. posthumously in 1966.

BEHAN, Dominic, b. Dublin 1928, brother of Brendan B. Left Ireland in 1947. Involved in Labour movement and active trades unionism in Dublin and London. Has written ballads, TV documentaries, a biography, *My Brother Brendan,* 1965, a play, *Posterity Be Damned,* and an autobiography, *Teems of Times and Happy Returns,* 1961.

BELL, Robert, b. Cork 1800, d. London 1867. Ed. TCD. Journalist in Dublin. Went to London 1828, edited *Atlas.* Wrote a *Life of Canning,* 1846, and edited a 24-volume edition of English poets. His reputation rests mainly on this work, but he wrote several comedies and two novels, *Hearts and Altars,* 1852, and *Ladder of Gold,* 1856.

BELL, Sam Hanna, b. Glasgow 1909, of an Ulster-Scots family. Brought to Co. Down 1918. Worked at wide variety of jobs, including night watchman, laboratory attendant, salesman and clerk. Began writing documentary scripts for BBC, and short stories, which appeared in *The Bell,* and were republished as *Summer Loanen and Other Stories,* Belfast 1943. Encouraged by Louis MacNeice, began to work full time for Northern Ireland radio as features producer 1945-69, as well as writing novels: *December Bride,* 1951, rep. Belfast 1982, and *The Hollow Ball,* 1961. Has also written on Ulster customs and folklore, *Erin's Orange Lily,* 1956, etc. Among the first to recognise the merits of Sam Thompson's work and encourage him to write for radio and stage. Recent work: *The Theatre in Ulster* (history), Dublin and London 1972; *Within Our Province* (prose anthology), Belfast 1972; *A Man Flourishing* (novel), 1973.

BELLINGS (sometimes Beling), Richard, b. Belingstown 1613, d. Dublin 1677. Ed. Lincoln's Inn. Secretary to Supreme Council of Confederation of Kilkenny 1642: Royalist Ambassador in Europe 1644. In exile in Europe 1649-60, returning at Restoration. During his exile wrote *Vindication,* 1654, and probably composed his *History of the Confederation,* unpublished until the MS was discovered by Sir J. T. Gilbert and published in 1882.

BENCE-JONES, Mark Adayre, b. 1930. Ed. Ampleforth, Cambridge. Lives Glenville, Co. Cork. Novelist and architectural historian. Novels: *All a Nonsense,* 1957; *Paradise Escaped,* 1958; *Nothing in the City,* 1965. Also, *The Remarkable Irish,* 1966; *Palaces of the Raj; Clive of India; Cavaliers; Burke's Guide to Country Houses Vol. I Ireland,* 1978. Consultant ed. *Burke's Irish Family Records,* 1976.

BENNETT, Douglas, b. Dublin 1930s. Ed. National College of Art. Past-Master of Company of Goldsmiths of Ireland. *Irish Georgian Silver,* 1972; *Collecting Irish Silver,* 1984.

BENNETT, Louie, b. Dublin 1870, d. Killiney 1956. Ed. privately and in London. Became a journalist with a particular interest in social questions, pacifism, the labour movement and women's rights. Travelled widely in Europe. In 1913 was passionately involved in the Dublin General Strike. Became first woman President of the Irish Trades Union Congress, 1932. Published several novels, including *Prisoner of His Word,* 1908.

BERESFORD, Charles William de la Poer, b. Phillipstown 1846, d. Caithness 1919. First Baron Metemmeh and Curraghmore 1916. Entered navy 1859, Admiral 1906. Engaged through much of a stormy career in fierce quarrels with the Admiralty, culminating in his angry book *The Betrayal,* 1912, dealing with the re-organisation of the fleet to counter German naval preparations. *Memoirs,* 2 vols, 1914.

BERKELEY, George, b. Co. Kilkenny 1685, d. Oxford 1753. Ed. Kilkenny and TCD, becoming Fellow 1707. Moving to London in 1713 he joined the circle headed by Swift, Pope and Addison, having already published in 1709 his *Essay towards a New Theory of Vision,* a psychological analysis of visual perception, the *Treatise concerning the Principles of Human Knowledge,* 1710, and *Dialogues between Hylas and Philonous,* 1713, which together began to establish him as a major European philosopher. Grossly misunderstood and misrepresented at the popular level, Berkeley's thought cannot be reduced to capsule form, but it develops from the central thesis that the material world depends for its actuality on being perceived.

Between 1714 and 1721 he travelled widely, in France and Italy, first as chaplain to the Earl of Peterborough and then as tutor to the son of the Bishop of Clogher. His travel *Letters* cover this period.

In 1721 he returned to Ireland and wrote his *Essay towards preventing the Ruine of Great Britain,* as an ethical-economic attack on the South Sea Bubble speculations. But his chief interest had become the founding of a college in the Bermudas for bringing Christian civilisation to America and in 1725 he went back to London to persuade Walpole to back the project. After three years lobbying he obtained a grant of £20,000 and sailed for the West Indies in September 1728. He stopped in Rhode Island and in the event never reached the Bermudas. His grant was withdrawn and in 1731 he sailed back to England.

The years in Rhode Island were not wasted, however. There he made disciples for his philosophical ideas, who later introduced them to America, and he brought back the MS of *Alciphron, or the Minute Philosopher*, 1732, considered by many critics the best of his writings. Patterned on the *Dialogues of Plato*, it debates the problems of personality in man and God.

In 1734 Berkeley was made Bishop of Cloyne and became absorbed in the state of Ireland's economy and society. The *Analyst*, 1734, designed to show that the higher mathematics touch mysteries as insoluble by reason as those of religion, was followed by the first part of the *Querist*, 3 vols, 1735-37, containing some five hundred questions arising from the condition of Ireland, with hints and suggestions as to their solution. In succeeding years he wrote in favour of religious toleration, pamphlets on many subjects from religion to politics; the great *Philosophical Reflections* and *Inquiries concerning the virtues of Tar Water*, 1744 (later known as *Siris*); *Maxims concerning Patriotism*, 1750; *Further thoughts on Tar Water*, 1752, etc.

His belief in the universal application of Tar Water as a panacea shows eccentricity, but he used it in *Siris* principally as a philosophical step-ladder, leading up to philosophical concepts. It has been called neo-Platonic in form, a development of Platonic idealism. Both Hume and Kant were stimulated by Berkeley's thought, although ironically both misunderstood it. In spite of such persistent misunderstandings all 19th and 20th century philosophy owes debts to Berkeley. In 1752 ill-health made him resign his bishopric and he retired to Oxford where he died the following January.

BERRY, James, b. Louisburgh 1842, d. Carna 1914. Ed. locally in hedge schools and spent his life in Mayo. His *Tales of the West of Ireland* appeared in the *Mayo News* 1910-13, repub. Dublin 1967, ed. Gertrude M. Hogan, and again 1984. They contain local anecdotes, legends and descriptions of great value to anyone studying Irish life in the 18th and 19th centuries.

BEWLEY, Charles, b. Dublin 1888, d. Rome 1969. Ed. Dublin and England, Bar, first made his name defending Republican soldiers at British courts martial, 1919-21. Represented Irish Provisional govt. in Berlin, 1921-23. Returned to Berlin as Irish Minister 1933, where he became acquainted with the leading figures in the Nazi govt. *Herman Goering and the Third Reich*, NY 1962, is his account of them.

BIBBY, Thomas, b. Kilkenny 1799, d. Kilkenny 1863. Ed. TCD. Fine Greek scholar, became an eccentric and recluse. Published two long dramatic poems, *Gerald of Kildare*, 1845, and *Silken Thomas*, 1859.

BICKERSTAFFE, Isaac, b. Dublin *c*. 1735, d. 1812. Probably the son of a locksmith. Became page to Lord Chesterfield who procured him a commission in the Marines. Wrote more than twenty plays all produced by Garrick, and a dramatic poem, *Leucothoe*, 1756. His best-known pieces are the comic operas, *Love in a Village*, 1763 and *The Maid of the Mill*, 1765. *The Hypocrite*, 1768, was based on Molière's *Tartuffe*. In 1772 he was accused of murder and fled the country, dying abroad. Two other plays, written or at least published and produced after his flight, *The Sultan*, 1775, and *The Spoiled Child*, 1805, are usually attributed to him.

BIGGER, Francis Joseph, b. Belfast 1863, d. Belfast 1926. Ed. Liverpool and Belfast: solicitor 1888. Best-known work, *Ulster Land War of 1770*, Dublin 1910. Wrote on northern archaeology and edited *Ulster Journal of Archaeology*, 1894-1914. Strong supporter of Language Revival and all aspects of Irish culture.

BINCHY, Daniel A., b. 1900. Ed. UCD, Munich. Senior Professor Dublin Inst. for Adv. Studies. Preceded Charles Bewley as Irish Minister to Berlin, 1929-32. Wrote *Church and State in Fascist Italy*, Oxford 1941, rep. 1970. Author of many scholarly articles on aspects of early Irish history and law. Editor of *Corpus Iuris Hibernici*, 6 vols, Dublin 1979, a collection of canonical texts of early Irish law.

BINCHY, Maeve, b. Dublin 1940. Ed. Killiney, UCD. School-teacher 1960-68. Journalist *Irish Times* since 1968. Plays: *End of Term*, one act, Dublin 1976; *Half Promised Land*, full length, Dublin Theatre Festival 1979. TV plays: *Deeply Regretted By*, RTE 1979, won Jacobs Award and Prague Television Award for best script 1979; *Ireland of the Welcomes*, RTE 1980. Books, non-fiction: *My First Book*, 1976; *Maeve's Diary*, 1980, both Dublin. Short stories: *Central Line*, 1977; *Victoria Line*, 1980; *Dublin 4*, Swords 1982. Achieved enormous success with first novel, *Light a Penny Candle*, 1982; also *The Lilac Bus*, Swords 1984; *Echoes*, 1985.

BIRMINGHAM, George A., pseud. of Canon James Owen Hannay, b. Belfast 1865, d. 1950. After ordination spent 21 years in Westport, Co. Mayo, from where he went to Budapest as chaplain to British Embassy. During the First World War he was chaplain with the British Army in France, 1916-17. His first novel had been published in 1904, *The Seething Pot*, and his best-known books were written shortly afterwards: *The Northern Iron*, 1907, and *Spanish Gold*, 1908. He wrote a large number of novels, popular in England but often looked at askance in Ireland as being Protestant and Ascendancy in inspiration. Other titles include: *The Search Party*, 1909; *Lalage's Lovers*, 1911; *The Grand Duchess*, 1924; *Millicent's Corner*, 1935; and *Appeasement*, 1939.

He was boycotted in his Westport parish after the local production of his successful (in London) play *General John Regan*, 1913. He had already published under his own name *The Spirit and Origin of Christian Monasticism*, 1903, and *The Wisdom of the Desert*, 1904. Afterwards, still under the name Hannay, he wrote *Connaught to Chicago*, 1914; *A Padre in*

France, 1918 (reminiscences of his war service); *A Wayfarer in Hungary*, 1925; and biographies of *Isaiah*, 1937 and *Jeremiah*, 1939. For some years he held a living in Somerset, and afterwards was in London. His autobiography, *Pleasant Places*, appeared in 1934.

BLACAM, Aodh de, see DE BLACAM, Aodh

BLACKBURN, Helen, b. Valentia Island 1842, d. London 1903. Brought to London 1859, became involved in early suffragette movement. Edited *Englishwoman's Review* from 1881. Wrote many books on women's rights and conditions: *The Condition of Working Women* (with E. J. Boucherett), 1897; *Women's Suffrage: A record of the Movement in the British Isles*, 1902; and *Women under the Factory Acts*, 1903, being the best-known.

BLACKBURNE, E. Owens, pseud. of Elizabeth O'B. Casey, b. Slane 1848, d. 1894. Went to London 1873, as journalist. Contributed *In at the Death* to *The Nation* soon afterwards. Republished in 1876 as *A Woman Scorned*. Several other novels: *The Way Women Love*, 1877; *The Glen of Silver Birches*, 1889, etc.

BLACKER, William, b. Armagh 1777, d. Carrickblaeker 1855. Became a colonel and military songsmith. His most famous song was the Orange ballad having for refrain 'So put your trust in God, my boys, and keep your powder dry'. Wrote a book, *Ardmagh*, 1848.

BLACKLEY, William Lavery, b. Dundalk 1830, d. London 1902. Ed. Brussels and TCD. Ordained C. of E. held livings in Surrey and London. His plans for a National Insurance Scheme and old age pensions were set out in many essays, particularly 'National Insurance a Cheap, Practical and Popular Way of Preventing Pauperism', Nov. 1878 in *Nineteenth Century*, and in his *Collected Essays*, 1880. His ideas were rejected in England, but taken up both in the British colonies and in Europe from where they returned to result in the establishment of state pensions for the old in Great Britain in 1908.

BLACKWOOD, Caroline, b. Ulster 1931, daughter of 4th Marquis of Dufferin and Ava. Married artist Lucien Freud, grandson of Sigmund. Third husband was Robert Lowell, the American poet. Collection of short stories and journalistic pieces and memoirs, *For All That I Found There*, 1974; first novel *The Stepdaughter*, 1976, won David Higham Fiction Prize; a novella, *Great Granny Webster*, 1977, was best seller. *Goodnight, Sweet Ladies*, 1983, a longer novel; *On the Perimeter*, 1984, reportage on occupation of Greenham Common by anti-nuclear feminists; *Corrigan*, 1984, a novel.

BLESSINGTON, Countess of, see POWER, Marguerite.

BLYTHE, Ernest, b. Lisburn 1889, d. Dublin 1975. Ed. locally. Recruited by Sean O'Casey into IRB 1906. Irish Volunteers organiser 1914. Minister of Finance Irish Free State 1923-31. Founded An Gúm to publish books in Irish for the government. Managing Director Abbey Theatre 1941-67. Poetry pub. 1938; *Briseadh na Teorann,* 1955; 2 vols autobiography, 1957-1970.

BODKIN, Matthias McDonnel, b. Tuam 1849, d. 1933. Ed. Jesuits and Catholic University, Dublin. Nationalist MP for North Roscommon, County Court Judge 1907. Novels include *Lord Edward Fitzgerald,* 1896; *The Rebels,*1899, etc. Pub. *Recollections of an Irish Judge,* 1915.

BODKIN, Thomas Patrick, b. Dublin 1887, d. Birmingham 1961. Ed. Dublin and Paris. Bar 1911. Director National Gallery of Ireland 1927-35; Barber Professor of Fine Arts, Birmingham, 1935-52. Knight of St Gregory 1952. Many other honours. One of the leading authorities on European painting. Nephew of Hugh Lane, the art collector. Best remembered for *Hugh Lane & His Pictures,* Paris 1932, repub. Dublin 1934 and 1956, and *My Uncle Frank* (Hugh Lane), 1941, which went into several editions. Also wrote *The Paintings of Jan Vermeer,* 1940; *The Wilton Diptych,* 1947, etc.

BOLAND, Eavan Aisling, b. Dublin 1944. Daughter of F. H. Boland, the Irish diplomat. Ed. London, New York and TCD. Junior lecturer TCD 1967-68. Macaulay Fellowship 1968. MIAL. Married to novelist and critic Kevin Casey. Poetry: *New Territory,* Dublin 1967; *The War Horse,* 1975; *In Her Own Image,* Dublin 1980; *Night Feed,* Dublin, London and Boston 1983. Criticism: with Micheál MacLiammóir, *W. B. Yeats and his world,* 1971.

BOLGER, Dermot, b. Finglas 1959. Runs Raven Arts Press publishing; literary director Grapevine Arts Centre. Poetry: *Finglas Watching the Night,* 1977; *Never a Dull Moment,* 1978; *The Habit of Flesh,* 1980; *Finglas Lilies,* 1981; *No Waiting America,* 1982; *Internal Exiles,* 1985; all pub. Dublin. Also a novel, *Night Shift,* Dingle and Washington 1985.

BOLGER, William, see SHARE, Bernard.

BORLASE (sometimes Borlace), Edmund, b. Dublin *c.* 1620, d. Chester 1682. Ed. TCD, Leyden 1650, and Oxford 1660. Practised medicine in Chester. Notorious for his biased and misleading *Reduction of Ireland,* 1675, and *History of Execrable Irish Rebellion of 1641,* 1680, which were in some part answered by the Earl of Castlehaven in *Brief Reflections on the Earl of C's memoirs of his engagements and carriage in the wars of Ireland,* 1682.

BOUCICAULT, Dionysius Lardner, b. Dublin 1820, d. New York 1890. Ed. University College London. Acted with Macready, considered excellent, particularly in parts requiring pathos. His first play, *London Assurance,* 1841, was a great success, and he turned to writing and stage management, usually adapting plays from books or other sources. Often accused of creating the 'stage Irishman'. Wrote and produced more than 140 plays, in London, Dublin, and America. Among his many successes; *The Corsican*

Brothers, 1848; *The School for Scheming; The Rapparee; Forbidden Fruit;* and his three most famous Irish plays, *The Colleen Bawn,* 1860 (adapted from *The Collegians* by Gerald Griffin); *Arrah na Pogue,* 1864; and *The Shaughraun,* 1875.

BOURKE, Patrick J., b. Dublin 1883, d. 1932. Actor and playwright in the Boucicault tradition, long associated with Queen's Theatre, Dublin, where his first play, *When Wexford Rose,* was performed 1910. Other plays include *For the Land She Loved; The Northern Insurgent; In the Dark and Evil Days,* etc. Set various plays to music, including *Kathleen Mavourneen* in which he himself acted in countless revivals until 1928. Father of Seamus de Burca. Another son, Lorcan, acted for many years in his father's plays and others, and is now an impresario.

BOURKE, Ulick, b. Co. Galway 1829, d. Claremorris 1887. Ed. Maynooth. Parish priest of Claremorris 1878. One of the most influential of the Irish Revivalists, through his teaching and writings. *College Irish Grammar,* Dublin 1856, and *Easy Lessons, or Self-Instruction in Irish* went through many editions. Also wrote *Pre-Christian Ireland,* Dublin 1887.

BOWEN, Elizabeth Dorothea Cole, b. Dublin 1900, d. London 1973. Daughter of Henry Cole Bowen of Bowenscourt, Co. Cork. Ed. Downe Kent, TCD, Oxford. Awarded CBE 1948, Hon. D.Lit., TCD, 1949; Oxon 1956. Among great names of modern Irish literature. Short story collections include *Encounters,* 1923; *Look at All Those Roses,* 1941; *The Demon Lover,* 1945; *The Collected Stories of Elizabeth Bowen,* 1980. Novels include *The Hotel,*1927; *The Last September,* 1929; *Friends and Relations,* 1931; *The Death of the Heart,* 1938; *The Heat of the Day,* 1949; *The Little Girls,* 1964; and finally *Eva Trout,* 1969, awarded a prize by the Irish Academy of Letters the following year. Other titles are *A World of Love; The House in Paris; To the North; The Cat Jumps;* and *Joining Charles.* She was also an essayist and local historian: *Bowen's Court,*1942, repub. 1964, 1984, is a family history, *The Shelbourne Hotel,* 1951, an institutional one; essays include *Collected Impressions,* 1950, and *A Time in Rome,* 1960.

In 1923 she married Alan Charles Cameron, Scottish educationist and broadcaster. He died 1952.

BOWMAN, John, b. 1942. Ed. Belvedere, TCD. Ph.D. 1980. Joined RE 1962 as current affairs broadcaster. Books: *De Valera and the Ulster Question 1917-1973,* Oxford 1982, rep. 1983; co-ed. with Ronan O'Donoghue, *Portraits: Belvedere College, Dublin 1832-1982,* Dublin 1982.

BOYCE, John, b. Co. Donegal 1810, d. US 1864. Ed. Maynooth, ordained 1837, went to US 1845. Became well known as a novelist under pseud. Paul Peppergrass. Novels include *Shandy Maguire,* 1848; *The Spaewife,* 1853; *Mary Lee,* 1864.

BOYD, Elizabeth, b. *c.* 1700. Wrote a thanksgiving for the English victory at Dettingen: 'Glory to the Highest', 1743. Had already written a novel *The Happy Unfortunate, or The Female Page,* 1732, and a ballad opera *Don Sancho,* 1739.

BOYD, Henry, b. Dromore, *c.* 1756, d. Ballintemple 1832. Ed. TCD. Chaplain to Earl of Charleville. Fled from rebels in 1798. Became vicar of Rathfriland. Wrote several volumes of poetry, but his reputation was made by his translations of Dante: *The Inferno,* 1785, and the remainder, 1802. He also translated Petrarch.

BOYD, Hugh Macauley, b. Co. Antrim 1746, d. India 1794. Believed by many well-informed contemporaries to be the true 'Junius' of the *Junius Letters,* Almoner, the bookseller who was prosecuted for selling a print of the famous 35th 'Revolution' letter, among them. He was certainly among the foremost political journalists of his day. Ed. Dublin, TCD, Bar, he went to London about 1766 and entered the Goldsmith-Garrick circle. At this time he was still known as Hugh Macauley, but a legacy persuaded him to change his name to Boyd, his mother's father being an O'Boyd. In 1781 went to India as secretary to Lord Macartney, Governor of Madras, was captured and imprisoned by the French; became Master-Attendant of Madras and later editor of various Anglo-Indian journals. *The Miscellaneous Works of Hugh Boyd,* 2 vols, 1800.

BOYD, Thomas, b. Co. Louth 1867, d. 1927. Spent much of his life in London and Manchester. Contributed poetry to *United Ireland,* etc. Regarded as a notable minor poet of the Edwardian period, and is represented in many good anthologies. A volume *Poems* was published in Dublin, 1906.

BOYLAN, Clare, b. Dublin 1948. Journalist and magazine editor to 1984. First novel *Holy Pictures,* 1983, and short-story collection *Nail On The Head,* 1983, were both well received by critics in England and Ireland; second novel, *Last Resorts,* 1984. Stories have been included in Elek Books *Best Irish Short Stories* and Macmillan's *Winter's Tales.*

BOYLAN, Eugene, b. 1904, d. 1964. Ed. UCD and Vienna, winning Rockefeller Fellowship for postgraduate work in atomic physics. Returned to Ireland and lectured on experimental physics. Entered Cistercian Order in Roscrea. Elected Superior of monastery on Caldey Island, 1953, returned to Roscrea, 1958, elected Abbot of Roscrea, 1962. Books include *A Mystic under Arms,* Cork 1945; *This Tremendous Lover,* Cork 1947 (translated into nine languages and a world best seller); *The Spiritual Life of the Priest,* Cork 1949; *The Priest's Way to God,* Dublin 1962; and *Partnership with Christ,* Holland 1964, rep. Cork 1966.

BOYLAN, Henry, b. Drogheda 1912. Ed. TCD. Distinguished public servant for many years, Radio Éireann, Gaeltarra Éireann, Dept of Lands, etc. Now Chairman of Arramara Teo. Has published *Eire To-day: A Survey of Life in Modern Ireland,* Dublin and London 1948; *A Dictionary of Irish*

BOYLE

biography, Dublin, London and NY 1978; *Theobald Wolfe Tone,* Dublin 1981; and *This Arrogant City,* 1984.

BOYLE, John, b. 1707, d. 1762. 5th Earl of Orrery 1731. 5th Earl of Cork 1753. Translated *The Letters of Pliny,* 1751, and the same year published the well-known *Remarks on the Life & Writings of Jonathan Swift.*

BOYLE, Patrick, b. Co. Antrim, d. Dublin 1982. Ed. Coleraine Academical Institution. With Ulster Bank for 45 years. MIAL. Achieved belated but instant fame with short stories *At Night All Cats Are Grey,* 1966, and a first novel, *Like Any Other Man,* 1966. Other short stories: *All Looks Yellow to the Jaundiced Eye,* 1969; *A View from Calvary,* 1976; *The Port Wine Stain* (selected), Dublin 1983.

BOYLE, Robert, b. 1627, fourteenth child of 1st Earl of Cork, d. London 1691. Ed. Eton and on Grand Tour of Europe. In England 1644 and precocious member of London intellectual group that in 1662 was formalised as the Royal Society. Experimenting in Oxford on vacuums with Robert Hooke, published *New Experiments Physico-Mechanical,* 1660, and the *Sceptical Chymist,* 1661, in which he dealt the death blow to the mediaeval chemistry of the 'four elements' and 'three principles'. He defined chemical elements as substances incapable of division into simpler constituents and restored the atomic theory to European science. His fame rests on *Boyle's Law,* that the pressure and volume of gas are inversely proportional, propounded 1662. His collected *Works,* 5 vols, 1744.

BOYLE, Roger, b. Lismore 1621, 3rd son of Earl of Cork, d. 1679. Created Baron Broghill in childhood. Ed. TCD. Fought in Civil War for Charles I until 1649. Joined Cromwell and campaigned for Parliament in Ireland. After Cromwell's death recovered his old sympathies and helped secure Ireland for Charles II, receiving earldom of Orrery as reward. Wrote poetry, a novel *Parthenissa,* 1654; a *Treatise on the Art of War,* 1677; and several plays, *Mustapha,* 1668; *The Black Prince,* 1669; *Henry V,* 1672, etc.

BOYLE, William, b. Dromiskin 1853, d. London 1922. Ed. Dundalk. Civil servant, friend of Parnell and Redmond. An authority on life and work of James Mangan. Wrote verse, and descriptions of Irish country life, published as *A Kish of Brogues.* But his fame is as a playwright, among the first to write for the Abbey Theatre. His plays include *The Building Fund,* 1905, one of his best-known and most successful plays; *The Eloquent Dempsey,* another great success; *The Tale of a Town;* and *The Mineral Workers,* all appearing in 1906.

BOYSE, Samuel, b. Dublin 1708, d. London 1747. Ed. Glasgow, went to London and lived in miserable circumstances, slightly alleviated by friendship with Dr Johnson. In 1739 published a long poem 'The Deity' which was highly praised by Fielding and other critics. In 1741 he put out a modernised version of the *Canterbury Tales,* and in 1742 *The Praise of Peace.* His *The Pantheon or the Fabulous History of the Heathen Gods* was extremely popular and all his poetry was reprinted many times. He also translated a considerable amount of Dutch poetry, but gained small benefit from his popularity or his industry, and died still poverty-stricken.

BRADY, Joseph, pseud. of Monsignor Maurice Browne, b. 1892, d. Co. Kildare 1979. Brother of Cardinal Browne and brother-in-law of Sean McEntee; was parish priest of Ballymore Eustace, Co. Kildare. Author of *The Big Sycamore*, Dublin 1958, repub. US 1959, an immensely popular novel in the Canon Sheehan tradition. Its sequel, *In Monavalla*, appeared Dublin 1963.

BRADY, Nicholas, b. Bandon 1659, d. 1726. Became vicar of Richmond in 1696, in which year he and Nahum Tate issued their metrical version of the Psalms. Also translated the *Aeneid* and wrote a tragedy *The Rape*.

BREEN, Dan, b. 1894, d. Dublin 1969. Joined the Irish Volunteers 1914, and became one of the leading Flying Column commanders in the south during the War of Independence. His book, *My Fight for Irish Freedom*, Dublin 1924, Tralee 1964 (paperback), is interesting as one of the very few accounts of the war by a man involved in it.

BRENNAN, Elizabeth, poet and writer for children. Books include *Out of the Darkness*, 1945; *Am I My Brother's Keeper?* 1946; *The Wind Fairies*, 1946; *Whispering Walls*, 1948; *Mystery of Hermits' Crest*, 1948; *Wind over the Bogs* (poetry), 1950; *The Children's Book of Irish Saints*, 1963.

BRENNAN, Elizabeth, b. Dublin 1907. Ed. Dublin. Lived in south of England before settling in Sligo. Has written ten light romantic novels, some translated into several languages, among them: *Patrick's Woman*, 1969; *Mountain of Desire*, 1970; *Innocent in Eden*, 1971. Her most recent novel *Girl on an Island*, 1984, won ICA Award. Plays: *Compassion*, Dublin; *The Parting of the Ways*, Tubbercurry and RE.

BRENNAN, Jan Herbie, b. Co. Down 1940. Ed. locally. Worked as journalist, magazine editor and advertising director. Writes short stories as Herbie Brennan, non-fiction as J.H. Brennan, novels as Jan Brennan. Non-fiction: *Astral Doorways*, 1968; *Experimental Magic*, 1969; *Five Keys to Past Lives*, 1971; *Occult Reich*, 1974; *Beyond the Fourth Dimension*, 1975 (US title *The Ultimate Elsewhere*); *Occult History of the World*, vol.I, 1976 (vol II in preparation); *Power Play*, 1977 (US title *Getting What You Want*), on business psychology; *The Good Con Guide*, 1978, humour. Novels: *The Greythorn Woman*, 1979; *Dark Moon*, 1980; *Dream of Destiny*, 1980.

BRENNAN, M. M., Abbey playwright of the 1920s and '30s; plays include *The Young Man from Rathmines*, 1922, his best-known play, whose title has passed into the stock of Irish satirical proverbs. Other titles include *One Hundred Pounds Reward* and *The Big Sweep*, 1932, another popular success. Also *Napoleon and the Triplets*, Dublin 1932; and *Fitzgerald and the Guns*, Dublin 1944.

BRENNAN, Robert, b. Wexford 1881, d. Dublin 1964. Surveyor and then journalist before Easter 1916. After the Rising became Director of Publicity for Revolutionary movement, and Under Secretary for Foreign Affairs for Revolutionary Government, 1920. Held many important political and diplomatic posts; became Director of *Irish Press*, 1930-34, returned to Diplomatic Service as Secretary to Irish Legation in Washington, becoming Envoy, 1938, and remaining as Minister Plenipotentiary up to 1947. Returned to become Director of Radio Éireann. Wrote plays, mystery stories and reminiscences, such as *Goodnight Mr O'Donnell, The Man Who Walked Like a Dancer;* and *Allegiance,* his autobiography, pub. Dublin 1950.

BRISCOE, Robert, b. Dublin 1894, d. Dublin 1969. Ed. Dublin. Joined IRB as boy, acted as courier, involved in gun-running operations of 1914. Interned in Germany during First World War, where he had been learning family business. Returned to Ireland and fought in the War of Independence, taking the Republican side in the succeeding Civil War of 1922-24. Founder member of Fianna Fáil, the parliamentary party which inherited the bulk of Republican support. A Zionist, he passed on his guerrilla war experience to Jabotinsky, who came to Ireland to see him and pioneered the so-called 'coffin ship' operation to bring Jews to Palestine after Second World War. Memoirs, *For the Life of Me,* 1959 (with Alden Hatch).

BRITTAINE, George, b. *c.* 1790, d. Dublin 1847. Became rector of Kilcormack, and wrote a number of novels, all first published anonymously, such as *Confessions of Honor Delany,* Dublin 1830, and *The Election,* Dublin 1840.

BROCK, Lynn, see McALLISTER, Alexander.

BRODERICK, John, b. Athlone 1927. For some time managed the family business there. Self-educated. MIAL. Has written a series of powerful novels set in the Irish midlands, Dublin and London: *The Pilgrimage,* 1961; *The Fugitives,* 1962; *Don Juaneen,* 1963; *The Waking of Willie Ryan,* 1965; *An Apology for Roses,* 1973; *Cité Pleine de Rêves,* Paris 1974; *The Pride of Summer,* 1976; *London Irish,* 1979; *The Trial of Father Dillingham,* 1981; *A Prayer for Fair Weather,* 1984, a spy story told in the bleakly realistic style of Le Carré, and a new departure for the author; *The Rose Tree,* 1985. Spent several years in France. Now lives in England.

BRONTË, Patrick, b. Co. Down 1777, d. 1861. Of a family originally called Brunty or Branty. Worked as a blacksmith's labourer before becoming a schoolmaster. A patron sent him to Cambridge where he was ordained in Church of England. Appointed to Haworth parsonage. In 1812 married the niece of a Cornish parson and became father to the most famous family of novelists in English literature – Charlotte, Emily and Anne. He wrote a good deal of verse; *Cottage Poems* published in Halifax 1811; *The Rural Minstrel,* Halifax 1813; and *The Maid of Killarney,* 1818. Mrs Gaskell's

Life of Charlotte Brontë presents him as a villain. This seems to have been an injustice, and if some of his eccentricities tormented his daughters and his son, he also provided them with the qualities they poured into their novels.

BROOKE, Charlotte, b. Co. Cavan 1740, d. 1793. One of the 22 children of Henry B. She wrote a tragedy *Belisarius,* apparently never printed, but deserves entry here for her *Reliques of Irish Poetry,* 1789, a collection of Irish poems which she gathered over many years, translated and published.

BROOKE, Henry, b. Co. Cavan 1703, d. Dublin 1783. Ed. TCD. Went to London and became friendly with Swift and Pope. He must also have known Samuel Boyse and is often credited with a share in, or even the whole of Boyse's *Canterbury Tales Modernised.* But this is merely one more of the many injustices suffered by Boyse. Prolific in every sense of the word Brooke wrote political pamphlets, novels, plays, an oratorio, an opera, and fathered 22 children, including Charlotte of *The Reliques.* His most famous work is the novel *The Fool of Quality* often reprinted throughout the century. It first appeared in 1766-67. His plays include *Gustavus Vasa,* 1739; *The Earl of Westmoreland,* 1741; *The Earl of Essex,* 1761.

BROUGHAM, John, b. Dublin 1814, d. New York 1880. Actor and theatre manager, wrote more than 70 plays and libretti for many operas. Is supposed to be the original of Lever's Harry Lorrequer.

BROWN, Christy, b. Dublin 1932, d. 1981. Almost completely paralysed, his mother taught him to read, and also to write using a pencil gripped between toes of his left foot. From this came the title of his autobiography, *My Left Foot,* 1954, repub. 1980 as *The Childhood Story of Christy Brown.* The book is of great interest for its insights into the mind of a handicapped child and its descriptions of working-class life in Dublin. Novels are *Down All the Days,* 1970; *A Shadow on Summer,* 1973; *Wild Grow the Lilies,* 1976; *A Promising Career,* 1982. All repub. NY. Poetry: *Come Softly to My Wake,* 1971; *Background Music,* 1973; *Of Snails and Skylarks,* 1973; *Inmates,* 1981.

BROWN, Frances, b. Stranorlar 1816, blind, d. London 1879. Educated herself by listening to other children recite their lessons. Went to London, where she became known as 'the blind poetess of Donegal'. Was granted a Civil List pension. Published several volumes of poetry: *The Star of Atteghei,* 1844; *Lyrics and Miscellaneous Poems,* Edinburgh 1848; and *Pictures and Songs of Home,* 1856. Many of her pieces appeared in the *Athenaeum* from 1841 onwards.

BROWN (sometimes Browne), Patrick, b. Mayo 1720, d. Mayo 1790. Ed. Leyden. Naturalist and friend of Linnaeus, he published a *Civil and Natural History of Jamaica,* 1756, and having settled in his native Mayo in 1774, wrote his famous *Fasciculus Plantorum Hiberniae,* 1788, in English, Latin and Irish.

BROWN, Peter, b. Co. Dublin 1935. Ed. Bray, Oxford. Elected Fellow of All Souls, 1957, the youngest ever. *Augustine of Hippo*, 1967, awarded Council of Britain Prize.

BROWN, Stephen James Meredith, b. Co. Down 1881, d. 1962. Ordained 1914, Jesuit. Founded the Catholic Library in Dublin, 1922; wrote *A Reader's Guide to Irish Fiction*, Dublin 1910; *A Guide to Books on Ireland*, Dublin 1912; and *Ireland in Fiction*, Dublin 1916. Also wrote on meditation, and edited *Catalogue of Tales and Novels by Irish Writers*, 1927, many editions.

BROWNE, Maurice (Monsignor), see BRADY, Joseph.

BROWNE, Peter, b. Dublin 1666, d. Cork 1735. Bishop of Cork and theological controversialist, best known for his attacks on Toland: *Procedure, Extent & Limits of Human Understanding*, 1728, etc. In general he argued against rationalism. He was also strongly opposed to toasts in remembrance of the dead, particularly to 'the Glorious and Immortal Memory' of King William III. In many volumes, beginning with *Drinking in Remembrance of the Dead*, 1713, he attacked such practices, earning Swift's sardonic notice as a 'whimsical gentleman'.

BRYANS, Robin, pseud. of Robert Harbinson, b. Belfast 1928. Worked in Belfast shipyards as young man, and then as a trapper and later a teacher in Canada. His travel books include *Summer Saga* (Iceland) 1960; *Danish Episode*, 1961; *Fanfare for Brazil*, 1962; *Morocco*, 1965; *Trinidad and Tobago*, 1967.

BULFIN, William, b. near Birr 1862, d. Birr, 1910. Ed. Galway. Emigrated to Argentina at 17, lived as a gaucho on the pampas, became editor and newspaper owner in Buenos Aires. Returned to Ireland 1902 and travelled all over the country on a bicycle. Published two books, *Tales of the Pampas* and *Rambles in Eirinn*, 1907, repub. 1981.

BULLOCK, Shan F., b. Co. Fermanagh 1865, d. 1935. Son of prosperous Protestant farmer. Worked as clerk in London. Wrote many novels of which the best is considered to be *The Loughsiders*, 1924. Published his autobiography *After Sixty Years*, 1931. Other books include *The Awkward Squads*, 1893; *By Thrasna River*, 1895; *The Red Leaguers*, 1904; *Master John*, 1910.

BUNBURY, Selina, b. Co. Louth 1802, d. Cheltenham 1882. Of a devout Methodist family. In 1819 the father's bankruptcy left the family in poverty and the mother and children moved to Dublin. Selina taught in a primary school, and began writing in secrecy because of her mother's disapproval. There was a family connection with the Burneys, and Selina appears to have modelled herself on Fanny. Her earlier travel books concern Ireland and are of interest for their portrait of country districts before the Famine. *A Visit to My Birthplace*, Dublin 1820; *Cabin Conversations*, Dublin 1827;

Early Recollections, Dublin 1829; *Tales of My Country,* 1833, are all of value. Later books include *The Pyrenees,* 1845; *Summer in Northern Europe,* 1856; and *Russia After the War,* 1857.

Her first books were published in Dublin, and made her a local reputation. About 1830 the family moved to Liverpool. Selina kept house for her twin brother, and seems to have supported both of them by her writings. After his marriage in 1845 she began to travel, and write the books which are the real basis of her reputation. But both before 1845 and later she wrote many novels which in their day were extremely popular, some reaching several editions. *The Star of the Court – A Story of Anne Boleyn,* 1844; *Evelyn,* 1849; *Sir Guy d'Esterre,* 1859; *Florence Manvers,* 1865; *Lady Flora,* 1870, etc. She has been credited with over a hundred volumes, but many of these are tracts and pamphlets. Her real output appears to be about thirty books.

BUNTING, Edward, b. Armagh 1773, d. Dublin 1843. Became a music teacher in Belfast at a very early age. In 1792 attended the famous gathering of harpers there and became passionately interested in early Irish traditional music. Published *A General Collection of the Ancient Irish Music etc.,* with a preface, Dublin 1796, repub. London. This helped to waken interest in the subject and inspired Thomas Moore. A 2nd vol came out 1809 with an essay on Irish, Egyptian and Scottish harps; 3rd vol, Dublin 1840.

BURKE, Edmund, b. Dublin 1729, d. Beaconsfield 1797. Ed. Dublin, TCD, Middle Temple; called to English Bar. Came to early prominence as a writer, with *A Vindication of Natural Society,* 1756, and *The Sublime and Beautiful,* 1757, becoming also a compiler of *The Annual Register.* The Whigs marked him as a useful man, and after a stay in Ireland as secretary to the Chief Secretary, he was made private secretary to Lord Rockingham, the Prime Minister, in 1765, and entered Parliament as member for Wendover. He remained a member of the London Parliament for the rest of his life, and one of its greatest figures, but he never held high office, nor any office for long.

He was severely handicapped by his humble origin as the son of a Dublin solicitor, in a political environment that counted aristocratic connections as the chief political virtue. He was also handicapped by disreputable relatives and his own difficult character. As a political philosopher he is sometimes given more credit than he deserves. While helping to shape modern parliamentary democracy he opposed parliamentary reform. One might say that while his vote was Whig his heart was Tory. He was a politician who used theory as a political weapon, rather than a theorist who happened also to be an active politician. But the theoretical sparks he struck off in the heat of election or debate are more valuable than most coherently constructed systems of political theory.

He defined the political party, the role of the member, and the nature of political society in terms that have not been bettered. He opposed the royal influence in politics, urged conciliation of the American colonies, lost his Bristol seat through arguing for Irish free trade, used his office as Paymaster to fight against corruption and sinecures instead of as a source of personal enrichment (the normal practice), favoured Catholic Emancipation although himself a devoted Protestant, fought against the Slave Trade and for Penal Reform, foresaw the excess of the French Revolution and denounced the oppression involved in Britain's possession of India, this last being one cause of his notorious attack on Warren Hastings.

On almost every major issue of the day he was right and his enemies were wrong, but too often he was right for the wrong reasons. He is one of the great paradoxes of the 18th century: a champion of democracy who distrusted the people; a defender of oligarchy whose partisan attacks on Hastings set out the pattern for a just and liberal Empire; a political failure who occupies a major place in British political history.

An orator rather than a writer, his speeches and writings are still worth reading for style as well as content. *Reflections on the Revolution in France,* 1790, and *Appeal from the New to the Old Whigs,* 1791, contain much of his mature political thinking, some of it in direct contradiction of his earlier writings, such as *Thoughts on the Cause of the Present Discontents,* 1770, in which he had attacked George III's abuse of the royal prerogatives. As oratory, critics have singled out his speeches on American questions of 1774 and 1775.

After his quarrel with Fox in 1791 he lost all political influence, and spent the last years of his life burdened by debts and disappointments. His *Works and Correspondence* were published 1852. A curious footnote to Burke's speeches is the use Karl Marx made of a phrase in one of them. Burke once said that 'any five agricultural labourers picked at random would do the same amount of work as any other five'. Colm Brogan points out that on such slender foundations as this Marx erected his theory of Labour Value.

BURKE, Helen Lucy, b. Dublin. Won Irish PEN award for short story 'Trio' 1970. Novels: *Close Connections,* 1979; *A Season for Mothers,* 1980, both pub. Swords.

BURKE, John, b. 1787 (probably in Tipperary), d. Aix-la-Chapelle 1848. Creator, with his son John Bernard B., of *Burke's Peerage,* first issued 1826 as *A Genealogical and Heraldic Dictionary of the Peerage and Baronetage of the United Kingdom,* and between 1833 and 1838 there followed *A Genealogical and Heraldic History of the Commoners of Great Britain and Ireland,* now known as *Burke's Landed Gentry.* Both volumes continue to be published.

John Bernard, b. London 1814, moved to Ireland in middle-age and continued his father's work, editing the *Peerage* and *Landed Gentry* and publishing many genealogical works; *The Book of the Orders of Knighthood,* 1858, and *Vicissitudes of Families,* 1859, being the best-known. He became Ulster King-of-Arms 1853, was knighted 1854, became Governor of the National Gallery of Ireland 1874. He was succeeded in his editorial work by his son Peter, not to be confused with his brother Peter, 1811-81, author of two valuable works on Edmund Burke and others on Celebrated Trials.

BURKE, Thomas (known sometimes as De Burgo), b. Dublin *c.* 1709, d. Kilkenny 1776. Ed. Rome, became a Dominican, reputedly at 14 by special dispensation, and returning to Ireland in 1743 was made Bishop of Ossory in 1759. His great work is the *Hibernia Dominicana,* 1762, published in Kilkenny, but described on title page as published in Cologne, perhaps to protect the printer. A history of the Dominicans in Ireland, it was a commissioned work, but failed to please the Bishop's Superiors. Some parts of it were removed on their instructions. The reasons were political rather than theological or historical, it being considered dangerously critical of the English authorities.

BURY, John Bagnell, b. Derry 1861, d. Dublin 1927. Professor of Modern History TCD 1893; Cambridge 1902; wrote mostly on Greek and Roman history, and edited Pindar and Gibbon. Best known works: *History of Rome,* 1899; *History of Greece,* 1900; *Life of St Patrick,* 1905; *The Ancient Greek Historians,* 1909; *A History of Freedom of Thought,* 1914; *A History of the Later Roman Empire from the Death of Theodosius I to the Death of Justinian,* 1923, etc. He was editor of the *Cambridge Ancient History* and one of the most distinguished historians of the century. He favoured the 'accident' theory of history, as against the 'determinism' of a Toynbee or Spengler, and in support of it once quoted (in a paper to the Rationalist Press Association's Annual of 1916) Pascal's famous remark on Cleopatra's nose, that if it had been shorter the whole face of the earth would have changed. As a consequence some writers have credited him with coining the phrase.

BUTLER, Hubert Marshal, b. Kilkenny 1900. Ed. Charterhouse, St John's Oxford. Gentleman-scholar, journalist, traveller. Revived Kilkenny Archaeological Society 1945. Trans. from Russian Leonid Leonov's *The Thief,* 1931, and Chekhov's *The Cherry Orchard,* Old Vic 1934, pub. same year. Review editor *The Bell* 1950. Books: *Ten Thousand Saints: A Study in Irish and European Origins,* Kilkenny 1972, and *Escape from the Anthill* (selected essays on literary and historical themes), Mullingar 1985.

BUTLER, Richard, b. Granard 1794, d. Trim 1862. Ed. Kilkenny, Reading, Oxford. Vicar of Trim 1819-62. Dean of Clonmacnoise 1847. MRIA. Wrote *Notices of Trim Castle,* 1835, 4th ed. 1861. Ed. several Irish Archaeological Society publications. Married Harriet Edgeworth, Maria's half-sister, who compiled 'A Memoir of the Very Rev. Richard Butler', printed privately in 1863.

BUTLER, William Francis, b. Co. Tipperary 1838, d. London 1911. Served in British Army in many African campaigns, becoming major-general, 1893, having received KCB, 1886, for his services in the Sudan under Wolseley. Wrote *The Great Lone Land*, 1872, *The Campaign of the Cataracts*, 1887, and other books, including a life of *Sir Charles Napier*, 1890.

BUTT, Isaac, b. Stranorlar 1813, d. Dublin 1879. Ed. TCD, Bar 1838; QC 1844; founded *Dublin University Magazine* 1833. Opposed O'Connell and in his early political career supported the Union with Great Britain. Changed his views and defended Smith O'Brien in 1848 and many of the Fenians 20 years later. In 1870 founded Home Rule Association or League, which won 60 seats in London Parliament in 1874. Became MP for Youghal and afterwards for Limerick. His methods were too conservative, however, and he was displaced by Parnell. Wrote novels and stories and many political and historical works: *The Handbook of the Land*, 1870, on the land question; *Land Tenure in Ireland; The Problem of Irish Education*, 1875, etc. Fiction includes *The Gap of Barnesmore; Chapters of College Romance;* and *Irish Life in Court and Castle*.

BYRNE, Donn, b. US 1889, d. 1928. Of Irish parents, his work is so dominated by Irish themes and attitudes that he requires a place here. It has been described as 'ersatz' but this is unjust. At its best it contains great power, marred by a neurotic sentimentality which is at times powerful in its own right. He wrote several factual works and some remarkable novels of which *Brother Saul* is a serious attempt to understand the kind of man Saint Paul may have been, whether or not one agrees. Other novels include *Destiny Bay*, 1928; *The Power of the Dog*, 1929; *The Golden Coat*, 1930.

BYRNE, Miles, b. 1780 Co. Wexford, d. Paris 1862. United Irishman, fought at Vinegar Hill in the '98 Rising, and went on the run in the Wicklow Mountains. Worked as clerk in a Dublin timber yard from 1799-1803, when he met Robert Emmet. Emmet sent him to Paris to support Robert's brother Thomas Addis, the United Irishmen's Agent to Napoleon. His efforts resulted in creation of the Irish Legion and after the collapse of Emmet's conspiracy Byrne remained as lieutenant and later captain with the Legion throughout the Napoleonic campaigns of 1804-15. His experiences are set out in *Memoirs of Miles Byrne*, 3 vols, Paris 1863.

BYRNE, Seamus, b. Dublin 1904, d. Dublin 1968. Practised law for several years in Leitrim. Imprisoned 1940 for IRA involvement but released nine months later after three-week hunger strike. Plays include *Design for a Headstone*, Abbey 1950, and *Little City*, Dublin Theatre Festival 1964.

C

CABALL, John, b. Tralee 1909, Ed. CBS and UCD. Headmaster in Tralee. Widely travelled in Europe. Novel: *The Singing Swordsman – The Story of Pierce Ferriter*, Monyihan, Dublin 1953. Play: *The Rose of Tralee*.

CADDELL, Celia Mary, b. Co. Meath 1813, d. 1877. A life-long invalid. Wrote for Catholic periodicals, and several novels. *Blind Agnes*, 1855, and *Nellie Netterville*, 1867, were translated into French and Italian.

CAIRNES, John Elliot, b. Co. Louth 1823, d. Blackheath 1875. The son of a brewer and intended for the family business, he insisted against his father's will in going to TCD. In 1856 appointed Whately Professor of Political Economy and in 1857 published *Character and Logical Method of Political Economy;* 1859 appointed to chair of Political Economy and Jurisprudence, Galway, and there wrote his influential *The Slave Power,* 1862. This book did much to persuade British opinion to support the North against the South in the American Civil War. It made his reputation and in 1866 he was called to the chair of Political Economy at University College, London. *Essays on Political Economy, Theoretical and Applied,* 1873, and *Some Leading Principles of Political Economy newly Expounded,* 1874, were his last major works. In 1860 a hunting accident had broken his health and was the cause of his death at 52. In economics he followed his friends Mill and Ricardo but brought a fresh and powerful mind to the subject and deserves attention on his own account.

CALLANAN, Jeremiah John (sometimes Joseph), b. Cork 1795, d. Lisbon 1829. At Maynooth until 1816, then entered TCD. Too poor to continue there, enlisted in British Army. Bought out and became assistant to Dr Maginn, who introduced his poems to Blackwood. Spent several years travelling throughout Ireland in search of ballads and legends, but his MSS of these were lost. Went to Lisbon as a tutor and died there. His only work published during his lifetime, apart from poems in *Blackwood's Magazine,*was *Gougane Barra*, 1826. *The Recluse of Inchidoney and other poems* appeared 1830, *The Lay of Mizen Head* in 1859; and his collected poems, 1861.

CAMPBELL, Lady Colin, neé Blood, b. Co. Clare 1861, d. London 1911. At 15 wrote the first book to be illustrated by Kate Greenaway.

CAMPBELL, Joseph (sometimes Seosamh Mac Cathmhaoil), b. Belfast 1879, d. 1944. Ed. locally. Contributed to the Ulster Literary Theatre in its early days, 1904 onwards, and to the contemporary journal *Uladh*. Spent much time collecting Ulster traditional songs, translating and setting them to music. Many of these, such as 'My Lagan Love', have become concert classics. Went to London and became Secretary of Irish National

Literary Society. Had already published several volumes of songs and poetry, *The Garden of the Bees*, Belfast and Dublin, 1905; *The Rush Light*, Dublin 1906; and in London he published *The Manchild*, 1907. Before the First World War he returned to Ireland and settled in County Wicklow. A play, *Judgement*, was performed at the Abbey 1912, and more poetry *Earth of Cualann* published in Dublin 1916, just after the Rising. Of pronounced Republican sympathies, he became a county councillor at the time of the Treaty, and spoke out strongly against the jobbery and corruption he saw springing up in the infant Free State. At the outbreak of the Civil War he was arrested and interned for two years. In 1923 he emigrated to New York, embittered by his treatment, and remained there and in Fordham University until 1935, when he returned to Wicklow, settling on a small farm near Glencree. He died there in 1944. His collected poetry was published as *Poems of Joseph Campbell* in Dublin, 1963.

CAMPBELL, Michael, 4th Baron Glenavy, brother to 3rd Baron, b. Dublin 1924, d. London 1984. Ed. St Columba's, TCD; Bar; journalist in London. Novels: *Peter Perry*, 1956 (trans. Italian); *Oh, Mary, this London*, 1959; *Across the Water*, 1961; *The Princess in England*, 1964; all repub. NY; *Lord Dismiss Us*, 1967, a novel of school life; *Nothing Doing*, 1970.

CAMPBELL, Patrick, 3rd Baron Glenavy, b. Dublin 1913, d. Cannes 1980. Ed. Rossall and Oxford, and also Germany and the Sorbonne. Served in Irish Navy 1941-44, journalist on *Irish Times* 1944-47, and afterwards on many London papers, principally as a humorous columnist. Has published many books, mainly of his collected newspaper pieces, but reached his widest public on BBC television, revealing a wit that was refreshing for being based on humanity rather than cruelty. Books: *A Long Drink of Cold Water*, 1950; *A Short Trot With a Cultured Mind*, 1952; *Life in Thin Slices*, 1954; *Patrick Campbell's Omnibus*, 1956; *Come Here Till I Tell You*, 1960; *Constantly in Pursuit*, 1962; *How to Become a Scratch Golfer*, 1963; *Brewing Up in the Basement*, 1963; *The P-p-penguin Patrick Campbell*, 1965 (the title based on his stammer, made famous on TV); *Rough Husbandry*, 1965; *The Highspeed Gas Works*, 1970; *35 Years on the Job*, 1973; and many others.

CAMPION, John Thomas, b. Kilkenny 1814, d. *c.* 1890. Practised as a doctor locally and contributed to *The Nation, The United Irishman, The Irish Felon*, etc. Wrote a number of historical novels of which *The Last Struggles of the Irish Sea Smugglers*, Glasgow 1869, is of particular interest.

CANNING, Bernard John, b. 1932. Ordained 1956. Is press officer in diocese of Paisley, Scotland. Works include *St James's, Renfrew 1903-1963. Diamond Jubilee*, 1963; *Padraig H. Pearse and Scotland*, 1979; *The Living Stone: St Aloysius', Springburn 1882-1982*, 1982.

CANNING, George, b. Garvagh 1730, d. 1771. Ed. TCD. Disinherited by his father, went to London and was called to English Bar 1764. Married in 1768 and died broken by various misfortunes. *Horace's first Satire, modernised,* 1762; and *Poems,* 1767. His son George became Prime Minister of England in 1827.

CANNY, Nicholas Patrick, b. 1944. Ed. UCD and Pennsylvania. MRIA. Now Professor of Modern History UCG. *The Elizabethan Conquest of Ireland,* Sussex 1976; *The Upstart Earl: A Study of the Social and Mental World of Richard Boyle, First Earl of Cork 1566-1643,* Cambridge 1982.

CANTILLON, Richard, b. Co. Kerry *c.* 1680, d. London 1734, murdered by his cook. His fame rests on one book, *Essai sur la Nature du Commerce en General,* 1755, published either in Holland or Paris, supposedly translated from English. A very poor English translation followed in 1759. The Essay was probably written in Paris about 1725. Cantillon was at the time a banker there, and made a fortune from the Mississippi speculations. With his fortune he retired to London, bringing with him a Frenchman as cook. In 1734 he dismissed this man for some fault, and a few days later the Frenchman returned to murder Cantillon, and rob and set fire to the house. He was never caught.

The Essay is in some senses the earliest scientific treatment of Economics, earning C. the title of the Father of Political Economy. It advances the theory that currency is a measure of wealth and not wealth itself; that wealth is simply production, and that only agriculture yields a true surplus over the costs of production. The Essay had immense influence on later economists such as Quesnay, and the Physiocrats.

CARBERY, Ethna, pseud. of Anna MacManus, neé Johnston. b. Ballymena, Co. Antrim 1866, d. 1911. Wrote many poems for *The Nation, United Ireland,* etc. Edited and wrote for the *The Shan van Vocht,* a Belfast magazine, 1896-99. Married Seumas MacManus the poet. Poetry: *The Four Winds of Eirinn,* Dublin 1902. Collected short stories: *The Passionate Hearts,* Dublin 1903, and *In the Celtic Past,* Dublin 1904.

CAREY, Matthew, b. Dublin 1760, d. Philadelphia 1839. Journalist and controversialist, founded the *Pennsylvania Herald,* 1785, and in 1795 published the first United States' Atlas, under the title *Carey's American Atlas,* a valuable and popular work. In 1819 wrote *Vindiciae Hibernicae, or Ireland Vindicated,* an attempt to counter the biased histories of Borlase, Hume and others.

CARLETON, William, b. Co. Tyrone 1794, d. Dublin 1869. His father was a poor tenant farmer, Gaelic speaking and with a rich knowledge of legends and stories. Mary Carleton, William's mother, also Gaelic speaking, was a well-known singer in the district. The youngest of 14 children, William hoped to become a priest, and picked up some exotic learning from many hedge schoolmasters. But money failed, the family was evicted, and William joined the Ribbonmen in 1813. Big, wild, a great drinker and womaniser, he was torn for years between his passion for education and the priesthood, and quite different passions. Failing to become either priest or hedge schoolmaster, and turned out of doors by a succession of relatives, he set out from Ulster for Dublin, via Lough Derg, Mullingar and Maynooth, 'a tall, gaunt, gawkish looking young man'. On the road he gathered more stories and characters who were to fill his books over the next 40 years. In 1819, travelling through Louth, he saw the bodies of Ribbonmen hanging on gibbets 'like black fruit', and learned that they were hanged there for murdering Catholic peasants who had refused to join the Society. Years later he told their story in *Wildgoose Lodge,* with its ghastly descriptions of children spitted on pitchforks and women slaughtered. Wherever he went the roads were full of evicted peasants, victims of famine, pilgrims, tricksters and story-tellers. It was a fine if terrible apprenticeship. He reached Dublin hungry, bitter over his reception in Maynooth, and by the Jesuits of Clongowes, and ready for any step that led to food and shelter. Falling in love with a Protestant girl, Jane Anderson, niece of Fox the proselytiser, he married her and became a Protestant. The Erasmus Schools employed him briefly, sent him to Mullingar where he was gaoled for debt, and then to Carlow where he lost his schoolmastership for unknown offences. Returning to Dublin in 1826 he fell in with Caesar Otway, a gaunt, mad zealot who edited the *Christian Examiner,* and wanted information about Popish abominations and superstitions. Carleton supplied it, found that he could write as fluently as he could talk, and began to pour his genius into the narrow bigotry of the *Examiner,* bursting its bounds in the process. Here appeared the first of his *Traits and Stories of the Irish Peasantry* later published in 5 volumes in Dublin, 1830-33.

In 1831 he left the *Examiner,* already famous, and began writing for anyone who would pay him: Tories, Nationalists, Unionists, Young Irelanders, skinning the peasantry in one book – *Rody the Rover* or *Parra Sastha* – and flaying the landlords in another, such as *Valentine M'Clutchy.* All three of these appeared in Dublin, in 1845. He was bitterly attacked as a turncoat, a Judas, a hired assassin by each party in turn, particularly when he accepted a Civil List pension of £200 to stop writing for *The Tribune,* a revolutionary paper run by Kevin O'Dogherty.

The point his attackers missed was that his mainspring was neither religion nor politics but the peasant's hunger for security. He farmed his talents as he might have farmed his fields if he had had any, putting in the crop that suited the market. He was a realist and seems almost unique among Irish 19th-century writers for being so. One immense value in his work is that he gives this normally inarticulate peasant's viewpoint, wishing Godspeed to the idealists and damnation to the foreigner while concentrating on getting in the hay. Few writers have ever presented this sordid common sense with more humour and genius than Carleton did. Never really a novelist, his finest work is in the *Traits and Stories,* and in sudden passages of the novels, which are like windows on the dark and secret peasant Ireland of the early 19th century. When he died, his talents were long since drunk into ruin. Major works other than those mentioned above include *Fardorougha, the Miser,* Dublin 1839; *The Black Prophet: A Tale of the Famine,* Belfast 1847; *The Tithe Proctor,* Belfast 1849.

CARLETON, William, son of preceding, b. Dublin *c.* 1830. Emigrated to New Zealand. Several books of verse published in Australia, including *The Warden of Galway,* 1868. Considered then and long afterwards as one of the best 'Australian' poets.

CARNEY, Frank, b. Co. Galway 1902. Ed. Tuam and NUI. Civil servant for many years in the Old Age Pensions Dept which gave him the opportunity to travel widely in rural Ireland. His plays include *They Went by Bus; Peeping Tom,* 1940; and *The Righteous Are Bold,* 1946, his most famous play, and a great Abbey success, often revived.

CARNEY, James, b. Portlaoise 1914. Ed. CBS Synge St, UCD, Bonn. Professor in Dublin Inst. for Adv. Studies. Best known as a scholarly translator and editor of Irish poetry, particularly *Poems on the Butlers,* 1945; *Poems on the O'Reillys,* Dublin 1950; *A Genealogical History of the O'Reillys* (trans. from Irish of Eoghan Ó Raghallaigh the 18th-century poet, see Part 2), 1959; *Early Irish Poetry,* Cork 1965; *Mediaeval Irish Lyrics,* Dublin 1967, rep. 1985. *Studies in Irish Literature & History,* Dublin 1956, rev. 1979; and *The Problem of St Patrick,* Dublin 1961, rep. 1973.

CARPENTER, Andrew, b. Surrey 1943, of Irish descent. Ed. Oxford and UCD. Lecturer in English in Canadian universities and in Portugal. Now lecturer UCD. Founded Cadenus Press in Dublin 1972, to publish limited, scholarly editions of 17th-century Irish and Anglo-Irish texts in a series *Irish Writings from the Age of Swift.* Among those so far published, *Adventure at Siena* by Charles Ford; *Sermon on Predestination* by Archbishop William King; and *Different Styles of Poetry,* being verses by Wentworth Dillon, Fourth Earl of Roscommon, Thomas Parnell, and Jonathan Swift. Own writings include *Place, Personality and the Irish Writer,* Gerrards Cross 1977; *Natural Journey* (poems), Dublin 1975; *The Irish Perspective of Jonathan Swift,* Wuppertal 1978; and *Irish Writings in English – A Guide (1550-1830),* Dublin 1980. Besides publishing and editing the Cadenus Press series, has ed. E. M. Stephen's biography of J. M. Synge, *My Uncle John,* Oxford 1974, and *The Writers: A Sense of Ireland,* Dublin 1980.

CARROLL, Paul Vincent, b. Dundalk 1900, d. Kent 1968. Ed. Dublin and Glasgow. Schoolmaster in Glasgow 1921-37. Director of Glasgow Citizens' Theatre of which he was a co-founder. Winner of many major theatrical awards and honours in America and Ireland. New York Drama Critics' Circle Award 1937 and 1939, Casement Award of Irish Academy of Letters 1934, etc. Plays include *The Watched Pot,* 1931; *Things that are Caesar's,* 1932; *Shadows and Substance,* 1937 (one of his most successful plays); *The White Steed,* 1939; *The Coggerers* and *Kindred,* both 1939; *The Old*

Foolishness, 1940; *The Strings, My Lord, Are False,* 1942; *The Wise Have Not Spoken,* 1944; *The Chuckeyhead Story,* 1950; *Green Cars Go East,* 1951; *The Devil Came from Dublin,* 1952; *The Wayward Saint,* 1955. Considered one of the handful of great dramatists fostered by the Abbey Theatre.

CARSON, Ciaran, b. Belfast 1948. Ed. QUB. Civil servant, teacher and musician; later Traditional Arts officer with the Arts Council of Northern Ireland. Poetry: *The New Estate,* Belfast 1976.

CARTY, James, b. Wexford 1901, d. Dublin 1959. Assistant Librarian National Library. Wrote two bibliographies: *Bibliography of Irish History, 1912-1921,* Dublin 1937; and *Bibliography of Irish History, 1870-1912,* Dublin 1941. He also wrote *Ireland from the Flight of the Earls to Grattan's Parliament,* Dublin 1944; *Ireland from Grattan's Parliament to the Great Famine,* Dublin 1949; and *Ireland from the Great Famine to the Treaty,* Dublin 1951.

CARY, Joyce, pseud. of Arthur Joyce Lunel, b. Derry 1888, d. 1957. Ed. England. In 1912 joined Red Cross unit at front in Balkan War. Then joined the Nigerian Service and was involved in Cameroons campaign 1915-16. Invalided out of Service in 1920, settled in Oxford and began writing, but developed slowly. He was in his mid-forties before his first novel, *Aissa Saved,* was published in 1932. After that he published a novel every second year or so until his death, and by the outbreak of the Second World War was accepted as a major novelist. In 1943 was sent by British government to East Africa to help make a race relations film *Men of Two Worlds,* and in 1946 went to India on a similar mission. Between 1949 and 1955 visited America often on lecture tours. Apart from novels, wrote poetry, short stories, and a volume of autobiography, *A House of Children,* 1941, which won the James Tait Black Memorial Prize. Of the novels, *Mister Johnson,* a compassionate study of an African caught between two worlds, white and black, is one of the best-known, although some critics now find its racial attitudes condescending. *Herself Surprised,* 1941; *To Be a Pilgrim,* 1942, were successful, but *The Horse's Mouth,* 1944, savage portrait of an outrageous artist, made critics consider Cary as one of the most important novelists of his time. *The Moonlight,* 1946; *A Fearful Joy,* 1949; *Prisoner of Grace,* 1952; *Except the Lord,* 1953; and *Not Honour More,* 1955, were his last books.

CASEMENT, Roger, b. Co.Antrim 1864, executed London 1916. British consul 1895-1911, when he acquired fame for exposing the terrible conditions in the Congo and the rubber plantations of South America. Received a knighthood for his public services. In 1913 identified himself with Irish Nationalism, and helped organise the Irish Volunteers. In October 1914 went to Germany to create an Irish Brigade among Irish prisoners of war and to secure German help for the Rising. His attempts achieved little practical result and on his return to Ireland by German submarine he was immediately captured, April 1916. Three months later he was executed for treason in London. To prevent American-Irish intervention on his behalf diaries were circulated purporting to be his, recording gross immoralities over a long period. Argument has raged since as to whether they were forged by his captors, or were genuine. They have been published as *The Black Diaries of Roger Casement*, ed. Maurice Girodias and Peter Singleton Gates, Paris, London, NY 1959. A year earlier his collected writings and poetry were published and edited by Herbert O. Mackey as *The Game Against Europe*, Dublin 1958.

CASEY, John Keegan, b. Mullingar 1846, d. 1870. Son of Catholic peasant farmer. Tradesman's clerk. Joined Fenians and imprisoned 1867. d. of consumption. Had contributed poems to *The Nation*, etc., from the age of 16 onwards. *Wreath of Shamrocks*, 1866; *The Rising of the Moon*, 1869; and *Reliques of J. K. Casey, 1878*.

CASEY, Juanita, b. England 1925, daughter of an Irish tinker, Annie Maloney, who died at her birth. Her father, Jobey Smith, an English gypsy, abandoned her a year later and benefactors sent her to private boarding schools between periods of circus life. Married first an English farmer, then a Swedish sculptor and next an Irish journalist. Short stories, illustrated by herself, *Hath the Rain a Father?* 1966. Poems: *Horse by the River*, Dublin 1968; *Eternity Smith*, 1985. Novels: *The Horse of Selene*, Dublin 1971, rep. 1985; *The Circus*, Dublin 1974.

CASEY, William Francis, b. Capetown 1884, d. London 1957. Ed. Dublin, TCD. Bar 1909. Soon after went to London to work as freelance journalist and then as sporting correspondent for *The Times*. Later became *The Times* foreign correspondent in Washington, Paris and elsewhere, before becoming editor until retirement 1952. Novels: *Zoe*, 1911; *Haphazard*, 1917; and *Private Life of a Successful Man*, 1935. Before leaving Ireland wrote two plays, *The Man Who Missed the Tide* and *The Suburban Grove*, both produced Abbey 1908.

CASEY, Kevin, b. Kells, Co. Meath 1940. Ed. CBS Kells, Blackrock. Married to poet Eavan Boland. Critic, novelist, playwright. Novels: *The Sinner's Bell*, 1968; *A Sense of Survival*, 1974, rep. 1985; *Dreams of Revenge*, 1977.

CASTILLO, John (sometimes Castello), b. 1792 Rathfarnham, d. Pickering 1845. Taken to England in childhood where he turned Protestant and became a celebrated Wesleyan preacher in Yorkshire. Wrote much poetry and was known as the 'Bard of the Dales', his collected poems appearing under that title in London 1850. He wrote mostly in dialect, and his *Poems in the North Yorkshire Dialect* were printed in Middlesborough 1878.

CASTLEREAGH, Viscount Robert Stewart, b. Ulster 1769, d. by suicide, Kent 1822. Notorious in Ireland as 'the executioner in enamel', represser of the Rising of '98 as Chief Secretary for Ireland, and the man who destroyed the Irish Parliament by forcing through the Act of Union in 1800, he has naturally received something less than justice from Irish students of his period. In England as well he has been overshadowed by the more sympathetic figure of Canning, his great rival, and opponent in the famous duel, and by the failure of Walcheren in the same year, 1809. But despite his failures and lack of sympathy with liberal and national aspirations, he was a great Irishman and deserving of attention. On the humane level he was always in favour of Catholic Emancipation, and pushed through the Act of Union only on the understanding that it would be granted as part of the same political deal. When the King's intransigence betrayed him he resigned. On the level of statesmanship he created and held together the Grand Alliance that defeated Napoleon, and was one of the chief architects of the longest peace Europe has known. In creating that peace he insisted on justice, against the popular and royal clamour for a 'Carthaginian peace' that would leave France prostrate. He prevented Prussia from taking Alsace and Lorraine, saying 'Our business is not to collect trophies, but to bring back the world to peaceful habits', and after 1815 was a moderating influence against the increasingly despotic tendencies of the Allies. If there had been any statesman of his influence and stature at Versailles the world would have been spared much. His half-brother Sir Charles Stewart edited his *Correspondence and Despatches,* 12 vols, 1847-53.

CHAIGNEAU, William, b. Dublin, 1709 of Huguenot family, d. Dublin 1781. Served in British Army in Flanders and became army agent in Dublin. Adapted and translated French farces for Tate Wilkinson, but is remembered for his novel *Jack Connor,* published anonymously in 1752, a bawdy, scandalous book, excluded from most works of reference.

CHAMBERS, Anne, b. Mayo 1950. Ed. Castlebar. Senior executive officer Central Bank of Ireland. *Granuaile: The Life and Times of Grace O'Malley (c. 1530-1603),* Dublin 1979; *Chieftain to Knight: Tibbott-ne-Long Bourke (1567-1629), First Viscount Mayo,* Dublin 1983.

CHEASTY, James, b. 1928 Co. Waterford. Ed. locally. Plays: *A Stranger Came,* Dublin 1956; *The Lost Years,* Dublin 1958; *Francey,* Dublin 1962 (trans. Irish 1964); *All Set for Birmingham,* Waterford 1968, pub. Waterford 1970; *Prisoners of Silence,* Dun Laoghaire 1971, pub. Waterford 1971. Novel: *The Captive,* Dublin 1965.

CHERRY, Andrew, b. Limerick 1762, d. 1812. Son of a printer and book-seller. Strolling player in Ireland and England, and an occasional play-wright, for example *The Soldier's Daughter,* 1804; *The Travellers,* 1806; *Peter the Great,* 1807. His main claim on Irish remembrance is for his story 'The Dear Little Shamrock'.

CHESNEY, Charles Cornwallis, b. Co. Down 1826, d. Aldershot 1876. Served in Royal Engineers till forced to retire from active service by ill-health. Became Professor of Military History, Sandhurst, and revolutionised the teaching of military history: *The Waterloo Lectures,*

1861; *Campaigns in Virginia and Maryland*, 1863; *The Tactical Use of Fortresses*, 1868; *The Military Resources of Prussia and France*, 1870 (with a Mr Reeve); and *Essays in Military Biography*, 1874, all became textbooks.

CHESNEY, Francis Rawdon, b. Co. Down 1789, d. 1872. Gazetted Royal Artillery 1805. Spent much of his military life in the Near and Far East, inspecting a proposed route for a Suez Canal in 1829, and exploring a continental route to India via Syria and the Euphrates several times in the 1830s. Wrote *Survey of the Euphrates and Tigris*, 1850; and *Narrative of the Euphrates Expedition*, 1868. Father of Col. Charles Cornwallis C.

CHEYNEY, Peter, pseud. of Major Reginald Evelyn Peter Southhouse Cheyney, b. Co. Clare 1896, d. 1951. Ed. The Mercers School and University of London. Became a law clerk before enlisting 1914. Severely wounded 1916, given special assignment 1917. Published two vols war poetry, *Poems of Love and War*, 1916 and *To Corona and Other Poems*, 1917. In the 1920s was active journalist and writer of lyrics and theatrical monologues. Also wrote in French. Became Editor of *St John's Ambulance Gazette*, 1928-43, and News editor of *Sunday Graphic*, 1933-34. In 1932 formed a private detective bureau, Cheyney Research and Investigations, and this, with his legal knowledge and wartime Intelligence experience gave him the foundations for his immense success as a thriller and crime writer. This success began with *This Man is Dangerous*, 1936,and was confirmed with more than 30 bestsellers in the next 15 years. *Dames Don't Care*, 1937; *Dangerous Curves*, 1939; *You Can't Hit a Woman*, 1940; *Mr Caution and Mr Callaghan*, 1941, introducing his two most famous characters; and the *Dark* series of spy novels, *Dark Duet*, 1942; *Dark Wanton*, 1948, etc.: *Lady Behave*, 1950; and *Ladies Won't Wait*, 1951, were the first English thrillers to adopt the American style. At his peak Cheyney was selling a million and a half copies a year in English alone. Swordsman, criminologist, traveller, sportsman, he was more like a character from Buchan or Sapper than one of his own books. Died after a lengthy illness, still working. His last book, *Velvet Johnnie*, was published in 1952.

CHICHESTER, Frederick Richard, Earl of Belfast. b. Belfast 1827, d. Naples 1853. Ed. Eton. Lectured to working men's clubs in Belfast on 'Poets and Poetry'. Wrote several novels, the best of which is *Two Generations*, 1851. Also published a book on Naples.

CHILDERS, Robert Erskine, b. 1870, d. Dublin 1922. Ed. Haileybury and Cambridge. Served in Boer War and wounded 1900. Brought a cargo of arms from Germany to Howth in his private yacht 1914. British Navy 1914, DSO 1916. In secretariat of Irish Convention 1917; Director of Publicity for Revolutionary Govt 1919-21; Chief Secretary Irish Peace Delegation 1921. He opposed the resulting peace treaty and during the Civil War was arrested for carrying a pistol given him by Michael Collins. He was court martialled, and shot in Beggars' Bush Barracks, 24 November 1922, while his appeal was being considered. He published a book on

Home Rule in 1912, but his literary fame rests on one prophetic thriller, *The Riddle of the Sands,* published in 1910, and foreshadowing the coming war. A military historian and theoretician of some distinction, he wrote vol. 5 *The Times History of War,* and also *War and the Arme Blanche,* 1910, and *German Influence on British Cavalry,* 1911, in both of which he exposed the folly of current British Army reliance on cavalry as an effective counter to machine guns. Unfortunately for many men then alive he was not believed. He also wrote *The Framework of Home Rule,* 1911.

CLARKE, Aidan, b. Hertfordshire 1933. Son of Austin C. Ed. TCD. MRIA. Lecturer in Modern History Magee 1959-65, then TCD. Vice-Provost TCD 1981–. *The Old English in Ireland 1625-1642,* 1966; *The Graces 1625-41,* 1968; chs VI-X of *A New History of Ireland, 1534-1691,* vol. 3, Oxford 1976.

CLARKE, Austin (Augustine Joseph), b. 1896, d. Dublin 1974. Ed. UCD, followed Thomas McDonagh as English lecturer there 1917-21. Won Tail-teann Award for poetry 1932. Foundation member Irish Academy of Letters, became its President 1952-54. Was President of Irish PEN 1939-42, and 1946-49. After the death of Yeats was considered Ireland's greatest living poet. Hon. D. Litt. TCD 1966; Gregory Medal 1968. Lived for many years in Templeogue, Co. Dublin, where he printed much of his own poetry on his own handset press. Many volumes include *Later Poems,* 1961; *Flight to Africa,* 1963; *Mnemosyne Lay in Dust* (an autobiographical poem), 1966. Also wrote novels: *The Bright Temptation,* 1932; and *The Singing Men at Cashel,* 1936; an autobiography in prose, *Twice Around the Black Church,* 1960; and *A Penny in the Clouds,* 1968. His *Collected Plays* were pub. Dublin 1963, and *Collected Poems,* Dublin and Oxford 1974.

CLARKE, Desmond, b. Mayo 1907, d. Mayo 1979. Ed. Dublin. Librarian RDS 1943-74. Past-President Library Association of Ireland. Secretary of Irish PEN 1965-75. Trustee National Library of Ireland. Wrote short stories, but is best known as biographer of minor 18th-century notables. *Thomas Prior, 1681-1751,* Dublin 1951; *Arthur Dobbs Esq., 1689-1765,* London and North Carolina 1958; *The Unfortunate Husbandman,* 1964; *The Ingenious Mr Edgeworth,* 1965; *Three Stories,* Dublin 1973; *Louison: The Life and Loves of Marie Louise O'Morphi,* Belfast 1979. Edited *An Leabharlann,* 1956-65, and *The Changing Face of Irish Literature,* Dublin 1971.

CLARKE, Thomas James, b. Isle of Wight 1857, executed Dublin 1916. Irish parentage, taken to S. Africa in infancy, to Ireland 1867. Went to US 1881 returning 1883 on Clan-na-Gael mission. Arrested that year and sentenced to life imprisonment. Served 15 years. Returned to America 1899, but came back to Dublin 1907 and started a tobacconist and newsagent shop which became a centre for nationalist activity. First signatory of *Proclamation of the Irish Republic.* He had been the Rising's chief planner since 1911. Taken prisoner and shot on 3rd May. *Glimpses of an Irish Felon's Prison Life,* London and Dublin 1922.

CLERKE, Agnes Mary, b. Skibbereen 1842, d. London 1907. Younger sister of Ellen Mary C. the novelist. A fine musician, she was one of the few women to achieve fame as an astronomer. Extraordinarily precocious, she began her *Popular History of Astronomy during the 19th Century,* Edinburgh 1885, when she was only 15, and some chapters in the existing text were written at that age. It became a standard work. She had studied in Italy before moving to London, 1877. In 1888 she was making observations at the Cape of Good Hope and published *System of the Stars,* 1890, and *Problems in Astrophysics,* 1903. She and her sister lived together all their lives and died within a year of one another in London.

CLERKE, Ellen Mary, b. Skibbereen 1840, d. London 1906. Sister of Agnes Mary Clerke the scientist. Novels include *The Flying Dutchman,* 1881; and *Flames of Fire,* 1902. Her *Fable and Song in Italy* was pub. 1899. She also wrote in German and Italian for various European papers.

CLIFFORD, Francis, pseud. of Arthur Leonard Bell Thompson, b. 1917, d. 1975. Ed. Christ's Hospital School. Went to work in Burma in 1930s and remained to serve there in 1939 war. Special Service operations behind the Japanese lines led him to Intelligence work and he finished the war at Special Operations Executive in London. In industry in England after war, and began to write in 1951. Early novels, *Honour the Shrine,* 1953; *The Trembling Earth,* 1955; and *Act of Mercy,* 1960 (filmed), encouraged him to give up industry for full-time writing. In 1965 was considering returning to a regular job as a result of a series of disappointments and disillusions, when his eleventh novel, *The Naked Runner,* was bought by Frank Sinatra for a film. Total receipts before publication estimated at £100,000. Other novels, mostly based on his own espionage and counter-intelligence, include *The Green Fields of Eden; A Battle Is Fought to be Won; The Hunting Ground,* 1964; *The Third Side of the Coin,* 1965; *All Men Are Lonely Now,* 1967; *Another Way of Dying,* 1968; *The Blindside,* 1971; *A Wild Justice,* 1972; *Amigo, Amigo,* 1973; *The Grosvenor Square Goodbye,* 1974; *Drummer in the Dark,* 1976; *Ten Minutes on a June Morning,* 1977; *Desperate Journey,* 1980. All distinguished for a literary style not often found in thrillers.

CLIFFORD, Sigerson, b. Cork 1913, d. Dublin 1985. Ed. CBS, Co. Kerry, he wrote poetry, plays and a reconstruction of the Colleen Bawn murder, *Death Sails the Shannon* (with W. MacLysaght), Tralee. Plays include *The Great Pacificator,* Abbey; *Nano; The Glassy Man; The Wild Colonial Boy.* Poetry: *Travelling Tinkers* (Dolmen Press's first publication, 13 August 1951) and *Lascar Rock,* Dublin; *Ballads of a Bogman,* London and New York. Many scripts and short stories for Radio Éireann and Irish journals.

CLIVE, Kitty, neé Rafter, b. Ulster 1711, d. Strawberry Hill 1785. Began acting in childhood, brought to London and acted at Drury Lane for years with Colley Cibber, Macklin and Garrick. Dr Johnson admired her as an actress, and so did Handel. She married a barrister, George C., and received a pension from Horace Walpole. As well as acting she wrote several pieces for the theatre, of which *The Rehearsal*, 1753, was most popular, and the only one printed.

COBBE, Frances Power, b. Co. Kildare 1822, d. 1904. After her father's death in 1857, left Ireland and travelled in Italy and Asia. She met Mary Carpenter, the reformer, and settling with her in Bristol, joined in her work for the establishment of Industrial Schools and improved conditions for young criminals. She also worked for women's suffrage and against vivisection. Her many books include *Friendless Girls*, 1861; *Criminals, Idiots, Women and Minors*, 1869, *Darwinism in Morals*, 1872; an *Autobiography*, 1894.

COCKBURN, Patricia Evangeline Anne, née Arbuthnot, b. Rosscarbery 1914. Worked on *The Week* for her 2nd husband, writer and journalist Claud C., as well as for Royal Geographical Society in Africa and Asia. Artist in sea-shell collages. Lives near Waterford. Books: *The Years of the Week; Figure of Eight* (autobiography), 1985.

COFFEY, Brian, b. Dublin 1905. Son of late President of UCD. Lived in Paris 1930s in James Joyce circle, then in US and England. Close friend, literary editor and executor of Denis Devlin. Poetry: *Selected Poems*, 1971; *Dice Thrown Never Will Annul Chance*, 1965, a trans. of Mallarmé; *Death of Hektor*, 1984; all pub. Dublin. *Irish University Review 5*, 1975, intro. James May, was a special issue devoted to his life and work.

COFFEY, Charles, b. Dublin *c.* 1700, d. London 1745. A cripple from birth, moved to London and wrote very successfully for the theatre. In his first piece *The Beggar's Wedding*, 1729, he introduced Irish traditional tunes onto the London stage for the first time. *The Devil to Pay*, 1731, was immensely popular and continued in the repertories and revivals for more than a hundred and fifty years. It was still being produced in 1900. Others include *A Wife and No Wife*, 1732; *The Boarding School*, 1933; *The Merry Cobbler*, 1735; and *The Devil Upon Two Sticks*, 1745.

COFFEY, George, b. Dublin 1857, d. Dublin 1916. Best known work *Origins of Prehistoric Ornament in Ireland*, 1897. Also wrote an interesting volume, *New Grange*, Dublin 1912; and *The Bronze Age in Ireland*, Dublin 1913.

COFFEY, Tom, b. Co. Clare 1925. Ed. Ennis, worked as librarian, entertainments officer in a holiday camp, tutor and many other jobs. Acted and sang in amateur dramatics, and began writing in Irish, winning two Oireachtas awards in 1954-55. Plays in English include *Stranger Beware*, Abbey 1959; *Anyone Could Rob a Bank*, Abbey 1960; *The Long Sorrow*, Abbey 1961; *Them*, Eblana Theatre 1962; *Gone Tomorrow*, Gate Theatre (winner of Irish Life Award) 1965; *Ties* and *The Call*, Abbey 1966. Many televised. A television play *Ship in the Night*, broadcast 1965 by RTE.

COGAN, James Joseph, b. Co. Wicklow 1875, d. Dublin 1941. Ed. Terenure College, UCD and Rome. Went to Australia as 'Bush missioner' 1900. In 1908 his novel *Old Irish Hearts and Homes*, Melbourne, had an immense success in Australia, and was widely read and translated in Europe.

COLE, Dorothea, see BOWEN, Elizabeth.

COLGAN, John, b. Donegal or Derry 1592, d. 1657 (?). Ed. Louvain, entered Franciscan Order 1618. Taught at Louvain and was then asked to prepare a history of Irish Saints. based on materials gathered by Fr Hugh Ward, much of it in Irish and Old Irish. *Acta Sanctorum Hiberniae,* Louvain 1645, contained the biographies of saints with feast days in Jan-March period. *Trias Thaumaturga,* Louvain 1647, contained lives of SS Patrick, Brigid and Columba, with material on Irish ecclesiastical antiquities. *Life of Duns Scotus,* Louvain 1655.

COLLINS, William, b. Co. Wicklow *c.* 1740, d. London 1812. Author of a curious *Memoir of George Morland* and *The Story of a Picture.* His son was William Collins the artist, and his grandson was William Wilkie Collins, the novelist.

COLLIS, John Stewart, b. Dublin 1900, d. 1984. Twin brother of Robert C. Ed. Bray, Rugby and abroad. Early life overshadowed by his mother's preference for Robert. Abandoned literary life in London, where he was acquainted with Yeats and Shaw, to devote himself to country life. Books include *Forward to Nature,* 1927; *Farewell to Argument,* 1935; *While Following the Plough,* 1946; *The Triumph of the Tree,* 1950; *Bound upon a Course* (autobiography), 1971; *The Carlyles* (Thomas and Jane), 1971; *The Worm Forgives the Plough,* 1973; *Christopher Columbus,* 1976; and *Living with a Stranger: A Discourse on the Human Body,* 1978.

COLLIS, Maurice Stewart, b. Dublin 1889, d. London 1973. Ed. Rugby, Oxford, but returned to Ireland for holidays, and through his mother was deeply influenced by the Literary Revival in Edwardian Dublin. He also held strong Nationalist opinions. An uncle, Sir George Grierson the Orientalist, turned his mind to the Far East, and he joined the Indian Civil Service. Posted to Burma he rose to District Magistrate of Rangoon by 1928. Sympathy with Burmese Nationalism threatened his further promotion and he retired to England in 1934 to write. His first book, *Siamese White,* 1934 is a study of the famous Samuel White, Burmese traveller and adventurer. Other biographical works: *Discovery of L. S. Lowry,* 1951; *Journey Outward,* 1952; *Into Hidden Burma* and *Land of the Great Image,* 1953; the very successful *Cortes and Montezuma,* 1954, trans. into 6 languages; *Last and First in Burma,* 1956, etc. and *Somerville and Ross,* 1968. His novels include *She was a Queen,* an historical novel; and *Mystery of Dead Lovers.* Brother-in-law to the late Joseph Hone and a close friend of Jack Yeats.

COLLIS, Robert, b. 1900, d. Co. Wicklow 1975. Brother of Maurice and Robert C. Served as a doctor in Africa and looked after refugee children following the Second World War. *The Silver Fleece* (autobiography), 1936; *Straight On,* 1947, with Han Hogerzeil, describes the liberation of Belsen Camp. C. adopted five orphan children from the camp, and in 1958 married Han H., a Dutch lawyer and fellow rescue-worker in Belsen; *The Ultimate Value* (refugee children), 1951; *A Doctor's Nigeria,* 1960; a second autobiography, *To Be a Pilgrim,* 1975.

COLUM, Mary, b. 1885, d. 1957. Taught in Patrick Pearse's school in Dublin. Married Padraic Colum 1912. Spent much of the remainder of her life in America. *Life and the Dream,* Dublin 1928, NY 1947, an autobiography; *From these Roots,* 1938, essays on modern literature. Best-known work, in collaboration with husband, *Our Friend James Joyce,* 1959.

COLUM, Padraic, b. Longford 1881, d. Connecticut 1972. One of the first Abbey playwrights, as well as a fine poet. His play *Broken Soil,* 1903, turned the infant theatre away from Yeats' Celtic visions towards peasant reality. *The Land,* 1905, and *Thomas Muskerry,* 1910, are his best known plays. In 1914 he went to America. In 1924 visited Hawaii at the invitation of the authorities there to investigate folklore and turn Hawaiian legends into stories for local children. Spent much of his life in America as lecturer and working for publishers. Major books include *Collected Poems,* 1932; *The Legend of St Columba; The Story of Lowry Maen,* a narrative poem, 1937; *Ten Poems,* 1959; *Our Friend James Joyce* written with Mary Colum, 1959; *The Poet's Circuits,* 1960; *Wild Earth; Dramatic Legends,* etc.. A revised and enlarged 3rd edition of *Irish Elegies,* Dublin 1963 (first ed. 1958). His two most famous poems are, for the general public, 'The Old Woman of the Roads' and 'She Moved Through the Fair'. Also wrote on travel, criticism, and biography: *A Half Day's Ride,* 1932, on Corsican travels; and *Ourselves Alone: The Story of Arthur Griffith & the Origin of the Irish Free State,* NY 1959 (the main title being a translation of the Irish slogan *Sinn Féin*).

COMERFORD, Maire, b. 1893, d. Dublin 1982. Wounded and imprisoned during Civil War she remained a passionate Republican and enemy of the Treaty and all that stemmed from it until her death. Her lasting memorial is one small but invaluable book, *The First Dáil,* Dublin 1969.

COMYN, James, Kt, b. Dublin 1921. Son of James C., later a QC. Ed. The Oratory, Oxford. President Oxford Union. English Bar 1942; Irish Bar 1945. High Court Judge; Chairman Bar Council England; QC. Lives Tara, Co. Meath, a keen farmer and writer of books on trials: *Dear Friends at Court,* 1973; *Irish at Law,* 1981, rep. 1983; and *Lost Causes,* 1982.

CONCANEN, Matthew, b. 1701, d. 1749. Among the earliest of the tribe of virulent Irish journalists to invade London. Was foolish enough to attack Pope, who lashed him, among many others, in the *Dunciad.* Became Attorney-General in Jamaica in return for his services to the government as a journalist, 1732, retired in 1748 to London, and died of consumption there. His work is interesting, particularly *A Match at Football*, a mock heroic poem, 1721. His best service to Irish letters was the making of the first anthology of Irish verse, much of it translated from the Gaelic. It appeared as *Miscellaneous Poems, Orig; and Trans; by Several Hands*, 1724.

CONCANNON, Helena, neé Walsh, b. Co. Derry 1878, d. 1952. Married Thomas C. 1906, a prominent figure in Gaelic League. She became a member of Dáil Éireann 1933, and Senator 1938. Wrote many books of a religious flavour, and much history. *Irish Nuns in Penal Days*, 1931; *Blessed Oliver Plunkett*, Dublin 1935, etc.

CONDON, Edward O'Meagher, b. Cork *c.* 1835, d. New York 1915. Emigrated to US where he fought in Civil War, and acquired US citizenship. Returned to Ireland as Fenian organiser with many other war veterans. Was in the famous attack on the prison van in Manchester, designed to release Fenian prisoners. Caught and condemned to death, was saved by his US citizenship. Served 10 years in prison, returned to US where he wrote *The Irish Race in America*, NY 1887. Became a Constitutionalist in old age.

CONGREVE, William, b. England 1670, d. 1729. Only connected with Ireland by the accident of his father's military service there. Ed. Kilkenny and TCD, being Swift's fellow student at both places. He remained friendly with Swift throughout his life. His comedies, *The Old Bachelor*, 1693, *The Double Dealer*, 1694, *Love for Love*, 1695, and *The Way of the World*, 1700, have a verbal firework quality that in some ways resembles Wilde and Shaw, and it might be possible to claim that they owed something to Irish influence. One of the great figures of the miscalled 'Restoration Drama', and indeed of English literature, he was never a professional writer, being eager instead to be a gentleman, and after 1700 and the comparative failure of *The Way of the World* (ironically his best play), he ceased writing.

CONNELL, Jim, b. Kilskyre, Co. Meath 1852, d. London 1929. Claimed to have been educated at least partly in one of the last hedge schools. Had a varied career as sheep farmer, labourer, journalist and self-taught lawyer. Involved in Irish revolutionary movement; later moved to London, joining the Social Democrat Federation, and becoming Secretary of the Workmen's Legal Friendly Society. Wrote a number of political works, and some rousing songs, of which one, 'The Red Flag', became world famous as the socialist anthem. Originally set to an Irish tune, 'The White Cockade', the British Labour movement changed the tune many years later to that of 'Tannenbaum', but the words remain as Connell wrote them. Also wrote *The Confessions of a Poacher; The Truth about the Game Laws; Brothers at Last;* and *Socialism and the Survival of the Fittest*.

CONNELL, Vivian, b. Cork 1905, d. Co. Wicklow 1981. Distinguished man of letters; work includes plays, *The Nineteenth Hole of Europe* and

Throng o' Scarlet, etc. but is principally known as a novelist, beginning with the famous *The Chinese Room,* 1943. Others include *Hounds of Cloneen,*1951; *September in Quinze,* 1952; *Peacock Is a Gentleman,* 1953; *Corinna Lang, Goodbye,* 1954; and *The Naked Rich.*

CONNELLAN, Owen, b. Co. Sligo 1800, d. Dublin 1869. Claimed descent from Laoghaire MacNeill, King of Ireland, and Mayo chiefs. An Irish scholar and one of the founders of the Irish Revival, he had some of the eccentricities as well as many of the great virtues of 19th-century scholarship. He was, for example, convinced that Irish and Etruscan were identical. Nevertheless his *Practical Grammar of the Irish Language,* 1844, has value, particularly for its North Connaught peculiarities. *The Annals of Ireland,* 1846, translated from the *Annals of the Four Masters,* was superseded by O'Donovan's great work. In 1860 pub. text and translation of *Imtheacht na Tromdhaimhe.*

CONNER, Rearden (Patrick Rearden Connor), b. Dublin 1907. Ed. Presentation Bros Cork. Went to London 1924 and worked as a landscape gardener. His first novel *Shake Hands with the Devil,* 1933, was a Literary Guild selection in US. Filmed in Dublin 1960. Wrote many novels, and under the pen-name 'Peter Malin', several boys' books. Main books: *Rude Earth,* 1934; *Salute to Aphrodite,* 1935; *Time to Kill,* 1936; *Men Must Live,* 1937; *The Sword of Love,* 1938; *The Devil Among the Tailors,* 1947; *My Love to the Gallows,* 1949; *Hunger of the Heart,* 1950; *The Singing Stone,* 1951; *The House of Cain,* 1952; also many short stories.

CONNOLLY, James, b. Glasgow 1868 of Irish parents. Executed Dublin 1916. As a boy tramped the roads, worked as labourer's boy, printer's devil and pedlar. Educated himself and in 1894 founded Irish Socialist Republican Party. In 1903 went to America, returning to Europe 1910. Trade union organiser, Belfast 1911-13. Joined Larkin in Dublin for Great Strike of 1913 and organised Citizen Army 1914. This was absorbed into the larger Volunteer force, created by the Nationalists, the two revolutionary armies and their leaders forming a close and loyal alliance. Nevertheless their fundamental aims were different and had Connolly survived, as de Valera did, both the War of Independence and the Civil War might have taken different directions. As it was, the Marxist element in the Republican movement was suppressed by the Nationalists and has almost vanished from the text-books. The pathetic Workers and Peasant Soviets, set up in Munster Creameries during the Civil War period, were in some ways Connolly's epitaph, rather than the present Irish Labour Movement.

Many legends surround Connolly's share in the planning of the Easter Rising of 1916. He is supposed to have been kidnapped on Pearse's orders, a few days before the Rising, in order to prevent his breaking the revolutionary alliance, and to have been released only on giving guarantees of continued loyalty to the Nationalists. This has been strongly contradicted, but obviously there were violent internal disagreements among all the leaders as to tactics and even strategy. In the event Connolly was appointed commandant of the force which occupied the GPO, was severely wounded and finally surrendered in order to save his men. He was executed in a chair on 12 May. His writings on labour and revolutionary socialism include *Erin's Hope; The End and the Means*, Dublin 1897; *Labour in Irish History*, Dublin 1910; and *The Reconquest of Ireland*, Dublin 1915. He also founded several trade union and Socialist journals: *The Harp, The Irish Worker*, and *The Worker's Republic*. In 1916 his play, *Under Which Flag?*was produced in Dublin. Apparently never printed. *Legacy and Songs of Freedom* was pub. 1917. A major figure in world Socialism.

CONNOR, Bernard (sometimes O'Connor), b. Kerry *c*. 1666, d. London 1698. Ed. privately, being a Catholic and so debarred from TCD. In 1686 at University of Montpellier and then Paris. Took MD, Rheims, 1691, gaining fame as anatomist. Travelled in N. Italy, S. Germany, Austria and Poland, becoming court physician to King John Sobieski. In 1694 travelled as doctor with king's daughter on her marriage journey to Bavaria. Continued to London where he conformed to Church of England requirements and became Fellow of Royal Society and lecturer at Oxford. Published *Evangelium Medici*, 1697, offering rational explanations of biblical miracles, and *A History of Poland*, 2 vols, 1698, long a standard work. Only the 1st volume is wholly Connor's, the 2nd being largely the work of Savage. The same year he caught a fever and died, doubly consoled for his doubts by Church of England and Catholic rites.

CONNOR, Elizabeth, b. Clonmel. Daughter of Judge Troy. Plays for the Abbey: *Mount Prospect*, 1940; *Swans and Geese*, 1941; *An Apple a Day*, 1942; *The Dark Road*, 1947. Publications include *Dead Stars' Light*, 1938. Since 1955 has written under pseud. 'Una Troy'.

CONWAY, Tom, see KEENAN, Thomas Patrick.

CONYERS, Minnie Dorothea Spaight, b. Limerick 1871, d. Limerick 1949. Daughter of Col. J. Blood Smyth. Husband Lt. Charles Conyers d. 1915; remarried Capt. Joseph White 1917. Wrote several popular, romantic Anglo-Irish novels, most of them centred on hunting and the difficulties of buying and selling horses: *Peter's Pedigree*, 1904; *The Boy, Some Horses, and a Girl*, 1908; *The Strayings of Sandy*, 1909; *Sally*, 1912; *Old Andy*, 1914; *A Mixed Pack*, 1915, etc.

CONYNGHAM, David Power, b. Killenaule *c*. 1825, d. 1883. Cousin of Charles Kickham, with whom he participated in 1848 Rising. Fought in American Civil War, rising to rank of major. Became journalist and wrote several novels, sometimes using pseud. 'Allen H. Clington'. Novels include *Sarsfield*, Boston 1871; *The O'Mahony, Chief of the Comeraghs*, NY 1879.

COOGAN, Timothy Patrick, b. Co. Dublin 1935. Ed. Blackrock. Editor *Irish Press*. His *Ireland Since the Rising*, 1966, is interesting as one of the first attempts by an historian born long after Independence was achieved to assess the results, not as a partisan but as an heir. *The I.R.A.*, 1970, rev. 1980; *The Irish: A Personal View*, 1975; *On the Blanket* (account of campaign for political status by IRA prisoners in Northern Ireland), Swords 1980.

COOKE, Emma, b. Portarlington, Co. Laois, 1934. Lives Limerick. Short stories: *Female Forms*, 1980. Novel: *A Single Sensation*, 1982. Both pub. Swords.

COOKE, William, b. Cork *c.* 1740, d. London 1824. In London knew Goldsmith and Burke, and wrote *Memoirs of Charles Macklin*, 1804.

COOPER, Bryan Ricco, b. India 1884, d. 1930. MP for S. Co. Dublin 1910, strong Unionist and supporter of Carson. Fought at Gallipoli, later publishing *The Tenth (Irish) Division in Gallipoli*, 1918. Appointed Press Censor in Dublin he was sickened by Black and Tan excesses and swung over to support Sinn Fein and the Republicans. But in the Civil War disputes he accepted the Treaty and the Free State, becoming a member of Dáil Éireann 1923. In 1920 he had published his interesting *A Rebel's Diary*.

COPE, Joan Penelope (Lady Grant), b. Paris 1926. Ed. privately. As a child wrote a best seller *Bramshill – being the memoirs of Joan Penelope Cope,* 1938. *Bygone Flowers,* 1940. Translated *Arabic Andalusian Casidas* from the Spanish, 1954, preface by Roy Campbell. Contributor to *Time and Tide* etc. Descended from old Dublin weaving family, Cope Street being named after an ancestor.

COPE, Paddy the, see GALLAGHER, Patrick.

CORKERY, Daniel, b. Cork 1878, d. 1964. Ed. by Presentation Brothers, Cork and UCC. Professor of English UCC 1931-47, elected to Irish Senate 1951. The greatest single influence on Irish prose writing of today, unhappily overshadowed by such pupils as Frank O'Connor. Both as teacher and writer shaped several generations of Irish novelists and short-story writers. His critical work was nationalist in vision, and his fiction was strictly provincial, which deepened its value but has unfortunately narrowed its appeal outside Ireland. His novel *The Threshold of Quiet* appeared in 1917. His plays include *The Labour Leader,* 1919; *The Yellow Bittern,* 1920; *The Onus of Ownership; Fohnam the Sculptor.* His collections of short stories are *A Munster Twilight,* 1916; *The Hounds of Banba,* 1920; *The Stormy Hills,* 1929; and *Earth out of Earth,* 1939. *The Hidden Ireland,* Dublin 1925, repub. several times, is essential reading for any student of Irish literature or life in the 18th century. It is the only book in English which shows truly what was lost in the great winter of Gaelic culture. Also, *Synge and Anglo-Irish Literature,* Cork 1931; *The Fortunes of the Irish Language,* Dublin 1954.

CORRY, John, b. Co. Louth *c.* 1770, date of death unknown, but probably in London after 1825. Besides many country and local histories, and lives of *Cowper, Joseph Priestley, George Washington,* etc., wrote some absorbing and valuable studies of turn-of-the-century London: *A Satirical View of London,* 1801, that went into many editions, and *The English Metropolis; or, London in 1820,* 1820. His *History of Lancashire,* 2 vols, came out 1825. Also *Poems,* 1797, and several novels including *The Suicide,* 1805.

COSGRAVE, Patrick, b. Dublin 1941. Ed. UCD and Cambridge. Political commentator. Married Ruth Dudley Edwards: now separated. Was Telefís Éireann's first London correspondent, and worked in Conservative Party's research department; 1975-79, was special adviser to Mrs Margaret Thatcher. Published *The Public Poetry of Robert Lowell,* 1970; *Churchill At War,* vol. 1, 1974; vol. 2 1979; *Cheyney's Law* (a thriller), 1977; *Margaret Thatcher: A Tory and Her Party,* 1978; *The Three Colonels,* 1979; *R. A. Butler, an English Life,* 1981; *Thatcher: The First Term,* 1985.

COSTELLO, Louisa Stuart, b. Ireland 1799, d. Boulogne 1870. Taken to France in childhood she became one of the most popular travel and historical writers of her time. *Memoirs of Eminent Englishwomen,* 1844; *Bearn and the Pyrenees,* 1844; *The Rose Garden of Persia,* 1845; *A Tour to and from Venice,* 1846, were among her most successful books. She was also a painter, studying in Paris after 1814, and when her father died early she helped to support the family by painting miniatures. She made it possible for her brother Dudley to remain at Sandhurst, and after he left the army on half-pay in 1828 he helped her by illustrating some of her books, particularly *The Rose Garden.* Between them they drew fashionable attention to the beauties of mediaeval illuminations, copying many of them in Paris and the British Museum themselves. Dudley became foreign correspondent to the *Daily News* and also wrote many popular travel books. His *Tour through the Valley of the Meuse,* 1845, remained in circulation into the present century.

COULTER, John, b. Belfast 1888, d. 1976. Emigrated to Canada 1936, becoming important influence in the theatre, with *Family Portrait,* produced Toronto 1937; *Holy Manhattan,* Toronto 1941, and *The Drums Are Out,* 1948. *Deirdre of the Sorrows,* retold for music by Healey Willan, pub. Toronto 1944, new ed. 1965. Also wrote biography of *Churchill,* Toronto 1944; a novel, *Turf Smoke,* Toronto 1945 (adapted from *Holy Manhattan),* and poetry, *The Blossoming Thorn,* Toronto 1946. In the 1970s his play *God's Ulsterman,* Toronto 1974, and the trilogy *Rich,* Toronto 1975, were given their first major productions.

COUSINS, James Henry Sproull, b. Belfast 1873, d. India 1956. Ed. Belfast. Private secretary to Lord Mayor of Belfast before moving to Dublin in 1897, where he acted minor parts for the newly formed Irish National Theatre Society. In 1905 taught English in Harcourt Street High School. In 1913 went to India as teacher. Had already written poetry in Ireland, *Ben Madigan and Other Poems,* Belfast 1894; *The Voice of One,* 1900; *The Quest,* Dublin 1906; *Etain the Beloved and Other Poems,* Dublin

1912; and continued to write in India, being published in Madras. Further volumes of poetry include *Sea-Change*, 1920, and *Collected Poems, 1894-1940*, also Madras 1940. Other work includes *Heathen Essays*, 1923, and autobiography, *We Two Together*, with Margaret E. Cousins, 1950.

COX, Walter, b. Westmeath 1770, d. 1837. Worked in Dublin as gunsmith, and later as journalist. Travelled in France and America. Suspected of acting as an informer in 1798. Founded *Irish Magazine* and *Asylum of Neglected Biography* in Dublin in early 1800s, and was frequently fined and imprisoned for sedition, scurrility and libel. Persisted in spite of punishment and threats until 1815 when he was granted a pension on condition he left Ireland. Left 1816, and forfeited the pension by returning 1835. Died two years later in presumably deserved poverty. Wrote a play *The Widow Dempsey's Funeral*, Dublin 1822, and a harsh attack on Daniel O'Connell, *The Cuckoo Calendar*, Dublin 1833.

COX, William Trevor, see TREVOR, William.

COYNE, Joseph Stirling, b. Birr 1803, d. London 1868. The son of an officer in the Commissariat. Ed. Dublin. Wrote farces for Theatre Royal in Dublin, and moved to London 1837 with an introduction from William Carleton to Croker. In London wrote for *Bentley's Miscellany*, etc., and also wrote about 60 farces and theatrical pieces, some of which were translated in French and German. His enduring fame is as a co-founder of *Punch*.

CRAIG, Maurice James, b. Belfast 1919. Ed. Castle Park, Shrewsbury, Magdalene College Cambridge, TCD. Inspector of Ancient Monuments with English Ministry of Works 1952-70. Adviser to An Foras Forbartha 1971-75. Hon. Fellow TCD and Royal Institute of the Architects of Ireland. MRIA. Best known as historian of Dublin. *The Volunteer Earl* (The Earl of Charlemont), 1948; *The Dublin City Churches* (with H. A. Wheeler), Dublin 1948; *Dublin 1660-1860*, 1952, rep. Dublin 1969, 1980; *Irish Bookbindings 1600-1800*, 1954 (a remarkable art form in the late 17th and early 18th centuries); *The Personality of Leinster*, Dublin 1961; *Architectural Drawings of Sir John Vanbrugh and Sir Edward Pearce*, (with Howard Colvin), Oxford 1964; ed. *The Life of James Gandon*, 1969; *Ireland Observed* (with the Knight of Glin), Cork 1970; *Classic Irish Houses of the Middle Size*, 1976; *Architecture of Ireland from the Earliest Times to 1880*, 1982. Poetry includes *Black Swans*, 1941; *Some Way for Reason*, 1948.

CRAWFORD, Julia, b. *c.* 1799 Co. Cavan, d. *c.* 1860. Immortal as authoress of the song 'Kathleen Mavourneen', which first appeared in the *Metropolitan Magazine*, London 1830. Published *Irish Songs, Set to Music by F. N. Crouch*, 1840. Also wrote several novels.

CRAWFORD, William, b. Co. Antrim 1739, d. Antrim 1800. Presbyterian minister and supporter of the Volunteer movement. His *Volunteer Sermons*, pub. 1779 and 1780. *History of Ireland*, 1783, is remarkable as being written in the form of letters.

CREAGH, Richard (also Crevagh, Crewe and O Mulchreibe), b. Limerick 1525, d. London 1585. Ed. Louvain. In Limerick as priest 1557-62, when he went to Rome. Appointed Archbishop of Armagh 1564, returning to Ireland that year. Arrested in Drogheda while saying Mass and sent to London in chains. Escaped from Tower of London and reached Louvain. Returned to Ireland via Spain and met Shane O'Neill in Armagh in 1566. Arrested in Connaught and imprisoned in Dublin he again escaped, but was recaptured later in 1567, transferred to London and imprisoned until his death in 1585, possibly by poison. He wrote in Irish (see Part 2), in Latin (an account of his escape from the Tower appearing in Cardinal Moran's *Spicilegium Ossoriensae)*, particularly *Topographia Hiberniae* and *De Lingua Hibernica,* unpublished but preserved in part in the TCD MSS collection. His principal work in English is *An Ecclesiastical History.*

CROFTON, Francis Blake, b. *c.* 1840, d. *c.* 1895. Author of humorous stories centred on 'Major Mendax', a Munchausen character of vast imagination. *The Hairbreadth Escapes of Major Mendax* was the best known.

CROKER, Mrs B. M., daughter of Rev. W. Shepherd, b. Co. Roscommon *c.* 1850, d. 1920. Ed. England, married an English/officer and spent many years in the Far East. Wrote a large number of novels and short stories, more than 40 volumes, including *Proper Pride,* 1882; *A Bird of Passage,* 1886; *A Nine Days' Wonder,* 1905; *Lismoyle,* 1914. Many of her books continued to be reprinted throughout the 1920s and '30s.

CROKER, John Wilson, b. Galway 1780, d. 1857 at Hampton. Some sources give Waterford as birthplace. Became MP for Downpatrick 1807 and a figure in London literature and politics. As First Secretary to the Admiralty 1809-30 he distinguished himself by refusing to sign fraudulent accounts, and to redress the balance defended the Duke of York's case in the scandal following Mrs Clarke's sale of army commissions. His fame today rests on his vicious review of Keats's *Endymion,* but he deserves more attention than that. *A Sketch of the State of Ireland Past & Present,* Dublin 1808, and his diaries published as *The Croker Papers,* 1884, are of great interest. He knew everyone who mattered in London politics, was a client of Wellington and the great Marquis of Hertford (Thackeray's Marquis of Steyne) and was left £21,000 in the latter's will. He was responsible for the erection of Nelson's Column in Dublin, opposed reform but favoured Catholic Emancipation, and foresaw the importance of railways before most contemparies. He was one of the founders and principal contributors to *The Quarterly Review,* along with Scott, Canning, Southey and Lockhart, although he brought little of the 'liberal, conciliatory' tone to it which Scott hoped would be its hallmark. He attacked Lady Morgan in a number of articles which appeared pathological to some contemporaries. Appears as 'Rigby' in Disraeli's *Coningsby* and Macaulay loathed him 'more than cold boiled veal'. Yet personally he seems to have been kind. For example he found a place in the Admiralty for his namesake John Wilson C., and was more than generous to his servants. Other books of his include *Stories for Children from English History*, 1817 (which inspired Scott's *Tales of a Grandfather); Suffolk Papers*, 1823; *Boswell's Johnson*, and *Military Events of the French Revolution of 1830*, both 1831; *Essays on the Early Period of the French Revolution*, 1857; and a history of the guillotine. It was Croker who first applied the label 'Conservative' to the Tory Party.

CROKER, Thomas Crofton, b. Cork 1798, d. London 1854. In youth travelled much in West of Ireland where he collected stories and songs, sending many of the latter to Thomas Moore. Became clerk in the Admiralty in 1818 but returned often to west and south of Ireland. Helped found Camden Society 1839, Percy Society 1840, and the British Archaeological Association 1843. Published *Fairy Legends & Traditions of the South West of Ireland*, 1825; *Legends of the Lakes*, 1829; and *Popular Songs of Ireland*, 1839. The Brothers Grimm translated *Fairy Legends* into German and it went into many editions in English. It was England's first view of Irish folklore and created a deep impression. He wrote two very popular humorous books, *Barney Mahoney*, and *My Village Versus Our Village*.

CROLY, George, b. Dublin 1780, d. London 1860. Ed. TCD. Ordained 1804. Moved to London 1810, became rector of St Stephen's, City of London. Gained a great reputation as a preacher, and also as a poet in the style of Byron and Moore. Poetry includes *Paris in 1815* and *The Modern Orlando*. His novels include *Salathiel*, 1829; *Marston*, 1846.

CROMMELIN, May de la Cherois, b. Co. Down *c*. 1850, d. *c*. 1910. One ancestor, a Huguenot refugee, was the founder of the linen trade in Ulster. She wrote more than 30 novels and many short stories: *Orange Lily and Other Stories*, 1879; *Black Abbey*, 1880; *The Golden Bow*, 1912, etc.

CRONE, Anne, b. Dublin 1915, d. Belfast 1972, of asthma. Teacher and novelist. *Bridie Steen*, NY 1948, rep. 1973 and 1984; *This Pleasant Lea*, NY 1951; *My Heart and I*, 1955.

CRONE, John Smyth, b. Belfast 1858, d. London 1945. Ed. Belfast, practised medicine in London. Founded and edited *Irish Book Lover*, 1909; elected Royal Irish Academy 1916; President Irish Literary Society, London 1918-25. Wrote *A Concise Dictionary of Irish Biography*, Dublin 1928, 2nd ed. 1937; and *Henry Bradshaw, His Life and Works*, Dublin 1931. With F. J. Bigger edited the latter's biographical, topographical and historical writings as *In Remembrance*, Dublin 1927.

CRONIN, Anthony, b. Co. Wexford 1926. Associate editor of *The Bell* and literary editor of *Time and Tide*. *Poems*, 1957 and *The Life of Riley*, 1964, repub. Dingle 1983 (novel). Highly regarded as critic. Cultural advisor to C. J. Haughey when Taoiseach: instigator of Aosdana scheme. Volume of essays, *A Question of Modernity*, 1966, contains his much-praised essay on *Ulysses; Collected Poems, 1950-1973*, Dublin 1973; *Dead as Doornails*, Dublin and London, 1976 (memoir of literary Dublin); *Identity Papers*, Dublin 1979 (novel); *Reductionist Poem*, Dublin 1980; *Heritage Now: Irish Literature in the English Language*, Dingle 1982; *New and Selected Poems*, Dublin 1982, received Marten Toonder Award, 1983; *An Irish Eye*, Dingle 1985 (collected journalism); *Letter to an Englishman* Dublin 1985 (poems).

CROOKSHANK, Anne, b. near Belfast 1927. Keeper of Art for Belfast Museum and Art Gallery (now Ulster Museum). Professor of the History of Art TCD. *Irish Portraits 1600-1860*, 1969, and *The Painters of Ireland c. 1660-1920*, 1978, both with the Knight of Glin; ed., with Eoin O'Brien and Gordon Wolstenholme, *A Portrait of Irish Medicine*, Swords 1984.

CROSS, Eric, b.Newry *c.* 1905, d.Co. Mayo 1980. Famous for one book of short stories *The Tailor and Ansty*, 1942. The book resulted in bitter controversy, but was swiftly recognised as a classic. One other collection, *Silence is Golden*, Dublin 1978.

CROWE, Eyre Evans, b. England 1799 of Irish parents, d. 1868. Ed. TCD. Usually regarded as an Irish writer, among the group of writers busily interpreting Ireland to England between the Act of Union and the Famine. Best-known works: *To-day in Ireland*, 1825; and *Yesterday in Ireland*, 1829.

CRUISE, William, b. Co. Westmeath *c.* 1750, d. London 1824. Bar 1773, but being Catholic was unable to practise. Acted as conveyancer with much success and a writer on law. *A Digest of the Laws of England respecting Real Property*, 1804, continued to be reprinted in England and America for 50 years.

CULLEN, Louis Michael, b. New Ross 1932. Ed. CBS, UCG, Paris, LSE. Associate lecturer Modern History TCD 1963-72, Professor 1972–. *Anglo-Irish Trade 1660-1800*, 1968; *Life in Ireland*, 1968, rev. 1979; *An Economic History of Ireland Since 1660*, 1972, rev. 1976; *The Emergence of Modern Ireland*, 1981, 1983.

CUMBERLAND, Marten, pseud. of Kevin O'Hara, b. London 1892, but long resident in Ireland, and prominent in Irish literary circles. Wrote several plays and a long series of detective novels, many of them centred on the character Saturnin Dax. Later titles include *Postscript to Death*, 1963; *The DiceWere Loaded*, 1965; *No Sentiment in Murder*, 1966; and, as Kevin O'Hara, *Don't Tell the Police*, 1963; *It's Your Funeral*, 1966.

CUMMINGS, James Sleator, b. Co. Monaghan 1819, d. Khyber Pass 1842, in action. His *Six Years Diary*, 1847, is a record of the life of a subaltern in India at the time.

CUMMINS, Geraldine Dorothy, b. Cork 1890, d. Cork 1969. Ed. privately. Married to Austin Clarke for ten days in 1920. Began writing career as playwright in collaboration with Suzanne R. Day: *Broken Faith*, 1912; *The Way of the World*, 1914; *Fox and Geese*, 1917 (all Abbey, the latter also Cork, London), etc. Turned to novels, including *The Land They Loved*, 1919; *Fires of Beltane*, 1936; *Childhood of Jesus*, 1937, rep. 1972. Short stories *Variety Show*, 1959. All these deal mainly with peasant life in Munster. Other works include biography and psychical research: *Beyond Human Personality*, 1935; *Dr E. Œ. Somerville* (a close friend), 1952; *Fate of Colonel Fawcett*, 1955; *Swan on a Black Sea* (a study of automatic writing), 1965. Left behind much unpublished material of a psychic nature which she claimed was dictated to her by a guiding spirit, Astor. One such book published was *Scripts of Cleophas*, an account of life in the early Christian communities. This became subject of a famous law case over the ownership of 'spirit writings'. Mr Justice Eve, deciding that spirits could have no property in this world, said that copyright belonged to the medium.

CUNNINGHAM, John, b. Dublin 1729, d. Newcastle-on-Tyne 1773. Son of a wine merchant. Wrote a successful farce *Love in a Mist* when only 17 and took to the stage and travelling theatres. His poetry was very popular and often reprinted before and after his death.

CURRAN, Constantine Peter, b. Dublin 1880, d. Dublin 1975. Ed. CBS O'Connell School, UCD. BL. Registrar of Supreme Court 1946-52. Classicist and scholar; friend to Joyce and Beckett; lover of paintings and music; well known for his Wednesday afternoon Dublin salons in 1930s. *The Rotunda Hospital: Its Architects and Craftsmen*, Dublin 1945; *Dublin Decorative Plasterwork of the Seventeenth and Eighteenth Centuries*, 1967; *James Joyce Remembered*, 1968; *Under the Receding Wave* (Dublin memoir), 1970. Many contributions to *Studies*.

CURRAN, Henry Grattan, b. 1800, d.1876. Natural son of John Philpot Curran. Barrister and writer. Best-known novel *Confessions of a Whitefoot*, 1884.

CURRY, Eugene, see O'CURRY, Eugene.

CURRY, John, b. *c.* 1710, d. 1780. A member of the O Corra family, made landless by the Irish wars. Ed. Paris and Rheims, returning to Dublin as a physician. He worked for Catholic Emancipation, founding the committee which became eventually the Catholic Association. Best-known work *An historical and critical Review of the Civil Wars in Ireland*, Dublin 1775.

CURTAYNE, Alice, b. Co. Kerry 1901, d. 1981. Ed. England. Married writer Stephen Rynne 1935. Best-known works include *Saint Catherine of Siena*, 1929, last rep. 1981; *Patrick Sarsfield*, Dublin 1934; *House of Cards*, Dublin 1940; *Irish Saints for Boys and Girls*, Dublin 1955; *Irish Story, A Survey of Irish History and Culture*, Dublin 1962; *Francis Ledwidge, A Life of the Poet*, 1972; and ed. *Complete Poems of Francis Ledwidge*, 1974.

CURTIN, Jeremiah, b. Detroit, US 1835, of Irish parents, d. Vermont, US

1906. One of the best-known collectors of Irish folktales. In US Government Service as translator, and served in St Petersburg 1864-70. On staff of Bureau of Ethnology, Smithsonian Institute 1883-91. Visited Ireland many times. *Tales of the Fairies and of the Ghost World* (collected in S. W. Munster), Boston and London 1893; *Myths and Folklore of Ireland,* Boston and London 1890 and 1911; *Hero Tales of Ireland,* Boston and London 1894, and *Memoirs of Jeremiah Curtin,* Wisconsin 1941. He also collected American and Mongol folktales and wrote *The Mongols: A History,* US 1908 (with a foreword by Theodore Roosevelt).

CURTIS, Edmund, b. Lancs 1881 of Irish emigrant parents, d. Dublin 1943. At 15 was working in a rubber factory. Published verses lamenting his unhappy destiny in a local newspaper. Interested readers helped him to return to school, and eventually to Oxford. Became Professor of Modern History Dublin University 1914, Lecky Professor 1939. Wrote *Roger of Sicily & the Normans in Lower Italy 1016-1154,* NY 1912; *A History of Mediaeval Ireland,* 1923; *Richard II in Ireland 1394-5,* Oxford 1927; *A History of Ireland,* 1936. His work has been criticised for inaccuracies of detail and lack of notice of current research, but it still has value and much of it was pioneer work. A Gaelic Nationalist by sympathy, he made use of Irish language sources.

CUSACK, Margaret Anne, b. 1832, probably near Kenmare, d. Leamington 1899. Of a Protestant family she became a convert and entered the Poor Clares at Kenmare as Sister Mary Francis Clare. She wrote a *History of Kerry,* 1871; an autobiography *The Nun of Kenmare,* 1889; and *The Black Pope: A History of the Jesuits,* 1896, among many other works. Having quarrelled with her bishop she reverted to Protestantism, about 1871, and went to America, where she published *Advice to Irish Girls in America,* NY 1872. This and her later writings reflect her altered opinions.

D

DABORNE, Robert, b. *c.* 1570, d. 1628. Clergyman and playwright, collaborator with Massinger and Field. Own plays include *A Christian turn'd Turke,* 1612. Dean of Lismore 1621.

DAIKEN, Leslie (Leslie H. YODAIKEN), b. Dublin 1912, d. 1964. Poetry: *Signatures of All Things,* 1945. Wrote mainly on children's games and toys in several countries, including *Children's Games Throughout the Year,* 1949; *Children's Games Throughout the Ages,* 1953; *The Lullaby Book,* 1959; *Out Goes She* (Dublin Street Rhymes, with commentary), Dublin 1963.

DALEY

DALEY, Victor James, b. Navan, Co. Armagh 1858, d. Sydney 1905. Became a journalist in Australia, where he was considered to be a major poet.

D'ALTON, John, b. Co. Westmeath 1792, d. 1867. Ed. TCD. Bar 1813. Expert genealogist and local historian of Dublin. *History of the County of Dublin,* and *Memoirs of the Archbishops of Dublin,* both appeared 1838. In 1855 he published *King James II's Irish Army Lists 1689* with historical and genealogical notes, a valuable source of information for family histories of the period.

D'ALTON, John Francis, b. Claremorris 1882, d. 1963. Ed. Blackrock, Rome. Professor and President, Maynooth. Cardinal 1953. Best-known work *Horace and his Age,* 1917. An authority on St John Chrysostom, see his *Selections from the Writings of St John Chrysostom,* 1940.

D'ALTON, Louis, b. Dublin 1900, d. London 1951. Son of Charles D'A., comedian and actor-manager. As a child was brought on constant tours with his father's travelling company, throughout Scotland, England and Ireland. As a young man he set up his own acting company, and wrote plays and produced them for his own actors, a gruelling apprenticeship that made him one of the most professional playwrights ever to write and work for the Abbey. His first play for the Abbey was *The Man in the Cloak,* based on the life of James Clarence Mangan. It immediately impressed the critics and was followed by *The Spanish Soldier,* 1940; *The Mousetrap; Lovers Meeting,* a powerful tragedy centred on the country practice of arranged marriages; *They Got What They Wanted,* one of his most popular plays; *Tomorrow Never Comes; This Other Eden; The Devil a Saint Would Be; The Money Doesn't Matter* which ran in the Abbey for 8 weeks in 1941 and then and later was one of the theatre's great successes. One of the Abbey's leading producers as well as playwrights, and often produced his own plays. In 1940 he took the Abbey's number 2 company on a tour of the provinces. In 1945 he published a novel, *Death Is So Fair,* based on the revolutionary period in Ireland, 1916-21.

DALTON, Maurice, author of *Sable and Gold,* a play about the 1916 Easter Rising, first performed at the Abbey 1918. Other plays include *Mary Margaret.*

DALY, Ita, b. Drumshanbo, Co. Leitrim 1955. Ed. Dublin, UCD. Married to literary editor David Marcus; one daughter. Winner of two Hennessy Awards. *The Lady With the Red Shoes* (short stories), Swords 1980; *Ellen* (novel), 1986.

DALY, Leo, b. Dublin 1920. Ed. Mullingar. Qualified as psychiatric nurse, became broadcaster and journalist. Has written *James Joyce and the Mullingar Connection,* Dublin 1975; the guide-book *Oileáin Árann,* Dublin 1975; essays, *Titles,* Mullingar 1981, and a novel, *The Rock Garden,* Mullingar 1984.

DALY, Mary E. Ed. Carrickmacross, UCD, Oxford. Lecturer in Modern Irish History UCD. Married with two children. *A Social and Economic History of Ireland Since 1800,* Dublin 1981; *Dublin The Deposed Capital: A Social and Economic History,* Cork 1984.

DALY, Padraig John, b. Dungarvan 1943. Joined Augustinians as novice 1961. Ed. Dublin and Gregorian University, Rome. Poems: *Nowhere but in Praise,* Dublin 1978, and, in Italian and English, on alternate pages, *Dall'orlo marino del mondo,* Rome 1981.

DANAHER, Kevin, b. Co. Limerick 1913. Ed. UCD and Berlin. Captain in Irish Army 1940-45. Followed Dr Hayes McCoy as editor of *The Irish Sword,* 1960–. Has written *In Ireland Long Ago,* Cork 1962; *Gentle Places and Simple Things,* Cork 1964; *Irish Country People,* Cork 1966; and *Folktales of the Irish Countryside,* Cork 1968; all dealing with Irish rural life and traditions. *A Bibliography of Irish Ethnology and Folk Tradition,* Dublin and Cork 1978; *That's How It Was,* Cork 1984. Now lecturer in ethnology, UCD, and President of Military History Society of Ireland.

DANBY, Frank, see FRANKAU, Julia.

DARLEY, George, b. Dublin 1795, d. London 1846. Used pseud. 'Guy Penseval' occasionally. Journalist in London, where his plays, poetry and mathematical works were much admired. His best story is considered to be 'Lillian of the Vale', which first appeared in *The London Magazine.* His complete poems were published in London 1908; *Selected Poems,* 1979.

DAUNT, William Joseph O'Neill, b. Tullamore 1807, d. Kilashin 1894. Wrote several volumes on Irish 19th-century history, but is best remembered for his *Personal Recollections of the Late Daniel O'Connell M.P.,* 1848.

DAVEY, Samuel, b. 1700, wrote several plays including an opera, *Whittington and His Cat,* 1739.

DAVIDSON, James Norris Goddard, b. 1908. Ed. Portora and Cambridge. Editor of *Granta.* Trained in documentary film making under John Grierson. Made first Irish edition of *March of Time.* Joined RE 1947. Novels: *Galore Park,* 1934; *The Soft Impeachment,* 1936. Many TV awards for scripts and programmes.

DAVIS, Francis, b. Cork 1810, d. Belfast 1885. Contributed to *The Nation,* etc. Became known as The Belfastman, and published several volumes of poetry in Belfast, where he was a muslin weaver. Collected poems pub. Belfast 1878.

DAVIS, Thomas Osborne, b. Mallow 1814, d. 1845. Ed. TCD and Bar. In 1842 founded *The Nation* with Charles Gavan Duffy and J. B. Dillon, and himself contributed many articles and verses to it. Swiftly came to be regarded as *the* national poet, and was the inspiration of the Young Ireland movement. His influence on his contempories was immense, and it continued long after his early death. In many aspects of Irish Nationalism it continues still. Collected poems pub. Dublin 1846 as *The Poems of T.D.*; *Literary and Historical Essays*, 1846; and *Collected Prose Writings of Thomas Davis*, 1891.

DAVISON, Philip, b. Dublin 1957. Novels: *The Book-Thief's Heartbeat*, Dublin 1981; *Twist and Shout*, Dingle 1983; *The Private Citizen*, Dingle 1985. Co-scripted films *Exposure*, 1978, and *Criminal Conversation*, 1980, both Dublin.

DAVITT, Michael, b. Co. Mayo 1846, d. Dublin 1906. His parents, evicted in 1852, emigrated to Lancashire where he became child-labourer in a mill. Lost his right arm in machinery, and being then useless for work was sent to a Wesleyan school. Joined Fenians 1865 and became organising secretary of Irish Republican Brotherhood 1868. Engaged in arms smuggling to Ireland 1870; was arrested and sentenced to 15 years. Served 7 and in 1878 followed parents to America. Returning to Ireland started Land League agitation, opposing Parnell. Arrested in 1881, was elected MP for Co. Meath while in Portland prison. Released 1882, and moving into alliance with Parnell after the assassination of Ld Frederick Cavendish, persuaded him to join the National League, successor to the Land League. Broke finally with Parnell over the divorce. In 1895 entered Parliament for S.Mayo (his first election being null because of his imprisonment at the time of election, and a second being declared void in 1892 on the grounds of clerical intimidation of the voters). In 1899 resigned his seat in protest against the Boer War and between 1903 and 1905 visited Russia several times as a journalist. Active in founding British Labour Party with Keir Hardie and others 1905. He died of blood poisoning. His writing covers a wide range, from anti-Semitism in Russia to convict life in Britain. He favoured Land Nationalisation and his programme was Socialistic. *The Prison Life of Michael Davitt*, Dublin 1882, incorporates his evidence before a House of Lords Commission on Convict Prison Life. *Leaves from a Prison Diary*, 1884, covers much the same ground, but also analyses the conditions which create criminals, suggests remedies social and political, and deals finally with Irish politics, 'How Ireland is ruled and ruined' and 'How the Anglo-Irish problem might be solved'. This is his most famous book, but it was followed by others worth attention even today. *The Defence of the Land League*, 1891; *Life and Progress in Australasia*, 1898; *The Boer Fight for Freedom*, NY 1902; *Within the Pale* (a study of anti-Semitism in Russia), 1903; and *The Fall of Feudalism in Ireland* (a history of land agitation), London and NY 1904.

DAVYS, Mary, b. Dublin *c.* 1670. Married the Reverend Peter Davys, master of the Free School of St Patrick's. Both she and her husband were reputed to be friends of Jonathan Swift. Her husband died in 1698 and she moved first to York, and then to Cambridge where she kept a coffee-house and wrote plays, novels, and her memoirs. Her *Complete Works* are published 2 vols, 1725.

DAWE, Gerald, b.Belfast 1952. Ed. Coleraine and Galway; tutor in Department of English UCG. Poetry includes *Heritages*, 1976; *Blood and Moon*, 1976; *Sheltering Places*, Belfast 1978. Ed. *The Younger Irish Poets*, Belfast 1982 (some of own work included). With Edna Longley, *Across a Roaring Hill: The Protestant Imagination in Modern Ireland* (essays), Belfast 1985.

DAY, Suzanne Rouvier, b. Cork *c*. 1890, d. London 1964. Keen ornithologist. Was in London Fire Service throughout the war. Collaborated with Geraldine Cummins in the play *Fox and Geese*, Abbey 1917, and several other plays produced at the Abbey before the First World War, including *The Way of the World* and *Broken Faith*, 1913.

DAY-LEWIS, Cecil, b. Ballintubber 1905, d. Herts 1972. Ed. Sherbourne and Oxford. One of the most distinguished poets of his day; Professor of Poetry, Oxford 1950-54; Vice-President Royal Society of Literature; member of Arts Council of Great Britain. Wrote a number of original and successful detective novels under the pseud. Nicholas Blake, such as *Whisper in the Gloom*, 1954; *Tangled Web*, 1956, etc. Translated the *Aeneid*, and published a large quantity of poetry; titles include *Italian Visit*, 1953; *Collected Poems*, 1954; *Requiem for the Living*, 1964; *The Room and Other Poems*, 1965. Published his autobiography *Buried Day*, 1960.

DEALE, Kenneth Edwin Lee, b. Dublin 1907, d. 1974. Bar 1935, took silk 1950; Judge of Circuit Court 1955; High Court 1974. Playwright: *The Case of the Damaged Chocolates*, BBC 1957; *The Alibi*, BBC 1958; *The Forger*, 1962; *The Conspiracy*, Abbey Theatre 1966. Also wrote on law; notably, *A Guide to High Court Practice*, Dublin 1941; *Landlord and Tenant Acts, 1931 and 1943*, Dublin 1952; *Memorable Irish Trials*, 1960, and *Beyond Any Reasonable Doubt* (murder trials), Dublin 1971.

DEANE, Seamus, b. Derry 1940. Ed. QUB and Cambridge. Fulbright lecturer and Woodrow Wilson Fellow at Reed College, Oregon, and Berkeley, California. Now Professor of Modern English and American Literature UCD. Poetry: *Gradual Wars*, 1972 (AE Memorial Award 1973); *Rumours*, 1977; *History Lessons*, 1983; all pub. Dublin. Field Day Pamphlets: *Civilians and Barbarians*, 1983; *Heroic Styles: the tradition of an idea*, 1984; both pub. Derry. Also, *Celtic Revivals: Essays in Modern Irish Literature 1880-1980*, 1985.

DEASE, Alice, b. Co. Westmeath *c*. 1875, date of death unknown. Wrote a number of patriotic novels and stories before the First World War, in which she served with the Red Cross. Books include *The Beckoning of the Wand*, 1908; *Good Men of Erin*, 1910; *The Lady of Mystery*, 1913; *Down West & Other Sketches of Irish Life*, 1914; *The Mass: Our Splendid Privilege*, Dublin 1931.

DE BLACAM, Aodh, b. London 1890, d. Dublin 1951. Son of Ulster family. Learned Irish in London from Robert Lynd. Went to Ireland as journalist 1915. Was interned by Black and Tans for his Nationalist writings. Well known as journalist under pseud. 'Roddy the Rover'. Wrote *The Story of Colmcille,* Dublin 1929; *Gaelic Literature Surveyed,* Dublin 1929; *The Life of Wolfe Tone,* Dublin 1935, etc.

DE BURCA, Seamus, b. Dublin 1912, son of the actor-playwright Patrick Bourke, Director of theatrical costumiers in Dublin. Plays include *Knocknagow,* 1944, adapted from the novel by Charles Kickham; *Thomas Davis,* 1948; *Limpid River,* 1956; *Mrs Howard's Husband,* 1959; *The Boys and Girls are Gone,* 1961. Has written one novel, *Limpid River,* 1962, and biography of Peadar Kearney, author of national anthem, 1957.

DE COURCY IRELAND, John Evan, b. Lucknow, India 1911. Irish parents. Ed. Marlborough, Oxford, between sea voyages as sailor. Journalist, teacher, Labour Party organiser in Ireland. Member of Maritime Institute of Ireland from 1943; Hon. Sec. Dun Laoghaire Life Boat from 1957; founder member of Military History Society of Ireland, and Inland Waterways Association. Publications: *Irish Sea Fisheries,* 1960; *The Sea and the Easter Rising,* 1966; *Ireland's Sea Fisheries: A History,* 1981; *Wreck and Rescue on the East Coast of Ireland,* 1983; *Ireland and The Irish in Maritime History,* 1985; all pub. Dublin.

DEEVY, Teresa, b. Waterford 1903, d. Waterford 1963. Suffered all her life from almost complete deafness, yet managed to write plays in which the sound as well as the sense of language was used with great authority and poetic value. *Temporal Powers,* 1932, *The King of Spain's Daughter* and *Katie Roche,* both 1935, and *The Wild Goose,* 1936, were all first performed at the Abbey; often revived and played numberless times by amateur companies throughout Ireland. After 1936 she wrote almost exclusively for radio. *Within A Marble City* was widely praised as a masterpiece when first broadcast. Elected to Irish Academy of Letters 1954.

DELANY, Frank, b. Tipperary 1942. Ed. Tipperary, Ross College Dublin. Bank of Ireland 1961-72; RTE 1972-75; BBC 1975-83, making name with 'Bookshelf'. Director of Century/Hutchinson. *James Joyce's Odyssey,* 1981; *Betjeman Country,* 1983. Is preparing 'Celts', a TV series and book 1986.

DELANY, Patrick, b. Ireland 1685 or 1686, d. Bath 1767. Ed. TCD. Friend of Thomas Sheridan and Swift, who admired him as 'the most eminent preacher we have'. His reputation rests on his *Observations upon Lord Orrery's Remarks upon the Life and Writings of Dr. Jonathan Swift,* 1754, which set out to vindicate Swift, and are of value as the only account of S. by a close friend who had known him in his full health. S. appointed Delany as one of his executors and left him a medal. Among contemporaries, however, D.'s fame, apart from his preaching, rested on his eccentric defences of polygamy, Old Testament dietary laws, and even those crimes of King David which David himself repented. These views were set out in *Revelations Examined with Candour,* vol.I, 1732; vol.II, 1734;

vol.III, 1763 (abstention from things strangled and from blood); *Reflections upon Polygamy* (and the encouragement given to that practice by the Scriptures of the Old Testament), 1738, 2nd ed. 1739 (with a preface arguing that polygamy does not favour population); and *An Historical Account of the Life & Reign of King David,* vol.I, 1740; vols II and III, 1742. In 1757 he founded *The Humanist,* a kindly journal in which he denounced many practices, including that of docking horses' tails.

DELAUNE, Thomas, b. Cork *c.* 1635, d. Newgate Prison 1685. Of Catholic farming family, became a Baptist and was obliged to leave Cork for England. Married the daughter of a Baptist Minister and worked at translations and teaching. His most famous work is *Plea for the Non-Conformist,* 1683, for which he was imprisoned and fined. Unable to pay the fine he remained in Newgate with his family, where they all starved to death during the next 18 months. The sum of £67 would have released the family, but while Dissenters read the *Plea* written on their behalf, they would not subscribe for the author's release. Reprinted often, one of the editions carries Daniel Defoe's indignant preface, scourging the Dissenters for their meanness. Delaune's *A Narrative of the Sufferings of T.D.,* 1684, was written during his imprisonment and describes his prison conditions.

DEMPSEY, Peter J. R., b. Nenagh 1914. Ed. UCC, Rome, Montreal. OFM Cap. Doctorate in psychology, and in theology from Gregorian University, Rome. Professor of Applied Psychology UCC 1964-82. *De Exegeticis Principiis Sancti Bonaventurae,* Rome 1946; *The Psychology of Sartre,* Cork 1950; *Psychology for All,* Cork 1952 (fifth printing 1965); *Freud, Psychoanalysis and Catholicism,* Cork 1956; ed. in English, *The Gospel Story: a Harmony of the Four Gospels (ed. in Italian by Pietro Vanetti SJ),* Cork 1962; *Psychology and the Manager,* 1973.

DENHAM, John, b. Dublin 1615, d. 1669. Read law at Gray's Inn. Royalist, knighted after the Restoration and made Surveyor-General. One of the architects of Burlington House and Greenwich Hospital. His poetry was highly regarded in his time, and he was buried in Westminster Abbey. His verse-plays include *The famous battle of the Catts in the Province of Ulster,* 1688. His poem *Cooper's Hill,* 1642, was his most admired work.

DENVIR, John, b. Bushmills 1834, d. London 1916. Lived mostly in Liverpool, where he founded the immensely popular *Denvir's Penny Library,* consisting of small volumes of Irish poetry, history and biography. Millions of copies were sold to immigrants and did much to maintain or create an interest in Irish Nationalism among them. His own writings include *The Irish in Britain,* 1892, and *Life Story of an Old Rebel,* Dublin 1910. He also published in Liverpool about 1877 a pamphlet *The Catalpa,* an account of the rescue of the military Fenians from Fremantle.

DE PAOR, Liam, b. Dublin 1926. Ed. Dublin, UCD. Joined National Monuments branch of Office of Public Works. Gained Travelling

Studentship of NUI, became lecturer in Archaeology UCD. UNESCO adviser for a year in Nepal, on conservation of historic monuments. Now college lecturer in history, UCD. Has taken part in excavations in Ireland and elsewhere. Co-author, with wife, Maire, of *Early Christian Ireland,* London and NY 1958 (German and Italian translations) and author of *Archaeology: an Illustrated Introduction,* 1967 (paperback). Contributed chapter *The Age of the Viking Wars* to *The Course of Irish History,* (ed. Moody and Martin), Cork 1967. Also wrote *Divided Ulster,* 1970.

DE PAOR, Máire, née MacDermott, b. Co. Donegal 1925. Ed. Buncrana, UCD; in Dept. Archaeology UCD for 12 years; Ph.D. Lectured abroad many times; on many archaeological expeditions in Ireland and Europe, and with husband in Nepal. Trans: *Art Irlandais* by F. Henry, 1954. Co-author with husband Liam de Paor of *Early Christian Ireland,* London and NY., 1958 (also German and Italian editions), paperback ed. 1978.

DERMODY, Thomas, b. Ennis 1775, d. England 1802. The son of a drunken schoolmaster. Precocious in every way, he assisted his father in school at 9 years old, teaching the classics; wrote poetry of merit at 10; and inspired by *Tom Jones* ran away from home at about 15 with 2/- in his pockets. In Dublin he found and lost a series of distinguished friends and patrons; the Reverend Gilbert Austin, rector of Maynooth, arranged the publication of his poems. The future Lord Kilwarden, then Attorney General, took him up, and offered to put him through University. Robert Owenson, Lady Morgan's father, the Dowager Countess of Moira; each in turn supported him for a time until they found that his vices outweighed his charms. Both must have been prodigious. Somewhere about 1800 Dermody made his way to England, where his excesses killed him, and he expired with the unforgettable words 'I am vicious because I like it'. His work includes *The Reform* (a poem), 1792, attached to his pamphlet *The Rights of Justice,* and his collected poems published in 1807 as *The Harp of Erin.*

DERMOTT, Laurence, b. Co. Roscommon 1720, d. London 1791. He arrived in London about 1750, perhaps already a member of the *Antient Masons,* later to become the *Grand Lodge of England.* He was made Grand Secretary in 1752 and Deputy Grand Master in 1771. In 1756 he published *Ahiman Rezon, or Help to a Brother,* regarded by many as the most remarkable book on Masonry in English. It sets out the laws of Masonry and the reasons for Masonry's existence. The book is known throughout the masonic world. A Dublin edition was printed in 1760.

DERRICK, Samuel, b. Dublin 1724, d. Tunbridge Wells 1769. Apprenticed to a liner-draper, but ran away to join travelling players. Moved to London and became friendly with Dr Johnson and Oliver Goldsmith. Succeeded Beau Nash as Master of Ceremonies at Bath. Wrote several popular plays, including *Sylla,* based on an original play by King Frederick of Prussia, and *A Voyage to the Moon,* both 1753; also an Ossianic poem, *The Battle of Lora,* 1762.

DE VALERA, Ruaidhri, b. Dublin 1916, d. Enniskillen 1978. Ed. UCD. Place-names and Archaeological Officer with Ordnance Survey, 1946-57; Professor of Celtic Archaeology UCD 1957-78. Most important work, with Seán Ó Nualláin, *Survey of the Megalithic Tombs of Ireland,* vol 1, 1961; vol.2, 1964; vol.3, 1972; vol.4, 1983. Shortly before his death he revised Seán Ó Ríordáin's *Antiquities of the Irish Countryside,* 1979.

DEVAS, Nicolette, b. Co. Clare 1912. Daughter of Francis MacNamara, sister of Caitlin, who married Dylan Thomas. Brought to England in childhood, she lived with Augustus John's family and knew many of the great figures of the 1920s art-world, including Yeats and T. E. Lawrence. She became a painter, and married the portraitist Anthony D. Her memoirs *Two Flamboyant Fathers,* 1966 (US 1967), give a good portrait of Augustus John. Novels: *Bonfire,* 1958; *Nightwatch,* 1961; *Black Eggs,* 1970. A further vol. of memoirs, *Susannah's Nightingales,* 1978.

DE VERE, Aubrey, b. Curragh Chase 1788, d. Curragh Chase 1846. Son of Sir Vere Hunt of Limerick. Succeeded to baronetcy 1818 and adopted name of De Vere. In 1807 he had married Mary Spring-Rice. He was a friend of Wordsworth and was a progressive and humane landlord. Wrote many long poems and some verse-tragedies including *The Lamentations of Ireland,* 1823, but his reputation rests on his sonnets, pub. 1875.

DE VERE, Aubrey Thomas, b. Curragh Chase 1814, d. Curragh Chase 1902. Son of Sir Aubrey and Mary, née Spring-Rice. Ed. TCD. Became Catholic 1851. Wrote a vast amount of poetry, including *The Foray of Queen Meave,* 1882. His *Recollections* were pub. 1897. His brother Stephen was the author of the famous song 'The Snowy Breasted Pearl'.

DEVLIN, Denis, b. 1908, d. Dublin 1959. Ed. UCD and Sorbonne. Spent some years in Paris before joining Irish Foreign Service 1935. In Washington Embassy 1938-46. Appointed Ambassador to Italy 1950. Poetry includes *Intercessions,* 1937; *Lough Derg,* NY 1964; and *Collected Poems,* Dublin 1964. His long poem *The Heavenly Foreigner,* ed. Brian Coffey, Dublin 1967.

DEVOY, John, b. Co. Kildare 1842, d. 1928. According to Pearse 'the greatest of the Fenians'. He served in Algeria in the French Foreign Legion and then in the British Army. Arrested in 1866 for organising Fenian cells, sentenced to 15 years, amnestied 1871 on condition that he left England and Ireland. Settled in America and joined Clan na Gael, swiftly becoming influential. Helped to bring about the alliance with the Irish Republican Brotherhood, during the planning of the expedition to rescue those Fenian prisoners still in prison camp in Australia. The success of this mission in 1876 gave the Clan enormous prestige and did much to restore the morale of all the Irish revolutionary movements, shattered by the failures of 1865-67. Devoy spent the rest of his life plotting and writing for Irish freedom, and through his editorship of the *Gaelic-American* became one of the main influences leading to 1916. But 45 years in exile had detached him from many Irish realities and when in 1919 de Valera met him in America the two men quarrelled bitterly. The point at issue was simply one of political strategy in America; whether Clan na Gael should attempt to persuade the American government to recognise the new Irish Republic, in defiance of its late ally Britain. Devoy told de Valera this was politically impossible and was obviously right. But behind this clash lay complex divisions, of temperament, of generation, and of the historic exile against the contemporary politician. It must have been hard for Devoy to accept that a new generation of leaders had taken over, and that decisions were now to be taken in Dublin rather than New York. These factors made the quarrel insoluble, and did incalculable damage in the following years. In 1924 Devoy visited Ireland and stood in Dáil Éireann to salute the new Free State and be saluted by its representatives. He was the only Fenian leader to survive and return to a free Ireland, bringing memories not only of the Fenian Rising, but even of the Famine. Devoy's principal writings outside of journalism are *The Land of Eire* and *The Irish Land League*, both NY 1882, and *Recollections of an Irish Rebel,* NY 1928. His letters were edited by W. O'Brien and D. Ryan and published as *John Devoy's Post Bag,* Dublin, 2 vols, 1948. The letters had been brought from America in 1938 by Frank Robbins.

DICKSON, Charles, b. Co. Down 1886, d. 1978. Ed. Belfast, MD. Joined civil service, Dublin 1912, retiring as Chief Medical Officer 1954. Served in France and Belgium 1915-19 with RAMC. MC 1917. Editor *Irish Journal of Medical Science* 1962-70. Authority on late 18th-century Ireland. *The Life of Michael Dwyer,* Dublin 1944 (reprinted); *The Wexford Rising in 1798,* Tralee 1955; *Revolt in the North,* Dublin 1960.

DIGBY, Kenelm Henry, b. Ireland 1800, d. London 1880. Son of Dean of Clonfert. Ed. Cambridge, converted to Catholicism and became a vastly admired writer of pious and moralistic works. *The Broadstone of Honour, or Rules for the Gentlemen of England* (on the Origin, Spirit and Institution of Christian Chivalry), 1822/3, revised in 4 vols, 1826-27, reissued 1845-48, was required reading for pious young men both Protestant and Catholic. *Mores Catholici, or Ages of Faith,* came out in 11 vols, 1831-40, and was followed by much also of the same kind. At one time some clergymen regarded Digby's work as next in value only to the Bible.

DILL, Edward Marcus, b. Derry 1810, d. Fethard 1862. Ed. Glasgow. Presbyterian minister of Cookstown 1835. In 1848 in America collecting money for Famine relief with great success. *The Mystery Solved or: Ireland's Miseries, the Grand Cause and Cure,* Edinburgh 1852.

DILLON, Eilis, b. Galway 1920. Ed. Sligo. Married Cormac Ó Cuilleanáin, Professor of Irish UCC; then, on his death, the critic Vivian Mercier. Writes novels, plays and stories for children. Books include *The Lost Island,* 1952; *The San Sebastian,* 1953; *Plover Hill,* 1957; *The Bitter Glass,* 1958; *The*

Singing Cave, 1959; *Bold John Henebry,* 1965; *Across the Bitter Sea* (best selling historical romance), 1973, and *Blood Relations* (its sequel), 1977; *Wild Geese,* 1981; *Inside Ireland* (autobiography), 1982; *Citizen Burke* (novel), 1984.

DILLON, John Blake, b. Co. Mayo 1816, d. Killarney 1866 of cholera. Bar 1841, after brief intention to enter priesthood. Associated with Thomas Davis and Gavan Duffy in founding *The Nation.* After the failure of the '48 Rising hid on the Aran Islands and escaped to France and then America. Returned to Ireland after amnesty of 1855 and entered constitutional politics. Helped found the National Association. MP for Tipperary 1865-66. His son John followed him in the Tipperary seat and became Redmond's successor in 1918, suffering total defeat at the hands of Sinn Fein in that year's elections.

DILLON, John Talbot, Bt, b. Co. Meath 1740, d. Dublin 1805. MP for Wicklow 1771. Made Baron of the Holy Roman Empire in Vienna by Emperor Joseph II in recognition of his services to Catholic interests in Parliament. Wrote much on Spain; *Travels through Spain,* 1780, several editions in English, trans. German 1782, is still a source on Spanish conditions of the period. But D.'s principal merit is his *Historical and Critical Memoirs of the General Revolution in France 1789,* 1790. This contains many contemporary documents and gives a contemporary's view of the early stages of the revolution unobscured by hindsight.

DILLON, Myles, b. Dublin 1900, d. Dublin 1972. 3rd son of Nationalist leader John D. Ed. Ireland, Germany, France. Reader in Sanskrit, TCD 1928-30, UCD 1930-37; Professor of Irish, Wisconsin University 1937-46; Senior Professor, School of Celtic Studies 1949; Director of Celtic School, Dublin Inst. for Adv. Studies 1960-68. *The Cycles of the Kings,* Oxford 1946; *Early Irish Literature,* Chicago 1948, rep. 1969; ed. *Early Irish Society,* Dublin 1954; *Irish Sagas,* Dublin 1959, rep. 1968, 1985. *The Book of Rights,* Dublin, 1962; *The Celtic Realms* (with Nora Chadwick) 1967; *Celts and Aryans,* Simla 1975.

DILLON, Wentworth, 4th Earl of Roscommon, b. Dublin 1633, d. London 1685. Ed. England. Lost estates under Commonwealth, regained at Restoration. Buried Westminster Abbey, 1685. *Poetical Works of the Rt. Hon. Wentworth Dillon, Earl of Roscommon,* 1701, ran to many editions. Dr Johnson included him in his 'Lives of the Poets'. His *Essay on Translated Verse* contains his celebrated praise of *Paradise Lost* and defence of blank verse, although these passages do not appear in the first edition of 1684. He was the first major critic to recognise the poem's genius.

DILLON-LEE, Henry Augustus, b. 1777, d. 1832. Succeeded as 13th Viscount Dillon. Published one novel which caused comment at the time: *The Life and Opinions of Sir Richard Maltravers,* 1822.

DOBBS, Francis, b. Co. Antrim 1750, d. 1811. Known as 'millenium

Dobbs' for his belief in the imminent destruction of the world. MP for Charlemont, spoke powerfully against the Act of Union, his printed speech selling 30,000 copies. *Memoirs of F. Dobbs Esq – also genuine reports of his Speech in Parliament on the subject of an union and prediction of the second coming of the Messiah, with extracts from his poem on the Millenium,* Dublin 1800. A comprehensive work.

DODDS, Eric Robertson, b. Belfast 1893, d. Oxford *c.* 1979. Ed. St Andrew's Dublin, Campbell College Belfast, Balliol College Oxford. Married 1923. Taught Classics in Reading and Birmingham University. Oxford Chair of Greek 1936-60. President of Society for Psychical Research 1961-63. Lecturer on Swan's Hellenic Cruises in 1960s. Friend to Stephen Mac-Kenna (ed. with Memoir his *Journals and Letters,* 1936), Louis MacNeice (literary executor, ed. autobiography *The Strings Are False,* 1965, and *Collected Poems,* 1966), and Wystan Auden. Books: *Select Passages illustrating Neoplatonism,* 1923; ed. *Proclus, The Elements of Theology,* 1933; *The Greeks and the Irrational,* 1951 (based on lectures given at University of Berkeley, California, 1949); *The Ancient Concept of Progress and Other Essays on Greek Literature and Belief,* 1973; and a remarkable autobiography, *Missing Persons,* 1979, winner of Duff Cooper Award.

DOGGETT, Thomas, b. Dublin *c.* 1660, d. Eltham 1721. A travelling actor, went to London and became well-known for his comic characters. Was playing at Drury Lane with great success in 1691. Returned to Dublin with a handsome fortune. His comedy *The Country Wake,* 1690, was often revived and has merit, but his fame rests on the Thames Sculling Prize which he founded and financed, 'Doggett's Coat and Badge', competed for by Thames boatmen every August 1st.

DOHENY, Michael, b. Co. Tipperary 1805, d. New York 1863. Self-educated, entered Gray's Inn 1834 and became legal adviser to borough of Cashel. Young Irelander, fled to America with James Stephens in 1848 and 1849 published there *The Felon's Track, History of the Attempted Outbreak in Ireland.* Later editions contained a preface by Arthur Griffiths, and appendices, including the Dublin Castle descriptions of the wanted Young Irelanders. Doheny's reads: 'Barrister; forty (sic) years of age; five feet eight inches in height; fair or sandy hair; grey eyes; coarse red face like a man given to drink; high cheek bones; wants several of his teeth; very vulgar appearance; peculiar coarse unpleasant voice; dress respectable; small short red whiskers'. This may not have been quite accurate as D. was esteemed as a most effective public speaker, but it is an interesting example of Castle style.

DONAGHY, John Lyle, b. 1902, d. 1947. Ed. Larne Grammar School and TCD. Schoolmaster for several years. Poetry includes *At Dawn above Aherlow,* 1926, and *Into the Light,* 1934.

DONLEAVY, James Patrick, b. Brooklyn, New York, 1926. Ed. locally.

Served US Navy, entering TCD 1946. At first a painter, married Valerie Heron and moved to London 1953. Now lives in Co. Westmeath with second wife Mary Wilson Price: two children from each marriage. Novels: *The Ginger Man*, Paris 1955 (dramatized 1959); *A Singular Man*, Boston 1963 (dramatized 1964); *The Beastly Beatitudes of Balthazar B.*, NY 1968 (dramatized 1981); *The Onion Eaters*, NY 1971; *A Fairy Tale of New York*, NY 1973 (dramatized 1980); *The Destinies of Darcy Dancer, Gentleman*, NY 1977; *Schultz*, NY 1979; *Leila*, NY 1983. Also: *Meet My Maker the Mad Molecule* (short stories), Boston 1964; *The Saddest Summer of Samuel S* (novella), NY 1966; *The Plays of J. P. Donleavy*, NY 1972; *The Unexpurgated Code – A Complete Manual of Survival*, NY 1975; *De Alfonce Tennis, The Superlative Game of Eccentric Champions. Its History, Accoutrements, Rules, Conduct and Regimen* (A Legend), 1984.

DONLEVY, Andrew, b. 1694, d. *c.* 1765. Titular Dean of Raphoe. Ed. Sligo and Paris, became Prefect of Irish College there. Famous for *The Catechism, or Christian Doctrine*, Paris 1742, printed in both Irish and English with an appendix on *The Elements of the Irish Language*. It was still being reprinted 100 years later, see 1848 ed. used in Maynooth.

DONNELLY, Charles, b. Tyrone 1910, d. Jarama 1937. Ed. UCD, considered brilliant in a circle including Denis Devlin, Brian Nolan (Flann O'Brien), Donagh MacDonagh, Niall Sheridan, Liam Redmond and Cyril Cusack. Contributed poems to *Comhthrom Feine*, a university magazine edited by Sheridan. A left-wing Republican, he went to London, 1936, to volunteer for war-service in Spain. Submitted a thesis on Military Strategy in 19th-century Spain to Captain Liddell Hart who was much impressed with Donnelly's thinking. Joined the Abraham Lincoln Battalion and was killed on the Jarama front. Poems appear in some anthologies. Ewart Milne and others regarded him before his death as likely to become a major poet.

DONNELLY, Neil, b. Tullamore, Co. Offaly 1948. Ed. local CBS. Labourer in England, then teacher. Plays include *The Station Master*, Edinburgh 1974; *Upstarts*, 1980; *The Silver Dollar Boys*, 1981 (both pub. Dublin); *Flying Home*, 1983; and *Chalk Farm Blues*, 1984; all produced Peacock, Dublin. Won Harveys Award 1982. *The Crack*, Gaiety1985.

DONOGHUE, Denis, b. Co. Carlow 1928. Ed. CBS Newry, UCD, Fellow King's College Cambridge. Professor of Modern English and American Literature UCD until 1980. Henry James Professor of English Letters, New York University 1981–. *The Third Voice*, 1959; *Connoisseurs of Chaos*, 1966; *The Ordinary Universe*, 1968; *Jonathan Swift*, 1969; *Emily Dickinson*, 1969; *Yeats*, 1971; *Thieves of Fire*, 1973; *The Sovereign Ghost* (a study of literary imagination), California 1976, London 1978; *Ferocious Alphabets* (about the art of criticism and communication), 1981; *The Arts Without Mystery* (his 1982 BBC Reith Lectures), 1983. Elected to American Academy of Arts and Science 1983.

DOUGLAS, James, b. Co. Wicklow 1929. Playwright and short-story writer, as well as part-time electrician. Came to notice 1961 with *North City Traffic Straight Ahead* in Dublin Theatre Festival. Other plays include *Carrie*, Dublin Theatre Festival 1963 (based on own short story); *The Ice Goddess*, Gate 1964; *The Savages*, Eblana 1970. His TV play *Babbi Joe*, adapted for theatre, was produced off-Broadway 1978. Other plays and TV serials include *The Riordans*. His play *What Is the Stars?* won the final Irish Life Award, withdrawn when Sean O'Casey's widow threatened legal action, claiming the play could injure her husband's memory. Also writes short stories in Irish for magazines.

DOWDEN, Edward, b.Cork 1843, d.1913. Professor of English Literature TCD 1867. Opponent of Home Rule. Edited many Shakespeare plays and established great reputation with *Shakespeare: A Critical Study of His Mind & Art,* 1875. His *Introduction to Shakespeare,* 1893 was widely read, and his *Life of Shelley,* 1886, became a standard work.

DOWLING, Richard, b. Clonmel 1846, d. London 1898. Ed. Limerick, worked on *The Nation,* and edited a Dublin comic paper *Zozimus.* Wrote several novels and collections of stories, such as *While London Sleeps.* His best book is *The Mystery of Killard,* 1879.

DOWLING, Vincent George, b. London 1785 of Irish parents, d. London 1852. Ed. Dublin. Journalist and editor of the annual *Bell's Life* from 1824. He published in it in 1827 details of a proposed new police system. Two years later Peel's Metropolitan Police Act adopted these details even to the names of various ranks, and Dowling claimed to be the effective author of the new force. But he had many parliamentary connections and may have taken the details from the minutes of some committee. In 1812 he had seized hold of Bellingham just after the murder of the Prime Minister, Percival, in the House of Commons. He had also acted as courier for Queen Caroline, whose cause he championed.

DOWSLEY, William George, b. Clonmel 1871, d. Capetown 1947. After various clerical jobs was ordained in Bristol, and went out to South Africa in 1903 as chaplain and master of St Andrew's College, Grahamstown. Wrote plays, books on farming and contributed to several Irish journals. His novel *The Travelling Men*, Dublin 1925, was republished in England and US and translated into Irish. *Far Away Cows Wear Long Horns* won the Bronze Medal at the 1930 Aonach Tailteann Games. Served for many years as rector of St Stephen's, Capetown.

DOYLE, James Warren, b. New Ross 1786, d. Carlow 1834. Ed. at seminary in New Ross and Coimbra University, his studies there interrupted by Napoleon's invasion. Became interpreter in Wellington's army. Returned to Ireland 1808, ordained priest 1809, became Professor of Rhetoric, Carlow College and in 1819 Bishop of Kildare and Leighlin, hence his famous 'pen-initials' JKL, attached to *Letters on the State of Ireland,* 1824-25, and many other political and religious essays. In 1825,

1830 and 1832 gave evidence before London parliamentary committees on the state of Ireland, and impressed his hearers immensely. During these years he restored Church discipline in his diocese, established schools and fought for a Poor Law.

DOYLE, Lynn, pseud. of Leslie Alexander Montgomery, b. Downpatrick 1873, d. 1961. Ed. Dundalk. Bank clerk and finally bank manager. Wrote many plays in the 1920s including *Love and Land,* 1927, but is chiefly remembered for his humorous stories centring on the imaginary district of Ballygullion and its inhabitants. The first collection, *Ballygullion,* appeared in 1908. Others are *Lobster Salad,* 1922; *Dear Ducks,* 1925; *Me and Mr Murphy,* 1930; *Rosabelle,* 1933; *The Shake of the Bag,* 1939; *A Bowl of Broth,* 1945; *Green Oranges,* 1947; *Back to Ballygullion,* 1953; *New Stories,* 1957, and in the same year a collection made up from previous volumes, *The Ballygullion Bus.* One of the best-known and loved comic writers with a pawky northern humour, more astringent and far less condescending than Somerville and Ross, he has often been dismissed by critics as merely a humorist, but in stories such as 'The Rapparee' he showed a more serious talent and historical insight.

The first Irish writer to be appointed to the Censorship Board, he resigned in 1937.

DOYLE, Martin, see HICKEY, William.

DRENNAN, William, b. Belfast 1754, d. Belfast 1820. MD Edinburgh 1778, practised in Newry and later in Dublin. Drew up prospectus for United Irelanders. Tried for sedition 1794 and acquitted. Wrote a great deal of much admired poetry, and is famous for coining the phrase 'the emerald isle' which first appeared in his poem 'When Erin First Rose'. Another famous poem of his is·'The Wail of the Women after the Battle', 1798. His poetry collected and published as *Fugitive Pieces,* 1815.

DRUMMOND, James, b. Dublin 1835, d. Oxford 1918. Ed. TCD. Unitarian minister in London and Oxford. Wrote in favour of women's suffrage and Home Rule, among other causes. *Life and Letters of Dr. Martineau,* and *The Jewish Messiah: A critical History of the Messianic Idea among the Jews,* 1877.

DRUMMOND, William Hamilton, b. Larne 1778, d. Dublin 1865. Ed. Belfast and Glasgow. Ordained Belfast 1800. Took parish in Dublin in 1815 and paraphrased many poems from old Irish sources. Books include *Ancient Irish Minstrelsy,* Dublin 1852.

DUFF, Francis Michael (Frank), b. Co. Dublin 1889, d. Dublin 1980. Ed. Blackrock. In civil service to 1934. Founded Legion of Mary, 1921, for which he wrote *The Legion of Mary Handbook,* and through it exerted a worldwide influence on the Church. His articles and speeches are collected in several volumes, including *The Spirit of the Legion of Mary,* 1956; *Walking with Mary,* 1961; *Mary Shall Reign,* 1961; all Glasgow.

DUFFERIN, Lady Helen Selina, b. 1807, d. 1867. The grand-daughter of Richard Brinsley Sheridan. Her most famous poem is 'I'm Sitting on the Style, Mary'. Mother of Marquis of Dufferin and Ava by the 4th Lord Dufferin, in Florence, 1826. Her son wrote a volume of poems *Letters from High Latitudes*, 1857, which inspired her *Lispings from Low Latitudes*, 1863, under the pseud. 'The Hon. Impulsia Gushington'. Shortly before her death she married the Earl of Gifford.

DUFFY, Bernard, b. *c.* 1884, d. 1952. Plays include *Fraternity; The Coiner; The Counter Charm*, all Abbey 1916; *The Piper of Tavran*, Dublin 1921 (adapted from a story by Douglas Hyde); *Cupboard Love*, and *The Plot*. Novels: *Oriel*, Dublin 1918; *The Rocky Road*, Dublin 1929.

DUFFY, Charles Gavan, b. Monaghan 1816 of poor parents who nevertheless managed to educate him, d. Nice 1903. Became a journalist and co-founder of *The Nation* with Thomas Davis and J. B. Dillon. Wrote for it under many pseuds. including 'Ben Herder' and 'The O'Donnell', etc. Entered Parliament 1852 after the ruin of the Young Ireland conspiracy and his own trial for sedition. But despairing of Ireland's future emigrated to Australia 1855 and became Prime Minister of Victoria 1871. Knighted KCMG 1873 and retired to South of France 1880, where he wrote accounts of the Young Ireland movement: *Young Ireland: A Fragment of Irish History 1840-50*, 1880, with its sequel, *Four Years of Irish History 1845-1849*, 1883, and *A Short Life of Thomas Davis*, London and Dublin 1895. Autobiography: *My Life in Two Hemispheres*, 2 vols, 1898, rep. Shannon 1969. *Irish Ballad Poetry*, 1843, remained a loved household book throughout the 19th century and longer. His daughter founded *Scoil Bride*, one of the first all-Irish schools in Dublin.

DUGGAN, Patrick, b. Dublin 1934. Ed. Belvedere College, and trained at Gate Theatre. He acted in Dublin and London, and on TV, and has written children's books: *The Travelling People*, 1964; and *The Travelling Boy*, 1965. Also lyrics and libretto for musicals, *How Now Brown Cow* and *The Golden Horseshoe*, 1967.

DUNKIN, William, b. 1709, d. 1765. Friend of Swift, who was at one time thought to be the author of Dunkin's *Vindication of the Libel*. Other works include *Boeotia*, 1747; *The Murphaeid* (a burlesque on the *Aeneid*); *The Poetical Mirror* and *The Parson's Revels* (comic sketches of country life). *Collected Works*, 2 vols, Dublin 1769.

DUNNE, Lee, b. Dublin 1934. Sailor, travelling actor, taxi driver. His first novel *Goodbye to the Hill*, 1965, caused him to be compared to Brendan Behan. Since then he has poured out novels, many as paperback originals, based on own adventures as taxi driver, such as *Midnight Cabbie, The Cabbie Who Came In from the Cold, The Cabfather, Virgin Cabbies*, etc. Novels with more serious intentions: *A Bed in the Sticks*, 1968; *Does Your Mother*, 1970; *Paddy Maguire Is Dead*, 1972; and *Ringleader* (a political thriller), NY 1980. Has also written plays adapted from own novels, of which *Goodbye to the Hill,* Dublin 1978, confounded the critics by its popular success; revived Dublin 1985, and repub. Swords.

DUNRAVEN, Edwin Richard Wyndham-Quin, 3rd Earl, b. 1812 in Limerick, according to some sources, and London in others, d. England 1871. Remembered for his *Notes of Architecture,* 1871-75, ed. Margaret Stokes, her father Dr William S. having been the earl's companion in his researches. A good landlord, he was himself a convert to Catholicism and restored many ruined churches to Catholic use. His mother Caroline Wyndham was author of *Memorials of Adare,* often attributed to him.

DUNRAVEN, Thomas Wyndham-Quin, 4th Earl, son of 3rd Earl, b. Adare 1841, d. London 1926. Ed. Rome, Paris, Oxford. Joined Life Guards 1862. War correspondent for *Daily Telegraph* in 1867 and in 1870 was one of a number of Irish war córrespondents covering Franco-Prussian War, another being William Howard Russell. Succeeding to earldom, made his home in Adare and worked for land reform, publishing *The Irish Question,* 1880, and *The Legacy of Past Years, A Study of Irish History,* 1911, in attempt to persuade all parties to a compromise. Elected member of first Senate of Irish Free State 1923. Apart from his sober distinctions as reformer and magnate, he was also a big game hunter, and his *The Great Divide: Travels in the Upper Yellowstone in the Summer of 1874,* 1876, is an interesting view of the newly opened Mid-West when there were still more buffalo than men in the area.

DUNSANY, Lord Edward John Moreton Drax Plunkett, 18th Baron, b. 1878, d. 1957. Ed. Eton. Patron of letters and the discoverer of Francis Ledwidge, gave great encouragement to Mary Lavin and Anne Crone among many others. Wrote copiously throughout his long life and has been regarded as not only a skilled entertainer but 'a master of the short story', by critics such as Sean O'Faolain. To the general public his best-known creation is Jorkens, a lying vulgarian who spins incredible yarns to sceptical listeners in a London club. But he wrote many plays, some of which were performed at the Abbey, for example *The Glittering Gates,* 1909. *The Gods of the Mountain; If; A Night at an Inn; The Tents of the Arabs,* are other well-known plays, many of which deal in supernatural forces. He wrote a number of successful novels. *The Sword of Welleran,* 1908, being regarded as one of the best. *The Chronicles of Rodriguez,* 1922; *The King of Elfand's Daughter,* 1924; *The Charwoman's Shadow,* 1926; *The Blessing of Pan,* 1927; *The Curse of the Wise Woman,* 1933; and *Guerilla,* 1944, are other titles. He also wrote memoirs and autobiographical works.

DURCAN, Paul, b. Dublin 1944, related to Sean MacBride. Ed. UCC. Poet and literary critic. Collection of poetry: *Endsville* (with Brian Lynch), Dublin 1967; *O Westport in the Light of Asia Minor,* Dublin 1975; *Teresa's Bar,* Dublin 1976; *Sam's Cross,* Dublin 1978; *Jesus Break His Fall,* Dublin 1980; *Ark of the North,* 1982; *Jumping the Train Tracks with Angela,*

1983. Included in *Penguin Book of Irish Verse,* 2nd ed. 1979. Patrick Kavanagh Award 1974.

E

EAGER, Alan Robert, b. Dublin 1926. Librarian RDS 1974 –. Principal work *A Guide to Irish Bibliographical Material, being a bibliography of Irish Bibliographies and some sources of information,* 1964, an immense and valuable work containing 4000 entries, the only guide of its kind in existence. Much enlarged revised ed. 1979, and again in 1981.

EDGEWORTH, Francis Ysidro, b. Edgeworthstown 1845, d. 1926. Nephew of Maria, and last of male Edgeworths. Ed. TCD and Oxford; English Bar 1877. Professor of Political Economy, London and later at Oxford, 1891. First editor and chief influence on *The Economic Journal* from 1890 to 1926. *Mathematical Psychics,* 1881, set out his theory on the application of mathematical method to social sciences. J. M. Keynes called book and theory 'eccentric', but from 1908 Keynes collaborated with him on the *Journal,* and other critics have described parts of his theory as 'classical', and of the highest importance. *Papers relating to Political Economy,* 1925, 3 vols, collect all his principal later writings. He did much valuable work on statistical theory.

EDGEWORTH, Henry Essex, b. Edgeworthstown 1745, d. Mitau 1807. Son of Protestant rector of Edgeworthstown and cousin of Richard Lovell E. Brought to France in childhood on his father's turning Catholic, he entered priesthood and became chaplain and confessor to both Louis XVI and the Princess Elizabeth, attending Louis to the guillotine. He escaped to England and became chaplain to Louis XVIII. He died of a fever caught caring for French prisoners in Mitau. *Memoirs,* ed. C. Sneyd Edgeworth, 1815. *Letters from Abbé Edgeworth to his friends, 1777-1807, with memoirs of his life,* 1818, was edited and the memoirs in part written by the Rev. Thomas Richard England, b. Cork 1790, d. Cork 1847.

EDGEWORTH, Maria, b. 1767 near Reading, d. Edgeworthstown 1849. Her father, Richard Lovell E., brought her to Ireland and Edgeworthstown in 1782, and soon made her his principal helper on the large estate. Among many other duties this involved preparing moral tales for her brothers and sisters in accordance with her father's theories of education. The first series of these was published in London in 1796 as *The Parent's Assistant,* and was not only popular but immensely influential in England and America. She had already published *Letters to Literary Ladies,* 1795, in defence of education for women. The 2-vol. *Practical Education* (based on Rousseau's theories and written in collaboration with her father), 1798, was followed by a new enlarged edition in 3 vols of the *Assistant,* 1800-1. *Moral Tales,* 1801; *Essay on Irish Bulls,* 1802; *Popular Tales,* and *The Modern Griselda,* 1804; *Memoirs* (of her father), 1820, are her principal non-fiction works, all except the last being educational or moralistic. Her father is usually thought to have had a dramatic influence on her work, giving it in Mme de Stael's phrase a 'sad utility'. But it is equally likely that she simply shared her father's moralising and utilitarian character. Her novel *Castle Rackrent,* 1800, had made her famous. Tracing the ruin of an Ascendancy family over several generations, as told by an old servant, it was both a moral tale and a superb fiction, an unlikely mixture. It set the pattern for most of her future work. *Ennui,* 1809, is overburdened by the morality, but the ending, in which a brutally illiterate peasant inherits the Big House, and burns it, was both a prophecy, a warning, and a powerful scene. In *The Absentee,* 1812, Maria E. handled her two intentions far better, flaying the vanity of the Irish absentee landowners in London, aping the English aristocracy; and pointing with cold anger to the results in Ireland of their absence. Her ending has been criticised for optimism, seeing the return of the 'Absentee's' son as the panacea for Ireland's ills. But she had her father's example in mind and had not yet realised that more was needed.

Ormond, 1817, her most ambitious work, shows a much deeper grasp of the realities of Irish life. It examines the whole range of Ireland's governing class, from the English landlord of newly bought or granted estates, to 'King Corny' of the Black Islands, the pathetic ruin of Gaelic splendour, and shows more clearly than most of her successors were to understand that the conflict between England and Ireland was not between two countries or even two religions, but between two irreconcilable cultures, one of which had to be destroyed. King Corny and his clan loyalties are out of the Iron Age and Maria, like her father, and Daniel O'Connell, knew that they had to disappear if Ireland was to survive. Her sentimental failure of nerve at the end of the book was to believe that by buying the Islands from the Wild Goose heir to King Corny, Ormond would preserve the best of the old and attach it to the new order. The unkind might see this same failure in many later idealists.

Ormond was Maria's last Irish novel. After 1817 events grew too terrible for moral fiction. She managed the estate for her brother, as she had for her father, protected the tenants from him, educated the peasant children, built a market house, lived as a great lady and a centre of civilised common sense in a darkening world. *Helen,* with an English setting, appeared in 1834. Then nothing. When the Famine came she fought desperately to feed her people, who had never truly been her people, and died of her efforts. Her influence on European literature, both directly, and through Sir Walter Scott, was immense. He credited her with being the inspiration of his own historical novels, and both the Russian and French realists of the 19th century owed a great debt to her.

EDGEWORTH, Michael Pakenham, b. Edgeworthstown 1812, d. Eigg

1881, youngest son of Richard Lovell E. Author of *A Grammar of Kashmiri*, 1878, and discoverer of many varieties of Asiatic plants.

EDGEWORTH, Richard Lovell, b. Bath 1744, d. 1817. Immortal as Maria's father, and criticised as an unfortunate influence on her work. This is almost certainly unjust. Her faults were her own as much as his, and it is unlikely that her work would have reached such wide and early success without his help. A good landlord, he devoted much of his life to his estates and tenants in Edgeworthstown, and another great part of it to educating the 19 of his 22 children by four marriages who survived infancy. Apart from these major interests he had an 18th-century hunger for knowledge, invention and improvement, and is far from the conceited bore of Byron's unkind description. He invented what may have been the first semaphore, to signal the winner at Newmarket to a friend some miles away. He invented a type of bicycle, a land-measuring instrument, and various methods of reclaiming bogs. He spoke and worked for parliamentary reform and Catholic Emancipation, and voted against the Act of Union. His ideas on education for children, although owing much to Rousseau, were valuable in themselves and through Maria's writings and his own had a vast influence on English and American education. He was a close and admired friend of such men as Humphry Davy (the chemist inventor of the miners' safety lamp) and Josiah Wedgewood. He experimented in aeronautics and seems to have reached the same conclusions as the Montgolfiers earlier than they did. He advanced intelligent theories on road-making which others took as their own much later.

One of his most enduring and endearing interests was women. At 15 he went through a mock marriage with his tutor's daughter during his sister's marriage festivities at Edgeworthstown, and his father thought it necessary to have the ceremony annulled. At Oxford in 1763, when he was still only 19, he eloped with Anna Maria Elers to Scotland. The marriage was less than ideal and in 1770 he fell into a passion for Honora Sneyd, a famous beauty. Thomas Day, author of *Sandford and Merton,* a close friend, persuaded him to fly from temptation to France, which he reluctantly did. There he enjoyed much French society and diverted the course of the Rhone in a mechanical experiment. In 1773 his wife died and he married his Honora, only to lose her in 1780. She begged him to marry her sister Elizabeth and he immediately obeyed on Honora's death. This caused a tremendous ecclesiastical scandal but he weathered it and gave Elizabeth seven children to follow the six he already had. She died in 1797 and the next year he married Frances Beaufort, who gave him six more, and survived him. When his last child was born he was already 68.

He collaborated with Maria on *Practical Education,* 2 vols, 1798; *Essay on Irish Bulls,* 1802; and she completed his *Memoirs of Richard Lovell Edgeworth,* 1820, rep. Shannon 1969, which he had brought up to the year 1782. He wrote *Poetry Explained for the Use of Young People,* 1802; *Essays on Professional Education,* 1809; and an *Essay on the Construction* *of Roads & Carriages,*1813.

EDWARDS, Owen Dudley, b. Dublin 1938. Ed. Belvedere, UCD, John Hopkins. Reader in History, Edinburgh University 1968–. *The Sins of Our Fathers: Roots of Conflict in Northern Ireland,* Dublin 1970; *The Mind of an Activist – James Connolly,* Dublin 1971; *P. G. Wodehouse: A Critical & Historical Essay,* 1977; with Gwynfor Evans, Ioan Rhys and Hugh MacDiarmid, *Celtic Nationalism,* 1968; *Burke and Hare,* 1981; *A Quest for Sherlock Holmes,* 1982; *Edinburgh,* Edinburgh 1983; ed. with Fergus Pyle, *1916. The Easter Rising,* 1968; ed. *Conor Cruise O'Brien Introduces Ireland,* 1969; ed. with Bernard Ransom, *James Connolly: Selected Political Writings,* 1973; ed. with George Shepperson, *Scotland, Europe and the American Revolution,* Edinburgh 1976.

EDWARDS, Robert Walter Dudley, b. Dublin 1909. Ed. UCD and King's College, London. Professor Modern Irish History UCD 1945-79. Works include *Church and State in Tudor Ireland. A History of the Penal Laws against Irish Catholics, 1534-1603,* Dublin 1935; ed. with Desmond Williams *The Great Famine, Studies in Irish History, 1845-52,* Dublin 1957; *A New History of Ireland,* Dublin and London 1972; *Daniel O'Connell and his world,* 1975; *Ireland in the Age of the Tudors, The Destruction of Hiberno-Norman Civilisation,* 1977; with Mary O'Dowd, *Sources for Early Modern Irish History 1543-1641,* 1985.

EDWARDS, Ruth Dudley, b. Dublin 1944. Ed. UCD. With Dept of Industry, London. *An Atlas of Irish History,* London 1973, 2nd ed. 1981; *Patrick Pearse: The Triumph of Failure,* 1977; *James Connolly,* 1981; *Corridors of Death,* 1982, and *The Saint Valentine's Day Murders,* 1984 (both thrillers).

EGAN, Desmond, b. Athlone 1936. Teacher, publisher, poet. Poetry: *Midland,* 1972; *Leaves,* 1974; *Siege* and *Woodcutter,* 1978; *Athlone?* 1980; *Collected Poems,* Maine 1983, won Muir Award 1983, and American Society of Poetry Award 1984; *Seeing Double,* 1984; all pub. Kildare. Ed. *Era,* a literary magazine, and runs Goldsmith Press. Married to cookery writer Vivienne Abbott.

EGAN, Pierce, b. 1772, d. London 1849. Became sports journalist in London and wrote verse, comic pieces for the theatre and one or two plays. Is remembered for his *Life in London,* sketches of London low life, 1822, as well as *Boxiana: Sketches of Antient and Modern Pugilism,* 1812-21.

EGERTON, George, pseud. of Mary Chavelita Dunne, b. Australia 1859, daughter of an Irish officer, d. 1945. Brought up in Ireland, her father's improvidence created endless hardships. A relative sent her to Germany for two years, but she returned to look after her family. In 1887 she became travelling companion to a Mr and Mrs Higginson, the wife being the widow of Whyte Melville the author. Chavelita eloped with Higginson to Norway, where she became deeply impressed by the Norwegian literary revolution.

After Higginson's death in 1889 she met Knut Hamsun and undertook to translate *Hunger*. Returning to London in 1891 she married George Egerton Clairmonte, settled in County Cork and wrote a collection of short stories based on her Norwegian adventures. Published in 1893 as *Keynotes* it was both a success and a sensation, the first appearance in English literature of the new, Ibsenite woman, of sensuality treated as a desirable factor in life. Tragically for 'George Egerton', this first book was the peak of her career and reputation; *Discords*, 1894; *Symphonies*, 1897; *The Wheel of God* (an autobiographical novel) and *Rosa Amorosa* (a volume of love letters), 1901, were mere repetitions of her one theme when others had gone beyond her.

In 1901, Clairmonte being dead, she married Golding Bright, a young literary agent, and turned to plays. None was successful; *His Wife's Family*, NY 1908, and *Camilla States Her Case*, London 1925, were laughed off stage. From writing little she came to write nothing at all, and her work and reputation were almost totally forgotten except by historians of the literary nineties. Her letters and diaries have been edited by Terence de Vere White in his *A Leaf from the Yellow Book*, 1958.

EGLINTON, John, pseud. of William Kirkpatrick Magee, b. Dublin 1868, d. Bournemouth 1961. Second son of Presbyterian minister. Ed. Dublin, TCD, worked in National Library 1895-1921. Acted for time as George Moore's secretary, and edited *Dana,* a literary magazine that published AE, Padraic Colum, George Moore, W.B. Yeats and James Joyce, who offered Eglinton *Portrait of the Artist as a Young Man* as a serial. Eglinton turned it down. Leaving Ireland after the Treaty to settle in London, E. is now remembered for *Irish Literary Portraits,* 1935 (rep. NY 1967); and *A Memoir of AE,* 1937. Also, *Anglo-Irish Essays,* Dublin 1917.

ELLIS, Conleth, b. Carlow 1937. Ed. UCD, UCG. Teacher, poet. *Poems* (in collaboration), Carlow 1961; *This Ripening Time,* Carlow 1966; *Under the Stone,* Dublin 1975; and a volume in Irish, *Fomhar na nGeanna,* Dublin 1975. *After Doomsday,* Dublin 1982, and *Aimsir Fhaistineach,* 1982.

ELLIS-FERMOR, Una Mary, b. 1894, d. 1958. Ed. Oxford, Professor of English, London University, 1947-58. *The Irish Dramatic Movement,* 1939, rep. 1964.

FMMET, Christopher Temple, b. 1761, d. 1788. Brother of Robert E. Ed. TCD. Bar. His allegorical poem 'Decree' prophesied the downfall of the British Empire unless Ireland's wrongs were righted, and forms an interesting sidelight on his brother's revolutionary concerns.

EMMET, Robert, b. Dublin 1778, executed Dublin 1803. The son of the Viceroy's physician, and younger brother of Thomas Addis E. Left TCD to join United Irishmen 1798, his name being struck off the rolls in consequence. Travelled in Europe and met Napoleon and Talleyrand to interest them in an Irish invasion. The next year, 1803, he returned to Dublin, spent his personal fortune of £3000 on weapons and hoped to seize Dublin Castle and the Viceroy in a swift blow which would rouse the country. The attempt failed and Emmet escaped to the Wicklow mountains, but he returned to see Sarah Curran for a last farewell, was betrayed by an informer, captured, and hanged. His *Speech from the Dock,* printed immediately after the event, and reprinted countless times as a broadsheet throughout the century, served as a passionate rallying cry that found its justification in 1916. See RIDGEWAY, William.

ENGLISH, William, b. about 1710, d. 1778. An Augustinian monk who wrote ballads, including the famous *Cashel of Munster.*

ENNIS, John, b. Westmeath 1944. Ed. Cork and Dublin. Poet and teacher. Won Patrick Kavanagh Award 1975. Volumes of poetry include *Night on Hibernia,* Dublin 1976; *Dolmen Hill,* Dublin 1977 (containing 'Orpheus' that won Open Poetry Competition at Listowel Writers' Week, a competition he had already won the previous year); *A Drink of Spring,* Dublin 1979.

ENSOR, George, b. Dublin 1769, d. Co. Armagh 1843. Ed. TCD. Political theorist widely read in his day. *Addresses to the People of Ireland on the Degradation & Misery of their Country,* Dublin 1823, and *Irish affairs at the close of 1825,* Dublin 1826, are both interesting. He also attacked Malthus in *An Inquiry Concerning the Population of Nations, containing a Refutation of Mr. Malthus's Essay on Population,* 1818. There is much irony in this attempted refutation, in view of the coming Famine, but Ensor died before 1847.

EOGAN, George, b. Nobber, Co.Meath. Ed. UCD. Professor of Archaeology UCD. Leading authority on Ireland's Bronze Age. With Michael Herity, *Ireland in Prehistory,* 1977; *Hoards of the Later Bronze Age,* Dublin 1983; *Excavation at Knowth,* vol. 1, Dublin 1984.

ERVINE, St John Greer, b. Belfast 1883, d. England 1971. Worked in a Belfast insurance office at 14. Three years later emigrated to London. Saw service in the First World War, but during 1915 returned to Ireland and was for a time manager of the Abbey Theatre, where his early plays had already had great success: *Mixed Marriage,* 1910; *June Clegg,* 1911; *John Ferguson,* 1914.

After the war he became influential as a dramatic critic and continued writing both plays and novels. The best-known of his later plays are *The first Mrs Fraser,* 1928; *Boyd's Shop,* 1935; *Robert's Wife,* 1937; *Friends and Relations,* 1940; *Private Enterprise,* 1947; *My Brother Tom,* 1952; and *Esperanza,* 1957.

His novels include *Mrs Martin's Men, The Wayward Man, Alice and a Family, Changing Winds, The Foolish Lovers, Sophie.* Also wrote on the theatre and several biographies. *How to Write a Play,* 1928; *The Theatre In My Time,* 1933; *God's Soldier* (a life of General Booth), 1934; *Craig-*

avon, Ulsterman, 1949; *Oscar Wilde, A Present Time Appraisal,* 1951; *Bernard Shaw: His Life, Work and Friends,* 1956, etc.

ESLER, Erminda, b. Co. Donegal about 1860, daughter of Rev. Alexander Rentoul. Became a popular novelist, *The Way of Transgressors,* 1890, etc. and short-story writer for English magazines.

EVANS, Emyr Estyn, b. Wales 1905. Honorary Irishman with life-long association with Department of Geography, Queen's University, Belfast, 1928 until retirement as Director of Institute of Irish Studies 1970. Publications include *Irish Heritage,* 1942; *Mourne Country,* 1951, both Dundalk; *Irish Folk Ways,* 1957; *Prehistoric and Early Christian Ireland,* 1966; *The Personality of Ireland,* Cambridge 1973, repub. Belfast 1981; *The Irishness of the Irish* (essay collection), Belfast 1985.

EVERETT, Katherine, née Herbert, b. Cahirnane 1872, d. after 1951. Her *Bricks and Flowers,* 1949, and *Walk With Me,* 1951, contain interesting glimpses of the Anglo-Irish gentry in its decline, and some insights as to why it declined.

F

FAIRLEY, James S., b. Belfast 1940. Ed. Campbell College and QUB. Lecturer in Zoology UCG. *An Irish Beast Book,* Belfast 1975, 2nd ed. 1984; *Irish Whales and Whaling,* Belfast 1981.

FALLER, Kevin, b. Galway 1920, d. Dublin 1983. Journalist in Dublin since 1945. Poetry includes *Island Lyrics,* Dublin 1963; *Lament for the Bull Island,* Dublin 1973; *The Lilac Tree and Other Poems,* Dublin 1979. Also a novel, *Genesis,* 1953, and many plays for radio and TV. Poems included in *Love Poems of the Irish* and *The Penguin Book of Irish Verse. Memoirs* (collected poems), Dublin 1984.

FALLON, Gabriel, b. 1898, d. Dublin 1980. Joined civil service and worked in London as young man. Returned to Dublin 1920, joined Abbey Theatre Company as spare-time actor (the general practice then) and acted in the first productions of O'Casey's plays. Left company in 1928, but remained interested in theatre as critic and from 1959 as a Director of the Abbey. *Sean O'Casey: The Man I Knew,* 1965; *The Abbey and the Actor,* Dublin 1969 (autobiography).

FALLON, Niall, b. Co. Wexford 1941, son of Padraic F. Ed. TCD. Journalist. *The Armada in Ireland,* 1978; *The Lusitania,* 1980; *Fly-fishing for Irish Trout,* 1983.

FALLON, Padraic, b. Athenry, Co. Galway, 1906, d. 1974. Ed. Roscrea, Ballinasloe. Joined Customs and Excise service and served in Wexford for many years, where he also farmed. A poet of great power, very reluctant to publish in volume form. Has written some of the most remarkable verse-plays ever broadcast from Radio Éireann, particularly the treatments of Irish legend, *Diarmuid and Grainne,* called at the time Radio Éireann's 'best production', and *The Vision of Mac Conglinne,* 1953, both re-broadcast several times. A stage play, *The Seventh Step,* a tragedy in Classical Greek form but set in 20th century Ireland, was performed in Cork and Dublin, 1954, and had great critical success. Much of his poetry appeared in *The Dublin Magazine* in the 1950s. *Poems,* Dublin 1973; *Poems and Versions,* Manchester and Dublin, 1983.

FALLON, Peter, b. Germany 1951 of Irish parents. Ed. Glenstal, TCD. Set up The Gallery Press 1970. Lecture tours and periods as poet-in-residence in America. Ed., with Sean Golden, *Soft Day* (anthology of contemporary Irish writing), Notre Dame 1980, and, with Andrew Carpenter, *The Writers, A Sense of Ireland,* Dublin 1980. Fiction editor to the O'Brien Press 1980–. Poetry: *Co-incidence of Flesh,* 1973; *The First Affair,* 1974; *The Speaking Stones,* 1978; *Winter Work,* 1983; all pub. Dublin.

FALLS, Cyril Bentham, b. Dublin 1888, d. 1971. Served in First World War with Inniskillings. Appointed Gen. Staff; liaison duties with French Army. Military Correspondent for *The Times,* 1939-53; Chichele Professor of the History of War, Oxford 1946-53. Wrote many books on war, including *The History of the 36th (Ulster) Division,* 1922; *The Birth of Ulster,* 1936; *Elizabeth's Irish Wars,* 1950; and *Mountjoy: Elizabethan General,* 1955.

FARQUHAR, George, b. Londonderry 1677, d. 1707. Expelled from TCD 1695. Worked as a corrector of the press, and then as an actor at Smock Alley Theatre, where he played the part of Othello among others. In Dryden's *Indian Emperor* he accidentally stabbed another actor who almost died. Shocked, Farquhar gave up the stage, and went to London in 1697. He began writing plays, both adaptations from French and earlier English comedies, and original work of his own. His second play ran 53 nights at Drury Lane, an immense run for the period. But he made little out of it, or spent it quickly, because even after several more successes he was glad to accept a commission from Lord Orrery in 1704. He went on a recruiting drive in the midlands, and wrote his famous comedy *The Recruiting Officer,* 1706,based on his experiences.

He served briefly in Holland, but poverty forced him to sell his commission. A friend, Wilks the actor, found him reduced almost to starvation and lent him 20 guineas, which gave him breathing space to write his best comedy, *The Beaux Stratagem,* 1707. He died later that year, still in dreadful straits, and leaving two very young daughters to the care of Wilks.

Commonly included with the 'Restoration' dramatists, he belongs really to the 18th century and the picaresque novelists such as Fielding and Smollett and Defoe are his true companions in literature. He had great influence in England and Europe. His plays include *Love and a Bottle*, 1698; *The Constant Couple*, 1699; *Sir Harry Wildair*, 1701; *The Inconstant* (based on Beaumont and Fletcher), 1702; *The Twin Rivals*, 1702; *The Stage Coach* (from the French), 1704. He also wrote essays, *Love and Business* (including 'The Discourse on Comedy'), 1702, and a poem, 'Barcelona', 1708.

FARRELL, Bernard, b. Sandycove 1939. Ed. Dublin, where he lives. Worked in Sealink 1960-79. Plays include *I Do Not Like Thee, Dr Fell*, Peacock 1979; *Canaries*, Abbey 1980; *All In Favour Said No!*, Abbey 1981; *Then Moses Met Marconi*, Project 1983. *All the Way Back*, Abbey 1985. Radio plays: *Gliding with Mr Gleeson* and *Scholarship Trio*, both RTE 1984. Won Rooney Prize 1980. Also writes short stories.

FARRELL, Brian, b. Manchester 1929. Ed. UCD and Harvard. Lecturer in Politics UCD; RTE presenter/commentator. Many articles and essays on Irish political system and political history, including 'Markievicz and the Women of the Revolution' in *Leaders and Men of the Easter Rising*, ed. F.X. Martin, 1967. Books: *Chairman or Chief? The Role of the Taoiseach in Irish Government*, 1971; and *The Founding of Dáil Éireann*, 1971; *Sean Lemass*, 1983; all pub. Dublin.

FARRELL, M. J., pseud of Molly Skrine, see KEANE, Molly.

FARRELL, Michael, b. 1900, d. 1962. Ed. UCD, where he studied medicine. Imprisoned during Troubles. After release made long walking tour of Continent, and then took a job in the Belgian Congo. Returned to Ireland 1930, and studied at TCD. In 1932 he left Dublin to live in the Wicklow hills, gave up medicine and devoted himself to a novel which became a legend in 'literary' Dublin; the archetypal Irish novel, endlessly talked about and never written. In the 1940s wrote for *The Bell* and for Radio Éireann. In the 1950s his novel had reached vast proportions. Even when a publisher had been found for it he could not bring himself to edit it to publishable length, and he died leaving a huge pile of MS. His long-time friend Dr Monk Gibbon edited the MS and it was published in London in 1963 as *Thy Tears Might Cease*, republished the same year in America. It was an immediate and overwhelming success, a best seller in both continents; the long, sensitive and moving study of a man very like the author, living through the first half of the century.

FARRELL, Michael, b. Co. Derry 1940s. One of the leaders of Northern Irish civil rights group, People's Democracy, late 1960s and early '70s. Now journalist in Dublin. *Northern Ireland, the Orange State*, 1976, revised ed. 1980; *Arming the Protestants: The Formation of the Ulster Special Constabulary and RUC 1920-27*, 1983.

FARREN, Robert, see Ó FARACHÁIN, Roibeard.

FARRINGTON, Conor Anthony, b. Dublin 1928. Ed. St Columba's and TCD. Scholarship to Yale Drama School 1959. Acted in England, toured to Malta and India, joined RE Rep. Co. 1955. Has written several radio plays, including *Death of Don Juan*, 1951; *The Tribunal*, 1959 (broadcast Ireland, Canada, Australia, Holland, etc.); *The Good Shepherd*, 1961. Stage plays include *The Last P.M.*, Dublin Theatre Festival 1963. Published plays include *The Ghostly Garden*, 1964, prize winner in ICA Drama Competition; *Aaron Thy Brother*, Dublin 1975.

FEEHAN, John, b. Birr, Co. Offaly, 1946. Ed. TCD. Fellow of Geological Society of London. Historical geographer. *The Landscape of Slieve Bloom*, Dublin 1979; *Laois: An Environmental History*, Laois 1983.

FEEHAN, Sean, b. Cashel 1916. Ed. Rockwell, UCG. Served in Irish Army until 1945, retiring as captain. Co-founder Mercier Press, Cork, in 1945, mainly for religious publications. Has written biography of his wife, *Tomorrow to be Brave*, 1972; several books on sailing, including *The Wind that Round the Fastnet Sweeps*, 1978; one on publishing, *An Irish Publisher and his World*, 1969; controversial books, *The Shooting of Michael Collins*, 1981; *Bobby Sands and the Tragedy of Northern Ireland*, 1983; *Operation Brogue*, Cork 1984, (detailing British Secret Service intrigues in Irish political life), all pub. Dublin and Cork. Wrote *The Comic History of Ireland* with E.J. Delaney, 1951, rep. in abbreviated ed. 1964, and ed. *The Irish Bedside Book*, 1980.

FEENEY, John, b. Dublin 1948, d. Sussex 1984 in air crash. Ed. UCD. Journalist and publisher (founder Egotist Press). *John Charles McQuaid* (biography), Cork 1974; *Worm Friday* (novel), Dublin 1974; *Mao Dies and Other Stories*, Dublin 1977. Founder-member Irish Writers' Co-Op.

FENNELL, Desmond Carolan, b. Belfast 1929. Ed. Belvedere, UCD, Bonn. Edited *Herder Correspondence*, 1964-68. 1976-82 Lectured in Political Science and Modern European History at UCG; now in Communications, College of Commerce, Dublin. Newspaper columnist, broadcaster. Books include *Mainly in Wonder*, 1959; *The State of the Nation: Ireland since the Sixties*, Swords 1983; *Beyond Nationalism*, Swords 1985. Also ed. *The Changing Face of Catholic Ireland* (foreword by K. Rahner SJ), 1968.

FERGUSON, Mary Catherine, née Guinness, b. Stillorgan 1823. d. 1905. Married Samuel Ferguson the poet and archaeologist. Pub. *The Story of the Irish Before the Conquest*, 1868, which went into many editions. In 1896 brought out *Sir Samuel Ferguson In the Ireland of His Day*.

FERGUSON, Samuel, b. Belfast 1810, d. Howth 1886. Ed. TCD. Bar 1838, QC 1859, LL.D. 1864. Founded Protestant Repeal Association in aid of Young Ireland movement, but later withdrew from active politics and devoted himself to scholarship and poetry. Became Deputy-Keeper of Public Records, Dublin, 1867, and President of the Royal Irish Academy 1881. In 1878 he was knighted for his public services. His most important antiquarian work is his famous *Ogham Inscriptions in Ireland Scotland & Wales*, Edinburgh 1887, edited by his widow.

His poetry includes both humorous verse and long narrative poems based on Gaelic legends. His most famous comic poem was written under the pseud. 'Mr Michael Heffernan, Master of the National School, Tallymactaggart, Co. Leitrim' and was titled 'Father Tom and the Pope, or a Night in the Vatican'.

Other books were *The Cromlech on Howth,* 1864; *Lays of the Western Gael,* 1865; *Congal,* 1872; *The Poems of Samuel Ferguson,* Dublin 1880; *The Forging of the Anchor,* 1883; *The Hibernian Night's Entertainment,* Dublin 1888. He contributed frequently to *Blackwood's Magazine,* for which he wrote some Irish stories, as well as articles.

FERRAR, John, b. Limerick *c.* 1740, d. Dublin *c.* 1800. Remembered chiefly for his *History of the City of Limerick,* 1767, published in Limerick where he was a bookseller and printer, probably by himself, and *A View of Ancient & Modern Dublin,* Dublin 1796.

FIACC, Padraic (Patrick Joseph O'Connor), b. Belfast 1924. Ed. New York where he studied briefly for priesthood before returning to Belfast and lay life 1946. Poem: *Woe to the Boy* appeared in part in *New Irish poets,* NY 1948; the same collection in full, still unpublished, won AE Memorial Prize 1957. *By the Black Stream* (poems 1947-67), Dublin and Oxford 1969; *Odour of Blood,* Kildare 1973, 2nd ed. 1983; *Nights in the Bad Place,* Belfast 1977. *Woe to the Boy* was finally pub. Belfast 1979.

FIGGIS, Darrell, b. Rathmines 1882, d. suicide London 1925. Taken to India as a child, later worked in London for tea importers. Joined the Irish Volunteers, and was involved in the Howth gun-running incident of 1914 with Erskine Childers and others. Drew up the Constitution of the Irish Free State, and was a member of Dáil Éireann for County Dublin. He wrote a play, *Queen Tara;* poetry, *A Vision of Life;* some fiction, and *The Return of the Hero* under the pseud. 'Michael Ireland'.

FINDLEY, William, b. N. Ireland 1741, d. Pennsylvania 1821. Went to America 1763 and fought in the American War of Independence. Elected member of first Congress in which he supported Jefferson and opposed the draft Constitution. His *History of Insurrection in Pennsylvania,* Philadelphia 1796, is interesting. He continued in Congress to 1817.

FINGLAS, Patrick, b. Ireland *c.* 1480, d. Dublin *c.* 1540. Appointed Baron of the Exchequer in Ireland 1520; Chief Justice of the King's Bench 1534; remembered for his *Breviat of the getting of Ireland, and of the decaie of the same,* printed in Harris's *Hibernica,* 1770. It describes the 'conquest of Ireland, the decay of that land, and measures proposed to remedy the grievances thereof arising from the oppressions of the Irish nobility'. The MS is reputedly in the Public Record Office.

FINNEGAN, Seamus, b. Belfast 1949. Ed. Belfast and Manchester. Teacher before becoming full-time playwright. Has written many plays including *Laws of God* and *Race,* 1978; *Paddy and Britannia,* 1979; *Act of Union,* 1980; *Soldiers,* and *Herself Alone,* 1981; *James Joyce and the Israelites,*

London and Tel Aviv 1982. *Beyond a Joke, North, Mary's Men, Tout* (RSC Thought Crimes Series), 1984, and *Gombeen,* 1985. Also wrote TV scripts for *Interrogation,* BBC 1 1981, *Doctors' Dilemmas,* BBC 2 1983, and *Beyond a Joke,* Channel 4 1983 (commissioned treatment on racism).

FINNERTY, Peter, b. Co. Galway 1766, d. Westminster 1822. Defended by Curran over a libel he had written for the *Dublin Press,* 1797, but condemned. Went as war correspondent on Walcheren Expedition and published highly critical bulletins in the *Morning Chronicle,* 1809. The government forced him to return to England in a warship to silence him, and when he accused Castlereagh of instigating this he was tried again for libel and imprisoned, 1811. Appears to have been the first active Irish war correspondent, although this honour is usually accorded to William Howard Russell. *The Case of Peter Finnerty, including a Full Report of all the Proceedings which took place in the Court of King's Bench, with notes and Preface comprehending an Essay upon the Law of Libel,* anon., but probably by Finnerty, went into four editions in 1811, an indication of the furious interest surrounding any controversy involving the freedom of the press. Finnerty deserves a place among those who fought to achieve it.

FITZGERALD, Brian, b. London 1909 of Irish father, d. London 1977. Historian biographer. *Emily, Duchess of Leinster: A Study of Her Life and Times, 1731-1814,* 1949; ed. *Correspondence of Emily, Duchess of Leinster,* vol.1, 1949, vol.2, 1954, vol.3, 1957; *Lady Luisa Connolly: An Anglo-Irish Biography,* 1950; *The Geraldines: An Experiment in Irish Government, 1169-1601,* 1951; *The Anglo-Irish: Three Representative Types, Cork, Ormonde, Swift, 1602-1745,* 1952; *Daniel Defoe: A Study in Conflict,* 1954.

FITZGERALD, Nigel. b. Co. Cork 1906. Ed. Clongowes and TCD. Toured with Anew McMaster's Shakespearean company. During Second World War served in Europe and Africa. Has written a number of popular thrillers; titles include *Midsummer Malice,* 1953; *The House is Falling,* 1955; *Imagine a Man,* 1956; *The Candles Are All Out,* 1960; *The Day of the Adder,* 1963.

FITZGERALD, Percy Hetherington, b. Co. Louth 1834, d. London 1925. Ed. Stonyhurst and TCD. Bar. Crown prosecutor, NE circuit, but moved to London and became a writer, publishing a reputed 200 volumes of fiction and history, as well as practising sculpture and painting. He is responsible for the statue of Dr Johnson in the Strand, a bust of Dickens at Bath, and a statue of Boswell at Lichfield. Among his better known books are *Beauty Talbot, The Dear Girl, Bella Donna, Diana Jay,* and *Death Jewels.* He also wrote several plays, some of which were printed.

FITZGIBBON, Edward, b. Limerick 1803, d. London 1857. One of the great fishermen of all time, writing on angling for *The Observer,* and *Bell's Life in London.* He had been brought to London at 14, and then to

Marseilles, returning to London in 1830 as House of Commons reporter for the *Morning Chronicle*. He once caught salmon and grilse in the one river during 55 hours continuous fishing. His *Handbook of Angling*, 1847, is a classic and went into many editions. *The Book of Salmon*, 1850, was written with Andrew Young. In 1853 he brought out the best edition of Walton's *Compleat Angler*. Unfortunately he drank heavily between bouts of abstinence, and died of it.

FITZGIBBON, Robert Louis Constantine, b. Massachusetts, US 1919, d. Dublin 1983. Ed. Munich, Sorbonne, Oxford. With British and Australian armies 1939-46. Teacher in Bermuda 1946-47. FRSL; MIAL. Fiction: *The Arabian Bird*, 1948; *The Iron Hoop*, 1949; *Dear Emily*, 1952; *The Holiday*, 1953; *The Fair Game*, 1956; *Paradise Lost and More*, 1959; *Watcher in Florence*, 1959; *When the Kissing Had to Stop*, 1960; *Going to the River*, 1963; *High Heroic*, 1969; *In the Bunker*, 1973; *The Golden Age*, 1975; *Man in Aspic*, 1977. Non-fiction: *The Blitz*, 1957; *The Life of Dylan Thomas*, 1966; *London's Burning*, 1970; *Red Hand: the Ulster Colony*, 1971; *The Life and Times of de Valera*, 1973; *Secret Intelligence in the Twentieth Century*, 1976; *Drink*, 1979; *The Irish in Ireland*, Newton Abbot 1983. A play, *The Devil at Work*, Abbey 1971. Also many translations from French, German and Italian.

FITZGIBBON, Theodora, née Rosling. b. London 1916 of Irish parents. Ed. Brussels, Paris, London. Widely travelled, living in India, America, France, Italy for several years. Best known as writer on international and Irish cookery: *The Food of the Western World*, US 1976; *A Taste of Ireland*, 1968; *Irish Traditional Food*, Dublin 1983; and many other cookery books. Winner of Glenfiddich Gold Medal Award 1977. Novel: *Flight of the Kingfisher*, 1968. Autobiography: *With Love*, 1982; *Love Lies a Loss*, 1985.

FITZMAURICE, George, b. Co. Kerry 1878, d. 1963. Entered civil service and was in Dept. of Agriculture until he retired on pension. Became well known as a playwright about 1900 and was one of the first 'names', apart from Yeats, to write for the Abbey. In 1907 his *The Country Dressmaker* was one of the theatre's first popular successes. He followed it with *The Pie dish*, 1908; *The Magic Glasses*, 1913; and *Twixt the Giltinans and the Carmodys*, 1923. Another play *The Moonlighters* was never produced. He wrote also for *The Dublin Magazine* whose editor Seumas O'Sullivan was his long-time friend. For many years he lived in deep seclusion.

FITZPATRICK, T., b. Co. Down 1845, d. Dublin 1912. School-teacher and historian. Novels include *Jabez Murdock* (under pseud. 'Banna Borka'), 1887, and *The King of Claddagh*, 1899. He published two interesting volumes on the Civil War period in the Waterford area: *The Bloody Bridge & other papers of 1641*, Dublin 1903, and *Waterford during the Civil War*, Waterford 1912.

FITZPATRICK, W. J., b. Co. Down 1902, d. Co. Down 1982. Ed. Kilkeel, became journalist and broadcaster with interest in folklore. *An Old-Timer Talking*, Mourne 1963, and *Margaret O'Mourne*, Mourne 1963, record local folk tales and superstitions from two singers and story-tellers of the district. *Sailing Ships of Mourne*, Mourne 1975; *A Mourne Man's Memoirs*, Mourne 1982.

FITZPATRICK, William John, b. Dublin 1830, d. Dublin 1895. Ed. Clongowes. First came to notice in 1856 in a pamphlet claiming that Thomas Scott, brother of Sir Walter, had written much of the Waverley novels. He published *The Friends, Foes and Adventures of Lady Morgan*, 1859, and *Lady Morgan, her Career, Literary & Personal*, 1860. He had also published *Lord Edward FitzGerald*, 1859, his first great success; *Life and Times of Bishop Doyle*, 1861; and then in 1866 his most famous book, *The Sham Squire*, continuing the story of FitzGerald and his betrayal. This sold 16,000 copies. In 1888 he published *Correspondence of Daniel O'Connell*, and in 1892 *Secret Service under Pitt*, of equal interest, and a study in historical detective work: Pope Leo XIII gave him the Order of St Gregory the Great in recognition of the O'Connell book, and he was made Hon. LL. D. of Royal University of Ireland.

FITZ-SIMON, Christopher, b. Belfast 1934. Ed. St Columba's, TCD. Drama director RTE; artistic director Irish Theatre Company; script editor National Theatre Society; lecturer in Theatre Studies TCD 1983-. Writes plays for radio and short stories. Books: *The Arts in Ireland, A Chronology*, Dublin 1982; *The Irish Theatre*, 1983.

FITZSIMON, Ellen O'Connell, b. Dublin 1805, d. 1883. Eldest daughter of Daniel O'Connell. Remembered for poem 'The Song of the Irish Emigrant in America', which contains the immortal line 'my ears are full of tears'. It appeared in the volume *Darrynane in Eighteen Hundred and Thirty-Two and Other Poems*, Dublin 1863.

FITZWILLIAM, Michael, pseud. of John Benignus Lyons, b. Co. Mayo 1922. Ed. UCD; MD 1949; FRCPI 1959. Travelled in Far East, Americas, Europe. Published *A Question of Surgery*, 1960 (also paperback); *South Downs General Hospital*, 1961 (paperback, Dutch and German trans.); *When Doctors Differ*, 1963 (paperback, Dutch and German trans.). For work under own name see LYONS, John Benignus.

FLECKNOE, Richard, b. *c.* 1600, d. probably 1678. In Rome 1645 where he became a Jesuit. Visited Constantinople 1647, and Portugal and Brazil 1648. *A Relation of Ten Years Travels in Europe Asia Afrique and America*, 1656. He knew many of the leading English poets, and Dryden satirised him as 'MacFlecknoe'. His verse drama *Loves Dominion*, 1654,was very popular and often reprinted. He wrote comedies, tragi-comedies, allegories and a great deal of comic verse.

FLATTISBURY, Philip, b. *c.* 1470 perhaps near Naas and died there about 1530. Drew up the *Red Book of the Earls of Kildare*, 1503, being a collection of title deeds and documents concerning land and property held by the Kildare Geraldines. In 1537 this book was searched for by the Tudor agents during the proceedings against the chief Kildare Geraldines, but it was kept concealed from them. It is still in the hands of the FitzGerald family and there is a photostat copy in the National Library of Ireland. The Irish MSS Commission published an edition of the MS as *The Red Book of the Earls of Kildare*, ed. and trans. Gearoid MacNiocaill, Dublin 1964.

FLEETWOOD, John Finlayson, b. 1917. Ed. Dublin, Brussels. Doctor. Pub. *A History of Medicine in Ireland*, Dublin 1951, rep. 1983.

FLEMING, James, b. Carlow 1830, d. London 1908. Appointed a Royal Chaplain 1876, his funeral sermon for the Duke of Clarence, published as *Recognition in Eternity*, 1892, achieved enormous sales, making a profit for Fleming of £1725, all of which he gave to charity. This figure goes some way to explaining the number of sermons printed in the 19th century.

FLEMING, Lionel, b. Cork, d. 1974. Journalist and broadcaster. His *Head or Harp*, 1965, is a nostalgic look at the Protestant gentry of the south of Ireland making its terms with the new Free State.

FLOOD, Joseph Mary, b. Longford 1882, d. *c.* 1954. Ed. Longford and Paris. Bar 1908. Professor of English and Roman Law UCG 1917-22; District Justice 1922, one of the first to be appointed after the Treaty. His *Ireland: Its Myths and Legends*, Dublin 1916, and its companion volume, *Ireland: Its Saints and Scholars*, Dublin 1917, still continue to be read. Other books include *The Abbé Edgeworth*, Dublin 1919; *Life of Chevalier Wogan*, Dublin 1922; *Five Saints of France*, Dublin 1937; *The Sieges of Limerick*, Limerick 1944. In 1950 F. was appointed to the Irish Film Censorship Appeal Board; resigned 1953.

FLOOD, William Henry Grattan, b. Co. Waterford 1859, d. Enniscorthy 1928. Became organist in Enniscorthy Cathedral 1895, was Irish correspondent of the *Tablet*, and was made Kt of St Gregory 1922. Wrote *History of Enniscorthy*, Enniscorthy 1898; *History of Irish Music*, Dublin 1905; *Story of the Bagpipe*, 1911; *John Field of Dublin, Inventor of the Nocturne*, Dublin 1920 (a 40 pp. booklet); *Introductory Sketch of Irish Musical History*, 1922; *Early Tudor Composers*, Oxford 1925.

FLYNN, Mannix, b. Dublin 1957. Ed. Dublin, Letterfrack, Mountjoy. A professional actor. Play: *He Who Laughs Wins*. His first novel, *Nothing To Say*, Swords 1983, received much critical attention and caused him to be nominated as one of the Twelve Great Irish Writers by a publishers' and booksellers' committee, which itself received some critical attention for the nomination, not least because its list of Twelve Greats consisted of thirteen names.

FORRISTAL, Desmond Timothy, b. Dublin 1930. Ed. Belvedere, UCD. Ordained priest 1955. Plays include *The True Story of the Horrid Popish Plot*, 1972; *Black Man's Country*, 1974; *The Seventh Sin*, 1976; *Captive*

Audience, 1979, all Gate, Dublin; *Kolbe*, Abbey 1982. Also *Maximilian of Auschwitz* (biography of Fr Kolbe), Swords 1982. PP of Dalkey 1985.

FOSTER, Robert Fitzroy, b. 1949. Ed. Newtown Waterford, Delaware US, TCD. Ph.D. 1975. Lecturer in History London University 1974-83; Reader 1983-. Married Aisling O'Conor Donelan 1972; one son Phineas Patrick. Executive committee member of British-Irish Association. Books: *Charles Stewart Parnell: The Man and his Family*, Brighton 1976; *Lord Randolph Churchill: A Political Life*, Oxford 1982; *Political Novels and Nineteenth Century History*, Winchester 1982.

FOSTER, Vere Henry Lewis, b. Copenhagen 1819, where his Irish father was British Minister, d. Belfast 1900. Ed. Eton, Oxford, entered diplomatic service; in South America 1844-47. In London in 1847 he heard of the Famine and went to investigate. Remained to work for Famine Relief, and afterwards for cheap passages for emigrants, travelling three times to US in the so-called coffin ships, to expose the racketeering of the owners and the miseries of the passengers.

Seeing that only education could improve the condition of the poor in Ireland he spent much of his fortune from 1865 onwards in the building of parish schools. He also helped set up the teachers' union which was to become the Irish National Teachers Organisation. In 1868 he designed and had published the first of the famous Vere Foster Copy books, as *Elementary Drawing Copybooks*. Innumerable editions followed, it being his belief that a good copper-plate hand was the first and most essential lesson a child could learn. These books remained in common use well into the time of the Free State.

In his last years Foster worked for the relief of the sick and poor in Belfast and died of self-neglect. All his money was gone and hardly a newspaper in Ireland gave two lines to his obituary.

FOX, Charlotte Milligan, b. Omagh 1864, d. London 1916. Founded the *Irish Folk Song Society*, 1904, and travelled through Ireland collecting folk songs and music on gramophone records. Wrote *Annals of the Irish Harpers*, 1911.

FOX, R. M., b. Leeds 1899. Worked in engineering shop in London, gained scholarship to Oxford 1914, delayed for five years by war. During war gave up exemption from military service in order to register protest as conscientious objector. Three years in prison. At Oxford 1919-22. Visited Russia 1921. Journalist in Dublin where he became involved in Irish Labour and Nationalist movements, and married Patricia Lynch 1922. Books include *Factory Echoes*, 1919 (essays, translated into Russian); *Smoky Crusade* (on being a C.O.), 1920; *The Triumphant Machine* (on industrial psychology); *Rebel Irishwomen*, Dublin 1935 (pub. in paperback); *Green Banners*, 1938; *History of the Citizen Army*, Dublin 1943; *James Connolly*, Tralee 1947; *Years of Freedom: Ireland 1921-48*, Cork 1948; *Jim Larkin*, 1957; *Louie Bennett*, Dublin 1958; *China Diary*, 1959 (following a journalists' invitation journey to China that year).

FRANCIS, M. E., pseud. of Mrs Francis Blundell, b. Killiney *c*. 1855, d. 1930. Went to Liverpool on her marriage. Contributed to *Irish Monthly* etc. and wrote a total of 30 novels: *Whither*, 1892; *The Story of Dan*, 1894; *Miss Erin*, 1898; *Children of Light and Other Stories*, 1908; *The Tender Passion*, 1910; *Dark Rosaleen*, 1915; *Beck of Beckford*, 1920, etc.

FRANCIS, Philip, Kt, b. Dublin 1740, d. London 1818. Son of Rev. Dr Philip F., the translator of Horace. Ed. Dublin and St Paul's School, London. Member of Bengal Council set up in 1773 to advise the Governor General, Warren Hastings. Conceived a jealous hatred for H., was wounded by him in a duel 1780, and retiring the next year to England with a fortune gained in India, set himself to ruin Hastings. He used Burke as his tool and between them they had H. impeached 1788, the impeachment failing only after six years of malignant attack and total ruin of H. Sheridan was also deeply involved in this sordid story of mainly Irish venom.

Francis was made KCB 1806, enjoyed the friendship of the Prince Regent, and at 74 married a young wife who doted on him. She, with many others, was convinced that he was Junius, of *The Junius Letters*, first published in *The Public Advertiser*, 1769-72, reprinted with 113 additional letters 1812. He never admitted the authorship, and although he is the most generally accepted candidate, others have been plausibly put forward. See BOYD, Hugh Macaulay, for example, in this volume.

FRANKAU, Julia, née Miss Davis, b. Dublin 1864, d. London 1916. Wrote sometimes under pseud. of Frank Danby. Although very popular as a novelist, her enduring work was in biography and art history. *Eighteenth Century Colour Prints*, 1900; *Life of J. R. Smith*, 1902; and *Lives of James & William Wand*, 1904, are regarded as her best work. Novels included *Pigs in Clover* and *Babes in Bohemia*.

FRANKLIN, Andrew, b. *c*. 1760, d. *c*. 1820. Emigrated to London. Ed. *Morning Post* in 1805. Wrote many operettas and comedies, including *The Mermaid*, 1792; *The Wandering Jew*, 1797; *The Counterfeit*, 1804.

FRAZER, John, b. Birr about 1804, d. Dublin 1852. Became a cabinet maker and wrote verse under the name Jean de Jean, de Jean being the original name of his family. Became editor of the *Trades Advocate* in Dublin, and contributed to *The Nation*, *The Irish Felon*, etc. *Poems by J. de Jean*, Dublin 1851.

FRENCH, Nicholas, b. Wexford 1604, d. Ghent 1678. Ed. Louvain. Ordained and became parish priest of Wexford about 1640, Bishop of Ferns 1643. One of the Wexford representatives at Confederation of Kilkenny, 1645, and well-informed as to the inner intrigues and failures of the Confederation. *The Unkinde Deserter or Royall Men & True Friends*, Brussels 1652, accuses the Duke of Ormonde of causing the failure of the previous year's mission to Brussels, intended to secure the Duke of

Lorraine's interest on behalf of Irish Catholics. In 1653 French was in Paris as coadjutor to the Archbishop. He was in Santiago 1662-65, and in 1670 became President of the Irish College, Louvain, where he had been for some time. In 1668 he had published there *The Settlement and Sale of Ireland*. In 1675 he moved to Ghent as coadjutor.

FRENCH, William Percy, b. Clooneyquin, Co. Roscommon 1854, d. Formby 1920. Ed. England and TCD. BA 1876; BE 1881. Wrote his most famous comic poem while still a student. 'Abdallah Bubbul Ameer' appeared under a pseud. and was never copyrighted. Many names have been suggested as the true author, but there is no reasonable doubt that Percy French wrote it. After leaving TCD he practised for six years as a civil engineer in Co. Cavan, and at the same time continued writing.

He became editor of a comic paper, *The Jarvey,* wrote libretti for musical comedies and opera, and began giving professional entertainments, singing his own songs. He was a great success, hitting off the English taste for stage Irishry, without offending his fellow countrymen to too great an extent; a remarkable feat. Many of his songs have passed into Irish folk music, such as 'The West Clare Railway' with its refrain 'Are you right there, Michael, are you right?' This song was based on real characters, and led to a famous libel case with the directors of the railway.

As well as writing and singing, French was also a talented painter, and painted several pictures of Irish scenes for King George V.

His books include *Chronicles and Poems, Racquety Rhymes, More Poems and Parodies*. His play *The Knight of the Road* was produced in Dublin 1891.

FRIEL, Brian, b. Co. Tyrone 1929. Ed. St Columb's College Derry, St Joseph's Training College Belfast. School-teacher until 1960, since when he relied entirely on writing. Received the Arts Council Macaulay Fellowship. Appointed shareholder of the Abbey Theatre 1965. Has written many short stories, mainly for *The New Yorker,* plays for radio and for the stage. Short-story collections: *The Saucer of Larks,* London 1962, US 1963; *The Gold in the Sea,* London and US 1966; *The Diviner* (a selection), Dublin and London 1983. Plays include *This doubtful paradise* first performed Belfast 1959; *The Enemy Within,* Abbey 1962. *The Blind Mice,* Eblana 1963; *Philadelphia, Here I come!* Gaiety 1964, published London 1965 and trans. into many languages, including German, Greek and Italian. Performed with great success NY 1966. *The Loves of Cass Maguire,* first performed Dublin 1966; *Lovers,* 1966; *The Gentle Island,* 1971; *The Freedom of the City,* 1973; *Volunteers,* 1974; *Faith Healer,* 1979; *Aristocrats,* 1979; *Translations,* 1980; trans. *Chekov's Three Sisters,* 1981; *The Communication Cord,* Derry 1982; and *Selected Plays of Brian Friel,* 1984. Founder and director of Field Day Theatre Company based Derry since 1980.

His plays are deeply rooted in Ireland, but concern themselves with much wider problems than those of being Irish.

FULLER, James Franklin, b. Denniquin, Kerry 1835, d. Dublin 1924. Spent some time as an actor before qualifying as an architect. Designed many churches and country mansions in Ireland, and wrote several novels which were highly praised at the time, and remain interesting. The best are probably *Culmshire Folk*, 1873, and *John Orlebar, Clerk*, 1878. He also wrote his autobiography *Omniana, The Autobiography of an Irish Octogenarian*, 1915.

FURLONG, Alice, b. Dublin *c.* 1875, d. 1946. Poems include *Roses and Rue*, 1899, and *Tales of Fairy Folk, Queens and Heroes*, Dublin 1907. Her elder sister Mary, who died 1898, also wrote poetry.

FURLONG, Nicholas, b. Wexford 1929. Ed. Wexford, Warrenstown and Dublin. Farmer and writer. *Dermot, King of Leinster and the Foreigners*, Tralee 1973; *Fifty Years A-Ploughing*, Athy 1981; *Loch Garman and Wexford*, Wexford 1982; *Guides to Kilkenny, Waterford, Carlow and Wexford*, Dublin 1984. Plays: *Insurrection '98*, 1965; *The Lunatic Fringe*, 1966; and *Purple and Gold*, 1984. All Wexford.

FURLONG, Thomas, b. Scarawalsh 1794, d. 1827. Son of a small farmer. Became a grocer's curate and then a journalist. Edited *New Irish Magazine*, 1822. Translated poetry from the Irish and wrote a great deal of verse in English for many journals, in Ireland and England. Hardiman included many of his translations in *Irish Minstrelsy*. Three collections of his poetry published: *The Misanthrope*, 1819; *The Doom of Derenzie*, 1829; and *The Plagues of Ireland*, 1834; the last two posthumously.

G

GAGE, Thomas, b. Ireland 1597, d. Kent *c.* 1655. Travelling in Spain joined Dominicans, in 1625 was sent as missionary to the Philippines, and afterwards to Central America. Went to England, renounced Catholicism, and was made Protestant rector of Deal in Kent. His *English-American, or New Survey of the West Indias*, 1648, was translated into French and German, republished many times in the next 60 years, and again in 1928. It deals with many interesting matters, including his experiences of sorcery and voodoo. He also wrote *A duell between a Jesuit and a Dominican*, 1651.

GAHAN, William, b. Dublin 1732, d. Dublin 1804. Augustinian friar and writer of influential spiritual works. Joined Augustinians 1748, ordained Louvain 1755, gaining Doctorate in Theology. Returned Dublin 1761 founding a school, St John's Lane, which still exists. Prior of Dublin Community 1770-78 and 1803-04. Provincial of Irish Augustinians 1782-86. As administrator was deeply involved in restoration of formal religious life and organisation after persecution of Catholics from 1691 to 1760.

Gained public fame over the Dr Butler case. Butler was a Catholic bishop who apostasized in 1787 and married a Protestant to obtain family estates and provide an heir. Nearing death in 1800, he returned to Catholic faith making his confession to Fr Gahan. Relatives contested Dr Butler's will and G. was subpoenaed as a witness in resulting law case. G. refused to break seal of confessional and was imprisoned for seven days for contempt of court. On G.'s death four years later he was buried in Protestant graveyard of St James, Dublin, Catholics being forbidden by law to possess own cemetries.

Major works include *A Manual of Catholic Piety*, Dublin 1788, repub. Dublin 1927; *Compendious Abstract of the History of the Church of Christ*, Dublin 1793, repub. NY 1871; also ed. Bourdaloue SJ, *Spiritual Retreat*, Dublin 1801, repub. Dublin 1893. His most popular work, the *Manual*, was republished in Scotland, England, Spain, India and America, with more than 50 editions over a 140-year period. It was used by Catholic soldiers in the British Army, Irish people in English prisons, and nuns in convents.

GALLAGHER, Frank, b. Cork 1893, d. 1962. Pseud. 'David Hogan' and 'David O'Neill'. Journalist. Joined Irish Volunteers and from 1919 worked under Erskine Childers on publicity staff of Republican Government. Edited the *Irish Bulletin*, the clandestine journal of the movement. Imprisoned 1920, inspired a lengthy hunger strike. Editor of *Irish Press* 1931; Head of Govt. Information Bureau, 1940; on staff of National Library 1954. Wrote *Days of Fear*, 1928 (on the War of Independence); *The Four Glorious Years*, Dublin 1953, under name David Hogan; and *The Indivisible Island*, 1957. A fellow member of the National Library staff, Thomas P. O'Neill assisted largely with that book.

GALLAGHER, Patrick (Paddy the Cope), b. Co. Donegal 1873, d. Co. Donegal 1966. Son of a poor peasant farmer went to work at 9 years old as a day labourer. In *My Story*, 1939, he describes the hardships of the labourers travelling from Donegal to Scotland for the potato harvest. From these experiences grew his determination to improve the lot of his neighbourhood by establishing a co-operative. Against the fierce opposition of the local middlemen he succeeded in establishing what came to be know as 'the Cope', and was himself to become nationally known as 'Paddy the Cope'. *My Story* gives an account of his difficulties in simple and often moving words.

GALLAHER, Lee, b. Co. Wicklow 1939. Painter and playwright. Plays: *Kiss Me, Mister Bogart*, Lantern 1970; *All the Candles in Your Head*, Lantern 1974; *The Velvet Abbatoir*, Project 1976 (incorporating his own collages). TV and radio plays include *Jutland; Errors and Omissions;* BBC and RTE 1983. Co-writer with Wesley Burrowes, of TV serial, *Glenroe*, RTE 1983-84.

GALLIVAN, G. P. (Gerry), b. Limerick 1920. Ed. locally, works with an

GALVIN

American airline. In 1953 his first play *Alas Poor Yorick* won Eire Society award in Boston, US. *Decision at Easter* produced Gate, 1959; *Mourn the Ivy Leaf,* 1960 Theatre Festival; *The Stepping Stone* produced Cork, Dublin, Belfast 1963; *Campobasso, 1965* Theatre Festival; *Watershed,* Dublin 1967; *A Beginning of Truth,* Dublin 1968; *The Treaty Debates,* Dublin 1972; *Dev,* Dublin 1977.

GALVIN, Patrick, b. Cork 1927. Ed. Presentation Brothers Cork. Lives Belfast. Poet and playwright. Poetry: *Heart of Grace,* 1957; *Christ in London,* 1960; *The Woodburners,* Dublin 1973; *Midnight and Other Poems,* 1979. Plays: *And Him Stretched,* Dublin 1963; *Cry the Believers,* 1965; *Nightfall to Belfast,* 1973; *The Last Burning,* 1974; *We Do It For Love,* 1975 (these last three all pub. Belfast 1977); *The Devil's Own People,* Dublin 1976; *Man on the Porch, Selected Poems,* 1979. Leverhulme Fellowship, Belfast 1974-76; Resident dramatist Lyric Theatre Belfast since 1974. Plays staged London and Glasgow as well as Belfast and Dublin.

GAMBLE, John, b. Strabane *c.* 1770, d. 1831. MD Edinburgh 1793. Army surgeon in Dutch campaign. Returned to Ireland and travelled the country on foot, writing some excellent travel sketches and stories based on his experiences. *Sarsfield, or Wanderings of Youth,* 1814; *Howard,* 1815; *Northern Irish Tales,* 1818.

GANLY, Andrew, b. Dublin, 1908, d. 1982. Ed. TCD, qualifying in dental science. Practised as dentist in Ireland and Malay States. Specialist on Greece and Greek Art. Acted as travel courier to Middle East, Greece and Far East. Wrote several plays in 1930s of which the one-act curtain-raiser, *The Dear Queen,* 1938, is the best-known. Often revived. Later plays failed to please and he turned to novels and short stories. *The Desolate Sky,* Dublin and London, 1966-67. *The Dear Queen,* Dublin 1976; its sequel, *The Dance in Nineteen Hundred and Ten,* 1977.

GANNON, Nicholas John, b. Sligo 1831, d. 1875. Ed. Clongowes. Became a JP. Wrote verse, novels and criticism, including *An Essay on the characteristic Errors of Our Most Distinguished Poets,* 1853. His poems include 'The O'Donoghue of the Lakes', 1858, apparently one of the most popular 19th-century subjects for poetry; and *Mary Desmond,* 1873. His novels include *Above and Below,* 1864.

GARDINER, Matthew, b. *c.* 1710, d. *c.* 1745. Wrote verse-plays and ballad operas including *The Sharpers,* 1740, and *The Parthian Hero,* 1741.

GAUGHAN, John Anthony, b. Kerry 1932. Ed. UCD and Maynooth. Ordained 1957. Teacher, 1957-60; tutor in philosophy UCD 1963-65. Now a curate in Dublin. *Doneraile,* Dublin 1968; *Listowel and Its Vicinity,* Dublin 1973; *Memoirs of Constable Jeremiah Mee, R.I.C.,* Dublin 1975; *Austin Stack: Portrait of a Separatist;* Dublin 1977; *The Knights of Glin,* Dublin 1978; *Thomas Johnson,* Dublin 1980; *A Political Odyssey: Thomas O'Donnell,* Dublin 1983.

GEBLER, Ernest, b. Dublin 1915. Spent some years in England and America. First novel, *He Had My Heart Scalded,* 1945, is about a Dublin childhood. *The Voyage of the Mayflower,* 1950, sold 4 million copies in America and was filmed. Since then has written *The Love Investigator, A Week in the Country, The Old Man and the Girl,* and *Hoffmann,* later turned into a film and a play, winning an Emmey Award. *Civilised Life,* 1979. Plays include *She Sits Smiling, Call Me Daddy, Cry for Help,* and *Eileen O'Roon.* Has written for TV and films. Was married to Edna O'Brien the novelist. Their son Carlo G.'s first novel *Eleventh Summer* pub. 1985. Lives in Dalkey.

GENTLEMAN, Francis, b. Dublin 1728, d. Dublin 1784. Became a lieutenant in the British Army but left it for the stage, both acting, and writing many plays. He published a much criticised edition of Shakespeare, and died after a long illness. His plays include *Fortune,* 1751; *Zaphira,* 1754; a version of *Oroonoko* (from the play by Thomas Southerne), 1760; an opera, *Orpheus and Eurydice,* 1783; and many more. *The Dramatic Censor,* 2 vols, 1770, published anonymously, criticises many plays of his time, and is his best-known work.

GEOGHEGAN, Arthur Gerald, b. Dublin 1810, d. London 1889. Civil servant and antiquarian. His verse-history *The Monks of Kilcrea* was translated into French.

GIBBINGS, Robert John, b. Cork 1889, d. Oxford 1958. Son of Canon of Cork Cathedral. Ed. UCC and the Slade School, London. Served with Royal Munster Fusiliers, Gallipoli. A skilled artist, G. was founder member of Society of Wood Engravers and ran the Golden Cockerel Press 1924-33, taught book production at Reading University 1936-42. Wrote many travel books, often illustrating them himself. *Coconut Island,* 1936; *Coming Down the Wye,* 1942; *Sweet Cork of Thee,* 1951, etc. His *John Graham, Convict,* 1937, repub. 1956, gives an absorbing account of Irish convict life in the Australian settlements early in the 19th century.

GIBBON, William Monk, b. Dublin 1896. Ed. St Columba's, and Oxford. Officer in RASC 1916-18. Studied farming but took up school-teaching after First World War and has taught in Switzerland, England and Ireland. Won Silver Medal for Poetry at Tailteann Games 1928. MIAL. Poetry includes *The Tremulous String,* 1926; *The Branch of Hawthorn Tree,* 1927; *For Daws to Peck At,* 1929; *Seventeen Sonnets,* 1932; *This Insubstantial Pageant* (collected poems), 1951; *The Velvet Bow and Other Poems,* 1972. Has published two remarkable autobiographical works: *Mount Ida,* 1948, rep. 1983; *The Climate of Love,* 1961. His first volume of autobiography was *The Seals,* 1935. A long-time friend of Michael Farrell, Dr Gibbon edited the MS of Farrell's epic novel, *Thy Tears Might Cease,* after the author's death. His other principal works are *The Red Shoes Ballet: A Critical Study,* 1948; *The Tales of Hoffmann: A Study of the Film,* 1951 (both included in the series *Classical Literature of the Film*, NY); *An Intruder at the Ballet*, 1952; *Austria*, 1953; *Western Germany*, 1955; *The Rhine and its Castles*, 1957; *The Masterpiece and the Man: Yeats as I Knew Him*, 1959; *Great Houses of Europe*, 1962; *Great Palaces of Europe*, 1964; and three further instalments of autobiography: *Inglorious Soldier*, 1968; *The Brahms Waltz*, 1970; *The Pupil*, Dublin 1981.

GIBSON, Ian, b. Dublin 1939. Ed. Quaker school, Waterford, and TCD. Lecturer in Spanish QUB 1962-68, and later at London University. Lives in Madrid. The *Death of Lorca*, Paris 1971, London 1973, banned in Spain. This received Prix International de la Presse at Nice Book Festival 1972. Translated into 13 languages. *The English Vice*, a study of flagellation as a sexual perversion, 1976, US 1984. Biography of *Jose Antonio*, 1980, won Spanish Planeta Prize. Working on a 2-vol. biography in Spanish of Federico Garcia Lorca, the first vol. pub. Madrid 1984. Has written a number of other books in Spanish on aspects of the Spanish Civil War of 1936-39, and *Un Irlandes en España,* being interviews with Spanish writers and politicians.

GILBERT, John Thomas, b. Dublin 1829, d. Dublin 1898. Established Public Record Office in Dublin 1867. In 1891 married Rosa Mulholland. Wrote *History of the City of Dublin*, 3 vols, 1854-59; *Ancient Historical Manuscripts*, 1861; and *History of the Viceroys of Ireland*. Knighted 1897.

GILBERT, Lady (Rosa Mulholland), b. Belfast 1841, d. Dublin 1921. In 1891 married Mr (later Sir) John Gilbert. Her sister became Lady Russell of Kilowen. Dickens encouraged her early work, printing many of her stories in *Household Words*. She wrote a large number of novels, from the early *Dumara*, 1864, published under the name 'Ruth Murray', to *The Return of Mary O'Murrough*, 1910. The best-known was probably *A Fair Emigrant*, 1888.

GILTINAN, Donal, spent some years in Irish Customs Service. Has written many plays for radio and for British television. His best-known stage plays are *Goldfish in the Sun*, Abbey 1950; and *Light in the Sky*. Novels include *Prince of Darkness*, 1955.

GINNELL, Laurence, b. Co. Westmeath 1854, d. US 1923. A self-educated man, he was called to both Irish and English Bars, became MP for Westmeath 1906-18. First among Irish party to turn to Sinn Fein. Pub. *The Brehon Laws*, 1894; *The Doubtful Grant of Ireland*, 1899; and *Land and Liberty*, 1908.

GLYNN, Joseph Aloysius, b. Gort 1869, d. 1951, knighted 1915. He was President of the Irish Council of the St Vincent de Paul Society for many years and wrote *Life of Matt Talbot*, 1928, which has been translated into 13 languages. It tells the story of the Dublin workman, now Venerable Matt Talbot, candidate for canonisation.

GOGARTY, Oliver St John, b. 1878, d. NY 1957. Ed. Stonyhurst, Clongowes, TCD. MD 1907. Senator of Irish Free State 1922-36. As celebrated for his life as for his poetry. Perhaps his most famous exploit was his escape from his executioners in a house beside the Liffey during the Irish Civil War. In Yeat's words, 'Pleading a natural necessity he got into the garden, plunged under a shower of revolver bullets and as he swam the ice-cold December stream promised it, should it land him in safety, two swans. I was present when he fulfilled that vow.' In the same essay Yeats called him 'one of the great lyric poets of our age'. Later critics have been less enthusiastic, perhaps for dislike of the things Yeats admired in him, the swashbuckling and the swift indifference. His many volumes of poetry include *The Ship*, 1918; *An Offering of Swans*, 1924; *Others to Adorn*, 1939. In 1937 he published a book of reminiscences, *As I Was Going Down Sackville Street*, which became the cause of a famous libel action. In 1954 he published his autobiography, *It Isn't This Time of Year At All*. Other books include *I Follow St Patrick*, 1938; *Tumbling in the Hay*, 1939; *Mr Petunia*, 1946; *Intimations*, 1950; *Mourning Became Mrs Spendlove*, 1952.

GOLDSMITH, Oliver, b. Co. Longford 1728, d. London 1774. Ed. Athlone and Edgeworthstown. Ran away from TCD 1744, but returned. Studied medicine at Edinburgh and Leyden. Travelled through Europe 1755-56, returning to London with no money and a very dubious degree. Its doubtfulness may explain his failure as a doctor and he turned to literature, becoming the friend of Dr Johnson and his 'Club'. He produced a great deal of hack work, including biographies of Voltaire and Beau Nash, and histories of Greece, Rome and England. His reputation rests on two comedies, *The Good Natured Man*, 1768; and *She Stoops to Conquer*, 1773, generally considered his masterpiece and regularly revived ever since. His novel *The Vicar of Wakefield*, 1766, is also regarded as a classic, although its delicate sentiment makes it less acceptable to modern taste than his plays, which are much harder and more realistic, owing a great deal to Shakespeare's style of comedy. For Irish readers his most interesting work is his long poem 'The Deserted Village', 1770, ostensibly an English village ruined by the Industrial Revolution, but quite clearly based on his memoirs of some village in Longford or Roscommon in the 1740s, ruined by the Penal Laws and a grasping landlord.

He also wrote many essays, including the famous *The Citizen of the World*, 1762. Shortly before his death he published another lengthy poem 'Retaliation', 1774.

GORHAM, Maurice Anthony Coneys, b. London 1902, of Galway family, d. Dublin 1975. Ed. Stonyhurst, Oxford. Journalist, joined BBC 1926. Became Head of BBC TV 1945-46. Appointed Director of Radio Éireann 1953-60. Has written *Broadcasting & Television since 1900*, 1952; *Forty Years of Irish Broadcasting*, 1967; *Ireland from Old Photographs*, 1971, rep. 1979, re-issued 1985 as *Ireland Yesterday*, as well as a number of books on London life and habits.

GRATTAN, Henry, b. Dublin 1746, d. London 1820. Lawyer and politician, the principal architect of the Irish Parliament of 1782-1800, often called Grattan's Parliament. With Burke raised oratory to a new level in English. Many volumes of his *Speeches* have been published. The best edition is *The Speeches of the Rt. Hon. Henry Grattan, to which is added his letter on the Union,* ed. D.O. Madden, Dublin 1845.

GRATTAN, Thomas Colley, b. 1792, Dublin, d. 1864. Studied law but never practised. British Consul in Boston, US. Wrote several travel books, a history of the Netherlands, and a number of novels of which the best is considered to be *The Heiress of Bruges,* 1830.

GRAVES, Alfred Perceval, b. Dublin 1846, d. Harlech 1931. Ed. England and TCD, Clerk in Home Office. Assistant editor of *Punch* for a time, and later Inspector of Schools. Contributed to many magazines, including the *Spectator,* and wrote a great deal of verse. His most famous song is 'Father O'Flynn'. Pub. *Songs of Killarney,* 1873; *Irish Songs and Ballads,* 1880; *Songs of Old Ireland* (set to music by Professor Stanford), 1883;*Father O'Flynn and other Irish Lyrics,* 1889. He also edited *Songs of Irish Wit and Humour,* 1884.

His first wife dying in 1886, he remarried after a few years and by his second wife he became the father of Robert (MIAL) and Charles Graves. The family is a remarkable example of inherited talent. Alfred Perceval's father, the Protestant Bishop of Limerick, published poetry; his uncle Robert was author of a life of Rowan Hamilton; his aunt Clara, his brothers Arnold and Charles and other relatives over three generations published poetry; and his son Robert is one of the major English poets of the century, while Charles is a well-known journalist and travel writer. He lived well into his nineties, and in the words of his son Robert, 'could dance a jig to the end'.

GRAVES, Arnold, b. 1846, brother of Alfred Perceval G. Wrote verse, plays and novels, including *Prince Patrick,* 1898.

GRAVES, Clotilde Inez Mary, b. Buttevant 1864, d. 1932. Studied art in Bloomsbury. A well-known playwright of her day, having 16 plays produced in New York and London, including *Nitocris* produced at Drury Lane 1887, and *The Lovers' Battle,* 1902, the latter based on Pope's 'Rape of the Lock'. She wrote a pantomime, *Puss in Boots,* Drury Lane 1898, and some novels, the most famous being *The Dop Doctor,* 1910, pub. under the pseud. 'Richard Dehan', and *Between Two Thieves,* 1914.

GRAY, Tony, b. Dublin 1922. Twenty years with *Irish Times,* succeeding Brian Inglis and Patrick Campbell as 'Quidnunc', the daily columnist. Left Ireland, 1959, to join *Daily Mirror* in London. In 1962 began script-writing for TV. His novels include *Starting from Tomorrow,* 1965; *The Real Professionals,* 1966; *Gone the Time,* 1967; *Interlude,* 1968; *The Last Laugh,* 1972; non-fiction includes *The Irish Answer,* 1966; *Psalms and Slaughter,* 1972; *The Orange Order,* 1972; *No Surrender, The Siege of Londonderry,*

1689, 1975; *Champions of Peace, The Story of Alfred Nobel, the Peace Prize and Its Laureates*, 1976; many translations.

GREACEN, Robert, b. Derry 1920. Ed. Belfast and TCD. Has written several volumes of verse that have been well received by critics: *The Bird*, 1941; *One Recent Evening*, 1944; *The Undying Day*, 1948; *A Garland for Captain Fox*, Dublin 1975; *Young Mr Gibbon*, Dublin 1979; *A Bright Mask*, Dublin 1985. Also *Even Without Irene* (autobiography), Dublin 1969. Domiciled in London since 1948.

GREEN, Alice Stopford, b. Kells 1847, d. Dublin 1929. Daughter of Archdeacon Stopford. Privately educated, she learned Greek to help her father's biblical researches, and was one of the first women students admitted to the College of Science. She married the English journalist and historian John Richard Green, author of the famous *Short History of the English People*, in 1877, and he crystallised her interest in history. She became his helper and when he died in 1883 she completed his *Conquest of England* and brought it out that year. Her own work began with *Henry II*, 1888, and her interest turned towards Irish affairs. Irish history was still much in the hands of English propagandists, and her great service to Ireland was to begin to redress the bias. *The Making of Ireland and its Undoing*, 1908, and *Irish Nationality*, 1911, set out to refute the assumption that Ireland had no civilisation before the Norman conquest in the 12th century, and that the clan system was synonymous with barbarism. *A History of the Irish State to 1014*, 1925, was her last major work.

She knew most of the great figures in Irish affairs, and fought hard to defend Casement. After the Treaty of 1921 she was elected to the Irish Senate.

GREGG, Tresham Dames, b. *c.* 1830, d. *c.* 1900. DD. Several historical verse-plays in Shakespearean style. Also *Queen Elizabeth, or the Origin of Shakespeare*, 1872.

GREGORY, Augusta, b. Co. Galway 1859, daughter of Dudley Persse, d. 1932. Married Sir William Gregory 1880; widowed 1892. Close friend of Yeats and Edward Martyn, founded Irish Literary Theatre movement with them in 1898, out of which grew the Abbey Theatre Company, 1904. Throughout the rest of her life she gave most of her energies to the theatre, writing plays for it and offering guidance and patronage to many playwrights, from Synge to O'Casey. Like Yeats, her ambition was to provide the new nationalist Ireland with a heroic literature, based on and developed from the old heroic legends, and the folk tales of the western peasantry. She provided an admirable counter-balance to Yeat's more visionary energies.

Her plays have been much smiled at by critics, particularly for their so-called 'Kiltartan' language, Irish dialect heard through a lady's hearing aid, but they were popular on the stage, and are the work of a writer who knew how a theatre worked. *Spreading the News, Kincora, The Workhouse*

Ward, The Rising of the Moon, have all been revived and well received by successive generations of Irish playgoers. Others are *The Golden Apple, Three lost Plays,* etc.

Published work includes *Poets and Dreamers; Gods and Fighting Men; Kiltartan Poetry Book; Cuchulain of Muirthemne; A Book of Saints & Wonders,* 1907; *Kiltartan History Book,* Dublin 1909; *Our Irish Theatre: A Chapter of Autobiography,* 1914; *Hugh Lane's Life & Achievement,* 1921 (Hugh Lane the picture collector was her nephew); and *Lady Gregory's Journals 1916-30,* ed. Lennox Robinson, 1946.

GRIFFIN, Gerald, b. Limerick 1803, d. Cork 1840. Went to London 1823. John Banim found him work as a hack, which he hated, and which ruined his health. In 1827 his collection of stories *Holland-Tide* was published in London, just as his health broke completely. His brother William brought him back to Limerick where he wrote *Tales of the Munster Festivals* which increased his already considerable reputation. But his major work is *The Collegians,* 1829, one of the most powerful Irish novels ever written, despite W.B.Yeats's preferring Banim to Griffin. The book is based on a notorious and squalid murder case in Limerick, transformed in the novel into something of deep social significance. It is possible to see similarities to Dostoevsky, and the book was immediately recognised in Ireland as being a masterpiece. Unfortunately for Griffin it was too successful, and later generations have been unable to see the novel clearly because of its vulgarisation and distortion by the stage version *The Colleen Bawn,* and the opera.

Always withdrawn, and religious, an unhappy love affair with a married woman, Lydia Fisher, made Griffin decide to enter the Christian Brothers. He burned several uncompleted MSS, gave up his career, and dedicated the remainder of his life to teaching poor children. He died in North Monastery, Cork. His works collected by his brother and pub. London 1842-43.

GRIFFITH, Arthur, b. Dublin 1872, d. Dublin 1922. First President of the Irish Free State. Founded Celtic Literary Society with William Rooney 1889, and belonged to many other Irish Revival organisations. Also joined the IRB. In 1896 went to Transvaal to work in the mines. Returned to Ireland 1899, and founded *The United Irishman,* which he edited until 1906. Used the paper to preach failure of Home Rule policy and demanded total separation from Britain. In 1904 published the famous series of 'Hungarian' articles in *The United Irishman,* calling for Irish revolutionaries to follow the Hungarian example of Kossuth and Deak after 1848. This was to set up a national assembly which would not recognise the British administration. Passive resistance to British was to follow. These articles were republished as *The Resurrection of Hungary or a Parallel for Ireland,* Dublin 1904, and it can be argued that this was the most influential booklet ever published in Ireland, outside the Catechism. A National Council was set up and at a meeting in the Rotunda, Dublin, in November 1905, the 'Sinn Fein' movement and party was created.

In 1906 Griffith left the IRB, and with *The United Irishman* closing over a libel action, he began a new paper, *Sinn Fein*. In 1910 elected President of Sinn Fein. Took no part in the 1916 Rising, but was imprisoned. After release elected for Cavan in the 'Sinn Fein Election', 1918. Arrested again in 1919, and a third time in 1920. Throughout this period his 'Hungarian policy' was the mainspring of the nationalist movement, with passive resistance giving way to guerilla warfare. In the Treaty negotiations of 1921 G. led the Irish delegation which eventually accepted and signed the Treaty. This led to a break with the de Valera-Republican faction, and in the following year to Civil War. Griffith meanwhile was elected President of the Free State set up under the Treaty. He died the same year.

GRIFFITH, Richard, b. Dublin (?) *c.* 1704, d. Naas 1788. Ed. TCD. Married an English woman from Glamorganshire, Elizabeth G., and collaborated with her in several popular novels written in the form of letters exchanged between lovers. *A series of Genuine Letters between Henry & Frances,* 1757 (ostensibly at least drawn from their own correspondence before their marriage in 1752); followed by *Delicate Distress* by 'Frances', 1769; and *The Gordian Knot* by 'Henry', 1770. Outside this collaboration Richard G. wrote *The Triumvirate,* 1764, an altogether more virile affair, full of bawdry, and a comedy *Variety* acted at Drury Lane 1782.

GRIMSHAW, Beatrice, b. Co. Antrim, *c.* 1880, d. 1953. Ed. Caen, Belfast and London. Travelled in the South Seas, enquiring into tropical colonisation. First white woman to penetrate several areas of Borneo and New Guinea, including notorious Sepik River and Fly River valleys. Wrote several travel books on her experiences: *In the Strange South Seas, From Fiji to the Cannibal Islands,* both 1907, and *The New New Guinea,* 1910. Novels included *When the Red Gods Call,* 1910; *Guinea Gold,* 1912; *The Beach of Terror* (short stories), 1931; *The Mystery of Tumbling Reef,* 1932; *South Sea Sarah,* 1940.

GROVES, Edward, b. *c.* 1775, d. *c.* 1850. Ed. TCD. Ordained *c.* 1800. Wrote several very popular plays, particularly *The Warden of Galway,* first acted in Dublin 1831, when it ran 45 nights, a remarkable success for the period. *Alomprah, or the Hunter of Burmah,* pub. 1832; *The O'Donoghue of the Lakes,* etc. His many other interests included a universal language and he published a book on it, *Pasilogia,* 1846. He was a friend and supporter of Daniel O'Connell.

GUINAN, Joseph, b. *c.* 1870, d. unknown. Priest in Liverpool for several years, and parish priest in County Longford. *Scenes and Sketches in an Irish Parish,* 1904; *The Soggarth Aroon,* 1907 (extremely popular novel about a priest); *The Island Parish,* 1908; *The Curate of Kilcloon,* 1913; etc.

GUINNESS, Bryan Walter, 2nd Baron Moyne, b. 1905. Ed. Eton, Oxford; called to English Bar 1930. Married Diana Mitford, who subsequently married Oswald Mosley. MIAL. Member of the famous brewing family; Vice-Chairman of the Company, Chairman of the Company's Iveagh

(Housing) Trust, a Governor of the National Gallery of Ireland, and a Commissioner of Irish Lights. An intelligent and forceful patron of arts, letters and culture in Ireland. Has written a considerable amount of prose and poetry of great merit, and has received Hon. D.Litt. from both TCD and NUI. Plays include *The Fragrant Concubine*, 1938, and *A Riverside Charade*, 1954. Books for children include *The Story of Johnny and Jemima*, 1936; *The Children in the Desert, 1947; The Animals' Breakfast*, 1950. Poetry includes *Twenty-three poems*, 1931; *Reflexions*, 1947; *Collected Poems*, 1956; *Selected Poems*, 1964; *The Clock*, 1973. Adult novels: *Singing Out of Tune*, 1933; *Landscape with Figures*, 1934; *A Week by the Sea*, 1936; *Lady Crushwell's Companion*, 1938; *A Fugue of Cinderellas*, 1956; *Leo and Rosabelle*, 1961; *The Giant's Eye*, 1964; *The Engagement*, 1969; *Hellenic Flirtation*, 1978. Also *The Girl with the Flower* (short stories), 1966; *Diary Not Kept* (autobiographical essays), 1975; *Potpourri* (memoirs), 1982.

GUINNESS, Desmond, the Hon., b. 1931. Son of Bryan G. Ed. Gordonstoun, Oxford. Founder and President of Georgian Society 1958. Lecturer and writer on Georgian architecture, particularly of Dublin. *A Portrait of Dublin*, 1967; *Irish Houses and Castles* (with William Ryan), 1971; *Mr Jefferson, Architect*, 1973; *The Palladian Style* (with Julius T. Sadler, Jr), 1976; *Georgian Dublin*, 1979; *The White House, An Architectural History*, US 1980.

GWYNN, Aubrey, b. 1892, d. 1983. Son of Stephen G. Ed. UCD, Oxford, Louvain, ordained SJ 1924; Lecturer UCD 1926; Professor of Mediaeval History UCD 1949-61. *Roman Education from Cicero to Quintilian*, Oxford 1926; *The English Austin Friars in the time of Wyclif*, Oxford 1940; *The Mediaeval Province of Armagh 1470-1545*, Dundalk 1946; *The Writings of Bishop Patrick 1074-84*, Dublin 1955.

GWYNN, Denis Rolleston, b. 1893, d. Dublin 1972. Son of Stephen G. Journalist and historian, became Research Professor of Modern Irish History UCC 1946-63. Books include *The Catholic Reaction in France*, NY 1924; *The Irish Free State 1922-27*, 1928; *A Hundred years of Catholic Emancipation*, 1929; *Edward Martyn and the Irish Revival*, 1930; *The Life and Death of Roger Casement*, 1930.

GWYNN, Stephen Lucius, b. Co. Donegal 1864, d. 1950. Grandson of William Smith O'Brien. Ed. Dublin and Oxford. Elected Nationalist MP for Galway 1906, and sat as leading member of Irish Parliamentary party under Redmond until 1919. Novels include *The Old Knowledge*, 1901; *John Maxwell's Marriage*, 1903; *The Glade in the Forest*, 1907; *Robert Emmet*, 1909. *Collected Poems* pub. 1923; a travel book in 1930; and *Aftermath*, 1946. An authority on 18th-century Ireland, wrote *Henry Grattan and His Times*, 1939, and work includes a number of biographies, including *Dean Swift*, 1933, and *Goldsmith*, 1935. During First World War served in France 1914-17, receiving Legion of Honour. Honoured by

Irish Academy of Letters shortly before his death. Hon. D.Litt. NUI.

H

HACKETT, Francis, b.Kilkenny 1883, d. Denmark 1962. Emigrated US 1901; worked in New York as a journalist 1920-23. Edited the left-wing *New Republic.* Returned to Ireland 1927. Wrote much history and criticism but is famous in Ireland for his novel *The Green Lion,* 1935, banned by the Irish censors. In anger at this decision H. moved to Denmark, where his wife the playwright Signe Toksvig came from, staying there until Second World War. Spent war in New York and returned to Denmark 1946. Other novels include *Queen Anne Boleyn,* 1939, and *The Senator's Last Night,* 1943. Books of criticism include *Horizons,* 1918; *Invisible Censor,* 1921; *On Judging Books,* 1947. History: *Personal History of Henry the Eighth,* 1929; *Francis the First,* 1934. Also, *Ireland: A Study in Nationalism,* NY 1918, and *I Choose Denmark* (autobiography), NY 1940.

HALIDAY, Charles, b. Dublin 1789, d. Monkstown 1866. Left vast collection of pamphlets and MSS relating to Irish history, now in Royal Irish Academy, comprising 25,000 items. Is remembered for his history of the *Scandinavian Kingdom of Dublin,* ed. J. P. Prendergast, 1881.

HALL, Anna Maria, née Fielding, b. Dublin 1800, d. E. Mousley 1881. Went with mother to London 1815; married S.C. Hall 1824, who sometimes collaborated with her. She wrote verse-plays, burlettas, opera, short stories and novels. Her work was immensely popular in England, remaining in print in various editions throughout the 19th century. Ireland never seemed to care for it to the same extent. Her best work is in *Stories of Irish Peasantry.* Other books were *Marian, or a Young Maid's Fortunes; The Buccaneer; Mabel's Curse,* 1825, one of her earliest works; *St. Pierre the Refugee,* 1837; *The Groves of Blarney,* 1838, etc.

HALLORAN, Laurence Hynes (sometimes Hallaran), b. 1766, d. 1831. Ordained about 1790. DD. Became a naval chaplain, and was on board HMS *Britannia* at Battle of Trafalgar. Later went out to Capetown as rector of the Grammar School and in 1818 was accused of forgery, convicted, and sentenced to transportation to Australia. In Sydney he became once more a successful schoolmaster, and continued there, protesting his innocence until his death. He wrote a good deal of verse, including *The Female Volunteer,* 1801, and *The Battle of Trafalgar,* 1806, intensely interesting as being the poetic account of an eye-witness.

HALPINE, Charles Graham, b. Co. Meath 1829, d. 1868. Ed. TCD, emigrated to America 1851, edited *New York Times* and other papers. Served in Civil War and rose to Brigadier-General. Wrote humorous and satiric sketches in prose and verse about the war, under pseud. 'Private Miles O'Reilly'. After the war became owner-editor of *New York Citizen;* elected Registrar of the Country of New York 1867, and died of chloroform poisoning. His books include verse, essays, and two historical novels both first published in Dublin: *Mountcashel's Brigade, or The Rescue of Cremona* and *The Patriot Brothers.* They ran to many editions. His poetry includes *Baked Meats of the Funeral, by Private Miles O'Reilly,* NY 1866.

HAMILTON, Anthony, b. Roscrea 1645, d. 1720. Nephew of Ormonde and connected to Abercorns. Taken to France in 1649 after the flight of his uncle, remaining there until the Restoration. In 1660 the family followed the king to London. In 1663 the Chevalier de Gramont came to London and married Anthony's sister Elizabeth, obtaining commissions from Louis XIV for Anthony and his brother George. Sent on a secret recruiting mission to Ireland, and then to the Low Countries, both being Catholics and sympathetic to the Catholic party. On James II's accession, 1685, Anthony returned to British Army and served as Military Governor of Limerick, 1685-87. Followed James into exile 1690, and in his enforced leisure took to writing, mostly in French. His *Contes* were well known at one time, being burlesques of the then popular fairy tales *à la Perrault,* and|Oriental stories in vogue at the same period. But his immortality was gained by taking down his brother-in-law's *Memoirs of the Count de Grammont* (sic), published in Cologne in French 1713, poorly translated into English the following year by Boyer, the French edition having been edited by Horace Walpole, and reprinted many times. Walter Scott produced a fine edition 1811, with many notes. Peter Quennell made a new translation 1931. The book gives a sometimes inaccurate, but always lively and often valuable portrait of the times at both the English and the French Courts. The first part of the book is presumed to be Gramont's dictation, the second part Hamilton's invention.

HAMILTON, Elizabeth, b. Belfast 1758, d. Harrogate 1816. Sister of Charles H. the Orientalist. Lived in Scotland for many years with relatives, and wrote on education, devoting herself to philanthropy. She also wrote novels, of which the best-known is *The Cottagers of Glenburnie,* 1808, that went into many editions.

HAMILTON, Elizabeth, b. Co. Wicklow 1906. Ed. US and England, London University 1925-32. Poet. Has also written travel books and biography, including *The Year Returns,* 1952; *River Full of Stars,* 1954; *Put Off Thy Shoes,* 1957; *The Great Teresa* (of Avila), 1960; *An Irish Childhood,* 1963; *Heloise,* 1966. Her mother, Mary H. (1875-1951) wrote an autobiography, *Green and Gold,* 1948.

HAMILTON, M., pseud. of Mrs Churchill-Luck, b. Spottiswood-Ashe, Co. Derry *c.* 1860. Novels include *Across an Ulster Bog,* 1896; *Beyond the Boundary,* 1902; *On an Ulster Farm,* 1904.

HAMILTON, William, b. Londonderry 1755, d. 1797, murdered by rapparees. Fellow TCD, and rector of Fanad, Co. Donegal. Attracted attention with *Letters Concerning Northern Coast of Antrim*, 1786, trans. German 1787; and *Letters on the Principles of the French Democracy & their influence on Britain and Ireland*, Dublin 1792; both supporting the government and established order against Nationalist and Catholic feeling. As a magistrate and Church of Ireland rector he had much power in Donegal and in the eyes of his Catholic neighbours he abused it. In 1797 he was killed by 'banditti' in the house of a friend. He is principally remembered as one of the founders of a society, the *Palaeosopheus* which with the *Neosopheus* became the Royal Irish Academy in 1786, to whose early *Transactions* he contributed several papers on antiquarian matters.

HAMILTON, William Rowan, b. Dublin 1805, d. Dunsink Observatory 1865. An infant prodigy, his uncle taught him to read Greek and Hebrew before he was 5, and at 10 he read Arabic, Persian and Sanskrit. His principal interest however was already mathematics and astronomy. He entered TCD 1823 and while still an undergraduate was made Professor of Astronomy 1827. In 1828 he published the first part of *A Theory of Systems of Rays*, a classic study in optics. In 1835 he was knighted and in 1837 made President of the Royal Irish Academy. He was also Astronomer Royal of Ireland. In 1834 he had published *A General Method in Dynamics*. His *Lectures on Quaternions* were published 1853, followed by the posthumous *The Elements of Quaternions*, 1866, edited by his son.

It is said that walking across a Dublin canal bridge he stopped to scribble calculations on the parapet, and this was in fact the central equation of the Quaternion theory. The theory itself is a system of vector algebra which Hamilton expected to have much the same value in mathematics as the differential calculus. This hope was disappointed, but the theory is still of great importance and H. remains a remarkable figure in the history of mathematics and of optics. *The Mathematical Papers of Sir William Rowan Hamilton*, pub. Royal Irish Academy, Dublin, vol. 1, 1931; vol. 2, 1940; vol. 3, 1967; vol. 4, not yet pub.

He was also deeply interested in poetry, and he and his sister both published poetry which their contemporaries admired. An intimate friend of Wordsworth, Hamilton accompanied him on his Irish journey. His verse is to be found in many 19th-century anthologies.

HANAGHAN, Jonathan, b. Cheshire 1887, d. 1967. Lived in Dublin for many years where he ran the Runa Press, succeeded by the Strongs. Volumes of poetry include *By Immortal Seas*, 1931; *Poems to Mary*, 1945; *Eve's Moods Unveiled*, 1955; *Society, Evolution and Revelation*, 1957; *Sayings of Jonathan Hanaghan*, 1960; *Freud & Jesus*, 1967; *The Wisdom of Jonty*, 1970; *Forging Passion into Power*, 1979. All pub. Dublin.

HANBURY-TENISON, Airling Robert, b. Co. Monaghan 1936. Ed. Eton, Oxford. Ecologist and traveller. Co-founder of Survival International and Chairman since 1969. Books include *A Question of Survival*, 1973; *A*

Pattern of Peoples, 1975; *Mulu: The Rain Forest,* 1980; *Worlds Apart,* 1985.

HANLEY, Gerald, b. Cork 1916. MIAL. Spent many years in East Africa during and after Second World War, and several of his novels deal with life in Kenya. They include *The Consul at Sunset; Monsoon Victory; The Year of the Lion,* 1953, repub. 1974; *Drinkers of Darkness; Without Love; The Journey Homeward,* 1961, repub. 1984; *Gilligan's Last Elephant,* 1962; *See You In Yasukini,* 1969; *Warriors and Strangers,* 1971; *Noble Descents,* 1982. Much admired by Ernest Hemingway as a writer combining action and thought in the same story, a rare accomplishment. Lives in Co. Wicklow.

HANLEY, James, b. Dublin 1901. Brother of Gerald H. Left Ireland for Liverpool aged ten. Canadian Navy in First World War. Merchant seaman, journalist, and prolific writer of novels, plays, short stories and other books. His novels have been compared to William Faulkner's and serious critics lament the popular neglect of his work. Much of his subject matter concerns the sea and the very poor. *Drift,* 1930, and *Ebb and Flood,* 1932, were among his earliest novels; then came a sequence set in Dublin in the early twentieth century – *The Furys,* 1935, repub. 1983; *Secret Journey,* 1936; *Our Time is Gone,* 1940; others include *A Sailor's Song,* 1943, repub. 1977; *Winter Song,* 1950; *The House in the Valley,* 1952, repub. as *Against the Stream,* 1982; *Welsh Sonata,* 1954, repub. 1978; *What Farrer Saw,* repub. 1984; recently, *Another World,* 1972; *A Woman in the Sky,* 1973; *A Dream Journey,* 1976; *A Kingdom,* 1978. His *Collected Stories* were pub. 1953, and an autobiography, *Broken Water,* 1937. Plays include *The Inner Journey,* NY 1965, and *Leave Us Alone,* produced London 1972. Also several successful TV and radio plays. Lived in Wales from 1931 to *c.* 1980. Now lives London.

HANLY, David, b. Limerick 1944. Ed. Limerick. With RTE 1964-71; Bord Fáilte 1971-76, when he resigned to write full-time. First novel, *In Guilt and In Glory,* 1979. Now a radio journalist.

HANNAY, James Owen, see BIRMINGHAM, George A.

HANNAY, Patrick, b. *c.* 1585, d. 1629, drowned at sea. Appointed Master of Irish Chancery Courts, 1627. His verse-play *The Happy Husband,* 1618, was pub. with some other poetry, 1622; facs. ed. 1875.

HARBINSON, Robert, b. Belfast 1928, has written a number of travel books under the name of 'Robin Bryans', and some distinguished short stories, *Up Spake the Cabin Boy, The Fair World and Other Stories,* etc. as well as volumes of autobiography, *No Surrender: An Ulster Childhood,* and *The Protégé.*

HARBISON, Peter Desmond, b. Dublin 1939. Ed. Glenstal, UCD, Germany. Archaeologist and P.R. executive to Bord Fáilte 1966–. *The Axes, Daggers and Halberds of the Early Bronze Age in Ireland,* 1969; *A Guide* to the National Monuments in the Republic of Ireland, Dublin and London 1970, rev. 1975, US 1979; The Archaeology of Ireland, 1976; with Jeanne Sheehy and Homan Potterton, Irish Art and Architecture from Prehistory to the Present, 1978. Is preparing a 2-vol. study of Irish High Crosses.

HARDIMAN, James, b. Mayo 1790, d. Galway 1855. A native Irish speaker, he became librarian of Queen's College Galway and is chiefly remembered for his work in collecting and saving Irish folk music. The History of the Town and Country of Galway, Dublin 1820, rep. Galway 1975; Irish Minstrelsy, or, Bardic Remains of Ireland, 1831; An Account of Two Irish Wills, Dublin 1843 (H. was for a time sub-commissioner of Public Records in Dublin Castle); and The Statutes of Kilkenny, Dublin 1843, are his best-known books.

HARDY, Elizabeth, b. 1794, d. 1854. A zealous Protestant, she published several novels, anonymously, of a tendentiously religious kind, such as The Confessor: a Jesuit Tale of the Times, 1854. Confined in Queen's Bench Prison, London, for a small debt, and died there after 18 months.

HARDY, Francis, b. near Mullingar 1751, d. 1812. Ed. TCD. Bar 1777. Member for Mullingar in Irish Parliament. Opposed Union against all pressures and bribes to support it. A close friend of Grattan and Lord Charlemont, and was a principal founder with the latter of the Royal Irish Academy, 1786 (see HAMILTON, William). Another friend, Richard Lovell Edgeworth, asked him to write Charlemont's biography, which he published as Memoirs of James Caulfeild, Earl of Charlemont, 1810, 2nd ed. 1812. These are interesting, and if read with caution, valuable.

HARMON, Maurice, b. 1930. Ed. UCD and Harvard. Assistant Professor of English Lewis and Clarke College, Oregon, 1958-63, and Notre Dame, Indiana, 1963-65. Lecturer in English UCD 1965-75; statutory lecturer 1976-. Ed. University Review, 1966-70, and Irish University Review, A Journal of Irish Studies, 1970-. Books include Modern Irish Literature 1800-1967, Dublin 1967; Sean O'Faolain: A Critical Introduction, US 1967, rev. Dublin 1984; The Celtic Master, Dublin, Oxford and Penn. 1969; ed. stories of William Carleton with introductions, Wildgoose Lodge, etc. 1973; co-ed. with Patrick Rafroidi, The Irish Novel in our Time, Lille 1976; Select Bibliography for the Study of Anglo-Irish Literature and Its Background, An Irish Studies Handbook, Dublin 1977; ed. Irish Poets after Yeats: Seven Poets, Dublin, Boston 1978; ed. Image and Illusion: Anglo-Irish Literature and Its Contexts, Dublin 1979; with Roger McHugh, A Short History of Anglo-Irish Literature, Dublin, NY 1982; and ed. The Irish Writer and the City, Gerrards Cross 1984.

HARRIS, (Frank) James Thomas, b. Galway 1855, d. France 1931. Son of naval lieutenant. Ed. Royal School Armagh and English grammar school. Ran away to America at 16 and became a cowboy. Returned to Europe and studied in Germany. Entered London literary scene as editor of Evening

News, 1882, and his principal achievements are in journalism and biography. His short stories, *Elder Conklin,* 1894; *Montes the Matador,* 1900; *The Yellow Ticket,* 1914, etc. were highly praised at the time, particularly by Meredith, and he also wrote several plays, of which the most successful was *Mr and Mrs Daventry* running for 160 performances in London (1899-1900). Others were *A New Commandment* and *The Bucket Shop.* Novels include *Great Days,* 1914, and *Pantopia,* NY 1930, almost his last writing.

In 1914 an apparently unjustified prison sentence for contempt of court in London made him leave Europe for America, where he edited *Pearson's,* 1916-22. Opposition to American war and peace policy made him unpopular there and he returned to Europe to write and publish privately *The Life and Loves of Frank Harris.* He died impoverished but impenitent at the scandalised fury this last work created in England and America. Also wrote biographies: *The Man Shakespeare,* 1909; *Contemporary Portraits,* 1915, followed by a second series, NY 1919; a third NY 1920, and a fourth NY 1927. *Life and Confessions of Oscar Wilde,* 1920, *Bernard Shaw,* NY 1931.

HARTNETT, Michael, b. Newcastle West 1941. Ed. locally. Lecturer in creative writing Thomond College, Limerick, 1976-78. Poetry includes *Anatomy of a Cliché,* 1968; *Hag of Beare,* 1969; *Gypsy Ballads* (trans. from Lorca), 1973; *A Farewell to English,* 1975; *Prisoners,* 1977; *Collected Poems in English,* 1984; *Inchicore Haiku,* 1985; all pub. Dublin. See also Part 2.

HAVARD, William, b. Dublin 1710, d. London 1778. Son of a vintner, became a surgeon's apprentice and then an actor. Wrote several very popular verse-tragedies including *Scanderbeg,* 1733; *King Charles I,* 1737; and *Regulus,* 1744. When he died Garrick wrote his epitaph.

HAY, Edward, b. Co. Wexford 1761, d. Dublin 1826. Suggested the first Irish census but failed to have his plan adopted. Tried for complicity in the '98 Rising, was acquitted and wrote *History of the Insurrection of the County of Wexford, A.D. 1798,* Dublin 1803.

HAYDN, Joseph Timothy, b. Limerick 1786, d. London 1856. Pub. *Dictionary of Dates,* 1841, which ran through 25 editions before 1900, and many since.

HAYES, Richard, b. Co. Limerick, d. Dublin 1958. Irish film censor 1940-54. Authority on Wild Geese. *Ireland and Irishmen in the French Revolution,* 1932; *Irish Swordsmen of France,* 1934; *The Last Invasion of Ireland: When Connacht Rose,* 1937, rep. 1939; *Old Irish Links with France,* 1940; *Biographical Dictionary of Irishmen in France,* 1949.

HAYES, Richard James, b. Co. Mayo 1902, d. Dublin 1976. Ed. Clongowes and TCD, where he was a brilliant student, gaining the unique distinction of a Moderatorship in three subjects, even two being rare. He afterwards qualified also as Doctor in Laws. He joined the National Library staff 1923, became Assistant Librarian 1929, Director 1940, being then the youngest Director of a National Library in the world. Retired 1967. He had published an introduction to the study of modern languages, *Comparative Idiom*, 1927, and the monumental *Catalogue of MSS relating to Irish History in Irish and Foreign Libraries*, 11 vols, US 1966. For his work in Irish see Part 2.

HAYES-McCOY, Gerard Anthony, b. Galway 1911, d. Galway 1975. Ed. Patrician Bros, UCG, Edinburgh and London. Co-founder Military History Society and first editor of its journal *The Irish Sword*, 1949-60. On staff of National Museum of Ireland 1939-58. Professor of History UCG 1958-75. Wrote principally for learned journals, but published *Scots Mercenary Forces in Ireland 1565-1603*, 1937; *Ulster and Other Irish Maps c. 1600*, 1964; *Sixteenth Century Irish Swords*, 1966; *Irish Battles*, 1969, rep. Dublin 1980; *History of Irish Flags from Earliest Times*, Dublin 1979 (posthumous); also ed. *The Irish at War*, Cork 1964.

HAYNES, James, b. Tipperary *c.* 1790, d. *c.* 1850. Ed. TCD. Journalist in London, among the apparently innumerable band of talented Irish hack-writers and entertainers who crossed the Irish Sea after the Act of Union. His plays had great success in both London and Dublin, including *Conscience, or the Bridal Night*, 1821; *Durazzo*, 1823; and *Mary Stuart*, 1840.

HAYWARD, Richard, b. Belfast 1898, d. 1964 in a car accident. Began career as dramatist and actor in Belfast, specialising in dialect monologues and stories. Became an expert on Ulster dialect and wrote a number of novels, plays, and a travel series on Ireland in 4 vols. *This is Ireland: Leinster*, 1949; *Ulster*, 1950; *Connacht*, 1952; and *Mayo, Sligo, Leitrim & Roscommon*, 1955. In 1954 pub. *The Story of the Irish Harp*.

HEAD, Richard, b. Carrickfergus *c.* 1637, d. 1686, drowned in the Solent. Son of a clergyman killed in the Rebellion of 1641. Sent to Oxford, he ruined himself there by gambling, and became a bookseller in London. He wrote poetry, a successful comedy, *The Humours of Dublin*, 1663; *The Life and Death of Mother Shipton*, 1684; *Nugae Venalis, or a Complaisant Companion*, 1686, which went into many editions, and several other works. His most famous book was *The English Rogue*, the robustly indecent story of a professional thief, told as his 'autobiography'.

HEALY, Dermot, b. Co. Westmeath 1947. Short stories: *Banished Misfortunes*, Dingle 1982. Novel: *Fighting with Shadows*, Dingle and London 1984. Wrote film script *Our Boys*, Dublin 1980. Hennessy Literary Awards 1974 and 1976. Tom Gallon Award 1983.

HEALY, Gerard, b. Dublin 1918, d. London 1963. Ed. Synge St. Acted at Gate and Abbey and on TV. He wrote two plays, both of which had great critical and popular success: *Thy Dear Father*, Abbey 1943, and *The Black Stranger*, 1945. Seriously ill with TB for several years he recovered to continue acting and had received enthusiastic notices for his part in Hugh Leonard's *Stephen D* in London, 1963, when he died suddenly in the theatre.

HEALY, John, b. 1930. Journalist and political commentator. Books include *Death of an Irish Town,* and *Nineteen Acres,* Galway 1978.

HEANEY, Seamus Justin, b. Co. Derry 1939. Ed. Anahorish, Derry, QUB. Teacher 1961-66; lecturer QUB 1966-72. Guest lecturer California, Harvard, etc. Broadcaster and major Irish poet. *Eleven Poems,* Belfast 1965; *Death of a Naturalist,* London and NY 1966; *Door Into the Dark,* London and NY 1969; *Wintering Out,* London and NY 1972; *Bog Poems,* 1975; *North,* London and NY 1975; *Stations,* Belfast 1976; *Fieldwork,* London and NY 1979; *Preoccupations: Selected Prose 1968-1978,* 1980; *An Open Letter,* Derry 1983; *Station Island,* 1984; *Hailstones,* Dublin 1984. Has edited several volumes of poetry and won numerous awards (Somerset Maugham 1966; Cholmondley 1968; Irish Academy of Letters 1971; Duff Cooper and W. H. Smith 1975, etc.).

HECTOR, Annie French (née French), b. Dublin 1825, d. London 1902. Went to London at 19 and married Alexander Hector, a merchant and explorer, hence her occasional pseud. of 'Mrs Alexander'. She became a vastly successful novelist, publishing over 40 books, translated into many languages from French to Polish. Her most famous books include *The Wooing O't,* 1873; *Blind Fate,* 1891; *A Choice of Evils,* 1895; and *Kitty Costello,* 1902, this last containing a good deal of autobiography.

HENN, Thomas Rice, b. Sligo 1901, d. Cambridge 1974. Ed. Cambridge. In Burmah 1923-25. Donnellan Lecturer TCD 1965. Served in British Army Second World War, ending as Brigadier, General Staff. Fellow St Catherine's College and senior lecturer in Anglo-Irish literature Cambridge 1926-69. For several years Director of Yeats International Summer School at Sligo. Wrote criticism and biography: *The Lonely Tower,* (on Yeats) 1950, rev. 1965; *The Harvest of Tragedy,* 1956; *Rudyard Kipling,* 1966; *Last Essays,* 1976.

HENNESSY, Maurice N., b. Youghal 1906. Ed. Roscrea. Colonial official Africa; battalion commander in Second World War; director of Adult Education for Bedford School district in New York; African Affairs consultant to American University in Washington DC; columnist for *Sunday Independent;* US correspondent for *Time Educational Supplement.* Principal books: *Congo,* 1961; *Africa Under My Heart,* 1965; *I'll Come Back in the Springtime: John F. Kennedy and the Irish,* 1966; *The Rajah from Tipperary,* 1972; *The Wild Geese: The Irish Soldier in Exile,* 1973, US 1975. Lives in Massachusetts.

HENRY, Augustine, b. Co. Antrim 1857, d. Dublin 1930. Served in Imperial Chinese Customs, and travelling in the interior collected many plants and seeds not then known in Europe. Collaborated with H. J. Elwes on the monumental *The Trees of Great Britain and Ireland,* 7 vols, 1906-13. Also wrote *Forests, Woods and Trees in Relation to Hygiene,* 1919. His collection of trees and plants was given to the National Botanical Gardens, and a catalogue published as *The Augustine Henry Forestry Herbarium at the National Botanic Gardens Glasnevin, a catalogue of the specimens,* Dublin 1957.

HERITY, Michael, b. Donegal 1929. Ed. UCD. RTE newsreader during 1960s. Associate Professor of Archaeology UCD. Dean of Celtic Studies 1984. Editor of *Journal of the Royal Society of Antiquaries of Ireland* since 1971. *Irish Passage Graves. Neolithic Tomb-Builders in Ireland and Britain 2500 BC,* Dublin 1974; and, with George Eogan, *Ireland in Prehistory,* 1977.

HERRON, Shaun, b. Co. Antrim 1912. Ed. QUB, Edinburgh and Princeton. Fought in Spanish Civil War and Second World War. Lecturer in Canadian and US universities. Journalist in London until 1957, before emigrating to Canada and becoming Canadian citizen. Left journalism to write novels, living in US, Spain and Ireland. Novels: *Miro,* 1968; *The Hound, the Fox and the Harper,* 1970; *Through the Dark and Hairy Wood,* 1972; *The Whore Mother,* 1973 (about the troubles in Belfast); *The Bird in Last Year's Nest,* 1974; *The MacDonnell,* 1978; *Aladale,* 1979; *The Pirate Queen of Connacht* (Grace O'Malley), 1980.

HETHERINGTON, George, b. Dublin 1916. Ed. England and TCD. Managing Director of a Dublin printers and Director of *Irish Times* until 1972. Has published a small amount of excellent verse in *The Bell, Envoy, Dublin Magazine,* and in several American and English anthologies.

HEWITT, John Harold, b. Belfast 1907. Ed. QUB. Curator Ulster Museum, Belfast, 1930-57; Art Director Herbert Art Gallery and Museum, Coventry, 1957-72; now writer-in-residence, QUB. MIAL. Major Ulster poet, widely published in Britain and America and included in many anthologies. Collections include *No Rebel Word,* 1948; *Collected Poems, 1932-1967,* 1968; *Out of My Time,* Belfast 1974; *Time Enough,* Belfast 1976 (Poetry Book Society Award); *The Rain Dance,* Belfast 1978; *The Selected John Hewitt,* Belfast 1981; *Mosaic,* 1982. His books of criticism include *Colin Middleton,* Dublin 1976; *Art in Ulster, 1,* Belfast 1977. Ed. *Rhyming Weavers and Other Country Poets of Antrim and Down,* Belfast 1974.

HICKEY, Elizabeth, b. Edinburgh 1917 of Irish family. Ed. Scotland, Ireland, TCD. Guide book to Tara, *The Legend of Tara,* 1954, has gone through many editions. *I Send My Love Along the Boyne,* Dublin 1966. *The Green Cockatrice,* written under pseud. 'Basil Iske', 1978.

HICKEY, William, b. Co. Cork 1787 or 1788, d. Dublin 1875. Ed. TCD and Cambridge. Protestant curate and later rector of Kilcormick, moving to Wexford and finally to Muilankin. His chief interest, apart from the Church, was educating the Irish peasantry in better farming methods. His first publication, under his pseud. of 'Martin Doyle', was *State of the Poor in Ireland,* Dublin (?) 1817. In the 1820s near Bannow he established an agricultural school with the help of Thomas Boyce of Bannow House, and with the same patron set up the South Wexford Agricultural Society, the first of its kind in Ireland. *Hints to Small Farmers* appeared first in the *Wexford Herald* as letters to the editor. Collected and published 1830, the book went into many editions up to 1867. It was followed by a whole series of *Hints:/on Road-work*, 1830; *Emigration to Upper Canada*, 1831; *The Flower Garden*, 1834; *A Cyclopaedia of Practical Husbandry*, 1839; *Farm and Garden Produce*, 1857; *Cottage Farming*, 1870. He also directed some of his writing at landlords: *An Address to the Landlords of Ireland on Subjects Connected with the Melioration of the Lower Classes*, 1831; *The Labouring Classes in Ireland: An Enquiry as to What Beneficial Changes May be Effected in their Condition*, 1846, among many other works.

HICKEY, William, b. Dublin (?) 1749 (?), d. 1830. Son of Joseph Hickey, who appears in Goldsmith's unfinished poem 'Retaliation', 1744. An attorney, he travelled to India several times and describes his voyages in his *Memoirs*, first pub. in several vols, 1913-25. The book is scandalous and amusing, describing his addiction to women and claret, and his fortunes and misfortunes as a lawyer.

HIFFERNAN, Paul, b. Dublin 1719, d. 1777. Ed. Ireland and France. Became a journalist of dissolute habits, and wrote much verse-drama, some of which was highly regarded in his time. *The Wishes of a Free People*, 1791, etc.

HIGGINS, Aidan Charles, b. Celbridge, Co. Kildare 1927. Ed. Clongowes. Worked in England and S.Africa. Short stories, *Felo de Se*, 1960 (repub. 1973 as *Asylum and Other Stories);* many translations; travel, *Images of Africa, (1956-60),* 1971; novels, *Langrishe Go Down*, 1966, NY 1967; *Balcony of Europe*, 1972, NY 1973; *Scenes from a Receding Past*, 1977; *Bornholm Night-Ferry*, Dingle and London 1983. Has also written children's stories and several plays for radio broadcast BBC and RE.

HIGGINS, Frederick Robert, b. 1896 Co. Mayo, d. 1941. Ed. locally. Went to work in Dublin as an office boy at 14 years old; became a trades union official and in 1920 editor of a succession of Irish journals, economic and literary. In 1935 was co-editor with W. B. Yeats of *Broadsides,* a poetry magazine. Foundation member of Irish Academy of Letters and Managing Director of Abbey Theatre, for which he wrote *A Deuce of Jacks*, 1935. His main literary reputation rests on his poetry, *Salt Air*, 1924; *Island ·Blood*, 1925; *The Dark Breed*, 1927; *Arable Holdings*, 1933; and *The Gap of Brightness*, 1940.

HINKSON, H. A., b. Dublin 1865, d. Ireland 1919. Ed. TCD and Germany. Called to English Bar 1902, but returned to Ireland in 1916 where he died three years later. In 1893 he had married the poet Katharjne Tynan and was the father of Pamela Hinkson. Wrote a number of novels, including

Golden Lads and Girls, 1895; *Up for the Green,* 1898; *Fan Fitzgerald,* 1902; *O'Grady of Trinity,* 1909; *The Considine Luck,* 1912, etc.

HINKSON, Pamela, b. London 1900, d. 1982. Daughter of Kathleen Tynan. Ed. privately in Ireland, where her father was a resident magistrate in Mayo until his death in 1919, and in Germany and France. Travelled widely as journalist in Europe, America and India. Worked for Ministry of Information 1939-45 and at Shamrock Club in London for Irish servicemen. In 1944 lectured in US on India. Lectured in Germany 1946-47. Also broadcast on radio. Her first book, *Irish Gold,* was written in Ireland. A few years later, in the mid-1930s, she collaborated with Lady Fingall on the latter's autobiography *Seventy Years Young,* 1937. Her first great success was *The Ladies' Road,* 1932, which sold 100,000 copies in the Penguin edition. Other books include *Indian Harvest,* on her visit to India in the late '30s, as a guest of the viceroy; *The Deeply Rooted,* 1934; *Golden Rose,* 1944, also widely praised and read; and *The Lonely Bride,* 1951. She returned to Ireland in 1959.

HITCHCOCK, Francis Clere, b. Dublin 1896, d. Beaconsfield 1962. Brother of Rex Ingram. Served in India First World War and in England Second World War. OBE, MC. Pub. *Stand To,* a diary of the trenches, and his famous *Saddle Up,* 1933, a manual of equitation, frequently reprinted. *To Horse,* 1933, concerns advanced management of stables and horses.

HOBHOUSE, Violet, b. Co. Antrim 1864, d. 1902. Eldest daughter of Edmund McNeill. Deeply interested in Irish folklore and traditions, but a strong Unionist, campaigning against Home Rule in English elections of 1887 and later. Wrote poetry and novels, *An Unknown Quantity,* 1898, and *Warp and Weft,* 1899.

HOEY, Frances Sarah, b. Johnston, Co. Dublin 1830, d. Essex 1908. Married A. M. Stewart at 16, widowed at 25 and went to London with a letter from Carleton, introducing her to Thackeray. Began a long and prolific career writing for magazines, publishing many serials and novels, under her second married name of Hoey, and also under name of Edmund Yates, editor of *The World,* for whom she wrote for 40 years. Novels include *The Question of Cain,* 1882, and *The Rover's Creed.*

HOGAN, David, see GALLAGHER, Frank.

HOGAN, Desmond, b. Ballinasloe, Co. Galway 1951. Ed. UCD. Actor and teacher. Now full-time writer in London. Plays, *A Short Walk to the Sea,* Dublin 1975; *Sanctified Distances,* Dublin 1976; radio play, *Jimmy,* BBC 1977. Novels: *The Ikon Maker,* Dublin 1976, repub. London and NY 1979, Swedish ed. 1980; *The Leaves on Grey,* London and NY 1980; and *A Curious Street,* 1984. Short stories: *The Diamonds at the Bottom of the Sea,* 1979; and *Children of Lir,* 1981.

HOGAN, Edmund Ignatius, b. Cork 1831, d. 1917. Jesuit; pub. the famous *Onomasticon Goedelicum* (on Gaelic place names), 1910, still the standard reference work. Had previously written an account of *The Irish Wolfdog*, 1897.

HOGAN, Ita Margaret. *Anglo-Irish Music 1780-1830*, Cork 1966, a guide containing an account of most of the musical activities in Ireland with biographies and bibliographies of musicians, composers and visiting singers.

HOLLOWAY, Joseph, b. Dublin 1861, d. 1944. Attended every play put on by the Abbey Theatre, as well as many of the rehearsals, and kept a diary of his impressions. The complete journal covers 50 years in 221 vols. A selection was pub. in 1967 as *Joseph Holloway's Abbey Theatre*, ed. Robert Hogan and Michael O'Neill. It includes H.'s account of the '16 Rising.

HOLWELL, John Zephaniah, b. Dublin 1711, d. near Harrow 1798. Went to India as surgeon 1732, helped defend Fort William against Suraja Dowlah 1756, and on its surrender was imprisoned in the Black Hole of Calcutta with 145 companions. The next morning he and 22 others were still alive. His *A Genuine Narrative of the Deaths etc. in the Black Hole*, 1758, is the only eye-witness account. Studied Hindu culture, almost the first Irishman to do so, and wrote much on India, including *An Account of the Method of Inoculating for the Smallpox in the East Indies*, 1767, 30 years before Jenner's successful experiments. But of course knowledge of vaccination had been introduced to England much earlier, by Lady Mary Wortley Montagu, who had learned of it in Turkey.

HONE, Joseph, b. London 1937, grandson of Joseph Maunsel H. Ed. Kilkenny College and St Columba's, Dublin. Worked in cinema, theatre, BBC and UN Secretariat, New York, until 1968, before career as writer. Lives Oxfordshire, England. Fiction includes *The Private Sector*, 1971; *The Parish Trap*, 1977; *The Valley of the Fox*, 1982. Travel: *The Dancing Waiters*, 1975; *Gone Tomorrow*, 1981; *Children of the Country*, 1986. Also ed. *Irish Ghost Stories*, 1975.

HONE, Joseph Maunsel, b. Ireland 1882, d. 1959. Ed. Cheam School and Cambridge; was a distinguished literary historian, becoming President of Irish Academy of Letters 1957. *W. B. Yeats: The Poet in Contemporary Ireland*, Dublin and London 1915; *Bishop Berkeley*, 1932; *Ireland Since 1922*, 1932; *Thomas Davis*, London and Dublin 1934; *Swift or the Egoist* (with Dr M. M. Rossi), 1935; *The Life of George Moore*, 1936; *The Moores of Moore Hall*, and *The Life of Henry Tonks*, 1939; *W. B. Yeats 1865-1939*, 1942; and *Selections from a Dictionary of Irish Writers* (this being a sadly brief work of less than 50 pages), Dublin 1944.

HORGAN, John Joseph, b. Co. Cork 1881; d. 1967. Solicitor, Chairman of Cork Harbour Commissioners; wrote what the *Manchester Guardian* described as 'a kind of anarchists' Bible', titled *The Complete Grammar of Anarchy, by members of the War Cabinet and their friends*, Dublin

1918, consisting largely of quotations from public speeches made by colleagues or supporters of Lloyd George. The British government confiscated the first edition.

HORNER, John, b. Belfast 1858, d. 1919. Engineer and industrialist, is remembered for *The Linen Trade of Europe During the Spinning-Wheel Period,* Oxford 1920, now a standard work.

HOULT, Norah, b. Dublin 1898, d. Ireland 1984. Quickly recognised as a fine writer with the publication of her first book of short stories, *Poor Women,* 1928. These have been reprinted many times and were immediately accepted as classics. Other works: *House Under Mars,* 1946; *Journey into Print,* 1954; *Father and Daughter,* 1957; *Husband and Wife,* 1959; *Last Days of Miss Jenkinson,* 1962; *A Poet's Pilgrimage,* 1965; *Only Fools and Horses Work,* 1969; *Not for Our Sins Alone,* 1972; *Two Girls in the Big Smoke,* 1977.

HOWARD, Alfred, b. Dublin *c.* 1800. Son of a vintner, a parentage which seems to have inspired many Irish writers. Journalist and comic writer, founder and editor of two Dublin comic papers, *Paddy Kelly's Budget,* 1832-38, Paddy Kelly being a pseud. he used, and in the 1840s, *Punch and Judy.* Among his other writings was a play on the popular theme of *The O'Donoghue of the Lakes; or, the Harlequin and the Leprechaun,* acted in Dublin 1840; pub. that year in Dublin, as being by Paddy Kelly.

HOWARD, Gorges Edmund, b. Coleraine 1715, d. 1786. Architect in Dublin. Protestant champion of Catholic Emancipation. Published some verse and several plays, *Almeyda, or the Rival Kings,* Dublin 1769, *The Female Gamester,* Dublin 1778, etc. *Miscellaneous Works in Prose and Verse,* Dublin 1782. His plays were much ridiculed at the time, but nevertheless held the stage. Also wrote legal works of more permanent value.

HULL, Eleanor, b. England 1860 of Co. Down family, d. 1935. Ed. Dublin. A serious journalist and Irish scholar, she founded the Irish Texts Society for the publication of early MSS in 1899, and was herself a student of Old Irish. Her books include *The Cuchulain Saga in Irish Literature,* 1898; *Pagan Ireland,* 1904; *Early Christian Ireland,* 1904; *A Textbook of Irish Literature,* 2 vols, 1906-08; *The Poem-Book of the Gael,* 1912; *The Northmen in Britain,* 1913; *Folklore of the British Isles,* 1928; and *A History of Ireland,* vol. I, 1926; vol. II, 1931.

HUNGERFORD, Margaret Wolfe, née Hamilton, b. Co. Cork 1855, d. Bandon 1897. Used pseud. 'The Duchess.' Popular romantic novelist, published about 30 books, such as *The O'Connors of Ballynahinch* and *An Unsatisfactory Lover,* 1894.

HUTCHINSON, Pearse, b. Glasgow 1927. Drama critic Radio Éireann 1957-61. Gregory Fellow in poetry, University of Leeds, 1971-73; Butler Award for Gaelic Writing 1969. Poetry: *Tongue Without Hands,* 1963;

Expansions, 1969; *Watching the Morning Grow,* 1973; *The Frost Is All Over,* 1975; *Selected Poems,* 1982; all pub. Dublin. For work in Irish see Part 2.

HYDE, Douglas, b. Sligo 1860, d. 1949. First President of Ireland 1937. Devoted his life to the restoration of the Irish language and culture. An authority on Irish folklore, he translated many legends from Irish and Scottish Gaelic. *Folklore of the Irish Celts,* 1890; *The Love-songs of Connacht,* 1893; *Beside the Fire* (Gaelic folk stories collected, translated & edited by D.H.), 1898, *Legends of Saints & Sinners,* 1915. But perhaps his most enduring monument is the Gaelic League which he founded in 1893. For work in Irish see Part 2.

HYDE, Harford Montgomery, b. Belfast 1907. Ed. QUB, Oxford. English Bar 1934. Intelligence Officer Second World War. Has written widely on criminal history, including *The Rise of Castlereagh,* 1933; *The Trials of Oscar Wilde,* 1948; *The Trial of Roger Casement,* 1960; *Rufus Isaacs,* 1967. One-time secretary to the Londonderrys, has written *The Londonderrys: A Family Portrait,* 1979. *Lord Alfred Douglas,* 1984, his 53rd book.

I

INGLIS, Brian, b. 1916. Ed. Shrewsbury, TCD, Oxford, RAF 1940-46. Editor of *Spectator* 1959-62. Has written particularly on medical subjects but also on Irish history: *The Freedom of the Press in Ireland,* 1954, *The Story of Ireland,* 1956; *Revolution in Medicine,* 1958; *Fringe Medicine,* 1964; *Private Conscience: Public Morality,* 1964; *Drugs, Doctors and Disease,* 1965, *A History of Medicine,* 1965; *Abdication,* 1966; *Poverty and the Industrial Revolution,* 1971; *Roger Casement,* 1973; *The Forbidden Game, the Social History of Drugs,* 1975; *The Opium War,* 1976; *Natural and Supernatural,* 1977; *Natural Medicine,* 1979; *The Diseases of Civilisation,* 1981; *Science and Parascience,* 1984. His autobiography, *West Briton,* 1962, is an interesting document of the surviving Anglo-Irish, Protestant community in the Irish Republic.

INGRAM, John Kells, b. Newry 1823, d. 1907. Professor of Greek TCD. President of the Royal Irish Academy 1892. His bibliography occupies 46 pages in *An Leabharlann,* vol. III, no.1, 1909 (this being the *Librarians Journal*). His major works include *A History of Political Economy,* 1888 (twice translated into French, 1893, 1908); *A History of Slavery and Serfdom,* 1895; *Outlines of the History of Religion,* 1900; *Practical Morals,* 1904; and *The Final Transition,* 1905. Was the author of the famous poem, 'Who Fears to Speak of '98?', which appeared anonymously in *The Nation* of April 1843, under the title 'The Memory of the Dead'.

INGRAM, Rex, pen-name of Rex Hitchcock, b. Dublin 1892, d. Los Angeles 1950. Ed. Dublin and Yale, trained as a sculptor and worked on Washington and Gettysburg monuments before turning to early films. Served in RFC during First World War, returned to Hollywood to become one of the best-known silent-film directors. His films include *The Four Horsemen of the Apocalypse* and *The Garden of Allah.* Among other stars he discovered Rudolph Valentino and Ramon Novarro. A friend of Vincent Blasco Ibanez and Robert Hitchens, he left Hollywood to give all his time to writing. Fluent in Arabic he travelled widely in North Africa and the Middle East, and several of his novels are set in these areas: *The Legion Advances,* 1934, etc. *Mars in the House of Death,* US 1939, deals with bullfighting.

IRELAND, Denis, b. Belfast 1894, d. 1974. Served in France and Greece during First World War. Journalist and broadcaster. Irish Senate 1948-51. On Irish delegation to Council of Europe. Wrote *From the Irish Shore* (autobiography), 1936; *Patriot Adventurer* (Wolfe Tone), 1936; *Statues Round the City Hall* (autobiography), 1939.

IREMONGER, Valentin, b. Dublin 1918. Ed. CBS Synge St and Colaiste Mhuire. Trained in Abbey Theatre School of Acting. Joined Abbey company 1939-40; Gate Theatre 1942-44. Entered Foreign Service 1946, and in 1964 was accredited Ambassador to Sweden, Norway and Finland. Irish Ambassador to Luxembourg, having been Ambassador in India 1968-73. In 1945 won AE Memorial Award. Poetry includes *On the Barricades* (with Robert Greacen, Bruce Williamson), 1944; *Reservations,* Dublin 1950; *Horan's Field and Other Reservations* (collected poems), Dublin 1972. Has translated Rilke into Irish, 1955; also two Irish novels into English, *The Hard Road to Klondyke,* 1962, and *An Irish Navvy,* 1964.

As editor with Robert Greacen, of *Contemporary Irish Poetry,* 1949, of *Envoy* (poetry) 1949-51, and of *Irish Short Stories,* 1960, has had a strong influence on many younger writers. Plays include *Wrap up my Green Jacket,* 1948.

IRVINE, Alexander, b. Co. Antrim *c.* 1860, d. *c.* 1926. Newsboy, coal miner, Royal Marine, emigrated to New York. Wrote the well-known novel *My Lady of the Chimney Corner,* 1914; *The Souls of Poor Folk,* and *The Man from World's End and Other Stories,* 1926.

IRVINE, John, b. Belfast 1903, d. 1964. Poet: *A Voice in the Dark,* Belfast 1932; *Willow Leaves: Lyrics in the Manner of the Early Chinese Poets,* Dublin 1941; *With No Changed Voice,* Dublin 1946; *By Winding Roads,* Belfast 1950; *Green Altars,* Belfast 1951; *Lost Sanctuary and Other Poems,* Belfast 1954; *Treasury of Irish Saints* (drawings by Ruth Brandt), Dublin 1964, pub. posthumously. Many of his poems have been set to music. Ed. *The Flowering Branch, an Anthology of Irish Poetry Past and Present,* Belfast 1945.

IRWIN, Thomas Caulfield, b. Co. Down 1823, d. Rathmines 1892, insane. Of a wealthy family. Lost his inheritance and took to journalism. Contributed to *The Nation*, etc. Wrote a biography of Swift for *The Shamrock*, and published some poetry in Dublin and Glasgow. His contemporaries regarded him as a major poet. *Irish Poems and Legends* Glasgow, 1869; *Songs and Romances*, Dublin 1878, etc.

IRWIN, Thomas P., b. Dublin 1901. Son of active trade union leader, was involved in the 1913 Dublin General Strike. Fought in War of Independence and Civil War; was interned, and released after 12-day hunger strike. Wrote *Benson's Flying Column*, Dublin 1935, several editions and great success, dealing with experiences in War of Independence. Worked as maintenance foreman with Dublin Corporation for 40 years.

ISDELL, Sarah, b. *c.* 1780, related to Oliver Goldsmith, d. unknown. Wrote a very successful comedy, *The Poor Gentleman*, acted in Dublin 1811, and often revived. Also a novel, *The Irish Recluse*, 1809.

J

JACKMAN, Isaac, b. *c.* 1750, d. unknown. One of the several Irishmen to become editor of *The Morning Post*, after practising law in Dublin. Wrote several farces and comic opera between 1777 and the end of the century, such as *The Milesian*, 1777, and the highly successful *The Man of Parts*, 1795.

JACKSON, Robert Wyse, b. 1908, d. Dublin 1976. Ed. Waterford, TCD, Manchester. Curate 1934-39; rector Limerick 1939-46; dean Cashel 1946-60. Bishop of Limerick, Ardfert and Aghadoe 1961-70. *Swift and His Circle*, 1945; *Oliver Goldsmith: Essays Towards an Interpretation*, 1954; *The Best of Swift*, 1967; *Irish Silver*, 1972; *The Story of Limerick*, 1973; *The Story of Kilkenny* and *Archbishop Magrath – The Scoundrel of Cashel*, 1974. Also a play, *Fair Liberty Was All His Cry*, and novels: *Spanish Man Hunt; The Journal of Corinna Brown*.

JAMESON, Anna, b. 1794, d. 1860. Highly regarded as a poet in the Regency period, but now remembered for her *Diary of an Ennuyée*.

JEBB, John, b. Drogheda 1775, d. Surrey 1833. Became Protestant Bishop of Limerick, Ardfert and Aghadoe 1822; was a pioneer in the High Church controversies which took shape after his death as the Oxford Movement. *Essays on Sacred Literature*, 1820, and *Practical Theology*, 1830, gave him a great reputation. His correspondence with Alexander Knox was pub. in 1836 in 2 vols and this too gave an impetus to the High Church movement. His nephew John pub. *A Literal Translation of the Book of Psalms,*

2 vols, 1846, which was valuable in its day for removing many errors from the accepted English versions.

JENNETT, Seán, b. 1912. Poet and expert on typography. Poetry includes *Always Adam*, 1943 *The Cloth of Flesh*, 1945; *The Sun and Old Stones*, 1961; *Deserts of England*, 1964. Also *The Making of Books*, 1974, and several travel books including *Connacht*, 1970; *Paris*, 1973; *Loire*, 1975.

JEPHSON, Robert, b. 1736, d. Blackrock 1803. Ed. Dublin. Captain in British Army and later Master of Horse to Viceroy. MP for Old Leighlin in Irish Parliament, 1778. Wrote for stage, and published some poetry. His long poem 'Roman Portraits', 1794, was illustrated by Bartolozzi. Plays include *Braganza*, a tragedy, 1775; *Two Strings to Your Bow*, a farce, 1791, etc.

JESSOP, George H., b. *c.* 1850, d. London 1915. Ed. TCD, emigrated to US 1873. Popular playwright and novelist. Books include *Where the Shamrock Grows*, 1911.

JKL, see DOYLE, James Warren.

JOHNSTON, Jennifer Prudence, b. Dublin 1930. Daughter of William Denis J. Ed. TCD. FRSL. Highly regarded novelist; *The Captains and the Kings*, 1972; *The Gates*, 1973; *How Many Miles to Babylon*, 1974; *Shadows on our Skin*, 1977; *The Old Jest*, 1979; *The Christmas Tree*, 1981; *The Railway Station Man*, 1984. A play, *Indian Summer*, 1984.

JOHNSTON, William Denis, b. Dublin 1901, d. Dublin 1984. Son of Hon. William Johnston, Judge of Supreme Court. Ed. St Andrew's, Dublin, Merchiston, Edinburgh, Christ's College, Cambridge. President of Union. Pugsley Scholar, Harvard. English Bar 1925, N. Ireland Bar 1926. Director Gate Theatre 1931-36. BBC War Correspondent 1942-45. Director of Programmes BBC 1946-47. English Dept, Mount Holyoke, Mass., 1952-60. Guggenheim Fellowship 1955. Head of Theatre Dept, Smith College, Mass., 1961. MIAL. Major Irish playwright, making an immediate reputation with the impressionistic *The Old Lady Says No*, 1929, revived countless times in Dublin and elsewhere. *The Moon on the Yellow River*, 1931, confirmed his reputation. *A Bride for the Unicorn*, 1933; *Storm Song*, 1934; *The Golden Cuckoo*, 1939; *A Fourth for Bridge*, 1948; *Strange Occurrence on Ireland's Eye*, 1956 (the reconstruction of a notorious crime); *The Scythe and the Sunset*, 1958. Has also written 2 vols of autobiography or 'speculative narrative': *Nine Rivers from Jordan* (based on experience as war correspondent), 1953; *The Brazen Horn*, Dublin 1976; and a biography, *In Search of Swift*, Dublin 1959.

JOHNSTONE (sometimes Johnson), Charles, b. Co. Limerick 1719, d. Calcutta *c.* 1800. Ed. TCD and called to Bar, but unable to practice because of deafness. Took to writing and became owner-editor of several newspapers. Published several books of which the most famous was a highly libellous novel *Chrysal, or the Adventures of a Guinea*, which came out in

4 vols in London, 1760-65. The book pretended to reveal political secrets and to expose the private lives of various public men. It was often reprinted. He also published *The Reverie*, 1762; *The Pilgrim*, 1775; and *The History of John Juniper Esq.*, 1781. In the following year, already a wealthy man of advanced middle-age, he went out to India, possibly to escape the enmity of men he had libelled.

JONES, Henry, b. near Drogheda 1721, d. *c.* 1770. Became a bricklayer, and wrote poetry in his leisure. Lord Chesterfield read some of it, and became his patron, bringing him to London, where he swiftly became a notable and admired figure. He published a great deal of poetry between 1746 and 1770, most of it frequently reprinted, but his greatest success was with plays. One or two of them, such as *The Earl of Essex*, 1753, and *The Heroine of the Cave*, 1775 (altered by Paul Hiffernan for publication), enjóyed a greater success than any other London playwright achieved throughout the 18th century, and all his plays were enormously popular. Like Hiffernan, he loved a bottle, and was run over by a carriage in London, probably when drunk. He died of his injuries a few weeks later.

According to some authorities the year of his accident and death was 1773.

JORDAN, John Edward, d. Dublin 1930. Ed. CBS Synge St, UCD, Oxford. Lecturer UCD 1959-69. Critic, poet, short-story writer. Poetry: *Patrician Stations*, 1971; *A Raft from Flotsam*, 1975; *Blood and Stations* (with prose), 1976; *With Whom Did I Share the Crystal?* 1980; all pub. Dublin. Also *Yarns* (short stories), Swords 1977, and (ed.) *The Pleasures of Gaelic Literature*, Cork 1977.

JORDAN, Neil, b. Sligo 1951. Ed. UCD. Worked as labourer and teacher. Began writing career with short stories, *Night in Tunisia and Other Stories*, Dublin 1976, London 1979 (winner of Guardian Fiction Prize), repub. Dingle 1982, and two novels, *The Past*, 1980, and *The Dream of a Beast*, 1983. Turned to the cinema with screen-plays *Travellers*, 1980, and *Angel* (also directed), 1983. *Company of Wolves*, 1984, adapted from the story by English novelist Angela Carter, won him 'Best Director' in the film section of British Critics Circle 1984.

JOY, Henry, b. Belfast 1754, d. Belfast 1835. Published anonymously *Historical Collections relative to the Town of Belfast*, now rare, but of interest to students of northern history.

JOYCE, James, b. Rathgar 1882, d. Zurich 1941. Ed. Clongowes, UCD; studied theology, medicine, and trained as a singer. Left Ireland in 1902, already convinced of his destiny as a great writer and interpreter of Ireland to itself. More than any other writer, his adult life and his work are inseparable, and he might be said to have lived merely to translate his adolescent impressions of Dublin into literature. He returned to Dublin very seldom, one visit being for the improbable-sounding purpose of managing a cinema.

In 1904 he had completed his first major prose work, the short stories of *Dubliners*, but mutual suspicions and obstinacies between himself and his publishers prevented publication for ten years. Meanwhile he published a volume of poems, *Chamber Music*, 1907, of a suprisingly slight and conventional kind. *Dubliners*, 1914, was quickly followed by the often rewritten *Portrait of the Artist as a Young Man*, 1916, almost purely autobiographical, of which *Stephen Hero* was an earlier version. *The Portrait* was immediately recognised, even in wartime England, as a masterpiece, and had enthusiastic reviews, including one by H. G. Wells, hailing Joyce as a major writer. In 1922 *Ulysses* was published in France, and became the subject of numerous court actions, customs seizures, bannings, burnings, smugglings, and learned articles. It describes 18 hours in the lives of various Dubliners, with a degree of physical detail that scandalised a generation that had survived the trenches largely unmoved, unless they happened to have been in the trenches themselves. It is popularly supposed that one character in the novel, 'plump, stately Buck Mulligan', is a pen-portrait of Oliver St John Gogarty, the poet.

Ulysses made famous the so-called 'stream of consciousness' technique, and helped to free the novel from the rigid and largely sterile forms in which it had hardened in the previous half-century. Needless to say, the technique was not new, and almost nothing in the novel is as revolutionary as its worshippers have sometimes claimed. Parallels have been convincingly demonstrated with the Classical Alexandrian poets, and innumerable other schools and periods, down to such contemporaries of Joyce as Dorothy Richardson. This is not to belittle the book. Newness of technique is almost valueless in itself. The book established itself in the 1920s and has remained a masterpiece and landmark in fiction, not for newness, but for content.

After 1922 Joyce remained in Paris, troubled still further by long-standing eye trouble, and obliged to undergo a series of terrible eye-operations. This made it necessary for him to use his friends as readers and secretaries, and any literary Irish visitor to Paris was likely to be pressed into service, first reading works indicated by Joyce, then discussing them on lengthy walks with him, and finally writing and rewriting the digested essence of the work for later inclusion into Joyce's *Work in Progress*.

In this all-embracing masterwork, ultimately published as *Finnegans Wake,* Joyce pushed the language to its limits, and many critics have said that he pushed it beyond them, creating not so much a work of literature as a gigantic puzzle, in which every sentence, and often each word bears two and three and more meanings, visual, aural, suggested, anagramatic, allusive, referring to other languages, previous sentences, folklore, historical anecdotes, popular ballads, ancient Dublin jokes and scandals, and almost anything that struck Joyce's compendious fancy.

Just as *Ulysses* is built on the foundation of the *Odyssey,* each part taking its symbolic meaning from the model-work, so *Finnegans Wake* is created

JOYCE

round and on the solipsist dream of Finnegan. But to attempt to explain the work is to pretend to understand it, and this would be a large claim. Parts of the work appeared separately: *Anna Livia Plurabelle* in 1930, and *Haveth Childers Everywhere* in 1931. The whole book was published in 1939.

JOYCE, Patrick Weston, b. Co. Limerick 1827, d. 1914. Wrote a number of works on Irish grammar and history, but is chiefly remembered for *Irish Names of Places*, vol. I, 1869; vol. II, 1875; and vol. III, 1913.

JOYCE, Robert Dwyer, b. Co. Limerick 1830, d. Dublin 1883. Became a civil servant and later studied medicine in Queen's College Cork. MD 1865. Emigrated to US to practise. He had already published *Ballads, Romances and Songs*, Dublin 1861. In Boston he published *Ballads of Irish Chivalry*, 1872, and the enormously popular *Deirdre*, 1876, which sold 10,000 copies in the week of publication. *Blanid*, 1879, was almost as successful. He returned to Ireland in 1883, and died in Dublin the same year. He also published some prose including *Legends of the Wars in Ireland*, Boston 1868, and *Irish Fireside Tales*, Boston 1871.

JOYCE, Stanislaus, b. Dublin 1884, d. Trieste 1955 (brother of James J.). Joined his brother in Trieste in 1905, taught in the Berlitz School there and became Professor in University of Trieste. Was expelled from Italy for opposing Fascists 1936. His relations with James cooled after 1914, and from 1920 onwards they rarely met. His *Recollections of James Joyce by his brother S.J.*, first written in Italian, were translated and published by S.J. in New York 1950. *My Brother's Keeper*, 1958, and the *The Dublin Diary of Stanislaus Joyce*, 1962, have an interest of their own, apart from their information about James.

JOYCE, Trevor, b. Dublin 1947. Ed. Dublin. Poetry includes *Sole Glum Trek*, 1967; *Watches*, 1969; *Pentahedron*, 1972; *The Poems of Sweeney Peregrine* (trans. of *Buile Suibhne*), 1976. All pub. Dublin.

JUDGE, Michael, b. Dublin 1921. Ed. UCD, College of Art. Teacher, playwright, short-story writer. Has written prize-winning plays for radio and television, including *The Chair*, RTE 1963, Belfast 1967, pub. in *Four Irish Plays*, ed. R. Hogan, Delaware 1982; *Saturday Night Woman*, Delaware 1978; *And Then Came Jonathan*, Dublin Theatre Festival 1980.

K

KANE, Robert John, b. Dublin 1809, d. Dublin 1890. Studied medicine first, but turned to chemistry. In 1832 founded the *Dublin Journal of Medical Science*. In 1845 was made President of Queen's College, Cork, and the next year formed the Museum of Industry in Ireland, becoming its Director and receiving a knighthood. He had already published *Elements of Chemistry,* 1842, and *Industrial Resources of Ireland,* 1844. The Young Irelanders seized on this latter book as an economic justification of their claims for Irish independence, proving, at least to their satisfaction, that if Ireland had control of her own resources she could become prosperous.

KAVANAGH, Julia, b. Thurles 1824, d. Nice 1877. Daughter of Morgan K. the philologist and poet. Spent part of her childhood in Paris, and went to London in 1844. Wrote many novels. The best-known were *Madeleine,* 1848; *Nathalie,* 1850; and *Daisy Burns,* 1853, of which a French translation was made in 1860. She travelled in Itlay and wrote *A Summer and Winter in the Two Sicilies.* She also published biographical sketches of English and French *Women of Letters* in 1862-63.

KAVANAGH, Morgan, b. Tipperary *c.* 1800, d. 1874. Father of Julia K. Held eccentric philological views, and wrote novels and poetry, *Wanderings of Lucan,* 1824; *The Reign of Lockrin,* 1839, etc.

KAVANAGH, Patrick, b. Monaghan 1906, d. Dublin 1967. Grew up on a small farm of the kind described in some of his work. A dedicated poet in the great tradition of Gaelic rather than English poetry, in which 'poetry' is a spiritual force to be served by the poet, rather than a means of communication, although this is not to suggest any lack of clarity in Kavanagh's poetry, which is free from all fashionable tricks. Accepted as a major Irish poet since the appearance of *Ploughman and Other Poems,* 1936; *The Great Hunger,* 1942; *A Soul for Sale,* 1947; *Come Dance with Kitty Stobling,* 1960; and *Collected Poems,* 1964, are other titles. Represented in all major anthologies and often reprinted in Ireland and England. His two novels, *The Green Fool,* 1938, and *Tarry Flynn,* 1948, are both regarded as classics. *Collected Pruse* appeared 1967, including a transcript of his unsuccessful libel action against *The Leinster Leader.* A novel, *By Night Unstarred,* was pub. 1977, but doubt exists as to the extent of his authorship.

KAVANAGH, Patrick, b. Wexford 1834, d. Wexford 1916. Ed. Wexford and Rome, ordained Rome 1856. He was a grand-nephew of Father Michael Murphy, the fighting priest of 1798, and wrote *A Popular History of the Insurrection of 1798,* based in part on family traditions.

KAVANAGH, Peter, b. Co. Monaghan, younger brother of Patrick K. Ph.D. TCD. Professor of English, Loyola University, Chicago; an authority on *The Irish Theatre,* Tralee 1946; *The Story of the Abbey Theatre 1899-1949,* NY 1950. In New York set up The Peter Kavanagh Handpress on which he printed *Irish Mythology: A Dictionary,* NY 1958-59, and *Saint Jerome,* NY 1961. In 1960 he printed from memory extracts from the *John Quinn MSS Collection* now held in the NY Public Library with an embargo on publication until 1988. As a result of a law case arising out of the embargo the bulk of the edition had to be destroyed. A few copies have survived. The extracts are of letters from Synge, Lady Gregory, James Joyce etc. In 1977 published his brother's posthumous novel, *By Night Unstarred;* and *Patrick Kavanagh: Sacred Keeper,* Dublin 1980.

KEANE, John Brendan, b. Listowel 1928. Ed. locally. Went to England 1951, where he worked as a street sweeper and a barman among other jobs. Returned to Kerry 1953, married, and bought a small public house in Listowel 1955. Tried writing short stories without success, and then, with almost no theatrical experience of any kind began writing plays. His first play *Sive,* 1959, was an immediate and outstanding success in Ireland, and has been produced in London and San Francisco. It was followed by *Sharon's Grave,* 1960, also produced in New York; *The Highest House on the Mountain,* 1960; *No More in Dust,* 1961; *Many Young Men of Twenty,* 1961; *Hut 42,* 1962, first produced at the Abbey; *The Year of the Hiker,* 1963; *The Field,* 1965; *Roses of Tralee,* 1966; *Big Maggie,* 1969; *The Change in Mame Fadden,* 1971; *Moll,* 1972; *The Crazy Wall,* 1974; *The Good Thing,* 1975; *The Buds of Ballybunion,* 1978; as well as a number of one-act plays. Most have been printed in Cork or US.

Has written poetry, *The Street,* Cork 1961; essays such as *Unlawful Sex,* Cork 1977, and an immensely popular series of *Letters of...* – books, consisting of an imaginary series of letters from a parish priest, a civic guard, etc. The series began with *Letters of a Successful T.D.,* Cork 1967, and still continues, annually. Also *Self-Portrait,* Cork 1964, rep. 1978; *Stories from a Kerry Fireside,* Cork 1980; *More Irish Short Stories,* Cork 1981. *Man of the Triple Name,* Dingle 1984, is the study of an Irish match-maker; *Owl Sandwiches,* Dingle 1985, a book of reminiscences.

His plays have had more success with the public than with the critics and there has been a curious flavour about the controversy aroused by his work, as if he were somehow the champion of the provincial against the metropolitan. A possible cause of critical unenthusiasm has been the excite-ment and poetry of his writing, presently unfashionable. Lives and works in Listowel, still as a licensee.

KEANE, Katherine, née Boylan, b. Drogheda 1904. Ed. locally. Has written many radio plays, broadcast between 1943-55, on RE. Two novels, *Who Goes Home,* Dublin 1947, and *So Ends My Dream,* Dublin 1950.

KEANE, Molly, née Mary Nesta Skrine, b. 1905. Her pen-name of M.J. Farrell was taken from a public house sign, writing being considered not the right thing for a member of her family and class, or so she felt. (One wonders why, in view of the long list of respectable and well-bred women who were already famous as novelists?) As Farrell she wrote a number of well-received comedies for the London theatre, such as *Spring Meeting,* produced by John Gielgud in the 1930s. Her novel, *Devoted Ladies,* 1934, rep. 1984, was highly praised by Compton McKenzie, and until the 1950s she was accepted as a figure in English (rather than Irish) literature. A savage attack on her last play in the late 1950s by a devotee of the new realist, *Look Back in Anger* school so hurt her that she gave up writing for 20 years. But in the 1970s she began a novel 'just for herself', which as *Good Behaviour*, 1981, became a publishing sensation, received everywhere as a masterpiece of black comedy about Anglo-Irish life of the 1920s. *Time After Time*, 1983, seemed less successful to most reviewers.

KEANEY, Marian, b. Sligo 1944. County Librarian Longford/Westmeath since 1974. Books include *Westmeath Authors,* Mullingar 1969, *Westmeath Local Studies,* Mullingar 1982, and *Irish Missionaries from the Golden Age to the 20th Century,* Dublin 1984.

KEARNEY, Colbert, b. Dublin 1945. Ed. UCD and Cambridge. Lecturer in English UCC. *The Writings of Brendan Behan,* Dublin and London 1977, listed among 'best academic books of the year' by *Choice,* US 1978.

KEARNEY, Peadar (sometimes Ó Cearnaigh) b. 1883, d. 1942. Ed. Dublin, and in the Mechanics' penny library. Worked in a bicycle shop, and at various labouring jobs, but early on was interested in theatre and writing, particularly patriotic songs, to be sung by the athletic clubs which were to form the nucleus of the Volunteers. In 1907 he wrote 'The Soldier's Song', set to music by Patrick Heeney, which is now the National Anthem of the Irish Republic. Sean Rogan also helped with the music. The first man to sing it, apart from the author, was Patrick Bourke, the playwright. The song was not printed until 1912, by Bulmer Hobson in *Irish Freedom.* On the formation of the Volunteers it became their marching song, was sung by the Republican soldiers during Easter Week 1916, and in the internment camps afterwards, by which time it had become the unofficial National Anthem. In 1916 in the US the song was arranged by Victor Herbert and published in New York. About 1907 Peadar K. was working in Wicklow and teaching Irish at night, to Sean O'Casey among others. By 1911 he was working as props man with the Abbey Theatre and toured in England with the company. He was also writing plays and poetry, and was a member of the IRB. He was again on tour with the Abbey in England in 1916, leaving hurriedly to take part in the Rising, against the wishes of St John Ervine, the tour manager. Arrested in 1920 and interned, he was released at the Treaty 1921, and served on the Free State side in the Civil War. A friend of Michael Collins and other leaders, he was a patriot who gained nothing from his patriotism. After the Civil War ended he returned to casual labour, mostly painting, and died in comparative poverty. Apart from the National Anthem he had written songs that every Irishman sings: *The Three-Coloured Ribbon; Down by the Glenside,* etc. rep. as *The Soldier's Song and Other Poems,* 1928. Related to Brendan Behan and Patrick Bourke.

KEARNEY, Richard, b. Cork 1954. Ed. Glenstal, McGill Montreal, University of Paris. Founder-editor, with Mark Patrick Hederman, of *The Crane Bag,* Dublin Spring 1977-, biannual review of arts, politics and philosophy. Ed. *The Irish Mind,* Dublin 1984, outlining intellectual trad-itions in Irish culture. Works: *Dialogues with Contemporary Continental Thinkers,* Manchester 1984; *Poetique du Possible,* Paris 1984; and *Modern Movements in European Philosophy,* Manchester 1985.

KEATING, Maurice Bagenal St Leger, b. near Kildare *c.* 1755, d. 1835. Served in Light Dragoons. Travelled in Spain and Morocco, 1784, and published *Travels in Europe and Africa,* 1816. Had already in 1800 pub-lished a good translation of Bernal Diaz' *The True History of the Conquest of Mexico.*

KEEGAN, John, b. Laois *c.* 1809, d. 1849. Self-educated. Contributed poems to *The Nation, The Irish Penny Journal, Dublin University Magazine* and many other papers. Became the most popular of the Irish 'peasant poets'. His collected *Legends and Poems* pub. Dublin 1907.

KEENAN, Thomas Patrick, b. Dublin *c.* 1860, d. 1927. Became profes-sional actor and entertainer under the name Tom Conway, and author of a vast number of songs, many of which still enjoy popularity, and some that have become world-famous: Mother Machree; If you're Irish Come Into the Parlour; Hello Patsy Fagan, etc. He acted in most of Dublin's music halls and theatres for over 50 years.

KEIGHTLEY, Samuel Robert, Kt , b. Belfast 1859, d. unknown. Ed. Queen's College Belfast. Bar. Member of University Senate. Poet and novelist; *The Pikemen,* 1903 etc.

KELL, Richard, b. Youghal 1927. Ed. Belfast and TCD. Lecturer, Isleworth Polytechnic, 1960-69. Senior lecturer English literature Newcastle-upon-Tyne Polytechnic since 1970. Poetry: *Fantasy Poets 35,* Oxford 1957; *Control Tower,* 1962; *Differences,* 1969; *Humours,* Sunderland 1978; and *Heartwood,* Newcastle-upon-Tyne 1978.

KELLEHER, Daniel Lawrence, b. Cork 1883, d. unknown. Ed. UCC, and became a school-teacher. Published many travel books, and several volumes of poetry, some of which has been reprinted in America and British anthologies. His play *Stephen Gray* was well received on its first Abbey performance.

KELLY, George, b. Connaught 1688, d. *c.* 1750. Ed. TCD. Took Deacon's orders and served in a Dublin church, where in 1718 he preached a fiery Jacobite sermon in favour of the Old Pretender. Threatened with prosecu-tion he fled to Paris, forgot about the Church and became involved in John Law's Mississippi Scheme, apparently with profit. At the same time he became involved in Jacobite plots, assuming the *alias* James Johnson. Atter-bury employed him as secretary and he was used on secret missions to and from the Pretender.

In 1722 such a mission took him to London, he was arrested, tried and condemned for treason. His defence was printed and sold emormously but he remained in the Tower 1723-36. In the latter year he escaped and reached

France, re-entering Jacobite circles. In 1744 he became Prince Charles Edward's secretary and was one of the 'Seven men of Moidart' to land at Eriska with the Young Pretender in June 1745. After Culloden and the Prince's escape Kelly rejoined him in Paris, becoming sole secretary to him 1747. He translated Castlenau's *Memoirs of the English Affairs*, 1724. These and his trial records are of value to the student of the period.

KELLY, Hugh, b. Dublin 1739, d. London 1777. Son of a publican. Emigrated to London 1760. Worked first as a staymaker and then as a journalist, becoming successively editor of the *Court Magazine*, the *Ladies' Museum*, and the *Public Ledger*. Wrote political pamphlets for the government, being rewarded with a pension. Wrote a popular account of a prostitute's life, *Louisa Mildmay, or the History of a Magdalen*, 1767, and the next year an immensely successful comedy, *False Delicacy*, produced in London by Garrick, and translated into French, Portuguese and German. His later plays were less successful. His *Works* published 1778.

KELLY, John, b. *c*. 1705, d. London 1751. Barrister and playwright. Translated from German. His best known work is *The Fall of Bob, or the Oracle of Gin*, 1739, one of the earliest examples of the temperance play.

KELLY, Maeve, b. Dundalk 1930. Poet and short-story writer. Collection of short stories, *A Life of Her Own*, Dublin 1976, rep. 1979. Won Hennessy Literary Award 1972. First novel, *Necessary Treasons*, 1985.

KELLY, Matthew, b. Kilkenny 1814, d. 1858. Ed. Maynooth. Professor at Irish College, Paris, 1839-41 and at Maynooth 1841-58. Wrote *Calendar of Irish Saints*, Dublin 1857.

KELLY, Michael, b. Dublin 1762, d. Margate 1826. Son of Master of Ceremonies at Dublin Castle. Michael sang as a child in Kane O'Hara's puppet shows in Capel Street, and then at 15 took over a major part in the Smock Alley Theatre, astonishing musical Dublin with his voice. Toured Europe and in Vienna sang *Don Curzio* and *Don Basilio* in the first performance of Mozart's *Marriage of Figaro*. After this K. sang principally in England and occasionally in Ireland. His *Reminiscences*, 1826, ghost-written by Theodore Hook, are full of theatrical gossip.

KELLY, Peter, b. Laois 1811, d. Dublin 1883. Ed. TCD. Well-known as a political orator and agitator, but became Clerk of the Peace for Queen's Co. Wrote a novel about evictions, *Glenmore, or the Irish Peasant*, 1839, published as by 'a member of the Irish Bar'.

KELLY, Thomas, b. Co. Sligo 1886, d. unknown. Spent 40 years in British Customs and Excise. Has written many short stories and plays. Stories chosen by Jonathan Cape for their anthologies of *Best British Short Stories* in 1926 and 1927. Plays include *The Schemer* produced Manchester 1931, and several broadcast plays, *Word of Honour, Promotion, The Ticket*, etc., which have been printed and often acted by repertory companies in Ireland and Britain.

KENEALY, Edward Vaughan Hyde, b. Cork 1819, d. London 1880. Ed. TCD. Bar. A scholar, translator from the Irish, an orator and poet, he is best known as the unfortunate defense counsel in the Tichborne Claimant case, going to gaol for his pains, and also being disbarred. He stood for Parliament and failed, and then started a weekly paper, *The Englishman.* It swiftly achieved the then impressive circulation of 160,000 copies a week, and with this as a springboard he successfully contested Stoke-on-Trent and entered Parliament 1875. His *Noah's Ark* pub. 1850, and collected *Poems and Translations,* 1864, among other books of verse and misc. writing.

KENNEDY, Maurice, b. Youghal 1925. Ed. Limerick and UCC. Civil servant. Author of several short stories of merit, but deserves entry here for one remarkable story, 'Vladivostok', first published in *Irish Writing,* 1954, reprinted in *Winter's Tales 2* and *Faber Book of Modern Short Stories;* translated into German; printed in Braille; featured in a volume for use in French schools.

KENNEDY, Patrick, b. Co. Wexford 1801, d. 1873. Moved to Dublin 1823 and became a bookseller in Anglesea St. Wrote for *Dublin University Magazine* and other papers and published some very popular books of legends, stories and folk tales, including *Fictions of our Forefathers,* Dublin and London 1860; *Legendary Fictions of the Irish Celts,* 1866; *The Fireside Stories of Ireland,* Dublin 1870; *The Bardic Stories of Ireland,* 1871, etc.

KENNELLY, Brendan, b. Co. Kerry 1936. Ed. TCD, Leeds. Professor of Modern Literature TCD since 1973. Novels: *The Crooked Cross,* 1963; *The Florentines,* 1967. Poetry includes *Let Fall No Burning Leaf,* 1963; *Dream of a Black Fox,* 1968; *Love Cry,* 1972; *A Kind of Trust,* 1975; *Islandman,* 1977; *The Boats are Home,* 1980; *Cromwell,* 1983; *Moloney Up and At It,* 1984. All pub. Dublin. Ed. *The Penguin Book of Irish Verse,* 1970.

KENNEY, James b. *c.* 1780, d. Paris 1849. The family moved to London about 1800 and the father became manager of Boodle's Club. He hoped to make James a banker, but the boy preferred the theatre and made an early success with the famous play *Raising the Wind,* 1803, highly popular then and for long afterwards. Other successful plays include *Too Many Cooks,* 1805; *Turn Out,* 1812; and *The Sicilian Vespers,* 1840. Byron knew and disliked him. Later in life James suffered from a nervous disease. His son was a translator and librettist for opera.

KENNY, Adrian, b. Dublin 1945. Teacher, short-story writer. Has appeared in *New Irish Writing* and other anthologies. *Arcady and Other Stories,* Dublin 1983. Has also written a novel, *The Feast of Michaelmas,* Dublin 1979.

KENNY, Louise M. Stacpoole, b. Co. Clare *c.* 1885, d. Bray 1933. Daughter of J. K. Dunne. Popular novelist just before First World War; *Carrow* *of Carrowduff,* 1911; *Our Own Country,* 1913, etc. Lived mostly in Limerick.

KEON, Miles Gerald, b. Leitrim 1821, d. Bermuda 1875. Ed. Stonyhurst, Gray's Inn. Journalist on *Morning Post* for 12 years, went to India 1858, returned and was made Secretary of Bermuda where he died. His novels were popular, some of them appearing first as serials, such as *Harding the Money Spinner* which ran in the *London Journal* of 1852, and was repub. 1879. His best-known book was *Dion and the Sybils: A Romance of the First Century,* 1866.

KETTLE, Tom, b. Dublin 1880, d. Somme 1916. MP for East Tyrone 1906-10. First Professor of Economics UCD. Joined the Irish Volunteers, 1913, and visited Belgium to buy arms for the Nationalist cause. But in 1914 saw Prussia as a greater threat than England, and joined Dublin Fusiliers. He was killed leading a bayonet charge in the battle of the Somme. His epitaph was taken from one of his own poems, 'Died not for flag, nor king, nor Emperor, But for a dream born in a herdsman's shed, And for the secret scripture of the poor', a moving sentiment hardly applicable to most of the casualties on the Somme. His writings include *Miscellaneous Essays,* on patriotic subjects; *The Open Secret of Ireland,* 1912; *The Ways of War,* 1917, and *The Day's Burden,* 1918.

KICKHAM, Charles Joseph, b. Mullinahone 1828, d. Blackrock 1882. A gun-powder accident in childhood injured his eyesight and hearing. As a young man he took part in the 'Young Ireland' movement, and joined the Fenians in 1860. Arrested in 1865 he was condemned to 14 years' penal servitude, but served only 4. He wrote verse and short stories, some of which were collected and published in 1870 as *Poems, Sketches and Narratives Illustrative of Irish Life.* He had already published some novels, including *Rory of the Hill,* 1857, and *Sally Cavanagh,* 1869, written while he was in prison. In 1879 he published *Knocknagow,* generally accepted as his finest work.

KIELY, Benedict T. J., b. Co. Tyrone 1919. Ed. CBS Omagh and UCD. Journalist 1945-64, several years literary editor of the *Irish Press.* Lectured in US universities 1964-68. MIAL. A fine critic and writer of short stories and novels. Novels: *Land Without Stars,* 1947; *In a Harbour Green,* 1949; *Call for a Miracle,* 1950; *The Cards of the Gambler,* 1953; *Honey Seems Bitter,* 1954; *There Was an Ancient House,* 1955; *The Captain with the Whiskers.* 1960; *Dogs Enjoy the Morning,* 1968; *Proxopera,* 1977; *Nothing Happens in Carmin Cross,* London and Boston 1985. Short-story collections: *A Journey to the Seven Streams,* 1963; *A Ball of Malt and Madame Butterfly,* 1973; *A Cow in the House,* 1978; *The State of Ireland,* Boston 1981. Criticism: *Poor Scholar: A Study of the Works and Days of William Carleton 1794-1869,* 1947; *Modern Irish Fiction - A Critique,* Dublin 1950. Also, *Countries of Contention: A Study of the Origins and Implications of the Partition of Ireland* (his first book), Cork 1945; *All the*

KIELY

Way to Bantry Bay and Other Irish Journeys (reminiscences), 1978; *Ireland from the Air,* 1985. A volume of memoirs in preparation (Oxford).

KIELY, Jerome, b. Kinsale 1925. Ed. locally and Maynooth. Ordained 1950. Has travelled in Africa and America and Near East. Poetry published in English and American magazines. Won Adam Prize for Poetry 1953, C.Day-Lewis adjudicating. Features in *New Poets of Ireland,* Denver 1963. Poetry collected in *The Griffon Sings,* 1966. *Seven Year Island* (a novel), 1969.

KILBRACKEN, 3rd Baron, John Raymond Godley, b. 1920. Ed. Eton, where on the strength of dreaming about racing winners he set up as a schoolboy bookie with much success. Journalist, traveller and landowner, has published reminiscences, *Living Like a Lord,* 1955; *A Peer behind the Curtain,* 1959 (travels to Moscow); *Shamrocks and Unicorns,* 1962; *Van Meejeren,* 1967 (biography); *Bring Back my Stringbag,* 1979 (autobiography); *The Easy Way to Bird/Tree/Flower Recognition,* 1982/83/84 respectively.

KILLANIN, 3rd Baron, Michael Morris, b. 1914. Ed. Eton, Sorbonne, Cambridge. London journalist 1935-8. Produced films with John Ford in Ireland 1950s. MRIA. LL.D. NUI 1975; D.Litt. NUU 1977. President of International Olympic Committee 1972-80. Innumerable decorations. Lives Dublin and Galway. Books: *Sir Godfrey Kneller,* 1962; with Michael V. Duignan, *The Shell Guide to Ireland,* 1962, 2nd ed. 1967, rev. 1969; *My Olympic Years,* 1983 (40,000 sold in Japanese ed.).

KILROY, Thomas, b. Callan, Co. Kilkenny 1934. Ed. Kilkenny, UCD. FRSL; MIAL. Visiting professor to American universities (Notre Dame, Vanderbilt, Dartmouth, McGill) in the sixties. Professor of Modern English UCG 1978-. Plays: *The Door,* BBC 1967, trans. French, Dutch, German, Flemish; *The Death and Resurrection of Mr Roche,* Dublin Theatre Festival 1968; *The O'Neill,* Peacock 1969; *Tea and Sex and Shakespeare,* 1976; *Talbot's Box,* 1977, and *The Seagull* (interpretation of Chekhov's comedy), 1981, both Dublin Theatre Festival. Novel, *The Big Chapel,* 1971, won Guardian Fiction Prize 1971 and Heinemann Literary Prize 1972. Ed. *Sean O'Casey: A Collection of Critical Essays,* New Jersey 1975.

KING, Richard Ashe, b. Co. Clare 1839, d. London 1932. Ordained in Church of England but gave up his living 1881 to concentrate on writing. Wrote a number of serials and popular novels, such as *The Wearing of the Green,* 1886; *A Geraldine,* 1893, as well as works on Swift and Goldsmith.

KING, William, b. Antrim 1650, d. Dublin 1729. Ed. TCD, ordained 1674, Chancellor of St Patrick's, Dublin, 1679, Bishop of Derry 1691, Archbishop of Dublin 1704. Philosopher, polemicist, and founder-member of Dublin Philosophical Society 1683. Wrote many tracts defending Anglicanism against Rome, and against Presbyterianism. *The State of the Protestants,* 1691, dealt with Anglican attitudes during the reign of James II. He wrote on scientific matters, contributed to *Philosophical Transactions,* but is remembered principally for *De Origine Mali,* 1702, trans. by Bishop Law as *The Origin of Evil,* 1730. His *Sermon on Predestination* repub. Cadenus Press, Dublin 1976. (See CARPENTER, Andrew.)

KINSELLA, Thomas, b. Dublin 1928. Ed. UCD. Influential not only as poet but as editor of literary magazines. Director Dolmen Press; MIAL. Won Guinness Poetry Award 1958 and Irish Arts Council Triennial Book Award 1961. His books include *The Starlit Eye,* 1952; *Poems,* 1956; *Another September,* 1958; *Moralities,* 1960; *Poems and Translations,* 1961; *Downstream,* 1962; *Wormwood,* 1966; *Nightwalker and Other Poems,* 1968; *A Selected Life,* 1972, and its sequel, *Vertical Man,* 1973; *One, A Sequence of poems,* 1974; *Fifteen Dead,* 1979, *Poems, 1956-1973,* Dublin 1980. He has translated *The Tain,* 1969, re-issue 1985; *St Patrick, Apostle of Ireland,* 1973; and *An Duanaire 1600-1900: Poems of the Dispossessed,* ed. by Seán Ó Tuama, 1981. All pub. Dublin.

KIRWAN, Richard, b. Co. Galway 1733, d. 1812. Remembered for his *Elements of Mineralogy,* 1784, trans. French, German, Russian, many editions. It was the first systematic treatment of the subject.

KNOWLES, James Sheridan, b. Cork 1784, d. Torquay 1862. Son of the lexicographer James K., and first cousin of Richard Brinsley Sheridan. Was taken to London 1793, and studied medicine. MD Aberdeen. After brief service in army began a successful theatrical career as actor, producer and author. Wrote more than 20 plays of which the best-known are *The Hunchback,* 1832, which apart from numerous revivals ran through nine editions in four years when published, and *The Lovechase,* 1837. In 1844 he became a Baptist preacher and was as popular a preacher as he had been a playwright. Other works include poetry and two novels, *George Lovell,* 1846, and *Fortescue,* 1847. Neither had anything like the appeal of his plays or sermons, and he was obviously born for the theatre and the spoken word. He was the most popular verse playwright of his generation.

KNOX, Robert Bent, b. Co. Tyrone 1808, d. Armagh 1893. Author of *Ecclesiastical Index* (of Ireland), 1839, an invaluable source of information. Became Archbishop of Armagh (Protestant), 1886.

KUHN, Joy, née Green, b. Limerick. Journalist in Ireland, England and Southern Africa. Woman editor of *Zambia Mail.* Scriptwriter BBC. *Twelve Shades of Black,* Cape Town 1976, London 1977, describes life in South African native townships from the inside. *Myth and Magic,* Cape Town 1978, deals with sculpture and beliefs of Shona tribesmen. *The Liar and the Pagan Lady,* 1980, a novel. Now Mrs Martin.

L

LALOR, James Fintan, b. 1807, d. 1849. Young Irelander and contributor to *The Nation* and the *Irish Felon* 1847-48. He had been a member of O'Connell's Repeal Association and being expelled from it with the other Young Irelanders, formed the Irish Confederation 1846/7. The two papers, *The Nation* and *Irish Felon,* were the principal voices of the group and in them he argued for the nationalisation of all land in Ireland and as a means of achieving this proposed a tenants' association to withold rents and fight the landlords by all possible means. His slogan was 'the land of Ireland for the people of Ireland'. After the failure of the '48 conspiracy he was imprisoned, and died the following year. His ideas were taken up and developed by Michael Davitt, and remained a constant thread in the complex weaving and inter-weaving of Irish Revolutionary movements. In some senses he was the ancestor of Connolly's Marxist element in the 1916 Rising and of some parts of the Republican side of the Civil War. The Donegal land-struggles of the 1920s and '30s against payment of annuities to English ex-landlords also owed some of their inspiration to his teaching. Much of his writing is contained in *James Fintan Lalor,* ed. L. Fogarty, Dublin and London 1918.

LAMB, Hilda, née Hawes, b. England of Irish descent. Settled in Ireland in the 1920s when very young. Close friend of the Bulmer Hobson family and other leaders of the National movement. Worked for many years on her first novel, *The Willing Heart,* 1958, based on 15th and 16th-century family papers. A second historical novel, *Daughter of Aragon,* 1965. Lives in Dublin.

LANE, Temple, pseud. of Mary Isabel Leslie, Ph.D., b. Dublin 1899, d. (?). Spent her childhood mostly in Tipperary. Ed. England and TCD, won the Large Gold Medal 1922. Wrote the famous poem *The Fairy Tree,* set to music by Dr Vincent O'Brien. Other verse includes *Fisherman's Wake,* Dublin and London, 1940, and *Curlews,* Dublin 1946. Has written many novels: *Burnt Bridges,* 1925; *The Bands of Orion,* 1929; *The Little Wood,* 1930, which won the Tailteann Gold Medal; *Blind Wedding,* 1931; *Sinner Anthony,* 1933; *The Trains Go South,* 1938; *Battle of the Warrior,* 1940; *House of My Pilgrimage,* London and Dublin 1941; *Friday's Well,* Dublin 1943; *Come Back,* Dublin 1945; and *My Bonny's Away,* Dublin 1947. *Friday's Well* was adapted for the stage by Frank Carney. As well as 'Temple Lane', Miss Leslie used the pseud. 'Jean Herbert'.

LANGBRIDGE, Rosamund, b. Co.Donegal 1880, d. unknown. Daughter of Rev. Frederick L. Ed. privately in Limerick. Contributed to *Manchester Guardian* and other papers. Wrote a number of novels including *The Flame and the Flood,* 1908, *Land of the Ever Young,* 1920, and *The Green Banks* *of Shannon,* 1929.

LANIGAN, John, b. Cashel 1758, d. Dublin 1828. Ordained Rome, taught in Pavia in the 1790s. Returning to Ireland 1796, became assistant librarian in the Royal Dublin Society 1799, and in 1808 with Edward O'Reilly founded the Gaelic Society in Dublin. *An Ecclesiastical History of Ireland from the first introduction of Christianity to the beginning of the 13th Century,* 4 vols, 1822, 2nd ed. 1829, is his principal work.

LARMINIE, William, b. Co. Mayo 1849, d. Bray 1900. Spent many years in civil service, wrote poetry, and collected folk stories. Books include *West Irish Folk-Tales and Romances,* 1898, and two volumes of poetry: *Glanlua,* 1889, and *Fand and Other Poems,* Dublin 1892.

LATIMER, William Thomas, b. Co. Tyrone 1842, d. Eglish 1919. Wrote many books on aspects of northern history, including *A History of the Irish Presbyterians,* 1893, which Lecky praised highly.

LAVERTY, Maura Kelly, b. Co. Kildare 1907, d. 1966. Ed. Tullow. Went to Spain 1925, as governess, became secretary to Princess Bibesco, and was finally a journalist in Madrid. Returned to Ireland 1928 as a journalist. First novel, *Never No More,* 1942, repub. 1984. Her second, *Touched By the Thorn,* was banned in Ireland, but received the Irish Women Writers Award. Other books include *Alone We Embark, 1943; No More Than Human,* 1944; *Lift Up Your Gates,* 1946, *Green Orchard,* 1949. Her play *Liffey Lane,* 1947, is a dramatisation of *Lift Up Your Gates.* Another play, *Tolka Row,* was adapted for RTE with great success. Also known for her cookbooks: *Flour Economy,* 1941; *Full and Plenty,* 1960, 2nd ed. 1966; all Dublin.

LAVIN, Mary, b. Massachusetts 1912. Ed. UCD. Lord Dunsany was the first to recognise her talent and encourage it, writing a foreword to her first collection of stories, *Tales from Bective Bridge,* 1942, which won the James Tait Black Memorial Prize. Other collections of stories include *The Long Ago,* 1944; *The Becker Wives,* 1946; *At Sally Gap,* Boston 1946; *Patriot Son,* and *A Single Lady,* 1956; *Selected Short Stories,* NY 1959; *The Great Wave,* 1961; *Short Stories of Mary Lavin,* 1964; *In the Middle of the Fields,* 1967; *Happiness,* 1969; *Collected Stories,* Boston 1971; *A Memory and Other Stories,* 1972; *The Shrine and Other Stories,* 1976. Her *Collected Stories* are due out 1985. Novels include *The House in Clewe Street,* 1945; *Mary O'Grady,* 1950; and *A Likely Story,* 1957. Contributes regularly to *The New Yorker.*

Regarded as among the greatest living Irish writers, she has been awarded many honours, such as the Katherine Mansfield Prize 1961, several Guggenheim Fellowships, the Eire Society Gold Medal 1974, and the Gregory Medal 1975, which W. B. Yeats called the supreme literary award of the Irish nation. President Irish Academy of Letters 1972-74. Lives in Dublin and Bective.

LAWLESS, Emily, the Honourable, b. Kildare 1845, d. Surrey 1913. Daughter of 3rd Lord Cloncurry, wrote historical studies, novels and poetry, receiving D.Litt. from TCD. Her best-known novels were *Grania,* 1892, and *Maelcho,* 2 vols, 1894. Her poetry was collected and republished in Dublin, 1965. Also *The Story of Ireland,* 1884, and a biography of *Maria Edgeworth,* 1904.

LAWLESS, John, b. Dublin 1773, d. London 1837. Belfast editor and agitator on behalf of Catholic Emancipation, he was one of the leading northern figures in the Catholic Association, and so violent a speaker and politician that O'Connell regarded him with considerable distaste as 'Mad Lawless'. But in the crisis over the monster demonstration at Ballybay in 1828 he acted with discretion, withdrawing from the meeting to avoid the inevitable bloodshed. This drew favourable comment from Wellington, who from having been wholly against Emancipation swung round to favouring it, in part because of the strength shown by such meetings as Ballybay, and in part because of the maturity shown by the Catholic Association's leaders.

His chief writings are *A Compendium of the History of Ireland,* Dublin 1814, and *An Address to the Catholics of Ireland,* 1825.

LAWRENCE, Vincent, b. Wexford 1940. Ed. Wexford and Dublin. Teacher and writer. Fiction reviewer *Sunday Press* since 1974. Short stories in *Introduction 4,* 1971; novel, *An End to Flight,* 1973; radio play, *Looking Back,* RE 1984. Hennessy Literary Award 1971; Robert Pitman Literary Prize 1973. Brother of writer John Banville.

LAWRENCE, William, b. Belfast 1862, d. 1940. Became best known as historian of Elizabethan stage. *Pre-Restoration Stage Studies,* 1927; *The Physical Conditions of the Elizabethan Public Playhouse,* 1927; *Shakespeare's Workshop,* 1928; *Those Nut-Cracking Elizabethans,* 1935; *Old Theatre Days and Ways,* 1935; *Speeding Up Shakespeare,* 1937. Lawrences's importance for Irish literature lies in his influence as drama critic for *The Stage.*

LEADBEATER, Mary, b. Ballitore, Co. Kildare 1758, d. Ballitore 1826. Daughter of Quaker family named Shackleton she received a good education and in 1784 was brought to London by her father. There she met Burke and visited Beaconsfield and remained his correspondent for many years. In 1791 she married a small farmer and became post-mistress of Ballitore. Many of her friends were involved in the '98 Rising and *The Annals of Ballitore,* generally called *The Leadbeater Papers,* are an invaluable source. The 1st vol. is a local history with much biographical material of the period 1766-1823. The 2nd vol. deals particularly with the Rising. These papers lay unpublished until 1862. During her lifetime she brought out a number of moral tales: *Dialogues among the Irish Peasantry,* Dublin 1811, instructed the poor, and *The Landlord's Friend,* 1813, hoped to instruct the rich, a more ambitious undertaking. *Tales for Cottagers,* 1814, written with her sister Elizabeth, continued the series. These have value as they reveal much about cottage life of the period, but *Cottage Biography being a Collection of Lives of the Irish Peasantry,* Dublin 1822, is invaluable, being almost the only material of its kind in existence. The *Lives* are of her Ballitore neighbours. The following year she published *Biographical Notices of members of the Society of Friends.*

LEAMY, Edmund, b. Waterford 1848, d. Pau 1904. Solicitor and MP. Edited *United Ireland.* Collected and published many Irish fairy stories and wrote some fiction and poetry. *Irish Fairy Tales,* Dublin 1889, etc.

LEARED, Arthur, b. Wexford 1822, d. London 1879. Doctor, invented the double stethoscope and wrote on the *Circulation of the Blood and on Digestion.* Also wrote a medical treatise in Icelandic, having visited Iceland several times. Travelled widely, his best-known travel books being *Morocco and the Moors,* 1876, revised by Sir Richard Burton, 1891, and *A Visit to the Court of Morocco,* 1879.

LEASK, Harold G., b. 1882, d. 1964. Architect; was Inspector of National Monuments 1923-49, and wrote guides and learned studies of many of the principal Irish monastic ruins. His great works were *Irish Castles and Castellated Houses,* 1941, and *Irish Churches and Monastic Buildings,* 3 vols, Dundalk 1955-60. Both widely acclaimed.

LECKY, William Edward Hartpole, b. Co. Dublin 1838, d. 1903. Principally a historian of ideas, he first published a series of essays *Leaders of Public Opinion in Ireland,* 1861, anonymously, and then turned to *History of the Rise and Influence of Rationalism in Europe,* 2 vols, 1865, and *History of European Morals from Augustus to Charlemagne,* 2 vols, 1869, which between them established him as a major historian. *A History of England in the 18th Century,* 8 vols, 1878-90, and *A History of Ireland in the Eighteenth Century,* 1892 (being vols 8-12 of a new 12-vol. ed. of *A History of England,* etc.) show great sympathy for Irish ambitions and contradict the Whig attitudes of Froude. In spite of this, Lecky was not a democrat in any modern sense, *vide: Democracy and Liberty,* 1896, and he opposed Home Rule as not in the best interests of Ireland. MP for TCD 1895-1903.

LEDWICH, Edward, b. Dublin 1738, d. Dublin 1823. Was vicar of Aghaboe, in the then Queen's Country, 1772-97. In 1789 published the ridiculous *Antiquities of Ireland,* Dublin, which drew much scorn on his head. But deserves remembrance for *A Statistical Account of the Parish of Aghaboe,* 1796. Here he knew what he was writing about. His grandson, Thomas Hawkesworth Ledwich, 1823-58, wrote *The Anatomy of the Human Body,* 1852, for many years a required text-book. The Dublin Original School of Medicine was renamed the Ledwich School of Medicine in his honour after his death, until its amalgamation in 1887 with the

College of Surgeons.

LEDWIDGE, Francis, b. Slane 1887, d. Flanders 1917. Had little formal education and worked on roads as a labourer. Lord Dunsany discovered his talent for poetry and encouraged him. Ledwidge joined the Inniskilling Fusiliers and was killed in action. Almost his entire work is contained in two volumes, *Songs of the Fields,* 1916, and *Songs of the Peace,* 1917. Also *Last Songs,* 1918.

LEEN, Edward, b. Co. Limerick, 1885, d. Kimmage 1944. Ed. Rockwell College, Paris, Rome. Holy Ghost Father; missionary in Nigeria 1920-22. Dean of Studies and then President Blackrock College 1922-31; Superior Holy Ghost Missionary College, Kimmage 1940-44. After a serious illness in 1935 began writing. *Progress Through Mental Prayer,* 1935; *In the Likeness of Christ,* 1936; *The Holy Ghost,* 1937; *Why the Cross,* 1938; *The True Vine and its Branches,* 1939; *The Church Before Pilate,* 1940; *What is Education,* 1944; and *Our Blessed Lady,* 1945, have been read throughout the Catholic world. See also *My Last Retreat,* Cork 1958, printed from notes of the last retreat and sermons given by Fr Leen.

LE FANU, Joseph Sheridan, b. Dublin 1814, d. Dublin 1873. Ed. TCD. Bar. Became a writer very early, publishing *The Purcell Papers* in the *Dublin University Magazine* while still in TCD. (It must be remembered that the *Magazine* had no connection with TCD and was not a student magazine.) These papers were later published as a volume, 1880, with a memoir of Le Fanu's life. In 1847 Le Fanu, a connection of the astonishing Sheridan family, published *Torlogh O'Brien,* considered by some critics as one of the best of Irish historical novels. A feature of all his subsequent novels, 16 of them, is a Gothic 'uncanniness' which he raises above mere ghostliness to a powerful literary and artistic factor in his books. The best of them deserve comparison with Wilkie Collins, himself the grandson of an Irish writer. *The House by the Churchyard,* 1863; *Uncle Silas,* 1864; and *In a Glass Darkly,* 1872, all have great merit. Le Fanu also wrote poetry and his collected *Poems* were edited and published by A.P. Graves, 1896.

A Peter Le Fanu had written *Smock Alley Secrets,* a play produced in Dublin in 1778.

LEITCH, Maurice, b. Co. Antrim 1933. Teacher and BBC features producer. Novels: *The Liberty Lad,* 1965, rep. Belfast 1985; *Poor Lazarus,* 1969 (won Guardian Fiction Prize); *Stamping Ground,* 1975; *Silver's City,* 1981.

LELAND, Jeremy, b. 1932. Descendant of Thomas L. Ed. Wellington, Slade. Farmed near Drogheda 1955-65. Now lives Norwich. Novels: *The River Decrees,* 1969; *The Jonah,* 1970; *The Tower,* 1972; *Lirri,* 1973. Short stories: *The Last Sandcastle,* Dublin 1983.

LELAND, Mary, b. Cork. Ed. South Presentation Covent Cork. Journalist and feature writer with *Cork Examiner* and *Irish Times.*Listowel Writers'

Week Prize for short story 1980. First novel, *The Killeen*, 1985. Lives in Cork with three children.

LELAND, Thomas, b. Dublin 1722, d. 1785. Probably son of John L. the non-Conformist minister who had written *View of the Principal Deistical Writers*, 1754-56. Ed. TCD, ordained 1748, he became Professor of Oratory, TCD, 1763 and vicar of Bray 1768 (although not the Bray of the song). Wrote *The Principles of Human Eloquence*, 1764, which has a period charm, but gained a permanent reputation with *The History of Ireland: From the Invasion of Henry II*, 3 vols, Dublin and London 1773. On publication was found by all sides to suffer from gross impartiality and was accordingly much attacked, but as time went by gained a following and is now a classic among Irish histories.

LENIHAN, Maurice, b. Waterford 1811, d. 1895. Ed. Carlow. Edited *Limerick Reporter* from 1841 for many years, in favour of Nationalism. Became Mayor of Limerick 1884. In 1866 published *Limerick, Its History and Antiquities*.

LEONARD, Hugh, pseud. of John Keyes Byrne, b. Dalkey, Co. Dublin 1926. Civil servant in Dublin for 14 years, began acting and writing for amateur theatre, and was first recognised as a professional playwright by the Abbey Theatre with *The Big Birthday*, 1956; *A Leap in the Dark*, 1957; *Madigan's Lock*, 1958; *A Walk on the Water*, 1960. Since then has written for London and New York theatres, and achieved immense success as a TV script-writer and dramatist. TV series and serials include *Country Matters, Nicholas Nickleby, Me Mammy, Strumpet City, Good Behaviour;* has also written film scripts, *Great Catherine, Herself Surprised, Troubles;* and books, *Leonard's Last Book*, 1978, and *Home Before Night*, 1979. Plays since 1960 include *Stephen D*, 1962; *The Poker Session*, 1963; *The Saints Go Cycling In* (dramatisation of Flann O'Brien *The Dalkey Archive*), 1965; *The Au Pair Man*, 1968; *The Patrick Pearse Motel*, 1971; *Da*, 1973; *Irishmen*, 1975; *Time Was*, 1976; *A Life*, 1979; *Weekend*, and *Kill*, 1982. In 1978 new productions of *Da* won wide praise (Drama Critics Award, four Tony Awards, etc.). *Some of My Best Friends Are Husbands* (adapted from Labiche farce), Dublin 1985.

LEPPER, John Heron, b. Belfast 1878, d. unknown. Ed. Scotland and TCD. Bar. Several novels, *A Tory in Arms*, 1916; *The North East Corner*, 1917 (he was a barrister on the NE circuit); short stories and a book on *Famous Secret Societies*. Moved to London 1914.

LESLIE, Anita, b. 1914. Daughter of Sir Shane Leslie, privately educated. Ambulance driver during Second World War in S. Africa, Syria, Italy, France, transferring to French Army 1944/5, entering Berlin with French troops. Received Croix de Guerre. Her war memoirs, *Train to Nowhere*, 1946, praised as best war book by a woman. She had already published *Life of Rodin*, 1939, and in 1951 published an account of sailing a small boat through the Caribbean, *Love in a Nutshell. The Fabulous Mr Leonard Jerome,* NY 1954, biography of Winston Churchill's American grandfather, was a best seller. Other biographies are *Mrs FitzHerbert,* NY 1958; *Mr Frewen of England,* 1965; *Jennie,* 1967; *Sir Francis Chichester,* 1975; *Cousin Clare,* 1976; *Madame Tussaud* (with Pauline Chapman), 1978. *Edwardians in Love* (a social history), 1972; *The Gilt and the Gingerbread: An Autobiography,* 1981; *A Story Half Told,* 1984; *Cousin Randolph,* 1985.

LESLIE, Desmond Peter Arthur, b. London 1921. Youngest son of Sir Shane Leslie. Ed. Ampleforth and TCD. RAF 1940-44, invalided out. Commissioned to write a science fiction, he produced instead a thesis on the Flying Saucer phenomenon, *Flying Saucers Have Landed,* 1953, which to date has been translated into 16 languages and been republished in many editions. Has also written *How Britain Won the Space Race* (with Patrick Moore), 1966, and *The Jesus File* (a novel), 1975.

LESLIE, Shane (John Randolph), 3rd Bt, b. Co. Monaghan 1885, d. Hove 1971. Ed. Eton and Cambridge, Knight Commander of Order of St Gregory. A life-long interest in ghosts and the supernatural had resulted in a number of books such as *Fifteen Odd Stories,* 1935; *Shane Leslie's Ghost Book,* 1955, etc. But his writing life began as a poet: *Songs of Oriel,* 1916; *Verses in Peace and War,* 1922; *The Poems of Shane Leslie,* 1928; *Poems and Ballads,* 1933. Other titles include *The Isle of Columkille; Doomsland,* 1923; and a play, *Lord Mulroy's Ghost,* Dublin 1954. Has written number of biographies and some history. In 1907 visited Russia and met Tolstoy, becoming in a sense his disciple. The following year became a Catholic. In 1918 was responsible for introducing Scott Fitzgerald to his editor Max Perkins of Scribners, New York. Books include *The End of a Chapter,* 1916; *Story of St Patrick's Purgatory,* 1917; *Life of Sir Mark Sykes,* 1922; *George the Fourth,* 1926; *The Skull of Swift,* 1928; *The Epic of Jutland,* 1930; *The Oxford Movement,* 1933; *The Film of Memory,* 1938; *Life of Mrs FitzHerbert,* 1939; *Letters of Mrs FitzHerbert,* 1940; *The Irish Tangle for English Readers,* 1946; *Cardinal Gasquet,* and *Cardinal Manning,* Dublin 1953. *The Long Shadows,* 1966, was another volume of autobiography.

LETTS, Winifred M., b. 1882, d. 1972. Ed. England and Dublin. Wrote a number of plays for the early Abbey, poetry, including *Songs from Leinster,* 1913, and several novels including *Christina's Son,* 1915.

LEVER, Charles James, b. Dublin 1806, d. Trieste 1872. Ed. TCD, Göttingen and Louvain, where he received his MD. In 1829 travelled in the backwoods of Canada and the US. These journeys provide the basis for his novels *Con Cregan* and *Arthur O'Leary.* In 1832 he practised as a doctor in Dublin throughout the cholera epidemic, and later in various Irish country towns. In 1840 he moved to Brussels, sending serial stories to the *Dublin University Magazine,* among other journals, as well as practising medicine. The *DUM* published his *Harry Lorrequer* in 1840 and

Charles O'Malley, 1841, the latter based on his student days in TCD and by far his most popular novel.

In 1842 he returned to Dublin, gave up his practice and became editor of the *DUM* until 1845. In these years he also wrote and published *Arthur O'Leary, Tom Burke of Ours,* and *The O'Donoghue.* In 1845 he returned to Brussels and later to Germany. In 1847 he wrote *The Knight of Gwynne.* Moving on to Italy he wrote *Roland Cashel, Luttrel of Arran, Con Cregan, Sir Jasper Carew,* and between 1852 and 1854 the popular humorous series *The Dodd Family Abroad.* These were followed by a quite different type of book, *The Fortunes of Glencore, The Martins of Cro-Martin,* and *The Daltons.*

In 1858 he became British consul at La Spezia where he continued to pour out novels, serials, cómic verse, and humorous essays for *Blackwood's* (under the name Cornelius O'Dowd) and other magazines. In 1867 he was promoted to the consulship at Trieste. Many of his novels were illustrated by the then famous comic artist Hablot Knight Browne ('Phiz'), and the illustrations as much as the contents of the books have infuriated generations of patriotic Irish readers. Lever has been accused of helping to create the 'stage Irishman,' of distorting the Irish scene and character for a despicable profit, and of sneering at his unhappy fellow-countrymen for a cheap popularity among his country's enemies.

This seems much too heavy a criticism to level at a comic writer, who was exercising the caricaturist's privilege of concentrating on the ridiculous features of his subject.

LEWIS, Clive Staples, b. Belfast 1898, d. 1963. Ed. Malvern, Oxford (Triple First). Fellow and Tutor, Magdalen, 1925-54, Professor of Mediaeval and Renaissance Literature, Cambridge, 1954-63. Achieved popular fame with *The Screwtape Letters,* 1942, ostensibly the letters of a devil to his apprentice nephew, but in fact essays on practical morality and theology. Wrote *The Allegory of Love,* Oxford 1936, and *Beyond Personality: the Christian idea of God,* 1944. *Suprised by Joy,* 1955, an autobiography telling of his conversion to a robustly intellectual Anglo-Catholicism; *Studies in Words,* Cambridge 1960; and *The Discarded Image* (mediaeval and Renaissance literature), Cambridge 1964, were others of his books. Also wrote a number of theological fairy stories for children. Increasingly recognised as a spiritual writer of significance.

LIDDIARD, Anna, b. Co. Meath *c.* 1785. Married Rev. William Liddiard and published many volumes of patriotic verse: *Poems,* Dublin 1810; *The Gye-Laiga,* 1811; *Mount Leinster,* Dublin 1819, etc. Her husband also wrote poetry and some travel books.

LIDDY, James, b. Kilkee 1934. Ed. UCD. Bar. An authority on James Joyce and an encourager of young poets as editor and adviser to a succession of poetry magazines. Own poetry collected in *Esau, My Kingdom for a drink,* Dublin 1962; *In a Blue Smoke,* Dublin 1964; *Blue Mountain,* Dublin and

LITTLE

NY 1968; *A Life of Stephen Dedalus*, San Francisco 1969; *A Munster Song of Love and War*, 1971; *Orpheus in the Ice-Cream Parlour*, Gorey 1975; *Baudelaire's Bar Room Flowers*, Santa Barbara 1975; *Corca Bascinn*, Dublin and NY 1977; *Comyn's Lay*, Fort Bragg 1978. Has appeared in *The Penguin Book of Irish Verse*, 1970, and many anthologies.

Now an American citizen, and Assistant Professor of English Wisconsin-Milwaukee University. Also Chairman of Gorey Arts Centre.

LITTLE, Arthur, b. Dublin 1897, d. Dublin 1949. Ed. Belvedere, TCD. Jesuit 1914. Taught philosophy at Tullabeg 1932-46. His books include *Philosophy without Tears*, and *The Nature of Art*, 1946, as well as some poetry, particularly *Christ Unconquered*, Dublin 1942.

LITTLE, George, A., b. Dublin 1899, d. 1965. Ed. RCSI. As a medical student in the War of Independence was appointed medical officer in 1st Dublin Brigade, becoming the friend of Michael Collins and other leaders. Wrote *The Ouzel Galley*, Dublin 1940; *Malachi Horan Remembers*, Dublin 1943 (folklore); *Brendan the Navigator*, Dublin 1945; and *Dublin before the Vikings*, Dublin 1957.

LLOYD, John (also Seán Luid), b. Co. Limerick 1741, d. Co. Clare 1786. A wandering school-teacher, he wrote poetry in Irish (see Part 2), but is best remembered in English for *A Short Tour; or an Impartial and Accurate Description of the County of Clare with some Particular & Historical Observations*, Ennis 1780. A facsimile reprint of this was published 1893, edited by Henry Henn.

LOBO, George Edmund, b. Dublin 1894, d. Dublin 1971. Novels: *Golden Desire*, 1925, and *Mandrake* (under pseud. Oliver Sherry), 1928. Also poetry including *Sacrifice of Love*, 1916, admired by Douglas Hyde, and *Clay Speaks of the Fire*, 1947, praised by many poets - Ralph Hodgson, de la Mare and Francis Meynell among others.

LOGAN, Patrick, b. Co. Leitrim 1911. Ed. UCD. Medical doctor with special interest in the history of medicine. *Making the Cure* (Irish folk medicine), Dublin 1972; *Irish Holy Wells and Pilgrimages*, 1981; *The Old Gods*, Belfast 1981; *Irish Country Cures*, Belfast 1981; and *Medical Dublin*, Belfast 1984.

LONGFIELD, Ada Kathleen (Mrs Harold Graham Leask), published *Anglo Irish Trade in the 16th Century*, 1929, and edited the *FitzWilliam Accounts 1560-65*, Dublin 1960.

LONGFORD, 6th Earl, Edward Arthur Henry Pakenham, b. 1902, d. 1961. Ed. Eton and Oxford, succeeded 1915. In 1930 joined Michael Mac-Liammoir and Hilton Edwards on the board of their recently established Gate Theatre, and devoted the rest of his life to the patronage of Irish theatre and culture. Wrote several plays, *The Melians*, 1931; *Carmilla* 1932 (based on Le Fanu story, produced in London 1937); and his most famous play *Yahoo*, based on the life of Dean Swift, 1933. Others include *Ascen-*

dancy, 1935; and *Armlet of Jade,* 1936; *The Vineyard,* 1943. For many seasons he took the Gate Company on tours of the Irish provinces, and spent a large part of his private fortune in subsidising the company, the only regular repertory company in the country apart from the Abbey with its own theatre. In 1956 when the theatre was threatened with closure by the Dublin Corporation as a fire hazard he personally collected money at the door of the theatre for a rebuilding fund, to which he also contributed many thousands of pounds. A classical scholar and fluent Irish speaker, he translated Aeschylus and Sophocles (in collaboration with his wife) and also classical Irish poetry, including 'The Midnight Court'. His translations of Molière and Beaumarchais were often staged. Appointed to the Senate by de Valera. Member of the Royal Irish Academy, and the Irish Academy of Letters. Hon. D.Litt. Dublin University and NUI.

LONGFORD, Lady, Christine Patti, née Trew, b. Somerset 1900. d. 1980. Ed. Oxford. Married 6th Earl of Longford 1925, came with him to Ireland and adopted it as her country. A distinguished figure in Irish theatrical life. After her husband's death in 1961 continued to run the Gate Theatre. MIAL. She wrote about 20 plays, beginning with *Queens and Emperors,* 1932, and including adaptations of Jane Austen's *Pride and Prejudice,* 1937; Maria Edgeworth's *The Absentee,* 1938, etc. Some of her best-known plays have been historical: *The United Brothers,* 1942; *Patrick Sarsfield,* 1943; and *The Earl of Straw,* 1944. Later plays include *Witch Hunt; Tankardstown; The Paragons; Mr Supple; The Hill of Quirke,* 1943; *Stop the Clock,* 1955; *Mount Lawless,* 1957; *Stephen Stoney,* 1960. Translated Aeschylus with her husband. She also wrote some well-received novels, of which the most successful were *Making Conversation,* 1931; *Country Places,* 1932; *Mr Jiggins of Jigginstown,* 1933; *Printed Cotton,* 1935; and *Sea Change,* 1940. Wrote *A Biography of Dublin,* 1936.

LONGFORD, 7th Earl, Frank Pakenham, b. 1905. British politician, Leader of House of Lords 1964, Lord Privy Seal 1966. Wrote the standard work on the Anglo-Irish Treaty negotiations and the surrounding circumstances, *Peace by Ordeal,* 1935. Has also written on crime and punishment, *The Idea of Punishment,* 1961; and biographies; *Eamon de Valera* (with Thomas P. O'Neill), 1970; *The Life of Jesus Christ,* 1974; *Abraham Lincoln,* 1974; *John Kennedy,* 1976; *St Francis of Assisi,* 1978; *Eleven at No. 10,* 1984. Several vols of autobiography, including *Born to Believe,* 1953; *The Grain of Wheat,* 1974.

LONGLEY, Michael, b. Belfast 1939. Ed. Royal Belfast Academical Institution, TCD. Married to critic Edna Longley. Teacher 1962-69. Arts Council of Northern Ireland 1970. Poetry includes *No Continuing City,* 1969; *An Exploded View,* 1973; *Man Lying on a Wall,* 1976; *The Echo Gate,* 1979; *Selected Poems 1963-1980,* US 1981; *Poems 1963-1983,* Dublin and London 1985.

LOVER, Samuel, b. Dublin 1797, d. Jersey 1868. Trained as a painter and for some years earned his living in Dublin painting sea-scapes and minia-tures. In 1828 he was elected to the Royal Hibernian Academy. He began writing ballads and sketches, publishing them with his own illustrations. Helped found the *Dublin University Magazine,* and contributed to it. His first major work was *Legends and Stories of Ireland,* 1831, although he had already written some plays, such as *Il Paddy Whack in Italia,* 1825, etc. Moved to London 1835, and wrote *Rory O'More,* 1836, and his most famous novel *Handy Andy,* 1842.

His eyesight was failing, forcing him to abandon art altogether by 1844, when as an alternative he began giving stage entertainments under the general title *An Irish Evening* or *Irish Evenings.* He toured England, and the US, and was very successful, presenting his own sketches and songs, much as Percy French was to do 50 years later. He produced altogether over 300 songs including favourites such as 'The Angel's Whisper', 'Molly Bawn', 'The Low-backed Car', and 'Fourleaved Shamrock', many of these forming part of musical plays. In 1856 he received a pension.

Like Lever, with whom he is always linked and often confused, he has been despised as a literary traitor to Ireland, sneering at everything Irish as ludicrously uncouth. And again this is largely unjust.

LUBY, Thomas Clarke, b. Dublin 1821, d. New York 1901. Arrested 1849, emigrated to Australia but returned to work with Fintan Lalor on the *Tribune,* and later to help James Stephens organise the Fenian conspi-racy in Ireland. He is said to have devised the Fenian oath. Again arrested 1865 and sentenced to 20 years. Released after 6, broken in health. Opposed Parnell and the Land League, and went to America. *Life of Daniel O'Con-nell,* NY 1872, and *Life and Times of Illustrious & Representative Irishmen,* NY 1878.

LUCAS, Charles, b. Co. Clare 1713, d. Dublin 1771. A surgeon in Dublin and fiery advocate of justice for Ireland, was twice threatened with im-prisonment for his speeches and had to escape the country. Chiefly remembered as the founder of *The Freeman's Journal,* 1763. Pub. *Divelina libera; an apology for the civil rights and liberties of the Commons and Citizens of Dublin,* 1744, and *Political Constitutions of Great Britain and Ireland,* 2 vols, 1751.

LUCE, Arthur Aston, b. Gloucester 1882, d. Dublin 1977 after an assault. Ed. Eastbourne, TCD. Royal Irish Rifles 1915-18. Professor of Moral Philosophy TCD 1934-49. Vice Provost TCD 1946-51; Precentor 1953-77. Wife and daughter drowned in Liffey at Celbridge 1940. Many books include, *Life of George Berkeley,* 1949; *Teach Yourself Logic,* 1958; *Fish-ing and Thinking,* 1959; *The Dialectic of Immaterialism,* 1963.

LUCY, Seán, b. Bombay 1931. Ed. Glenstal, UCC. Lt. RAEC 1954-57. Professor of Modern English UCC 1967-. *T. S. Eliot and the Idea of Trad-ition,* 1960; ed. anthologies, *Love Poems of the Irish,* 1968; *Five Irish Poets,* 1970; *Irish Poets in English: The Thomas Davis Lectures on Anglo-*

Irish Poetry, 1972; *Goldsmith, The Gentle Master*, 1984; all pub. Cork. Also *Unfinished Sequence and Other Poems*, Dublin 1979.

LYNAM, William Francis, b. Co. Galway *c.* 1845, d. Clontarf 1894. Lieutenant Lancs Militia 1867, Major 1881. Wrote a vast number of serials for magazines, of which the most famous and successful was *Mick McQuaid*. It appeared in the *Shamrock* of 1867 ff., and was enormously popular.

LYNCH, Hannah, b. Dublin 1862, d. Paris 1904. As a young girl joined the 'Ladies'Land League' and when *United Ireland* was suppressed she took the type over to France and printed it in Paris, where, after various travels, she eventually settled. She wrote many travel books and some novels, of which the best-known were *The Prince of the Glades* and *Clare Monroe*.

LYNCH, Liam, b. Dublin 1937. Novels: *Shell, Sea Shell,* 1982; *Tenebrae,* 1985, both Dublin. Plays include *Do Thrushes Sing in Birmingham?* Abbey 1963; *Soldier,* Peacock 1969; *Strange Dreams Unending,* RE 1973; *Krieg,* Project 1981; and *Voids,* Dublin Theatre Festival 1982.

LYNCH, Martin, b. Belfast 1950. Worked in Belfast's docklands, writing through involvement with community groups in early 1970s. Period as Writer in Residence Lyric Theatre, Belfast. Plays include *Dockers,* 1980; *The Interrogation of Ambrose Fogarty,* 1982, pub. Belfast; *Castles in the Air,* 1982; *Oul Delph and False Teeth,* 1983.

LYNCH, Patricia, b. Cork 1898, d. Dublin 1972. Ed. Ireland, Britain and Belgium. As a young journalist wrote the first eye-witness account from the Irish view point of the 1916 Rising. Settled in Dublin 1920 and swiftly became recognised as one of the world's finest writers of children's books. Her stories have been translated into most European languages, serialised, broadcast, printed in braille; in 1932 she was awarded the Tailteann Silver Medal for Literature. In 1965 the International Youth Library, sponsored by UNESCO, organised an exhibition of her books in Munich. She published over 50 volumes, all of them reprinted many times in England and America.

Her most famous creation *The Turf Cutter's Donkey,* appeared in 1934, illustrated by Jack Yeats. It was chosen as Junior Book Club selection. In 1941 *The Grey Goose of Kilnevin* was chosen by the Cardinal Hayes Literature Committee as one of the best 100 books, adult or juvenile, published in America that year.

Long Ears, 1943, and now in Puffin Books; *The Brogeen* Series, 1947 onwards; *Fiona Leaps the Bonfire,* 1957; *Back of Beyond,* 1966 and *The Kerry Caravan,* 1967, are among her other better-known books. Lived in Dublin and was married to R. M. Fox the writer. MIAL 1967.

LYNCH, Stanislaus, b. Co. Cavan 1907, d. 1983. Authority on hunting and Irish horses. Published several volumes of hunting poems, including

Rhymes of an Irish Huntsman, London and NY 1937, and *Hoofprints on Parchment,* Dublin 1956, illustrated by Tom Carr. Fiction includes *From Foal to Tallyho,* Dundalk 1948, illustrated by Olive Whitmore. His work has been translated into many languages. Achieved the unique distinction of two Olympic Diplomas for Literature for his books on hunting, at London Olympics 1948 and Helsinki 1952. Essays: *Echoes of the Hunting Horn,* Dublin and NY 1947; *A Hunting Man's Rambles,* Oxford 1951. Appointed 1966 as Inspector of all equestrian facilities in Ireland by Bord Fáilte.

LYND, Robert Wilson, b. Belfast 1879, d. London 1949. Ed. Belfast. Journalist in London and famous as essayist under the pseud. 'Y.Y.' Volumes include *Home Life in Ireland,* 1909; *Ireland a Nation,* 1919, which reflect his strong nationalist sympathies; *The Blue Lion,* 1923; *Dr Johnson & Company,* 1927; and some 31 others.

LYONS, Francis Steward Leland, b. Londonderry 1923, d. Dublin 1983. Ed. TCD. Fellow 1951-64, then Professor of Modern History University of Kent. Provost of Trinity until 1981. *The Irish Parliamentary Party 1890-1910,* 1951; *The Fall of Parnell 1890-1,* 1960; *Parnell,* 1965; *John Dillon: A Biography,* 1968; *Ireland Since the Famine,* 1971, rev. 1973; *Charles Stewart Parnell,* 1977 (Heinemann Prize 1978); *Culture and Anarchy in Ireland, 1890-1939,* Oxford 1979; ed. (with R. Hawkins) *Ireland under the Union: Varieties of Tension,* Oxford 1979.

LYONS, John Benignus, b. Co. Mayo 1922. Ed. UCD. MD 1949, FRCPI 1959. Travelled in Far East, Americas, Europe. For work under pseud. see FITZWILLIAM, Michael. Under own name wrote *The Citizen Surgeon,* (a life of Sir Victor Horsley) 1966; *James Joyce andMedicine,* 1973; *Brief Lives of Irish Doctors,* 1978; *The Mystery of Oliver Goldsmith's Medical Degree,* 1979; *Oliver St John Gogarty,* 1979; *Tom Kettle,* 1983; all pub. Dublin.

LYONS, John Charles, b. Mullingar 1792, d. Mullingar 1874. Ed. Pembroke College Oxford. Gardener, antiquary. High Sheriff of Westmeath 1816. Founded Ledeston Press 1837. Publications include *Remarks on the Management of Orchidaceous Plants,* 1843 (facsimile ed. 1983); *The Book of Surveys and Distribution of the Estates of the County of Westmeath Forfeited in the Year 1641,* 1852; *The Grand Juries of the County of Westmeath from the Year 1727 to the Year 1853,* 2 vols, 1853: all pub. Mullingar.

LYSAGHT, Charles Edward, b. Dublin 1942. Ed. Gonzaga College, UCD, Cambridge (President of the Union 1964). BL. Taught law London University; moved to Dublin 1970. Research Counsellor at Irish Law Reform Commission. Founder member of British-Irish Association. Legal publications, and a much-praised biography, *Brendan Bracken,* 1979.

LYSAGHT, Edward, see MacLYSAGHT, Edward.

LYSAGHT, Edward, b. Co. Clare 1763, d. 1810. Ed. TCD and Oxford. English and Irish Bar. A Volunteer, and opponent of Union. His *Poems of the late Edward Lysaght* pub. 1811.

LYSAGHT, Sidney Royse, b. Co. Cork *c*. 1860, d. 1941. Became an ironmaster in Bristol. Wrote poetry, *A Modern Ideal*, 1886; *Horizons and Landmarks*, 1911, etc.; novels, including *Her Majesty's Rebels*, 1907; and a play, *The Immortal Jew*.

LYTTON, Rosina, Lady, née Wheeler, b. Co. Limerick 1802, d. near London 1882. Married the 1st Baron against his mother's wishes, and was bitterly unhappy, soon getting a legal separation from him. He figures as the villain of several of her novels, of which the best and best-known is *Cheveley, or the Man of Honour*, 1839. Incessant quarrels and intrigues managed to get her confined to an asylum, but this was done illegally, and she was released.

M

MacALISTER, Robert Alexander Stewart, b. Dublin 1870, d. 1950. Ed. Dublin, Germany, Cambridge. Became one of the leading figures in European archaeology. Was Director of Excavations for the Palestine Exploration Fund, 1900-9, and Professor of Celtic Archaeology UCD 1909-43. Received many honorary doctorates. His principal monument is *The Archaeology of Ireland*, 1927. He revised this extensively for the 2nd ed. of 1944, and in the opinion of most archaeologists his revisions were unfortunate, offering a number of untenable theories. The first edition is still of great practical value to students. Other books include *Excavations in Palestine*, 1902; *Ireland in Pre-Celtic Times*, 1921; *Ancient Ireland*, 1935; *The Secret Language of Ireland*, 1937. The last title contains the only available study of Shelta, the language of the Irish tinkers or travelling people.

McALLISTER, Alexander, b. Dublin 1877, d. Surrey 1944. Ed. Clongowes and Royal University. Chief clerk in National University 1908-14, also Librarian. Began writing plays about 1900 under pseud. 'Henry Alexander' and sometimes 'Anthony P. Wharton'. His play *Irene Wycherly*, 1906, was very successful in London and on tour. *At the Barn*, 1912, had Marie Tempest in a leading role and was also successful, but for some reason succeeding plays were failures. McAllister served throughout the First World War in the machine-gun corps and was twice wounded. After 1918 he lived in England, turning to novels under the name Anthony Wharton. *The Man on the Hill*, 1923, was a serious study of society breaking up under the stress of war conditions. In 1925 he began writing detective novels under still another pseud., 'Lynn Brock', beginning with *The Deduc-*

tions of Colonel Gore. In 1926 a last 'serious' novel, *The Two of Diamonds,* came out, followed by a long series of very successful and professional detective stories by 'Lynn Brock', most of them centred on *Colonel Gore,* his *Second Case, Third Case, The Kink, The Mendip Mystery,* etc, many of them often reprinted and translated. Dorothy Sayers regarded him as one of the best detective story-writers of the period, on a level with Ronald Knox. But at the end of his life he returned to the theatre with a last play, *The O'Cuddy,* produced at the Abbey 1943, with Cyril Cusack, F. J. McCormick, Gerard Healy. The critics praised it but the public stayed away and it closed after a week.

MacAONGHUSA, Proinsias, b. Galway 1933. Brought up speaking only Irish until age 13. Ed. Galway and Dublin. Abbey theatre actor 1951-53. Broadcaster, journalist; active in socialist and republican politics, and civil rights movements in Ireland and elsewhere. United Nations Special Consultant on Namibia 1974-75. Chairman Irish International Peace Movement since 1978. Books include *The Best of Connolly,* 1966; *The Best of Pearse,* 1967; *The Best of Tone,* 1972; all with Liam Ó Reagáin, pub. Cork. Most recently, *Quotations from P. H. Pearse,* Dublin 1979.

MACARDLE, Dorothy, b. 1889, d. 1958. Ed. UCD. Taught in Alexandra College and was arrested in her classroom by British troops during the 'Troubles' for her Republican activities. Chose Republican side in Civil War. Visited Geneva as journalist to cover sessions of League of Nations under Presidency of her friend, de Valera. In Second World War devoted herself to the cause of refugee children. Wrote short stories, *Earthbound,* 1924; plays, *Atonement,* 1918; *Ann Kavanagh,* 1922; *The Old Man,* 1925; *Dark Waters,* etc; and novels, including *Uneasy Freehold; The Seed was Kind; Fantastic Summer,* 1946; *The Uninvited* (filmed); and *Dark Enchantment,* 1953.

Her principal historical work was *The Irish Republic,* 1937, repub. 1968, a standard reference book on the events leading up to the establishment of the Irish State. Also *Children of Europe,* 1949, on the needs of displaced and refugee children after Second World War.

McARDLE, Joseph Ardle, b. Dublin 1934. Ed. Monaghan, Limerick and Dublin. Barrister, former international civil servant. Now lecturer and business consultant. Founder and director of Co-Op Books. Has translated from Polish into English (works of Cardinal Wyszinski) and from French, *The Year with the Liturgy. How the Law Works,* 1963, and a novel, *Closing Time,* Dublin 1983.

MACARTNEY, George, 1st Earl, b. Co. Antrim 1737, d. London 1806. Ambassador to Russia as young man, became Chief Secretary for Ireland 1769-72. Created Earl 1792 and sent to Peking as ambassador, from which arose his *Journal of the Embassy to China* included in the *Memoir* by John Barrow, 1807. This contains the famous description of his reception by the Chinese Emperor as the messenger of a barbarian vassal (i.e. George

III), bringing tribute. He wrote *An Account of an Embassy to Russia*, 1768, and *A Political Account of Ireland*, 1773, also reprinted in Barrow's *Memoir*.

McAUGHTRY, Sam, b. Belfast 1921. Left school at 14. Joined RAF 1940 as aircraft rigger, became flying officer. After war worked in London as builder's labourer, then joined Ministry of Agriculture in Belfast 1947; retired as Deputy Principal. Autobiographical novel, *The Sinking of the Kenbane Head*, Belfast 1977. Short stories: *Play It Again, Sam*, Belfast 1978. *Blind Spot and Other Stories*, Belfast 1979; and *Belfast No. 1*, Belfast 1981. Also well known as journalist.

McAULEY, James J., b. Dublin 1935. Journalist, critic and poet. *Observations*, Dublin 1960; *A New Address*, Dublin 1965; *Draft Balance Sheet: Poems 1963-1969*, Dublin 1970; *After the Blizzard*, Columbia, US 1975; *Recital: Poems 1972-1980*, Dublin 1982.

McBRIDE, John Joseph, b. Belfast 1898. Wrote a number of plays: *Bean of Ballyamin; The Yellow Rose; The Colorado Beetle; Down by the Glenside*.

McCABE, Eugene, b. Co. Monaghan 1930. Ed. Kildare, worked as farm manager, Co. Wicklow, now farms family holding in Monaghan. His play *The King of the Castle* was the major success of the Dublin Theatre Festival 1964; also *Breakdown*, 1966; *Swift*, 1969; both produced Dublin. *Roma*, a play for TV, RTE 1979. *Pull Down a Horseman* and *Gale Day* (plays about James Connolly and Patrick Pearse), pub. Dublin 1979. A novel, *Victims*, 1976 (about the troubles in the North and the best evocation of them yet published, comparable in ways to O'Flaherty's *The Informer*); *Heritage and Other Stories*, 1978.

MacCABE, William Bernard, b. Dublin 1801, d. Donnybrook 1891. Journalist in Dublin and London and prolific writer of historical romances, such as *Agnes Arnold*, 1861.

McCALL, Patrick Joseph, b. Dublin 1861, d. 1919. Well known at the turn of the century as poet, song-writer, and translator from the Irish. Best-known collection: *Irish Fireside Songs*, Dublin 1911.

MacCALL, Seamus, b. at sea 1892, d. Dalkey 1964. Ran away to South America as a schoolboy and worked on first railway crossing of Andes. Served in British Army in First World War, and later on Republican side in Civil War. Journalist, wrote a number of volumes of history and biography: *Thomas Moore*, Dublin 1935; *Irish Mitchel*, 1937; *And So Began the Irish Nation*, etc.

MacCANA, Proinsias, b. Belfast 1926. Ed. QUB, Sorbonne. MRIA. Professor of Early Irish Language and Literature UCD 1971-. Has written *Branwen, Daughter of Llyr*, Cardiff 1958; *Celtic Mythology*, London 1970, rep. 1983; *The Mabinogi*, Cardiff 1977; *Literature in Irish*, 1981.

For works in Irish see Part 2.

McCANN, John, b. Dublin 1905, d. Dublin 1980. Ed. Christian Brothers, Synge St. Practised journalism for several years and wrote plays for radio and short stories. In 1930 his play *The Dreamer* was performed at the Peacock but he was more involved in politics than literature. He entered Dail Eireann 1939 and was Lord Mayor of Dublin, 1946-47. He lost his Dail seat in 1954, and that year the Abbey put on his play *Twenty Years A-Wooing*, a kindly satire on the typical lengthy Irish engagement. It proved an enormous success and established McCann as the best money-spinner then writing for the Abbey. *Give Me a Bed of Roses*, 1957, and *I Know Where I'm Going*, 1959, confirmed his success. *Put a Beggar of Horseback*, 1961, and *A Jew Called Sammy*, 1962, followed.

McCANN, Sean, b. Dublin 1929. Left Ireland 1945, and was for a time in Egypt. Journalist in England, and now in Dublin. Writes for radio and TV, as well as for press. Ed. *The World of Brendan Behan*, 1965, NY 1966; *The World of Sean O'Casey*, 1966; *The Story of the Abbey Theatre*, 1967. Author of *Four Square Guide to Ireland*, 1967; *The Wit of the Irish*, 1968; *The Wit of Oscar Wilde*, 1969; *The Fighting Irish*, 1972; *The Irish in Love*, 1973; *All the World's Roses*, 1974; *We are the Champions*, 1975.

MacCARTHY, Callaghan, b. Co. Cork 1879, d. unknown. Wrote *The Causes of Poverty*, Dublin and London 1908.

McCARTHY, Denis Florence, b. Dublin 1817, d. 1882. Bar. Journalist, contributing to *The Nation*, etc. Professor of English Literature at Catholic University, Dublin. Translated Calderon, *The Dramas of Calderon*, 1853, etc., and published some original poetry, such as *The Bell Founder*, 1857.

McCARTHY, J. Bernard, b. Crosshaven 1888, d. 1979. Ed. privately. Published a novel, *Possessions*, 1926, but is known for his plays, many of which were first produced by the Abbey. Have been revived and reproduced by professional and amateur companies throughout Ireland. Among the most successful are *Kinship*, 1914; *The Crusaders*, 1917; *The Long Road to Gurranabraher*, 1923; and *The Able Dealer*, 1928.

McCARTHY, Justin, b. Cork 1830, d. Kent 1912. Began as a journalist in Cork when only 18, moved to Liverpool 1852 and to London 1860, becoming editor of the *Morning Star* 1864. Entered Parliament for Longford 1879 and after the Parnellite split of 1890 led the majority faction. Resigned 1896.

Novels include *A Fair Saxon*, 1873; *The Comet of a Season*, 1881; *Mononia*, 1901. Wrote much biography, and history. *George Sand*, 1870; *Modern Leaders*, 1872; *A History of Our Own Times*, 5 vols, 1879-97; *The Epoch of Reform*, 1882; *History of the Four Georges*, 2 vols, 1889-90; *Sir Robert Peel*, 1891, were all brought out while he was either a working journalist or an active politician. *Mr Gladstone*, 1898; *Reminiscences*, 1889; *The Story of an Irishman*, NY 1904. He was also co-editor of the

10 vol. anthology *Irish Literature*, published the same year.

McCARTHY, Thomas, b. Co. Waterford 1954. Ed. UCC. Poet and librarian. Fellow of International Writing Programme at University of Iowa 1978-79. Poems: *Shattered Frost*, 1975; *Warm Circle*, 1976; *The First Convention*, 1977 (won Patrick Kavanagh Award); *The Sorrow Garden*, 1978; *The Non-Aligned Story-teller*, 1984. Won Irish American Literary Foundation Award 1984. Currently editor of *Poetry Ireland*.

McCLINTOCK, Francis Leopold, b. Dundalk 1819, d. London 1907. Navy 1831. Was in the Arctic 1848-52 and made various improvements to Arctic equipment for travelling on ice. During these years some 15 expeditions to the Arctic had been searching for Sir John Franklin's lost expedition. Information found by some of them led Lady Franklin to equip *The Fox* and McClintock was given command, July 1857. He found evidence in King William's Land that Franklin had died in 1847, after his ships had been locked in pack ice for nine months. The ships were later abandoned by their crews, who died in trying to reach civilisation. Returning to London McClintock was knighted 1860 and given the Freedom of the City. Vice-Admiral 1877, KCB 1891. Wrote *The Voyage of the 'Fox' in the Arctic Seas*, 1859, and *Fate of Sir John Franklin*, 1860.

McCLURE, Robert John Le Mesurier, b. Wexford 1807, d. 1873. Arctic explorer and first white man to make the North-West Passage, partly by ship, partly on foot, in 1854. He had entered the Navy 1824, and had been on several Arctic expeditions previously. He was in command of the *Investigation* 1850-54, and it being trapped in ice for two years he left it and completed the journey on foot. He and his men were eventually rescued by Captain Kellett. KCB. Admiral. His *Voyages*, 2 vols, 1884.

McCORMACK, William John, b. Co. Wicklow 1947. Ed. TCD. Taught English University of Leeds. Visiting Professor of English at Clamson University, South Carolina. Poetry (under pseud. 'Hugh Maxton'): *Stones*, 1970; *The Noise of the Fields*, 1976; *Jubilee for Renegades*, 1982; *At the Protestant Museum*, 1985; all pub. Dublin. Literary history: *Sheridan Le Fanu and Victorian Ireland*, 1980; *Ascendancy and Tradition in Anglo-Irish History from 1789 to 1939*, 1985; both Oxford.

MacDERMOT, Frank, b. Dublin 1886, d. 1975. Ed. Oxford. Bar 1911. Served in British Army during First World War 4 times mentioned in despatches. Banker in New York 1919-27. Returned to Ireland and stood as Nationalist candidate in W. Belfast 1929. Defeated, but elected independent TD for Roscommon 1932. Became leader of Centre Party in Dáil Éireann 1933; Senator 1938-43. During Second World War criticised Irish neutrality. In 1945 became Paris correspondent for *Sunday Times*. Had written a life of *Theobald Wolfe Tone*, 1939.

MacDERMOTT, W. R., b. Co. Monaghan 1838, d. Armagh 1918. Ed. TCD and practised medicine in Armagh. His best-known novel was *The

MacDONAGH

Green Republic, 1902.

MacDONAGH, Donagh, b. 1912, d. 1968. Son of Thomas MacD. the Irish patriot and 1916 leader. A District Justice and broadcaster, as well as poet and playwright. His poems appear in several anthologies, including *The Oxford Book of Irish Verse,* of which he was co-editor with Lennox Robinson. Best-known for his verse-plays *Happy as Larry,* 1946, and *Step-in-the-Hollow,* Gaiety 1957.

MacDONAGH, Michael, b. Limerick 1860, d. 1946. Ed. Christian Brothers, journalist on *Freeman's Journal* and London *Times.* Became Chairman of Press Gallery, House of Commons, 1924. Wrote a number of books on Parliament, *The Speaker of the House,* 1914, etc. Also wrote on the First World War, *The Irish at the Front,* 1916 (with a foreword by John Redmond), and *The Irish on the Somme,* 1917; and several biographies, including *The Life of William O'Brien,* 1928, and *Daniel O'Connell and Catholic Emancipation,* 1929.

MacDONAGH, Oliver Ormond Gerard, b. Carlow 1924. Ed. CBS Roscommon, Clongowes, UCD, King's Inns, Cambridge. Taught history Cambridge 1950-64, South Australia 1964-68. Professor of Modern History UCC 1968-70, visiting Yale 1970-71, and with Inst. for Adv. Studies, Australian National University, 1973-. *Irish Overseas Emigration During the Famine,* 1955; *A Pattern of Government Growth,* 1961; *Ireland: The Union and Its Aftermath,* 1967, rev. 1977; ed. *Irish Culture and Nationalism 1750-1950,* 1983; *States of Mind: A Study of Anglo-Irish Conflict 1780-1980,* 1983, paperback ed. 1985.

MacDONAGH, Patrick (sometimes spelled MacDONOGH), b. 1902, d. 1961. Poetry: *A Leaf in the Wind,* 1929, *Shamrock Leaves,* 1936, both pub. Belfast; *The Vestal Fire,* 1941, *One Landscape Still,* 1958, both pub. Dublin.

MacDONAGH, Thomas, b. Cloughjordan 1878, d. 1916. Lecturer in English Literature UCD. Helped Padraic Pearse found St Enda's College, 1908. Prominent in Irish Volunteer movement. One of the signatories of the Proclamation of the Irish Republic, 1916. Shot after the Easter Rising. As a natural development of his political and national beliefs he had been a co-founder of the Irish Theatre in Hardwicke St, Dublin, in 1914, with Edward Martyn and Joseph Plunkett, and was himself a poet and playwright. His volumes of poetry include *Through the Ivory Gate,* 1903; *Lyrical Poems,* 1913; and *Poetical Works,* 1916. His play *When the Dawn Is Come* was produced at the Abbey 1908.

MacDONALD, Walter, b. Co. Kilkenny 1854, d. Maynooth 1920. Priest and Professor of Theology Maynooth for 40 years. A brilliant and controversial teacher, he attacked obscurantism in every form, including the need to teach through Latin. Advocated entry of Catholic students into TCD (forbidden by hierarchy), and urged the laity to take part in Church affairs.

Many of his writings were refused the Imprimatur or condemned outright by Rome, including his *Motion, Its Origin and Conservation*, Dublin 1898. Also wrote *Reminiscences of a Maynooth Professor*, ed. Denis Gwynn, 1924, reissued 1967.

McDONNELL, Eneas, b. Westport 1783, d. Laragh 1858. Ed. Tuam and Maynooth. Edited *Cork Chronicle* 1816, and as a result of an article in the paper was sentenced to six months imprisonment. Later became Parliamentary agent in London for the Catholic Association, and a prolific pamphleteer on their behalf. Wrote one successful novel, *The Hermit of Glenconella*, 1820.

MacDONNELL, Randall William, b. Dublin 1870, d. unknown. Ed. TCD. An engineer who wrote handbooks on engineering. Wrote several novels, including the well-known *Kathleen Mavourneen*, 1898, and *When Cromwell Came to Drogheda*, 1906.

MacDONOGH, Stephen, b. Dublin 1949. Ed. Rugby. Co-founder of Irish Writers' Co-Op 1976 and Chairperson 1977-81. Set up Brandon Books publishing with Bernard Goggins 1984. Poetry: *York Poems*, York 1972; *My Tribe*, Dublin 1982. Also *Green and Gold: The Wrenboys of Dingle*, 1983; *A Visitors' Guide to the Dingle Peninsula*, 1985; both pub. Dingle.

McDOWELL, Robert Brendan, b. Co. Louth 1914. Ed. Belfast and TCD. Fellow TCD 1951. Junior Dean and Registrar of Chambers TCD 1956-69; Associate Professor Modern History 1967-82. Now Professor Emeritus. *Public Opinion and Government Policy in Ireland 1801-1846*, 1952; *British Conservatism 1832-1914*, 1959; and *The Irish Administration 1801-1914*, 1964, are his principal books. Has also written *Irish Public Opinion 1750-1800*, 1944; *Alice Stopford Green: A Passionate Historian*, Dublin 1967; *The Irish Convention 1917-1918*, 1970; *The Church of Ireland 1869-1969*, 1975; with W. B. Stanford, *Mahaffy* (biography), 1971; *Ireland in the Age of Imperialism and Revolution 1760-1801*, Oxford 1979; with D. A. Webb, *Trinity College, Dublin 1592-1952: An Academic History*, Cambridge 1982. Has edited *Social Life in Ireland 1800-45*, Dublin 1957, and *Correspondence of Edmund Burke*, vol. 8, Cambridge 1969, and, with J. A. Woods, vol. 9, Cambridge 1970.

McDUNPHY, Michael, b. 1890. Entered civil service 1912, dismissed 1918 for refusing to take Oath of Allegiance. Bar 1928. Secretary to the President 1937-54. Wrote an authoritative study on the powers, functions and duties of *The President of Ireland*, Dublin 1945.

McELLIGOTT, Thomas James, b. Cork 1914. Ed. UCC. M.Litt. TCD 1968; Ph.D. UCC 1978. Many teaching posts throughout Ireland; played handball for four counties. Ed. *The European Teacher* 1962-77. Books: *Education in Ireland*, 1967; *Secondary Education in Ireland*, 1981; *The Story of Handball*, 1983; all pub. Dublin.

McENTEE, Máire, b. 1922. Daughter of Sean McEntee. A poetess of great merit, married to Conor Cruise O'Brien. For her principal works in Irish see Part 2.

McENTEE, Sean, b. 1899, d. 1984. Ed. Belfast. Took part in Easter Rising 1916, and sentenced to death; commuted to life imprisonment. Served in English prisons until general amnesty of 1917. Elected Sinn Fein member for Monaghan 1918, and continued a distinguished political career, holding many ministerial posts until the 1960s. Published *Poems*, 1918. Father of Maire McEntee.

MacEOIN, Gary, b. Ireland 1909. Entered Redemptorist novitiate but was refused ordination. Became a journalist in Dublin and US. *Cervantes*, Milwaukee 1950; *Nothing is Quite Enough*, 1954; an autobiography telling of his spiritual conflicts.

McFADDEN, Roy, b. Belfast 1921. Practises as a solicitor. His verse is included in many anthologies including *The Oxford Book of Irish Verse*. Poetry: *Swords and Ploughshares*, 1943; *Flowers for a Lady*, 1945; *The Heart's Townland*, 1947; *Elegy for the Dead of the Princess Victoria*, 1953. More recently, *The Garryowen*, 1971; *Verifications*, 1977; *A Watching Brief*, 1979, all Belfast. *The Selected Roy MacFadden*, ed. John Boyd, Dundonald 1983.

McGAHERN, John, b. Dublin 1935. Son of a senior Garda officer. Brought up in the West of Ireland. Ed. Presentation Brothers, Carrick-on-Shannon. Trained as a school-teacher and taught in Clontarf 1957-64. His first novel, *The Barracks*, 1963, won the AE Memorial Award and a Macaulay Fellowship. Granted leave of absence from his school to take up the Fellowship he completed his second novel, *The Dark*, 1965. This dealt with the problems of adolescence and clerical celibacy in a way that roused furious controversy in Ireland, before the book was banned by the Censorship Board. Early in 1966 McGahern was informed that his contract as a teacher would not be renewed. Now lives in Co. Leitrim. Short stories: *Nightlines*, 1971; *Getting Through*, 1978; *High Ground*, 1985. Novels: *The Leavetaking*, 1974 (won Society of Authors Award 1975), revised 1984; *The Pornographer*, 1979. Award of American Irish Foundation 1985.

McGEE, James E., b. Cushendall 1830, d. New York 1880. Ed. Wexford. On staff of *The Nation* 1847, emigrated to US 1849, became a colonel in Civil War. Wrote several books about Irish history and biographical sketches of well-known patriots. Best known for his *The Men of '48* .

MacGEE, Thomas d'Arcy, b. Co. Louth 1825, d. Montreal 1868. Went to US as a young journalist, returned to Ireland and joined Young Irelanders. Returned to America 1848, moved to Canada and became MP for Montreal 1857 and a constitutionalist. As a cabinet minister the federation of the Canadian provinces was largely his work. He denounced the Fenians, particularly for their proposed invasion of Canada. He was shot by one of them in Montreal. Wrote poetry and a novel, and several volumes of Irish history: *Irish Writers of the 17th Century*, and a *Life of Art MacMurrough*, both Dublin 1847, among others.

MacGILL, Patrick, b. Glenties 1891, d. New York 1963. Left school at 12, emigrated to Scotland at 14 and worked as a navvy. Served as a private with the London Irish Rifles during First World War. Wrote an account of his war experiences, *The Amateur Army;* some poetry, *Songs of a Navvy, Soldier Songs,* etc., but was best known for a series of realistic and savagely bitter novels about the war, or the Irish migrant labourers in Scotland. They were very popular at the time of publication and have been republished in the 1980s. They include *Children of the Dead End,* 1914; *The Rat Pit,* 1915; *Glenmornan,* 1919; *Lanty Hanlon,* 1922; *The Glen of Carra,* 1934; and *Helen Spenser,* 1937.

McGINLEY, Patrick, b. Donegal 1937. Ed. UCG. Taught in Ireland. Went to England mid-60s. Now journalist and publisher. Novels include *Bogmail,* 1978; *Goosefoot,* 1983; *Foggage,* 1984; *The Trick of the Ga Bolga.*

McGRATH, Fergal, b. Dublin 1895. Ed. UCD and Oxford. Entered Jesuit Order 1913, ordained 1927; has written boys' stories including *Adventure Island,* Dublin and NY 1932 (French trans. banned by Nazis during Occupation); short stories, *Tenement Angel,* Dublin 1934; *Fr John Sullivan, SJ* (a biography), 1941; *Newman's University: Idea and Reality,* 1951 (for this awarded D.Phil,Oxon); *More Memories of Fr John Sullivan,* 1976; *Education in Ancient and Mediaeval Ireland,* 1979.

MacGREEVY, Thomas, b. Co. Kerry 1893, d. Dublin 1967. Poet and critic, served in First World War as artillery officer. Helped found Irish Central Library for Students, lectured in Paris University 1926-33, and remained as a journalist of the arts there until the war. Was with Joyce when he died. Returned to Dublin 1941, made Director of National Gallery 1950. Principal works include *Introduction to the Method of Leonardo da Vinci,* 1929, trans. from French of Paul Valéry; *Jack B. Yeats,* 1945; *Pictures in the Irish National Gallery,* 1945; *Nicolas Poussin,* 1960; *Collected Poems,* Dublin 1971.

McGUCKIAN, Medbh, b. Belfast 1950. Teacher. Poetry: *Portrait of Joanna,* Belfast 1980; *The Flower Master,* Oxford 1982; *Venus and the Rain,* Oxford 1984. Her poem, 'The Flitting', won first prize in National Poetry Competition. Won Rooney Prize 1982.

McGUINNESS, Frank, b. Buncrana, Co. Donegal 1953. Ed. UCD. Poet, short-story writer, playwright, teacher. Plays: *The Factory Girls,* Peacock 1982, Australia 1983; *Borderlands,* TEAM 1983; *Observe the Sons of Ulster Marching Towards the Somme,* Peacock 1985; *Baglady,* Peacock 1985; *Gatherers,* TEAM 1985. Won Rooney Prize 1985.

McHENRY, James, b. Larne 1785, d. Larne 1845. Ed. Dublin and Glasgow, where he paid part of his fees by writing verse. Emigrated to US 1817, and in 1824 settled in Philadelphia as a doctor, and also a trader and journalist, editing the *American Monthly Magazine* which published his best-known novel *O'Halloran,* 1824. In 1842 he became US consul in Derry. Other novels include *The Wilderness,* NY 1823, and *Meredith,* 1831.

McHUGH, Roger Joseph, b. Dublin 1908, Ed.UCD. Professor of English UCD 1965-67; Professor of Anglo-Irish Literature 1967-78; Professor Emeritus 1979. Visiting Professor Pittsburgh 1969-70; Berg Professor NYU 1972 and 1975. Plays: *Trial at Green Street Court House,* Dublin 1945; *Rossa,* Tralee 1948. Ed. *Carlow in Ninety-Eight,* Dublin 1949; *Letters of W. B. Yeats to Katharine Tynan,* Dublin and NY 1953; *Dublin 1916,* Dublin 1966; *Ah, Sweet Dancer,* London and NY 1972 (the letters of W. B. Yeats and Margot Ruddock); has also written *Henry Grattan,* Dublin 1936, NY 1937; *Universities and European Unity,* Dublin 1955; with Maurice Harmon, *A Short History of Anglo-Irish Literature,* Dublin and NY 1982.

McILROY, Archibald, b. Co. Antrim 1860, d. at sea 1915. Worked in insurance and banks. Wrote stories and novels with a distinct Ulster flavour, including *A Banker's Love Story,* 1901. Died on the *Lusitania.*

MacINTYRE, Tom, b. Cavan 1931. Taught at Clongowes and in US (University of Michigan; Williams College, Mass.). Writes in many forms: novel, *The Charollais,* 1969; short story, *Dance the Dance,* 1969, and *The Harper's Turn,* Dublin 1982; reportage, *Through the Bridewell Gate,* 1971; free-verse translation from the Irish, *Blood Relations,* 1972; and drama, *Eye Winker Tom Tinker,* 1972; *Jack Be Nimble,* 1976; *Find the Lady,* 1977; all Peacock, Dublin; *Doobally Black Way,* Paris and Dublin 1979; *The Great Hunger* (adaptation of Kavanagh's poem), 1983; *The Bearded Lady* (on Swift), 1984.

MACKAY, John Cosby, b. Carrick-on-Suir *c.* 1868, d. 1941. A solicitor in Gorey and Clonmel, his chief private interest was forestry and he deserves remembrance for *Trodden Gold,* Dublin 1928; *Forestry in Ireland,* 1934; and *The Rape of Ireland,* Dublin 1940.

MacKAY, William, b. Belfast 1846, d. unknown. Journalist, novelist, one of three literary brothers, the others being Wallis and Joseph William, both of whom wrote plays and verse. William wrote several novels, of which the best-known was *Beside Still Waters.*

MACKEN, Walter, b. 1916 Galway, d. 1967. Ed. Patrician Brothers. Spent three years with Abbey Theatre Company as actor; later returned to Galway to manage the Gaelic language theatre, An Taidhbhearc, which he helped to develop into a national institution. In 1965 was invited to come back to Abbey Theatre as assistant manager and artistic adviser. Several plays, including *Mungo's Mansions,* 1946; *Vacant Possession,* 1948; *Home is the Hero,* 1953 (a long run at the Abbey and later filmed); and *Twilight* *of a Warrior*, 1956. But his greatest reputation rests on his novels: *Quench the Moon*, 1948; *I Am Alone*, 1949; *Rain On the Wind*, 1950; *Sunset on the Window Panes*, 1954; and particularly the historical trilogy, *Seek the Fair Land*, 1959, *The Silent People*, 1962, and *The Scorching Wind*, 1964, dealing respectively with the Cromwellian invasion, the Famine, and the Easter Rebellion. Short stories: *Green Hills*, 1956, and *God Made Sunday*, 1962 etc. Died shortly after his last novel appeared, *Brown Lord of the Mountain*, 1967.

McKENNA, James, b. Dublin 1933. Playwright and sculptor. Macaulay Fellowship, sculpture, 1960. *The Scatterin'* (teddy-boy muscial), Dublin Theatre Festival 1960; *At Bantry*, Peacock 1967.

McKENNA, Nial, b. *c.* 1670, d. *c.* 1740. Harper and poet, author of the famous song 'Little Celia Connellan'.

MacKENNA, Stephen, b. 1872, d. London 1934. Ed. Ratcliffe College, Leicestershire. Translator, scholar, Gaelic revivalist, republican. Friend to J. M. Synge in his Paris period (as to Osborn Bergin, Edmund Curtis and James Stephens later), entered journalism covering European affairs for *The New York World*, resigning 1907, returning to Dublin as leader-writer for *The Freeman's Journal* for a time. After Easter Week, 1916, wrote *Memories of the Dead* under *nom de plume* 'Martin Daly'. Backed by E. R. Debenham (of the London store), began his life-work translating Plotinus's *Enneads* (5 vols, 1917-1930), described by George Steiner as 'one of the masterpieces of modern English prose and formal sensibility' (*After Babel*, 1975). Struck by double blow of Anglo-Irish Treaty in 1922 and his wife's death in 1923, he went to England in 1924 to suffer penury and ill health thereafter. His witty *Journals and Letters*, edited with a Memoir by E. R. Dodds, was published in 1936.

MACKEY, Herbert O., b. Ennis 1894, d. Dublin 1966. A lifelong champion of Roger Casement. Wrote *The Life and Times of Roger Casement*, Dublin 1954, and *Roger Casement: A Guide to the Forged Diaries*, Dublin 1962, to prove that Casement was not guilty of the immoralities alleged against his character. Also wrote *The Life of Thomas Moore*, Dublin 1951.

MACKLIN, Charles, b. in Northern Ireland *c.* 1697, d. 1797. Accused of murdering a fellow-actor, but acquitted. Considered the finest actor of his generation. Famous for his study of Shylock. Also wrote several comedies which were well thought of and often revived; including *Love à la Mode*, 1759 and *The Man of the World*, 1781. Died reputedly one hundred years old.

McKOWEN, James, b. Ulster 1814, d. 1889. His best-known song 'Ould Irish Jig' has remained popular in Ireland for over 100 years.

MacLAVERTY, Bernard, b. Belfast 1942. Ed. locally. Worked in QUB as laboratory technician and took degree there. Now teaching in Scotland. Fiction includes *Secrets and Other Stories*, Belfast 1977; *Lamb,* Belfast and

London 1980, *A Time to Dance and Other Stories*, 1982, and *Cal*, 1983 (made into successful film, 1984). Has written plays for radio and TV, such as *My Dear Palestrina*, BBC 1980, a subtly understated view of Ulster Catholic bigotry, and the kind of background that led to the peculiarly venomous character of modern Northern Irish politics; also a book for children, *A Man in Search of a Pet*, Belfast 1978.

McLAVERTY, Michael Francis, b. Monaghan 1907. Ed. Belfast and London. Became a schoolmaster and later headmaster in Belfast. MIAL. Novels: *Call My Brother Back*, 1939; *Lost Fields*, 1942; *In This Thy Day*, 1945 (these three repub., successively, Swords 1979-81); *The Three Brothers*, 1948; *Truth in the Night*, 1951; *School for Hope*, 1954; *The Choice*, 1958; *The Brightening Day*, 1965; all London and NY. Short stories: *The White Mare*, 1943; *The Game Cock & Other Stories*, 1949; *The Road to the Shore*, Swords 1976; *Collected Short Stories*, Swords 1978.

MacLIAMMÓIR, Mícheál, b. Cork 1899, d. 1978. Ed. privately. Went on stage in London as a boy, 1911, and remained in West End productions for four years. In 1915 began studying art at Slade School, and after the war designed and painted for the Irish Theatre and for the Dublin Drama League. Went abroad again to study further, until 1927, returning to Ireland to join Anew MacMaster's Shakespearean touring company. One of the founders of the Galway Gaelic Theatre, and in 1928 founded the Gate Theatre Company in Dublin with the English actor Hilton Edwards. The Gate became for the Irish theatre what the Abbey was then ceasing to be, and did much to revive the reputation of Irish acting and theatrical writing abroad. The company toured in England, America, Europe and Egypt, and MacLiammoir himself gained an international reputation as an actor. He also continued to design and paint, and to write plays and poetry in both English and Irish, as well as autobiography, *All for Hecuba*, 1946; *Put Money in Thy Purse*, 1952; *Each Actor on His Ass*, 1960; *Memoirs of an Irish Actor, Young and Old*, 1977; plays including *Ill Met by Moonlight*, 1957, and *Where Stars Walk*, 1961, both often revived; and the dramatic monologues with which in the 1960s he achieved world-wide fame and critical praise. *The Importance of being Oscar*, 1963; *I must be Talking to My Friends*, 1965. MIAL. For writings in Irish see Part 2.

MacLYSAGHT, Edward Anthony, b. at sea 1887, of old Clare family, on voyage to Australia. The family had dropped the Mac from their name in an earlier generation and he was baptised and educated as Lysaght, under which name he published a novel, *The Gael*, 1919. The following year many Lysaght families in Clare and Limerick restored the Mac and he became MacL. Ed. Rugby, Oxford and UCC. Was a member of Irish Senate 1922-25, and of governing body UCC 1927-31. In S.Africa as journalist 1932-37. Returned to Ireland to join Manuscripts Commission. Chief Genealogical Officer and Keeper of Manuscripts National Library until 1955. His principal historical work was on genealogy and surnames, but

MacMANUS

he also wrote *Irish Life in the Seventeenth Century*, 1939, rev. 1950, rep. Dublin 1979, and *East Clare 1916-1921*, Ennis 1954. *Irish Families, Their Names, Arms and Origins*, Dublin 1957, rev. 1972, 4th rev. ed. 1985; *More Irish Families*, Dublin and Galway, 1960, rev. Dublin 1983; *Supplement to Irish Families*, Dublin 1964; and the invaluable *Guide to Irish Surnames*, Dublin 1964, 2nd enlarged ed. 1965, new ed. *The Surnames of Ireland*, Dublin 1978, 6th rev. 1985. Also *Forth the Banners Go* (reminiscences of William O'Brien as told to Edward MacLysaght), Dublin 1969; and *Changing Times: Ireland Since 1898*, Gerrards Cross 1978. Has edited *Calendar of the Orrery Papers*, Dublin 1941; *The Kenmare Manuscripts*, Dublin 1942, rep. 1970; *The Wardenship of Galway*, Dublin 1944; *Seventeenth Century Hearth Money Rolls*, Dublin 1967.

MacMAHON, Bryan Michael, b. Listowel 1909. Was principal teacher there. MIAL. Appointed shareholder in New Abbey Theatre Company by Irish government. Represented Ireland at Harvard International Seminar 1963. Has written historical pageants for national commemorative events. Is best known for his short stories, which appear in most good anthologies of Irish writing, but has also written several successful plays: *The Bugle in the Blood*, 1949; *The Song of the Anvil*, 1960; and *The Honey Spike* 1961, all first acted at the Abbey. Wrote *Jackomoora and the King of Ireland's Son*, US 1950 for children. His novel *Children of the Rainbow*, 1952, was republished in the US and Canada, chosen as a Book Find Club Selection translated into German and rep. Dublin 1982. His short-story collections include *The Lion Tamer and Other Stories*, 1948, repub. US four editions. *The End of the World*, Swords 1977; *The Sound of Hooves*, 1985. Travel, *Here's Ireland*, London and NY 1971, Dublin 1982. Translated *Peig* (the autobiography of Peig Sayers of the Great Blasket) from Irish into English, Dublin and US 1973.

An authority on Shelta, the language of the travelling people or tinkers. Introduced Writers' Workshop concept to Ireland from Iowa where he was visiting lecturer. Hon. LL.D. NUI. President Irish PEN 1972-73.

McMAHON, Sean, b. Derry 1931. Ed. St Columb's College Derry (where he teaches mathematics), QUB. Editor and compiler of *The Best of the Bell*, Dublin 1978; with Brian M. Walker and Art Ó Broin, *Faces of Ireland 1875-1925*, Belfast 1980; *A Book of Irish Quotations*, Dublin 1984; *Rich and Rare*, Swords 1984, rev. 1985; *This England*, Swords 1986.

MacMANUS, Charlotte Elisabeth, b. *c.* 1850, d. 1941. Worked in Gaelic League and wrote a number of popular serials and patriotic novels, many of which had great success: *Lally of the Brigade*, 1899; *Nessa*, 1904; *In Sarsfield's Days*, 1907, etc.

MacMANUS, Francis, b. Kilkenny 1909, d. Dublin 1965. Ed. CBS, UCD. Widely travelled in Europe. School-teacher until becoming Director of Talks and Features in Irish radio, 1947. Wrote travel books, short stories, essays, biography and history, and a play. The novels include *Stand and*

Give Challenge, 1935; *Candle for the Proud,* 1936; *Men Withering,* 1939, rep. Cork 1981; *The Wild Garden,* 1940; *Flow on Lovely River,* 1941; *Watergate,* 1942, rep. Swords 1981; *The Greatest of These,* 1943, rep. Cork 1979; *Statue for a Square,* 1945; *The Fire in the Dust,* 1951; *American Son,* 1959. Creator of Thomas Davis Lecture series on Irish radio, one of the formative influences in Irish adult education. Wrote several biographies, *Boccaccio,* 1947; *St Columban,* 1962; and histories, *The Irish Struggle 1916-26,* 1966, and ed. *The Years of the Great Test: Ireland 1926-37,* Cork, 1966. Also ed. *The Yeats We Knew,* Cork 1965.

MacMANUS, Michael Joseph, b. Leitrim 1888, d. Donegal 1951. Ed. London University. Taught in Lancashire 1907. Freelance journalist in Fleet Street. Returned to Ireland 1916. Literary editor of *Irish Press* from its foundation in 1931 to his death. *So This is Dublin,* 1927; *Dublin Diversions,* 1928; *The Green Jackdaw; Irish Cavalcade,* 1939; *Rackrent Hall,* 1941; *Biography of Eamon de Valera,* 1944. President of Bibliographical Society of Ireland, and Book Association of Ireland.

MacMANUS, Seumas, b. Co. Donegal 1861, d. New York 1960. A National school-teacher for several years, before moving to US in 1899. Married Anna Johnston (the poetess Ethna Carbery). Published a large number of collections of short stories, including *The Leadin' Road to Donegal,* 1896; *Through the Turf Smoke,* 1900; *The Miracle of Father Peter; Orange and Green; A Lad of the O'Friels,* 1906; *The Humours of Donegal; Lo and Behold Ye!,* 1919; *Top of the Morning,* 1920; *Bold Blades of Donegal,* 1937 etc. Also wrote some plays: *The Townland of Tawney,* 1904, and *The Hard Hearted Man,* 1905, for the early Abbey Theatre. Published his autobiography, *The Rocky Road to Dublin,* NY 1938. In 1917 Notre Dame University conferred an LL.D. on him.

McNALLY, Leonard, b. Dublin 1752, d. 1820. Ed. TCD. Bar. Joined United Irishmen, and defended many of them as counsel at several treason trials. It only became known after his death that in fact he betrayed them, procuring their secrets and passing these on the the British government. He wrote a number of verse-plays and comic opera, including *The Apotheosis of Punch,* 1779; *Tristram Shandy,* 1783; *Critic upon Critic,* 1792; and several songs which long remained popular, the best-known being 'Sweet Lass of Richmond Hill'. Rewarded for his treachery by a government pension, he died in prosperity.

MacNAMARA, Brinsley, pen-name of John Weldon, b. Delvin, Co. Westmeath 1890, d. 1963. Joined Abbey Theatre company 1909 and toured with it in US. Left the company in 1912 to give all his time to writing. Became a centre of national controversy with his first novel, *The Valley of the Squinting Windows,* 1918, widely supposed to be based on his birthplace. The next year the Abbey produced his first play, *The Rebellion in Ballycullion,* and he published a second novel, *The Clanking of Chains,* 1920, the account of a patriot disillusioned and embittered by the struggle for Irish freedom.

MacNamara became Director of the Abbey Theatre and wrote several more plays for the company, of which the best-known include *Look at the Heffernans!*, *Margaret Gillan*, *The Glorious Uncertainty* and *The Grand House in the City*. He also published other novels: *The Mirror in the Dusk*, 1921; *The Various Lives of Marcus Igoe*, 1929; *Return to Ebontheever*, 1930; *Michael Caravan*, 1948; and two collections of short stories, *The Smiling Faces and Other Stories*, 1929; *Some Curious People*, 1945. A play *The Master* (Abbey Theatre) had Barry Fitzgerald in the cast.

MacNEICE, Louis, b. Belfast 1907, d. 1963. Ed. Dorset, Oxford. Went to Spain towards the end of the Civil War, and has usually been considered an integral part of the 'left-wing political' school of English poets, led by Auden and Spender. But appears never to have been as politically motivated as they were, and to have considered himself an Irish rather than an English poet. Worked for the BBC for many years, and wrote many radio plays, such as *Christopher Columbus*, 1944, *The Mad Islands* and *The Administrator*. Also wrote plays *Out of the Picture*, when still a student, and *One for the Grave*, Dublin 1966. But his reputation rests on his poetry, once very highly regarded by critics, and now undergoing the usual reassessment which closely follows a writer's death. It has been described as 'dry' and 'casual,' both in praise and denigration. Collections of poetry include *Autumn Journal*, 1938-39; *Holes in the sky*, 1947; *Collected Poems 1925-48*; *Autumn Sequel*, 1954; *Visitations*, 1957. His autobiography covering his life up to 1940, *The Strings are False*, pub. posthumously, 1965; *Collected Poems*, ed. E. R. Dodds, 1966, rep. 1979.

MacNEILL, Eoin (sometimes John), b. Co. Antrim 1867, d. Dublin 1945. Civil servant. One of founders of Gaelic League 1893. Professor of Early Irish History UCD 1908-45. Helped organise and became commander of Irish Volunteers 1913. In 1916 countermanded the orders for the Easter Rising on ground that it could not succeed. This disorganised the plans and resulted in many districts failing to act. Nevertheless was imprisoned by British, released 1917. Served in Free State Parliament and became Minister of Education 1922-25. *Phases of Irish History*, Dublin 1919; *Celtic Ireland*, Dublin 1921, repub. Dublin 1981; *St Patrick*, 1934; *Early Irish Laws and Institutions*, 1935.

McNEILL, Janet, b. Dublin 1907. Ed. England and St Andrew's University. Journalist in Belfast. Married Robert Alexander 1933, and lived in Lisburn. Chairman Belfast centre of Irish PEN, 1956-57; BBC Advisory Council 1959-64. Now living in Bristol. Has written novels, children's books, radio plays and two stage plays, *Signs and Wonders*, acted Belfast 1951, and *Gospel Truth* pub. Belfast 1951. Children's books include *My Friend Specs McCann*, 1955; *This Happy Morning*, 1959; *Tom's Tower*, 1965. Adult novels include *A Child in the House*, 1955; *The Other Side of the Wall*, 1957; *As Strangers Here*, 1960; *The Early Harvest*, 1962; *The Maiden*

Dinosaur, 1964 (repub. in US as *The Belfast Friends,* 1966); *Talk to Me,* 1965 (also broadcast by RE). Since 1966 has concentrated on novels for children, among many recent titles, *Wait For It,* 1972, and *We Three Kings,* 1974.

MacNEILL, Máire. Daughter of Eoin MacNeill. Ed. UCD. Staff of Irish Folklore Commission 1939-45. Author of magisterial *The Festival of Lughnasa,* Oxford 1962, rep. in 2 vols Dublin 1982. Lives in Co. Clare, married to John Sweeney.

Mac NIOCAILL, Geroid, see FLATTISBURY, Philip.

McNULTY, Edward Matthew, b. Antrim 1856, d. 1943. At school with George Bernard Shaw in Dublin and became his close friend for many years. Wrote several stage-Irish novels, *Misther O'Ryan,* 1894, etc., and two plays, *The Lord Mayor,* 1914, and *The Courting of Mary Doyle,* 1921, leaving behind, after his death, an unpublished memoir of G.B.S., since become famous in American academic circles.

McSPARRAN, Archibald, b. Co. Derry 1786, d. Philadelphia 1848. Schoolmaster at Glenkeen 1802-16. Entered TCD as pensioner 1816. Wrote a very successful book, *MacDonnell and the Norman de Burgos,* 1829. Emigrated to America soon after, where he wrote *Tales of the Alleghanies, The Hermit of the Rocky Mountains,* etc.

MacSWINEY, Owen, b. *c.* 1675, d. 1754. Went to London as a young man and became manager first of Drury Lane Theatre and later of the Queen's Theatre, Haymarket. George II made him Keeper of the King's Mews. He was a close friend of Peg Woffington, the Irish actress, and left her the large fortune he had made in theatre management. He wrote several popular plays, including *The Quacks, or Love the Physician,* 1705; *Camilla* (an opera), 1707; and another opera, *Pyrrhus and Demetrius,* 1709.

MacSWINEY, Terence, b. Cork 1883, d. 1920. Ed. Royal University. Taught himself Irish. Active in the Volunteer movement. Interned 1916, elected MP for mid-Cork 1918, and also Lord Mayor of Cork. Arrested, deported, and kept in Brixton Prison where he died after a hunger strike lasting 74 days. Wrote several volumes of poetry, including *Battle Cries,* 1918; and *Despite Fools' Laughter.* Also wrote plays, *The Revolutionist,* performed at the Abbey, 1921, and essays, *Principles of Freedom,* NY 1921.

MADDEN, Richard Robert, b. Dublin 1798, d. Dublin 1886. Ed. Dublin, studied medicine Paris, Naples and London. Travelled in Near East 1824-27, practised as surgeon in London until 1833. That year appointed a special magistrate to administer Abolition of Slavery Statute in Jamaica. After bitter quarrels with the planters resigned 1834, but returned to similar work in Havana 1836-40. Held govt office in W. Australia 1847, but returned to Ireland 1848, and took up the cause of the Irish peasantry with the same passion he had shown for the freed slaves and the exploited Australian settlers. In some ways his career and character foreshadowed that of Casement. *A Twelve Months Residence in the West Indies*, 1835, describes the troubles following Abolition; *An Address on Slavery in Cuba*, 1840; *Egypt and Mohammed Ali*, 1841; *History of the Penal Laws*, 1847; *The Island of Cuba*, 1849; *The History of Irish Periodical Literature from the end of the 17th to the middle of the 19th century*, 1867, are all of interest. He also collected materials for a history of the Rising of '98 which J. Bowles Daly later edited as *Ireland in '98*. But Madden's principal work and monument, as far as the student of Irish history is concerned, is *The United Irishmen, Their Lives & Times*, 7 vols, 1843-46.

MADDEN, Samuel, b. Dublin 1686, d. 1765. A friend of Dr Johnson and Swift he is much more than the figure of fun commonly thought. The author of a successful tragedy, *Themistocles, the Lover of His Country*, 1729, he became famous in Ireland where he held a Dublin living, for his scheme of premiums to encourage learning. He set this out in *A Proposal for the General Encouragement of Learning in Dublin College*, Dublin 1731, 2nd ed. 1732, and *A Letter to the Dublin Society on the improving of their Fund; & the Manufacturers Tillage etc in Ireland*, Dublin 1739. He became known from these as Premium Madden. But his principal work appeared in 1738, *Reflections and Resolutions Proper for the Gentlemen of Ireland as to their conduct for the service of their Country*. In this he blamed Ireland's misfortunes on the idleness and extravagance of the people; recommended the useful employment of criminals within the country instead of the wasteful system of transportation outside it; and more to the point recommended travelling teachers of agriculture who would improve the state of farming; the setting up of agricultural schools in country towns, etc. He and others had earlier founded the Dublin Society for much the same purposes.

MAGEE, Heno, b. Dublin 1939. Left school at 14, became messenger boy, later enlisted in RAF. Now living in Dublin. Plays: *Hatchet*, Dublin 1972 (brought to England 1978); *Red Biddy*, Dublin 1974; both successfully revived. *I'm Getting Out of this Kip*, RTE 1972; all raw, authentic working-class plays. Awarded Rooney Prize for Irish Literature 1976.

MAGEE, William Kirkpatrick, see EGLINTON, John.

MAGENNIS, Peter, b. Co. Fermanagh 1817, d. Co. Fermanagh 1910. Farmer's son, became National school-teacher. Wrote poetry and novels of which the most successful was *The Ribbon Informer*, 1874, based on childhood knowledge of the Ribbon conspiracies.

MAGINN, William, b. Cork 1793, d. Walton-on-Thames 1842. School-master's son. Ed. Cork and TCD. Went to London and became known as journalist and wit. Famous for his creation of the immensely successful magazine dialogues *Noctes Ambrosianae* which ran in *Blackwood's* 1822-35. He originated the idea and wrote some of the dialogues. After 1830 became editor of *Frazer's Magazine*. Is credited with several novels including *Whitehall, or the days of George IV,* 1827, and *John Manesty,* 1846, but it seems impossible to be certain how much he wrote of them. He died in poverty. *Miscellaneous Writings,* ed. R. S. Mackenzie, 5 vols, NY 1855-57; *Miscellanies: Prose and Verse,* ed. R. W. Montague, 2 vols, 1885, includes famous Pendennis and Polyglott sketches; *Ten Tales,* 1933, is a selection of his Irish stories.

MAHAFFY, John Pentland, b. Switzerland 1839, d. 1919. Provost of Trinity from 1914, and one of the great 'characters' of Dublin life. His father was British Chaplain at Vevay, but in 1848 the family returned to Donegal. Mahaffy was ed. privately and TCD where he was 1st Sen. Mod. 1859; Fellow 1864; Professor of Ancient History 1869-99. He founded the Georgian Society for the preservation of Georgian Dublin, and in a sense he belonged to the 18th rather than the 19th century. His sardonic tongue earned him many enemies, which astonished him, and a great reputation as a wit, which consoled him.

On a more serious level he had a reputation as a scholar, damaged by the fact that his interests were too widespread. In 1866 he published *Commentary on Kant,* which earned Mill's notice, and *Kant's Philosophy,* 1872, philosophy being his early study. He also published *Descartes,* London and Edinburgh 1880, but his mind had already turned to Ancient, and particularly Classical Greek, History. *Prologomena to Ancient History,* 1871, although out-dated, is still regarded as a fine book. *Greek Social Life from Homer to Menander,* 1874; *A History of Classical Greek Literature,* 2 vols, 1880, *Greek Life and Thought,* London and NY 1887; *The Empire of the Ptolemies,* 1895, were his principal historical works.

In 1887 he brought out *Principles of the Art of Conversation,* London and NY, which he was well qualified to write. In 1903 he published *An Epoch in Irish History* (TCD, its foundations and early fortunes), and the next year *The Particular Book of Trinity College.* In politics he was a patriot, but of an 18th-century Ascendancy kind. He would have been at home with Burke and perhaps with Swift. He scorned the Nationalists of his day as provincial, and was caustic about Patrick Pearse. In 1916 he directed the defence of TCD against the insurgents, but in 1917 proposed at the Irish Convention to which he and Trinity were host, that Ireland should have a Federal Constitution on the Swiss model, with Ulster as an autonomous province.

MAHER, James, b. Co. Kilkenny. Vice-President, American-Irish Historical Society, authority on Charles Kickham. Has published several anthologies: *Chief of the Comeraghs* (John O'Mahony the Fenian), Mullinahone 1957; *Ormonde Castle,* Thurles 1970, etc.

MAHER, Sean, b. Tullamore 1932 of itinerant parents. Lived a hard life travelling the roads, with spells in industrial school and prison, in Ireland and England, before writing *The Road to God Knows Where,* Dublin 1972, a rare and valuable account of the itinerant way of life and its traditions.

MALONE

MAHER, William. An 18th-century ballad monger in Waterford, by profession a clothier. Is credited with having written the immortal song, 'The Night Before Larry was Stretched.'

MAHON, Derek, b. Belfast 1941 to family of shipyard engineers. Ed. Royal Belfast Academical Institution and TCD. Travelled North Amercia, returning Ireland 1967. Married Doreen Douglas. Moved to London 1970 where he now lives. Poetry: *Night-Crossing,* 1969; *Lives,* 1972; *The Snow Party,* 1975; *Poems 1962-1978,* 1980; *The Hunt by Night,* 1983; all Oxford. Won Eric Gregory Award 1967; Denis Devlin Memorial Award 1975. Numerous TV adaptations of Irish works by Jennifer Johnston, John Montague, Elizabeth Bowen; also adapted Molière's *School for Husbands* for stage as *High Time,* Derry 1984.

MAHONY, Francis Sylvester, b. Cork 1804, d. Paris 1866. Ed. France, became a Jesuit, taught at Clongowes where his pupils included the future Canon Sheehan, but was dismissed for allegedly leading his seminarians on a drunken school outing, and expelled from the Society of Jesus. Turned to journalism, writing for *The Daily News, Frazer's Magazine,* etc. His famous pen-name, Father Prout, Parish Priest of Watergrasshill, Co. Cork, first appeared in *Frazer's* in April 1831. Lived for many years in Rome and Paris as a foreign correspondent for London journals. His volumes of humorous poetry include *The Reliques of Father Prout,* 1836. His *Roman Letters by Don Jeremy Savonarola,* first sent from Rome to London papers as satirical sketches,were collected and pub. 1847.

MAHONY, Martin Francis, b. Cork 1831, d. 1885. Nephew of Francis Sylvester M. Wrote several political and legal satires in the form of novels: *The Irish Bar Sinister,* Dublin 1871; *Cheap John's Auction,* Dublin 1873; and *Jerpoint,* Dublin 1875.

MALONE, Edmund or Edmond, b. Dublin 1741, d. London 1812. Ed. TCD. Bar 1767. In 1774 sat for Sir Joshua Reynolds. Moved to London permanently 1777, having already begun an edition of Goldsmith's works, which came out in London 1780. Published, 1778, his *Attempts to ascertain the order in which the plays of Shakespeare were written,* and this immediately established him as a critic and man of letters. He became an intimate of the Johnson-Boswell circle, helped revise the *Tour to the Hebrides,* 1785, and 1789-90 worked with Boswell revising the *Life of Samuel Johnson,* 1791, reading half of the proof sheets and helping in many ways. Boswell dying in 1795, Malone edited the 3rd, 4th, 5th and 6th editions between 1799 and 1811, with notes.

While still working with Boswell he had in 1790 brought out his own greatest work, *Shakespeare,* swiftly recognised as the finest edition of the plays to that date, and for long after. Malone has been called the first scholarly editor of Shakespeare, setting all Shakespearean criticism on a new level. In the same year he published *An Historical Account of the Rise and Progress of the English Stage.* In 1796 he published an *Exposure of the Ireland Forgeries,* these being pretended Shakespearean autograph MSS, *The Works of Sir Joshua Reynolds with a memoir,* 1797, and *The Critical and Miscellaneous Prose Work of John Dryden,* 1800, followed, and he spent his last years gathering notes and material for the vast *Variorum Shakespeare.* He died before he could put these in order, and left them to Boswell's younger son, also James, who edited and brought them out in 21 vols, 1821.

MANGAN, James Clarence, b. Dublin 1803, d. 1849. Son of a poor grocer. Ed. by a charitable priest who taught him German among other things. Worked as a lawyer's clerk, where he broke his health copying documents, and later in the Ordnance Survey. Wrote for *The Nation* under several pen names, and translated German poetry, as well as writing poetry under his own name. His main publications include the two volume *German Anthology,* Dublin 1845, *Poets and Poetry of Munster* and *The Tribes of Ireland.* He died in the cholera epidemic of 1849, after a life of almost unrelieved poverty and unhappiness. His most famous poem is 'Dark Rosaleen,' in which, in the old Gaelic tradition of the *aisling* or vision poem, he sees Ireland as a beautiful and sorrowing woman, his Dark Rose, and images her salvation coming from across the sea. John Mitchel brought out an edition of his *Poems* in New York, 1870, and Imogen Guiney another in 1897. A bronze bust of the poet stands in St Stephen's Green, Dublin.

MANIFOLD, Deirdre, b. Galway. Interested in the realities behind the façade of world politics, she wrote *Fatima and the Great Conspiracy,* Galway 1982 (4 printings within 18 months), proposing that the conflict between American capitalism and Russian communism is a cover for a plan to produce tyrannical world government.

MANNING, Mary, b. Dublin 1906. Lived many years in US, returned to Dublin 1970, resettling in Massachusetts. Plays: *Youth's the Season,* Dublin 1931; *Happy Family,* Dublin 1934; adaptation of *Finnegans Wake,* produced Cambridge, Mass. 1955, Irish Theatre Festival 1960, also London and Paris; adaption of Frank O'Connor's *The Saint and Mary Kate,* Dublin 1968; *Ah Well It Won't be Long Now,* Dublin 1972. Novels: *Mount Venus,* Boston 1938; *Lovely People,* Boston 1953; *Last Chronicles of Ballyfungus,* Boston and London 1978.

MANT, Richard, b. Southampton 1776, d. Co. Antrim 1848. Ed. Oxford. Bishop of Down, Connor and Dromore 1823. Voted against Catholic Emancipation in the Lords in 1821 and 1825. Wrote *History of the Church of Ireland,* 1840.

MARCUS, David, b. Cork 1924. Ed. Presentation Bros, UCC, King's Inns Dublin. Founder and editor, with Terence Smith, of literary magazine *Irish Writing,* 1946-54; and ed. *Poetry Ireland* 1948-54. Pioneered 'New Irish Writing' page in *Irish Press* as Literary Editor 1968–. *Six Poems,* Dublin

1952; *To Next Year in Jerusalem* (novel), 1954. Ed. *Sphere Book of Modern Irish Short Stories*, 1972; *Modern Irish Love Stories*, 1974; *Irish Poets 1924-1974*, 1975; *New Irish Writing*, 1978; *Body and Soul*, Swords 1979; *Bodley Head Book of Irish Short Stories*, 1980, paperbacked in 2 vols 1982.

MARMION, Joseph, b. Dublin 1858, d. Namur 1923. Ed. Dublin and Rome. Ordained Rome 1881. After year as parish curate appointed to teach philosophy at Clonliffe. Increasingly drawn to monastic life, entered Benedictine Order at Maredsous, Namur 1886. In 1899 was sent to Mont Cesar Monastery, Louvain, as Prior and Professor of Theology, remaining there until elected Abbot of Maredsous 1909-23. He had no interest in publication, but a number of his students drafted three volumes from notes taken at his lectures and submitted them to him for correction. The result was *Le Christ, vie de l'âme*, Belgium 1918; *Le Christ dans ses mystères*, 1919; and *Le Christ, idéal du moine*, 1922. These books swiftly reached and influenced an enormous audience, being translated into nine languages and achieving popularity not only with Catholics but also among Greek Orthodox readers.

MARTIN, Francis Xavier, b. Co. Kerry 1922. Ed. UCD, Rome, Cambridge. Joined Augustinian Order 1941. Professor of Mediaeval History UCD 1962-. MRIA. Edited radio and TV series on Irish History. Founder chairman of Friends of Medieval Dublin since 1977. Main works: *Friar Nugent, Agent of the Counter-Reformation 1569-1635*, London and Rome 1962; *No Hero in the House: Diarmait Mac Murchada and the Coming of the Normans to Ireland*, Dublin 1977; as editor, *The Irish Volunteers 1913-1915*, Dublin 1963; *The Howth Gun-Running 1914*, Dublin 1964; *Leaders and Men of the Easter Rising: Dublin 1916*, London and Ithaca 1967; *Eoin MacNeill: Scholar and Man of Action, 1867-1945*, by Professor Michael Tierney, Oxford 1980; and as co-editor, *The Course of Irish History*, Cork 1967, rev. 1984; *The Scholar Revolutionary: Eoin MacNeill 1867-1945 and the Making of the New Ireland*, Shannon 1973; *A New History of Ireland*, vol. 3 1976, vol. 8 1983, vol. 9 1984, all pub. Oxford.

MARTIN, Mary Letitia, b. Co. Galway 1815 of a great land-owning family, d. New York 1850. She herself inherited 200,000 acres in 1847 and was known locally as 'The Princess of Connemara'. The land was so heavily mortgaged she was left nearly penniless and emigrated to Belgium, where she supported herself and her husband by writing romances, and then sailed for America in 1850. She was prematurely confined on board ship and died as a result of childbirth on reaching New York. Her first novel, *St Etienne,* appeared 1845. Her most interesting work is *Julia Howard*, 1850, not for its literary merit, which is small, but for its autobiographical content, dealing with the West of Ireland and the Famine.

MARTIN, Thomas Augustine, b. Leitrim 1935. Ed. Roscrea, UCD. Professor of Anglo-Irish Literature and Drama UCD. Director of Yeats International Summer School 1978. Senate member 1973-80. Broadcaster and critic. *James Stephens*, Dublin and London 1977; ed. *Winter's Tales from Ireland*, vol. I, Dublin and London 1971; and *The Charwoman's Daughter* by James Stephens, Dublin and London 1972. *Anglo-Irish Literature*, 1981; *W. B. Yeats*, Dublin 1983. Ed. *The Genius of Irish Prose*, Cork 1985.

MARTIN, William David, b. Belfast 1937. Ed. Belfast, Keele and Warwick. Royal Navy 1955-62. Lectured in English at Northern Ireland Polytechnic, Co. Antrim, 1971-75. Since 1976 senior lecturer in English at N. I. Polytech. Novels: *The Task*, 1975; *The Ceremony of Innocence*, 1977; *The Road to Ballyshannon*, 1981.

MARTYN, Edward, b. Co. Galway 1859, d. 1923. Ed. Dublin and Oxford. Unusual in being both a Catholic and a wealthy landlord. He became prominent in every aspect of the Irish Revival, from the language, which he learned to speak and write fluently, to traditional music, being a founder of the now annual Feis Ceoil (music festival). He established the Palestrina Choir in Dublin's pro-Cathedral, and discovered John McCormack as one of the choristers. His name is best remembered as co-founder with Yeats and Lady Gregory of the Irish Literary Theatre, in 1898, the amateur group which became the Abbey Theatre Company. His own plays were among the first modest successes of the group, and of the theatre: *The Heather Field; Maeve; Grangecolman; The Tale of a Town;* and *The Dream Physician.* The character George Augustus Moon in this last play is a caricature of George Augustus Moore, and Martyn's revenge for Moore's cruel portrait of Martyn in *Hail and Farewell.* The two men, ill-assorted friends for many years, broke finally over these mutual dagger thrusts.

Martyn also broke with many other friends. More intolerant of 'popular' theatre even than Yeats, he withdrew from the Abbey and devoted himself to an amateur group which would produce literary and symbolic plays by himself and others of like mind. In 1914 he founded the Irish Theatre in Hardwicke Street, with Joseph Plunkett and Thomas MacDonagh. Gradually weakened by ill-health he withdrew more and more to Galway and the life of a recluse. Before he died, he willed his body to a Dublin hospital for dissection, insisting on a pauper's burial for the remains. Much laughed at for his eccentricities, he remains one of the founders of modern Irish culture.

MATHEW, Frank, b. 1865. Nephew of the famous Father Mathew, apostle of temperance. Ed. in England. Wrote stories and some novels: *At the Rising of the Moon* (short stories), 1893; *The Wood of the Brambles*, 1896; *The Spanish Wine*, 1898; and *Love of Comrades*, 1900, all novels.

MATHEWS, Aidan Carl, b. Dublin 1956. Poetry includes *Windfalls,* 1977, and *Minding Ruth*, Dublin 1983. Plays: *The Diamond Body; Exit-Entrance* (about double suicide of Arthur Koestler and his wife) won Listowel Drama Award 1984; *The Antigone*, 1984. Ed. *Immediate Man*, a commemoration of Cearbhall O Dalaigh, Dublin 1983. Currently a producer with RTE.

MATURIN, Charles Robert, b. Dublin 1782, d. Dublin 1824. Ed. TCD.

Ordained in Church of Ireland and served as curate in Loughrea and Dublin. Began a school, and wrote plays and novels: *The Fatal Revenge*, 1807; *The Wild Irish Boy*, 1808 (in answer to Lady Morgan's *Wild Irish Girl* of 1806); *The Milesian Chief*, 1812, imitated by Walter Scott in *The Bride of Lammermoor; Women*, 1818, the only one of his books to deal with contemporary Irish society; *Melmoth the Wanderer*, 1820, his masterpiece; and *The Albigenses*, all being novels of a Gothic kind, written at least in part as an escape from the terrible poverty and degradation surrounding him in his Dublin parish, St Peter's. His first play, *Bertram*, was a success at Drury Lane, London. His next two plays, *Manuel* and *Fredolfo*, failed badly. He wrote much of his work under the pseud. 'Dennis Jasper Murphy'.

He was one of the strangest among the many strange characters in Irish letters, and deserves more attention than he has ever received. Even during his lifetime, when his books created a considerable stir of interest, they were comparatively little read, none reaching a second edition before his death.

MATURIN, Edward, b. Dublin 1812, d. New York 1881. Son of the Reverend Charles Robert M. Ed. TCD. Emigrated to US and became Professor of Greek first in Charleston and then in New York. Helped revise the translation of St Mark's Gospel for the American Bible Union. Novels include *The Irish Chieftain*, 1848; *Bianca*, 1852, etc; also wrote poetry, publishing *Lyrics of Spain and Erin*, 1850, in Boston.

MAXTON, Hugh, see McCORMACK, William John.

MAXWELL, Constantia Elizabeth, b. Dublin 1886, d. Kent 1962. Ed. Scotland and TCD. First woman member of TCD staff, assistant to Professor of History. Became doyenne of Irish historians, detached and ironic. Lecky Professor of Modern History, TCD, 1945-51. Her many books include *Irish History from Contemporary Sources (1509-1610)*, 1923, reprinted often, still in use; *Dublin under the Georges*, 1936, probably her most famous book, and revolutionary at the time, offering a new kind of social approach to history many years before Trevelyan made it fashionable; also *Country and Town in Ireland under the Georges*, 1940, revised ed. Dundalk 1949; *The Stranger in Ireland from the reign of Elizabeth to the Great Famine*, 1954, rep. Dublin 1979.

MAXWELL, William Hamilton, b. Co. Down 1792, d. near Edinburgh 1850. Ed. TCD. Fought in the Peninsular campaigns and at Waterloo. Became Rector of Balla in Connemara, 1820. Wrote travel and contemporary history: *Life of the Duke of Wellington*, 3 vols, 1839-41; *Wanderings in the Highlands and Islands*, 2 vols, 1844; *History of the Rebellion in 1798*, 1845; *Hints To a Soldier on Service*, 2 vols, 1845; *The Irish Movements*, 1848; and *Erin-go-Bragh, or Irish Life Pictures*, 2 vols, 1859. Contributed articles and stories to *Bentley's Miscellany* and *Dublin University Magazine*. Wrote several popular novels, some of them based on his war experiences, such as *Stories of Waterloo*. They include *Hector O'Halloran; Captain Blake; O'Hara, or 1798*, 1825; *Wild Sports of the West*, 1832; *The Dark Lady of Doona*, 1834; and *Barry O'Linn*, 1848.

MAYNE, Rutherford, pseud. of Samuel Waddell, b. Japan 1878, d. 1967, brother of Helen Waddell. Ed. Belfast. Joined Ulster Literary Theatre 1904 as actor and soon as writer. A great-great nephew of Mayne Reid, the boy's adventure-story writer, he took 'Mayne' as a pseudonym. His first play, *The Turn of the Road*, 1906, was accepted as a hard attack on Puritanism, but he preferred to regard its target as 'Philistinism'. *The Drone* in 1908 was regarded as his masterpiece and was followed by a large number of plays, including *The Truth; Bridge Head; The Red Turf; Plays of Changing Ireland; Peter*, etc., mostly for Ulster theatres, but some for the Abbey. For many years he continued to act as an amateur, and toured abroad with amateur companies. His career was in the Irish Land Commission, and he retired as Commissioner.

MAYNE, Thomas Ekenhead, b. Belfast 1867, d. 1899, son of a bookseller. Wrote stories and poetry. *Blackthorn Blossoms*, 1897, *Belfast and The Heart o' the Peat* (short stories), Belfast 1899.

MEADE, Elizabeth Thomasina, b. Bandon, 1850, d. Oxford 1915. Went to London 1874. Edited *Atlanta* magazine for 6 years. Wrote a vast number of novels, some with Irish settings, such as *The O'Donnells of Inchfawn* and *The Wild Irish Girl* (not to be confused with Lady Morgan's novel of the same title).

MEAGHER, Thomas Francis, b. Waterford 1823, d. Missouri River 1867. Son of a wealthy business man and MP. Ed. Clongowes and Stonyhurst. Joined Young Irelanders and became famous as an orator. Arrested in 1848 and condemned to death, reprieved, and transported for life to Van Diemen's Land. Escaped 1852 to America where he helped found the *Citizen* newspaper and lectured widely. Organised the Irish Brigade for the North in the American Civil War and fought with distinction at Richmond, Bull Run and other battles. After the war appointed Secretary (in effect governor) of Montana Territory by President Johnson. On a river journey fell from the steamboat and was drowned. There are strong grounds for suspecting that he was murdered for reasons of local Montana politics. His *Speeches on the Legislative Independence of Ireland*, 1853, repub. as *Meagher of the Sword*, ed. Mrs Arthur Griffith, 1916.

MEANY, Stephen Joseph, b. Co. Clare 1825, d. New York 1888. Journalist in Clare and Dublin. Worked on *Freeman's Journal*. Imprisoned in 1848 after the Young Ireland disturbances. Moved to Liverpool and became first President of the Liverpool Press Association. Emigrated to America, 1860, and became owner-editor of the *Commercial*, Toledo, Ohio. Returned to England and was arrested in 1867 on charge of Fenianism. Sentenced to 15 years. Returned to America at the end of his sentence, and died there.

Paradoxically, for a convicted Young Irelander and Fenian his main claim to literary fame is the passionately British and loyal song 'Three Cheers for the Red White and Blue'. Published some poetry, and a novel, *The Terry Alt.*

MELDON, Maurice, b. 1926, d. 1958. Ed. Dundalk, and worked in civil service. Won the Radio Eireann play competition in 1947 with *Song of the Parakeet.* The House Under Green Shadows* was produced at the Abbey, 1951, and his dream fantasy *Aisling* was first performed in 1953, in a small theatre club. It was revived afterwards at the Gate, and published in 1959. Meldon himself was killed in a road accident.

MICHAEL of Kildare, born at end of 13th century, *c.* 1280. Interesting as the first 'Anglo-Irish' poet. He travelled widely in Ireland as a mendicant friar, almost certainly a Franciscan, and wrote poetry in both Latin and English. Dr Heuser includes one of his poems in the *Kildare-Gedichte,* and he is also mentioned in Croker's *Popular Songs of Ireland,* 1839.

MICHELBURNE, John, b. 1646, d. Derry 1721. One of the Governors of Derry during the siege. Wrote a tragi-comedy based on his eyewitness knowledge, *Ireland Preserved, or the Siege of Londonderry,* 1705.

MILEY, John, b. Co. Kildare *c.* 1805, d. Bray 1861. Famous as the man who carried O'Connell's heart to Rome and brought the Liberator's body back from Italy to Ireland. Became rector of Irish College, Paris, 1849, and then parish priest of Bray, 1859. Published several histories of episodes in papal history, particularly *History of the Papal States,* 1850.

MILLAR, Florence Norah, b. Co. Dublin 1920, related to Sheridan Le Fanu. Ed. Dublin and England. Studied music RIAM. Has written many stories, and some novels and plays. Novels include *Fishing is Dangerous,* 1946; *Grant's Overture,* 1947; and *The Lone Kiwi* (for boys), 1948. Her *Pageant of St Columba* was staged at Raphoe, 1963.

MILLIGAN, Alice, b. Co. Tyrone 1866, d. Omagh 1953. Ed. Belfast and London. Daughter of Seaton M. the Irish antiquary. Wrote poetry for *United Irishman, Sinn Fein,* etc.; founded and edited *Shan Van Vocht,* with Ethna Carbery, 1896-99. Wrote a novel, *A Royal Democrat,* 1892, and was one of the first 'Abbey' playwrights, writing *The Last Feast of the Fianna* for the Irish Literary Theatre, 1900. She wrote another play for the Abbey proper, *The Daughter of Donagh,* 1920. Collaborated with her father in *Glimpses of Erin* and with her brother W. H. M. in *Sons of the Sea Kings,* based on Scandinavian sagas. Also published a *Life of Wolfe Tone,* 1898.

MILLIKEN, Richard Alfred, b. Co. Cork 1767, d. 1815. With his sister founded *The Casket or Hesperian Magazine* in Cork. Fought against the rebels in 1798. Wrote poetry, songs, plays, and a novel, *The Slave of Surinam,* Cork 1810. Plays include *Macha* and *Anaconda.* Most famous song is 'The Groves of Blarney'. Many of his songs were extremely popular.

His sister also wrote novels.

MILLINGEN, John Gideon, b. Ireland 1792, d. London 1862. Of Dutch parentage, he claimed to have been born in Ireland, and published an autobiographical novel *Adventures of an Irish Gentleman*, 1830. As a child was taken to Paris where he later qualified MD. In 1802 he joined the British Army, serving in Egypt, the Peninsula, at Waterloo and in the West Indies. In 1823 settled in Boulogne and published *Sketches of Ancient and Modern Boulogne*, Boulogne 1826. In the 1830s was medical officer to the Military Lunatic Asylum at Chatham and then to the Middlesex Pauper Lunatic Asylum. Wrote a *History of Duelling*, 2 vols, 1841; *Jack Hornet, or the March of Intellect*, 1845; and the interesting if highly coloured *Recollections of Republican France*, 1848.

MILNE, Ewart, b. Dublin 1903. Ed. Ashford and Dublin. A sailor during the 1920s. Served in Spanish Civil War with Spanish Medical Aid, 1936-38. Became a farm worker in England, 1942-46. Has long been recognised as one of the major Irish poets, and appears in many English and American anthologies. His books include *Listen Mangan*, Dublin, 1941; *Jubilo*, 1945; *Boding Day*, 1947; *Diamond Cut Diamond*, 1950; *Galion*, Dublin, 1953; *Once More to Tourney*, 1958; *A Garland for the Green*, 1962; *Time Stopped*, 1967; *Drift of Pinions*, 1976; *Cantata Under Orion*, 1977; *The Folded Leaf*, 1983.

MITCHEL, John, b. Co. Derry 1815, son of a Presbyterian minister, d. Newry 1875. Ed. TCD. Solicitor 1840. Becoming Davis's friend, joined him in editing *The Nation* and in 1848 founded *The United Irishman*. Condemned to 14 years transportation the same year for treasonous articles, he was sent to Bermuda and then Van Diemen's Land. He escaped 1853, went to San Francisco, and later New York. There he published his most famous work, *Jail Journal, or Five Years in British Prisons*, 1854. But he lost much of his American popularity by founding a series of unsuccessful newspapers whose main policy was the defence of slavery. In 1874 he returned to Ireland and the next year was elected MP for Tipperary. The election was declared invalid, he was re-elected, and died soon after. Apart from the *Jail Journal* his main works are the *Life of Hugh O'Neill, Prince of Ulster*, 1845; *History of Ireland from the Treaty of Limerick*, Glasgow, 1868; his edition of the *Poems* of Mangan, 1859, with a memoir of Mangan; and the *Poems* of Davis, 1868.

MITCHELL, Susan Langstaff, b. Carrick-on-Shannon, Co. Leitrim 1866, d. Dublin 1926. Ed. Dublin. Journalist. Assistant editor 1901 on *Irish Homestead* and *Irish Statesman*, its successor. Books include *Aids to Immortality of Certain Persons in Ireland*, 1908; *The Living Chalice*, 1908; *George Moore*, 1916; *Secret Springs of Dublin Song*, 1918.

MOFFAT, William, b. *c.* 1675, d. *c.* 1735. Author of immensely popular rhyming *History of Ireland*, constantly read and reprinted in Ireland and

England under different titles for 100 years. A good edition is *The Irish Hudibras*, 1755.

MOLESWORTH, Robert, 1st Viscount, b. Dublin 1656, d. near Dublin 1725. As Ambassador to Denmark offended the Danish Court and was obliged to leave abruptly, 1694. Wrote *An Account of Denmark as it was in the year 1692*, which increased the offence, preaching anti-clerical and revolutionary doctrines. In Ireland 1695, became MP for Dublin. In 1723 published *Considerations for Promoting Agriculture* (in Ireland) which Swift at the time and Lecky 150 years later described as full of good sense, exposing the gross faults of Irish agriculture and proposing ways of mending it. 'If they had been carried out,' Lecky wrote, 'they might have made Ireland a happy properous country.' One of the *Drapier's Letters* (see SWIFT) is dedicated to Molesworth as an Irish patriot. He was made Viscount 1719.

MOLINES (sometimes Multen), Alan, b. Ballycoulter 1654, d. Barbadoes 1690, allegedly of too much rum. FRS 1683. A discreditable love affair obliged him to leave Dublin for London, 1686, from where he went with Lord Inchiquin to the West Indies. He published the sad *Anatomical Account of the Elephant Accidentally Burned to Death in Dublin on 17th June 1661, Together with a Relation of New Anatomical Observations on the Eyes of Animals*, Dublin 1682. His examination was so accurate that it was quoted for many years afterwards in zoological quarters.

MOLLOY, Charles, b. in then King's County 1646, d. London *c*. 1710. Author of *De Jure Maritimo et Navali*, 1676, a standard work on maritime law for more than a century.

MOLLOY, Charles, b. Dublin about 1690, d. 1767. Married an heiress. Practised as barrister in London and also wrote for magazines and newpapers. Author of several very popular comedies: *The Perplexed Couple*, 1715; *The Coquet*, 1718; and *The Half-pay Officer*, 1720. His plays went on being revived and reprinted at least to the end of the century.

MOLLOY, James Lynam, b. Cornelare 1837, d. 1909. Ed. Dublin and abroad. Barrister, but never practised. Wrote many extremely popular songs, of which the most enduring have been 'Just a Song at Twilight' and 'Kerry Dance'.

MOLLOY, Joseph FitzGerald, b. New Ross 1858, d. London 1908. Went to London 1878 where he worked in the New Zealand Agent-General's office for four years. Besides poetry and many novels he wrote some very successful volumes of history and biography. His best-known books are *Court Life Below Stairs*, 2 vols, 1882-3, an account of London under the Georges; *The Life and Adventures of Peg Woffington*, 1884; *Royalty Restored*, 1885 (London under Charles II); *The Life and Adventures of Edmund Kean*, 1888; *The Most Gorgeous Lady Blessington*, 1896; *Romance of the Irish Stage*, 1897; *The Russian Court in the 18th Century*,

1905; and *Sir Joshua and His Circle*, 1906.

MOLLOY, Michael J., b. Co. Galway 1917, son of a village school-teacher. Was taken to see an Abbey play as a boy and determined to be a playwright, with Synge as his ideal. His first work was written for local amateur groups. Since then has written a number of highly regarded plays for the Abbey, beginning with *The Old Road*, 1943, and including *The Visiting House*, 1946; *The King of Friday's Men*, 1948, his best-known play, a powerful historical melodrama; *The Wood of the Whispering*, 1953; *The Will and the Way*, 1955; *Daughter from over the Water; A Right Rose Tree*, 1958; *The Wooing of Duvesa*, 1964; *The Bride of Fontebranda*, 1975; *Petticoat Loose*, 1979; all pub. Dublin. Most are based on folk traditions and deal with the decay of the West of Ireland caused by emigration.

MOLYNEUX, Thomas, Bt, b. Dublin 1661, d. Dublin 1733. Ed. TCD. Friend of Locke, Newton and many leading figures of the day. Published in 1696 the first scientific *Account of the Irish Elk*. Also wrote on the Giant's Causeway, and Danish forts. Founded the Blind Asylum, 1711.

MOLYNEUX, William, b. Dublin 1656, d. 1698. Ed. TCD, Middle Temple. Brother of Thomas M. Like his brother, a friend of Locke, and of Flamstead. Founded Dublin Philosophical Society 1683. FRS 1685. Contributed to *Philosophical Transactions* and author of two famous treatises, *Sciothericum Telescopicum*, Dublin 1686, and *Dioptrica Nova*, Dublin 1692. He posed the famous question, 'What knowledge of the visual world can a blind man have?' which fascinated many 18th-century philosphers, including Bishop Berkeley. *The Case of Ireland Stated*, Dublin 1698, set out Ireland's claims to nationhood and independence with force and clarity, and in 1782 Grattan said at the opening of the new Irish 'sovereign' Parliament, 'Spirit of Swift, spirit of Molyneux, your genius has prevailed.'

MONTAGUE, John Patrick, b. Brooklyn, NY 1929. Ed. Armagh, UCD, Yale, Iowa. Lived in Paris for many years. Went to California, teaching at Berkeley. Now lives Cork and teaches UCC. MIAL. One of Ireland's principal poets. A volume of short stories, *Death of a Chieftain*, 1964, was well received. Poetry includes *Forms of Exile*, Dublin 1958; *Poisoned Lands*, 1961; *Patriotic Suite*, Dublin 1966; *A Chosen Light*, 1967; *Tides*, Dublin 1970; *The Rough Field*, 1972; *A Slow Dance*, 1975; *The Great Cloak*, 1978; *Selected Poems*, 1982; *The Dead Kingdom*, 1984; all pub. Dublin and Oxford. Also ed. *Dolmen Miscellany of Irish Writing*, Dublin 1962; *The Faber Book of Irish Verse*, 1974.

MONTEZ, Lola (properly Marie Dolores Eliza Rosanna Gilbert), b. Limerick 1818, d. New York 1861. Living with her mother at Bath, eloped with an army captain back to Ireland 1837, married him and went out to India. Divorced in 1842 she took up dancing as a career, studying in Spain and touring Europe. In Munich 1846 captivated the king and was created by him Countess of Landsfeld with an income of £5000 a year. She used her influence against the Jesuits and in favour of liberal democracy. But in 1848 the revolution ended her Bavarian interlude and she continued touring, with several unfortunate marriages on the way. In 1858 in New York she published *The Art of Beauty*, trans. French 1862. In 1859 a school friend converted her to a life of charity and she spent her last years visiting the ex-prostitutes and outcasts in the Magdalen Asylum near New York. Struck with paralysis 1861, she died after a few months suffering. *Autobiography and Lectures of Lola Montez,* NY and London 1858. These were probably ghost-written for her by the Rev. C. C. Burr.

MOODY, Theodore William, b. Belfast 1907, d. 1984. Ed. Royal Belfast Academical Institution, QUB. Professor of Modern History TCD 1939-77, Emeritus Fellow 1977. Joint ed. and contributor *Irish Historical Studies* 1938-77; *The Londonderry Plantation, 1609-41,* Belfast 1939; with J.C. Beckett, *Thomas Davis, 1814-45,* Dublin 1945; *Ulster since 1800, 1955* and 1957; with J. C. Beckett, *Queens Belfast, 1845-49: the History of a University,* 2 vols, 1959; ed., with F. X. Martin and F. J. Byrne, *A New History of Ireland, 1534-1691,* vol. 3, Oxford 1976; *A Chronology of Irish History to 1976,* vol. 8, Oxford 1983; and *Maps, Genealogies, Lists,* vol. 9, Oxford 1984; ed. and contributor, *Nationality and the Pursuit of National Independence,* Belfast 1978. Final work: *Davitt and Irish Revolution 1846-82,* Oxford 1982, paperback ed. 1984.

MOORE, Brian, b. Belfast 1921. Ed. locally. Served with British Ministry of War Transport as a civilian employee 1943-46. Was in Warsaw with UNRRA mission 1946-47. Freelance reporter in Western Europe 1947-48. Emigrated to Canada and worked in a construction camp in northern Ontario before returning to journalism in Montreal. Wrote best seller *Judith Hearne,* 1955, widely praised, and has followed it with further successes, both critical and popular: *The Feast of Lupercal,* 1957; *The Luck of Ginger Coffey,* 1960 (made into a film); and *An Answer from Limbo,* 1962. Won Guggenheim Fellowships in 1959 and 1961, and the Governor General of Canada's Literary Award for 1960. Other novels: *The Emperor of Ice-Cream,* 1965; *I Am Mary Dunne,* 1968; *Fergus,* 1970; *The Revolution Script,* 1972; *Catholics,* 1972 (W. H. Smith Literary Award 1973); *The Great Victorian Collection,* 1975; *The Doctor's Wife,* 1976; *The Mangan Inheritance,* 1979; *The Temptation of Eileen Hughes,* 1981; *Cold Heaven,* 1983; and *Black Robe,* 1985.

MOORE, Francis Frankfort, b. Belfast 1850, d. 1931. Ed. locally. Journalist, wrote novels, plays, poetry. *Flying from Shadows* (verse), 1871. His play *The Queen's Rooms* was a success in London 1891.

MOORE, George Augustus, b. Co. Mayo 1852, d. 1933. His father was a wealthy landowner with a racing stable, who died when Moore was 18. Already in revolt against his family traditions and obligations, Moore went to Paris, trying to become an artist. Returned to Mayo 1879, and moved restlessly between his estate and London. His first novel *A Modern Lover,*

1883, was in the French 'realist' style of Zola, but is generally thought a failure. His second, *A Mummer's Wife*, 1885, shocked Victorian London and made Moore's reputation as a serious writer. In his next books such as the novel, *A Drama in Muslin*, 1887 (rewritten as *Muslin*, 1915), he showed a development of technique rather than of content, but *Esther Waters*, 1894, regarded by many as his greatest book, was an advance in both. For its background he drew on his knowledge of the racing world.

Memoirs of My Dead Life, 1906, and *Hail and Farewell* (trilogy), 1911-14, established him as a Great Author, and for many tastes he lived the role too consciously. In the early 1900s he had returned to Dublin to help Yeats and Lady Gregory establish the Abbey Theatre, but the collaboration led to bitter misunderstandings. However the return to Ireland rekindled his interest in his own country as a source of material, for example *The Untilled Field*, 1903 (translated into Irish by Padraic O'Sullivan as *As an tUr gort, Scéalta*, Dublin 1902); a short novel, *The Lake*, 1905, repub. 1981, and *A Storyteller's Holiday*, 1918. Some of his Irish short stories are as penetrating and genuine as any by the acknowledged great Irish short-story writers. Yet for a variety of reasons Moore has never been popular in Ireland. *In Minor Keys*, his uncollected stories, appeared in 1985.

His later books, after *Avowals*, 1919, began to take on a glassy smoothness of style that became a trade mark. It had already shown itself in *The Brook Kerith*, 1916, which seems to point backwards to the 1890s, rather than forward. Although Moore lived until 1933, still writing (*Aphrodite in Aulis*, 1930), he seemed even then an historical figure rather than a contemporary writer.

MOORE, Thomas, b. Dublin, 1779, d. 1852. Like Mangan, the son of a grocer. Ed. TCD and Middle Temple. His translation of Anacreon, 1800, dedicated to the Prince Regent, won instant success; followed by *The Poetical Work of the late Thomas Little*, 1801. In 1803 appointed Registrar of Admiralty Court in Bermuda, and travelled out to appoint a resident deputy. Visited the US and Canada on the way home. *Epistles, Odes and Other Poems*, 1806, was bitterly attacked in the *Edinburgh Review*. As a result he fought a duel with the reviewer, but some music lover avoided loading the pistols and no one was killed. Began publishing the series *Irish Melodies* in 1808 and found himself both rich and famous almost overnight. His royalties on the *Melodies* have been estimated at £15,000, which by the day's values must be reckoned a large fortune. In spite of this, and the almost equal success of his Oriental, Byronic poem, *Lalla Rookh*, 1817, he was virtually bankrupt by 1819. He blamed his Bermuda deputy for his troubles, the latter being a swindler certainly. But the total embezzlement in Bermuda came only to £6000, and Moore was finally held responsible for only £1000. In 1819 he fled to the Continent with his wife; travelled in Italy, meeting Byron, and in France, where he stayed until 1822. He then returned to his wife's home in Wiltshire and spent the rest of his life there. He continued to bring out the *Irish Melodies*, wrote lives of Byron (whose memoirs he destroyed for obscure reasons), Sheridan, Lord Edward Fitzgerald, and wrote several other books: *The Memoirs of Captain Rock,* 1824, and *The Epicurean,* 1827. In 1835 he was granted a pension of £300 a year, and lived on until 1852, suffering for many years from a mental illness.

In Ireland his reputation is almost that of 'the' national poet, an Irish equivalent to Burns, among the plainer sorts of reader. Intellectuals and Nationalists have tended to see him differently, as a stage-Irish warbler who debased Irish airs and covered them in sugar for the futile delight of London society; a versifier who sold his birthright for a dish of tea; a social climber of the nastiest sort who helped to distort the English view of Ireland. But this is to shoot a canary with a cannon.

MORAN, Michael, b. Dublin 1794, d. Dublin 1846. Blind almost from birth. Grew up in the neighbourhood of 'the Coombe' on Dublin's south side, singing in the streets for pennies. Adopted the name of 'Zozimus' under which he composed a large number of street ballads, many of them surviving in Dublin to the present day, such as 'Whiskey and Water'. He was also know as 'The last Gleeman', and for years was a well known figure and 'character' in the city.

MORGAN, Lady (Sydney Owenson), b. *c.* 1775 supposedly at sea, d. 1859. Her father was Robert Owenson, formerly MacOwen, the actor manager. He sent her to the Huguenot school, Clontarf, but losing his money was forced to become a strolling actor, while Sydney became a governess. She had learned Gaelic songs and dances from Gaelic-speaking cousins in Connacht, and found that the Ascendancy families she now worked for were fascinated by them. In 1805 Alicia Lefanu helped her publish *Twelve Original Hibernian Melodies in London.* She had already published a novel in 1803, *St Clair: or, the Heiress of Desmond.* In the year of the *Melodies* she published another, *The Novice of St Dominick,* and began to have a reputation.

In 1806 she became famous, with *The Wild Irish Girl.* It contained everything which polite England wished to hear about Ireland; a beautiful, windswept heroine playing a harp on the ruined battlements of a romantic castle; a dispossessed Gaelic nobleman, and an even more noble Englishman. The thing is ridiculous, but powerfully ridiculous, and had the same effect that *Ossian* had had for an earlier generation. Sydney 'Glorvina' Owenson became the social rage.

In 1809 she was taken up by the Marquess and Marchioness of Abercorn, who for peculiar reasons bullied her into marrying their doctor, Charles Morgan, the marquess knighting him for a wedding present.

Lady Morgan set up her salon in Kildare St and for a time was a centre for Dublin's political and literary life. *O'Donnel,* 1814, is the first novel to have an Irish Catholic hero, and gained her the vicious enmity of John Wilson Croker. *Florence Macarthy,* 1819, is a far better book than any of her previous novels and has a serious intention; it has some similarity to

Faulkner's purpose in his novels of the Deep South. Her Crawleys are equivalent to his carpet-bagging Snopeses. In 1827 she published her best novel, The O'Briens and the O'Flahertys, with its beautifully observed analysis of the layers of old and new gentry in Connacht, from the vanished Gaelic O'Flahertys to the dreadful Hunkses. The book is also valuable for the character of Fitzwalter, based on that of Lord Edward Fitzgerald.

In 1815 she was in France and published her impressions, France, 1817. This was savagely reviewed but eagerly read, going through four editions in two years.

She published Italy, 1821, which was again attacked by critics, but Byron found it 'fearless and excellent'. In Italy it was banned by the Pope, the King of Sardinia and Piedmont, and the Emperor of Austria, but it was widely read in England, and translated into French. (A second volume of France appeared 1830.)

In 1837 Melbourne granted her a pension and she left Dublin for London, hoping for a larger stage. But her great days were past, and she died long after her fame. Her other books include a Life of Salvator Rosa; Absenteeism, 1825; Passages from my Autobiography, 1859; her memoirs and diaries were edited by W. Hepworth Dixon as Lady Morgan's Memoirs: Autobiography, Diaries, and Correspondence, 1862.

MORIARTY, Christopher, b. Dublin 1936. Ed. TCD. Biologist in Irish civil service. Published Guide to Irish Birds, Cork 1967; A Natural History of Ireland, Cork, 1976; Eels, 1978.

MORRIS, William O'Connor, b. 1824, d. 1904. Ed. Oxford. Bar. Professor of Law at King's Inns 1862. County Court Judge in Louth 1872. Wrote a great deal; his best-known book is the fictional reconstruction of the events leading to the Treaty of Limerick, and all that followed, told through the Memoirs of Gerald O'Connor (1671-1748).

MORROW, John, b. Belfast 1930. Community Arts Officer, Arts Council of Northern Ireland. Novels: The Confessions of Proinsias O'Toole, 1977; The Essex Factor, 1981. Short stories: Northern Myths, 1979; all pub. Belfast.

MOULD, Daphne D.C. Pochin, b. England 1920. Ed. Edinburgh University. Ireland's first woman flying instructor. Many books on Irish history and travel in Ireland. Among them Ireland of the Saints, 1953; Irish Pilgrimage, Dublin 1955; The Irish Saints, Dublin 1964; The Aran Islands, Newton Abbot 1972; The Monasteries of Ireland, 1976; Valentia: Portrait of an Island, Dublin 1978; Discovering Cork, Cork 1985.

MOYLAN, Thomas King, b. 1885, d. 1958. Became chief clerk to Grangegorman Mental Hospital near Dublin. Wrote a number of highly popular comedies which remained favourites with amateur companies for half a century; Paid In His Own Coin; Tactics; Naboclish; Uncle Pat, Dublin 1913; The Curse of the Country, 1917; Movies and Oh Lawsy me,

MURPHY

1918; *A Damsel from Dublin*, 1945.

MULDOON, Paul, b. Co. Armagh 1951. Ed. QUB. Now radio producer, Belfast. Poetry: *New Weather*, 1973; *Mules*, 1975; *Why Brownlee Left*, Dublin and London 1980; *Quoof*, 1983; *The Wishbone*, Dublin 1984.

MULKERNS, Val, b. Dublin 1925. Ed. Dominican College Dublin. Civil servant 1945-49; assistant editor *The Bell* 1952-54. Short stories: *Antiquities*, 1978; *A Friend of Don Juan*, 1979; *An Idle Woman*, Swords 1980. Novels: *A Time Outworn*, 1951; *A Peacock Cry*, 1954; *The Summerhouse*, 1984; *Very Like a Whale*, 1986.

MULLEN, Barbara, b. 1914, d. London 1979. Daughter of Pat Mullen of the Aran Islands. The family went to America but early in her childhood her father returned to Aran. She was brought up in Boston, until able to rejoin her father in her twenties. Actress in England, famous in the TV series 'Doctor Finlay's Casebook'. *Life is My Adventure*, 1937.

MURDOCH, Jean Iris, b. Dublin 1920. Ed. Somerville College, Oxford. Entered Treasury 1942 as temporary civil servant. Joined UNRRA 1944, and in 1945 began working in Europe for displaced persons. Returned to Oxford as Tutor and Fellow St Anne's College 1948. MIAL; MRIA; Litt.D. TCD 1985. Married critic John Bayley 1956. Has written a series of highly distinguished and successful intellectual novels, which belong naturally and exclusively to English fiction. But in 1965 *The Red and the Green* appeared, a novel dealing with the 1916-23 period in Ireland and the conflicting loyalties of Anglo-Irish families such as her own. Other works include *Under the Net*, 1954; *A Severed Head*, 1961; *An Unofficial Rose*, 1962; *The Italian Girl*, 1964. With J. B. Priestley adapted *A Severed Head* as a play, 1964. *Bruno's Dream*, 1969; *The Black Prince*, 1973; *A Word Child*, 1975; *The Sea, the Sea*, 1978 (won Booker Prize); *Nuns and Soldiers*, 1980; *The Philosopher's Pupil*, 1983; *The Good Apprentice*, 1985. Plays include *The Servants and the Snow*, 1970; *The Three Arrows*, 1973. Poetry: *Year of Birds*, illustrated Raymond Stone, 1984.

MURPHY, Arthur, b. Clooniquin, Co. Roscommon 1727, d. London 1805. Ed. St Omer. Worked as a clerk in Cork. Moved to London, became a journalist, and then an actor-playwright. Called to the Bar 1762, and appointed a Commissioner of Bankruptcy 1798. He was a close friend of Dr Johnson and of Garrick and Henry Fielding. A good Classical translator of Tacitus and Sallust. Tragedies include *The Orphan of China*, 1759; *Zenobia*, 1768 etc. but his reputation rests on his comedies, such as *The Apprentice*, 1756; *The Way to Keep Him*, 1760; *The Grecian Daughter*, 1772; and *Know Your Own Mind*, 1778. These were extremely popular and constantly revived for many years and even modern critics have set them beside Sheridan as examples of the best in 18th-century humour.

MURPHY, Dervla, b. 1931. Ed. at the Ursuline Convent in Waterford, reached immediate fame with *Full Tilt*, an account of her bicycle journey from Dublin to India. Alternative Book Society Choice. 2nd printing in same year, 1965, paperback, translations. *Tibetan Foothold*, 1966, tells of her experiences in a refugee camp in India. *The Waiting Land*, 1967, is about Nepal. Has since written *In Ethiopia with a Mule*, 1968; *On a Shoestring to Coorg: an Experience of South India*, 1976; *Where the Indus is Young: a Winter in Baltistan*, 1977; *A Place Apart*, 1978, about Northern Ireland, awarded the second Christopher Ewart-Biggs Memorial Prize. *Wheels within Wheels*, 1979, is the story of her childhood. *Race to the Finish*, 1982, concerns the threat to mankind posed by the arms industry; *Eight Feet in the Andes*, 1983; *Changing the Problem: Post-Forum Reflections*, Mullingar 1984, addresses the political future of Northern Ireland.

MURPHY, Gerard, b. Co. Monaghan 1900, d. 1959. Professor of the History of Celtic Literature, UCD, 1938-59. *Tales from Ireland*, Dublin 1947; *Ossianic Lore and Romantic Tales of Medieval Ireland*, Dublin 1955; *Saga and Myth in Ancient Ireland*, Dublin 1955; *Early Irish Lyrics*, ed. and trans., Oxford 1956; *Early Irish Metrics* (with vocabulary), Dublin 1961. Also translated parts II and III of *The Book of the Lays of Finn* for ITS, 1953.

MURPHY, James, b. Co. Carlow 1839, d. Dublin, 1921. Teacher and later Professor of Mathematics in Catholic University, Dublin. Wrote a number of novels based on episodes in Irish history, all published in Dublin: *The Forge of Clohogue*, 1885; *The Shan Van Vocht; Hugh Roach the Ribbonman*, 1887, etc.

MURPHY, Michael J., b. Liverpool 1913 of South Armagh parents. Brought back to South Armagh 1922. Ed. Dromintee National School, left school aged 14 to work for local farmers. Began freelancing and broadcasting for BBC and Radio Eireann. Joined Irish Folklore Commission 1942, now on staff of Dept. of Irish Folklore UCD. Has collected folk tales and traditions (over 100 volumes) throughout Old Ulster. Publications include *At Slieve Gullion's Foot*, Dundalk 1941; *Mountain Year*, Dublin 1964; *Tyrone Folkquest*, Belfast 1973; *Now You're Talking* (folktales), Belfast 1975; *Mountainy Crack* (story of a Slieve Gullion family), Belfast, 1976. Plays: *The Hard Man*, Dublin 1949; *Culprit of the Shadows*, 1951; *Dust Under Our Feet*, Belfast 1953; *Men on the Wall*, Belfast 1956.

MURPHY, Richard, b. Co. Mayo 1927. Part of childhood in Ceylon. Demy scholar, Magdalen College Oxford, 1948. Also at Sorbonne. Director of English School Canea, Crete, 1953-54. Lived for several years in Connemara, where he restored two Galway hookers, using them in the summer to bring tourists to Inishbofin. Lectures in England and America on poetry. Most of his own poetry deals with the sea. Won AE Memorial Prize 1951, Guinness Poetry Prize 1962. *Archaeology of Love*, Dublin 1955; *Sailing to an Island*, 1963 (Poetry Book Society Choice Spring 1963, repub. US 1964); *Penguin Modern Poets, 7*, 1966; *The Battle of Aughrim*, London and NY, 1968; *High Island*, London and NY, 1975; *Selected Poems*, 1979.

MURRAY

The Price of Stone, 1983, is a sonnet sequence, repub. with additions 1985.

MURPHY, Seamus, b. Mallow 1910, d. Cork 1975. Studied in School of Art, Cork, and in France. Sculptor and author of much praised autobiography, *Stone Mad,* 1950, republished 1966, with additional material.

MURPHY, Thomas, b. Co. Galway 1936. Ed. CBS Tuam and Dublin. Vocational School teacher 1957-62, when he became full-time playwright. Has written several plays for BBC TV, and for the stage, including *The Fly Sham, The Fooleen,* and *Morning After Optimism.* But his reputation rests on one play, *Whistle in the Dark,* 1961, which had a sensational impact in Dublin and England, and was later filmed. It deals with the raw violence of immigrant Irishmen in Coventry, and impressed most critics as the best Irish play for many years. Since then has written *A Crucial Week in the Life of a Grocer's Assistant* (revision of *The Fooleen*), 1969; *The White House,* 1973; *On the Outside* and *On the Inside,* two one-act plays, 1974; *The Vicar of Wakefield,* adaptation, 1974; *The Sanctuary Lamp,* 1975; *The Blue Macushla,* 1980; *The Informer,* adaptation, 1981; *The Gigli Concert,* 1983 (Harveys Award 1984); all Dublin.

MURRAY, John Fisher, b. Belfast 1811, d. Dublin 1865. Son of Dr Murray, discoverer of Fluid Magnesia. Ed. Belfast and TCD, taking MD. Contributed to *Blackwood's Magazine* and many Dublin journals. A Young Irelander, chivalrous, witty. Defended Lady Flora Hastings against her slanderers. His best works are *The Irish Oyster Eater* first published in *Blackwood's,* 1840, and *The Viceroy,* 1841, a satirical novel about Dublin society.

MURRAY, Patrick Joseph, b. Athlone 1937. Ed. locally and UCG. Taught English Athlone 1960-71, Maynooth 1971–. *Milton – the Modern Phase,* 1967, re-establishes Milton against the criticisms of Pound and Eliot; *The Shakespearean Scene,* 1969; *The Tragic Comedian: A Study of Samuel Beckett,* Cork 1970; *Maria Edgeworth: A Study of the Novelist,* Cork 1971.

MURRAY, T. C. (Thomas), b. Macroom 1873, d. 1959. Became a teacher, and eventually Headmaster of the Inchicore Model Schools, Dublin. Was encouraged by Daniel Corkery to write plays, and submitted a comedy *Wheel of Fortune* to a Cork dramatic society. It was acted in 1909, and the following year he offered a much more powerful play, *Birthright,* to the Abbey. For the remainder of his long writing life he was regarded as one of the leading Abbey playwrights. *Maurice Harte,* 1912, was one of the plays chosen by the Abbey for their London tour. *Sovereign Love,* 1913, *The Briery Gap* and *Spring, Aftermath,* 1922, all showed an increase in power, culminating in *Autumn Fire,* 1924, accepted as his masterpiece. In it a headstrong widower marries a young wife, becomes a cripple through attempting to show himself still young, and sees her fall in love with his son. There are echoes of Ibsen in the situation and the power of the play. His later plays seem to most critics less powerful: *The Pipe in the Fields;*

173

Michaelmas Eve; Illuminations, etc.

MURRAY, William Cotter, b. Co. Clare 1929. Went to US 1949. Served in US Army, afterwards worked at various jobs including teaching. Obtained B.Sc. and Ph.D. While teaching began to write *Michael Joe,* a novel of Irish life, first pub. US 1965, winner of Meredith-Iowa Writers' Award valued at $15,000. Repub. England and Ireland, 1965.

MUSGRAVE, Richard B, b. Dungarvan *c.* 1757, d. Dublin 1818. Interesting for his *Letter on the Present Situation of Public Affairs,* 1795, which gave warning of the approaching rebellion of 1798. Also wrote *Memoir of the Different Rebellions in Ireland,* 1801, which ran through 3 editions 1801-2.

N

NALLY, Thomas Henry, b. Mayo *c.* 1869, d. 1932. Had a varied career including service on the first Free State government's Agricultural Commission. In 1916 his play *The Spancel of Death* was accepted by the Abbey and due for its first performance the day after Easter Monday. The performance was cancelled because of the Rising, and when theatres opened again the directors decided not to produce the play at all. The following year Nally's pantomine, *Finn Varra Maa,* was produced in Dublin, and heavily criticised in 'loyalist' circles for its subversive Irish patriotism. This was apparently the first occasion on which a truly Irish legend was made the basis of a pantomime, a practice later commonplace with the Abbey.

In 1924 Nally submitted *The Spancel of Death* for the Tailteann Games literary competition in which it received 'honourable mention'. See REDDIN, Kenneth, for winning play. The play was never subsequently produced or printed, and remains almost the only play in literary history to be renowned for not being performed. It deals with witchcraft and kindred superstitions in a West of Ireland setting. *The Spancel* was a strip of human flesh, used as a death token in the same way that English and Scottish covens used a garter or lace. Nally appears to have been well-informed about the folklore of the subject.

NARY, Cornelius, b. Co. Kildare 1660, d. Dublin 1728. Ordained 1682 in Paris, taught in Irish College there until 1696, when he moved to London to become tutor to Earl of Antrim. In 1702 was imprisoned in Dublin for an infraction of the Penal Laws against Catholics, being then the parish priest of St Michan's. On his release began publishing devotional works for Irish Catholics and, of more permanent interest, *A Brief History of St Patrick's Purgatory,* Dublin 1718, and *The Case of the Catholics in Ireland,* Dublin 1724.

NAUGHTON, Bill, b. Co. Mayo 1910, raised Lancashire, England. Ed. locally. Civil defence driver Second World War. Worked as lorry driver, weaver, coal bagger. Novels: *Rafe Granite,* 1947; *One Small Boy,* 1957; *Alfie,* 1966; *Alfie Darling,* 1970. Short stories: *Late Night in Watling Street and Other Stories,* 1959; *The Goalkeeper's Revenge and Spit Nolan,* 1974; *Bees Have Stopped Working and Other Stories,* 1976. Plays: *Spring and Port Wine,* Birmingham 1964; *June Evening,* Birmingham 1966; *Alfie,* London 1963; *All in Good Time,* London 1963; *He Was Gone When We Got There* (music by Leonard Salzedo), London 1966; *Annie and Fanny,* Bolton 1967; and *Lighthearted Intercourse,* Bolton 1971. Many award-winning plays written for TV and radio. He won Screenwriters' Guild Awards and Prix Italia.

NEARY, Bernard, b. Dublin 1950. Ed. CBS Cabra. Civil servant in the Dept of Fisheries. *A History of Cabra and Phibsboro,* 1983; *North of the Liffey* (sketches of well-known Dublin characters), 1984; *The Life and Times of Jim Branigan: 'Lugs',* 1985; all pub. Dublin.

NEESON, Eoin, b. Cork 1927. Ed. CBS Cork, Dominican College Kildare. Air Army Corps 1944-46. Provincial editor/journalist 1950s. RTE 1961-68. Civil servant with Dept of Forestry and Wildlife 1972. Director Government Information Bureau 1968. Two novels under pseud. 'Desmond O'Neill': *Life Has No Price,* 1960, repub. NY 1960; *Red Diamonds,* 1968. A number of plays for radio and TV: *The Face of Treason* (in collaboration), Dublin 1965. Volumes on Irish folklore and history: *The Civil War in Ireland, 1921-23,* 1966; *Book of Irish Myths and Legends,* 2 vols, 1965-66; *The Book of Irish Saints,* 1967; *The Life and Death of Michael Collins,* 1968; all pub. Cork. Under pseud. 'Donal O'Neill', is embarking upon ambitious series of Irish historical novels, 'March of a Nation'.

NEVIN, May, b. Dublin, d. 1980. Prolific writer of short stories for Catholic journals in US and Ireland. Novels: *The Girls of Sunnyside,* Dublin, repub. NY 1935; *Over the Hills,* Dublin 1935.

NÍ CHUILLEANAIN, Eilean, b. Cork 1942, daughter of Eilis Dillon. Ed. Cork, Oxford. Lecturer in Renaissance English TCD 1966–. Poetry: *Acts and Monuments,* 1973; *Site of Ambush,* 1975; *Second Voyage,* North Carolina, 1977; *Cork,* 1977; *The Rose Geranium,* 1981; all pub. Dublin. Ed. *Irish Women: Image and Achievement.* Dublin 1985. Joint-ed. of *Cyphers,* a Dublin literary magazine.

NOLAN, Christopher, b. Mullingar 1965. Due to accident at birth was severely brain damaged and physically crippled, but with mother's help learned to type with stick attached to forehead. *Damburst of Dreams,* 1981, a collection of poetry and short stories, has been highly praised by critics.

NOLAN, William, b. Co. Tipperary 1946. Ed. UCD. Assistant lecturer Geography UCG 1971. Ph.D. NUI 1975. Lecturer in Geography Carysfort

College, Co. Dublin. President of Geographical Society of Ireland 1982-84. Books: *Northwest Clare*, 1973; *Sources for Local Studies*, Dublin 1979, rev. 1982 as *Tracing the Past; Fassadinin: Land, Settlement and Society*, Dublin 1982; ed. with Thomas G. McGrath, *Tipperary: History and Society*, Dublin 1985.

NOLAN, Winefride, b. Wales 1913. Irish parentage. Ed. University of Wales, taught in Scotland. Has written a number of novels, mostly for children, and a book on farming in Wicklow, *Seven Fat Kine*, Dublin 1966, which described a way of life now vanishing. Also *The New Invasion*, 1953, an autobiography, and *The Night of the Wolf*, Dublin 1969.

NOWLAN, Kevin B., b. Dublin 1921. Ed. UCD and Cambridge. Professor of Modern History UCD. Lectured extensively abroad; holder of French and German government awards. Works include *Charles Gavan Duffy and the Repeal Movement*, Dublin 1963; *The Politics of Repeal 1841-50*, London and Toronto, 1965, rep. 1975; with R. Dudley Edwards and Desmond Williams, *Ireland and the Italian Risorgimento*, Dublin 1960; ed. with T. D. Williams, *Ireland in the War Years and after, 1939-51*, Dublin 1969; ed. *The Making of 1916: Studies in the History of the Rising*, Dublin 1969; ed. *Travel and Transport in Ireland*, Dublin 1973; ed. *The Materialistic Messiah*, Cork 1984; ed. with Maurice R. O'Connell, *Daniel O'Connell: Portrait of a Radical*, Belfast 1984.

NORTON, Caroline, the Honourable, b. 1807, d. 1877. Grand-daughter of Richard Brinsley Sheridan, sister of Lady Dufferin. Married a wastrel in 1829 and supported him until his death in 1869, mainly by writing novels. These were very popular, particularly *The Lady of La Guraye*, 1862. Also published verse, and some short stories, *Tales and Sketches*, 1850, etc.

O

O'BEIRNE, Michael, b. Dublin 1910. Assistant ed. *Woman's Life*, 1936. *People People Marry, People People Don't*, Dublin 1976, describes the setting up of a marriage bureau in Dublin. *Mister* (autobiography), Belfast 1979; *And the Moon at Night* (a sequel), Belfast 1981.

O'BRIEN, Charlotte Grace, b. Cahirmoyle 1845, d. 1909. Daughter of Smith O'Brien. Spent much of her childhood abroad with her father. As a young woman accompanied emigrants on 'coffin ships' to America and urged better conditions and better organised emigration schemes. Took active share in politics and in foundation and promotion of Gaelic League. Became a Catholic. Wrote novels, *Light and Shade*, 1878, etc; a play, *A Tale of Venice*, 1881; and poetry, *Lyrics*, 1887.

O'BRIEN

O'BRIEN, Conor Cruise, b. 1917. Ed. Dublin, TCD. MRIA. Joined Dept External Affairs 1944; Counsellor, Paris Embassy, 1955-56; member Irish delegation at UN 1955-60. Assistant Secretary Dept External Affairs 1960, chosen by Dag Hamarskjold as UN representative in Katanga 1961, at height of Congo crisis. Involved in fighting with the Tshombe forces, and in December 1961 resigned from UN and Irish civil service. Published his account of this episode in *To Katanga and Back,* 1962. Became Vice-Chancellor Ghana University under Nkrumah 1962-65, then became Albert Schweitzer Professor of Humanities, New York University. Irish Minister Posts and Telegraphs 1973-77, and Editor-in-Chief, *The Observer,* 1977-80. *Neighbours,* Ewart Biggs Memorial Lectures, 1980. Teaching in US 1980-85.

First achieved notice with *Maria Cross,* a collection of essays on Catholic writers, 1953, under the pseud. 'Donat O'Donnell'; repub. 1962 under his own name. Wrote *Parnell and His Party,* Oxford 1957; *Writers and Politics,* 1965. Also edited *The Shaping of Modern Ireland, 1960,* and published his Montague Burton Lectures: *Conflicting Concepts of the United Nations,* Leeds 1964; *Collected Essays,* 1966; *Camus* (critical essay), 1970; *States of Ireland,* 1972; *Herod: Reflections on Political Violence,* 1978; a play, *Murderous Angels,* 1969; with Maire Cruise O'Brien, *A Concise History of Ireland,* 1972; *The Siege, a Study of Zionism and Israel,* 1985.

O'BRIEN, Dillon, b. Co. Roscommon 1817, d. 1882. Ed. Tullabeg. Emigrated to US and settled in St Paul, Minn. Wrote verse and some popular novels, interesting as representatives of Irish-American literature, describing the Irish communities in America just after the great immigrations of the Famine years. His books include *The Dalys of Dalystown,* St Paul 1866; *Frank Blake,* St Paul 1876.

O'BRIEN, Edna, b. Co. Clare 1932. Brought up on a farm, educated at local National School and at Convent of Mercy, Loughrea. Studied pharmacy in Dublin. Moved to England 1958, published her first novel, *The Country Girls,* 1960. This was an immediate success in England, as was *The Lonely Girl,* 1962, filmed as *The Girl with Green Eyes; Girls in their Married Bliss,* 1964; *August is a Wicked Month,* 1965; *Casualties of Peace,* 1966; *The Love Object* (short stories), 1968; *A Pagan Place,* 1970; *Night,* 1972; *A Scandalous Woman and Other Stories,* 1974; *Mother Ireland,* 1976; *Johnny I Hardly Knew You,* 1977; *Mrs Reinhardt and Other Stories,* 1978; *Returning,* 1982; *A Fanatic Heart* (selected stories), 1985. Has written for cinema, *Zee & Co,* 1971; and the theatre, *The Gathering,* 1974; *Virginia,* 1981.

O'BRIEN, Fitzjames, b. Limerick 1828, d. 1862. Ed. TCD. Wrote verse for Irish magazines and went to London as a journalist, where he quickly ran through a large inheritance. Emigrated to America and wrote short stories for *Scribner's, Harper's* and the *Atlantic Monthly.* His play *A Gentleman from Ireland* was very well received. Volunteered for the northern

177

army in the Civil War and died in it from a wound. His short stories were collected and published as *The Diamond Lens and Other Stories*, Boston and London. Also *The Poems and Stories of F. O'B.*, Boston 1881.

O'BRIEN, Flann, the novel and playwrighting name of Brian Ó Nuallain, b. Strabane 1912, d. Dublin 1966. A civil servant for many years, and satirical columnist for the *Irish Times* under the pseud. 'Myles na Gopaleen'. His first novel *At Swim-Two-Birds*, 1939, repub. 1960, was recognised by a small circle, including William Saroyan, as a masterpiece in the tradition of *Ulysses*, and has been regarded as the only true successor to that book. In a dazzling cascade of wit, scholarship and prose-poetry it follows the picaresque adventures of a number of human and mythological characters through an enchanted Ireland. A play, *Faustus Kelly*, was produced at the Abbey 1943, but for many years after the best of his writing went into his daily newspaper column, castigating stupidity and pomposity, bad Irish and bad manners, and sporadically chronicling the adventures of Keats and Chapman, dissolute poet companions. In 1961 *The Hard Life* appeared, in 1965 *The Dalkey Archive* (dramatised by Hugh Leonard that year for the Dublin Theatre Festival as *The Saints Go Cycling In*) and in 1967 *The Third Policeman*. Widely revered as 'The Sage of Santry', he lived near Dublin. *The Poor Mouth (An Bheal Bhocht)* appeared 1973 (for this and other work in Irish see Part 2) among many posthumously published writings, from *The Best of Myles*, 1968, to *Myles Away from Dublin*, 1985.

O'BRIEN, George, b. Dublin 1892, d. 1973. Ed. UCD. Professor of Economics UCD 1926-61; member of many government committees. *Labour Organisation,* 1921; *An Essay on the Economic Effects of the Reformation*, 1923; *Agricultural Economics,* 1929; *The Four Green Fields,* Dublin and Cork, 1936; and *The Phantom of Plenty,* Dublin 1948. His best-known work is *The Economic History of Ireland*, 3 vols, London and Dublin, 1918-21.

O'BRIEN, Henry, b. Co. Kerry 1808, d. Middlesex 1835. Ed. TCD. Remarkable only as an example of the extravagances of Irish archaeology in the early 19th century, *The Round Towers of Ireland*, 1834, attempted to show that they were Buddhistic remains. Petrie condemned him at the time.

O'BRIEN, James J., b. New Ross 1792, d. London 1874. Ed. TCD. Bishop of Ossory, Ferns and Leighlin 1842. Wrote and preached against the Oxford Movement, and against the disestablishment of the Church of Ireland. When it was disestablished he was one of its main reorganisers. His *Attempt to explain the Doctrine of Justification,* 1833, went into 5 editions. *The Irish Education Question,* 1855; *The Case of the Established Church in Ireland,* 1867; and *The Disestablishment and Disendowment of the Irish branch of the United Church,* 1869, are his other main works.

O'BRIEN, Kate b. 1897, Limerick, d. 1974. Ed. locally and UCD. Journalist and translator for several years, deeply interested in Spain and Spanish literature and history. Her first work was a play, *Distinguished Villa*, 1926, which ran for three months in London. Her book *Without My Cloak*, 1931, won the Hawthornden Prize and established her as an important new name in Irish fiction. Other plays include *The Bridge*, 1927. Books include *The Ante-Room*, 1934, rep. Dublin 1981; *Mary Lavelle*, 1936; *The Schoolroom Window*, 1937; *Pray for the Wanderer*, 1938; *The Land of Spices*, 1941, rep. Dublin 1982; *The Last of Summer*, 1943; and *That Lady*, 1946, which for general readers is her best-known book. An historical novel set in Spain, it tells the tragic love story of King Philip's mistress, referred to by royal command, after her fall from favour, and hideous imprisonment, as 'that lady'. *The Flower of May*, 1953; *As Music and Splendour*, 1958; and *Presentation Parlour*, 1963, are among her later novels. Travel books and biography: *Farewell Spain*, 1937; *English Diaries & Journals*, 1943; *Teresa of Avila*, 1951; *My Ireland*, 1962.

O'BRIEN, Kate Cruise, b. Dublin 1948, daughter of Conor Cruise O'B. Ed. TCD. Hennessy Award 1971. *A Gift Horse and Other Stories*, Swords 1978.

O'BRIEN, Margaret, b. Cork 1908. Ed. Cork and Vienna, 1927-32. Returned to Cork, published *A Modern Wonder Worker*, Monaghan 1944, Dublin 1946, a life of Sister Maria Fortunata Viti. *As the Crow Flies*, 1967, is an autobiographical novel.

O'BRIEN, Richard Baptist, b. Carrick-on-Suir 1809, d. 1885. Priest and later Dean of Limerick. Wrote serval novels of which the most famous is *Jack Hazlitt*. Other include *Ailey Moore* and *The D'Altons of Crag*.

O'BRIEN, William, b. *c.* 1740 of the Inchiquin family, d. Dorsetshire *c.* 1815. Ran away to London where he became an actor and writer of farces. His wit and acting charmed the daughter of the Earl of Ilchester into marriage. Made respectable by his wife he became Receiver-General of Dorsetshire, and died there in high esteem. His plays include *Cross Purposes*, 1772, and *The Duel*, 1773, and his songs and essays were published as *O'Brien's Lusorium*, 1782, and often reprinted. Some of his humorous writing, in spite of or because of his aristocratic connections, was strong meat even for the 18th century, and so shocked my 19th-century predecessor O'Donoghue that he piously hoped that an Earl's son-in-law had not truly written it.

O'BRIEN, William, b. Mallow 1852, d. 1928. Journalist and later MP for Mallow and then Cork. Wrote verse and novels, his *When We Were Boys*, 1890, being regarded as the best of his books.

O'BRIEN, William Smith, b. Co. Clare 1803, d. Armagh 1864. Son of Sir Edward O'B., began his political career in the Tory interest, as MP for Ennis, 1828. Swung over to the Whigs and finally, via the Repeal Association, to the Young Irelanders. In 1847 was a founder of the Irish Confederation, and in 1848 took part in the abortive Young Ireland insurrection. Was sentenced to hanging, drawing and quartering for High Treason, one of the last men in Britain to receive such a sentence. Commuted to transportation for life, to Maria Island, Tasmania. Pardoned 1854, he travelled in America and Europe and wrote *Principles of Government*, 2 vols, Dublin 1856.

Ó BROIN, Leon, b. Dublin 1902. Ed. King's Inns. Involved in War of Independence. Bar 1924. Civil servant 1925-67, becoming secretary Dept Posts and Telegraphs 1948-67. MRIA. President Irish Historical Society 1973. Books include *Parnell*, Dublin 1937; *The Unfortunate Mr Robert Emmett*, 1958; *Dublin Castle and the 1916 Rising*, 1966; *The Chief Secretary, Augustine Birrell in Ireland*, 1969; *Fenian Fever*, 1971; *Michael Collins*, Dublin and London 1980; *Frank Duff*, Dublin and London 1982. Also ed. *In Great Haste: The Letters of Michael Collins and Kitty Kiernan*, Dublin and London 1983. For work in Irish see Part 2.

O'BYRNE, Brendan, b. Dublin 1912. Ed. Pearse St Library. Worked as lather boy in barber's shop before writing stories for *Dublin Evening Mail*. To England late 1930s; joined Royal Navy, 25 years at sea; joined London Electricity Board. Freelance journalist; historical adviser for BBC 2's 'Ireland: A Televison History'. First novel, *Wilson Place*, Swords 1985, describes growing up in 1920s Dublin.

O'BYRNE, William Richard, b. Co. Wicklow 1823, d. London 1898. Published a *Naval Biographical Dictionary*, 1849, being in effect a Navy List, giving the service record of every living officer. New editions until 1883, when the Navy's own record-keeping service was modernised, making O'Byrne's work no longer necessary.

O'CALLAGHAN, John Cornelius, b. Dublin 1805, d. Dublin 1883. Ed. Clongowes. Bar 1829. One of O'Connell's most loyal supporters, who with Hogan the sculptor crowned O'Connell at a monster meeting on the Hill of Tara. His miscellaneous writings for *The Nation* etc. pub. as *The Green Book*, Dublin 1840. His *History of the Irish Brigades in the Service of France*, Glasgow 1869, is a standard work. In 1846 he edited Charles O'Kelly's *Macariae Excidium*.

O'CASEY, Sean, b. Dublin 1884 as John Casey, d. Devon 1964. Worked as a labourer; self-educated. Deeply involved in the Labour Movement in Ireland before 1916, as a journalist pamphleteer. Secretary of the Irish Citizen Army under James Connolly. Representative of the Marxist element in the revolution which was later to be defeated by the Nationalist element and wither away into oblivion. This defeat and his disillusion with the results of independence probably played a large part in O'Casey's eventual decision to leave Ireland, quite apart from quarrels with the Abbey Theatre over his play *The Silver Tassie*.

O'Casey had been writing and submitting plays to the Abbey for several years without success before *The Shadow of a Gunman*, 1923. This immediately marked him as the new great voice of Irish theatre. *Juno and the Paycock*, 1924, was not only a tremendous personal success for O'Casey but restored the Abbey to financial and artistic health after years of near bankruptcy. *The Plough and the Stars*, 1926, caused the most dramatic row in Ireland since Synge's *Playboy of the Western World*, partly because it showed the revolutionary flag being taken into a public house.

In 1928 O'Casey submitted *The Silver Tassie* and Lady Gregory, Yeats, and Lennox Robinson all agreed that it was unsuitable for the Abbey and unworthy of O'Casey, being quite different in style to the three realist plays of the previous years. It was poetical-expressionist, particularly in the last act, rather than realist, and dealt with a theme, 'war', rather than human characters and a particular situation. Argument about the rejection still rages. The play has never been successfuly acted, but O'Casey felt that the Abbey should have given him the chance to fail, having lined its pockets with his successes. Already in London, O'Casey decided to stay in England permanently. He wrote many plays thereafter, *Within the Gates*, 1933; *Red Roses for Me*, 1946; *The Drums of Father Ned; The Bishop's Bonfire* etc. but none of them created the impact of his early masterpieces. His subject was Ireland and he was cut off from it. It is possible that had he stayed in Dublin he might have developed differently, but some serious critics consider this unlikely, feeling that he could not have gone on rewriting *Juno* and *The Plough*, and had really nothing else to say. Others regard his later 'poetical' plays as his true masterpieces, and feel they could not have been written without the width of experience and pain that emigration gave him. They see the *Tassie* and *Red Roses* as forerunners of the new experimental English theatre, without which writers like Pinter (trained in Irish repertory) would not have enjoyed the artistic freedom that they do.

As well as plays O'Casey wrote an autobiography, *I Knock at the Door*, 1939; *Pictures in the Hallway*, 1942; *Drums under the Windows*, 1945, describing his childhood in the slums of Dublin's north side, and his formation as a revolutionary and writer while working as a labourer and railway ganger. *Inishfallen, Fare Thee Well*, 1949; *Rose and Crown*, 1952; *Sunset and Evening Star*, 1954, recreate the days of Ireland's independence and Civil War, Abbey Theatre politics, departure for England, America, marriage, friendship, life in Devon during and after the Second World War. Repub. as a 3-vol. set 1963, and frequently since.

O'CLERY, Helen, b. Co. Donegal 1910. Ed. locally and in France. Trained as nurse and physiotherapist. Began writing children's books to occupy her son during a long illness. *Sparks Fly*, 1948; *Spring Show*, 1949; *Swiss Adventure*, 1951; *Rebel Sea Queen*, NY 1965, etc. Has also written on travel, *Pegasus Book of Ireland*, 1967, and books on Egypt. And has compiled anthologies for children, *Queens, Queens, Queens*, 1965, and others.

O'CONNELL, Charles C. Author of several remarkable novels: *Light over*

Fatima, 1947; *The Vanishing Island,* 1957; *The Miracle Maker,* 1960; *The Stubborn Heart,* 1964, all pub. Dublin.

O'CONNOR, Frank, pseud. of Michael O'Donovan, b. Cork 1903, d. 1966. Ed. Christian Brothers. Librarian Cork Co. Library 1925-28; Ballsbridge Dublin 1928-38. Influenced by Daniel Corkery towards a kind of writing rooted in his own background, 'an outward looking provincialism'. His first story collection, *Guests of the Nation,* 1931, sets out the conflict between England and Ireland in terms of a handful of men who but for history and politics would have been friends and instead must kill each other. Powerful and moving, it is in a sense the seminal story of modern Irish literature. Brendan Behan and Joseph O'Conor among others were directly influenced by it.

Two novels, *The Saint and Mary Kate,* 1932, and *Dutch Interior,* 1940, are still read and admired, but never created the impact of his short stories. *Bones of Contention,* 1936; *Crab Apple Jelly,* 1944; *The Common Chord,* 1947; *The Stories of Frank O'Connor,* 1953; *More Stories by Frank O'Connor,* 1954; *Selected Stories,* 1956; *Collection Two,* 1964. For many years O'Connor has been regarded in Ireland and abroad as one of the great masters of short story writing, to be equalled with Chekhov, de Maupassant and only a handful more. His translations of Irish poetry, particularly of *The Midnight Court,* 1945, by Brian Merriman, and of early Irish poetry as in *King, Lords & Commons,* US 1959, London 1961, Dublin 1970, are valuable as translations and as poetry in their own right.

He had two plays produced at the Abbey: *In the Train,* 1937, and *Moses' Rock,* 1938. From 1936-39 was a director of the Abbey. A life of Michael Collins, *The Big Fellow,* 1937; autobiography, *An Only Child,* 1961, and *My Father's Son,* 1968; criticism, *Towards an Appreciation of Literature,* 1945; *The Art of the Theatre,* Dublin 1947; *The Road to Stratford,* 1948; *The Mirror in the Roadway* (on the novel), 1957; *The Lonely Voice* (on the short story), 1963; *The Backward Look* (on Irish Literature), 1967; were some of his other major books. For his writing in Irish see Part 2.

O'CONNOR, John, b. 1913. Short stories published in *The Bell: Come Day-Go Day,* Dublin 1948; *Pattern of People,* 1959.

O'CONNOR, Joseph, author of novels including *The Norwayman,* 1949.

O'CONNOR, Kevin, b. Limerick 1941. Ed. locally. Worked in theatre and in publishing before becoming a producer in Irish radio. Has written *The Irish in Britain,* 1971, and a play *Friends,* Dublin 1976. Also radio documentaries: *The Limerick Soviet,* 1974, dealing with the little-known attempt by Limerick socialists in 1919 to imitate the Russian Revolution, and *A Death in January,* 1984, on the life of Sean Bourke.

O'CONNOR, Michael P., b. Loughrea 1896, d. Dublin 1967. Served with Irish Regiment in France First World War. Qualified in medicine UCD 1925. In Malayan Medical Service 1927-49, being interned by Japanese in

Sarawak 1941-45. Has written a number of novels and short stories based on his experiences and some historical material on the Singapore collapse of 1941 in collaboration with G. P. Willis. Fiction includes *Dreamer Awake*, Dublin 1946, and *Vile Repose*, 1950.

O'CONNOR, Thomas Power, b. Athlone 1848, d. London 1929. Ed. Athlone, Galway, went to London 1870 as journalist. A supporter of Parnell, entered Parliament as MP for Galway 1880. Founded and edited *The Star*, 1887, and the famous *T.P.'s Weekly*, 1902. In 1885 he had stood for Liverpool and represented the Scotland division there for the rest of his life. Made Film Censor 1917, Privy Councillor 1924, he was for many years the 'father' of the House of Commons, being the longest-sitting member. Wrote several biographies, and some parliamentary histories: *Lord Beaconsfield*, 1879; *Gladstone's House of Commons*, 1885; *The Parnell Movement*, 1886; *Memoirs of an Old Parliamentarian*, 1929.

O'CONNOR, Ulick, b. 1929. Ed. Dublin and New Orleans. Bar 1951. Poet, sportman and journalist, was a friend of St John Gogarty and was asked by him to undertake his biography. *Oliver St John Gogarty*, NY and London 1964. Next wrote *Travels with Ulick*, and ed. *The Joyce We Knew*, both Cork 1967; *Brendan Behan*, 1970; *Lifestyles* (poems), 1973; *A Terrible Beauty Is Born* (the troubles in Ireland), 1975; *Irish Tales and Sagas*, 1981; *Celtic Dawn* and *Sport is My Lifeline*, 1984; *Celtic Dawn* was pub. in the US as *All the Olympians: a biographical portrait of the Irish Literary Renaissance*, NY 1984; *A Critic at Large*, Cork 1985. Plays: *The Dream Box*, 1969; *The Dark Lovers* (Dean Swift and Stella), 1974; *Three Noh Plays*, 1981; *Execution*, 1985; all Dublin. Has also written and presented one-man shows on Behan, 1972, and Gogarty, 1975.

O'CONOR, Charles, b. Co. Sligo 1710, d. Belanagare, Co. Roscommon 1791. Gaelic scholar and enthusiast, and friend of Carolan, whose harp he kept in his house after Carolan's death. Published *Dissertations on the Ancient History of Ireland*, 1753.

O'CONOR, Charles, b. Belanagare 1764, d. 1828. Ed. Rome 1779-91; ordained, parish priest Co. Roscommon 1792-98. In 1796 published a memoir of his grandfather, *Memoirs of the Life & Writing of the Late Charles O'Connor*, which is of great interest to historians, showing the first steps taken by Irish Catholics of substance to obtain the constitutional repeal of the Penal Laws. The first ed. was suppressed as dangerous to the family, and the MS of a second vol. was burned by the author. Copies survive of the first vol. in TCD and British Museum. In 1798 became chaplain to Marchioness of Buckingham and librarian to Richard Grenville, later Duke of Buckingham and Chandos, at Stowe, where he assembled his major work, *Rerum Hibernicarium Scriptores*, 4 vols, 1814-28, from his patron's Irish MSS.

Charles' younger brother Matthew, 1773-1844, wrote a *History of Irish Catholics from the Settlement in 1691*, Dublin 1813, which has many faults but is based on documents inherited from his grandfather.

O'CONOR, Joseph, b. Dublin 1916. Went to London 1939. Served in British forces Second World War. Became an actor after the war and has written several plays of which the best-known is *The Iron Harp*, first performed at Bristol Old Vic 1955, winner of Foyle Award 1955, and published in Penguin Plays, 1959.

O'CURRY, Eugene, b. Co. Clare 1796, d. Dublin 1862. Self-educated, joined Ordnance Survey of Ireland 1834. Worked on cataloguing Irish MSS in British Museum, and then on the same task in TCD and the Royal Irish Academy. With his brother-in-law John O'Donovan founded Archaeological Society 1840. His MSS *Materials of Ancient Irish History*, Dublin 1861, is invaluable, as is *Manner and Customs of the Ancient Irish*, 3 vols, 1873, rep. NY 1971. With O'Donovan he was one of the small devoted band of 19th century Irish scholars who laid the foundations not only for the revival of Irish learning but for the revival of Irish pride and nationhood after the disasters of the '98 Rising, the Act of Union and the Famine.

O'DALY, John, b. Co. Waterford 1800, d. Dublin 1878. Ed. hedge school, became teacher of Irish in Wesleyan College, Kilkenny. Moved to Dublin and set up as bookseller, printing and selling many books of great value and interest to the Language Revival. Translated much poetry from the Irish, Mangan versifying the prose translations. *Reliques of Irish Jacobite Poetry*, Dublin 1844 (in this instance Walsh supplying the versification); *The Poets and Poetry of Munster*, Dublin 1849 (Mangan's verses), etc. Also *Key to the Study of Gaelic*, Boston 1899.

O'DONNELL, Donat, see O'BRIEN, Conor Cruise.

O'DONNELL, Joseph, b. Limerick 1934. Writes for stage and TV, also for puppet theatre and plays: *Let the Ravens Feed*, Dublin 1968; *The Lads*, Belfast 1972; *No-one*, Dublin 1973; *The Inside Trap*, Limerick 1973; *Cage*, Dublin 1973; *Bonfire*, Dublin 1978; *Zoz*, Dublin 1980; Novel: *Big Push*, Dublin 1982.

O'DONNELL, Peadar, b. Donegal 1893. One of 11 children. Ed. locally and St Patrick's College, Dublin. Became school-teacher in Donegal. In 1916 gave up teaching to become organiser in the Irish Transport and General Workers Union. Spoke against conscription in 1918, and joined IRA. Commanding officer Donegal Brigade 1921. Republican side in Civil War, captured in battle of Four Courts, Dublin, and sentenced to death by the Free State. Went on hunger strike for 41 days, and finally escaped from Harepark Camp in Kildare, 1924. Had begun writing in gaol, and first novel, *Storm*, about the Anglo-Irish war, was pub. 1925. Gaoled in 1927 for part in the Land Annuities agitation. On release went to South of France, and wrote *The Way It Was With Them*. Became involved in European agrarian movement and presided at Berlin over European Peasant Congress 1930. Supported de Valera 1932, broke with him shortly afterwards over social questions. In 1934 left the IRA believing it to have Fascist leanings. Founded Irish Republican Congress. Business manager of *The Bell* from 1940; editor 1946-54. MIAL, currently President.

Wrote one play, *Wrack*, performed at Abbey 1932. Other books include *Adrigoole*, 1928; *The Knife*, 1930; *The Gates Flew Open*, 1934, about his prison experiences; *On The Edge of the Stream*, 1934; *Salud! An Irishman in Spain*, 1937; *The Big Windows*, 1955; as well as his most famous books, *Islanders*, 1928; *There will be Another Day*, Dublin and Oxford, 1963, and *Proud Island*, Dublin 1975. His sympathies were always left wing, and his deepest interest was in the welfare of the peasant farmers and day labourers of the north-west of Ireland, exploited by the old landlords and apparently no better off under the Free State.

O'DONOGHUE, David James, b. London 1866, of Cork parentage, d. Dublin 1917. Came to Dublin in 1896 and set up as a bookseller. Librarian UCD 1909. Chiefly remembered for his *Poets of Ireland*, 1892, enlarged ed. 1912, to which this *Dictionary* owes much. Wrote *The Humour of Ireland*, 1894. Also ed. *Life and Writings of J. C. Mangan*, Edinburgh 1897, and wrote lives of *William Carleton*, 2 vols, 1896, and *Emmet*, Dublin 1903.

O'DONOGHUE, Florence, b. Co. Kerry 1894, d. 1967. Served in 1st Cork Brigade of Irish Republican Army 1917-21. Became Adjutant General 1922. Has written *No Other Law*, 1954; *Tomas MacCurtain*, 1958 and 1971; ed. *Mystery of the Casement Ship*, by Karl Spindler, 1965.

O'DONOGHUE, John, b. Co. Kerry 1900, d. London 1964. Son of a small farmer. Self-educated. Served in Garda Siochana, the new Irish Free State police force, 1924-31. Entered monastery, but left to emigrate to England. Worked as a labourer and in his spare time wrote and rewrote an autobiographical novel, eventually published as *In a Quiet Land*, 1957. Followed by *In a Strange Land*, 1958, and *In Kerry Long Ago*, 1960. The first of the three was particularly successful, in spite of having been rejected by many publishers. It was a Book Society recommendation and republished in the US, as was *In Kerry Long Ago*. He died while working on a fourth book about the life he saw as a guard.

O'DONOVAN, Edmund, b. Dublin 1844, d. Sudan 1883. Studied medicine at TCD but never graduated. Journalist from 1866, served with French Army in Franco-Prussian War, 1870, writing for Irish and English papers on his experiences. In Asia Minor 1876 as reporter for *Daily News* on Russo-Turkish war, and in 1879 travelled to Merv in Central Asia. Taken for a Russian spy he was imprisoned, but escaped after several months, and in 1882 published *The Merv Oasis: Travels and Adventures East of the Caspian 1879-81*, 2 vols, abridged ed. 1883. In that year he went with Hicks Pasha to the Sudan and died there.

O'DONOVAN, Gerald, b. Co. Down 1871, d. Surrey 1942. Catholic priest involved in the disputes over 'Modernism'. Left the priesthood and went to London, where he became a successful businessman and a popular and talented novelist. Books include *Father Ralph*, 1913; *How They Did It*, 1920; *Vocations*, 1921. Largely forgotten, his novels deserve renewed attention, giving an accurate and interesting account of Ireland in late Victorian and Edwardian times, from the vantage point of a priest. His admirers included Frank O'Connor.

O'DONOVAN, Jeremiah (Rossa), b. Rosscarbery 1831, d. New York 1915. He was tried for his share in the Phoenix Conspiracy, but released in 1859, becoming business manager of the *Irish People*, 1863-65. Involved in the main Fenian Conspiracy, he was arrested in 1865 and sentenced to penal servitude for life. Cruelly treated in prison he was amnestied 1871 with other leaders on condition that he left England and Ireland. Went to America and edited the *United Irishman*. Wrote *Prison Life*, NY 1874; *Irish Rebels in English Prisons*, NY 1882; and *Recollections 1838-98*, NY 1898. The return of his body to Ireland and his burial in Glasnevin were national events of much emotional significance, being the occasion for a celebrated funeral oration by Patrick Pearse.

O'DONOVAN, John, b. Co. Kilkenny 1809, d. Dublin 1861. Brought to Dublin 1817 on death of his father and well educated. Worked in Irish Record Office and then with O'Curry under George Petrie in the Ordnance Survey. In the course of his Survey work visited every parish in Ireland to learn the correct Irish place-names. His *Letters* concerning these and other antiquarian questions are an important source of information. Edited in 50 vols, 1924-32, by Fr Michael O'Flanagan. In 1836 he began the analytical catalogue of Irish MSS in TCD, almost the first scientific approach to such matters. With O'Curry founded Archaeological Society 1840. He translated and edited many Irish MSS and collaborated with Todd and O'Curry on *Irish Grammar*, Dublin 1845. His great monument is his fine edition of *The Annals of the Four Masters*, 6 vols, Dublin 1848-57, English and Irish texts on facing pages. One of the landmarks in Irish scholarship and a foundation stone for the Irish Revival. In 1850 he had become Professor of Celtic Studies, Queen's College, Belfast, and in 1852 joined the newly established commission for the translation of the *Senchus Mor*, the ancient laws of Ireland. No dictionary entry of any length could do justice to O'Donovan's importance.

O'DONOVAN, John Purcell, b. Dublin 1921. Ed. Synge St and by reading in. National Library. Worked at various jobs in Dublin and Belfast, including Fire Service, before settling on journalism. Music critic, and acknowledged in England and US as an authority on Bernard Shaw. *Shaw and the Charlatan Genius*, Dublin and Oxford 1966. Stage plays include *The Half Millionaire*, Abbey 1954; *The Less We Are Together*, Abbey 1957 (one of the longest runs in the history of the Abbey), pub. US 1966; *A Change of Mind*, Abbey 1958; *The Shaws of Synge Street*, Abbey 1960,

O'FAOLAIN

pub. US 1966; *Copperfaced Jack,* Abbey 1962, pub. US 1966; *Dearly Beloved Roger,* Abbey 1967. Founder-member of Society of Irish Playwrights; Senior Vice-President Royal Irish Academy of Music. Has also written *Wheels and Deals, People and Place in Irish Motoring,* 1983, and *G. B. Shaw,* Dublin 1983. Recent plays: *Devil's Daughter,* RTE 1981; *Carlotta,* Dublin Theatre Festival 1985; and a series of 11 *Famous Irish Trials,* RTE 1984-85. *Oh God,Oh Dublin,* Dublin and London 1985, is a social account of the city.

O'DONOVAN, Mrs Mary Jane, b. Irwin in Co. Cork 1845. Third wife of O'Donovan Rossa, she published *Irish Lyrical Poems,* NY, 1868.

O'DONOVAN, Michael, see O'CONNOR, Frank.

O'DUFFY, Emar Ultan, b. Dublin 1893, d. Surrey, 1935. Father was dentist to several Viceroys. Ed. Stonyhurst and UCD. Qualified as a dentist but disliked it and never practised. Joined Irish Volunteers but on practical grounds opposed the 1916 Rising. Sent by MacNeill to Belfast to prevent Volunteers from rising there. Went to England in 1925 when he had lost his post in Department of External Affairs and concerned himself with writing rather than with politics. Novels include *The Wasted Island; The Lion and the Fox; The Secret Enemy; Head of a Girl; The Bird Cage; Miss Rudd and Some Lovers.* He also wrote scathing and inventive satire, the *Cuandine Trilogy,* 1926-33: *King Goshawk and the Birds; The Spacious Adventures of the Man in the Street; Asses in Clover;* and a book on economics, *Life and Money,* which went into three editions in as many years.

O'FAOLAIN, Eileen, née Gould, b. Cork. Wife of Sean O'F. Distinguished writer of children's stories: *The Little Black Hen; The King of the Cats; The Children of Crooked Castle; The Fairy Hen; Irish Sagas and Folk-Tales,* 1954, rep. Swords 1983; *High Sang the Sword; Children of the Salmon,* 1965, rep. Swords 1984. Lives Dun Laoghaire.

O'FAOLAIN, Julia, b. London 1932. Daughter of Sean O'F. Ed. UCD, Rome, Sorbonne. Novelist and short-story writer. Novels: *Godded and Codded,* 1970 (as *Three Lovers,* NY 1971); *Women in the Wall,* 1975; *No Country for Young Men,* 1980; *The Obedient Wife,* 1982; *The Irish Signorina,* 1984. Short stories: *We Might See Sights! and Other Stories,* 1968; *Man In the Cellar,* 1974; *Melancholy Baby and Other Stories,* Swords 1978. Ed. with husband Lauro Martines, *Not in God's Image: Women in History from the Greeks to the Victorians,* London and NY 1973; and trans. *A Man of Parts* by Piero Chiara, Boston 1968. As Julia Martines, trans. *Two Memoirs of Renaissance Florence: the Diaries of Buonaccorso Pitti and Gregorio Dati* (ed. Gene Brucker), NY 1967.

O'FAOLAIN, Sean, b. John Whelan, Cork 1900. Ed. Presentation College, UCC and Harvard. Sold books for a year as commercial traveller. Fought with Republicans in Civil War and remained active for several years after.

Ó FARACHÁIN

Left Ireland to study at Harvard. Taught English Boston College 1929 and Strawberry Hill Teachers' Training College 1929-33. Returned to Ireland after marriage. Edited *The Bell* 1940-46. Recognised as another of the new voices in Irish writing with his first short-story collection, *Midsummer Night Madness*, 1932, which earned critical praise and clerical disapproval. Other collections: *A Purse of Coppers*, 1937; *The Finest Stories of Sean O'Faolain*, 1958; *I Remember! I Remember!*, 1961; *The Heat of the Sun*, 1966; *The Talking Trees*, 1971; *Foreign Affairs*, 1976; *Selected Stories*, 1978; and *Collected Stories*, 1980, 1981, 1982.

Four novels: *A Nest of Simple Folk*, 1934; *Bird Alone*, 1936; *Come Back to Erin*, 1940; *And Again?* 1979. A play: *She Had to Do Something*, Abbey 1937. Biographies: *Constance Markievicz*, 1934; *King of the Beggars* (a life of Daniel O'Connell), 1938; *De Valera*, 1939; *The Great O'Neill*, 1942; *Newman's Way*, 1952. Autobiography: *Vive Moi!*, 1964. Travel: *An Irish Journey*, 1940; *A Summer in Italy*, 1949; *South to Sicily*, 1953. Literary criticism: *The Short Story*, 1948; *The Vanishing Hero* (on the novelists of the twenties), 1956. *The Irish*, 1948, is an analysis of the national character.

Ó FARACHÁIN, Roibeárd (originally Riobárd), b. Robert Farren, Dublin 1909, d. Dublin 1984. Of working-class origins. Master's degree in Thomistic philosphy. Distinguished Irish poet and man of letters. MIAL. Co-founder with Austin Clarke of Irish Lyric Theatre 1944. Director of Abbey Theatre 1940-73. Talks Officer for Radio Eireann 1939-43; features editor, deputy-director, then Controller of Programmes 1953-74. Plays include *Assembly at Druim Ceat* and *Lost Light*, both performed Abbey 1943. Poetry in English: *Thronging Feet*, 1936; *Time's Wall Asunder*, 1939; *Rime Gentlemen, Please; Selected Poems;* and, his major work, an epic 4000-line poem on the life of St Colmcille, *The First Exile*, 1944, pub. US as *This Man Was Ireland;* also *Towards an Appreication of Poetry*, 1947, and *The Course of Irish Verse*, 1948; all pub. Dublin. See also Part 2.

O'FARRELL, Padraic, b. Co. Kildare 1932. Ed. Military College Curragh. Lt. Col., O.C. 4th Field Artillery Regiment, Columb Barracks, Mullingar. Fourteen books on aspects of life in Ireland: *Superstitions of the Irish Country People*, 1978; *How the Irish Speak English* and *Who's Who in the Irish War of Independence*, 1980; *The Sean MacEoin Story*, 1981; *The Ernie O'Malley Story*, 1983; *Shannon – Through Her Literature*, 1984; all pub. Cork. Also *Fore – The Fact and The Fantasy*, Mullingar 1984.

O'FLAHERTY, Liam, b. Aran Islands 1897, d. Dublin 1984. Born and brought up in an Irish-speaking family and community. A visiting priest of the Holy Ghost Order persuaded him as a boy that he should become a priest and sponsored his education, in Rockwell, Blackrock, and UCD. Finding that he had no vocation O'Flaherty left university with some hard feelings on all sides. He served in the British Army during the latter part of the First World War, was invalided out and eventually returned to Dublin to take some part in the Revolution and the Civil War. Finding himself out of sympathy with Irish society as it then was he went to London and endured some hardship there. His first, now almost unknown book, *Thy Neighbour's Wife,* appeared 1923, and *The Black Soul,* 1924, repub. 1981, Dublin. *The Informer,* 1925, repub. 1980, established him as a major new writer. The books tells the story of a modern Judas, a semi-literate traitor whose tortured mind reflects much greater things than his own squalid betrayal of a comrade and death. *Mr Gilhooley,* 1926; *The Assassin,* 1928; *The House of Gold,* 1929; *The Puritan,* 1932; *Hollywood Cemetery,* 1935; *Famine,* 1937, repub. Dublin 1980; *Insurrection; The Martyr; Skerrett,* repub. Dublin 1978; and *Land* are other novels. Three autobiographical books, *Two Years; I Went to Russia* and *Shame the Devil.* MIAL.

In spite of the large number of novels and the immense and deserved success of some of them, particularly *The Informer,* O'Flaherty is best known as a short-story writer, and in a sense *The Informer* itself is really a long short story rather than a novel. Collections include *Spring Sowing, 1924; The Tent, 1926; The Mountain Tavern,* 1929; *Two Lovely Beasts,* 1948; *The Wounded Cormorant and Other Stories,* NY 1973; *The Pedlar's Revenge,* Dublin 1976 (a collection of early stories). A short novel, *The Wilderness,* pub. Dublin 1978 (for the first time in book form having been serialised previously). *The Ecstasy of Angus,* a novella of a few pages, privately printed in 1931, was also rep. Dublin 1978.

O'FLANAGAN, James Roderick, b. Fermoy 1814, d. Fermoy 1900. Bar 1838; Crown Prosecutor, Cork, 1846. Founded the *Fermoy Journal.* His principal work was *Lives of the Lord Chancellors of Ireland,* 2 vols, 1870, but also wrote several lesser yet interesting books on Irish legal history. *Bar Life of O'Connell,* Dublin, 1875; *The Irish Bar,* 1879; *The Munster Circuit,* 1880, etc. Also wrote novels, including *Bryan O'Regan,* 1866; *Gentle Blood;* and *Captain O'Shaughnessy's Sporting Career,* 1872.

O'FLANAGAN, Michael, b. Co. Roscommon, 1876, d. Dublin 1942. Ed. locally and Maynooth College. Ordained 1900. Sent to US 1904 to preach for funds for diocese and became remarkable as preacher and fund-raiser. On one tour took 32 turf sods, one from each country of Ireland, charging Irish-Americans a dollar 'to tread once more on their native sod'. In spare time began fund-raising for Republican causes. In 1914 in Co. Mayo involved in tenant-right agitation, with marked success. By 1916 a prominent Republican speaker and organiser, he was almost the sole nationally known Republican figure left active after the Rising. In 1917 he managed the victorious Roscommon election campaign for Count Plunkett and during de Valera's imprisonment in Lincoln Gaol was acting President of Sinn Fein. His best-known action during the War of Independence was a telegram sent to Lloyd George stating 'Ireland is also willing to make peace'. Widely misunderstood then and since, it was an attempt to establish Ll. G.'s lack of honesty.

Always a Republican, his main political career ended with the Civil War, and his interests turned to historical research. With a small staff headed by Mary Nelson, later Mrs Elliott, he edited *The John O'Donovan Archaeological Survey* in 50 vols, county by county, between 1924-32. This in turn formed the basis of his *County Histories,* prepared 1932-1942, and almost completed by his death. These works contain irreplaceable information about local history, archaeology, place and family names, and have already provided many later researchers with much material, not always receiving credit in return.

Silenced many times by his ecclesiastical superiors and re-instated, he was silenced finally in 1932 for again taking up unacceptable political attitudes. Cathal Brugha differed from the hierarchy in calling him 'the staunchest priest who ever lived in Ireland'.

O'FLYNN (Ó FLOINN), Críostóir, b. Limerick 1927. Ed. locally, TCD. Playwright, short-story writer, teacher, broadcaster, journalist. Two plays, *Land of the Living* and *The Order of Melchizedek. Sanctuary Island* (short stories), 1971; *Banana,* 1977, and *At Dun Laoghaire Lighthouse,* 1978, both poetry; all pub. Dublin. *Centenary,* 1985, is an epic poem. For work in Irish see Part 2.

O'GRADY, Desmond James Bernard, b. Limerick 1935. Ed. Jesuits, Cistercians, Harvard. Lived Paris and Rome, and was for a time secretary to Pound. Poetry includes *Chords and Orchestrations,* Limerick 1956; *Reilly* 1961; *The Dark Edge of Europe,* 1967; *The Dying Gaul, Separations,* Dublin 1973; *The Gododdin* (trans. from Middle Welsh), Dublin 1977; *Sing Me Creation,* Dublin 1977; *The Headgear of the Tribe* (selected poems), 1978; *A Limerick Rake* (from the Irish), Dublin 1978.

O'GRADY, Standish, b. Castletown Bere 1846, d. 1928. Son of Viscount Guillamore. Ed. TCD, called to Bar, but turned to journalism. A talented historian, most of his novels had an historical basis; *The Chieftain's Last Rally; Red Hugh's Captivity,* 1889; *Lost on Du Corrig,* 1894; *In the Gates of the North; The Coming of Cuchullain,* 1894; *The Chain of Gold,* 1895 (one of his many boys' books); *Ulrick the Ready,* 1896; *In the Wake of King James,* 1896; *The Flight of the Eagle,* 1897, etc. His passionate interest in the heroic aspects of Irish history made him a strong influence on the generation growing up between 1890 and 1916, and he has been called 'the Father of the Irish Revival'. Works include *History of Ireland's Heroic Period,* 1878-80; *The Crisis in Ireland,* Dublin 1882; *Red Hugh's Captivity,* 1889; *The Story of Ireland,* 1894.

O'GRADY, Standish Hayes, b. Co. Limerick 1832, d. Cheshire 1915. Ed. Rugby and TCD. Friend of O'Donovan and O'Curry and copied some of the MSS in TCD library under their guidance. Went to US as Civil Engineer and remained there many years. Returned to London and compiled a *Catalogue of Irish MSS in the British Museum,* unfinished at his death and completed by Robin Flower. His principal work was *Silva Gadelica,* vol. I: Irish texts, vol. II: translations and notes, 1892, being tales from ancient

Irish MSS.

O'HAGAN, John, b. Newry 1822, d. 1890. Barrister and judge. Defended Gavan Duffy after the 1848 Rising. Trans. *Song of Roland,* 1883. Contributor to *The Nation.*

O'HALLORAN, Sylvester, b. Limerick 1728, d. Limerick 1807. Studied medicine Paris and Leyden, practised in Limerick from 1750. That year published *A New Treatise on the Glaucoma, or Cataract in Ireland* and created a stir with it. Wrote also on gangrene and amputations, 1756, and head injuries, 1791. It was said that he knew as much as he did about such matters because of the number of victims of faction fights brought to his surgery. Head injuries from blunt weapons were of course the chief wounds in such arguments. Founded the Co. Limerick Infirmary 1760 and encouraged the foundation of the Royal College of Surgeons 1784. *Insula Sacra,* 1770, was a plea for the preservation of ancient Irish MSS and annals, and in 1774 he published *Ierne Defended* and his *General History of Ireland to close of 12th century.*

O'HANLON, H. B., b. *c.* 1890. Encouraged to write plays by Edward Martyn, who considered him the chief discovery of his Irish Theatre, founded in 1914. His plays include *Tomorrow, Speculations,* and *The All Alone.* These were in line with Martyn's intellectual theories of drama, and seem never to have reached the professional stage.

O'HANLON, John, b. Stradbally 1821, d. Dublin 1905. In US 1842-53 where he was ordained 1847. Wrote much on Irish saints and folklore, and on Irish-American history. *The Irish Emigrant's Guide for the US,* Boston 1853, is interesting, as is the *Irish American History of the US,* Dublin 1903. His major work was *Lives of the Irish Saints,* 10 vols, Dublin, London, NY 1875-1903.

O'HANRAHAN, Michael, or Mícheál Ó hAnnracháin, b. New Ross 1877, d. 1916. Ed. locally. Enthusiast for Irish Language Revival and active in the Volunteer movement from 1914 onwards. Played a leading role in the Easter Rising of 1916, and was executed in Dublin that year. His novels include *A Swordsman of the Brigade,* Edinburgh and London 1914, and *When the Normans Came,* Dublin 1918.

O hAODHA, Mícheál, b. Clare 1918. For writing in Irish see Part 2. A play *The Weaver's Grave,* adapted from a story by Seumas O'Kelly, produced Dublin 1969. Has written *The Abbey – Then and Now* (an illustrated guide), Dublin 1969, and *Theatre in Ireland,* Oxford 1974.

O'HARA, Kane or Kean, b. Sligo 1714, d. 1782. Closely related to Lord Tyrawley. Lived mostly in Dublin where he was noted for his great height and distracted manner. Dublin street boys used to yell 'St Patrick's Steeple' after him, and more elegant wits described him as 'Cruel Tall O'Hara'. He is credited with the invention of burlesque, which is surely wrong, but he seems to have introduced it to Dublin with comic pieces such as his translation of the Italian burletta *Midas,* and with original burlesques such as *The Golden Pippin,* 1773, and *The Two Misers,* 1775. These were constantly revived and reprinted for many years after his death.

O'HARA, Kevin, see CUMBERLAND, Marten.

O'HEGARTY, Partrick Sarsfield, b. Cork 1879, d. 1955. Law clerk and then post office clerk until 1913, edited several Nationalist papers and became Secretary of the GPO 1922-45. *The Indestructible Nation* (Irish history), Dublin and London 1918; *John Mitchel,* Dublin 1917; *A Short Memoir of Terence MacSwiney,* Dublin 1922; *A History of Ireland Under the Union 1801-1922,* 1922; *The Victory of Sinn Fein,* Dublin 1924.

O'KEEFE, John, b. Dublin 1747, d. Southampton 1833. Trained as a painter and exhibited at the Royal Academy London. Preferred the theatre and became first an actor in Dublin and then a playwright in London, Becoming blind in 1790, his daughter Adelaide, herself an admired poet in her day, acted as his secretary. He wrote an immense number of highly successful plays in prose and verse, including *Tony Lumpkin in Town,* 1778; *The Castle of Andalusia,* 1789; and *Wild Oats,* the most popular of all his works, which remained in the repertoires all over Britain throughout the 19th century and well into the 20th. His comic opera *Merry Sherwood* contained the famous song 'I am a Friar of Orders Grey' which achieved a separate life of its own, down to the present day. He published his *Recollections,* 2 vols, 1826.

O'KELLY, Charles, b. Co. Galway 1621, d. Aughrane 1695. Ed. St. Omer, returned to Ireland 1642 to fight for Charles I in Civil War in Ireland. Went to Spain in 1649, returning to Ireland on Restoration. Became Lord of Manor of Screen 1674 and in 1689 sat for Roscommon in James II's Dublin Parliament. Commissioned to raise a regiment for service under Patrick Sarsfield, and despite his age served 1689-91, ending on Inish Bofin at the capitulation. Lived at Aughrane from 1691 to his death, and there wrote his curious account of the Williamite War in Latin, disguising it as an account of the conquest of Cyprus: *Macariae Excidium; or the Destruction of Cyprus containing the last Warr & Conquest of that Kingdom.* He also translated this work himself, pretending the original to have been in Syriac by 'Philotas Phylocypkes' translated into Latin by Gratianus Ragallus P.R., and 'now made into English by Col. Charles O'Kelly', 1692.

Crofton Croker edited this extraordinary work in 1841, but a better edition was prepared a few years later by John Cornelius O'Callaghan 'from 4 English copies & a Latin MS in the RIA'; O'C's notes and references being as valuable as the main text. The date of this edition is 1846 but it appears to have been reprinted by the Irish Archaeological Society, 1850.

O'Kelly also wrote his *Memoirs,* but the MS is lost.

O'KELLY, M. J., b. Co. Limerick 1915, d. 1982. Ed. Rockwell, UCC. Professor of Archaeology UCC 1946-82. One of Ireland's leading archaeologists and author of numerous scholarly papers and excavation reports. Major work: *Newgrange, Archaeology, Art and Legend,* 1982.

O'KELLY, Seumas, b. Loughrea 1881, d. 1918. Ed. locally. Journalist and editor first on provincial and later on Dublin papers. Close friend of Arthur Griffith, and other leaders of the revolutionary movement. Wrote several plays: *The Shuiler's Child,* 1909; *The Parnellite,* 1911; *Meadowsweet,* 1912; and *The Bribe,* 1913, all produced at the Abbey; *Driftwood* produced in London, 1913, by Miss Horniman. Two novels, *The Lady of Deerpark,* 1917, and *Wet Clay,* 1919, were published in London. But his reputation rests on his short stories. *The Weaver's Grave* is generally regarded as his masterpiece among these, and has been adapted for stage and radio, winning the Italia Prize in 1961 for Radio Éireann. Collections of his stories include *By the Stream of Kilmeen,* 1910; *Waysiders,* 1917; *Hillsiders,* 1917; *The Golden Barque; The Weaver's Grave;* and *The Leprechaun of Kilmeen,* 1920, the latter reprinted in Ireland in 1965, the former in 1984.

In 1918 O'Kelly was deputy for Arthur Griffith as editor of *Nationality* and on November 14th died of a heart attack. His work was neglected for many years and almost forgotten, but the Italia Prize revived interest in it.

O'LEARY, Con, b. Cork 1887, d. London 1958. Wrote plays for Abbey Theatre, *The Crossing,* 1914, *Queer Ones,* 1919, as well as a number of books, including the novel *Passage West,* 1945, and *Wayfarer in Ireland,* 1935.

O'LEARY, Ellen, b. Tipperary 1831, d. Cork 1889. Sister of the Fenian leader and herself active in revolutionary politics. Contributed poems to *The Nation* and other magazines in Ireland and America. W. B. Yeats respected her poetry. T. W. Rolleston edited her *Lays of Country, Home and Friends,* Dublin 1891. The volume had an introduction by Sir Charles Gavan Duffy.

O'LEARY, John, b. Tipperary 1830, d. Dublin 1907. Son of well-to-do shopkeeper, was intended first for law and then for medicine, but influenced by Davis turned to revolutionary journalism. Devoy called him one of the three most prominent men in the Fenian movement in Ireland after James Stephens but he was never an active revolutionary fighter. Edited *The Irish People.* Arrested 1865 in the great wave of Fenian arrests, and sentenced to 20 years, but served only 9. Exiled, chose Paris for a home until allowed to return to Ireland 1885. There he made friends with the Yeats family and deeply impressed the young W. B., who later wrote of 'O'Leary's noble head'. He devoted himself to writing and literary movements. Principal books are *Young Ireland,* 1885; *What Irishmen Should Read,* 1889; *Recollections of Fenians and Fenianism,* 1896.

O'LEARY, Liam, b. Youghal 1910. Ex-civil servant. Producer at Abbey Theatre in early 1940s, worked in films in Europe and Africa. Film archivist at National Film Archive, London, 1953-66. Worked in RTE film department for many years. *An Invitation to the Film*, 1945; *The Silent Cinema*, 1965; *The Spirit and the Clay*, 1967. The last is a biography of Rex Ingram the Irish film producer and novelist; also *Rex Ingram: Master of the Silent Cinema*, Dublin 1979.

O'LEARY, Margaret. Playwright and novelist much admired by Yeats. Plays include *The Woman*, 1929 and *The Coloured Balloon*, 1944, both performed at the Abbey; novels include *The House I Made*, 1935, and *Lightning Flash*, 1939, based on a play particularly loved by Yeats.

Ó LÚING, Seán Breandán, b. Kerry, 1917. Ed. UCD. School-teacher, then joined translation staff of Dáil Éireann. For Irish writing see Part 2. In English, *The Fremantle Mission*, Tralee 1965, an account of the rescue of Fenian prisoners from Australia in 1876. Contributed 'Arthur Griffith and Sinn Fein' to *Leaders and Men of the Easter Rising: Dublin 1916*, ed. Fr F. X. Martin, 1967. *I Die In a Good Cause*, biography of Thomas Ashe, Tralee 1970.

O'MAHONY, John, b. Co. Limerick 1819, d. New York 1877, buried Glasnevin, Dublin. Ed. TCD, involved in abortive 1848 conspiracy, emigrated to US 1852 and there with James Stephens founded the Fenian Brotherhood of which he became Head Centre. But the quarrels of exiles told on his mind, he had a mental breakdown and died in the obscurest poverty. Trans. Keating's *History of Ireland*, NY 1857.

O'MAHONY, Norah Tynan, b. 1865. Sister of Kathleen Tynan; wrote poetry, *The Field of Heaven*, 1915, etc. and some novels, including *Mrs Desmond's Foster-child*, Dublin 1915.

O'MAHONY, T. P., b. Cork 1939. Journalist (*Irish Press* commentator on religious affairs). Novels: *Sex and Sanctity*, Swords 1979; *The Vatican Caper*, Swords 1981.

O'MALLEY, Ernest, b. Co. Mayo 1898, d. Howth, 1957. As a medical student joined the Irish Volunteers 1917 and became their organiser for N.W. Ulster with rank of Captain on GHQ Staff. Wounded many times, he was captured and tortured by Black and Tans near Kilkenny 1920. Interned with other Republican sympathisers at outbreak of Civil War, escaped and fought with distinction. Surrounded in a Dublin house by Free State soldiers in 1922, received 21 bullet wounds. Imprisoned, was in the great hunger strike of 1923. Last Republican prisoner to be released in Civil War, told by doctor he would never walk again. But in Spain recovered and travelled widely in Europe and America. Collected funds for establishment of *Irish Press* 1927, became a school-teacher in New Mexico and a cab driver in New York. Returned to Ireland and published autobiographical account of War of Independence and Civil War, *On Another Man's Wound*, Dublin 1936, rep. 1979, hailed as a classic, repub. in US as *Army without Banners*, NY 1937 (also in paperback in US and UK under that title). A sequel *The Singing Flame*, Dublin 1978. Also, *Raids and Rallies*

(1950s pieces from *The Sunday Press*), Dublin 1982. Elected MIAL 1947.

O'MEARA, Barry Edward, b. probably Dublin 1786, d. London 1836. Studied medicine in Dublin and London, joining British Army as surgeon. Served in Mediterranean area and having engaged in a duel was cashiered 1808. Joined Navy and in July 1815 was surgeon on board *Bellerophon* when Napoleon surrendered to Captain Maitland. Went with Napoleon to St Helena as his private doctor. The Governor, Sir Hudson Lowe, asked him to spy on Napoleon to discover if there were designs to rescue him from the island. O'Meara read into this request a suggestion that he murder his imperial patient and quarrelled with Lowe so fiercely that he was obliged to resign 1818. He made his accusations against Lowe public and was thereupon dismissed from the Navy, thus having the unique distinction of being cashiered from both Army and Navy within ten years. He used his new leisure to write *Napoleon in Exile; or A Voice from St Helena*, 2 vols, 1822. This caused an enormous sensation at the time and is still of great interest. Mystery surrounds every factor in Napoleon's last exile and O'Meara is one of the very few friendly eye-witnesses.

O'MEARA, John Joseph, b. Co. Galway 1915. Ed. Cashel and UCD. Took Classics Doctorate at Oxford and played Rugby for the University 1943-44. Became Professor of Latin UCD 1948. Has written much on later Classical literature, particularly on Augustine, translating and editing *Against the Academics,* 1950, and writing *The Young Augustine: The Growth of St Augustine's Mind Up To His Conversion,* 1954, French trans. 1958, US 1964. In French with others, *Recherches Augustiniennes,* Paris 1958; with Odile de Montfort, *Ordeal at Lourdes,* 1959, and *Charter of Christendom: the Significance of St Augustine's 'City of God',* NY 1962. Among his other work is a translation of Giraldus Cambrensis, *Topography of Ireland,* Dundalk 1951, rep. Dublin 1978, the unflattering but fascinating travel book by the 12th-century priest Gerald de Barri, cousin of most of the Norman knights who conquered Ireland in the 1170s.

Later works include *Porphyry's Philosophy from Oracles,* and *Augustine's Dialogues of Cassiciacum,* both pub. in *Études Augustiniennes,* Paris 1969; *Navigatio Sancti Brendani Abbatis,* translated into English, Dublin 1976; *Saint Augustine on the Question of Man,* Philadelphia 1978. Has edited works on Eriugena and St Augustine.

O'MEARA, Kathleen, b. Dublin 1839, d. Paris 1888. Granddaughter of Barry Edward O'M. Taken to Paris as a child, and remained there until her death. Wrote novels, *A Woman's Trials,* 1867, and *The Battle of Connemara,* 1878, among others. Biographies include *Madame Mohl, Her Salon and Her Friends, a Study of Social Life in Paris,* 1885; and *The Curé d'Ars,* 1891. Both these are still of interest.

O'NEILL, Colman, b. 1929, ordained OP Dublin 1954. Professor Dogmatic Theology, Lateran University, Rome, 1958-63; Fribourg University 1963. *Meeting Christ in the Sacraments,* Cork 1965.

O'NEILL, David, see GALLAGHER, Frank.

O'NEILL, Desmond, see NEESON Eoin.

O'NEILL, Henry, b. Dundalk 1800, d. Dublin 1880, remembered for his controversy with Petrie over Round Towers, O'N. maintaining they had a pagan origin; but more valuably for *The Most Interesting of the Sculptured Crosses of Ancient Ireland*, 1857, with 36 lithographs by the author.

O'NEILL, John, b. Waterford 1777, d. *c.* 1860. A shoemaker in Carrick-on-Suir from where he moved to London. Wrote a novel *Mary of Avonmore*, some plays, and some temperance poetry, including the famous *The Drunkard*, 1840, illustrated by Cruikshank.

O'NEILL, Joseph, b. 1886, d. 1953. Ed. Galway, Manchester and Germany. Began career as Inspector of Primary Schools in Ireland 1907 and became Permanent Secretary to Dept of Education in 1923. In 1934 his novel *Wind from the North* won the Harmsworth Award of Irish Academy of Letters, and he was elected to the Academy 1936. *Land under England*, 1935, was a best seller, and was translated into French. It dealt with a fantastic discovery of the descendants of Roman legions still living in a vast network of caves beneath Hadrian's Wall. *Day of Wrath*, 1936; *Philip*, 1940; *Chosen by the Queen*, 1947, are among his other novels.

O'NEILL, Mary Devenport, b. Galway *c.* 1900, d. 1867. Ed. National College of Art. Married Joseph O'Neill. Verse-plays, *Bluebeard*, 1933, and *Cain*, 1945. Poetry includes *Prometheus*, 1929.

O'NEILL, Moira, pseud. of Agnes Nesta Shakespeare Skrine, née Higginson, b. *c.* 1870. Poetry includes *An Easter Vacation*, 1893; *Songs of the Glens of Antrim*, Edinburgh 1901. Mother of Molly Keane.

O'RAHILLY, Alfred J., b. Listowel 1884, d. 1969. Younger brother of Thomas Francis O'R., became President of UCC. Was ordained late in life, 1955, and appointed Domestic Prelate 1960. His books include a *Life of Father William Doyle SJ, 1873-1917*, 1920; *Case for the Treaty*, Dublin 1922; *Case for a Flour Tariff*, 1928; *Thoughts on the Constitution*, Dublin 1937; *Electromagnetics: A Discussion on Fundamentals* London and Cork 1948; *Aquinas versus Marx*, Cork 1948; *Gospel Studies I: the Family at Bethane*, Cork 1949, and *Gospel Meditations*, Dublin 1958.

O'RAHILLY, Thomas Francis, b. Listowel 1882, d. 1953. Ed. Dublin, Professor of Irish TCD 1919-29; Director for School of Celtic Studies, Dublin Inst. for Adv. Studies 1942-53. Wrote a vast number of papers on Irish-language questions, many of them putting forward the theory that Q-Celtic or Goidelic dialects were preceded in Ireland by varieties of P-Celtic, and suggesting a date as early as the 8th century B C for the introduction of some form of Celtic. The former theory is not widely accepted, but O'Rahilly remains an important figure in Irish studies. *Irish Dialects, Past and Present*, Dublin 1932; *The Goidels and their Predecessors* (Rhys Memorial Lecture), Oxford 1936; *The Two Patricks*, Dublin 1942; and *Early Irish History and Mythology*, Dublin 1946, are among his works of general interest.

O'REILLY, Edward, b. probably Co. Cavan *c.* 1770, d. Dublin 1829. Learned Irish in Dublin, curiously enough, about 1790. Published *Irish-English Dictionary*, Dublin 1817, by subscription, reissued 1821, and with a supplement by John O'Donovan 1864. His *Chronological Account of nearly 400 Irish Writers*, Dublin 1820, was based partly on notes gathered by William Haliday and appears to be the first *Dictionary of Irish Writers*. O'Curry criticised his work in *Manners and Customs of the Ancient Irish*, 1873.

O'REILLY, John Boyle, b. Dowth 1844, d. Boston 1890. Printer's apprentice. Joined IRB and enlisted in British Army as IRB agent. Court-martialled and sentenced to death, 1866. Sentence commuted to penal servitude and transportation. Escaped from Autralian convict settlement, 1869, and reached US, settling in Boston. Edited *The Pilot*. In 1875 helped in planning the rescue from Fremantle gaol of the six remaining Fenian convicts. Notre Dame University conferred Hon. Doctorate of Laws on him, but perhaps not for this particular exploit. Wrote a powerful novel, *Moondyne*, 1880, about the convict settlements. It ran to 12 editions within a short time. His poetry was also extremely popular.

O'REILLY, Miles, see under HALPINE, Charles Graham

Ó RIORDÁIN, Seán P., b. Cork 1905, d. 1957. National teacher. Later studied in Europe, and became Professor of Archaeology, UCD. Internationally known for his excavations on the Hill of Tara. Wrote *Antiquities of the Irish Countryside*, Cork 1942, London 1964, and *Tara: the Monuments on the Hill* (a pamphlet), Dundalk 1954. With Glyn Daniel wrote his major work, published after his death, *New Grange and the Bend of the Boyne*, 1964, a description of one of the greatest megalithic monuments in Europe.

O'RIORDAN, Conal Holmes O'Connell, b. Dublin 1874, d. 1948. Ed. Clongowes. Hoped to obtain commission in army but a riding accident left him with a spine injury, and he went on the stage, and also began writing plays and novels. In 1909 became Managing Director of Abbey Theatre, Dublin, and revived Synge's *Playboy of the Western World* in the teeth of universal opposition. Tried to enlist in 1914. Rejected, and made his way to the frontlines as Head of a YMCA Rest Hut. After the war gave up his pseud. of Norreys Connell which he had used from 1891-1920, and concentrated on novels which still had a strong theatrical quality, so that they have been accused of reading like 'unfinished plays'. Gained many honours. Fellow of Royal Society of Literature; Shute Lecturer Liverpool University; Hon. Examiner History Society, TCD; Council Member PEN.

Served as air raid warden in Second World War.

His early plays include *The Piper*, 1908; *An Imaginary Conversation*, 1909; and *Time*, 1909, all of which were acted at the Abbey, as well as in London. His long list of novels begins with *In the Green Park*, 1894; *The House of the Strange Woman*, 1895; and *The Fool and His Heart*, 1896. These and their successors were all hailed by critics as witty, lively, spirited, and he was called 'the boldest literary Irishman of his day'. Many of his books were historical novels, and his series *Soldier Born*, 1927; *Soldier of Waterloo*, 1928; *Soldier's Wife*, 1935; and *Soldier's End*, 1938, taking the story of David Quinn from the end of the 18th century to the 1880s, through Waterloo, the Famine in Ireland, and the American Civil War, was very well received, as were his Adam novels, *Adam of Dublin*, 1920; *Adam and Caroline*, 1921, etc. Both his books and plays were highly praised by critics such as Compton MacKenzie, Ivor Brown, Lady Gregory and Robert Lynd, and it is sad that they are now almost unremembered.

ORMSBY, Frank, b. Co. Fermanagh 1947. Ed. QUB. Teaches English at the Royal Belfast Academical Institution. Ed. *The Honest Ulsterman* (founded 1968 by James Simmons) with Michael Foley 1969-72, alone 1972-84, and now with Robert Johnstone. Eric Gregory Award for poetry 1974. Poems, *A Store of Candles*, 1977 (Poetry Book Society Choice); ed. *Poets from the North of Ireland*, 1979.

O'ROURKE, Edmund, b. Dublin 1814, d. London 1879. Became an actor in childhood, using name Edmund Falconer. Manager of Lyceum Theatre 1858, joint lessee of Drury Lane 1864-66. Acted in first production of *Colleen Bawn*, creating part of Danny Mann. Wrote plays and songs, including the immortal 'Killarney'. His play *The Cagot*, 1856, was very successful and so was *Peep o' Day*, 1861.

ORPEN, William, b. Co. Dublin 1878, d. London 1931. Ed. Dublin Metropolitan School of Art and Slade School, London. R.A. 1919. Had served in First World War as official war artist and in 1919 was official artist at Versailles. *An Onlooker in France*, 1921; *Outline of Art*, 1923; *Stories of old Ireland and Myself*, 1924.

ORR, James, B. Co. Antrim 1770, d. Co. Antrim 1816. Wrote verse for *Northern Star*, was involved in 1798 Rising and left an account of events at Donegore in verse. Mainly remembered for a song, 'The Irishman'.

O'SHEA, John Augustus (pseud. 'The Irish Bohemian'), b. Nenagh 1840, d. London 1905. Ed. Dublin; settled in Paris as foreign correspondent for *The Irishman*, 1860; wrote a number of books of journalistic reminiscence, but is chiefly remembered for his account of Paris under siege in the Franco-Prussian War of 1870, *An Iron Bound City*, 2 vols, 1886.

Ó SÚILLEABHÁIN, Seán, see O'SULLIVAN, Sean.

O'SULLIVAN, Daniel James, b. Cork 1906 of a lighthousekeeper's family. Became a keeper and also a field naturalist of great distinction, particularly with regard to Inistrahull. Poetry: *Lighthousekeeper's Lyrics,* Dundalk 1947.

O'SULLIVAN, Donal, b. Liverpool 1893 of Kerry parentage, d. 1973. Ed. Liverpool and London. Served as officer in British Navy during First World War and as civil servant in Dublin 1920, becoming assistant Secretary to Senate of Free State and Clerk to the Senate 1925-36. Senator 1943-44. President of Irish Council of European Movement and Director of Studies in Irish Folk Music and Song at UCD. Ed. journal of Irish Folk Song Society and *The Bunting collection of Irish Folk Music,* 6 vols, 1927. Wrote *The Irish Free State and its Senate,* 1940; *The Spice of Life and other Essays,* Dublin 1948; *Irish Folk Music and Song,* Dublin 1952; *Carolan: The Life, Times and Music of an Irish Harper,* 2 vols, 1958; *Songs of the Irish,* 1960, repub. Cork 1981; *Irish Folk Music, Song and Dance,* Dublin 1971 (*Irish Folk Music and Song* rev.).

O'SULLIVAN, Mary, b. Galway 1887, d. 1966. Ed. UCG and Germany. Professor of History UCG 1916-58, and Emeritus. *Old Galway,* Cambridge 1942, is a standard work on mediaeval city life in Ireland. *Italian Merchant Bankers in Ireland,* Dublin 1962, is a social and economic history of mediaeval Ireland.

O'SULLIVAN, Michael John, b. Cork 1794. Ed. locally. Bar. Journalist. Edited *Freeman's Journal* 1818. Wrote opera, plays and poetry. His play *Lalla Rookh* ran 100 nights in Dublin in 1815, an almost unheard of achievement for the period.

O'SULLIVAN, Mortimer, b. Clonmel 1791, d. Dublin 1859. Of Catholic parentage, became Protestant clergyman. Attacked landlordism in *Captain Rock Detected,* 1824, but also defended the Established Church. The title was a reference to Thomas Moore's *Captain Rock,* and ten years later he again answered Moore (*Travels of an Irish Gentleman in search of a religion*) with *Guide to an Irish Gentleman in search of a religion.* But his principal interest for the historian is his *Digest of Evidence on the State of Ireland,* 2 vols, 1826, being evidence he had given to a select parliamentary committee in 1825.

O'SULLIVAN, Sean (also as Ó Súilleabháin, Seán), b. Co. Kerry 1905. Joined Folklore Commission 1935. Travelled widely in Europe and US lecturing and gathering comparative material. Native Irish speaker. Principal works: *Handbook of Irish Folklore,* 1942; *Religious Folktales, The Types of Irish Folktale, Folktales of Ireland,* 1967, *Irish Wake Amusements,* Cork 1967 (trans. from author's own Irish edition of 1961), rep. 1979; many contributions to the *Encyclopaedia of Ireland,* Dublin 1968; and to learned journals in Ireland, America, Germany, Sweden, England.

O'SULLIVAN, Seumas, pseud. of James Sullivan Starkey, b. Dublin 1879, d. 1958. From university age onwards he was a leading and influential figure in the Irish Literary Revival; a friend of Arthur Griffith, James Joyce,

OTWAY

'AE', Oliver Gogarty and Yeats. He was one of the frequent literary visitors to the Martello tower at Sandycove beside the 'forty-foot', immortalised in the first pages of Joyce's *Ulysses*. He appeared as the Blind Man in Yeats' *On Baile's Strand*, December 27th 1904, the opening night of the first play staged in the Abbey Theatre.

In 1913 he support AE strongly in the latter's campaign against the employers during the Dublin strike. In 1923 he founded *The Dublin Magazine*. No one except himself expected it to survive the year. Torn by the Civil War, Ireland seemed an unlikely place for a literary magazine to survive. But it became one of the most influential ever published in Ireland, and over the next 30 years almost every Irish writer of merit contributed to it. In 1939 he was given an Hon. D Lit. by TCD. For many years he was President of Irish PEN and he was a member of the Irish Academy of Letters. His many volumes of poetry include *Twilight People*, 1905; *Verse Sacred and Profane*, 1908; *The Earth Lover*, 1909; *Selected Lyrics*, 1910; *Collected Poems*, 1912; *An Epilogue*, 1914; *Requiem*, 1917; *The Rosses*, 1918; *The Lamplighters*, 1929; *At Christmas*, 1934; *Personal Talk*, 1936; *Collected Poems*, 1940. In 1946 *Dublin Poems* was published in New York. His prose work includes *Mud and Purple*, 1917; *Common Adventures*, 1926; *Essays and Recollections*, 1944, etc. In 1938 a special issue of the *Neuphilologische Monatschrift* was devoted to a critical appraisal of his work, by Heinz Hopf'l, who regarded it as in the front rank of not only Irish but English poetry.

OTWAY, Caesar, b. Co. Tipperary 1780, d. Dublin 1842. Ed. TCD. Famous as the discoverer of William Carleton who wrote his first pieces in Otway's journal *The Christian Examiner*. *O's Sketches in Ireland*, Dublin 1827, give a picture of conditions then. Also *A Tour in Connaught*, Dublin 1839.

OULTON, Walley Chamberlain, b. Dublin 1750, d. Dublin 1820. Wrote many burlettas, opera and musical plays popular at the time. *The Haunted Castle*, 1784 etc. Also a long poem, *The Death of Abel*, 1814.

P

PAKENHAM, Frank, see LONGFORD, 7th Earl.

PAKENHAM, Thomas Frank Dermot, b. 1933. Eldest son of 7th Earl of Longford. Ed. Ampleforth, Belvedere, Oxford. Journalist and historian. *The Mountains of Rasselas: An Ethiopian Adventure*, NY 1959; *The Year of Liberty* (story of Irish Rebellion in 1798), 1969; *The Boer War*, 1979.

PALMER, William, b. Dublin 1803, d. London 1885. Ed. TCD, Oxford. Married Sophia Beaufort, daughter of the admiral who invented the

Beaufort Scale. His chief interest is his association with Keble, Newman and others in the first phases of the Tractarian Movement. His *Narrative of Events connected with the publications of Tracts for the Times,* 1843, was the decisive point leading to Newman's secession from the Anglican Tractarian Movement and his eventual conversion to Catholicism.

PARKER, Stewart, b. Belfast 1941. Ed. QUB. Poetry: *The Casualty's Meditation,* 1966; *Maw,* 1968; both pub. Belfast. Plays: *Spokesong,* 1976; *I'm a Dreamer Montreal* (for radio); *Iris in the Traffic, Ruby in the Rain* (for TV), 1982; *Northern Star,* 1984; *The Traveller* (for radio), 1985.

PARNELL, Thomas, b. Dublin 1679, d. Chester 1718. Ed. TCD, DD 1712. Befriended by Swift who secured his promotion in church to Archdeaconry of Finglas. His poetry was highly regarded for long after his death. *Poems on Several Occasions,* 1722, and *The Hermit* were long popular, being last reprinted in 1894. Collaborated often with Pope, writing the introduction to Pope's *Iliad* and helping him with the translation. In return Pope revised much of Parnell's most successful poetry.

PARNELL, William (later Parnell-Hayes), b. Avondale *c.* 1780, d. Avondale 1821. Was grandfather of Charles Stewart P., and was himself an MP for Wicklow 1817-21. *An Enquiry into the Causes of the Popular Discontents in Ireland,* London and Dublin 1804, and *An Historical Apology for the Irish Catholics,* were his main works. He opposed the Union and was a good landlord and a friend to the Catholics.

PAULIN, Tom, b. Leeds 1949. Ed. Belfast, Hull and Oxford. Lecturer in English Nottingham University 1972. Poetry: *A State of Justice,* 1977; *The Strange Museum,* 1980; *The Book of Juniper,* 1982; *Liberty Tree,* 1983. Criticism: *Thomas Hardy, the Poetry of Perception,* 1975; *A New Look at the Language Question,* Derry 1983; *Ireland and the English Crisis,* Newcastle-upon-Tyne 1984.

PAYNE, Basil, b. Dublin 1928. Ed. CBS Synge St and UCD. Travelled widely in Europe, and has translated much modern German poetry. Won Guiness Award for poetry at Cheltenham, 1964. Volumes include *Sunlight on a Square,* Dublin 1961, and *Aspects of Love,* Dublin 1966, retitled *Love in the Afternoon,* 1971; *Another Kind of Optimism,* Dublin and London 1974; *Voyage à Deux,* Geneva 1974; *Why are there so many Blind People in Philadelphia,* and *Aspects of Love* (not the same book as the 1966 title), US and London 1979. Writes short stories and plays (for one player): *In Dublin's Quare City; My Dublin, my America;* and *I Celebrate Myself and You,* produced Dublin 1973-75 and elsewhere. As well as being poet-in-residence at English and American universities, has served as 'artist afloat' on *QE2* and the S.S. *France.*

PAYNE, Robert, b. Nottinghamshire *c.* 1550, d. *c.* 1620. Was induced by government promises to emigrate to Munster with a group of farming neighbours after the Desmond Rebellion. Sent ahead to report, *A Briefe*

Description of Ireland, 1590, ed. Irish Archaeological Society, Dublin 1841, is of the first importance as a document of conditions at the time. He settled at Payne's End, Co. Cork, and apparently died there.

PEARSE, Padraic Henry, b. Dublin 1879 of an English father, executed 3 May 1916. Ed. CBS Westland Row, Royal University. Bar. Journalist and editor for Gaelic League 1903-8. Founded and ran St Enda's School, Rathfarnham 1908-16, with the ideal of producing Irishmen who loved Ireland, rather than imitation Englishmen. Leader of the Irish Republican Brotherhood and the Irish Volunteers, and helped to plan the Rising of 1916, forcing his plan through in the teeth of practical objections of men who thought in terms of military victory. An idealist in politics as in education, Pearse thought in terms of sacrifice and was to be proved right by political events.

Translated much Irish poetry and wrote plays, poetry and stories in English as well as Irish. *Collected Works* pub. 1917. His play *The Singer* produced at the Abbey 1942. He himself was taken prisoner after the Rising, during which he had been chosen President of the Provisional Republican Government. Also wrote on education and set out his theories in *The Story of a Success,* ed. Desmond Ryan, Dublin 1917, the record of St Enda's College. For writing in Irish see Part 2.

PENDER, Margaret T., née O'Doherty, b. Co. Antrim 1865, d. unknown. Daughter of a farmer. Ed. locally and Belfast. Wrote poetry for newspapers, short stories and some patriotic historical novels which had great popularity: *The Green Cockade: A Tale of Ulster in '98; The Last of the Irish Chiefs; The Outlaw; Spearmen of the North,* etc.

PEPPERGRASS, Paul see BOYCE, John.

PETRIE, George, b. Dublin 1790, d. Dublin 1866. Ed. Dublin, he was an artist and musician as well as an antiquarian, exhibiting regularly in the RHA of which he became President 1857, and collecting a large number of native Irish airs which he had published 1855, as *The Petrie Collection of the Native Music of Ireland.* As an antiquarian it is difficult to overestimate his importance. His great contribution to the study of Irish antiquities was his realisation that the key to them lay with the peasantry. He first began touring Ireland as an illustrator of guide books, and in Clonmacnoise in 1820 was so struck by the ruined splendour there that he decided to make Irish researches his life work. In 1833 he wrote his famous *Essay on the Round Towers of Ireland,* Dublin, for which he won the Gold Medal of the Royal Irish Academy, against Henry O'Brien's fanciful essay on the same subject. A special prize of £30 was voted for O'Brien, which indicated the kind of atmosphere in which Petrie had to work.

Also in 1833 the government sponsored the Ordnance Topographical Survey and he was employed on it, with O'Donovan and O'Curry as his assistants, until an economy drive ended the work after the first volume appeared in 1839. Like his assistants he continued as best he could, saving an enormous amount of the material remains of the past, some of which was to form the nucleus of the National Museum, and writing in the *Dublin Penny Journal* and the *Irish Penny Journal* eloquent pleas for the preservation and appreciation of Ireland's monuments and culture. Among his many books, *On the History and Antiquities of Tara Hill*, 1839, and *The Ecclesiastical Architecture of Ireland*, 1845, are of particular interest.

PHELAN, James Leo (Jim), b. 1895, d. *c.* 1960. Lived as a gypsy for most of his life, but was also an actor, blacksmith, film script writer, novelist, journalist and tramp, as well as being imprisoned. Wrote many short stories, some of which appeared in *Argosy* in England. His books are an unclassifiable mixture of fact and fiction, half novel and half reminiscence, such as *Green Volcano*, 1938 set in Ireland during the 1916-22 revolutionary period. Others include *Murder by Numbers*, 1941; *Turf Fire Tales*, 1947; *We Follow the Roads*, 1949; *Vagabond Cavalry*, 1951; *The Underworld*, 1953; *Tramps at Anchor*, 1954; *Tramping the Toby*, 1955; *Criminals in Real Life*, 1956; as well as his best-known book, *Wagon Wheels*.

PHILIBIN, An, pseud. of POLLOCK, John Hackett.

PHILLIPS, Charles, b. Sligo 1787, d. London 1859. Ed. TCD. Bar 1812, English Bar 1821; Commissioner of Bankruptcy Court in Liverpool 1842. He began to practise on the Connaught circuit and swiftly won a reputation as a powerful man with juries. Spoke warmly on behalf of Catholic Emancipation and received a national testimonial 1813. O'Connell thought much of him. Moving to London 1821 he soon became leader of the Old Bailey Bar. He had already become famous in London for his *The Queen's Case Stated*, 1820, a defence of the unhappy Queen Caroline, which ran into 20 editions in the year of publication. Also published his *Speeches*, 1816-17; *Curran and his Contemporaries*, 1818; writings on Napoleon and Napoleon III; and *Vacation thoughts on Capital Punishment*, 1857, which is an early blow in the long struggle against hanging in England and Ireland. The Quakers had this reprinted for their own use.

PHILIPS, William, b. Derry *c.* 1675, of old Anglo-Irish family, d. 1734. Playwright and soldier. *The Revengeful Queen*, 1698 (an historical tragedy, set in Italy), and *St Stephen's Green*, 1700 (a comedy of manners set in Dublin). Apparently then left Ireland to serve in the British Army on the Continent. Returned to write *Hibernia Freed*, 1722 (tragedy based on Irish history and myth, dedicated to the Earl of Thomond), and *Belisarius*, 1724 (a tragedy in blank verse).

PIGOTT, Richard, b. Co. Meath 1828, d. Madrid, suicide, 1889. Journalist, forger and blackmailer, notorious in Irish history for his share in the ruin of Parnell. The editor and manager of *The Irishman*, he had some inside knowledge of the Land League and its leaders. Selling his newspaper interests to the League in 1881, he took to blackmail and forgery. His articles 'Parnellism and Crime' in the London *Times*, 1886, accused Parnell of complicity in the Phoenix Park murders. As a witness before the Special Commission to investigate the charges Pigott was shown to be a perjurer. He fled to Madrid where he shot himself.

PILKINGTON, Laetitia, b. Dublin 1712, d. Dublin 1750. Daughter of Dr Van Lewen, of Holland. Something of a child prodigy, her early poetry won her local fame. She married Matthew Pilkington, a poor Irish parson, himself a poet, and immediately suffered from his jealousy of her talents. Finding her in bed with a gentleman at two o'clock one morning Matthew refused to believe her explanation that it was 'the attractive charms of a new book, which the gentleman would not lend me, but consented to stay till I read it through, that was the sole motive of my detaining him'. The couple separated and Laetitia went to London where after some time she was imprisoned for debt. Colley Cibber rescued her, and became a good friend, and she set up a print shop in St James's Street. She was eventually able to return to Dublin, in comfortable circumstances, but died soon after.

Her defence of her reputation alone gives her claim to a place here, but she was as one might guess a writer of forceful imagination. Her fame rests on her *Memoirs,* full of wit and insights into human nature, pub. in 2 vols, Dublin 1748. She also wrote plays; *The Turkish Court, or London Apprentice,* Dublin 1748, and a tragedy, *The Roman Father. The Celebrated Mrs Pilkington's Jests,* 1751, are supposed to have amused Swift highly when they were read to him in MS some years earlier. Her poetry delighted Pope.

PILKINGTON, Matthew, b. Dublin 1700, d. Donabate 1784. Ed. TCD. Vicar of Donabate and Portrahane. Compiled *Gentleman's & Connoisseur's Dictionary of Painters,* 1770. This was the first of its kind and contained 14,000 entries. Many editions appeared until in 1813 Bryan began bringing out his *Dictionary of Painters & Engravers* which was itself partly based on Pilkington's work. Not the Matthew P. married to Laetitia.

PILON, Frederick, b. Cork 1750, d. London 1788. Went to London and became an actor-playwright. Plays include *The Invasion,* 1778; *The Fair American,* 1782, etc.

PIM, Herbert Moore, b. Northern Ireland 1883, d. unknown. Poetry includes *Selected Poems,* 1917; *Songs from an Ulster Valley,* 1920; *New Poems,* 1927. Novels: *A Vampire of Souls,* 1903; *The Man with Thirty Lives,* 1909. Other works: *The Pessimist, A Study of the Problem of Pain* (part autobiography), 1914, under pseud. 'A. Newman'; *Unknown Immortals in the Northern City of Success,* 1917; *Unconquerable Ulster* (foreword by Sir Edward Carson, MP), 1919; *A Short History of Celtic Philosophy,* 1920.

PIM, Sheila, b. Dublin 1909. Ed. Dublin, Lausanne and Cambridge. Has written many detective novels and books with a gardening interest, including a biography of Augustine Henry, *The Wood and the Trees,* 1966, rep. Kilkenny 1984; *Common or Garden Crime,* 1945; *Creeping Venom,*

1946; *The Flowering Shamrock,* 1949 (a more serious novel); *A Brush with Death,* 1950; *A Hive of Suspects,* 1952; *Other People's Business* (a novel), 1957; and *The Sheltered Garden* (a novel), 1964.

PINDAR, Peter, pseud. of the Irish satirist C.F. Lawler, *fl. c.* 1810. Under his pseud. he published a series of biting attacks on the Prince Regent and other members of the Royal Family, all in verse, and all immensely successful. His satires normally went into 10 and more editions and his most famous satire, *The R–L blood, or An Illustrious Hen and Her Pretty Chickens,* went into at least 15 editions within a short period, at the end of the Napoleonic Wars.

PLUNKETT, George Noble, b. Dublin 1851, d. 1948. Ed. Clongowes and France. Bar 1886. Leo XIII created him Papal Count. For several years Director of Science and Arts Museum, Dublin. Wrote poetry, *God's Chosen Festival,* 1877, etc. Father of the 1916 leader, Joseph Mary P.

PLUNKETT, Horace, b. Gloucestershire 1854, d. Weybridge 1932. 3rd son of 16th Baron Dunsany. Ed. Eton, Oxford. Because of weak lungs was sent to farm in Wyoming 1879-89, but visited Ireland each year. The campaign for agricultural co-operation was gathering strength at this period and P. organised dairy co-operatives in southern Ireland. In 1891 the Congested Districts Board was set up and P. was appointed a member. Became Unionist MP for Dublin 1892. These two interests dominated his life: to improve Irish agriculture and to keep a united Ireland within the Commonwealth as it came to be called after 1919. Made a Senator of the Free State, 1922, his house was burned by Republican extremists 1923, and he moved to England. Continued his work for agricultural co-operatives there. Wrote much on agriculture. *Ireland in the New Century,* 1904, rep. 1982, and *The Rural Life Problem of the U.S.,* 1910, are two of his main works.

PLUNKETT, James, pseud. of James Plunkett Kelly, b. Dublin 1920. Ed. CBS Synge St. Became trade union official. Joined Radio Éireann as Assistant Programme Head 1955; transferred to Telefís Éireann 1961 as producer. Now Executive Producer, Special Projects. MIAL. Has written three radio plays, *Homecoming, Farewell Harper,* and *Big Jim,* the last based on the 1913 strike in Dublin and the career of James Larkin; the play was pub. Dublin 1955. It formed the basis of a stage play, *The Risen People,* first performed Abbey, 1958, revived in Dublin, Cork, Belfast and London. Short stories: *The Eagles and the Trumpets,* Dublin 1954; *The Trusting and the Maimed,* NY 1955; *Collected Stories,* Swords 1977; and novels, *Strumpet City,* 1969 (widely acclaimed novel of Dublin life in early 20th century, many translations including Russian; televised RTE); and *Farewell Companions,* 1977 (Dublin in '20s and '30s); *The Gems She Wore,* 1978, was a book of Irish places.

PLUNKETT, Joseph Mary, b. 1887, executed 1916. Son of Count Plunkett the poet. Became a journalist and revolutionary poet. In 1913 was a prominent member of the Irish Volunteers and became responsible for drawing up the military plans for a rising. In 1914 he was associated with Edward Martyn and Thomas MacDonagh in founding the Irish Theatre, Hardwicke St, Dublin. In 1916 he was one of the signatories of the Republican Proclamation, was court-martialled and sentenced to death. He married Grace Gifford in his cell on the eve of his execution (4th May 1916). He had published a volume of poetry, *The Circle and the Sword*, 1911, and his *Complete Poems* were collected and published after his death.

POLLOCK, John Hackett, b. Dublin 1887, d. 1964. Ed. CBS, Royal University and NUI. MD and pathologist in several Dublin hospitals. Founder member of Gate Theatre and prominent in Irish literary and cultural life. Wrote novels, poetry and plays, all published in Ireland under pseudonym 'An Philibin'. Plays include *The Fourth Wise Man*, a nativity play, later trans. Irish. Poetry: *Athens Aflame; The Secret Altar; Tristram and Iseult; Grass of Parnassus;* and *Lost Nightingale*, 1951. Novels include *The Valley of the Wild Swans*, 1932; *Peter and Paul*, 1933; *The Moth and the Star*, 1937; *Mount Kestrel* (a fantasy), 1945. Also a study of *William Butler Yeats*, 1935.

POLSON, Thomas R.J., b. Inniskillen *c.* 1820, d. 1908. Wrote a 3-volume historical novel set in the late 18th-century Ireland, probably based on family knowledge of the events: *The Fortune Teller's Intrigue*, Dublin 1848.

PORTER, James, b. Strabane 1753, d. 1798. School-teacher, Presbyterian minister, United Irishman, and the only Irishman on record as having been hanged for writing a satire. He had been concerned in the United Irishmen agitations in Ulster leading up to the Rising of 1798 and was in very bad odour with the authorities, particularly at Grey Abbey, where he was a preacher. In 1796 he published his satire, *Billy Bluff and Squire Firebrand*, in which he lacerated the dignitaries of Grey Abbey, and by implication the whole British system in Ireland. It was regarded as treasonable, and he was tried for it, and hanged in front of his own Meeting House in July 1798. The satire continued to be highly popular.

POWER, Marguerite, b. Clonmel 1789, d. Paris 1849. Daughter of Catholic family, her father was unpopular for his. attempts to put down the '98 Rising in his neighbourhood. Regarded as a traitor to the Catholic cause he was also a wastrel. He pushed Marguerite into marriage with a Captain Farmer when she was less than 15, presumably for money. She left the Captain after 3 months and returned home. Blossoming into beauty she caught the heart of the 1st Earl of Blessington, and a few months after Captain Farmer's death married the Earl in 1818. The couple travelled in Europe 1822-29, meeting Byron in Genoa, and bringing the Count D'Orsay with them first as a friend and then as the Earl's son-in-law. In 1829 the Earl died, D'Orsay separated from his wife, the Earl's daughter, and set up house in London next door to Lady B., their liaison causing much scandal for many years. Impoverished on the Earl's death, Lady B. turned to writing and became a fashionable journalist and travel writer, editing *The Book of Beauty and Keepsake*, and writing many books, including *Conversations with Lord Byron*, 1834, and *The Idler in Italy*, 3 vols, 1839-40. She also wrote novels such as *Grace Cassidy* and *The Two Friends*. Despite large earnings she went bankrupt in 1849, fled to Paris and died there the same year of apoplexy. Her niece Margaret P. also wrote novels.

POWER, Richard, b. Dublin 1928, d. Bray 1970. Ed. CBS, TCD and University of Iowa. Worked in Dept of Local Govt in Ireland, and scripted films for Dept, two of which won prizes at International Film Festivals, in Cork and Milan. Wrote mostly in Irish (see Part 2), but also wrote short stories and poetry in English and novels: *The Land of Youth*, US 1964, UK 1966, chosen as Book of the Month for July 1964 by Booksellers Guild of America, trans. Spanish; *The Hungry Grass*, US 1966, UK 1969; *Apple on the Treetop*, Swords 1980.

POWER, William Grattan Tyrone, b. Co. Waterford 1797, d. at sea 1841. Taken to Cardiff by his widowed mother in childhood. Joined strolling players when only 14. Became immensely successful as a comic actor in the late 1820s, touring England, Ireland and America. Was always known as Tyrone Power (the film actor was his great-grandson). Wrote several pleasant comedies and three novels including *The Lost Heir*, 1830, and *The King's Secret*, 1831. Also wrote *Impressions of America*, 1836. Drowned in the wreck of the *President* returning from America 1841.

PRAEGER, Robert Lloyd, b. Co. Down 1865, d. 1953. Son of a Dutch linen merchant. Ed. Belfast. Assistant Librarian and Librarian of National Library, 1893-1924, spent most of his leisure as a botanist and became a leading authority. President of Royal Irish Academy 1931-34. His *Natural History of Ireland*, 1950, is invaluable. Also wrote *The Way I Went*, 1937, rep. 1980, a classic of Irish topography, and *A Populous Solitude*, 1942.

PRENDERGAST, John Patrick, b. Dublin 1808, d. Dublin 1892. Ed. TCD. Bar 1830. Administered Lord Clifden's estates, 1836–. Published *The History of the Cromwellian Settlement in Ireland*, 1863, and as a result was asked to select official papers from the Carte MSS in the Bodleian Library which dealt with Irish affairs. Worked on these until 1880, and bequeathed many MSS to King's Inn Library, Dublin. Also wrote *The Tory War in Ulster*, 1868, and *Ireland from the Restoration to the Revolution*, 1887.

PRESTON, William, b. Dublin 1753, d. Dublin 1807. Ed. TCD. Bar. Judge of Appeals. Wrote poetry and many plays, including *Offa and Ethelbert, or the Saxon Princess*, 1791. Favoured Catholic Emancipation.

PRONE, Terry, b. Dublin 1949. Ed. UCD. Actress and journalist. Director of Arlen House, the Women's Press. Books: *Write and Get Paid for It!* 1979, 2nd ed. 1980; *Getting It Across*, 1980; *The Scattering of Mrs Blake and Related Matters* (a 1980 TV play adapted as a novel), 1985.

PROUT, Father, see MAHONY, Francis Sylvester.

PURCELL, Mary, b. Carrigeen 1906. Ed. Monaghan and Dublin. National teacher 1928-58. Has lectured in US and Europe. Biographies include *The Halo on the Sword* (Joan of Arc), Dublin 1950, US 1952, trans. etc. Awarded Palmes Academiques by French govt. *Matt Talbot and His Times,* Dublin 1954, US 1955; *The First Jesuit: St Ignatius Loyola,* Dublin 1956, US 1957; *The Great Captain* (Gonzalo de Cordoba), US 1962, London 1963; *The World of Monsieur Vincent* (St Vincent de Paul), NY and London 1963; *The Quiet Companion* (Peter Favre SJ), Dublin 1970; *The Vincentians* (history of Order in Ireland), Dublin 1973; *A Time for Sowing* (St John of God Brothers), Dublin 1979.

PURCELL, Patrick Joseph, b. Co. Kilkenny 1914. Ed. St Kieran's Kilkenny and UCD. Became a sports journalist in Dublin and an authority on the Gaelic Athletic Association. Novels: *Hanrahan's Daughter,* Dublin 1942, and *The Quiet Man,* Dublin 1945, both repub. in the US and chosen by the Catholic Book Club of American as monthly choices. The latter also chosen as alternate book by the Book of the Month Club. Trans. into Dutch and German. Not to be confused with the short story by Maurice Walsh filmed under that title. Other novels, *A Keeper of Swans,* 1944, and *Fiddler's Green,* 1949. Also *Sixty Glorious Years* (the story of the GAA), Dublin 1945, and *The Guinness Book of Hurling Records,* with David Guiney, Dublin 1965.

Q

QUAIN, Jones, b. Mallow 1796, d. London 1865. Half-brother to Sir John Q. the judge and co-author of *New System of Common Law Procedure.* Jones Q. went to London to teach anatomy and when less than 32 years old wrote *The Elements of Anatomy,* 1828, which became and remained for 80 years the standard text-book in English on the subject. Some later editions were ed. by his full brother Richard Q., also a doctor and medical writer, who later became a Surgeon Extraordinary to Queen Victoria. Strangely enough the Quains' cousin, another Richard Q. (1816-98) became Physician Extraordinary to the Queen in 1890, and was also a medical writer of note, editing the *Dictionary of Medicine,* 1882, which became the most successful medical publication of the period.

QUIGLEY, Hugh, b. Co. Clare 1818, d. Troy, NY 1883. Ed. Rome, ordained for American Mission. Rector of University of St Mary, Chicago; resigned to work among Chippewa Indians and Californian gold miners. Wrote two novels, *The Cross and the Shamrock,* Boston 1853, and *The Prophet of the Ruined Abbey,* Dublin 1863, and also *The Irish Race in California,* San Francisco 1878.

R

RATTAZZI, Marie Studholmine Bonaparte, Princess, b. Waterford 1833. Daughter of Sir Thomas Wyse and Princess Letitia Bonaparte, the daughter of Lucien B. She settled in Paris where she wrote poetry, novels and plays. She owned a theatre where she acted leading parts in her own plays. Married Urbano R. the Italian politician and opponent of Garibaldi. After his death in 1874 published *Rattazzi et Son Temps*, 1881-87.

RAY, R. J., pseud. of R. J. Brophy, b. Cork *c*. 1865. Journalist in Cork and Dublin. Wrote plays for the Abbey, *The White Feather*, 1909; *The Casting out of Martin Whelan*, 1910; and *The Gombeen Man*, 1913. Lennox Robinson admired them as being powerful and realistic.

READ, Charles Anderson, b. Sligo 1841, d. Surrey 1878. Failed in business locally and went to London where he wrote stories and serials for Young Folks, etc. His novels *Savourneen Dheelish*, 1869, and *Aileen Aroon*, 1870, were very successful, but his fame rests on his preparation of *The Cabinet of Irish Literature*, 4 vols, 1893, finished by T. P. O'Connor after Read's death, rev. ed. by Katharine Tynan Hinkson pub. 1906.

REDDIN, Kenneth, b. near Dublin 1895, d. 1967. Ed. Belvedere College, Dublin, Clongowes, and St Enda's, under Padraic Pearse. UCD 1918, and soon after leaving appointed Justice of the Districts Court 1922, a remarkable appointment for a man of 27; remained on Bench for over 37 years. Soon after 1922 had two plays performed at the Abbey, *Old Mag*, and *The Passing*, both pub. Dublin 1924. *The Passing* won the Gold Medal at the Tailteann Games that year, T. C. Murray's *Autumn Fire* being placed 2nd. In 1927 published a children's book, *The White Bolle Trie*, and another, *Mary Ann and the Old Party*, 1946, both in Dublin. Adult novels include *Somewhere to the Sea*, 1936, and *Another Shore*, 1945, republished in US 1946, as *Young Man With a Dream*. Under its English title it was filmed in Ealing Studios, 1947. Occasional pseud. 'Kenneth Sarr'.

REEVES, William, b. Co. Cork 1815, d. Dublin 1892. Ed. TCD. Ordained Derry 1839. Wished to be able to practise medicine among poor of his parish. Bishop of Down, Connor and Dromore 1886. His most famous work is *The Life of St Columba*, 1857, enthusiastically received by scholars throughout Europe; it still remains the best and fullest collection of materials on the early Irish Church in one volume. *Ecclesiastical Antiquities of Down, Connor and Dromore* which he had published in 1847 is narrower in scope but is also an essential reference book for its subject.

REID, Forrest, b. Belfast 1876, d. 1947. Ed. locally and Cambridge. Wrote a large number of popular novels and some critical essays, including *W. B. Yeats, A Critical Study*, 1915, rep. US 1982. Also wrote 2 vols. of autobiography, *Apostate*, 1926, and *Private Road*, 1940. Best-known novels include *The Kingdom of Twilight*, 1904; *The Garden Gods*, 1905; *Following Darkness*, 1912; *At the Door of the Gate*, 1915; *Pender Among the Residents*, 1922; *Uncle Stephen*, 1931; *The Retreat*, 1936; *Peter Waring*, 1937, rep. Belfast 1976; *Young Tom*, 1944.

REID, Graham J., b. Belfast. Ed. QUB 1977-80, later to be Writer in Residence. From a Protestant working-class family. Left school at 15. Several jobs including period in British Army. Returned Belfast and qualified as teacher, working in Stranmills |College of Education. Plays: *The Death of Humpty Dumpty*, 1979; *The Closed Door*, 1980; *The Hidden Curriculum*, 1982; *Callers*, 1985; all performed Peacock, Dublin. TV trilogy won Samuel Beckett Award 1982, pub. London as *Billy: Three Plays for Television*, 1984. Also *Remembrance,*1985.

REID, Thomas Mayne, b. Co. Down 1819, d. London 1883. Intended by his family for the Presbyterian ministry, but emigrated to America and led an extremely varied and adventurous life. Served in Mexican War and distinguished himself at Chapultepec where he was seriously wounded and left for dead. While convalescing wrote his first novel, *Scalp Hunters*, based on earlier adventures in the south-west territories of the US. Moved to London in 1849 and delighted generations of boys with series of adventure stories: *Rifle Rangers*, 1850; *Boy Hunter*, 1853; *War Trail*, 1857; *Boy Tar*, 1859; *Headless Horseman*, 1865; *The Castaways*, 1870; *The Death Shot*, 1874.

REILY, Hugh (sometimes Reilly), b. Cavan *c.* 1630, d. France 1695. Master in Chancery and Clerk of the Council in Ireland under James II, accompanied James into exile, where he wrote *Ireland's Case Briefly Stated*, 1695, an account of the state of Catholics in Ireland throughout the reigns of Elizabeth and the Stuarts, particularly noting the neglect of their interests by Charles II. James II, offended by the critical tone of the book, dismissed Reily, who died soon after. The book was for a 100 or more years almost the only printed defence of Irish Catholicism. Reprinted 1720, and again in 1754 in London as *Impartial History of Ireland*, it was then often reprinted in Dublin as *Genuine History of Ireland*, 1787, 1799, 1837, etc.

RIDDELL, Charlotte Eliza Lawson, née Cowan, b. Carrickfergus 1832, d. Middlesex 1906. Began writing as a girl and published over 30 novels and books of short stories: *The Race for Wealth*, *Above Suspicion*, *The Banshee's Warning*, etc.

RIDGEWAY, William, b. Dublin 1765, d. Trim 1817. Ed. TCD. Bar. He became the first successful Irish Law reporter, making accurate notes of famous Irish cases, in many of which he had appeared, mostly for the prosecution. One famous case in which he defended was that for assault and false imprisonment brought by John Hevey against the infamous Major Sirr, in 1802. In the following year he acted in and reported the series of trials arising from the Robert Emmet conspiracy, printing them as *A Report of the Proceedings in Cases of High Teason, at a Court of Oyer and Terminer, Held at the New Sessions House under a Special Commission, in the Month (sic) of August and September 1803.* The half title reads, *A Report of the Trial of Robert Emmet upon an Indictment for High Treason.*

ROBERTSON, Olivia, the Hon., b. London 1917. Ed. England and Dublin. Trained as painter. Nursed in London, 1940-41. Worked as playleader in Dublin Corporation playgrounds, 1941-45. Her book *St Malachy's Court,* 1946, is based on these playground experiences. *Field of the Stranger,* 1948, was a Book Society Choice, and a braille edition was published. Other novels are *The Golden Eye,* 1949, and *Miranda Speaks,* 1950. Two books on Dublin: *It's an Old Irish Custom,* 1954, and *Dublin Phoenix,* 1957, both illustrated by herself. More recently *The Call of Isis,* 1975; *The Isis Wedding Rite,* 1976; *Ordination of a Priestess,* 1977; and *Rite of Rebirth,* 1977; all pub. Enniscorthy for The Fellowship of Isis.

ROBINSON, Esmé Stuart Lennox, b. Cork 1886, d. 1958. Ed. Brandon. Interested in music, but his mind turned to theatre by seeing the Abbey Company perform in Cork in 1907. The same visit also made him an ardent Nationalist and in 1914 he joined the Volunteers. But long before then he had become a dramatist. His first play, *The Clancy Name,* 1908, ran three months. Chosen as manager of the Abbey Theatre by Yeats in 1910, he was sent to London to study theatre with Bernard Shaw. Resigning from the Abbey to write full time he found it less rewarding than he had hoped and became Organising Librarian for Carnegie Trust in Ireland, 1915, a job which took him all over Ireland. He wrote *The Dreamers* and then *The Whiteheaded Boy.* Yeats accepted this without enthusiasm, but it proved one of the great successes of the Abbey. In 1919 he returned to manage the theatre and was the chief discoverer and encourager of Sean O'Casey. In 1923 became a director of Abbey and remained one until 1956. In that year he made a controversial visit to China at the invitation of the Communist government, to celebrate Bernard Shaw's centenary. Among his many successful plays were *Never the Time and the Place; The Big House; Drama at Inish; The Far-Off Hills; Church Street; The Lost Leader; Killycregs at Twilight,* etc. He also wrote a novel, *A Young Man from the South,* short stories, criticism and biography, and edited several anthologies of poetry. *A Little Anthology of Modern Irish Verse,* 1929; *Oxford Book of Irish Verse,* 1958, etc. Ed. *J. B. Yeats' Letters,* 1920, and *Lady Gregory's Journals,* 1946.

The Irish Theatre, 1939; *Towards an Appreciation of the Theatre,* Dublin, 1945; *Ireland's Abbey Theatre,* 1951, are all essential reference books for a study of the subject. His own autobiography, *In Three Homes,* Dublin 1938 (written with his brother and sister), and *Curtain Up,* 1941, tell part of the story of a man who did as much as anyone, including Yeats, to create the Abbey, and the modern Irish theatre.

ROCHE, Regina Mary, née Dalton, b. Co. Waterford 1764, d. Waterford

1845. Published 15 or more novels, of which some were translated into French. Fame rests on one remarkable four-volume novel, *The Children of the Abbey*, 1798, which went into many editions and was enormously popular.

RODDY THE ROVER, see de BLACAM, Aodh.

RODGERS, William Robert, b. Belfast 1909, d. 1969. Presbyterian minister in Armagh 1934-46, BBC producer and script-writer 1946-52, elected to Irish Academy of Letters as a distinguished Irish and Ulster poet 1951. Collaborated with Louis MacNeice in the unpublished 'The Character of Ireland'. Volumes include *Awake*, 1941; *Europa and the Bull*, 1952; *Ireland in Colour*, 1956; and *Collected Poems*, Oxford 1971. Ed. *Irish Literary Portraits* (from broadcast conversations), 1972, NY 1973.

ROLLESTON, Thomas William Hazen, b. Shinrone 1857, d. Hampstead 1920. Ed. TCD and Germany. Translated German, and wrote on German Classical and Irish literature, including *The Teachings of Epictetus*, 1886, and *A Life of Lessing*, 1889. Founded *Dublin University Review* 1885. First Secretary of the Irish Literary Society in London where he settled in 1908. Published much poetry; also *Sea Spray*, 1909; *The High Deeds of Finn*, 1910; *Myths and Legends of the Celtic Race*, 1911, repub. 1985.

ROONEY, Philip, b. Co. Sligo 1907, d. Dublin 1962. Ed. Limerick. Worked as a bank clerk in Irish midlands for 15 years, during which time he wrote short stories. One of these, 'Irish Fortune', won him first prize in a Hospitals Sweeps competition. He published his first novel *All Out to Win*, Dublin 1935, *Red Sky at Dawn*, Dublin 1938; and *North Road*, Dublin 1940. Illness forced him to retire from banking and for the rest of his life he worked as a journalist, novelist and radio and TV scriptwriter. His best-known radio play was *The Quest for Matt Talbot*, chosen as Catholic Radio Play of the Year. Another was *The Three Mad Schoolmasters* based on Brinsley MacNamara's story and often rebroadcast. But his fame rests on his novels, which continued with *Singing River*, 1944; *Captain Boycott*, 1946, rep. 1966 and 1984, trans. in Scandinavia, repub. in America, filmed in Ireland, chosen as Book of the Month by American Catholic Literary Guild; *The Golden Coast*, 1947, and *The Long Day*, 1951, were his last books, published in Dublin.

ROS, Amanda McKittrick, b. Co. Down 1860 as Anna Margaret McKittrick, d. 1939. She trained as a teacher in Dublin, and later married Andrew Ross, stationmaster of Larne. In 1897 she published at her own expense *Irene Iddlesleigh* and followed it with two more novels, *Delina Delaney* and *Donald Dudley*, famed among critics and admirers as the worst novels ever published. Her admirers formed a club which met periodically in London to exchange quotations from her works, the membership including Lord Beveridge, Desmond MacCarthy, E. V. Lucas, and F. Anstey. Her poetry was as eccentric as her prose; *Poems of Puncture* and *Fumes of*

Formation are the principal collections.

ROSS, John, b. London 1917. Brought to Ireland 1919. Ed. Mountjoy School Dublin. The nephew of Barry FitzGerald and Arthur Shields, he began acting as a child with Gerald Fay in the Gate and Abbey companies. In 1939 his first thriller *The Moccasin Men* was published in London and was swiftly followed by eight more highly successful murder and spy stories, including *The Black Spot, Federal Agent, The Major, The Tall Man,* etc. In 1945 he gave up writing books to become a film scriptwriter, working on many Rank films including *Scott of the Antarctic.* Joined Radio Eireann as news scriptwriter in 1953. His novels have been translated into many languages, among them French, German and Danish. Also contributed to the *New Yorker, Saturday Evening Post, Colliers,* etc.

ROSS, Martin, pseud. of Martin, Violet Florence, b. Ross, Co. Galway 1861, d. 1915. Ed. Alexandra College Dublin. Collaborator with her forceful cousin Edith Œ. Somerville in several highly popular 'Anglo-Irish' novels. Their most famous creations were *Some Experiences of an Irish R.M.,* 1899; *Further Experiences of an Irish R.M.,* 1908 (R.M. standing for Resident Magistrate); and *Mr Knox's Country,* 1915. In these they sketched with cruelly humorous accuracy an Irish district such as West Cork at the end of the 19th century, sparing neither their own class of arrogantly decaying landowners, nor any other. Nationalists have hated these books for much the same reason that they hate Lover and Lever and others of their kind; and with as little and as much reason. Somerville and Ross had no interest in and probably no knowledge of 'the hidden Ireland' loved by their close contemporary and fellow Munsterman, Daniel Corkery. But what they saw they drew accurately with a happy malice, and it remains no less true for being an incomplete portrait. One need only compare it with the Ireland of Carleton and Barrington to find the same vein running consistently through the national character. It is generally considered that Violet Martin supplied the sense of humour to the partnership. The character of 'Mrs Knox of Aussolas' in the R.M. books was based on her mother, Mrs Martin of Ross. Other books by the partners include *The Real Charlotte,* 1894, now accepted as a masterpiece, on a minor scale, and *Dan Russel the Fox,* 1911. In 1932 she was awarded a posthumous Hon. D.Litt. by TCD.

ROTHERY, Brian, b. Dublin 1934. Ed. Dublin. Communications Officer, Institute for Industrial Research and Standards. Novels: *The Crossing,* London, NY and Germany 1970. *The Storm,* 1972; *The Celtic Queen,* with Ollie Petrocelli, NY 1974. Other works include *How to Organise Your Time and Resources,* London, NY 1972 (many trans.); *Survival by Competence,* London, NY 1972; *What Europe Means to the Irish,* Dublin 1973; *Men of Enterprise,* Dublin 1977.

ROTHERY, Sean, b. Dublin 1928. Ed. UCD. Architect and lecturer in College of Technology, Dublin. *Everyday Buildings of Ireland,* 1976; *The*

Shops of Ireland, 1978, both pub. Dublin.

ROWLEY, Richard, pseud. of Richard Valentine Williams, b. Belfast 1877, d. Loughgall, Co. Armagh 1947. Poet and playwright. Family firm McBride & Williams collapsed 1931. From 1934-43 Chairman of Northern Ireland Unemployment Assistance Board. During Second World War ran the Mourne Press. Poetry includes *The City Refuge,* Dublin 1917; *Workers,* 1923; *Sonnets for Felicity,* Co. Down 1942, etc. Best-known for *Apollo in Mourne,* 1926, rep. Belfast 1977, a mock-heroic play on the lines of *The Playboy of the Western World.*

RUSSELL, George William, b. Lurgan 1867, d. Bournemouth 1935. Was clerk in Dublin and studied art in his spare time. Began writing poetry, and both his mystical poems and similarly inspired paintings gained him an early reputation as an Irish William Blake. From 1899 was an official of the Irish Agricultural Organisation Society under Sir Horace Plunkett and edited its journal, *The Irish Homestead,* from 1905-23.

As a poet he became a guiding influence for many younger men and Yeats deeply admired him. His rooms in Dublin became a centre for artistic and intellectual discussion, and a focus for the 'Irish Renaissance' of late Victorian and Edwardian times. His play *Deirdre,* 1902, was one of the first to be put on by the Irish Literary Society, forerunner of the Abbey. It was followed by a large number of books of poetry and stories, all with a fantastic or mystical flavour. *New Poems* and *The Divine Vision,* 1904; *The Mask of Apollo and Other Stories,* 1905; *By Still Waters,* 1906; *The Hero in Man,* 1909; *The Renewal of Youth,* 1911; *Gods of War,* 1915; *The Candle of Vision,* 1919; *The Interpreters,* 1922; *Midsummer Eve,* 1928; *Enchantment,* 1930; *The Avatars,* 1933, etc.

From 1923-30 he was editor of *The Irish Statesman.* His famous pen-name 'AE' was shortening of an earlier pen-name 'Aeon', which utterly defeated a compositor. Russell thought that AE might be less liable to error. Yeats called his poetry 'the most delicate and subtle' that any Irishman had written in his time. He was also a painter of merit. Today a good Russell will fetch £1000 or more; in his own day he sold his paintings for as little as £2.

RUSSELL, Thomas O'Neill, b. Co. Westmeath 1828, d. Dublin 1908. Gaelic Revivalist who spent 30 years in America lecturing and writing on the language. Returned to Ireland 1895. Most famous book *Dick Massey: A Tale of Irish Life,* 1860, went into many editions.

RUSSELL, Violet, wife of George R. (AE). Published a famous collection of legendary stories based on the Finn cycle, *Heroes of the Dawn,* Dublin 1913.

RUSSELL, William Howard, b. Co. Dublin 1821, d. London 1907. Often called the first and greatest of war correspondents, although he was certainly not the first. As a very young man he reported the Irish general election of 1841 for the *Times* and so impressed the editor that he was asked to cover the repeal agitation of 1843. His accounts of meetings with Daniel O'Connell are of great interest. Although called to the English Bar, 1850, he was by then a professional journalist, covering the Schleswig-Holstein revolution of that year, again for the *Times*.

In the Crimean War his dispatches revealing the appalling inefficiency of the staff and commissariat led to the fall of the Aberdeen government in February 1855 and also brought Florence Nightingale out to the Crimea. Russell for the first time reported war as a business of the common soldier and showed him as a hero. His phrase 'the thin red streak topped with a line of steel', has passed into the language as 'the thin red line'.

In the Indian Mutiny his reports ended the atrocities being practised by the British against the defeated mutineers. In the American Civil War his unbiased reporting angered both sides so much that he felt obliged to leave America. He covered the Austro-Prussian War of 1856 and the Franco-Prussian War of 1870-71, and finally the Zulu War of 1879. In 1860 he had established the *Army and Navy Gazette* and gave this much of his time, leaving active journalism in 1880.

His books include *The Great War with Russia,* 1895. His *Letters from the Crimea* were published in book form, 1856. Repub. 1966.

RYAN, Cornelius, b. Dublin 1920, d. 1974. Ed. CBS Synge St. War correspondent, 1941-45, worked for many American news magazines. US citizen 1951. Achieved great success with *The Longest Day,* 1959 (the invasion of Normandy), *The Last Battle,* 1960 (the capture of Berlin), the best popular accounts of two key incidents in Second World War. Had already written *One Minute to Ditch,* 1957, and collaborated on several other works concerning the space programme, and a life of *MacArthur,* 1951 (with Frank Kelly); *A Bridge Too Far,* 1974, dealt with the abortive parachute attack on Arnhem. His last book, written with his wife Kathryn Morgan R. on the subject of his terminal illness, is *A Private Battle,* NY 1979.

RYAN, Desmond, b. London 1893, d. Dublin 1964. Son of W.P.R. Ed. in Pearse's school, and acted as his secretary before 1916. Fought in the GPO during the Rising. After release from internment became a journalist. Wrote *The Man called Pearse,* Dublin 1919; *James Connolly,* Dublin 1924; *Remembering Sion* (autobiography), 1934; *Unique Dictator* (de Valera), 1936; *The Phoenix Flame* (Fenianism and John Devoy), 1937; *The Rising* (1916), Dublin 1949, etc.

RYAN, Frederick, b. 1876, d. England 1913. Secretary to the Irish National Theatre Society in 1903, shortly after its foundation by Yeats. His best play *The Laying of the Foundations* had been produced by Yeats' company, 1902.

RYAN, John, b. 1925. Ed. Clongowes and National College of Art Dublin. Broadcaster, critic, editor, painter; one-time publican and publisher. Founder-editor of *Envoy*, 1949-51; editor of *The Dublin Magazine*, 1970-75; secretary of James Joyce Society of Ireland, 1970-74, and Irish Academy of Letters. Ed. *A Bash in the Tunnel* (James Joyce by the Irish), 1970. Two works: *Remembering How We Stood* (Bohemian Dublin at the Mid-Century), Dublin 1975; *A Wave of the Sea* (marine memoir), Swords 1981.

RYAN, William Patrick, b. Templemore 1867, d. London 1942. Journalist in London for most of his working life, but returned to Dublin 1906-11 to edit Nationalist journals. Returned to London to become assistant editor *Daily Herald*. Wrote *The Irish Literary Revival*, 1894; *The Pope's Green Island*, 1912; and *The Irish Labour Movement*, Dublin 1919. Also wrote a number of novels, plays and some poetry in Irish and English. Father of Desmond R.

RYNNE, Stephen b. Hampshire 1901 of Irish parents, d. Dublin 1980. Brought to Ireland 1907. Farmer and freelance journalist. *Green Fields*, 1938 (autobiography); *All Ireland*, 1956 (travel); *Father John Hayes* (founder of Muintir na Tir), Dublin 1960. Husband of Alice Curtayne.

RYVES, Elizabeth, b. 1750, d. London 1797. Cheated out of her inheritance, went to London and earned her living as a translator from French and as a journalist. Wrote plays and poetry, and one novel, supposedly autobiographical: *The Hermit of Snowden*. Died in bitter poverty. Isaac Disraeli mentions her in his *Calamities of Authors*.

S

SADLIER, Mary Anne, née Madden, b. Cootehill 1820, d. 1903. Emigrated to Canada 1844 and in 1846 married the well-known American publisher D. J. Sadlier. Her historical novels had a considerable success for many years: they include *Hermit of the Rock of Cashel; The Confederate Chieftains; The Blakes and Flanegans; The Old House by the Boyne,* etc.

SALKELD, Blanaid, b. India 1880, d. Dublin 1959. *Hello Eternity,* 1933, and *A Dubliner,* 1942. Also poetry: *The Fox's Covert,* 1935 and *Experiment in Error,* 1956. Older son became artist Cecil ffrench Salkeld; granddaughter Beatrice married Brendan Behan.

SALMON, George, b. Dublin 1819, d. Dublin 1904. Provost of TCD 1888. Wrote on theology and mathematics. His *Conic Sections,* 1847, written when he was still in his twenties, remained the leading text-book on the subject for 50 years. *Higher Plane Curves,* 1852; *Lessons Introductory to the New Algebra,* 1859; and *Geometry of three Dimensions,* 1862, all went into many editions, and as a body of work advanced the science of mathematics. He was not an inspired mathematician, but with tireless energy worked his way to original and valuable conclusions.

SAMPSON, William, b. Londonderry 1764, d. New York 1836. United Irishman, imprisoned in '98 and again in '99, was then banished to France where he began his *Memoirs*, NY 1807, finished in New York. His great achievement was in American law, his *Discourse showing the origin, progress, antiquities, curiosities & natures of the Common Law*, NY 1824, led eventually to much amendment and codification of laws inherited by the US from Britain.

SANDFORD, Francis, b. Co. Wicklow 1630, d. Newgate Prison 1694. Ed. TCD, he became Rouge-dragon Poursuivant in the College of Arms 1661, and Lancaster Herald 1676. The following year he published his masterpiece, *Genealogical History of Kings of England*, 1677, compiled at the urging of Charles II. But like many things urged by kings the undertaking brought more fame than profit. S. fell into debt, was put into Newgate, and there died.

SARR, Kenneth, see REDDIN, Kenneth.

SAVAGE, Marmion, b. Dublin 1803, d. Torquay 1872. Clerk to Council, Dublin Castle. Moved to London in 1856 as journalist. Married Lady Morgan's niece Olivia and published six novels of a satirical and witty flavour, including *The Falcon Family, or Young Ireland*, 1845; *My Uncle the Curate*, 1849; and *The Woman of Business*, 1870.

SCANLAN, Michael, b. Co. Limerick 1836. Emigrated to US as a young man. Author of a number of patriotic songs of which the most famous is 'The Fenian Men.'

SCOTT, Michael Peter, b. Dublin 1959. Ed. St Aidan's. Antiquarian bookseller and Irish folklore collector. *Irish Folk and Fairy Tales*, 3 vols, 1982-83; *Song of Children of Lir*, Skerries 1983; *Hall's Ireland*, 2 vols, 1984; *Celtic Odyssey; Tales from the Land of Erin* (trans. Voyage of Maeldún), 3 vols, 1985.

SCULLY, Denys, b. Co. Tipperary 1773, d. Tipperary 1830. Ed. Trinity College Cambridge, being only the second Catholic student there in 200 years. Barrister Leinster Circuit. His *Statement of the Penal Laws*, Dublin 1812, resulted in the imprisonment of the printer, but caused a great stir and ran through many editions.

SHANNON, Edward N,. b. *c.* 1790, d. Galway 1860. Byronic poet, some of whose poetry was thought by critics to be actually by Byron. Volumes include *The Crazed Maid of Venice*, 1826, etc.

SHARE, Bernard Vivian, b. 1930. Ed. TCD. Taught English Literature Newcastle University College, NSW Australia, 1954-57. Dublin journalist and writer of children's books, designed by William Bolger. Wrote highly successful and original *The Bed that went WHOOSH*, 1964, and *The Bed that went WHOOSH to* – (a series of Irish places), all pub. Dublin 1965.

Novels: *Inish*, 1966; *Merciful Hour*, 1970. Also *The Moon Is Upside Down* (travel), 1962; *Irish Lives* (biography), 1971; *And Nelson on His Pillar*, 1976; *The Emergency*, Dublin 1978. Editor of *Books Ireland*, a monthly trade journal.

SHAW, George Bernard, b. Dublin 1856, d. 1950. Son of an unsuccessful merchant. Ed. Wesley College. Worked as a clerk in a land agent's office after leaving school at 15. At this time he was deeply influenced by Vandeleur Lee the singing master, close friend of his mother and for several years a paying guest in the house. Critics have suggested that he sometimes feared that Lee was his actual father, although this appears to have been impossible, *vide Shaw and the Charlatan Genius* by John O'Donovan, 1965.

In 1876 he followed his mother and sister to London, where he did hack journalism for Lee, and wrote five novels of which the best-known is *Cashel Byron's Profession*, the hero being a professional boxer. In this unconventional choice of a hero one can see the embryo of all Shaw's playwrighting. In 1884 he joined the Fabian Society and developed from a shy young man into a political orator of skill and power. He first achieved literary notice as 'Corno di Bassetto' for *The Star* in 1888, and later as 'GBS' for *The World*, one of his achievements being to secure recognition in London for Wagner. In 1895 Frank Harris appointed him dramatic critic to *The Saturday Review*, where he made a second reputation by defending Ibsen. He had already produced his first play in 1892, *Widowers' Houses;* in 1893 *The Philanderer* failed to find a theatre, and in the same year *Mrs Warren's Profession* was refused a licence by the Lord Chamberlain. Shaw was advised on all sides to forget about trying to write plays and to stick to what he could really do well, which was criticism. He ignored the advice, and continued with playwrighting, still without success. *Arms and the Man, Candida, Caesar and Cleopatra* and the other plays of these years all failed to please, and it was not until about 1905 that Shaw began to be recognised as a major dramatist. Meanwhile, he continued in politics, serving as vestryman on the St Pancras local authority, 1897-1903. With Sydney Webb he was one of the principal workers in transforming the Fabian movement into the Parliamentary Labour Party, after a break with the Liberals in the 1890s.

As a Socialist he was against war in principle and practice, but was never a pacifist in the accepted sense. *War Issues for Irishmen,* 1918, contains many of his articles and letters on the war. A year earlier he had published *How to Settle the Irish Question.* As on every other subject his writings on war and Ireland were provocative, mocking, intelligent and widely misunderstood. He defended Casement with a passion that deeply injured his reputation in England, just as his war-recruiting play had offended his friends in Ireland.

At the end of the war his tone of cool rationalism and sardonic paradox began to match the mood of the times, and of a generation disillusioned with hypocrisy and flag waving. In *St Joan*, 1923, he wrote what many consider to be his masterpiece. Plays such as *St Joan; Androcles and the Lion*, 1912; *The Doctor's Dilemma*, 1906; *Man and Superman*, 1901-3; *Back to Methuselah*, 1921; and *The Apple Cart*, 1929, are his monument. He brought back intelligence to the theatre, and after the intellectual Sahara of 19th-century drama this was a vast achievement.

Other books include *The Quintessence of Ibsenism*, 1891; *The Sanity of Art*, 1895; *The Perfect Wagnerite*, 1898, and *Our Theatres in the Nineties*, 2 vols, 1906. *The Intelligent Woman's Guide to Socialism*, 1928, set out to describe every possible political system and prove its inadequacy, leaving only Socialism as a practical form of government. The book has been described as naïve, and a waste of a great man's talents, having taken three years to write, but it contains much good sense and is readable, which cannot always be said of books on political theory. It was reissued with revisions as *Everybody's Political What's What*, 1944.

What I Really Wrote About the War, 1930, contains his letters and articles to English and American papers, 1914-19. *Music in London*, 1932, is a collection of his music reviews as 'Corno di Bassetto', 1888-90, and as GBS, 1890-94. *London Music*, 1937, completed the collection. In 1932 he brought out *The Adventures of the Black Girl in her Search for God*, which irritated the orthodox to an extraordinary extent, the girl of the title finishing her search in the arms of a red-headed Irishman.

In 1933 he published *The Political Madhouse in America and Nearer Home*, after an unsatisfactory lecture tour of America, on which he was indignant to find himself addressing audiences of old ladies.

As well as these books, he published prefaces to his plays, the preface sometimes outweighing the play itself in length and substance. In them he said why he wrote the play, and expanded on the themes that had prompted him to write it. Particularly notable prefaces were written for *Man and Superman*, 1903; *John Bull's Other Island*, 1904; and *Back to Methuselah*, 1921.

SHEEHAN, Patrick Augustine, b. Mallow 1852, d. Doneraile 1913. Ed. Fermoy and Maynooth. Ordained 1875. Curate in England and then in Cobh and Mallow. Parish priest Doneraile 1895. DD 1902. Canon 1903. Wrote poetry, and many novels which achieved a vast popularity in Ireland and abroad. The best-known of them, still loved today by many Irish readers, include *My New Curate; Miriam Lucas; The Blindness of Dr Gray; The Queens' Fillet* and *Glenanaar. The Literary Life and Other Essays*, Dublin 1921.

SHEEHAN, Ronan, b. 1953. Short-story writer and novelist. *Tennis Players*, 1977; *Boy with an Injured Eye*, Dingle 1983 (short stories, of which 'Optics' won Hennessy Award 1974). Editor of *The Crane Bag*, and special editor of Latin-American issue 1983. Won Rooney Prize 1984.

SHEEHY, Edward, b. Co. Kerry about 1910, d. 1956. Wrote a number of excellent stories, many published in *The Bell* in the 1940s. Dogged by ill-health for many years. Collections include *God Send Sunday*, Dublin 1939.

SHEEHY, Jeanne, b. 1940s. Ed. UCD and TCD. Teaches Art History at Oxford Polytechnic. *Walter Osborne*, 1974; *J. J. McCarthy and the Gothic Revival in Ireland*, 1977; with Peter Harbison and Homan Potterton, *Irish Art and Architecture, from Prehistory to the Present*, 1978; *The Rediscovery of Ireland's past: The Celtic Revival 1830-1930*, 1980.

SHEIL, Richard Lalor, b. Kilkenny 1791, d. Florence 1851. Ed. TCD. Bar 1814. MP 1831. Master of the Mint 1846-60. Ambassador. Wrote several verse-tragedies, of which *Evadne, or the Statue*, 1819, was the most popular. Friend of John Banim's and his collaborator in *Damon and Pythias*.

SHERIDAN, Frances, née Chamberlaine, b. Dublin 1724, d. Blois 1766. Her father, the Rev. Dr Philip Chamberlaine, disapproved of female emancipation and particularly of education for women. He refused to allow her to be taught even to read and write but she learned both accomplishments in secret from her brother Walter, and when only 15 wrote a novel *Eugenia and Adelaide* although it remained unpublished until after her death.

During a serious theatre riot in 1745 instigated by a man named Kelly, Frances C. came to the aid of the manager, Thomas Sheridan. Two years later she married him. Thomas himself had written a *Life of Swift*, and between them they founded a literary dynasty spreading over many generations, and one of the most remarkable in the history of letters. Their second son was Richard Brinsley S., the playwright, born in 1751.

In 1754 they moved to London where Samuel Richardson encouraged Frances to continue writing. In 1761 she published her masterpiece, *Memoirs of Miss Sidney Biddulph*. It was enthusiastically received; Dr Johnson praised it; the Abbé Prevost adapted it into French; it was translated into German the next year. She followed this novel with several comedies, of which *The Discovery* was the most successful. In 1764 she retired to France.

SHERIDAN, John Desmond, b. 1903, d. Dublin 1980. Humorous essayist and novelist, most popular in his day; published a large number of collections of essays and sketches such as *I Laugh to Think*, 1946, and poetry, *Joe's No Saint*, 1949. His novels include *Paradise Alley*, 1945; *The Rest Is Silence; The Magnificent MacDarney*, 1949; *God Made Little Apples*, 1962; *Include Me Out*, 1968; all Dublin; and *The Hungry Sheep* (Catholic doctrine restated), NY 1973.

SHERIDAN, Niall Joseph, b. Co. Meath 1912. Ed. UCD. Edited *Cothrom Féinne*, contributors including Denis Devlin, Charles Donnelly, Donagh MacDonagh, and Brian Nolan (Flann O'Brien). Published *20 Poems*, 1934, with Donagh MacDonagh, contributed poetry to magazines in England, Ireland and America in the 1930s and short stories to *Esquire, Atlantic*

Monthly, etc in 1940s. His comedy, *Seven Men and a Dog,* Abbey 1958. Worked for Tourist Board for several years. Became senior executive in Telefís Éireann.

SHERIDAN, Richard Brinsley, b. Dublin 1751, d. 1816. Son of Thomas S. and Frances Chamberlaine, see above. Ed. Harrow, and immediately after leaving school wrote a three-act farce, *Jupiter,* with a schoolfriend. In 1771 the family moved to Bath where they met the composer Linley and his family. Richard fell in love with Miss Elizabeth Linley, eloped with her to France and after some romantic delay married her in 1773. Returning to London they settled down to live beyond their means. In 1775 he wrote *The Rivals,* which was very well received at Covent Garden. In the same year, desperate for funds, he produced two more farces, *St Patrick's Day* and *The Duenna,* neither of which were worthwhile.

In 1776, fortified by the success of *The Rivals,* and more still by large loans from his father-in-law and another friend, he bought half the patent of Drury Lane Theatre from Garrick for £35,000, a gigantic sum for the period. In 1778 he bought the remaining half share for £45,000. He put on a version of Vanbrugh's *Relapse,* and then his own masterpiece, *The School for Scandal.* In 1779 he produced *The Critic,* the last of his three great comedies. In 1780 he turned to politics, became an Under-Secretary in 1782 and held ministerial posts for the next thirty years. He made his reputation by his share in the impeachment of Warren Hastings in 1788, and increased it in 1794 in fierce debates concerning the French Revolution. But shortly before this, having lost his first wife, he married again, and unwisely, his new wife being more extravagant and far sillier than the first. His money affairs declined as his political reputation grew. In 1809 Drury Lane, renovated in 1794 at vast expense, burned to the ground and Sheridan was ruined. In 1812 he lost his seat in Parliament. His parliamentary leader and hero, Charles James Fox, was already dead, and the Prince Regent, his friend in prosperous days, was of little help in his ruin. He lived on in pathetic circumstances for four years and died in great poverty , 1816. He was given a magnificent funeral in Westminster Abbey.

SHERIDAN, Thomas, b. Co. Meath 1646, d. Paris (?) *c.* 1700. Ed. TCD, and Fellow of the Royal Society 1679. Visited James Duke of York in his Brussels retirement, 1679, and on James's accession received many favours, becoming Chief Secretary and Commissioner of the Revenue of Ireland, 1687. Went into exile with James, as his private secretary. He left a MS *History of his Own Times,* which passed into the Royal Library at Windsor, and the famous *Discourse on Rise & Power of Parliaments,* 1677 (reprinted as *Some Revelations in Irish History,* 1879), which is remarkable both for its information on political questions of Carolean Ireland, and for the politics of conciliation it put forward. If James II had followed them Irish and English history might have taken a different course. Great-uncle of Thomas S. below.

SHERIDAN, Thomas, b. Co. Cavan 1719, d. London 1788. Actor, lecturer and author, Swift's godson and biographer, he is chiefly famous as the father of Richard Brinsley S. His *General Dictionary of the English Language*, 2 vols, 1780, was highly successful. He brought out *The Works of Swift with Life* in 18 vols, 1784. Wrote many works on elocution and kindred subjects, and one play at least, when he was an undergraduate, *Captain O'Blunder or the Brave Irishman*, 1754. Managed the Smock Alley Theatre in Dublin for some years, and quarrelled with a section of the public for attempting to reform the manners of theatre-goers. This led to several theatrical riots, as a result of one of which a Miss Frances Chamberlaine became his friend, and soon his wife (see SHERIDAN, Frances). They moved to England in 1754, leaving young Richard S. at Doctor White's school in Grafton Street for several years more.

In England S. became the close friend of Dr Johnson, securing pensions for both J. and himself.

SHIELS, George, b. Ballymoney 1881, d. 1949. Ed. locally. Emigrated to Canada after leaving school and was injured in a railway accident, crippling him for life. Returning to Ireland he began writing, at first using pseud. of 'George Morshiel'. His first play was *Bedmates*, 1921, followed the same year by *Insurance Money* at the Abbey. *Paul Twyning*, 1922, was his first real success, and for more than 20 years he continued to write successfully for the Abbey, although his invalid state kept him housebound in the country. T. C. Murray the dramatist was a long-time friend by correspondence although they met only once; Murray sent him firsthand accounts of the openings of all plays at the theatre. Lennox Robinson called Shiels 'the Thomas Moore of the Irish Theatre,'and his plays had the warm-hearted simplicity of Moore's poetry, although he could also write tragedy, such as the often-revived *Passing Day*. Most of his plays are comedies and all of them have been revived many times: *Professor Tim; The Fort Field; The New Gossoon; Cartney and Kevney; The Summit*, etc. *The Rugged Path*, 1940, ran 8 weeks, and was seen by 25,000 people in its first run, a record for the Abbey then.

SHORTER, Dora Sigerson, b. Dublin 1866, d. 1918. Eldest daughter of George Sigerson. Well known as a poet under the name Dora Sigerson. Collections include *Sad Years*, 1918, and *The Tricolour*, 1922.

SIGERSON, Dora, see SHORTER, Dora Sigerson.

SIGERSON, George, b. Strabane 1836, d. 1925. Ed. Cork and Paris. Scientist and man of letters, wrote on medicine, geography, land tenure and was a distinguished translator of Irish poetry: *The Bards of the Gael and the Gall*, 1897, perhaps his best-known book. *Modern Ireland*, 1868 (Dublin ed. 1869); *History of Land Tenure and Land Classes of Ireland*, 1871; and *The Last Independent Parliament of Ireland*, 1918, were among his other principal works.

SIMMONS, James Stewart Alexander, b. Derry 1933. Ed. Campbell College and Leeds University. Lecturer Nigeria 1963-67, Coleraine 1968–. Founded and edited the magazine *The Honest Ulsterman,* 1968. Poetry includes *Energy to Burn,* 1971; *The Long Summer Still to Come,* 1973; *West Strand Visions,* 1974; *The Selected James Simmons,* 1978; *Constantly Singing,* 1980; *From the Irish,* 1985; all pub. Belfast.

SIMMS, John Gerald, b. Lifford, Co. Donegal 1904, d. 1979. Ed. Winchester, Oxford. Career in Indian civil service before entering TCD 1950. Lectured in modern history and elected Fellow 1966. Keeper of Marsh's Library, Dublin, 1974. MRIA. *The Williamite Confiscation in Ireland 1690-1703,* 1956; *Jacobite Ireland 1685-91,* 1969; *William Molyneux of Dublin* (ed. P. H. Kelly), Dublin 1982.

SKEFFINGTON, Francis Sheehy, b. Ballieborough 1878, d. Dublin 1916. Ed. UCD. Journalist, idealist and reformer. Editor of *The Nationalist* and *The Irish Citizen,* a feminist weekly. Wrote a *Life of Michael Davitt,* 1908, and a novel *In Dark and Evil Days,* but before it could be published he had been shot by a British officer during the Easter Rising of 1916. Captain Bowen-Colthurst was later found to be insane. *In Dark and Evil Days* was published posthumously.

SKELTON, Philip, b. near Lisburn 1707, d. Dublin 1787. Was given the living of Templecarn, near Lough Derg, and published an interesting *Description of Lough Derg,* 1759. Involved in many controversies over Deism, *Some Proposals for the Revival of Christianity,* 1736, was at first thought to be by Swift, having some of Swift's irony. In his parish he was notable for charity, selling his books to feed his people in the great Famine of 1757. He was noted for his attempts to teach his people theology, and someone kindly said that when he failed to feed his people books, he sold the books to feed them bread. He also had a curious habit of summoning the parish to what he supposed was his death bed. This happened often, until a parishioner said 'make it a day, sir, and don't always be disappointing us thus.' This cured him of his hypochondria and when he finally died he did it privately, in Dublin. Immortalized in his friend Samuel Burdy's *Life,* Dublin 1792, rep. Oxford 1914.

SLINGSBY, Freke, see under WALLER, John Francis.

SLOANE, Hans, b. Co. Down 1660, d. London 1753. Ed. London and France. Bt 1716. During travels 1685-89, collected the materials for his great works *The Natural History of Jamaica* and *A Voyage to the Islands of Madeira,* both of which came out in several volumes, 1707-25. *The Natural History* is regarded as his masterpiece. In 1732 S. was one of the promoters of the colony of Georgia. His museum, and library of 50,000 printed books and more than 3500 MSS (the Sloane Collection), formed the nucleus of the British Museum Library, his family receiving £20,000 in return.

SMITH, Brendan John, b. Essex 1917. In Ireland since 1921. Ed. Belvedere.

SMITH

Between 1941 and 1945 wrote nine plays and three revues, produced Dublin. Among them *You are Invited, No More Culture, Private Hotel, The Solving of Charlie,* and *One Man's Heaven.* Since 1950 has concentrated on production and teaching. In 1956 produced the National Pageant *Cuchulainn* in Dublin, and has been creator and Director of Dublin Theatre Festival since 1957. Awarded Le Croix de Chevalier de l'Ordre des Arts et des Lettres by French government, 1964.

SMITH, Charles, b. Waterford 1715 (?), d. Bristol 1762. Pioneered Irish topography. Wrote a series of county and city histories: *The Antient & Present State of the County of Down* (with Walter Harris), 1744; *The Antient (etc) of the County and City of Waterford,* 1746; *The Antient (etc) of the County & City of Cork,* 1750; and *The Antient (etc) of the County of Kerry,* 1756. Macaulay praised them.

SMITH, Paul, b. Dublin 1932. Worked at odd jobs from eight years old, but continued visiting school on occasions until he was thirteen. Messenger, factory worker, waiter, dancer, costume designer in Dublin theatres; travelled widely in Europe, Australia and North America. His first novel, *Esther's Altar,* London and NY 1959, was compared by Dorothy Parker to O'Casey. Other novels include *The Countrywoman,* 1962; *The Stubborn Season,* 1962; both pub. America and London; *Stravaganza,* 1963; *Annie,* NY 1972, repub. as *Summer Sang in Me,* 1975. *Esther's Altar* repub. as *Come Trailing Blood,* 1977.

SMITHSON, Annie M.P., b. Sandymount Dublin 1873, d. 1948. Ed. Dublin and Liverpool. Trained as nurse and midwife and practised as district nurse all over Ireland, becoming, 1929-42, Secretary and organiser of the Irish Nurses' Organisation. Born of a Protestant family she became a Catholic after an unhappy love affair, and on discovering that her father had been a Fenian involved in the Rising of 1867 her patriotism became strongly Nationalist and Republican. In the Civil War she took the Republican side and was in the dramatic siege of Moran's Hotel as a nurse.

Her writing life began late, her first novel, *Her Irish Heritage,* appearing in Dublin in 1917. Patriotic, frankly sentimental, her writing had a freshness and innocence that soon made her a bestseller in Ireland, the most successful of all Irish romantic novelists. Fifty years later her first novel, and those that followed, were still being reprinted and read. Other titles include *By Strange Paths; By Shadowed Ways; For God and Ireland; Wicklow Heather; The Walk of a Queen; The Marriage of Nurse Harding,* etc. Her autobiography, *Myself and Others* was published in 1944, in Dublin, as were all her novels. She is buried in Rathfarnham.

SMYTH, Alfred P., b. Co. Meath 1942. Ed. UCD. Fellow of Society of Antiquaries and Royal Geographical Society. Senior lecturer in history at University of Kent. *Scandinavian York and Dublin: the History and Archaeology of Two Related Viking Kingdoms,* 2 vols, 1975 and 1981; *Scandinavian Kings in the British Isles,* 1977; *Celtic Leinster,* Dublin 1982;

Warlords and Holy Men: Scotland AD 80-1000, 1984.

SMYTH, William, b. Dublin 1813, d. London 1878. Son of an alderman. Served as midshipman in British Navy and became Public Treasurer of Dublin. Exhibited paintings in RHA as well as acting and writing for the stage with great popular success. He was a close friend of both Thackeray and 'Father Prout.' His plays include *Old Carlisle Bridge,* Dublin 1862; *Hurrah! the Fleet,* Dublin 1863 etc.

SMYTHE, Percy Clinton Sydney, b. 1780, d. 1869. Ed. TCD. British Diplomatic Service, becoming Ambassador. Inherited title as 6th Viscount Strangford 1801. Translated *Poems from the Portuguese of Camoens,* 1803, which was very well received, going into at least six editions. After service in Portugal, Sweden, Turkey and Russia was given additional title of Baron Penshurst 1825. His brother Percy-William also served in the Diplomatic Corps, and became Oriental Secretary to the FO during the Crimean War. He contributed articles to many English journals. The 6th Viscount died 1855. Percy-William became 8th Viscount.

SOMERVILLE, Edith Oenone, b. Island of Corfu 1858, d. 1949. Ed. privately in her parents' house in County Cork. Studied art in London and Paris. In 1886 met her second cousin, Violet Martin (see ROSS, Martin) and struck both a friendship and a literary partnership of great value. In 1889 they produced a light, humorous book, *An Irish Cousin,* which pleased the public and secured them commissions to write travel articles. Violet Martin supplied most of the text and Edith Somerville the illustrations. In 1894 they published *The Real Charlotte,* a serious novel compared by many contemporary critics to Balzac. Irish connections who saw themselves mirrored in the book were less admiring. In 1899 they published *Some Experiences of an Irish R.M.* and became one of the most famous patnerships in literary history. *Some Irish Yesterdays,* 1906; *Further Experiences of an Irish R.M.,* 1908; *Dan Russel the Fox,* 1911; *The Discontented Little Elephant,* 1912 (a rather frightening children's book); and in 1915 the third of the R.M. books *In Mr Knox's Country.* That year Violet Martin died, but Edith Somerville was convinced, or claimed to be, that her dead friend remained invisibly with her, and continued to publish her books with the dual signature 'Somerville and Ross': *Irish Memories,* 1917; *Wheel Tracks,* 1923; *The Big House at Inver,* 1925; *French Leave,* 1928; *The States through Irish Eyes,* 1931; *An Incorruptible Irishman,* 1932 (a biography of her great-grandfather Charles Kendal Burke, Lord Chief Justice of Ireland in the early 1800s). In 1932 TCD conferred Hon. D. Litt. on Edith S. and posthumously on Violet Martin. Other books were *The Smile and the Tear,* 1933; *The Sweet Cry of Hounds,* 1936; *Sarah's Youth,* 1938; and *Notions in Garrison,* 1942.

SOMERVILLE-LARGE, Peter, b. 1929. Ed. TCD. Travel writer. Spent ten years in Arabia as army officer. Lives West Cork, married to critic Gillian S-L. *A Tribe's Tribulations,* 1967, on the Yemen; *Caviar Coast,* 1968, on

SOUTHERNE

Iran; *The Coast of West Cork*, 1972; *From Bantry Bay to Leitrim*, 1974; *Irish Eccentrics*, 1975; *Dublin*, 1979, rep. 1981; *A Living Dog*, 1981; *The Grand Irish Tour*, 1982; *Hang Glider* and *Cappaghglass* (study of a West Cork village), both 1985.

SOUTHERNE (or Southern), Thomas, b. Co. Dublin 1660, d. 1746. Ed. TCD and Middle Temple. Served in British Army. Collaborated with Dryden in at least two plays, of which *The Loyal Brother* addressed as a compliment to the Duke of York in 1682 was mainly his, Dryden providing prologue and epilogue. Served under the Duke of Berwick and at his request wrote *The Spartan Dame*. Neither of them are very good plays but he appears to have done well from them. His serious claim to standing consists of his two tragedies, *The Fatal Marriage*, 1694, and more particularly *Oroonoko*, 1696, based on Aphra Behn's novel and aimed against the Slave Trade. The novel and play are the first literary expression of the campaign in England against the trade, which was to culminate 100 years later in its abolition. Based on Aphra Behn's early years in Surinam, it tells the story of an African Prince and his love, Imoinda. After many adventures both find each other again as slaves in the East Indies. The Prince Oroonoko organises a mass escape, but the attempt is defeated and all ends in tragedy. The plot of both play and novel is strong and good, and the play held the stage for the whole of the 18th century and beyond.

Southerne died in 1746, leaving a large fortune. He is credited by Pope and others with having vastly increased the amount a playwright might expect to receive from a successful play. He himself reckoned on £700 as an average payment, where Dryden for example never got more than £100.

STACPOOLE, Henry de Vere, b. Kingstown (now Dun Laoghaire) 1863, d. 1951. Son of Rev. William S. Ed. Malvern and St Mary's Hospital. Qualified as a doctor but ceased practising shortly afterwards. His most famous novel is *The Blue Lagoon*, 1915; other novels include *Patsy*, 1908; *Garryowen*, 1910; *Father O'Flynn*, 1914. In 1915 he published *The North Sea and Other Poems*, and in 1916 *François Villon: His Life and Times*. Later books include *Men and Mice*, 1942; *Oxford Goes to War*, 1943; *The Story of My Village*, 1947; *The Land of Little Horses*, 1948. His books were immensely successful; translated into most European languages, and reprinted often. Apart from writing and medicine he had a life-long interest in sea-birds and founded the Penguin Club for their study and protection.

STANFORD, William Bedell, b. Belfast 1910, d. Dublin 1984. Ed. TCD. Regius Professor of Greek TCD 1940-80. Pro-Chancellor 1974-82. Chancellor 1982-4. Senator 1948-69. Chairman Dublin Inst. for Adv. Studies 1972-80. Among many works on Greek Literature he edited *The Odyssey*, 2 vols, 1947-48; *Sophocles' Ajax*, 1963, etc. Wrote *Greek Metaphor*, Oxford 1936; *Aeschylus in his Style*, Dublin 1942; *The Sound of Greek*, US 1967; *Ireland and the Classical Tradition*, Dublin and US, 1976; *Enemies of Poetry*, 1980; *Greek Tragedy and the Emotions*, 1983; and, with R. B. McDowell, *Mahaffy,* 1971, paperback ed. 1975.

STANIHURST, Richard, b. Dublin 1545, d. Brussels 1618. Became Speaker of Irish House of Commons. Converted to Catholicism by his wife, he became a Jesuit after her death. With tutor Edmund Campion, contributed a *Description* and a *History* of Ireland to Holinshed's *Chronicles,* 1577. His translation of the first four books of Virgil's *Aeneid* into English verse, 1583, was very popular and often reprinted, although regarded as vulgar burlesque by later poets and scholars.

STARKIE, Walter Fitzwilliam, b. 1894, d. Madrid 1976. Ed. Shrewsbury, TCD. Served with YMCA, First World War, attached to British troops in Italy. Director of Abbey Theatre 1927-42. Lecturer in Romance Languages TCD 1920; went to Madrid in 1940 as head of British Institute ; lectured in Madrid University 1948-56; Professor in Residence, University of California, 1962-70. Studied music as a young man and played the violin all over Europe, using his skill to acquire the friendship of gypsies, and to study their music and folklore. From this came *Raggle Taggle,* 1933, an account of his adventures in the Balkans. *Spanish Raggle Taggle,* 1934; *Gypsy Folklore and Music,* 1935; *The Waveless Plain* (an Italian memoir), 1938; *In Sara's Tents,* 1953; *The Road to Santiago,* 1957; *Scholars & Gypsies* (autobiography), 1963; all reflect this lifelong interest. Kt of Order of Alfonso XII; Chevalier of the Legion of Honour; Kt of Order of Crown of Italy; CBE; CMG; MIAL.

STEELE, Richard, b. Dublin 1672, d. Carmarthen 1729. Ed. Charterhouse and Oxford. Enlisted in Horse Guards 1694 and published a poem on the death of the Queen which secured him a commission in the Coldstreams. In 1700 he fought a duel with another Irishman, Kelly, and seriously wounded him. This so impressed his mind that he wrote *The Christian Hero* as a gesture of remorse, 1701, criticising the Military Life as being conducive to unwarrantable pleasures; advocating greater reliance on the Bible, and greater chivalry towards women. The public welcomed it, but his fellow officers thought him a milksop for it and in an attempt to redress the balance he wrote *The Funeral,* 1701; *The Lying Lover* and *The Tender Husband,* 1705. But virtue kept breaking out in all these and none were successful. Marriage to a rich widow in 1705 was far more beneficial and he secured promotion the same year. The widow quickly died and he married Mary (dear Prue) Scurlock, 1707, and became 'gazetteer,' a court appointment of some value. In 1709 he started *The Tatler* magazine with his schooldays friend Joseph Addison, and in 1711-12 ran *The Spectator.* It was followed by *The Guardian,* and next by *The Englishman,* 1713. In that year he became MP for Stockbridge in the Whig interest and campaigned for the Hanoverian Succession in Parliament and print. His pamphlet *The Crisis,* 1714, got him the enmity of Swift and expulsion from Parliament. With George I's accession he was restored to fortune, appointed supervisor of Drury Lane and granted other sinecures. In 1715 he was knighted. But in 1718 he fell out with the government and with Addison over the Peerage Bill, lost his Drury Lane job and the royal favour. In 1720 he wrote against the South Sea investment boom, which made him few friends when the bubble was rising, and fewer still when it burst, as he said it would. In 1724 money troubles forced him to leave London for Wales where he died.

It is easy to laugh at his moralising, but in most of the moral, social and economic disputes of the day Steele was right and his smart contemporaries were wrong. His plays, from *The Funeral*, 1701, to *The Conscious Lovers*, 1722, had a moral and social viewpoint, the lack of which is the great weakness of most Restoration and early 18th-century drama. With Addison he created the magazine and its 'journalism of ideas,' a new form in which comment, news, wit and wisdom were shrewdly blended, providing essayists with a convenient means of reaching a wide public. It is difficult to overestimate his influence on this branch of letters. His own essays were models for the whole of the 18th century and beyond.

STEPHENS, Henry Pottinger, b. Dublin *c.* 1850. Popular writer of operettas and burlesques in late Victorian London. *Virginia and Paul*, 1883; *The Red Hussar*, 1889, etc.

STEPHENS, James, b. Dublin 1882, d. 1950. Worked for years as a solicitor's clerk. Later became Registrar of the National Gallery of Ireland. Lived in Paris for a time, and in London, where be became a popular broadcaster. Wrote short stories, essays, poetry and criticism and in all fields secured the admiration of intelligent readers. But his public popularity rests on one remarkable book, *The Crock of Gold*, part fantasy, part fairy story, part pamphlet in the eternal Irish war of the sexes. The only Irish novel which can claim kinship with it is *At Swim-two-Birds* by Flann O'Brien. Other books are *The Demi-Gods; The Charwoman's Daughter; Irish Fairy Tales; Here Are Ladies; Deirdre*, 1923; *In the Land of Youth*, 1924; *Etched in Moonlight*, 1928; *Insurrections* (an early volume of poetry); and *The Hill of Visions* (also poetry), 1912. His eye-witness account of the Easter Rising, *The Insurrection in Dublin*, NY 1916, was reprinted in 1965. In his later years Stephens spent much of his genius in good talk rather than writing, both privately and in broadcasts. *Desire and Other Stories*, selected and introduced by Augustine Martin, Swords 1981.

STERNE, Laurence, b. Clonmel 1713, d. London 1768. An Irish writer only by accident of birth. His father was a junior officer in the British Army, himself the grandson of an Archbishop of York. Laurence spent the first few years of his life in garrison towns in Ireland, and may have absorbed some Irishness from nurses and street companions. Educated in Yorkshire and Cambridge he became a clergyman of rather liberal view, giving 'small, quiet attentions' to many women besides his long-suffering wife. His masterpiece is the long extravaganza *Tristram Shandy*, 1759-67. Some critics have seen it as the embryo of much modern 'advanced literature' from Proust to Joyce. Other works, all of similar humorous, romantic-psychological nature; *Sermon of Mr Yorick*, 1760; *Sentimental Journey* (of Mr Yorick in France), 1768; *Letters of Yorick to Eliza* (to Mrs Eliza Draper), 1775; *Collected Works* (with letters, and illustrated by Hogarth), 1780.

It is interesting as an example of critical blindness even in men of genius that *Tristram Shandy* was violently condemned as immoral and bad as literature by Dr Johnson, Horace Walpole, Richardson and Goldsmith among others. Sterne died penniless.

STOCK, Joseph, b. Dublin 1740, d. 1813. Became Bishop of Killala 1798, in which year he was captured by General Humbert, the commander of the French invasion force. His account, *Narrative of what passed at Killala in the summer of 1798. By an Eye-Witness*, 1799, is the best contemporary record of the invasion, and it's impartiality is believed to have prevented Stock from becoming Archbishop. In 1776 he had published a *Life of George Berkeley*, the only memoir by someone who knew B.

STOKER, Abraham, b. Dublin 1847, d. 1912. Ed. TCD. Bar. In civil service for some years. Wrote dramatic criticism and became editor of *The Evening Mail*. In 1878 Sir Henry Irving engaged him as private secretary and he stayed for 27 years until Irving's death in 1905. During this time Stoker, known generally as 'Bram' Stoker, wrote a dozen novels, of which *Dracula*, 1897, was the masterpiece. Others include *The Mystery of the Sea, The Jewel of the Seven Stars, The Lair of the White Worm*, and *The Lady of the Shroud;* all are still worth reading. But *Dracula* touched some universal and apparently timeless nerve of horror in the world's readers. It has been reprinted and translated countless times, often filmed, serialised, turned into comic strips, and has passed into the world's folklore.

STOKES, George Thomas, b. Athlone 1843, d. Dublin 1898. Librarian of St Patrick's library, Dublin, and vicar of All Saints. *Ireland and the Celtic Church*, 1886; *Ireland and the Anglo-Norman Church*, 1888.

STRONG, Eithne, née O'Connell, b. Co. Limerick 1923. Ed. TCD. Teacher and civil servant before marriage to Rupert Strong. Poetry: *Songs of Living*, 1961: *Sarah, in Passing*, 1974; *Flesh – the Greatest Sin*, 1980; *My Darling Neighbour*, 1985. Short stories, *Patterns*, 1981; also, in Irish, *Cirt Óibre*, 1980; *Fúil agus Fállai*, 1983. All pub. Dublin.

STRONG, Leonard Alfred George, b. Plymouth 1896, d. 1958. Son of Irish parents who brought him often to Ireland as a child. Ed. Brighton and Oxford, where he was an Open Classical Scholar. He became a broadcaster in the BBC's early days. MIAL; FRSL. Wrote verse: *Dublin Days*, 1921; *Lowery Road*, 1924; *At Glenan Cross*, 1928; *Northern Light*, 1930; *Call to the Swans*, 1936; and short stories: *Doyle's Rock*, 1925; *The English Captain*, 1929; *Tuesday Afternoon*, 1935; *The Travellers*, 1945 (winner of James Tait Black Memorial Prize); *Darling Tom*, 1952, etc. Novels include *The Jealous Ghost; The Garden*, 1931; *The Brothers*, 1932; *Sea Wall*, 1933; *Trevannion*, 1945; *The Bay; The Director; Corporal Tune; Laughter in the West; Mr Sheridan's Umbrella; King Richard's Land*, etc. He also wrote works of criticism, biography and local history, including *Instructions to Young Writers; Dr Quicksilver; Hill of Howth;* and an autobiography, *Green Memory*, 1961.

He was deeply interested in dialects; a great walker and lover of the West of Ireland, gathering dialect material wherever he went.

STRONG, Rupert, b. London 1911, d. Dublin 1984. Cousin of L.A.G. Strong. Ed. TCD. Dublin journalist and psychoanalyst from 1945. Poetry: *Jonathan of Birkenhead*, 1953; *From Inner Fires*, 1962; *Selected Poems*, 1974; *Come When You Can*, 1981; *Pre-Requiem for a Clown*, 1983; all pub. Dublin.

STUART, Henry Francis Montgomery, b. Australia 1902 of Ulster parents. Ed. Rugby. Married Iseult Gonne, daughter of Maude Gonne, 1920. Early poetry won critical praise in America and Ireland, and the patronage of W. B. Yeats, who hailed him as one of the great new names of Irish writing. MIAL. Poetry includes *We Have Kept the Faith*, Dublin 1923, new enlarged ed. 1982. Also wrote plays, *Men Crowd Me Round,* 1933, and *Strange Guest*, 1940, both produced at the Abbey.

His fame was secured by his novels, beginning with *Women and God*, 1931. Others include *The Coloured Dome*, 1932; *The Angel of Pity*, 1935; *The Great Squire*, 1939. At the outbreak of war he was employed in Germany and he spent the war principally in Berlin, in a strictly civilian capacity. His experiences there form the background of some of his later novels and are recounted in a memoir by his second wife, Madeline Stuart, *Manna in the Morning*, Dublin and Gerrards Cross 1984. Since the war he has written *The Pillar of Cloud*, 1948; *Redemption*, 1949; *The Flowering Cross*, 1950; *The Pilgrimage*, 1955; *Victors and Vanquished*, 1958; *Angels of Providence*, 1959; *Black List, Section H*, Illinois 1971, London 1975; *Memorial*, 1973; *A Hole in the Head*, 1977; *The High Consistory*, 1981; *Faillandia*, Dublin 1985. Also *States of Mind* (short prose writings 1938-83), Dublin 1983.

STUART, James, b. Armagh 1764, d. Belfast 1842, journalist, and author of *Historical Memoirs of the City of Armagh*, Belfast 1819.

SULLIVAN, Alexander Martin, b. Bantry 1830, d. Dublin 1884. In 1855 became assistant editor of *The Nation*, which at this period was against all revolutionary methods and favoured a constitutional struggle. For his opposition to the Fenians S. was sentenced to death by them in 1865, but escaped. Ironically he was sentenced three years later to imprisonment by the British authorities for an article on the execution of the Fenian 'Manchester Martyrs'. Released after 3 months he used £400 collected on his behalf in Ireland to erect the statue of Henry Grattan now in College Green Dublin. Formed the Home Rule party with Isaac Butt, but turned to Parnell in 1877. His *Story of Ireland,* 1870, was popular for many years. Also *New Ireland,* 1877, etc.

SULLIVAN, Timothy Daniel, b. Bantry 1827, d. 1914. Elder brother to A.M.S. above. Became well known as a journalist and poet for *The Nation,* where his most famous song 'God save Ireland' appeared in 1867 in commemoration of the Manchester Martyrs. Another of his songs to achieve immortality was 'The Song of the Canadian Backwoods', usually referred to as 'Ireland Boys Hooray'. A favourite with Irish emigrants in Canada and America, it was sung by the northern troops on the eve of the Battle of Fredericksburg in 1862. The southern troops took up the chorus and for half an hour the two armies sang in the darkness 'Here's to Ireland, dear old Ireland, Ireland boys, hooray.'

In 1880 'TD' as he was universally known was elected MP for Westmeath. In 1886 he became Lord Mayor of Dublin, defied the Castle over some edict and was gaoled. In prison he wrote *Lays of Tullamore Prison,* 1888. In 1890 he visited America to collect funds, but opposed the Parnell faction in the 'split'. In 1905 he published his *Recollections.* Other volumes of verse include *Greenleaves,* Dublin 1868; *Dunboy and Other Poems,* 1868; *Death of King Connor MacNessa; Lays of the Land League,* 1887; *Poems,* 1888; *Blanaid and Other Poems,* 1892.

SUPPLE, Gerald Henry, b. Dublin 1825. A coach-builder and poet, he emigrated to Australia in 1858 where he studied for the Bar, but having committed a murder was sentenced to 20 years imprisonment. His poetry first appeared in *The Nation,* and later in many Irish and Australian anthologies. His *The Dream of Dampier* was published in Melbourne, 1879, and he also wrote a *History of the Anglo-Norman invasion of Ireland,* Dublin 1856.

SWIFT, Jonathan, b. Dublin 1667, d. 1745. Much argument surrounds his birth but it seems likely that his father was one of the Temple family. He was a cousin of Dryden, and was at Kilkenny Grammar School with Congreve. In TCD he was accused of 'indiscipline' and almost refused a degree. In 1689 he became secretary to Sir William Temple. Ordained in 1694 in Ireland, he returned to the Temple house, 1696, and in 1697 wrote *The Battle of the Books,* his first major work. He also met Esther Johnson, the 'Stella' of his writings, ostensibly the daughter of a servant in the house, but most likely the child of Sir William Temple's sister, and therefore a close blood relative of Swift's if his own illegitimacy is accepted. This may explain the curious relationship between the two. In 1699 Sir William died and Swift returned to Ireland, becoming a prebendary of St Patrick's. In 1704 he published *A Tale of a Tub,* written much earlier. This is a satire on the main divisions of Christianity, and cost Swift all chance of a bishopric. He visited London often, mixed with the literary society of the day, poured out satires on religion and politics and less serious matters such as astrology; wrote poetry, and in 1710 quarrelled with the Whigs over Dissent and became an active Tory. The *Conduct of the Allies*, 1711, denouncing the war, sold 11,000 copies in 2 months and led to the fall of Marlborough and the Peace of Utrecht in 1712-13.

In 1713 he was made Dean of St Patrick's, Queen Anne's hostility to the 'irreligious satirist' preventing a better appointment. Sometime before this he had begun his *Journal to Stella* (1710-13) and had met the other principal woman in his life, Esther Vanhomrigh, whom he nicknamed 'Vanessa.' He seems to have been her lover and may have given her a child. In 1714 occurred the quarrel with Steele, in *The Public Spirit of the Whigs*. The fall of the Tory ministry ruined all his political hopes and with the accession of George I and the Whig government he retired to Dublin and became involved in Irish affairs. He wrote a number of pamphlets protesting at the ill-treatment and neglect of Ireland practised by successive English ministries. The most famous, and influential, of these were the *Drapier's Letters*, 1724, purporting to be by a Dublin draper prophesying the ruin of Ireland if a debased copper coinage (Wood's ha'pence) was circulated. Partly due to these letters the scheme was dropped. Another was *A Modest Proposal* – that the children of the poor should be fattened to feed the rich instead of being wastefully allowed to starve, 1729.

Vanessa died in 1723, at least partly because of Swift's cruel treatment of her. Stella died in 1728. Swift himself suffered increasing attacks of vertigo, and by 1738, all hope of Church preferment long vanished, he had begun to sink into alleged madness, having suffered most of his life from bilateral Ménière's disease, with symptoms of giddiness, nausea and deafness. In 1742 he had a stroke with aphasia, leaving him speechless while able to understand. His last few years appear to have been terrible, and for much of the time he had to be protected from himself by his servants. He died in 1745 and was buried in St Patrick's beside Stella. His truest mourners must have been the poor of Dublin. For many years a third of his income and most of his energies had been given for their welfare. Another third of his money was saved year by year to found St Patrick's Hospital for Imbeciles, opened 1757, and the first of its kind in Ireland.

His most-read book is *Gulliver's Travels*, 1726. *Directions to Servants*, 1745, was his last major work, attacking the menials as savagely as he had ever attacked their masters. In 1757 his *History of the Last Four Years of Queen Anne* was published. He had written the bulk of this, 1712-14, and then left it unfinished and unprinted till his death.

SYNGE, John Millington, b. Rathfarnham 1871, d. 1909. Ed. TCD, RIAM. Lived for a time in Paris where in 1899 he met W. B. Yeats. He had already visited the Aran Islands and Yeats persuaded him that the Irish peasantry and countryside were worthy subjects for a writer. He returned to Aran several times, and also tramped the Wicklow valleys and hills, gathering material. He later claimed, when his plays were attacked as 'pseudo-Irish', that he had never employed a word or phrase he had not first overheard in some peasant's kitchen. His first play, in 1903, *The Shadow of the Glen*, is set in Wicklow, and was enthusiastically greeted by the Irish newspapers as an 'insult to every decent woman in Ireland'. In 1904 came *Riders to the Sea,* called by the *Irish Times* 'quite unfit for presentation on the stage.' In 1905 *The Well of the Saints,* and then in 1907 *The Playboy of the Western World,* confirmed the author's reputation as a dangerous trouble-maker. By the end of the first week of the *Playboy's* opening run it required 500 policemen to control the audience, which in the Abbey Theatre numbered just under 500. The actors fought with the audience as well, and the audience screamed 'Kill the author,' 'Filth,' 'Sinn fein Amhain' and 'Take it off' so loudly that the play was inaudible, and nobody who had not read the script could have known why they hated it. In the same year the Abbey put on Synge's *The Tinkers' Wedding,* and Synge published *The Aran Islands.* In 1909 Synge died, the greatest playwright the Abbey had dis-covered, one of the greatest Ireland has ever produced, and the first who might be called truly Irish. All previous Irish playwrights, like his contem-poraries Wilde and Shaw, wrote primarily for English audiences and either ignored or distorted Irish affairs to please the Haymarket or Drury Lane. Synge wrote for an Irish audience about Irish things, and the measure of his success is the fury that his plays aroused. Of them all the *Playboy* is the masterpiece and most often revived, although all of them have been played countless times in many countries. The *Playboy* takes Ireland's dearest legends and illusions, stands them on their heads and mocks them, and the wonder is that Yeats, whose illusions were mocked along with everyone else's, not only put the play on, but kept it on at some risk to his career and even his physical safety.

In 1910 Synge's last play, *Deirdre,* appeared, still uncompleted at his death. His *Works,* including essays and poetry, were published the same year.

T

TATE, Nahum, b. Dublin 1652, d. London 1715. Son of a Puritan divine who was briefly Provost of TCD. Ed. TCD, described by a contemporary as a 'free, good-natured, fuddling companion.' Wrote several plays of little merit, such as *A Duke and no Duke,* 1685 and *Injured Innocence,* 1707. Also adapted Shakespeare's *King Lear* to current tastes, and wrote much poetry, which secured him the Poet Laureateship in succession to Shadwell in 1692. His poetry was of the neo-Classical kind, being written for public occasions rather than any private prompting, and although he was not the worst Laureate, this is faint praise. His pleasantest poetry is the *Panacea, or A Poem upon Tea,* 1700, and *The Innocent Epicure, or the Art of Angling.* His reputation rests on his metrical version of the Psalms, done with Nicholas Brady, fellow Irishman from County Cork, and an even worse poet than himself. The *Supplement to the New Version* (of the Psalms) was done in 1703 by Tate alone, and the hymn contained in it, 'While Shepherds Watched Their Flocks by Night', remains one of the most famous pieces of Christian poetry in English.

TAUTPHOEUS, Baroness von, originally Jemina Montgomery, b. Co. Donegal 1807, d. Munich 1893. Married the Baron von T. in 1838. He was Chamberlain to the King of Bavaria and she spent the remainder of her life in Germany. She wrote several novels, set in Bavaria: *The Initials*, 1850; *Cyrilla*, 1857; *Quits*, 1857; and *At Odds*, 1863.

TAYLOR, Geoffrey Basil, b. Norfolk 1900, raised Sligo, d. Dublin 1956. Ed.Haileybury/TCD. Worked in Carnegie Libraries in Wicklow and Sligo. Taught English in Cairo after 1929 divorce from artist Norah McGuinness and involvement with Robert Graves's ménage. Disinherited by father 1932 and so changed name from Phibbs to T. (his mother's). Remarried 1935. Literary editor of *The Bell* for several years. Poetry: *Withering of the Figleaf*, 1927; *A Dash of Garlic*, 1933. Also, *Insect Life in Britain* 1945; *Some Nineteenth Century Gardeners*, 1951; *Irish Poets of the Nineteeth Century* 1952; *The Victorian Flower Garden*, 1952.

TEELING, Charles Hamilton, b. Lisburn (?) 1778, d. Dublin 1850. Northern journalist, famous for his *Personal Narrative of the Rebellion of 1798*, Belfast 1828; *Sequel to, etc.*, Belfast 1832. Ineffective as literature, but important as eye-witness history.

THOMAS, Caitlin, Daughter of Francis MacNamara, and sister of Nicolette Devas. Married the poet Dylan Thomas and has published controversial books on their life together: *Leftover Life to kill*, 1957; *Not Quite Posthumous Letter to my Daughter*, 1963.

THOMPSON, Samuel (Sam), b. 1916 Belfast, d. 1965. Ed. locally, went to work in shipyards as a painter. Began writing documentary scripts on the shipyards for BBC, under the encouragement of Sam Hanna Bell. His first play, *Over the Bridge*, 1957, was accepted for performance in Belfast, and then rejected on the grounds that it would cause a public disturbance. Thompson sued the individual responsible and won his case, but the play was not performed until 1960, when it enjoyed successful and trouble-free runs in Belfast and Dublin. It deals with the bitter hostilities of religious groups in the industrial north. *The Evangelist*, 1963 approached bigotry from a different direction. Thompson died suddenly in 1965, leaving one more play, *Cemented with Love*, performed on Irish TV 1966. His body of work was small, but has been immensely influential. One or two previous playwrights had dealt with working-class Belfast from the inside, but not with his strength and talent. Questions which had been considered impossible for public dramatic debate appeared in his plays, and all succeeding northern playwrights must benefit from his trail-blazing.

THOMPSON, William, b. Rosscarbery 1785 (?), d. 1833. One of the principal figures in the creation of 'Scientific Socialism', he was a disciple of Robert Owen and spent much of his fortune in attempts to set on foot Owenite experiments in Ireland. A wealthy landowner, his interest in Socialism was born out of his knowledge of the poverty of his tenants, and he came to the view that all wealth is the product of labour. He set out his views in *An Inquiry into the Principles of the Distribution of Wealth most conducive to Human Happiness*, 1824, 2nd ed. 1850, 3rd 1869. This book had a great influence on European Socialism and Marx drew much inspiration from it, particularly on the theory of Surplus Value. T. also had strong views on sex equality, and in 1825 published an *Appeal of one Half of the Human Race, Women, against the Pretentions of the Other Half, Men, to retain them in Political, and thence, in Civil & Domestic, Slavery.*

Other publications were *Labour Rewarded: The Claims of Labour & Capital Conciliated, or how to secure to Labour the whole Products of its Exertions. By one of the Idle Classes*, 1827, and *Practical Directions for the Establishment of Communities on the Principles of Mutual Co-operation*, 1830. He intended to leave his fortune for the propagation of the co-operative movement, but his heirs-at-law disputed the will and eventually had it set aside.

THOMSON, William, Lord Kelvin, b. Belfast 1824, d. London 1907. Brought to Scotland as a child, he entered Glasgow University at 11 years old. His work on electric currents in submarine cables led to the success of the Atlantic Cable, for which he was knighted 1866. Invented various measuring devices, amp-metres, volt-metres, etc., and did important work in many branches of electrical research. Made Baron Kelvin of Largs 1892. His many papers collected as *Mathematical and Physical Papers*, several vols, 1882-1911.

THORNLEY, David Andrew Taylor, b. Surrey 1935, of an Irish mother (like his hero Pearse), d. 1978. Ed. St Paul's London, TCD. Journalist, broadcaster and politician. Associate Professor of Political Science TCD 1968-69. Labour TD 1969-77. Delegate to European Parliament 1974-77. *Isaac Butt and Home Rule*, 1964, US 1976. Many articles and short stories.

THURSTON, Katherine Cecil, née Madden. b. Cork 1875, d. Cork 1911. Married the novelist E. Temple Thurston 1901, but divorced him not long afterwards. Her novels were extremely popular: *John Chilcote*, 1904, was dramatised the next year, and *The Gambler* and *The Fly On the Wheel* also did well.

TIERNEY, Michael, b. Co. Galway 1894, d. Dublin 1975. Ed. UCD, Paris, Athens, Berlin. Professor of Greek UCD 1923-47. President UCD 1947-64. Kt of St Gregory 1955. Wrote and edited many learned papers, and *A Tribute to Newman*, Dublin 1945; *Hecuba*, Dublin 1946; *Daniel O'Connell*, 1949; *Struggle with Fortune*, Dublin 1954 (on the centenary of the

Catholic University of Ireland); *Eoin MacNeill: Scholar and Man of Action, 1867-1945*, ed. F. X. Martin, 1981.

TIGHE, Mary, née Blatchford, b. Co. Wicklow 1772, d. 1810. Her long poem, *Psyche, or the Legend of Love*, 1795, was popular in both the US and England, being reprinted many times, and deeply impressed and influenced Keats.

TODD, James Henthorn, b. Dublin 1805, d. Dublin 1869. Regius Professor of Hebrew TCD, his fame came from his work on Irish MSS. Worked with O'Donovan and O'Curry on classifying these. Edited *The Martyrology of Donegal* by Michael O'Clery (with William Reeves), and in 1867 pub. text and translation, with notes, of *The War of the Gaedhil with the Gaill* in the Rolls series.

TODHUNTER, John, b. Dublin 1839, of a Quaker family, d. Chiswick 1916. Ed. Mountmellick and York. At 16 began as clerk in Dublin for Pim's and Bewley's, but entered TCD to study medicine. M. Chir. 1868. MD 1871. Studied in Vienna and Paris, returning to practise in Dublin. Having always wanted to write he also became Professor of English Literature in Alexandra College, and in 1872 published *A Theory of the Beautiful* which caused favourable comment in intellectual circles in Germany as well as Britain. He had already contributed poetry to Thackeray's *Cornhill Magazine*, and in 1874 he gave up medicine, moved to London and devoted himself to literature. Influenced by Standish O'Grady, he wrote *The Banshee*, 1888; *The Life of Patrick Sarsfield*, 1894; and *Three Irish Bardic Tales*, 1896. *The Banshee* contains one of his best-known Irish poems, 'Aghadoe.' At the same time he had begun writing plays: *Helena in Troas*, 1886, with Beerbohm Tree and his wife in the lead; *A Sicilian Idyll*, 1890; *The Black Cat*, 1893, almost the first English production of an 'Ibsenite' play; *Mary Queen of Scots* and *The Poison Flower*. He also translated Heine and Goethe and wrote *A Study of Shelley*, 1880. Other books include *The True Tragedy of Rienzi*, 1881; *Sounds and Sweet Airs*, 1905; *From the Land of Oceans*, 1918; and *Selected Poems*, 1929.

TOLAND, John, b. Inishowen 1669, d. Putney 1722. Raised Catholic, turned Protestant at 16. Ed. Scotland, Leyden, Oxford. Famous for his *Christianity Not Mysterious*, 1696. This argued for a rational religion and was the first shot fired in England in the war of the Deists against the orthodox forces. The book caused a sensation and in Ireland was burned by the public hangman. *Amyntor*, 1699, dealt with the evidence for canonical as against apocryphal books of scripture. *Nazarenus*, 1718, concerned the possibility of a Pauline-Jewish schism in the primitive Church, and foreshadows the so-called Tübingen controversy. T. also wrote a *Life of Milton*, 1698; a *History of the Druids*, 1726; and an *Account of Prussia and Hanover*, 1705, in support of the Hanoverian succession.

TOMELTY, Joseph, b. Portaferry near Belfast 1911. Son of a house painter.

236

Apprenticed to his father, he began writing for radio in his spare time. In 1935 he was concerned with the beginnings of the Ulster Group Theatre, first as an actor and then in 1941 as General Manager. He resigned in 1951 to join Tyrone Guthrie's company for the Festival of Britain. His plays include *The End House*, Abbey 1944; *Right Again, Barnum*, Ulster Theatre 1946, which had a record-breaking run; *All Souls' Night* and *Is the Priest at Home?*, 1949; and *Mugs and Money*, 1953. He has written two novels, *Red Is thePort Light*, 1948, rep. Belfast 1984, and *The Apprentice*, 1953, rep. Belfast 1983. In 1955 a serious accident almost killed him, but he recovered to act again both in films and on the stage.

TONE, Theobald Wolfe, b. Dublin 1763, d. Dublin 1798. Son of a Dublin coachmaker, entered TCD 1781, eloped with Mathilda Witherington and neglected his studies. But received BA 1785 and called to Bar 1789. Had already made a curious proposal to British govt for a military colony in the South Seas. In 1790 published *A Review of the Conduct of the Administration* attacking British policies towards Ireland, and became a fiery Republican. *An Argument on behalf of the Catholics of Ireland*, 1791, called for a union of non-conformists and Catholics against the British authorities. In the same year he founded the Society of United Irishmen in Belfast and Dublin, and was assistant secretary to the Catholic Committee, 1792. Prominent at great Catholic Convention held at the Tailor's Hall, and in the delegation to petition George III, he found himself in advance of most of his colleagues and turned to France for help. In 1794 his dealings with the French Republic through Jackson were discovered and he was obliged to leave Ireland for America, 1795. Went to France 1796, and spent the rest of his life trying to organise a French invasion of Ireland. Hoche's expedition failed, as did a Dutch one the following year. Sailed with a third under Hardy that reached Lough Swilly and was captured. Court-martialled and condemned to death, some mystery surrounds his actual death, which is usually considered to have been suicide. His journals were published by his son William in America, 1826.

TONE, William Theobald Wolfe, b. Dublin 1791, d. New York 1828. In childhood was adopted 'a son of the French Republic' after his father Theobald Wolfe T.'s death in 1798. Wrote a history of *The Goths in Italy* of no great merit, and a much more interesting *School of Cavalry*, Georgetown, 1824, having settled in the US in 1816. But his main interest for Ireland is his edition of his father's papers, with a *Life of Theobald Wolfe Tone*, 2 vols, Washington 1826.

TORRENS, Robert, b. Co. Derry 1780, d. 1851. Served in Dutch campaign in Royal Marines and in the Spanish Legion in Peninsular War, rising to Colonel. Retired from army 1836 and became MP. Elected FRS. A classical economist in most respects, he added to the science by his work, particularly in stressing the role of land, labour and capital as factors in the production equation, and also in formulating the law of diminishing returns. *An Essay on the External Corn Trade,* 1815, went through several editions and had great influence on Peel. *An Essay on the Production of Wealth,* 1821, etc. Interested in Australian colonisation. Lake and River Torrens named after him. Wrote two novels, *Celebia Choosing a Husband,* 1809, and *The Victim of Intolerance, or the Hermit of Killarney: A Catholic Tale,* 1814.

TORRENS, William, b. McCullagh, Co. Dublin 1813. d. 1894. His mother was niece to Robert Torrens. and in 1863 he assumed her maiden name. Spent some years in Colonial Service in S. Australia. Became MP at Westminster. Wrote *Life of Lord Melbourne,* 1878; *Life of Lord Wellesley,* 1880; and *Twenty Years in Parliament,* 1883.

TOWNSHEND, Horatio, b. Co. Cork 1750, d. Co. Cork 1837. Vicar of Rosscarbery and author of the *Statistical Survey of the County of Cork,* 1 vol., Dublin 1819, 2nd ed. in 2 vols, Cork 1815.

TREACY, Maura, b. Kilkenny 1946. Short stories, *Sixpence in Her Shoe,* Swords 1977; novel, *Scenes from a Country Wedding,* Swords 1982.

TRENCH, Charles Chenevix, b. India 1914. Ed. Winchester, Oxford. Indian Army 1936-47. Colonial service Kenya 1948-63. Runs smallholding in North Tipperary. Books include *My Mother Told Me,* Edinburgh 1959; *Portrait of a Patriot* (biography of John Wilkes), 1963; *The Desert's Dusty Face,* 1964; *A History of Horsemanship,* 1970; *Charlie Gordon,* 1978; *The Great Dan* (biography of Daniel O'Connell), 1984; *The Frontier Scouts,* 1985.

TRENCH, Melasina, b. Dublin 1768, d. Galway 1837. Daughter of Philip Chenevix. Married Colonel St George 1786, who died two years later in Portugal. In 1798 she began her journal, travelling in Europe. In 1802 she married Richard Trench of Moate, Co. Galway. Her son Richard Chenevix T. edited her journal and letters as *Remains,* 1862. They are deeply interesting and have been compared to Walpole's *Letters* for quality.

TRENCH, Richard Chenevix, b. Dublin 1807, d. London 1886. Ed. Harrow, Cambridge. Ordained Norwich 1832. Professor of Divinity King's College London 1846. Dean of Westminster 1856. Archbishop of Dublin 1864. This literary churchman had over 40 published works, including *On the Study of Words,* 1851; *English Past and Present,* 1856; *Collected Poems,* 1885. Is credited with the genesis of the *Oxford English Dictionary* in a resolution moved at the Philological Society on 7 January 1858.

TRENCH, William Stuart, b. 1808 near Portarlington, d. Carrickmacross 1872. Cousin of Richard Chenevix T., became land agent for the Marquises of Lansdowne and Bath, and Lord Digby shortly before the Famine, and left the best contemporary account of an Irish district during it: *Realities of Irish Life,* 1868. It ran through 5 editions in the year of publication. An abridged edition in 1966 had an introduction by Patrick Kavanagh. He also contributed an equally interesting series of sketches and stories to the *Evening Hours,* a monthly magazine, 1871-72, but these were never reprinted in book form.

TREVOR, William, pseud. of Cox, Trevor, b. Co. Cork 1928. Ed. St Columba's, TCD. Practised as a sculptor before turning to writing. Joint winner of Irish section of Unknown Political Prisoner sculpture competition. MIAL. Novels: *A Standard of Behaviour,* 1958; *The Old Boys,* 1964, winner of Hawthornden Prize 1965; *The Boarding House,* 1965; *The Love Department,* 1966; *Mrs Eckdorf in O'Neill's Hotel,* 1968; *Miss Gomez and the Brethren,* 1971; *Elizabeth Alone,* 1973; *The Children of Dynmouth,* 1976 (Whitbread Prize), *Other People's Worlds,* 1980; *Fools of Fortune,* 1983 (Whitbread Prize – only writer to win it twice). Short-story collections: *The Day We Got Drunk on Cake,* 1967; *The Ballroom of Romance,* 1972; *Angels at the Ritz,* 1975 (Royal Society of Literature Prize); *Lovers of Their Time,* 1978; *The Distant Past,* Dublin 1979; *Beyond the Pale,* 1981; Plays: *The Elephant's Foot,* Nottingham 1965; *The Old Boys,* 1971; *Scenes from an Album,* Dublin 1981. Novels and stories widely translated. Allied Irish Banks' Prize for Literature 1976. Also *A Writer's Ireland. Landscape in Literature,* 1984.

TROY, Una, b. Co. Cork, see CONNOR, Elizabeth. Novelist. Many novels include *We are Seven,* 1955; *The Other End of the Bridge,* 1960; *The Benefactors,* 1969; *Out of the Everywhere,* 1976; and *Caught in the Furze,* 1977. Has also written several plays, all produced Dublin. Her books have been serialised in Britain and US, and translated into Dutch, Danish, Flemish, German, Slovene, etc.

TYNAN, Katharine, b. Dublin 1861, d. Wimbledon 1931. Ed. Drogheda. As a very young woman joined the Ladies' Land League and like her father supported Parnell both before and after the 'split' occasioned by the O'Shea scandal. But she was always more interested in literature than politics. Her first volume of poetry, *Louise de la Vallière,* 1885, won her a reputation and the friendship of the leading figures in the Irish Revival. From that time on she spent her life writing, and published more than 160 volumes of prose and poetry, including 4 vols of memoirs, from *Twenty-Five Years,* 1913, to *The Wandering Years,* 1922, which give valuable portraits of the major Irish figures of her time. She married H. A. Hinkson the writer and lawyer in 1883 and spent some years in England, but in 1916 returned to Ireland, where her husband was already Resident Magistrate in Mayo. After his death in 1919 she travelled on the Continent and in England and Ireland. A well-known portrait of her by John B. Yeats painted in 1896 is in the National Gallery, Dublin. She was one of the major poets of her generation. Volumes include *Shamrocks,* 1887; *Irish Love Songs,* 1892; *Flower of Youth,* 1915; *The Holy War,* 1926; *Collected Poems,* 1930. Stories include *A Cluster of Nuts,* 1894; *Countrymen All,* 1915; *A Fine Gentleman,* 1929.

TYNDALL, John, b. Co. Carlow 1820, d. 1893, of overdose of chloral. Friend of Huxley, did more than any writer of his time to spread scientific knowledge among educated laymen. Succeeded Faraday as Superintendent of Royal Institution, 1867-87. Investigated the 'plastic theory' with Huxley and published their findings in *The Glaciers of the Alps*, 1860. Wrote much on magnetism, light, heat, optics, *Heat Considered as a Mode of Motion*, 1863, being considered his finest work. His books were translated into most European and many Asiatic languages. He was also a pioneer Alpinist, making the first ascent of the Weisshorn, 1861, in which year he published *Mountaineering*. Wrote *Hours of Exercise in the Alps*, 1873. Also a biography, *Faraday as a Discoverer*, 1868.

U

USSHER, Percival Arland, b. London 1899, d. Dublin 1980. Ed. Abbotsholme, TCD, Cambridge. Moved from family home Cappoquin, Co. Waterford, to Dublin 1943. Self-taught Irish scholar, trans. Merriman's *The Midnight Court,* with preface by W. B. Yeats, 1926. MIAL. Philosophical belletrist, produced many books: *The Face and Mind of Ireland,* 1949; *The Magic People* (the Jews), 1952; *Three Great Irishmen* (Shaw, Yeats, Joyce), 1952; *Journey Through Dread* (a study of existentialism – Kierkegaard, Heidegger, Sartre), 1955; *The XXII Keys of Tarot,* Dublin 1957; *Spanish Mercy,* 1959; *Sages and Schoolmen* (on Greek schools of philosophy), Dublin 1967. Kept a 14-vol. diary 1943-77. Extracts published in *The Journal of Arland Ussher,* 1981, and *The Juggler,* 1982, both Dublin.

USSHER, (sometimes Usher), James, b. Dublin 1581, d. Cardiff 1656. Son of a Dublin lawyer, he was the second student admitted to TCD at its foundation, 1594. In 1635 became Archbishop of Armagh although he was a Calvinist by conviction and hostile to the extreme episcopal pretensions of Laud. He used his authority to condemn the use of Irish in the Church of Ireland, a decision of great significance for the language. He also drew up the articles or canons for the Church in 1634. In 1640 he went to England where he attempted a compromise between the Puritans and Episcopalians, and also tried to save Strafford. Spent some years in London, refusing episcopal privileges, and then withdrew to Cardiff. Appears to have died a Catholic. His chief popular monument is the *Biblical Chronology* or *Annales Veteris et Novi Testamenti,* 2 vols, 1650-54, setting the creation of the world at the year 4004 BC.

He is thus now considered a figure of fun in England and of malice in Ireland, a ferocious suppressor of native schools and an enemy of the language. But in personal character he appears to have been both wise, learned and charitable, with a good knowledge of early Irish history. *Works,* 17 vols, Dublin 1847-64.

His library was bought by the govt at his death and placed in TCD Library 1661.

V

VERSCHOYLE, Moira, b. Co. Limerick 1904. Ed. privately. Novels include *Children in Love,* 1961, and her best-known book, *Daughters of the General,* 1963. In 1960 she published her autobiography, *So Long to Wait.*

VOYNICH, Ethel Lilian, b. Cork 1867, d. *c.* 1947. Youngest daughter of Professor George Boole, author of *The Laws of Thought.* She married the Polish Count Voynich and through him was introduced to revolutionary Europe. Her first novel, *The Gadfly,* 1897, is set in Italy and its hero is a revolutionary patriot. The book achieved immense success all over the world, selling 2,500,000 copies in English and American editions alone over a period of 60 years. Communist critics have regarded her as one of the greatest 'American' novelists (she spent the last half of her life in America) and the book was a bestseller in both Russian and Chinese translations.

Her other novels, increasingly sombre in tone, had less success. *An Interrupted Friendship* also set in Italy; *Olive Latham* set in revolutionary Poland, and *Frank Raymond* are the best known. Her last novel, *Put Off Thy Shoes,* NY 1947, was a comparative failure. She died shortly after it appeared.

W

WADDELL, Helen Jane, b. Tokyo 1889, d. 1965. Ed. QUB. Sister of 'Rutherford Mayne', the playwright. Was a distinguished Latinist, specialising in the mediaeval poets. *The Wandering Scholars,* 1927, and *Mediaeval Latin Lyrics,* 1929, are her two best-known works and have been often republished. *Beasts and Saints,* 1934, and *The Desert Fathers,* 1936, are translations from Latin. Also wrote *Stories from Holy Writ,* 1949. Her novel *Peter Abelard,* 1933 almost a by-product of her historical researches, is one of the most remarkable, and most read, historical novels of all time, having reached well over 30 editions and many translations.

WADDING, Luke, b. Co. Waterford 1588, d. Rome 1657. Entered Franciscan Order in Portugal, studied at Coimbra and Lisbon, ordained 1613. Professor at Salamanca. In 1618 was appointed theologian to a Spanish Embassy, sent to Rome to promote the definition of the Dogma of the Immaculate Conception. For this purpose he prepared and published

Legatio Philippi III et IV pro definienda controversia Immaculatae Conceptionis, 1624. The following year he founded the College of St Isidore for Irish Franciscans in Rome, and in 1627 the Ludovisi College for Irish secular clergy. He published *Annales Ordinis Minorum,* 8 vols, Rome 1625-54, repub. in 25 vols, 1931-35. He edited the works of *Duns Scotus,* 16 vols, 1639, the works of *John Guallensis,* 1655, and wrote the *Life of St Anselm of Lucca,* 1657. Fr Anthony Hickey, of Clare, ed. Louvain, later Professor of Philosophy there, annotated and edited some of the volumes of *Duns Scotus.* He was a close friend of Fr Wadding, who wrote his epitaph when Fr H. died in Rome 1641.

WADE, John Augustine, b. Dublin 1796, d. London 1845. Made a fortune from songs and operettas such as *The Two Houses of Granada,* 1826; *Songs of the Flowers,* 1827; and volumes such as *Polish Melodies,* 1831, but spent the lot on drink, along with his wife's dowry.

WALL, Mervyn Eugene Welply, b. Dublin 1908. Ed. Belvedere, UCD, Bonn, living in Bonn 1922-24 and travelling in Europe. Civil servant 1934; Programme assistant in Radio Eireann 1948-57; Secretary of the Irish Arts Council 1957 onwards. MIAL. Married to music critic Fanny Feehan. Has written some widely praised short stories, published in America and Europe; three plays, *Alarm Among the Clerks,* 1940; *The Lady in the Twilight,* Abbey 1941; and *The Shadow,* 1945. His chief fame rests on his novels and particularly on *The Unfortunate Fursey,* 1946, the sad story of a lamentable monk in mediaeval Ireland. Republished in America and translated into French and Hungarian, it was the basis of a musical comedy produced at the Dublin Theatre Festival 1964. *The Return of Fursey* took place in 1948, and was followed by *Leaves for the Burning,* 1952, pub. in New York the same year and trans. Danish 1953. It was voted the best European novel of the year in Denmark. *No Trophies Raise,* 1956, was followed by a slim volume of local history, *Forty Foot Gentlemen Only,* Dublin 1962, the title being a reference to a famous bathing place near Joyce's Tower, Sandycove, where gentlemen, and even priests, had long bathed in naked seclusion and safety from women. Subsequent publications: *A Flutter of Wings,* short stories, Dublin 1974; *Hermitage,* a novel, serialised in *The Journal of Irish Literature,* Newark 1978-79, pub. Dublin 1982; *The Complete Fursey,* Dublin 1985.

WALLER, John Francis, b. Limerick 1809, d. 1894. Ed. TCD. Bar. Followed Charles Lever as editor of *Dublin University Magazine.* Served in Court of Chancery. Published *Ravenscroft Hall* in 1852, and under the pseud. 'Freke Slingsby' a volume of poems in the same year, *The Slingsby Papers,* all of which had previously appeared in the *DUM.* TCD conferred LL.B. and LL.D. on him for his scholarly and legal work. Many of the entries in the *Imperial Dictionary of Universal Biography* are by him, and he supervised its publication. He also edited *Goldsmith's Works.* Other volumes of poetry include *The Dead Bridal,* 1856, and *Peter Brown,* 1872.

WALSH, Edward, b. Derry 1805, d. Cork 1850. Became a teacher in government school, but was dismissed for his articles in *The Nation*. Imprisoned during the Tithe War, was briefly a journalist in Dublin, and then given a new teaching post on Spike Island, the convict island in Cork Harbour. But for saying goodbye to John Mitchel before his transportation in 1848 was dismissed again, becoming finally teacher in the Cork Workhouse.

Supplied versification for O'Daly's *Reliques*. Published on own account *Irish Popular Songs*, Dublin 1847.

WALSH, John, b. Cappoquin 1835, d. 1881. Ed. Mt Melleray. National School teacher and poet. His scattered poems were collected in 1892 by Father Hickey and published in successive issues of the *Waterford Star*. His son Michael Paul W. followed him both as a teacher and poet, and died in 1892. Father and son are buried on the Rock of Cashel.

WALSH, John Edward, b. Dublin 1816, d. 1869. Attorney General of Ireland and Master of the Rolls. *Rakes and Ruffians: The Underworld of Georgian Dublin*, Dublin 1979, first pub. 1847 under title *Ireland Sixty Years Ago*, rep. from 3rd revised ed. 1851, but with preface and last 3 chapters omitted. Subsequent typographically inferior eds pub. under titles *Ireland Ninety Years Ago* and *Ireland One Hundred and Twenty Years Ago*, the latter ed. by Dillon Cosgrave, Dublin 1911.

WALSH, Louis, b. Co. Derry 1880, d. 1942. Solicitor and later District Justice in Co. Donegal, the first to be appointed in Ireland. Extracts from his unpublished autobiography appeared in the *Irish Times*, 1967, describing the Sinn Fein courts during the War of Independence 1920-21. He wrote a number of books based on his experiences: *Yarns of a Country Attorney*, 1917; *The Next Time*, 1919 (trans. Dutch); *Memories of Men, Places* etc. Also *The Life of John Mitchel* and a number of plays.

WALSH, Maurice, b. Co. Kerry 1879, d. 1964. Ed. locally. Entered Customs and Excise service 1901. Spent 20 years in Scottish Highlands, where he acquired a connoisseur's taste for whisky. In 1922 transferred to Irish Service, and began writing again. In 1899 he sold a serial story for £20. In 1927 entered a competition with *The Key Above the Door*, written out of nostalgia for Scotland. Failed in the competition, but published in 1926, the book went on to sell 250,000 copies. It was followed by a number of best sellers, mostly set in Scotland, or a romantically seen West of Ireland. *While Rivers Run, The Small Dark Man, Blackcock's Feather*, etc. have pleased millions of readers in England and America. Also wrote a number of short stories, many centred on an unreliable gardener, Thomasheen James. A short story of a different kind, *The Quiet Man*, was filmed in Ireland and widely distributed.

Other books include *The Road to Nowhere*, 1932; *And No Quarter*, 1937; *Sons of the Swordmaker*, 1938; *Son of Apple*, 1947; *Castle Gillian*,

1948; *Trouble in the Glen,* 1951; *Son of a Tinker,* 1952.

WALSH, Paul, b. near Mullingar 1885, d. Multyfarnham 1941. Ed. locally and Maynooth. Ordained 1909. Professor in Latin St Finian's College, Navan; lecturer in Welsh Maynooth. Parish priest of Multyfarnham 1932. D.Lit. NUI 1941. Copious papers, articles, reviews on aspects of Irish language, literature, topography, hagiography and general history. *Irish Men of Learning,* 1947; *Placenames of Westmeath,* 1957; *Irish Chiefs and Leaders,* 1960; all ed. Colm Ó Lochlainn and pub. Dublin.

WALSH, Peter, b. Co. Kildare *c.* 1618, d.London 1688. Irish Franciscan, in the Civil Wars of 1642-49 he defended the Royalist cause and particularly the rights of the English Kings in Ireland. After the Restoration he published *A Loyal Remonstrance* denouncing papal infallibility and promising Irish Catholic allegiance to the Crown, and canvassed in favour of this remonstrance among Catholics in London and Dublin 1661-65. Opposition from Rome nullified his efforts, which were aimed at securing relief for Ireland and Catholics together. Settled in London 1669 and published *The History of the Remonstrance,* 1674, described as 'indispensable to the student of the period', although in many ways an incomplete picture. He had already, 1670, been excommunicated. Published *The Controversial Letters* (against the claims of Pope Gregory VII), 1673-74, and various other works. Supported in his last years by a pension from the Duke of Ormonde.

WALSH, Richard Hussey, b. Kilduff 1825, d.1862. The first economist to write an adequate treatment of metal currencies. *An Elementary Treatise on Metallic Currency,* 1853. John Stuart Mill in particular praised this book. Became a govt official in Mauritius 1857, and died there.

WALSH, Robert, b. Waterford 1772, d.1852. Wrote *An Essay on Ancient Coins, Medals and Gems,* 1828; *Notices of Brazil in 1828-9,* London 1830, US 1831; and *Residence at Constantinople during the Greek & Turkish Revolutions,* 2 vols, 1836. Also completed Warburton's and Whitelaw's *History of Dublin,* 2 vols, 1818.

WARBURTON, Bartholomew Elliott George (usually known as Elliott W.), b. near Tullamore 1810, d. at sea 1852. Ed. Cambridge. Bar 1837. Charles Lever persuaded him to make a book of his travel articles written for the *Dublin University Magazine.* The result, *The Crescent & the Cross, or Romance & Realities of Eastern Travel,* 2 vols, 1844, ran through 17 editions. Wrote *Memoirs of Prince Rupert & the Cavaliers,* 3 vols, 1849, trans. French 1851. Edited *Memoirs of Horace Walpole & his Contemporaries,* 1851, and wrote a number of historical novels of no great merit. But by an extraordinary coincidence, one of these, titled *Darien, or the Merchant Prince,* 1852, described the horrors of a fire at sea. In the year it was published W. died in a fire at sea on a voyage to the Isthmus of Darien.

His brother George (1816-57) published *The Conquest of Canada,* 1850, 2 vols, London and NY. It went through several editions.

WEBB, Alfred John, b. Dublin 1834, d. Shetlands 1908. Of a Quaker printing family. Travelled India and America, speaking against slavery. MP for West Waterford 1890-95. Wrote *A Compendium of Irish Biography*, Dublin 1878, rep. NY 1970.

WELCOME, John, pseud. of J. N. H. Brennan, b. Wexford 1914. Ed. Sedbergh and Oxford. Bar. Has edited several collections of 'Best' stories, Crime, Legal, Secret Service, etc., and has written a number of highly regarded thrillers, including *Run for Cover; Stop at Nothing; Beware of Midnight; Hard to Handle* and *Wanted for Killing*. Recent novels: *On the Stretch*, 1969; *Go For Broke*, 1972; *Grand National*, 1977; *Bellary Bay*, 1979; *A Call to Arms*, 1985. Also, *The Life and Times of Fred Archer*, 1967; *Neck or Nothing: The Life of Bob Sievier*, 1970; *The Sporting Empress* (Elizabeth of Austria), 1975; *Infamous Occasions* (racing scandals), 1980.

WEST, Anthony Cathcot Muir, b. Co. Down. Served in RAF during Second World War. Lives and farms in Anglesey, North Wales. Novels: *The Native Moment*, 1961; *Rebel to Judgement*, NY 1962, making his name with *The Ferret Fancier*, NY 1963, repub. Dublin 1983; *As Towns with Fire*, 1968, repub. 1985. Short stories: *River's End and Other Stories*, NY 1985; *All the King's Horses*, Swords 1981.

WESTROPP, Michael Seymour Dudley, b. Cork 1868, d. Dublin 1954. Resigned British Army commission 1898 and began long association with NMI 1899; Keeper of Art Division 1930-36. Also well known as entomologist. *Irish Glass*, Dublin 1920, repub. 1978.

WHARTON, Anthony P., see McALLISTER, Alexander.

WHITE, Herbert Terence de Vere, b. Dublin 1912. Senior Moderator TCD. Auditor Historical Society. Solicitor 1933. Always interested in literature, won a short-story competition organised by the Irish Academy of Letters in 1943. MIAL. Literary ed. *Irish Times* 1963-78. Novels: *An Affair with the Moon*, 1959; *Prenez Garde*, 1961; *The Remainder Man*, 1963; *Lucifer Falling*, 1966; *Tara*, 1967; *The Lambert Rule*, 1969; *The March Hare*, 1970; *Mr Stephen*, 1971; *The Distance and the Dark*, 1973; *The Radish Memoirs*, 1974; *My Name is Norval*, 1978; *Johnnie Cross*, 1983, a fictional account of the marriage of George Eliot and Johnnie Cross. Short stories: *Big Fleas and Little Fleas, and Other Stories*, 1976; *Chimes at Midnight*, 1978; *Birds of Prey*, 1980. Biographies: *The Road of Excess* (Isaac Butt), Dublin 1946; *Kevin O'Higgins*, Dublin 1948, rep. 1966; *The Story of the Royal Dublin Society*, Tralee 1955; ed. *A Leaf from the Yellow Book* (correspondence of George Egerton), 1958; *The Parents of Oscar Wilde*, 1967; and *Tom Moore: The Irish Poet*, 1977. Also, *A Fretful Midge* (autobiography), 1959; *Leinster* and *Ireland*, both 1968; *The Anglo-Irish*, 1972.

WHITE, James, b. Dublin 1759, d. Gloucestershire 1799. Fine Greek scholar who wrote poetry and several popular historical novels, some of which were translated into German. Eccentricity overtook him and he died in poverty. Novels include *Earl Strongbow*, 1789.

WHITE, James, b. Dublin 1913. Ed. Belvedere. Art critic *Standard* 1950, *Irish Press* 1950-59, *Irish Times* 1959-62. Extern. lecturer UCD and TCD 1955-62. Curator Municipal Gallery of Modern Art Dublin 1961-64. Director NGI 1964-80. With Michael Wynne, *Irish Stained Glass*, 1963; *National Gallery of Ireland*, Dublin 1968; with Hilary Pyle, *Jack B. Yeats*, 1971; *John Butler Yeats and the Irish Renaissance*, Dublin 1972; introduction to *Brian Bourke – A Catalogue*, Kildare 1981.

WHITE, William John 'Jack', b. Cork 1920, d. Germany 1980. Ed. Cork and TCD. Found. Scholar 1940. LL.B. 1942. Journalist Dublin, *Irish Times* 1942, London Editor 1946. Features and Literary Editor 1952. Irish correspondent *Observer* and *Manchester Guardian*. Head of Public Affairs Programmes, Telefis Eireann 1962, Assistant Controller Programmes 1963, Controller 1974-77. Director Broadcasting Resources 1977-80. Widely travelled in Europe and Africa. Wrote three Irish novels, exploring the Dublin middle classes, an almost virgin territory for serious writers. *One for the Road*, 1956; *The Hard Man* 1958; and *The Devil You Know*, 1962. Plays: *The Last Eleven*, Dublin 1968, Irish Life and Drama Award, pub. Newark 1979; *To-day the Bullfinch*, Dublin 1970. Contrib. to *Myles: Portraits of Brian O'Nolan*, 1973. Also *Minority Report: The Protestant Community in the Irish Republic*, Dublin 1975.

WHITELAW, James, b. Co. Leitrim 1749, d. Dublin 1813. Ed. TCD. Held various Dublin livings, and began in 1798 the famous census of the city's population, published as *Essays on the Population of Dublin in 1798*, Dublin 1805. Previously there had been no sound estimate, let alone a census. In some cases he found more than 100 persons living in one ruinous tenement. He then began the *History of Dublin* with John Warburton, uncompleted at their deaths, and finished by Robert Walsh, 2 vols, 1818.

WHITTY, Michael James, b. Wexford 1795, d. 1873. Son of a local shopowner. Intended for priesthood but went to London to become a writer. His *Tales of Irish Life*, 1822-24, illustrated by his friend Cruikshank, were an enormous success, repub. US, trans. French and German. He became editor of the *Liverpool Journal;* Chief Constable of Liverpool and organiser of the first English Police Force outside of London, in 1836; and finally owner-editor of the *Liverpool Daily Post*, forerunner of the 'popular' press, in 1855.

WHYTE, John Henry, b. Penang 1928. Ed. Ampleforth, Oxford. Lecturer in history Uganda 1958-61; in politics UCD 1961-66; in political science QUB 1966-71. *The Independent Irish Party 1850-9*, 1958; *Church and State in Modern Ireland 1923-70*, Dublin and London 1971, 2nd ed. (*C&SMI 1923-79*), 1979; *Catholics in Western Democracies. A Study in*

Political Behaviour, Dublin and London 1981.

WHYTE, Samuel, b. Dublin 1733, d. 1811. As a schoolmaster in Dublin his pupils included the future Duke of Wellington and his brother; Richard Brinsley Sheridan; and Thomas Moore. He himself wrote several volumes of poetry, and his *Poems on Various Occasions* was particularly successful, going into 3 editions in the year of issue, 1795.

WILDE, Jane Francesca, b. Wexford 1826 (although some suggest 1820), d. 1896. Daughter of Archdeacon Elgee. Contributed to *The Nation* from 1844, often using the pen name 'Speranza'. This pseud. was also used by another contributor over a poem 'Ugo Bassi' which became famous, and is often erroneously attributed to Jane Wilde. Married Sir William Wilde in 1851. Much older than her he was already a distinguished surgeon and President of the Irish Academy. Under her pen-name she published *Poems* 1864, and as Lady Jane Wilde a succession of works on folklore, *Driftwood from Scandinavia,* 1884; *Ancient Legends of Ireland,* 1887; *Ancient Cures,* 1891; and also *Men, Women and Books,* 1891; and *Social Studies,* 1893. Widowed in 1876 she moved to London, and in spite of the good reception of her scholarly work, and the fame of her son Oscar, she sank into poverty and died in very narrow circumstances, in the year of her son's public disgrace.

WILDE, Oscar Fingal O'Flahertie Wills, b. Dublin 1856, d. Paris 1900. Ed. TCD and Oxford where he won the Newdigate Poetry Prize with a poem 'Ravenna'. Published a volume of poetry 1881 and toured America 1882, causing something of a sensation with his cult of aestheticism. In 1883 he produced his first play *Vera, or the Nihilists,* which showed little promise of better things to come. It was eight years before he produced another, *The Duchess of Padua,* which was hardly more successful. In 1892 he wrote *Salomé* in French, and had it translated into English by Lord Alfred Douglas in 1893, with illustrations by Aubrey Beardsley. Richard Strauss used it as libretto for an opera, and the play itself has often been performed, in both languages, first in Paris in 1896, but not in England until 1931. The play has a hothouse beauty of language but no great dramatic value.

Long before this Wilde had acquired London fame as a personality, based on bizarre conduct, and witty conversation designed to shock the intellect rather than the feelings. His only claim to literary recognition was his novel *The Picture of Dorian Gray,* 1891, in whose hero some fashionable hostesses, with nervous fascination, saw Wilde himself, and a brilliant collection of critical essays, *Intentions,* published the same year. But in 1892 Wilde produced *Lady Windermere's Fan,* on the surface a commonplace comedy about a woman of uncertain reputation, but rescued from mediocrity by brilliance of dialogue. Into this, as into *A Woman of No Importance,* 1893, *An Ideal Husband* and *The Importance of being Earnest,* both 1895, Wilde poured all his usually ill-disciplined genius; genius of a kind which London accepted as peculiarly Irish, consisting of paradox, verbal conjuring, of turning clichés inside out to make an original witticism, such as 'Divorces are made in Heaven.' Some shafts were merely clever; others were also true. On his plane of casual elegance and fun Wilde was doing what Shaw was also beginning to do in his plays: challenging accepted, conventional thoughts, and offering fresh ones. But in 1895 he was pilloried for his homosexual attachment to Lord Alfred Douglas, by Alfred's father the Marquess of Queensberry, and was foolish enough to take a libel action against the marquess. Losing it exposed him automatically to prosecution under the quite recent legislation making such practices punishable when committed by men (although not by women) and after a dramatic trial he was sentenced to two years imprisonment. After his release he published *The Ballad of Reading Gaol* in 1898, and some critics profess to find it a true masterpiece. Others consider it mawkish doggerel, filled with self-pity. In recent times Brendan Behan's *The Quare Fellow* appears to owe something to its study of a prison awaiting the execution of a murderer.

Wilde left England for France but malice pursued him, and the French, who had no law against his 'English crime', allowed the English authorities to prompt them into persecuting him. He moved to Italy, where despite protestations to the contrary he took up once more with Alfred Douglas. The meeting brought neither of them happiness. Wilde returned to Paris and died there, broken in purse but not in humour, and joking even about his death. In 1905 his 'testament' *De Profundis* was published (full text given in *The Letters of Oscar Wilde*, ed. Rupert Hart-Davis, 1962), and again critics of a particular stamp have found it moving and spiritual in the extreme. Others find it sickens them, and there seems little doubt that Wilde's reputation must rest on his four great comedies.

WILDE, William Robert Wills, b. Co. Roscommon 1815, d. Dublin 1876. Father of Oscar and husband of Jane Francesca, whom he married 1851. He had already pub. *Narrative of a Voyage to Madeira Teneriffe & along the Shores of the Mediterranean*, 2 vols, Dublin 1840. Studied London, Berlin and Vienna, 1838-41; returned to Dublin to become its leading eye and ear specialist. Served as medical commissioner for Irish Census 1841 and 1851, publishing a Blue Book, *The Epidemics of Ireland*, 1851. In 1864 was knighted for service to Irish census. Wrote on eye and ear surgery, and invented the now general operation for mastoiditis, as well as an opthalmoscope.

In 1858 published a 3 vol. descriptive *Catalogue of the contents of the Museum of the RIA;* and wrote several Irish travel books, *The Beauties of the Boyne & the Blackwater*, 1849, and *Lough Corrib & Lough Mask*, 1867. In 1849 he published a booklet, *The Closing Years of the Life of Dean Swift*, attempting to prove that Swift was not insane in his last years.

A man of great generosity, he gave his services free to the poor, and used the first £1000 he earned to found St Mark's Opthalmic Hospital in Dublin. His warmth of heart also led him astray at times. He had three illegitimate children before his marriage, and kept one with him in later years as his assistant. A liaison with a Miss Travers, a patient, beginning in 1859, led to an expensive libel case which cost him only a halfpenny in damages, but many thousand pounds in costs. In the last ten years he let his practice decline and when he died he left his widow in comparative poverty.

WILKINS, Maurice, b. Dublin 1885. Ed. TCD. Headmaster Bangor Grammar School 1923-47. *Sonnets of Love and Friendship,* Hull 1958; *The Seeker,* Dublin 1960.

WILLIAMS, Charles, b. Coleraine 1838, d.1904. Founder of the Press Club in London. Published one novel, *John Thaddeus Mackay,* 1889.

WILLIAMS, Richard D'Alton, b. Dublin 1822, d.Thibodeaux 1862. Young Irelander. Wrote verse for *The Nation* under pseud. 'Shamrock'. Co-founder of *The Irish Tribune* 1848. Acquitted of treason-felony after the 1848 Rising, emigrated to US 1851, teaching in Mobile and practising medicine in New Orleans.

WILLIAMS, Richard Valentine, see ROWLEY, Richard.

WILLIAMS, T. Desmond, b. Dublin 1921. Ed. privately and UCD. Bar. Travelling Studentship of NUI to Cambridge 1943. Research Fellow 1947. Appointed by British Foreign Office 1948 to examine captured German govt papers in Berlin. Professor of Modern History UCD 1949-83. Co-ed. *The Great Famine,* 1956; ed. *The Irish Struggle 1916-1926,* 1966; ed. with Kevin B. Nowlan, *Ireland in the War Years and After, 1939-51,* Dublin 1969; ed. *Secret Societies in Ireland,* Dublin 1973; contributed with Kevin B. Nowlan and Robert Dudley Edwards to *Ireland and the Italian Risorgimento,* Dublin 1960.

WILLS, James, b. Roscommon 1790, d.1868. A friend of Charles Maturin, he gave him the MS of a poem, 'The Universe', to publish as his own, 1821, which made a great deal of money for M. and saved him from financial disaster. Wrote other poetry under his own name, but his chief monument is *Lives of Illustrious Irishmen,* Dublin 1840-47.

WILLS, William Gorman, b. Kilkenny 1828, d.1891. Son of James Wills the biographer. Cousin of Violet Martin and Edith Somerville the writers. Practised as a painter before turning to writing. Wrote novels, poetry and plays, mostly on historical subjects; plays include *Charles I,* 1872; *Jane Shore,* 1876; and *Olivia* (based on Goldsmith's *Vicar of Wakefield),* 1885. Henry Irving acted the leading part in *Charles I* and *Olivia,* making both plays far more successful than they might otherwise have been.

WILMOT, Barbarina, b. *c.* 1790, a cousin of Richard Brinsley Sheridan. Wrote many novels and plays, the best-known of which is her tragedy, *Ina,* 1815.

WILMOT, Catherine, b. Drogheda 1773, d.France 1824. With her sister Martha (b. Co. Cork 1775, d.Dublin 1873) wrote several remarkable journals concerning their European travels. Catherine's diary of Grand Tour made as companion to the Mount Cashell family was edited and published by Thomas Sadleir as *An Irish Peer on the Continent 1801-1803*, 1920. *The Russian Journals of Martha and Catherine Wilmot, 1803-1808*, edited and published by Marchioness of Londonderry and Montgomery Hyde, 1934, with *More Letters from Martha Wilmot; Vienna 1819-29*, 1935. Some of the Russian journey was spent with Princess Daschkaw (Daschkoff), then an elderly woman, and the *Journals* are of interest for their portrait of her, as well as of Russia at the time. The Viennese *Letters* were written when Martha's husband, the Rev. William Bradford, was chaplain to the British Embassy in Vienna, then the centre of Europe. It is this doubly central position of the writer that gives them their value.

WILSON, Andrew Patrick, b. Dublin (?) *c.* 1880, involved in Irish labour troubles culminating in the 1913 Strike led by James Larkin. Wrote a play with this as background, *The Plough*, 1914, mentioned admiringly in the *Great Soviet Encyclopaedia*, 1948 edition.

WILSON, John, b. *c.* 1635, probably near Londonderry, where he became Recorder in 1680, d. 1695. Wrote several plays; his comedy *The Cheats*, 1671, seems to have been the most popular, many editions being printed up to the end of the 17th century.

WILSON, John Crawford, b. Mallow 1825, d. 1901. Popular mid-Victorian novelist, books including *The Village Pearl*, 1852; *Elsie*, 1864; *Lost and Found*, 1865, etc.

WILSON, Robert Arthur, b. Co. Donegal 1820, d. Belfast 1875. Spent some years in America as a young man. Returned to Ulster and wrote for *The Nation* and other papers. Made reputation as humorous writer in *Morning News* under pseud. 'Barney Maglone'. Verse published 1894.

WINDELE, John, b. Cork 1801, d. Cork 1865. Author of *Guides* to Cork and Killarney, 1849; an antiquarian who saved many Ogham inscriptions from destruction by removing them to his home from the fields where they were in danger of being broken up for building materials. Collected many ancient Irish MSS| which were bought by the RIA 1865.

WINGFIELD, Lewis Strange, the Hon., b. Powerscourt 1842, d. London 1891. Son of 6th Viscount Powerscourt. Ed. Eton and Bonn. Led an extraordinary life: was in Paris during the siege of 1870, in the Sudan during Gordon's campaign; travelled in the Far East and North Africa, writing travel books about both areas; acted in London theatres, designed theatre costumes at the Lyceum; was an attendant in a lunatic asylum, a journalist, and a painter good enough to exhibit at the Royal Academy and be elected RHA. Wrote many novels, including *My Lords of Strogue*, 1879, and *The Maid of Honour*, 1891. His travel books on North Africa and China include *Wanderings of a Globetrotter in the Far East*, 1889. Was also one of the apparent regiment of Irish war correspondents covering the Franco-Prussian War, 1870-71, during which he not only wrote his dispatches, getting them out to the *Times* and *Daily News* by balloon, but also tended the wounded and qualified as a surgeon.

WINSTANLEY, John, b. Dublin 1676, d. Dublin 1750. Son of a lawyer. Ed. TCD but did not graduate. Poet. *Poems,* Dublin 1742; 2nd vol. ed. by his son 1751.

WOLFE, Charles, b. Dublin 1791, d. *c.* 1825. Cousin of both Wolfe Tone and General Wolfe of Quebec. In 1817 he published anonymously in *The Newry Telegraph* an ode, 'The Burial of Sir John Moore'. It created a sensation and many writers claimed the authorship before he established the truth. Byron, somewhat extravagantly, called it 'the finest Ode in the English language'. He never reached such heights again. A parson, his collected sermons and some poetry were published in 1825, shortly after his death, as *Remains of the Rev. C. W.,* Dublin.

WYCKHAM, Helen, pseud. of Pamela Evans, b. *c.* 1933. Raised Lusk, Co. Dublin. Ed. Cambridge. Lives Dyfed, South Wales. Novels: *Ribstone Pippins,* Dublin and London 1974; *Cavan,* 1977; *Ottoline Atlantica,* 1981.

WYSE, William Charles Buonaparte, b. Waterford 1826, d. Cannes 1892. Brother of Marie Studholmine, later Princess Rattazzi. Lived most of his life in France, like his sister, and wrote poetry in English and Provençale, being one of the group dedicated to restore that dialect to literary use. His elegy, 'In Memoriam of the Prince Imperial of France', appeared in 1879.

Y

YEATS, Jack Butler, b. London 1871, d. Dublin 1957. Brother of W. B. Y. Main reputation is as a painter, one of the most famous of all Irish artists; but he wrote a number of plays, novels and volumes of poetry, all of merit. Novels include *Sailing, Sailing Swiftly,* 1933, and *The Careless Flower,* 1947. Plays include *La La Noo; Apparitions; The Old Sea Road,* and *Rattle.*

YEATS, John Butler, b. Tullylish, Co. Down 1839, d. New York 1922. Painter and critic. Ed. Isle of Man, TCD. Bar 1866, never practising. RHA 1892. Married Susan Pollexfen; 5 children, 4 surviving: W.B.Y., J.B.Y., Lily and Lolly. Lived London 1887-1901; moved to New York 1908 under patronage of lawyer John Quinn. Writings: *Passages from the Letters of J.B.Y.,* ed. Ezra Pound, Dublin 1917; *Essays Irish and American,* Dublin and London 1918; *Further Letters,* ed. Lennox Robinson, Dublin 1920; *Early Memories,* Dublin 1923.

YEATS, William Butler, b. Sandymount 1865, d. France 1939. Son of John

Butler Y. RHA, but connected with the Ormonde family, an aristocratic link which was of deep influence throughout his life. Ed. Dublin and London, and studied art, but from 1887 he knew that he must be a poet before all else. In 1889, after some dabbling with Oriental themes, he also decided that Ireland and her heroic past must be the subject of his poetry, and that he must express 'certain ardent ideas and a high attitude of mind which were the nation itself to our belief', the 'our' including other poets of the Irish renaissance, a movement of which he was to become the head and centre through the Abbey Theatre. In 1892 he wrote a play *The Countess Cathleen* and in 1899 formed an amateur literary society which produced it. Helped in this by Lady Gregory and Edward Martyn, the society became the Abbey Theatre in 1904, finance being provided by Miss Annie Horniman, an English woman who had acted as his secretary in London. By then Yeats was already famous as a poet: *Poems*, 1895; *The Wind Among the Reeds* 1899; *In the Seven Woods*, 1903. He had also written a great deal of prose, and several plays, one of his books *The Celtic Twilight*, 1893, giving rise to an expression that was to describe, and ultimately condemn, the whole romantic, idealistic literary movement surrounding him.

At the same time, as a member of the Golden Dawn Society, he had become immersed in the curious mixture of spiritualism and mysticism which he developed over many years into a personal religion and the key-theme of his poetry. In the Abbey his greatest achievement was not the large body of plays he himself wrote; these are of greater value as poetry than as stage-plays; but the encouragement of Synge and a number of lesser but still considerable dramatists.

Suspected by the Castle as a revolutionary influence, and by many Anglo-Irish friends as a traitor to his class, he in fact kept himself deliberately clear of all real political involvement. His close friend and ideal of beauty, Maude Gonne, lost patience with his attitude, throwing herself into active political struggles for the poor of Ireland. Yeats felt that for him his best service was to give them a vision of what Ireland had been and might be again. Ireland received the gift with large indifference or active hatred.

Poems: Second Series, 1910, and *Later Poems*, 1922, are landmarks in his development as a poet of world importance. This importance was recognised in 1923 with the Nobel Prize, and in Ireland he was made a Senator of the Irish Free State, serving from 1922-28 and making some remarkable orations that deserve comparison with Burke and Grattan. During the 1920s he also discovered and developed his second great Abbey dramatist, Sean O'Casey. In 1928 they quarrelled, the fault lying partly with O'Casey, but also in great measure with Yeats. Even in such small things as calling the playwright 'Casey' instead of 'O'Casey', he displayed an arrogant insensitivity that was central to the worst side of his nature.

In the 1930s, at an age when most poets have ceased to produce creative work, Yeats reached the height of his powers. *The Tower, The Winding Stair* and *Last Poems* contain some of his finest poetry. He still continued to write plays, for example *A Full Moon in March*, 1935, but had long given up hope of reaching a popular audience with them.

At this period he allowed himself to become involved, to a slight extent, in political controversy, if not in politics. His aristocratic leanings and his intellectual and artistic arrogance naturally inclined him to authoritarian governments. But if he praised Mussolini and Hitler and Franco, so, at much the same times, did many democratic politicians in Europe and America. Winston Churchill at one time regarded Mussolini as the saviour of Italy. Moreover, Yeats's so-called 'approval' of Fascism was never unqualified, and at most was based on the partial knowledge then available to ordinary men. When an attempt was made to secure Yeats's backing for the Irish Blue Shirt movement in the later 1930s he refused it. Small minds now take pleasure in tarnishing his name with the cry 'Fascist', but this has no bearing on his grandeur. He died at Roquebrune in the south of France in 1939, but after the war in September 1948 his body was returned for reburial in the West of Ireland, in Drumcliff churchyard, Co. Sligo.

Z

ZOZIMUS, see MORAN, Michael.

ADDENDUM

Part 1

BECKETT, Mary, b. Belfast 1926. Ed. Belfast. Teacher in Ardoyne until 1956. Married, lives in Dublin. In *A Belfast Woman*, Swords 1980, she tells sombre, powerful stories in the tradition of O'Connor and O'Faolain.

DEANE, John F., b. Achill, Co. Mayo 1943. Teacher, poet. Founder of *Poetry Ireland* and *Poetry Ireland Review*; director of Aquila Press. Has published several text books. Poetry includes *Stalking After Time*, 1977, High Sacrifice, 1981, both pub. Dublin; and *Voices*, Edinburgh 1983.

DEVLIN, Polly, b. Tyrone 1944. Broadcaster and journalist in London. *The Vogue Book of Fashion: Photography*, 1979, rep. 1984; *All of Us There* (a childhood memoir) and *The Far Side of the Lough* (children's), both 1983.

HOPKIN, Alannah, b. Singapore 1949, raised Cork, London. Ed. Queen Mary College London. Journalist and author. Novels: *A Joke Goes a Long Way in the Country*, 1982; *The Outhaul*, 1985.

LEVINE, June, b. Dublin. Journalist, feminist. Cub reporter *Irish Times* at 15. Emigrated Canada 1956. Ed. *Irish Woman's Journal* 1960s, and researcher RTE's 'Late Late Show'. Best seller *Sisters*, Swords 1982, rep. 1985.

LYNAM, Shevawn, b. Dublin, raised Co. Galway. Ed. Madrid. Lives Wicklow. Ed. *NATO Letter* 1958-63. Irish Tourist Board 1963-71; Historic Irish Tourist Houses and Gardens Assn 1971–. *The Spirit and the Clay* (on Basque Resistance), 1954; *Humanity Dick* (on Richard Martin MP), 1975.

McCAFFERTY, Nell, b. Derry 1944. Ed. QUB. Journalist and broadcaster. Travelled Europe, Middle East. Part of Derry civil rights group 1968. Moved to Dublin with *Irish Times* 1970. *The Best of Nell* (14 years' writings), 1984; *A Woman to Blame: The Kerry Baby Story*, 1985.

MacLOCHLAINN, Alf, b. Dublin 1926. Ed. UCD. Director National Library of Ireland to 1982, now Librarian UCG. Novel: *Out of Focus*, Dublin 1977.

POWER, M. S., b. Dublin 1935. Ed. Ireland and France. Worked as TV producer in US. Lives England. Won Hennessy Short Story Award 1983. Two novels: *Hunt for the Autumn Clowns*, 1983; *The Killing of Yesterday's Children*, 1985.

Part 2

Ó MADAGÁIN, Breandán, b. Limerick 1932. Ed. Maynooth and UCD. Schools Inspector 1962-66. Lecturer in Modern Irish UCD 1966-75. Professor Modern Irish UCG 1975–. Books include *Teagasc ar an Sean-Tiomna*, 1974; *An Ghaeilge i Luimneach 1700-1900*, 1974; *An Dialann Dúlra*, 1978; all pub. Dublin.

Part 2

WRITERS IN IRISH AND LATIN

A

ADAMNÁN, Son of Rónán, b. Donegal *c.* 624, d. 704. Of the same family as the great Columba he entered the community of Iona and became its ninth abbot in 679. In 686 he visited Aldfrith, King of Northumbria, who had studied on Iona, perhaps under Adamnán. The king converted the abbot to the Roman view in the controversy over the date of Easter and kindred matters. Adamnán returned to Iona to try and convert his monks to the same opinion, but without great success. In northern Ireland he had a better reception, and was prominent at a great ecclesiastical gathering at Birr in 697, where he won acceptance for his 'law of the innocents,' protecting non-combatants in war. His draft of the law is preserved as *Cáin Adamnáin.*

His greatest work was his life of St Columba, *Vita Sancti Columbae* (ed. W. Reeves 1857), which besides much legendary material contains an invaluable record of the early Irish Church as well as a charming account of the saint.

Adamnán also wrote *De Locis Sanctis,* published in the series *Scriptores Latini Hiberniae,* an account of a pilgrimage to the Holy Land by the Gallic bishop Arculf, who was shipwrecked on one of the Western Isles on his return. Arculf is supposed to have dictated the story to him personally, and it is of great interest as being one of the earliest western, post-Roman accounts of Palestine and the eastern Mediterranean. There is also *Fis Adamnáin* (Adamnán's Vision), preserved in a 12th-century MS, and long believed to be by Adamnán. It is now regarded as a much later work.

AENGUS THE CULDEE, see OENGUS.

ÁGHAS, Pádraig, b. 1885, Co. Kerry. Learned Irish from Micheál Ó Conchubhair. Taught Irish in Co. Waterford, 1905-10. During 1920s wrote essays and stories published by Connradh na Gaedhilge, and a book *Gnath-Éolas ar Nadúir,* 1922, published by Comhlucht Oideachais na h-Éireann. His play *Toirmeasg Sidhe* was published by Máire Ní Raghallaigh, 1929.

ANNALS OF CONNACHT *(Annála Connacht)* chronicle Irish affairs from 1224-1554. The MS was compiled in Irish and is closely related to the *Annals of Loch Cé.* Both MSS appear to depend on a common source although the *Annals of Connacht* contain much that is earlier in date than the earliest parts of the other MS. The text has been edited and translated by A. Martin Freeman for Dublin Inst. for Adv. Studies, 1944.

ANNALS OF INNISFALLEN, compiled and transcribed at different periods between 11th and 14th centuries. Tradition claims the first portion to have been written on the island, Innisfallen, in the Lower Lake of Killarney, by Maelsuthan Ua Cerbaill, d. 1010, tutor to Brian Bóroimhe and himself a chief in the Killarney district. After the 11th century the entries change character, ceasing to be transcriptions of earlier material, and becoming notes made by different scribes at the times of the happenings the notes describe. These entries continue to 1326, and the *Annals* form the oldest substantial body of Irish chronicles, *The Annals of Tighernach* being older, but no more than a fragment.

Sir James Ware is the first known owner of the volume, probably acquiring it through Dubhaltach Mac Firbisigh, his Irish-speaking assistant. Rawlinson owned it in the 18th century and left it to the Bodleian Library. An English translation made by Mac Firbisigh for Ware is in the library of TCD. The *Annals* give a fuller and in some cases a different version of the history of early kings from that appearing elsewhere. A facsimile edition was edited with descriptive introduction by R. I. Best and Eoin Mac Néill for the RIA, Dublin 1933. Another edition with translation and index was prepared for Dublin Inst. for Adv. Studies by Seán Mac Airt, Dublin 1951. A very inaccurate edition was published by the Rev. Charles O'Conor, Dublin 1825.

ANNALS OF LOCH CÉ *(Annals of Lough Cé)* are a chronicle of Irish events from 1014-1590. Brian MacDermott was one of the several compilers. The MS was written in Irish and it is closely related to the *Annals of Connacht*. An edition with translation by William M. Hennessy was published in London, 1871, 2 vols.

ANNALS OF THE FOUR MASTERS (properly *Annales Rioghachta Éireann),* compiled between 1632 and 1636 by a number of historians led by the Franciscan brother, Micheál Ó Cléirigh. He and his three principal assistants are the Four Masters of the popular title, given to the *Annals* by Father John Colgan of Louvain. The compilation was a deliberate work of rescue of old material in danger of destruction by the English and by neglect of Irish learning after the defeat of Kinsale and the Flight of the Earls. See Ó CLÉIRIGH, Micheál. The *Annals* begin 'forty days before the Flood' or 'the Year 2242 of the world's age,' and the last entry is for AD 1616. From the 5th century AD the *Annals* are considered substantially accurate. They were edited by John O'Donovan as *Annals of the Kingdom of Ireland,* with trans. and notes, in 7 vols, Dublin 1849-51, 2nd ed 1856. Owen Connellan had brought out a trans. as *The Annals of Ireland,* Dublin 1846. See *The Four Masters and their Work,* Rev. Paul Walsh, Dublin 1944.

ANNALS OF TIGHERNACH, composed in the late 11th century at Clonmacnoise, according to tradition by the Abbot Tighernach, although this has been disputed in 'Irish Men of Learning', Rev. Paul Walsh, *Studies,* 1947. A later annalist, Augustine Mac Gradoigh, carried on the *Annals* from the year 1088 to 1405 and others made still later entries. The *Annals* form the oldest surviving native historical records and are also the most reliable. Fragments of early copies of the MSS are in the Bodleian Library.

ANNALS OF ULSTER, compiled 1498 by Cathal Mac Magnus, or Mac Magnusa Mheg Uidhir, Archdeacon of Clogher, the entries in the original

version ending in that year. Other scribes continued the *Annals* into the
16th and 17th centuries. The *Annals* give an account of the history of Ulster
from the mission of Palladius AD 431, and from the 7th century they quote
contemporary documents. Up to the beginning of the 10th century the
entries are in Latin, with few exceptions. After that period they continue
in Irish. The Four Masters used the *Annals* as a source. O'Donovan in the
19th century praised their 'veracious simplicity'. See Tomás Ó Máille, *The
Language of the Annals of Ulster*, Dublin 1910; and the edition with trans.
and notes by W. M. Hennessy (vol. I) and B. MacCarthy (vols II, III and
IV), pub. Dublin 1887, 1893, 1895, 1901. New ed. Gearóid MacNiocaill,
Dublin 1984.

ANONYMOUS. Sadly, this heading must conceal the authorship of some
of the greatest works in Irish literature, from the creator of the *Táin Bó
Cúailgne*, to the Christian monk who as a relief from his studies wrote the
famous poem in praise of his little white cat, *Pangur Bán*.

The enormous wealth of Irish myth and legend and epic poetry has been
recognised for a century and a half, brought to the notice of European
scholars by the researches and popularisations of such oddly assorted
people as Sydney Owenson, Edward Bunting, James Hardiman, Thomas
Crofton Croker (whose *Fairy Legends* caught the attention of the brothers
Grimm), Eugene O'Curry, John O'Donovan and perhaps greatest of all
and least recognised, George Petrie. Many other devoted students and local
specialists contributed by saving manuscripts, collecting oral versions of
tales and poems, noting down music and songs which themselves had a
bearing on old stories, and all of them salvaging at almost the twelfth hour
an irreplaceable treasure. Their work stands with that of Micheál Ó Cléirigh
and his helpers as the two greatest contributions to Irish culture.

The gathered material, oral and manuscript, falls into a few well defined
classes: tales of the gods; tales of the kings; tales of the heroes; and in
general much later than any of these, tales of the fairies. The earliest versions
of any of these types of story were in prose, with occasional verses inserted,
and this style of story-telling survived into the latest Gaelic period. But in
general the fashion changed about the 12th century from prose to ballad
form, perhaps under Norman influence, since this ballad form was already
popular in Western Europe.

The old stories were told and retold many times in constantly evolving
styles and versions, and it is sometimes possible to attach a name to the
'author' of one or another version, but in no case is there a known author
of the earliest, 'original' version. This of course is to be expected with
stories which however sophisticated they appear, derive from the earliest
period of the Gaelic occupation of Ireland and perhaps earlier still. Elements
in many stories suggest a pre-Celtic origin, and other elements which may
indeed be Celtic seem to belong to the period of the folk-wandering across
Europe in the early Iron Age.

It is this immense age and unbroken continuity of tradition that give the literature, oral and written, its unique value. Other traditions in Europe reach back as far, German and Greek for example; but in both cases the early strata have been obliterated by over-sophistication. 'Homer' even had been so worked and reworked between the likely time of origin and the crystallising of the poems in Classical Greek that it is impossible to restore from it the kind of barbaric epic that must underlie it.

Even Scandinavian literature was too much in the hands of Christian literary men for it to survive in what must have been its true wealth and shape. (It is legitimate to ask if some of the stylistic wealth that does survive there, all of which derives from Iceland, was not injected into it by Irish influence. Something like one-third of the early population of Iceland was Irish, brought there in the train of Norse chieftains, and there must have been tale-tellers and poets among the slaves. It would go a long way towards explaining an otherwise inexplicable change for the better in Scandinavian literature during the High Middle Ages.)

Early Irish literature on the other hand gives clear indications of what primitive story-telling and poetry must have been. Even in the *Táin Bó Cúailgne*, which Professor David Greene says (in *Early Irish Society*, ed. Myles Dillon, Dublin 1954) 'appears to have been a conscious attempt to provide Ireland with an epic comparable to the *Aeneid*', and which its translator Thomas Kinsella has compared to the *Iliad*, there are fragments which clearly belong to an earlier order of literature. Cú Chulainn has striking similarities to Achilles, but he is a far more primitive figure. It is easy to believe, reading the *Táin*, that this is what the Celtic chariot warriors who swept across Europe were truly like. And that it is what Achilles himself was truly like before Classical taste began to polish some of his rougher surfaces.

The principal collections of legendary tales in Irish are the *Leabhar Gabhála*, or *Book of Invasions*, describing the invasions of Ireland and the origins of the peoples who came there; the *Ulster Cycle* of the tales of the Northern Heroes, centring on Cú Chulainn and the *Táin Bó Cúailgne; The Fenian Cycle*, centring on the doings of Fionn Mac Cumhaill (this cycle is sometimes referred to as Ossianic, from Oisín, Fionn's grandson, and in legend the poet-narrator of all the stories, which in one version of the cycle he tells to St Patrick, having himself returned to Ireland from the Land of Youth to find all his comrades not only dead but long-forgotten, and the race of men grown small and miserable in the grey twilight of Christianity); *The Mythological Cycle*, telling of the deeds of the Tuatha Dé Danann, the invading gods and their conquest of the Fomorians, with their later adventures; and *The Cycles of the Kings*, which of their nature have no one central theme or character, but deal with the adventures of a number of kings, mostly of Leinster and the east of Ireland, as opposed to the Ulster Cycle which has a northern origin and bias.

Within these several collections, certain stories stand out and have taken on individual reputations for excellence and interest; among them the love-

story of *Diarmaid and Grainne;* the story of *Fled Bricrenn* (The Feast of
Bricriu); the *Táin* itself; the love story of Deirdre and the sons of Uisnech,
Longes Macc n-Uisnig; the story of the great fight at Da Derga's Hostel,
Togail Bruidne Da Derga; the story of Mac Da Thó's Pig, *Scéla Muicce
Meicc Da Thó,* called by Nora Chadwick in *Irish Sagas* 'one of the most
brilliantly told of the early Irish sagas'; the story of Cú Chulainn's boyhood,
of Oisín in the Land of Youth, of the Children of Lir, of the Wooing of
Étain and the Battle of Moytura; all these and a dozen more have a deserved
place on the highest level of the world's story-telling.

The reader without Irish will find an easy introduction to this area of
Gaelic literature in the series *Irish Life and Culture* brought out in Dublin
for the Cultural Relations Committee of Ireland. In particular *Early Irish
Society,* ed. Myles Dillon and already noted above; *Saga and Myth in
Ancient Ireland,* Gerard Murphy, 1955; *The Ossianic Lore and Romantic
Tales of Mediaeval Ireland;* and outside this series, *Irish Sagas,* ed. Myles
Dillon, Dublin 1959, being a series of lectures first delivered on Radio
Éireann. See also *The Gaelic Story-teller,* James H. Delargy, London 1945,
being the Sir John Rhys Memorial Lecture to the British Academy for that
year; *The Cycles of the Kings,* Myles Dillon, NY and London 1946; *Early
Irish History and Mythology,* Thomas F. O'Rahilly, Dublin 1946; *Early
Irish Literature,* Myles Dillon, Chicago 1948; *Studies in Irish Literature
and History,* James Carney, Dublin 1959; *The Táin,* trans. Thomas Kinsella, Dublin 1969; and in German the classic work on the subject, *Die
Irische Helden und Königsage,* Rudolph Thurneysen, Halle 1921, still
astonishingly untranslated into English (or Irish).

For other publications the reader should turn to the *Bibliography of Irish
Philology and of Printed Irish Literature,* R.I. Best, 1913; and *Bibliography
of Irish Philology and Manuscript Literature, Publications 1913-1941,* R.I.
Best, 1942; *Catalogue of MSS relating to Irish History in Irish and Foreign
Libraries,* 11 vols, Richard James Hayes, US 1966; *A Text-Book of Irish
Literature,* 2 vols, Eleanor Hull, London 1906-8, with the same author's
The Cuchulain Saga in Irish Literature, 1898.

Irish fairy tales, dealing not with gods, kings and heroes, but with simpler
aspects of the supernatural; ghosts and revenants and witches and supernatural beings reduced from gods to 'the good people' and 'the little people';
the kind of story that suggests a reduction in the status of the literature
and of the story-teller from the entertainment of chieftains to the amusement of peasants; these too have been collected and translated by many
enthusiasts from Lady Wilde and Jeremiah Curtin and Douglas Hyde to
the folklorists of today, and if many of the stories betray a later surface
than the epics and hero-tales, they may also contain elements that are older
still than the oldest of the epics. And old or not so old, they are worth
reading as folk literature, in Irish for preference but also in English. Part
2 of this *Dictionary* gives under the above headings and those mentioned
in the second paragraph of this entry a number of book titles where Irish

fairy tales may be found in translation. The Irish Folklore Commission's records and indexes provide all possible information about the tales in Irish. A member of the Folklore Commission's staff, Kevin Danaher, has published *Folktales of the Irish Countryside*, Cork 1967.

The remaining category of anonymous work is the poem. Some of these are clearly poetic fragments from prose tales, which have gained a life and identity of their own. Others, like *Pangur Bán* noticed above, are the work of scribes and monks who jotted them in the margins of more serious manuscripts or inserted them in chronicles without thinking it worth while to establish their authorship. Others again are anonymous from the accidents of time and of a poetry transmitted more by recitation than by reading. Examples of all these kinds of anonymous verse may be found in translation in *Kings, Lords & Commons*, Frank O'Connor, NY 1959, London 1961.

For a description of the MSS in which the major part of the above literature is to be found, see under BOOKS.

B

BAIRÉAD, Risteárd (Barrett), b. Co. Mayo 1729, d. Co. Mayo 1819. Famous for one satire-poem on the death of an evil bailiff, *Eoghan Cóir*. Although he spent all his life in Mayo as a school-teacher and later as a farmer, he is supposed to have been in political contact with Irish exiles, and to have been imprisoned for this. His poetry is popular rather than formal, and most of it is ironically humorous. Sections of it appear in James Hardiman's edition of O'Flaherty's *A Chorographical Description of West or H-Iar Connaught*, Dublin 1846, and in Michael Timony's *Abhráin Ghaedhilge an Iarthair* (Gaelic Songs of the West), Dublin 1906. An essay, *Richard Barrett, the Bard of Mayo*, by J. Karney, appears in *Gaelic Journal* V, 136-8, 1894.

BAIRÉAD, Tomás, b. Co. Galway, d. 1973. Published several volumes of short stories, of which the best known are *An Geall a Briseadh*, Dublin 1938, *Cruithneacht agus Ceannabháin* (short stories), Dublin 1940; *Ór na h·Áitinne*, Dublin 1949; and *Dán*, Dublin 1973; *Gan Baisteadh* (autobiography), Dublin 1972.

BÉASLAÍ, Piaras (Pierce Beasley), b. Liverpool 1881, d.1965. Ed. Jesuits, Liverpool. Journalist in England and after 1904 in Dublin. From 1911 devoted his life to the Language Revival founding Gaelic Speakers' League, *An Fáinne*, and The Society of Gaelic Writers. He saw the language as a weapon in the Nationalist struggle for independence and it was on his motion proposing that the Gaelic League stood for a Free and Gaelic Ireland, free from foreign influences, that Douglas Hyde was defeated in the

1915 Congress. It was natural for Béaslaí to take part in the fighting of 1916, when he was vice-commandant of the 1st Btn Volunteers in the North King St. area. Pen and rifle were simply alternate weapons in the struggle, and he was of one mind with Patrick Pearse in this. It was from Béaslaí's motion at the 1915 Congress in fact that Pearse took his cry of Ireland not only free but Gaelic, incorporating the thought in his great O'Donovan Rossa speech in that same week.

Arrested, condemned to penal servitude after 1916, Béaslaí escaped from gaol in Ireland and again from Strangeways gaol in Manchester, to become head of the publicity dept. of the IRA. He toured the USA on a publicity campaign after the Treaty, explaining its provisions to Irish Americans, and returned to become chief of the Press Censorship Dept. during the Civil War. He had been elected for East Kerry in the 1918 Dáil and also held the rank of major-general in the Free State Army. In 1922 he was asked to write the life of Michael Collins which appeared as *Michael Collins and the Making of the New Ireland*, 2 vols, Dublin 1925. He resigned from the Dáil in 1923 and from the army in 1924 and his principal interest for the remainder of his life was the Language Movement and literature.

He translated from English, French and German into Irish and his own writings include a novel, plays and poetry. He won the Gold Medal for a play in Irish at the 1929 Tailteann Games. Main works include *Fear na Milliún Púnt*, Dublin 1915 (a play); *Bealtaine 1916 agus Dánta Eile*, Dublin 1920; *Astronár*, Dublin 1928 (a novel); *An Danar*, Dublin 1929 (a play); *Éigse nua-Ghaedhilge*, Dublin 1933-34 (plays and poetry 1600-1850); *An Fear Fograidheachta*, Dublin 1938 (a farce); *Earc agus Áine agus Scéalta Eile*, Dublin 1946.

BEASLEY, Pierce, see BÉASLAÍ, Piaras.

BEDELL, William, b. Essex 1571, d. Druinlor 1642. Ed. Cambridge, ordained 1597, Provost of TCD 1627, Bishop of Kilmore and Ardagh 1629. He resigned the latter see in 1633 and in 1641 was driven from his home by the Catholic forces and died the following year in the house of his friend Dennis Sheridan. He is famous in Irish literature as the supervisor of an Irish translation of the Old Testament. Combined with Archbishop Daniel's translation of the New Testament and printed in London 1685, it was known as *Bedell's Bible*. The style is admirable, but being in the Protestant interest the translation found few readers. Most Irish Catholics who gave up their Catholicism also gave up their language, or at least preferred not to parade it.

BEHAN, Brendan (Breandán Ó Beachain), b. Dublin 1923, d. Dublin 1964. For his work in English, see Part 1. His writing career began in Irish and many critics have claimed that his Irish was better than his English, and that *An Giall* is a better play than its English version, *The Hostage*. It is certainly a different one, containing none of the farcical, song and dance elements of the successful London production. Besides *An Giall* Behan wrote articles for *Comhar* and some of his Irish poetry appears in *Nua-Bhéarsíocht,* 1939-49, Dublin 1950. However, in spite of his vigorous command of the language and his loving use of it, his writing in Irish betrays that fact that it was a language he had only learned as an adult. His work in it needed grammatical revision by an editor before publication.

Sean O'Sullivan the portrait painter was one of several people to interest Behan in Irish.

BENEDICT, An tAth. ODC. Pen-name 'Maol Íosa'. b. Offaly 1897, d. Dublin 1980. Entered the Carmelite Monastery of St Joseph, Loughrea, 1914. Sent to Dublin 1916 to study philosophy. His first work in Irish was an essay on Descartes, *Scrúdú ar Theagasc Dhescartes,* written for the Oireachtas of 1920 and published in *Gaethe Greine,* II. In the same year his essay *Éire – Náisiún Céasta* was published in the December issue of *Síoladóir* 1, 3. In 1926 he translated St Thérèse's autobiography from French into Irish and also wrote his own account of her life as *Sgéal Anama* – a biography of St Teresa of the Child Jesus, published by Muintir Chathail. *Lorcán Naomhtha Ua Tuathail* – a biography of St Lawrence O'Toole, was published by the Irish Department of Education 1929. Fr Benedict also wrote *Páis Chríost* – the Passion of Christ, Dublin 1941 and *An Leabhar Aifrinn* – an Irish and Latin version of the Missal, Dublin 1952.

BERGIN, Osborn Joseph (Ó hAimhirgín), b. Co. Cork 1872, d. Dublin 1950. Ed. UCC and Germany. Became Professor of Old Irish, UCD, 1908, and one of the foremost Irish scholars of the century. Edited many Old Irish texts. Maintained an attitude of reserve towards modern Irish and the Revival. *Maidin i mBéarra agus Dánta Eile,* Dublin 1918; *Táin Bó Cúailnge,* Dublin 1928; *Lebor na hUidre: Book of the Dun Cow,* ed. R.I. Best and O.J. Bergin, Dublin 1929.

Many articles on early Irish poetry in *Studies,* 1918-25.

BEST, Richard Irvine, b. N. Ireland 1872, d. Dublin 1959. Studied Old Irish in Paris under Arbois de Jubainville, some of whose work he translated into English. In Paris became friendly with Synge and Stephen MacKenna, and about 1903 met Kuno Meyer. In 1904 became Assistant Director of National Library of Ireland, and Director 1924-40. Senior Professor of Celtic Studies, Dublin Inst. for Adv. Studies, 1940-47, and Chairman of Irish MSS Commission. The outstanding authority on Irish Palaeography and Philology. His portrait as a young librarian is unflatteringly drawn in *Ulysses,* James Joyce having apparently had some grudge against him.

His first work was *The Irish Mythological Cycle and Celtic Mythology* from the French of Arbois de Jubainville, 1903. *Bibliography of the Publications of Whitley Stokes,* Halle 1911; *Bibliography of the Publications of Kuno Meyer,* Halle 1923; *Lebor na hUidre: Book of the Dun Cow,* ed. R.I. Best and Osborn Bergin, Dublin 1929, Best proving it to be the work of more than one hand; *Bibliography of Irish Philology and Printed Irish Literature,* Dublin 1913, *The Annals of Innisfallen,* facsimile from MSS in

Bodleian, descriptive introduction by R.I. Best and Eoin Mac Néill, Dublin 1933 for RIA; *Senchus Már, the Ancient Laws of Ireland, Facsimile of oldest fragments from MSS in TCD*, with descriptive introduction by R. I. Best and Rudolph Thurneysen, Dublin 1931; *The Martyrology of Tallaght*, ed. R.I. Best and H.J. Lawlor, Dublin 1931; *Bibliography of Irish Philology and MSS Literature, Publications 1913-41*, Dublin 1942/1969 for Inst. for Adv. Studies; *The Book of Leinster, formerly Lebar na Núachongbála*, ed. R.I. Best and O. Bergin, vol. I, 1954; vols II-V, ed. R.I. Best and O'Brien, Dublin 1956, 1957, 1965, 1967.

BHELDON, Riobárd, b. the Déise 1838, d. 1915. His poems appear in several collections, *Fiche Duain*, ed. Shán Ó Cuív, and *File an Chomaraigh*, Dublin 1903, among others.

BLATHMAC, son of Cú Brettan, *fl.* 750-70. Cú Brettan was a prominent supporter of the High King Fergal, at the Battle of Allen, 718, and wrote verses about the fighting. Blathmac became a monk and wrote a long, two-part poem addressed to the Blessed Virgin Mary, concerned in large part with her sufferings and the death of her Son. He used an easy, natural language which besides its poetic quality gives a valuable indication of the Irish of the period. The manuscript is in the National Library of Ireland, numbered G.50. The final stanzas of the second part of the poem are lost through damage to the MSS. *The Poems of Blathmac*, ed. and trans. James Carney, Dublin 1964.

BLYTHE, Ernest (Earnán de Blaghd), b. Lisburn 1889, d. Dublin 1975. Expelled from the local National School at 11 for insubordination, studied Irish in Dublin with Gaelic League, 1905-08, and later worked as a farm labourer in the Kerry Gaeltacht to perfect his knowledge of the language. At different periods before the Rising was an organiser for the IRB in the north, for the Irish Volunteers in Munster and South Connacht and for the Gaelic League in Co. Cork. Also worked as a journalist for Sinn Féin. Was restricted for more than two years during the First World War under the Defence of the Realm Act and during the War of Independence had numerous spells of imprisonment in Ireland and England. Became a Minister in the Free State government after 1923 and earned a place in Irish artistic history as Minister of Finance, when he was responsible for granting an annual subsidy to the Abbey Theatre. He confirmed this place by his long reign as Managing Director of the same theatre from 1939 to his retirement in 1967. His critics accuse him of destroying the Abbey as a National Theatre and a centre of dramatic life, turning it into a meagre and spiritless repertory company capable of neither justice to the past nor giving rise to new inspiration in the present. It is certainly true that since 1939 most Irish playwrights of any stature have presented most of their work, and often their first work, elsewhere than the Abbey. But this was often of their own choice, and Blythe was unjustly castigated at times for refusing plays he had never been offered, or that he had been offered under conditions no manager in his senses could accept. And attacks on a man who did at least keep a theatre open come very ill from a public which will do almost anything to a theatre except pay to sit in it.

One of Blythe's principal interests in the theatre was to make it a vehicle, or possible vehicle, for plays in Irish and it has been said that he was more interested in a player's Irish than in his or her ability to act. If this is true he may have been misguided, but he could reasonably claim to have been misguided by the Irish people, who at all opportunities have claimed to desire the revival of Irish. The only reservation they have is a steadfast refusal to read it or speak it or listen to it being spoken. In general the most savage attacks on Blythe and his politics were made by people who offered no evidence that they could do better.

Blythe's real importance in Irish literature is what he did and failed to do as master of the major outlet for Irish drama for 30 years. He also wrote poetry, political essays and a volume of autobiography in Irish, as well as much polemical journalism in English.

Fraoch agus Fothannáin, Dublin 1938 (poetry); *Briseadh na Teorann*, Dublin 1955 (a study of the causes and solutions of partition, arguing for conciliation and persuasion); *Trasna na Bóinne*, Dublin 1957 (his life up to 24); *Slán le hUltaibh*, Dublin 1969, and *Gaeil á Muscailt*, Dublin 1973, continue the story. For work in English see Part 1.

BOOKS. Most of what survives of early Irish literature is contained in a number of so-called 'Books,' collections of manuscripts which in some cases form one-volume libraries for the use of a monastery or great family. The more important of these are described in succeeding entries under their names, usually drawn from the place of compilation, such as Ballymote or Lismore or Lecan.

The existence of written material in Ireland almost certainly pre-dates the coming of St Patrick, but this material would have been in Latin, and imported. It is likely to have included copies of the Gospels. The earliest manuscripts written in Ireland were likewise copies of the Gospels, such as that contained in the *Domnach Airgid*, or *Silver Shrine*, of the 10th century, but itself dating from far earlier, perhaps even the 6th century. The fragment that remains is in the National Museum of Ireland. The *Cathach* or *Battler* is also traditionally ascribed to the 6th century, and to the hand of St Columba himself. It is supposedly the copy of the Psalms that he made from a copy owned by St Finnian of Moville, sitting up all night to complete it. On St Finnian's complaint that this was tantamount to robbery, Columba appealed to the king, who gave the famous judgment in favour of Finnian: 'To every cow its calf, to every book its copy.' Columba resisted this judgment, and the ensuing quarrel played a part in his exile. The manuscript itself passed into the keeping of Columba's family, the O'Donnells, who carried it into battle as a talisman, hence its name.

Already Irish writing had gone beyond the strict copying of Testament material. St Patrick's *Confessions* must have been written in the 5th century, although the manuscript copies that survive are much later. St Patrick also brought about the written codification of the already ancient Brehon Laws, setting up a committee of three kings, three clerics, and three poets, to bring them into line with the new Christian ethic, and write them down for posterity. Their work resulted in the *Senchus Már* and the *Book of Aicill,* which again survive only in much later copies.

St Patrick's disciple, St Benignus, is traditionally responsible for the *Leabhar na gCeart,* the *Book of Rights,* which describes the political constitutions of the Irish states as they existed in the 5th and 6th centuries. This is the earliest treatise of its kind in Europe. A copy of the work was incorporated in the lost *Saltair of Caiseal,* a 10th-century manuscript collection. It survives in the early 15th-century *Book of Lecan.*

The earliest manuscript collection containing substantial passages in Irish is the *Book of Armagh,* compiled by Feardomhnach in 807, and containing the oldest surviving copy of the *Confessions* of St Patrick, with lives of St Patrick and St Martin of Tours, and a copy of the New Testament.

It was long believed this book was written in St Patrick's own hand, and it was revered as *Canóin Phádraig.* It is certainly possible that Feardomhnach worked from St Patrick's own manuscripts. It was in the book that Brian Bóroimhe caused his scribe to insert the description of Brian as *Imperator Scotorum.*

The *Liber Hymnorum,* belonging to the late 9th or early 10th century, also contains Gaelic material, along with Latin.

From these centuries, the 7th to 10th, scraps of Gaelic writing survive in the margins if MSS compiled in other languages in European monasteries such as St Gall, and this material was gathered and commented on by the founder of Celtic philology, Johann Kaspar Zeuss (1806-1856), in his great *Grammatica Celtica,* 1853. It contains the earliest Irish known, and provides invaluable clues for the dating of old material bedded in later manuscripts, such as the early material in the *Lebor na hUidre, The Book of the Dun Cow.*

This Book was compiled in the late 11th or early 12th century and is the oldest Irish manuscript entirely in Irish, and containing literary rather than purely religious material. Much of its language belongs to 8th-century Irish and certain mystical verses appear older still, perhaps belonging even to the 6th century. It therefore seems certain that the scribe making the Book about the year 1200 was himself copying from MSS of a much earlier date and not merely writing down things recited to him orally.

This in turn suggests that while only religious, and primarily Latin material survives from before the 12th century, secular manuscripts were written and the practice of writing them may have begun almost as early as the copying of the Gospels and the writing of saints' Lives. The monastic scribes are very likely to have been drawn from exactly the classes that traditionally possessed knowledge of legends and stories, together with history, genealogies and law and medicine.

While before the coming of Christianity it had been considered wrong to commit such knowledge to writing, Christian practice must very soon have broken down this tabu and it is reasonable to suppose that at latest by the 7th century manuscript versions of the earliest epics and cycles were already in existence, drawn from oral traditions. These MSS would have provided the basis at first or second or third hand for the copies that still survive in manuscript books of the 12th and later centuries.

See also ANONYMOUS.

BOOK OF ARMAGH, compiled by Feardomhnach the scribe about 807, containing Latin versions of the *Confessions* of St Patrick, lives of the saint and of St Martin of Tours and a copy of the New Testament. Substantial passages are in Gaelic, the earliest such passages that survive. For many centuries the book was supposed to be in the handwriting of St Patrick and it was accordingly revered as *Canóin Phádraig*. An 11th-century insertion describes Brian Bóroimhe as *Imperator Scotorum*. The MS is in TCD. *Liber Ardmachanus,* ed. John Gwynn, for RIA, Dublin 1913; *Book of Armagh,* facs. ed. for Irish MSS Commission, Dublin 1937.

BOOK OF BALLYMOTE, compiled 1390 in Sligo by Maghnus Ó Duibhgeánnáin and helpers, for Mac Donogh of Tír Oiliolla. Contains the Ogham alphabet and provided the key to the numerous inscriptions on standing stones carved in this form of 'stroke' alphabet. Also contains the Irish version of the *Aeneid* and other classical matter; genealogies; bardic tracts on metre and grammar; and a copy of *The Book of Rights,* pub. by RIA, Dublin 1887.

BOOK OF DUNIRY, more properly *Speckled Book of Duniry,* the *Leabhar Breac,* written by the Mac Egan family *c.* 1400, mostly consisting of religious material drawn from earlier MSS. Remarkable for the purity of its Irish. Contains fragments of the *Senchus Mór,* the ancient Law Code of Ireland. Facs. ed. pub. by RIA, ed. B. O'Looney, in 2 vols, Dublin 1872, 1876.

BOOK OF GENEALOGIES, a massive compilation of the mid-17th century, giving the descents of all the principal clans of Ireland.

See MAC FIRBISIGH, Dubhaltach.

BOOK OF INVASIONS, the *Leabhar Gabhála,* an account of the early invasions of Ireland, mostly mythological. The earliest manuscript fragments of this work survive in the *Book of Leinster,* 12th century.

BOOK (GREAT) OF LECAN, compiled *c.* 1400 by Giolla Íosa Mór Mac Firbis. With *The Yellow Book of Lecan,* compiled by the same scribe at the same period, it contains genealogical material, and the earliest surviving version of the *Book of Rights,* the political treatise on the constitutions of the Irish states of the 6th century, drawn up by St Benignus. *The Yellow Book of Lecan* also contains part of the early version of the *Táin Bó Cúailgne.* The MS is now in TCD. *Leabhar Mór Mhic Fhir Bhisigh Leccain,* facs.ed. for Irish Commission, Introduction and MSS index, Kathleen Mulchrone, Dublin 1937. *The Yellow Book of Lecan, Leabhar Buidhe Lecain,* ed. Robert Atkinson, Dublin 1896.

BOOK OF LEINSTER (sometimes *Book of Glendalough* and in earlier times *Lebar na Nuachonghbala*), an anthology of stories and poetry compiled about 1150 by Fionn MacGormain, a bishop, in Glendalough. It contains part of a version of the *Táin,* less simply and forcefully written that the older version in the *Book of the Dun Cow,* parts of the *Dindshenchas* and of the *Leabhar Gabhála* or *Book of Invasions.* The RIA published a facs.ed., Dublin 1880, and it was edited for the Dublin Inst. for Adv. Studies by R.I. Best, Osborn Bergin, and M. A. O'Brien. Vol 1 (Best and Bergin), 1954; vols 2-5 (Best and O'Brien), 1956, 1957, 1965, 1967. The original MSS are divided between TCD and the Franciscan Library, Dublin.

BOOK OF RIGHTS *(Leabhar na gCeart,* sometimes *Lebor na Cert),* an account of the rights of the Irish kings, and the dues owed to them by their sub-kings. According to tradition this book was drawn up by St Benignus about 450 and was revised and enlarged by Cormac Mac Cuileannain, King of Cashel, about 900. The two earliest surviving copies are to be found in the *Book of Ballymote* and the *Book of Lecan.* John O'Donovan edited and translated the best version, Dublin, 1847. See also *Lebor na Cert,* ed. Myles Dillon, for ITS, Dublin 1962.

BOOK OF THE DUN COW *(Leabhar na hUidri,* sometimes *Lebor na hUidre),* named from the tradition that its vellum was cut from the hide of St Ciaran's dun cow. The earliest use of the name appears to be about 1470. The MS is the oldest written entirely in Irish and was compiled at Clonmacnoise *c.* 1100, for which reason the Four Masters call it *The Book of Clonmacnoise.* The MS is now incomplete, but still contains a large quantity of important material; an incomplete version of the *Táin,* fragments of the *Book of Invasions,* stories from the Red Branch Cycle of legends, poems attributed to St Colmcille and others. The chief scribe was Mael Muire Mac Ceileachair, who died 1106.

After the Cromwellian invasion the MS disappeared until 1837 when it came into the hands of the bookseller George Smith in Dublin. The RIA acquired it in 1844 when O'Curry catalogued its contents. It was transcribed by Joseph O'Longan and edited by Sir John T. Gilbert for the RIA, and published in facsimile, Dublin 1870. The RIA again published it, edited by R.I. Best and Osborn Bergin, Dublin 1929.

BREATHNACH, Breandán, b. Dublin 1912. Retired civil servant; Editor and publisher of *Ceol,* a journal of Irish music, since 1963. Chairman of Na Píobairí Uilleann since 1968. *Ceol Rince na hÉireann,* 1963; vol. 2, 1976; vol. 3, 1985. *The Folk Music and Dances of Ireland,* 1971.

BREATHNACH, Micheál (Cois Fhairrge), b. Co. Galway 1881, d. Dublin 1908. Prompted by Tomás Bán (Tomás Ua Concheanáinn) he joined the Gaelic League as a schoolboy and in 1902 became Vice-Secretary of the

League in London, where he was working. In 1905 he returned to the west of Ireland because of ill-health, and taught in Tuam. He spent the winters in Switzerland, but in 1908 his health deteriorated still further, and he died in Dublin. He published a number of stories and essays in *An Claidheamh Soluis* and *Irisleabhar na Gaeilge* in the last four years of his life and a history of Ireland, published by Connradh na Gaeilge, 1910-11. His travel book, *Seilg i measc na nAep* rep. 1980.

BREATHNACH, Micheál (Tóchar Mhairtin), b. Co, Galway 1886, native Irish speaker. Ed. Galway, and Royal University of Ireland. Became a teacher in Roscrea and later in Dublin; National School Inspector, 1922, Secondary School Inspector, 1923, Assistant Chief Inspector of Secondary Schools, 1932; Secretary of Dept of Education, 1944. Published essays, plays, anthologies, text-books and translations. *Trom agus Éadtrom*, Dublin 1927 (collected essays); *Cor in aghaidh an Chaim*, Dublin 1931 (a play, produced at the Abbey the same year); *Draoidheacht Chaitlín* (play, produced at Peacock Theatre, Dublin 1933); *Fion na Filidheachta*, Dublin 1931 (anthology of Irish poetry, rep. 1947 and 1953); *Prós na Fiannaidheachta*, Dublin 1932 (anthology of Fenian prose); and *Cuimhne an tSeanpháiste*, Dublin 1966.

BREATHNACH, Pádraic, b. Co. Galway 1942. Ed. UCG, teacher in Galway and Dublin. Lecturer in College of Education, Limerick from 1969. Has written short stories: *Bean Aonair & Scéalta Eile*, 1974, rep. 1984. *Buicéad Poitín & Scéalta Eile*, 1978; *An Lánúin & Scéalta Eile*, 1979. *Na Déithe Luachmhara Deiridh*, 1980; *Lilí agus Fraoch*, 1983.

BROWNE, Patrick, Monsignor; see DE BRÚN, An tAth.

C

CAROLAN, Turlough (Ó Cearbhalláin Toirdhealbhac), b. Nobber, Co. Meath 1670, d. Co. Roscommon 1738. The most famous of Irish harpers and like many of his kind both composer and poet as well as musician. Of good but impoverished family, his father migrated westwards to Leitrim, presumably in search of cheaper land to rent. Young Turlough was blinded by smallpox as a child and this tragedy had the compensation of freeing him from field-work to become a harper. The McDermott family of Alderford in Co. Roscommon took him under its protection and Mrs McDermott remained his patroness all his life. A great lover of women and whiskey, his best songs were inspired by one or the other, or both, such as 'Bridget Cruise' or the famous 'Receipt for Drinking'.

As a harper he travelled a wide area visiting houses that would give him hospitality in return for entertainment, and in this respect his life followed the ancient pattern. But he also seems to have been well acquainted with contemporary European music, particularly Italian. At the age of 50 he married a Miss Mary Maguire and took a farm at Mosshill in Co. Leitrim. They were both extravagant, and after her death in 1733 he returned to the road. His 'Lament' for his dead wife is one of his best poems. He found increasing consolation in whiskey and was finally warned by doctors, apparently much to his surprise, that whiskey would kill him. He had been drinking it by the pint tumbler, but he gave it up entirely for at least six weeks. He fell into a depression and was at last driven to go into a grocer's shop in Boyle, where he was staying, to beg the shop-boy for at least the smell of a glass. In a short while he was drinking again. At home with the McDermotts in 1738, he fell into his last illness, and died holding a bowl of whiskey he no longer had the strength to empty. It was hard, he said, 'that two such friends should part, at least without kissing'.

His fame swiftly turned into legends, one legend often contradicting another. He is alternately spoken of as a fine harper and mediocre poet, and as an indifferent harper but a splendid poet. His poetry, which is all that can now be judged, has a courteous dignity and here and there the genuine flame of humanity, like a pre-echo of Burns. Like some Irish writers since it is possible that his chief genius was for living. For the student his life and work are of great interest because they are among the last spasms of the dying world of Gaelic culture.

There are a number of MSS of Carolan's poems in the RIA. Some of his songs are included in James Hardiman's *Irish Minstrelsy*, Dublin 1831. Tomás Ó Máille edited *Amhráin Chearbhalláin*, containing his known songs and poems for the ITS, 1916.

CARVE, Thomas, alternatively Carue, Carew and Ó Corráin, b. Co. Tipperary 1590, d. after 1672, probably in Germany. A protégé of the Ormonde family he became a priest. He went to Germany in 1626 and serving in the Thirty Years' War as an army chaplain, rose to become Chaplain-General of the Irish, Scottish and English forces engaged in the war. His *Itinerarium*, vols 1 and 2, Mainz 1639-41, vol. 3, Spires 1646, contain eye-witness accounts of events during the war, and are a valuable source of information on it. The three parts were reprinted in one volume in a 100-copy edition, London 1859. He also wrote *Rerum Germanicarum ab Anno 1617 ad Annum 1641 Gestarum Epitome*, 1641, and *Lyra, seu Anacephalaeosis Hibernica*, Vienna 1651; 2nd revised ed. Sulzbach 1666, the latter being an account of Ireland and Irish customs. Carve was apparently fluent in Irish, but preferred English, and this is a reflection of his political sympathies. His *Galateus*, Nordhausen 1669, and *Enchiridion Apologeticum*, Noribergae 1670, were among his last works. He was still living in Sulzbach in 1672.

CASÁIN, An tAth. OFM Cap., b. Co. Cork 1897, d. California 1981. Son of Pádraig Ó Seaghdha. Ed. Cork and Rome, published a number of short stories in *Éarna I* and *II* and in *Capuchin Annual*. Other works include

Gleann an Uaignis, 1922; *An Londubh agus Scéalta Eile,* Dublin 1937.

CÉITINN, Seathrún, see KEATING, Geoffrey.

CLOCH LABHRÁIS, see Ó CIARGHUSA, Seán.

COIMÍN, Micheál, b. Co. Clare 1688, d. Co. Clare 1760. The family was supposedly descended from the Scots Comyns, Earls of Buchan in the Middle Ages, but of a branch long settled in Clare, and wealthy. Micheál's father, Patrick, lost his estate during the Cromwellian invasion, but was granted a substantial farm after the Restoration, and the family being Protestant, Micheál's circumstances were much easier and more secure than any of his contemporary Irish poets. The extraordinary thing is that he chose to be an Irish poet, writing in Irish. In some respects he was very much a member of his Ascendancy class, small squireens more interested in horses than in culture or justice. He is supposed to have abducted a young woman, Harriet Stacpoole, very much as Jonah Barrington describes his own acquaintances doing 70 years laters. He is also supposed to have married when only 14.

After his death his son Edward, entirely a squireen and with none of his father's love of Irish culture, burned his father's manuscripts, considering them evidence of treasonable thinking, or at least weak-mindedness, and therefore only a handful of Micheál Coimín's work survives, a few poems of which three deal with Harriet's abduction, and a very few stories. The stories are his finest work and remarkable not only because of what their author was but because they are in prose, an almost unused medium for Irish writers in the 18th century, presumably because it was so difficult to get any book in Irish printed. Poems at least could be memorised, and being mostly short could be copied.

The best story is *Eachtra Thoirdhealbhaigh Mhic Stairn,* written about 1740 and available in a modern edition under that title, edited by Eoghan Ó Neachtain, Dublin 1922. It is the old folk story of a king's son falling in love with a woman seen once and then lost and searching the world for her.

In his own time and for most of the 18th century, he was remembered for an Ossianic poem, *Laoi Oisín,* composed about 1750, translated into English as *Tir na nÓg,* Dublin 1863, and another edition and translation by David Comyn, *Laoidh Oisín air Thír na n-Óg,* Dublin 1880. Thomas Flannery brought out an edition in 1896. In manuscript copies, and taken orally from place to place, the poem in its time reached even the Hebrides, and may have been among the many genuine Ossianic verses and traditional stories that MacPherson discovered in the Highlands a few years later, to inspire his supposed translation, *Fingal,* in 1762.

COLGAN, John, b. Donegal *c.* 1590, d. Louvain 1658. He became a Franciscan friar and Professor of Theology at Louvain. His chief work is only a fragment of what he intended it to be, a six volume compendium of early Irish history and the lives of the Irish saints. Volume 1, containing the history, remained unpublished. Volume 4 according to Fr Luke Wadding, was in the press at the time of Colgan's death, but never appeared, and volumes 5 and 6 were presumably unwritten. Volume 2, entitled *Trias Thaumaturga*, which contains lives of SS. Patrick, Brigid and Columba, appeared in 1647, published in Louvain. Curiously, volume 3 was published in Louvain two years earlier, under the title *Acta Sanctorum Veteris et Majoris Scotiae seu Hiberniae*, and contains lives of the Irish saints whose feast days occur in January, February and March. Volumes 4, 5 and 6 were to continue the series of lives through the rest of the calendar. It seems possible that Colgan prepared the four volumes in MS some years previous to 1645 and then published volume 3 first. In 1655 he published in Antwerp a brief *Tractatus de Joannis Scoti. . . Vita*, claiming Duns Scotus as Irish rather than Scottish.

Although Colgan wrote in Latin his language for correspondence was Irish. It was he who gave the name 'The Four Masters' to the last great Irish Annalists. Even in fragmentary form, his two volumes of Irish saints' lives are a most valuable work. He was encouraged and helped in his writing by his predecessor as Louvain Professor of Theology, Aodh Buidhe Mac an Bhaird. Colgan himself retired from the Chair in 1645 and if this was on account of his age, rather than to free him for further writing, he may have been born much earlier than the suggested date of 1590. See entries MAC AN BHAIRD, Aodh Buidhe, and Ó CLÉIRIGH, Micheál.

COLMÁN MOCCU CLUSAIG, *fl.* 7th century. Probably a native of Cork. His most famous poem is the hymn *Sén Dé* (The Blessing of God) and it is in both Latin and Old Irish. Written during the great plague of 664 it is based on the prayer for the Commendation of the Soul from the Breviary. Some of his poetry appears in *Annals of Ireland*, John O'Donovan, Dublin 1860, and in *Goidelica – Eight Hymns from the Liber Hymnorum*, Whitley Stokes, Calcutta 1866, 2nd ed. London 1872.

COLMÁN, Saint, son of Lenene, b. 522, d. 600. Patron Saint of Cloyne and of the O'Daly family of hereditary bards. He was already a famous poet before taking Holy Orders, and on being tonsured he bequeathed his skill as a poet to his fosterling and pupil, Dálach, founder of the clan of Ó Dálaigh. Poems attributed to Colmán are in the *Book of Lismore,* and were edited by Whitley Stokes in *Lives of the Saints from the Book of Lismore,* 1890.

COLMAN, the Irishman, *fl.* 9th century. Remembered for his poem written to a younger priest of the same name, who longs to return to Ireland. It is likely that they were both in a monastery in the north of France. Helen Waddell gives the Latin text with a translation in *Mediaeval Latin Lyrics,* 1929, and 1952.

COLMCILLE, An tAth. (Colm Ó Labhra), b. Clonmel, joined Cistercians 1930. Under his lay name of Colm Ó Labhra published *Trodairí na Treas Briogáide,* Cló Úi Mheára 1955; and *Comhcheilg na Mainistreach Móire,*

Dublin 1968, a Club Leabhar selection. Under his name in religion, Colmcille, he has translated the Rule of St Benedict into Irish as *Noamh-Athar Beiniadhacht,* Dublin 1958; and written about his patron saint in *Deoraí Chríost,* Dublin 1960.

COLUMBA (Columcille, Colmcille), major Irish saint, b. Co. Donegal 521, d. Iona 597. Of royal birth and related to ruling princes in both Ulster and western Scotland he entered the Church as a prince and did much to confirm the aristocratic character of the Irish Church. He studied under St Finnian of Moville and also under St Finnian of Clonard. Returning from near what would later become Dublin, to the north, he founded monasteries at Derry, 546, and at Durrow, about 553. *The Book of Durrow* now in TCD library was long supposed to have been written by Columba's own hand. Certainly the colophon is in a very early Irish, and the whole MS was already venerated as an ancient relic at the beginning of the 10th century.

The Battle of Cuildremhne in 561 was believed to be his responsibility and the Irish ecclesiastical synod accordingly censured him. In 563 he went into exile with 12 followers and established himself on the island of Hy, later known as I Columcille, and later still as Iona. From there he organised many missionary journeys to the Picts of northern Scotland. He met St Kentigern in Glasgow, returned several times to Ireland, and shaped his new foundations in northern Britain and the Pictish territories on the Irish pattern, which meant that the bishops were largely subordinate to the abbots of the great monasteries, who in turn were subordinate to the mother house of Iona; a monastic rather than diocesan system. This, with differences in the date on which Easter was celebrated, and details of tonsure and liturgy, began to create a chasm if not a schism between the Irish and Roman versions of Catholicism and for more than 60 years after Columba's death it seemed possible that all of northern England would belong to the Irish system. It was only at the Synod of Whitby in 664 that the Roman cause defeated the Columban influence.

Columba's writings are a matter of legend and controversy. Much that in early centuries was ascribed to his authorship was simply work transcribed by him or under his direction. He is reputed to have 'written', that is copied, 300 books with his own hand. But he is likely to have composed at least the *Altus* traditionally ascribed to him and printed in the *Liber Hymnorum* of Dr James Todd, and John Colgan ascribes a number of works to him in Latin and Irish, including three Latin hymns; these last being almost certainly Columba's.

The chief source for details of Columba's Life is Adamnán, one of Columba's successors as Abbot of Iona, and a distant relative, but there had been an earlier Life by Cuimine, also an Abbot of Iona, and Adamnán incorporated much of the earlier Life in his own work.

There are a number of editions of Adamnán, ed. W. Reeves, 1857, and J. T. Fowler, 1894, among others.

COLUMBAN (also COLUMBANUS), b. Leinster 543, d. Bobbio 615.

Studied in Bangor under Congall. Went as a missionary to Britain, and then, between 585 and 590, to Gaul. He settled in the Vosges, founding the monasteries of Annegray, Luxeuil and Fontaine. The Rule he drew up for his monks was approved by the Council of Macon, 627, and is extant, but was soon replaced by the Benedictine Rule. Columban established good relations with several of the Frankish rulers, Hlothair II of Soissons and Theodebert II of Metz among them, but this did not save him from expulsion from Gaul when his long-running differences with the Gaulish bishops came to a crisis in 610. He was expelled from Frankish territory by Theodoric II, of Burgundy, who was the readier to act because of Columban's fierce criticisms of his court's immorality. The quarrel with the bishops arose over the differences between Celtic and Roman dating of Easter, and similar matters.

Columban moved into what is now Switzerland, where he left his pupil Gall, he himself crossing the Alps southwards into Lombardy. There in the Appenines he founded his last and greatest monastery at Bobbio, where he died in the winter of 615. With his almost namesake Columba he was among the first of the great Irish missionary saints who brought the Celtic version of Catholicism to the still pagan areas of Europe.

Columban's writings, all in Latin, include the Rule, six letters in prose, four in verse; a penitential supplement to the Rule, listing the punishments for infractions; a handful of sermons (all that are left as authentic from the seventeen once ascribed to him); and a Commentary on the Psalms which may or may not be his.

Among the letters are ones to Gregory the Great and Boniface III and IV. There is also some poetry, including a 'boat-song' and poems on vanity and life's vexations. All of the known works with some apocryphal matter is in the *Collectanea Sacra,* ed. Patrick Fleming, Augsburg 1621, rep. Louvain 1667. There is a *Vita* by Jonas of Susa, a monk of Bobbio, translated into English by D.C. Munro, 1896.

COMYN, David (Daithí Coimín), b. Co. Clare 1854, d. Dublin 1907. As a bank-clerk in Dublin in the 1870s he studied Irish and in 1876 helped to found the Society for the Preservation of the Irish Language. In 1879 he and Fr Nolan broke away to form the Gaelic Union. Comyn's great contribution to the Revival Movement was to press the government to include Irish as a subject in the curricula of the National and Intermediate Schools. This was achieved in 1878, and among the first text-books were Comyn's own *First* and *Second Irish Books.*

Comyn's next concern was Gaelic journalism. He wrote Irish columns for *The Irishman* and the *Shamrock* between 1878 and 1882, and became the first editor of the *Gaelic Journal,* founded by the Gaelic Union in November 1882. He edited a number of Irish MSS in the '80s and '90s, and collected a large library of MSS and books bearing on the Irish language and Irish history and archaeology. These were presented to the National Library of Ireland in 1907 as the Comyn Bequest. His work as editor includes *Mac-Ghníomhartha Fhinn,* published by Gill, Dublin 1881; *Díon-bhrollach Foras Feasa ar Éirinn,* for the ITS, 1898, and what was to have been his master work, Keating's History. Of this he brought out only the first volume as *Foras Feasa ar Éirinn,* vol. I, ITS, 1902. He had also printed the unpublished poems of Peadar Ó Doirnín in the *Gaelic Journal* in issues of 1895-96. He was already in poor health when working on Keating, and this prevented his continuing.

CONALL CEARNACH, see O'CONNELL, Frederick.

CONÁN MAOL, see Ó SÉAGHDHA, Pádraig.

CONCANNON, Thomas, see UA CONCHEANAINN.

CONNELLAN, Owen, b. Co. Sligo 1800, d. Dublin 1869. A founder of the Irish Revival movement and an eccentric scholar, see Part 1. His *Grammar of the Irish Language,* 1844, has a Connacht bias. In 1860 he published the Irish text, with English translation, of *Imtheacht na Tromdháimhe.*

CORMACÁN EIGEAS (the Learned) **MAC MAELBRIGDE,** d. 946. Became chief poet to Muirchertach, King of Ulster. In a poem celebrating a triumphal circuit of Ireland by his king, Cormacán gave him the name Muirchertach of the Leather Cloaks, because of the winter cloaks worn by his warriors. The circuit was made in the winter of 941-42, and the poem was written in the latter year. Editions are *A Mhuircheartaig Mhic Neill Nair* ed. *John O'Donovan – (The Circuit of Ireland by Muircheartach Mac Neill, Prince of Aileach; a poem written in the year DCCCCXLII by Cormacan Eigeas, chief poet of the North of Ireland. Now for the first time printed [from the Lebar Gebála of O'Clery] with transl. & notes),* Dublin, Irish Archaeological Society (Tracts Relating to Ireland, I) 1841; H. Morris, 'On the Circuit of Ireland by Muirchertach no gCochall gCroiceann, AD 941', *Journal of the Royal Society of Antiquaries of Ireland,* LXVI 9-31, 1936; LXVIII 291-93, 1938; and H.C. Lawlor, 'The Circuit of Muirchertach' *(Ibid.* LXVI 128-30, 1937).

CORMAC MAC CUILEANNÁIN, b. Cashel 836, d. in battle Co. Kildare 908. King and Bishop of Cashel, betrothed to Gormflaith, daughter of Flann Sionna the High King. Despite this, he found himself at war with Flann Sionna and was killed at the Battle of Bealach Mughna, the man responsible for his death being King Cearbhall of Leinster. Cormac was a poet and one of his lyrics is in *The Book of Leinster.* Its subject is death. But Cormac's literary fame arises from his authorship of *Sanas Chormaic* (Cormac's Glossary), listing a large number of old and rare words. He was also responsible for the compilation known in English as *The Psalter of Cashel* and playing a part in Irish law and history almost equivalent to that of the *Domesday Book* in England. It contains the genealogies of leading families of the period. A separate section, known as *The Book of Rights,* sets out in mnemonic verses the privileges, tributes and duties of each of the chieftains of Ireland. It was revised 200 years later in the reign of King Brian Bóroimhe and for centuries was in use in Gaelic Ireland. It is still of immense value as an historical source. See *Three Irish Glossaries,* Whitley Stokes, 1862; *Sanas Chormaic,* trans. and annotated John O'Donovan, ed. Whitley Stokes, Calcutta 1868; *Sanas Cormaic* (ed. from copy in *Yellow Book of Lecan),* Kuno Meyer, Halle 1912; *Leabhar na gCeart – or The Book of Rights,* ed. with trans. and notes, John O'Donovan, Dublin 1847; *Selections from Early Irish Poetry,* Kuno Meyer, Dublin 1909.

CRAOIBHÍN AOIBHINN, AN, see HYDE, Douglas.

CREAGH, Richard, see Ó MULCHRÉIBE, Ristéard.

CUMINE (sometimes CUIMINE) AILBHE, b. Ireland *c.* 600, d. Iona 669. He was a nephew of Seghine, 5th Abbot of Iona, and joined his uncle there, himself becoming 7th Abbot in 657. He was involved in the attempt to bring the Roman system regarding Easter to the Celtic Church and a letter addressed to *Segienus, Abbot of Hy,* is likely to have been his. It deals with the controversy over the rival 532-year and 84-year cycles used in calculating the date of Easter. Cumine chose the Roman side in the argument, but had small success in Iona.

He wrote a Life of St Columba which had a curious history. Believed lost for centuries, it was found at Compiégne in the early 18th century and published by Mabillon in his *Acta Sanctorum,* 1733. It was then seen to be identical with Colgan's Life of Colmcille published at Louvain, 1647, in his *Trias Thaumaturga.* Colgan had found the MS without any author's name, in Antwerp.

Cumine's Life of the saint, *De Virtutibus Sancti Columbae,* was used by Adamnán and is the basis for the third book of his *Vita Sancti Columbae.*

Cumine also wrote *De Poenitentiarum Mensura* which was again lost to view, for well over 1000 years in fact, until found in the monastery of St Gall by John Fleming in the 19th century.

CUSSEN, Cliodna, b. Limerick. Ed. UCD, studied art in Dublin and Florence, now a professional sculptor in Dublin. *Éire ins an 18d Aois,* London 1969. *Trupall, trapall,* 1972; *Síle Bhuí,* 1975; *Buile Shuibhne,* 1976; *Tomhais,* 1977; *Gearóid Iarla,* 1978; *Ealó ón gcaisleán,* 1978; *An Drochshaol,* 1980; all pub. Dublin. Has also ed. *Moírín,* Dunquin 1973.

CÚ ULADH see MAC FHIONNGHAILE, Peadar.

D

DALLAN FORGAILL, b. *c.* 540, d. Connacht 596. Chief of the poets of Ireland. According to the story *Imtheacht na Tromdhaimhe* (the Proceed-

DANIEL HUA LIATHÁIDE

ings of the Great Bardic Assembly), he was supposed to have instigated the Assembly's extortion of excessive hospitality from Guaire the Hospitable, the King of Connacht. Dallan is said to have been killed as a result, and avenged by his successor, Seanchán Torpéist, who extorted even more from the unhappy Guaire. The surviving poetry of Dallan Forgaill has been edited by G.O'B. Crowe, *The Amra Choluim Chilli* (a poem in praise of St Columcille), Dublin 1871; and Whitley Stokes, 'The Bodleian Amra Choluimb Chille', *Revue Celtique, XX, 1899, XXI, 1900. Irish Minstrelsy,* James Hardiman, Dublin 1831, gives translations of Dallan's odes to Aodh Mac Duach.

DANIEL HUA LIATHÁIDE, b. *c.* 810, d. of wounds 861. Abbot of Cork and Lismore. His poem of advice to a woman soliciting him has been edited and translated by Kuno Meyer in *Ériu I & II,* Dublin 1904, pp. 67-9.

DANIEL, William (Uilliam Ó Domhnuill), b. Kilkenny *c.* 1570, d. Tuam 1628. Fellow of TCD 1593. Archbishop of Tuam. More tolerant of Catholic rights than most of his fellow Protestant bishops, he did not join in their protest of 1626 against the toleration of Catholicism. While in TCD he had begun a translation into Irish of the New Testament, completing it in 1602. This was later combined with Bedell's version of the Old Testament in Irish form *Bedell's Bible,* London 1685. His *New Testament* was first printed, alone, Dublin 1602. He also translated the *Book of Common Prayer* into Irish, Dublin 1608.

DAVITT, Michael, b. Cork 1950. Ed. Cork. Poet and businessman (typesetting). Editor of *Innti* since 1970. Poetry: *Gleann ar Ghleann,* Dublin 1982; *Bligeard Sráide,* Dublin 1983, both collections.

DE BHAILIS, Colm, b. Lettermullen 1796, d. 1906. A folk poet. His collected verse pub. Connradh na Gaeilge, Dublin 1904.

DE BHALDRAITHE, Tomás, b. Co. Limerick 1916. Ed. Dublin and Paris. Became Professor of Modern Irish Language and Literature UCD 1960; has been editor of *Comhar* and consultant editor of the *Irish-English Dictionary,* Dublin 1978. His *English-Irish Dictionary,* Dublin 1959, is a standard work. Has also written *The Irish of Cois Fhairrge: A Phonetic Study,* Dublin Inst. for Adv. Studies 1945; *Gaeilge Chois Fhairrge: An Deilbhíocht,* Dublin Inst. for Adv. Studies 1953. Ed. of *Nuascéalaíocht,* Sáirséal agus Dill 1952; *Scothscéalaíocht,* Pádraic Ó Conaire (Sáirséal agus Dill) 1956; and *Seacht mBua an Éirí Amach,* Pádraic Ó Conaire (Sáirséal agus Dill) 1967. Since then has published *Cín Lae Amhlaoibh,* 1970, being the diary of an early 19th-century hedge schoolmaster; and *Seanchas Thomáis Laighléis,* 1977, being the memoirs of an octogenarian living in east Galway. Co-editor with Niall Ó Dónaill of *Irish-English Dictionary,* 1978. Ed. *Padraig Ó Conaire: Clocha ar a Charn,* 1982. All pub. Dublin.

DE BHFAL, (sometimes de Bhál), Eamon, b. Co. Cork *c.* 1670, d. 1755. A member of the famous Blarney Academy of Irish poets. In the poetic

278

controversy over patronage he sided with Diarmuid Bhuidhe Mac Cárrthaigh. His poetry was edited by Ristéard Ó Foghludha, *Cois Caoin Reathaighe*, Dublin 1946.

DE BHIAL, Tomás, b. near Ring, Co. Waterford 1886, d. Holycross 1954. *Gleann an Áir*, 1931, *Tóraithe agus Ropairí*, 1955, etc. Best known as translator of Canon Sheehan, Alice Stopford Green and others. Taught in Ring College for many years. In charge of College courses 1918-19.

DE BHILMOT, Séamus, b. Listowel 1902, d. Dublin 1977. Ed. Dublin. Town Clerk of Galway 1935-38, and Chairman of the Taidhbhearc Gaelic Theatre in Galway for the same period. Appointed Registrar of the National University of Ireland 1952 and became also a director of the Abbey Theatre 1958. Has written several plays including *Grádh Níos Mó*, Cork 1946, and other works in English and Irish: *The Splendid Pretence*, Dublin 1947; *Prólóg don Réim Nua*, Dublin 1954; *Eochair na Sráide* (short stories), Dublin 1967, etc. Also a novel, *Mise Méara*, Cork 1946.

DE BLAGHD, Earnán, see BLYTHE, Ernest.

DE BRÚN, An tAth. (Monsignor Patrick Browne), b. Co. Tipperary 1889, d. 1960. Ed. Dublin, Paris, Göttingen, ordained 1913; Professor of Mathematics, Maynooth, 1914; became President of University College Galway, Chairman of the Inst. for Adv. Studies and Director of the Arts Council. As a scholar he devoted much time to broadening the contacts between Irish and continental literatures. He translated from Greek, Latin, French and Italian into Irish, and was working on a translation of Dante's *Divine Comedy* when he died. *The Inferno* was published 1963.

During his lifetime he published translations of Shakespearean songs and poems, portions of the *Iliad*, three Sophoclean tragedies: *Antigone,* Dublin 1926; *Oedipus Rex*, Maynooth 1928; *Oedipus at Colonus*, Dublin 1929; Racine's *Athalie*, Dublin 1930, and Corneille's *Polyeucte*, Dublin 1932. With Father Ó Baoighealláin he wrote a Life of Christ, *Beatha Íosa Críost*, Dublin 1929. Long poem *Miserere*, ed. Máire Mhac an tSaoi, Dublin 1971.

DE BÚRCA, An tAth. Uileog (Canon Ulick J. Burke), b. Co. Mayo 1829, d. 1887. As a student in Maynooth wrote an Irish grammar, and published simple lessons in Irish in *The Nation*, an early step in the Language Revival movement. Became Professor in Tuam College, 1859 and President 1865. Later appointed to a parish in Mayo. Wrote a Life of Archbishop John MacHale as a serial in the *Gaelic Journal*, 1882-83, which was translated into English and published as *The Life & Times of the Most Rev. John MacHale*, 1882.

DE FREÍNE, Seán, b. Dublin 1927. Now a civil servant. Author of *Saoirse gan Só*, Dublin 1960. *The Great Silence*, rep. Cork, 1978.

DE hÍDE, Dubhghlas, see HYDE, Douglas.

DE HINDEBERG, An tAth. Risteárd (Rev. Richard Henebry), b. Co.

DE hÓRDHA

Waterford 1863, d. 1916. Ed. Maynooth, ordained 1892. He became interested in Old Irish through the influence of John Strachan, and studied in Germany under Professors Thurneysen and Zimmer, leading authorities on the language. He wrote his doctoral thesis on the Irish of the Decies of Munster. He spent some years as Professor of Celtic Studies in American Universities, returning to Ireland in 1906 to teach in the Irish Language College at Ring, Co. Waterford. In 1908 he became Professor of Celtic Studies in UCC. His books include *Sounds of Munster Irish*, Dublin 1898, and *Greas Fuirseoireachta*, Tralee 1910. His works ed. by Seán Ó Cuirrín, *Sgríbhne Ristéird de Hindeberg*, Dublin, Dollard 1924. His *Handbook of Irish Music* was brought out by Cork University Press 1928.

DE hÓRDHA, Seán, b. *c.* 1710, probably in Co. Cork, d. Co. Clare 1780. Came as a young blacksmith to Clare, and was taken under the patronage of Somhairle Mac Domhnaill of Kilkee. De hÓrdha's poetry was long cherished in Clare, and his 'repentance' poem, *Aithrighe*, written shortly before his death, was particularly loved by the people of Clare. It is still considered his best work. His poems occur in a number of 19th-century miscellanies, and his works were edited by Brian Mac Cumhghaill, *Seán de Hóra*, Dublin 1956.

DELARGY, James Hamilton (Séamas Ó Duilearga), b. Co. Antrim 1899, d. Dublin 1980. Director of Irish Folklore Commission 1935, later Hon. Director. Professor of Irish Folklore UCD 1946. *The Gaelic Storyteller*, 1945; *Leabhar Sheáin Í Chonaill* (stories of an Irish seanchaí, with English summary; Seán Ó Conaill being one of the last of the Gaelic story-tellers, and famous as such), Dublin 1948. Edited Tomás Ó Criomhthain's *Seanchas ó'n Oileán Thiar*, Dublin 1956.

DENN, Pádraig, b. Decies, Co. Waterford 1756, d. 1828. The son of a schoolmaster, became master of large school in Cappoquin. Also taught catechism in local church. Best known for religious poetry, especially his *Eachtra an Bháis* and *Siosma an Anama leis an gColainn*. Some of his poetry still forms part of the oral tradition.

DENVIR, Gearóid, b. Dublin 1950. Ed. UCD. Lecturer at UCD and University of Hamburg. Now in UCG, as well as being founder-headmaster of Coláiste Chamuis in Connemara Gaeltacht. Has published poetry; *Iomramh Aigne*, Dublin 1974. And ed. *Duanta Aneas* (critical ed. of poetry of Pádraig O Miléadha), Chois Fharraige 1977; *Aistí Phadraic Ui Chonaire* (annotated ed. of essays of P. Ó C.), Chois Fharraige 1978. Won Donncadh Ó Laoghaire Commemorative Prize, Oireachtas, 1978. *Pádraig Ó Conaire: Léachtaí Cuimhneacháin*, 1983; and poetry *Trudaireacht*, 1983.

DE RÍS, Seán, b. Belfast 1926. Ed. QUB. Did MA thesis on the Ulster poet *Peadar Ó Doirnín: a bheatha agus a shaothar*, 1969.

DE SIÚNTA, Earnán (Ernest Joynt, pseud. 'An Buachaillín Buidhe'), b. Co. Mayo 1875, d. Dublin 1955. A leading member of Connradh na

DONELLAN

Gaedhilge for many years. Translated the *Pilgrim's Progress* as *Turas an Oilithrigh*, Dublin 1928. Contributed short stories to many Irish publications, and also wrote in French. *Histoire de L'Irlande*, Rennes 1935.

DESMOND, Gerald, Third Earl of Desmond, the Poet Earl. See GEARÓID IARLA.

DE VALERA, Sinéad, b. Flanagan 1878, d. Dublin 1975. Was a primary school-teacher before marrying Éamon de Valera, President of the Irish Republic. She translated and retold a number of fairy stories and children's stories from English into Irish. Her best-known work includes *Coinneal na Nodlag agus Sgéalta Eile*, Dublin 1944, and *Áilleacht agus an Beithidheach* (Beauty and the Beast), Dublin 1946. She also wrote a number of short plays for reading and performance by schoolchildren.

DICUIL, b. Ireland *c.* 775, d. somewhere in Frankish territory *c.* 850. A monk and a learned geographer, drawing on Pliny, Solinus, Orosius, Isidore of Seville and other sources now known only through his writing. He seemed to have had first-hand acquaintance with the western and northern islands off the Irish and Scottish coasts.

He knew of the existence of the 'midnight sun' and writes knowledgeably of the sea-birds that nest in the Faroes. He had heard descriptions of the Nile as far south as Ethiopia, and writes of crocodiles. Some of his information undoubtedly came from travellers rather than simply from books; as a young student he listened to Brother Fidelis who had been to Egypt and measured a pyramid (with great accuracy). When taking his information from books he was always critical of what seemed unreasonable.

His *De Mensura Orbis Terrae* was based in some degree on the *Mensuratio Orbis* prepared in 435 for Theodosius II. His work was edited by C. A. Walckenaer, Paris 1807, and G. Parthey, Berlin 1870. Dicuil also wrote a grammar, now lost, and an astronomical work in prose and verse, of which the MS is preserved at Valenciennes.

DINDSHENCHAS, a 12th-century compilation of Irish place-names, with anecdotes explaining how each place received its name. The tradition of such name-lists is much older than the 12th century. Both prose and verse versions exist. See *The Metrical Dindschenchas* ed., trans. and notes, Edward Gwynn, vols 7-12 of Todd Lecture Series of RIA, 1900-35.

DONELLAN, Nehemias (Fearganimh Ó Domhnalláin), b. Tuam *c.* 1560, d. Tuam 1609. Ed. Cambridge, returning to Ireland as coadjutor to Archbishop of Tuam, succeeding to Archbishopric 1595. Fluent in Irish, translated the *Communion Book* into the language, and helped with the translation of the New Testament published in 1602 by William Daniel. All the biblical translations carried out by the Protestant hierarchy were intended as blows against the influence of the Catholic Church over the native Irish. It was confidently believed, for example, that this translation, *Tiomna Nuadh ár dTighearna agus ár Slanaightheora Íosa Críosd. . .,*

DONLEVY

would be the weapon to destroy 'the Roman Church in Ireland'.

DONLEVY, Andrew, b. 1694, d. *c.* 1765 (see Part 1). Probably born in Sligo, where he was educated first. In 1710 he was sent to Paris to study in the Irish College there, where he took a law degree and became prefect. His fame rests on his publication in 1742 of *The Catechism, or Christian Doctrine,* in both English and Irish versions, the Irish being *An Teagasg Críosduidhe.* The work has an appendix, 'The Elements of the Irish Language', principally concerned with orthography. Donlevy also included Bonaventure O'Hussey's *Abridgement of Christian Doctrine* in Irish verse, composed in the mid-17th century. Later edition by John McEnroe and Edward O'Reilly (author of the *Irish Dictionary)* in Dublin 1822, this edition including a 14th-century poem on the Passion by Donncha Mór Ó Dálaigh, Abbot of Boyle, and a compendium of Irish grammar by McEnroe. A third edition was published in 1848 for St Patrick's College, Maynooth. Donlevy became titular Dean of Raphoe.

DUBHDALETHE, b.c. 990, d.Armagh 1064. Became Archbishop of Armagh 1049, and in 1055 made war on the Abbot of Clonard over a property dispute. The Four Masters omit all reference to this disreputable episode. Dubhdalethe was himself an Annalist, among the first in Ireland to make use of the continental method of dating events by the year of the Christian era, in his *Annals of Ireland.* He must have begun their composition before 1020, because the *Annals of Ulster* in 1021 quote them. He also composed a chronology of the Archbishops of Armagh, a work now lost.

DUBTHACH MACCU LUGIR, *fl.* 430-50. Chief poet and brehon of Laoghaire, King of Ireland. Supposed to have been baptised by St Patrick. The *Book of Leinster* gives three of his poems and there is another poem attributed to him in the *Book of Rights.* He is one of the nine law interpreters who drew up the law code *Senchus Már,* completed in 441.

E

ELÁIR, An tAth (Hilary McDonagh), b. Co. Carlow 1900, d. 1967. Ed. CBS Kildare, Roscrea, UCC, Rome. *Cuimhne 700 Bliain San. Proinsias agus Bliain Nua,* 1928; *Ár nAthair,* 1953; *At God's Feet,* 1954; all pub. Dublin.

ELLIS, Conleth, b. Carlow 1937. Ed. Carlow, Dublin and Galway. Teacher, poet and critic. (For work in English see Part 1.) Poetry: *Fomhar na nGéanna,* 1975, *Aimsir Fhaistineach,* 1981; *Nead Lán Sneachta,* 1982; *Táin,* 1983; *Seabhac ag Guairdeall,* 1985; all pub. Dublin.

EOCHAID UA FLAINN, *fl.* 950, d.984. One of the contributors to the

Leabhar Gabhála, the *Book of Invasions.*

ERARD MAC COISE, b.*c.* 960, d. Clonmacnoise 1022. Chief poet to Malachy II, the High King deposed by Brian Bóroimhe and who resumed the kingship after Brian's death at Clontarf. He possessed a castle in Westmeath, at Clartha, which was destroyed in a raid by the O'Neills. He is supposed to have won compensation from Donnell O'Neill in Donegal by reciting a poem to him. Erard was present at the Battle of Clontarf, 1014, and brought news of it to Brian Bóroimhe's chief poet Mac Liag at Kincora. He and Mac Liag composed a dialogue poem about the fallen princes at the battle. He is also credited with a share in writing with Mac Liag *The War of the Gael with the Gall.* See *Fianaigecht,* Kuno Meyer, Dublin 1910; 'Elegy of Erard Mac Coise, Chief Chronicler of the Gaels, Pronounced over the Tomb of Fergal O'Ruairc, Chief of Brefny, at Clonmacnoise,' *Kilkenny Archaeological Society Journal,* New Series I, 1857; Kuno Meyer *Selections from Ancient Irish Poetry,* 1911.

ERIUGENA, Johannes Scotus (often Erigena in reference works), b. Ireland *c.* 810, d. England *c.* 880. Educated in Ireland, he went to the court of Charles the Bald in Western France some time after 840 and in 847 was appointed head of the palace school. His early fame rested on his learning as grammarian, linguist and dialectician. He was the supreme Greek scholar of his period in Western Europe and between 860-64 translated five major works of the 'Pseudo-Dionysius' from Greek into Latin: *De Caelesti Hierarchia; De Ecclesiastica Hierarchia; De Divinis Nominibus; De Mystica Theologia;* and *Epistolae* (the famous *Ten Letters of the 'Pseudo-Dionysius' the Areopagite);* the *Ambigua* of St Maximus the Confessor, the *De Imagine* of St Gregory of Nyssa, and the *Ancoratus* of St Epiphanius. He also wrote commentaries on the *De Caelesti Hierarchia* and on *St John's Gospel,* the latter commentary surviving only in fragments.

It was after completing this already remarkable body of work – more than remarkable given the period – that Eriugena (meaning the Eire-born) turned to what was to become his master-work, the *Peri Physeon,* generally kown as *De Divisione Naturae,* completed about 866. It is in the usual Carolingian renaissance form of a learned dialogue and has been called 'the only philosophical and theological synthesis of the early middle ages.' On misreadings of this work Eriugena was to become accused of pantheism, free-thinking, and rationalism. He was also considered a monist, with the suggestion that his was a type of monism inconsistent with orthodoxy. Careful reading disproves this charge, and his philosophy and theology are in fact drawn largely from Augustine, in particular the neo-Platonic portions of the Father's writings.

Equally Eriugena was thought to give the supremacy to reason in any conflict between reason and revelation. In fact he did not accept that such a conflict could truly exist. He suggests only that where conflicting interpretations of Revelation exist, apparently both of great authority and weight, reason be used to judge the conflict between the interpreters.

His style more than his content gave excuses to his attackers. He loved paradox and the pursuit of theories to their limits, and also striking and unusual images and terms. This allied to great learning frightened many of the less imaginative upholders of orthodoxy, and continued to do so for centuries.

At the end of the 12th and the beginning of the 13th cnturies, when Amalric of Bena and neo-Platonism in general were being condemned, Eriugena's work came under renewed scrutiny, and was condemned and burned by order of the Council of Paris, 1210, and again by Honorius III, 1225, who ordered all copies of De Divisione Naturae to be destroyed. It was placed on the Index in 1685.

The purpose of De Divisione was to describe and define the structure of the Universe, beginning with God as Divine Origin of all things, and ending with the assumption of all creatures into God. In this last lay the chief fault of the work for its critics, implying as it does the non-existence of Evil as an eternal phenomenon. Curiously enough, Eriugena's first exploration of this theory occured in a most orthodox context, the predestination controversy between Hincmar and Gottschalk. Hincmar enlisted Eriugena's aid as a controversialist against the 'predestinarians' and Eriugena accordingly wrote De Praedestinatione, 850-51. In this work he described Evil as that which in fact has no real existence, but is a failure to fulfill the divine purpose, and asserted that damnation is simply consciousness of this failure. The Council of Valence resoundingly condemned his theories in 855 as 'pultes Scotorum' or Scotch porridge, and he was again condemned by the Council of Langres in 859. If the tortured body and tormented mind of Gottschalk had been capable of laughter he might have enjoyed a very bitter laugh at the fall of his 'orthodox' opponent and at Hincmar's strange choice of champion. But Gottschalk had already been defeated and condemned before the victors turned on Eriugena.

And while Gottschalk died in prison, excommunicate to the last, Eriugena flourished in France as an Irishman should. It was not until theologians had enough learning to understand De Divisione Naturae, or to believe that they did, that they condemned it. From the end of the 12th century to the beginning of the 20th, Eriugena was almost continually under attack as a heretic of one kind or another. It is only in the present generation that he has been restored to some kind of orthodox acceptance.

Besides his theological writings Eriugena wrote some Latin verse, competent rather than inspired, and mostly in praise of his patron, Charles the Bald. But he was never a sycophant. There is a famous story of Charles, at dinner, asking Eriugena what the difference was between Sottum and Scottum. 'The breadth of the table, Sire,' Eriugena answered.

There is a legend, which may contain an element of truth, that on Charles's death in 877 Eriugena went to England and taught at Malmesbury, where he was killed by enraged students. Helen Waddell suggests he may have tried to make them think.

His *Works* were edited by H. J. Floss for Migne's *Patrologia Latina*, Vol. CXXII, 1853. There are several major German and French studies of his thinking, one of the most recent being *Jean Scot Érigène, sa Vie, son Oeuvre, sa Pensée*, 1933.

F

FEARGUS MAC ROIGH, see Ó MUIRGHEASA, Énrí.

FEIRITÉIR, Piaras, see FERRITER, Pierce.

FERRITER, Pierce (Phiaras Feiritéir), b. Co. Kerry *c*. 1610, d. Killarney, by hanging, 1653. Involved in the Rising of 1641 from religious rather than political motives; he was one of the leaders of the Catholic party in West Kerry and led the assault on Tralee Castle. His invention of an adaptation of the Trojan horse, in the form of an artificial sow, ended in disaster, but the castle surrendered in March 1642 and Ferriter held it until 1653 when he surrendered under safe conduct to Brigadier-General Nelson at Killarney. Despite the safe conduct, he was arrested and hanged without trial.

As a poet he is one of the major figures of 17th-century poetry in Irish. He wrote in both the old syllabic verse and the newer assonantal metre. Much of his poetry is in the courtly love tradition, but his long elegy in the assonantal metre is one of the first to use that form. He was held in great esteem by his contemporary poets and a number of poems were written in his honour. His poetry has been edited by P. Ó Duinnín, *Dánta Phiarais Feiritéir*, Gaelic League Series, Irish Texts 5, Dublin 1903.

FIACHRA, An tAth. OFM Cap., b. Co. Cork 1914. Ed. UCC, Ph.D. in modern philosophy, 1945, presenting his thesis in Irish. Since 1947 lecturing on Theology. Has published two philosophical works in Irish: *An Bheatha Phoiblí* and *An Bheatha Phléisiúrtha*, Dublin 1955. Under pseud. 'Donncha Ó Corcora', *Sonaíocht agus Smaointe*, Dublin 1977.

FIACHRA EILGEACH, see Ó FOGHLUDHA, Risteárd.

FLANN FIONN (FLANN FÍNA), Irish pseud. of King Aldfrith of Northumbria, b.*c*. 665, d.705. Sent to Iona as a boy, perhaps with the idea of making him a monk, he studied under Adamnán. In 685 he was recalled to Northumbria to become king, and the following year Adamnán visited him there, partly for friendship and partly to secure the release of some Irish captives. It was on this visit that Adamnán's conversion to the Roman usage regarding Easter and tonsures must have begun.

Aldfrith had learned Irish on Iona and wrote, in Irish, a famous praise poem on the beauties and attraction of Ireland. It appears in *Irish*

FLANN MAC LONÁIN

Minstrelsy, James Hardiman, Dublin 1831, and John O'Donovan translated it for the *Dublin Penny Journal,* vol. 1, 1832. See also 'The Wise sayings of Flann Fína – Aldfrith of Northumbria,' V. E. Hull, *Speculum,* IV, 1929, and 'Fithel & Flann Fina', R. M. Smith, *Revue Celtique,* XLVII, 1930.

FLANN MAC LONÁIN, b. Clare *c.* 850, d. Decies of Munster, in battle, 918. Poet to the O'Brien family and chief poet of Munster, and spent his prime at Kincora, the palace of Lorcan, King of West Munster and grandfather of Brian Bóroimhe. The Four Masters, who quote some of his poetry in the *Annals,* called him the 'Virgil of the race of Scotia.' Others, because of his avarice and the ferocity of his satires, called him the Devil's son and visualised him in hell after his death. See J. G. O'Keeffe's translation of the Irish MS, 'Flann Mac Lonáin in Repentant Mood the Day after his Death,' *Irish Texts,* I, 22-24, 1931. Despite these opinions the chief poet was buried in the Monastery of Terryglass. See also O'Keeffe's trans. 'Eulogy on Echnechan son of Dálach, King of Tir Conaill,' *ibid.;* O. J. Bergin, 'A Story of Flann Mac Lonáin. From the Yellow Book of Lecan col. 917,' *Anecdota from Irish MSS,* 1907; and T. Ó Donnchadha, *An Leabhar Muimhneach,* Dublin 1940.

FLANN MAINISTREACH (Flann of the Monastery), b. *c.* 1000, d. Co. Louth 1056. He was the headmaster of the great school of Monasterboice, and also a poet-historian. Most of his histories are contained in the *Book of Leinster,* and the best edition of his work is 'Poems of Flann Mainistreach on the Dynasties of Ailech, Mide & Brega' (ed. by E. MacNeill from the Book of Leinster with trans. & notes), *Archivium Hibernicum II,* 1913).

Other histories by Flann deal with the burial places of the Tuatha Dé Danann, the deaths of the pagan kings of Tara, the deaths of the Christian kings of Ireland, the names and descents of the Great Bardic Company of the 7th century, the household of St Patrick, and universal history. One of his sons followed him in Monasterboice as a teacher.

FLEMING, John (Seagan Pléimion), b. Clonea *c.* 1815, d. Dublin 1895. At school in Rathcormac under Dr O'Hickey and fluent in Irish from his earliest years. Became assistant to David Comyn in editing the *Gaelic Journal,* 1882-92. He was involved in the Gaelic Revival from its first steps and published Irish lessons in the *National Teachers' Journal* between 1872-77. In 1881 he published a *Life of Donncadh Ruadh Mac Conmara* in *The Irishman* and this was reprinted in 1882. The 2nd vol. of *The Gaelic Journal,* 1884, printed an edition of Mac Conmara's poems prepared by Fleming.

FLEMING, Patrick (baptised Christopher), b. Co. Louth 1599, d. Prague, murdered, 1631. Ed. Douai and Louvain, entered Franciscan Order 1618, taking name Patrick. Studied further in Rome, returning to Louvain to teach philosophy, and finally going to Prague as first Superior of the Irish College there. During the siege of 1631 he was murdered by peasants. He collected much Irish material on the lives of early abbots and saints, supplying information to Hugh Ward. Some appears in *Collectanea Sacra,* ed. Thos. Sirini, Louvain 1667. He also left a MS compendium of the *Chronicle of the Monastery of St Peter at Regensburg,* of particular interest because of the early Irish missionary influence on Regensburg. His *Letters on Irish Hagiography* to Hugh Ward, have been printed in the *Irish Ecclesiastical Record.* He also wrote a life of his master at Louvain, Aodh Mac Aingil, *Vita Reverendi Patris Hugonis Cavelli,* Louvain 1626.

FOTHADH NA CANOÍNE (Fothadh of the Canon), b. *c.* 810, d. 876. A cleric as well as a poet, he secured the acceptance of an ecclesiastical canon exempting the clergy from warfare. *Atduis Daíb a n-Aic ned Fir* in Kuno Meyer's 'Mitteilungen aus Irischen Handschriften', *Zeitschrift für Celtische Philologie,* VII, 299, 1910. Also see *Eclas Débhi,* in *Annals of the Four Masters,* John O'Donovan, Dublin 1848-51. And *Cert Cech Rig co Réil,* Tadhg O'Donoghue, in *Miscellany Presented to Kuno Meyer,* Halle 1912.

G

GEARNON, Antoin, b. *c.* 1600, d. after 1667. Ed. in Franciscan College in Prague, taught at Louvain and returned to Ireland to become Guardian of the Franciscans, first in Dundalk and later in Dublin. He was for a time Chaplain to Queen Henrietta. His fame rests on his book of religious instruction in Irish, *Párrthas an Anma* (The Paradise of the Soul), long admired for its beauty of style and expression.

GEARÓID IARLA (Gerald the Rhymer), 3rd Earl of Desmond, known in English as the Poet Earl, born *c.* 1335, d. 1398. Son of the 1st earl, Justiciar of Ireland, 1367-69, and a leading figure in the gaelicisation of the Norman-Irish dynasties. Although he fought against the Gaelic chiefs on many occasions, it is typical that when imprisoned by Brian O'Brien of Thomond in 1370 he spent his time in prison composing love-poems in Irish, and one of his sons, James, was fostered with the O'Briens in 1388. As well as poetry he was credited with deep knowledge of mathematics and magic. The Annalists called him 'a nobleman of wonderful bounty... easy of access... a witty and ingenious composer of Irish poetry, learned and profound chronicler.' The Gaelic peasantry long believed that he was not dead, but was sleeping beneath Lough Gur, from where he would come again on an enchanted horse to his castle.

It was after Gerald's time that the Geraldines abandoned French entirely as their court language and spoke Gaelic for pleasure among themselves as well as for administrative necessity.

Gerald himself has been credited with introducing the French tradition of courtly love-poetry into Irish, and is certainly the author of the oldest surviving example. Some of his poems are included in *Reliquiae Celticae,* vol. 1, 1892, edited by Alexander Cameron. The Earl of Longford translated one of his poems, 'Against Blame of Women' in *Poems from the Irish,* Dublin and Oxford 1945.

GENEALOGIES. These compilations purport to trace the ancestry of tribes and individuals in early Christian and mediaeval Ireland. They are often fabrications designed to lend a spurious authenticity and the sanction of tradition to some recently acquired rights or privileges. They were written down in the 7th and 8th centuries, and were often compiled in the monasteries which flourished at that time. Many of the most important texts are collected in M. A. O'Brien (ed.), *Corpus Genealogiarum Hibernicarum,* Dublin 1962. Also Paul Walsh (ed.), *Genealogiae Regnum et Sanctorum Hiberniae,* Maynooth 1918. V.H.

GILLA COEMÁIN, *fl.* 1025-1075, poet and chronicler. Poems of his, a king-list from the earliest times to Brian Bóroimhe, and on world chronology to 1072, are in the *Book of Leinster.*

GODINEZ, see WADDING, Michael.

GÓGAN, L. S. b. Dublin 1891, d. Dublin 1979. Son of member of IRB and the old Sinn Féin. Assistant Secretary to Committee establishing Irish Volunteers 1913. Close friend of Roger Casement. Visited US to buy arms from Germans there for 1916 Rising. Assistant in the Irish Antiquities Division, National Museum, 1914-16, 1922-36. Keeper of Art and Industrial Division, 1936-57. Poetry: *Nuadhánta,* 1919; *Dánta agus Duanóga* (Tailteann Gold Medal), 1930; *Dánta an Lae Inniu,* 1936; *Dánta Eile,* 1939; *Dánta agus Duanta,* 1948; *Duanaire a Sé,* 1966.

GORMFLAITH, daughter of Flann Sionna, b. *c.* 870, d. 919. Her father was King of Ireland, 879-914, and she was first bethrothed to Cormac Mac Cuileannáin, King-Bishop of Cashel. Cormac was killed by King Cearbhall of Leinster who became Gormflaith's second husband. Her third marriage was to Niall Glundubh who succeeded her father as High King in 914, and was killed by Danes in 917. After his death legend tells that Gormflaith became a beggar-woman and died in want. She is credited with laments on the deaths of her husbands and her son, and her poetry in quoted in the *Annals:* 'Evil to me the compliment of the two foreigners who slew Niall and Cearbhall; Cearbhall (was slain) by Hulb, a great deed: Niall Glundubh by Amhlaidhe.' The name Amhlaidhe is an Irish transliteration of Norse Olaf, and it has been suggested by Sir Israel Gollancz that this transliteration is the basis of the otherwise unexplained appearance of the name Amloda-Amlethus-Hamlet in Scandinavian and European literature. Certainly the poet Snaebjorn, first known source for the name Amloda, was a second cousin of Queen Gormflaith and visited Ireland where he may have read her poetry.

For an edition of her known poetry, see O. J. Bergin, 'Poems attributed to Gormliath', *Miscellany presented to Kuno Meyer*, pp. 343-369, Halle 1912. See also Eleanor Knott, *Irish Syllabic Poetry*, 1928.

GREENE, David William, b. Dublin 1915, d. Dublin 1981. Ed. TCD. Assistant Librarian, National Library, 1941-48. Professor of Irish, TCD, 1955-67, then Senior Professor, Dublin Inst. for Adv. Studies. Contributed to *Dictionary of the Irish Language;* Lexicographer to Royal Irish Academy's *Irish Dictionary;* author of the articles on Irish Language and Irish Literature in *Encyclopaedia Britannica;* editor for Cumann Merriman of *Cúirt an Mheán Oíche*, Dublin 1968. With Frank O'Connor, edited and translated *A Golden Treasury of Irish Poetry,\ A.D. 600–1200,* 1967. Edited with Fergus Kelly, Osborn Bergin's *Irish Bardic poetry; texts and translations, together with introd. lecture,* 1970; *Duanaire Mhéig Uidhir* (from the Copenhagen MS), 1972; and again with Fergus Kelly, *The Irish Adam & Eve story from Saltair na Rann,* vol. 1, text and trans., 1976. All pub. Dublin Inst. for Adv. Studies. Also *Writing in Irish to-day*, Dublin 1972.

GRUAGACH AN TOBAIR, see Ó SÉAGHDHA, Pádraig.

H

HAGIOGRAPHY (SAINTS' LIVES). The Saints' Lives are not biographies in the modern sense. They are often fabulous tales recounting the wonders and miracles allegedly performed by the early Irish saints. Often written many centuries after the events recounted are supposed to have occurred, they were usually compiled in the principal monastery associated with the saint, which thus sought to perpetuate his/her tradition. Many of them acted as charters through which a large monestery sought to claim control over lesser monasteries by the simple pretext of stating that the saint had also founded or been given control over the lesser monastery. The majority of the lives date to the 11th and 12th centuries, though some are earlier.

The principal collections are: C. Plummer (ed.), *Vitae Sanctorum Hiberniae*, 2 vols, Oxford 1910 (lives in Latin) ; C.Plummer (ed.), *Bethada Náem nÉrenn*, 2 vols, Oxford 1922 (lives in Old Irish) ; C. Plummer, *Miscellanea Hagiographica Hibernica*, Bruxelles 1925; Whitley Stokes (ed.), *Lives of the Saints from the Book of Lismore*, 1890; and W. W. Heist, *Vitae Sanctorum Hibernicae ex Codice olim Salamanticensi nunc Bruxellensi*, Bruxelles 1965 (lives in Latin written in the 12th century and preserved in the Irish College in Salamanca, Spain). V.H.

HAICÉAD, An tAth Pádraigín, b. Co. Tipperary c. 1600, d. Cashel 1654. Ed. Ireland and Louvain. Entered Dominican Order. Became Prior of Cashel about 1637. Involved in peace-making efforts after the Rising of 1641 and in ecclesiastical quarrels. In pursuit of the latter he returned to Louvain in 1651 and conducted a political correspondence with Rinuccini the Papal Nuncio in Ireland. In 1654 was involved in a quarrel with the head of the Dominican Order in Ireland and died shortly before publication of a judgment against him. Much of his poetry dealt with political matters. *An t-Athair Pádraigín Haicéad*, ed. Tadhg Ó Donnchadha, Dublin 1916. And ed. *Filíocht Phádraigín Haicéad,* ed. Máire Ní Cheallacháin, Dublin 1962.

HICKEY, Anthony, OFM, b. Co. Clare 1586, d. Rome 1641. Ed. Louvain. Entered Franciscan Order 1607, and taught at Louvain and Cologne. Called to Rome 1619 to help Fr Luke Wadding in preparing *Franciscan Annals* and editing Duns Scotus. He remained in Rome for the rest of his life, and took part in the work of revising the Roman Breviary, and was also engaged in the debate over the doctrine of the Immaculate Conception. In 1639 he became Definitòr General of the Franciscans. Works: *Commentarii,* Lyons 1639; a share in the Luke Wadding edition of Duns Scotus, with commentary, also 1639; and writings on the Immaculate Conception, the Stigmata of St Catherine of Siena, etc. Many of his MSS, including a letter on the Irish Language, are preserved by the Franciscan Order in Dublin.

HUTCHINSON, Pearse, b. Glasgow 1927, brought to Ireland at five years of age. See also Part 1. Has written in *Comhar* and *Scéala Éireann.* Poems in Irish, collected as *Faoistin Bhacach,* Dublin 1968.

HYDE, Douglas (Dubhghlas de hÍde and 'An Craoibhín Aoibhinn'), b. Co. Roscommon 1862, d. Dublin 1949. First President of Ireland, founder of the Gaelic League and with de Valera and perhaps one or two more, the creator of modern Ireland. Which is not to say that he, any more than de Valera, would have wished it to become what it has. Unlike his fellow creators, he was intensely apolitical, and to this extent impractical. He saw the language as a beautiful and powerful vehicle of culture and the spirit of Irishness that would render politics almost irrelevant. But the more powerful and instrumental he made the language seem to his contemporaries, the more inevitable it became that they should make use of it for political ends. This was the paradox and tragedy of his lifework.

The son of a Protestant clergyman he was educated at home and at TCD, becoming immediately noted as a scholar. LL.D. 1888, he became Professor of Modern Languages in New Brunswick State University in 1891. In 1893 he founded the Gaelic League and remained its President until 1915. Both the Irish Parliamentary Party and the Nationalists offered inducements to Hyde to place the League in their camp, and these efforts became greater as Hyde and the League increased in stature. In 1899 Hyde became President of the ITS.

In 1906 he was a member of the Royal Commission on Irish University Education. In the same year he returned from America with £11,000 gathered as a fund for the League and became a Freeman of Dublin, Cork and Kilkenny. He was appointed to the Senate of the National University in 1909 and was made a Professor of Modern Irish in UCD.

During this time he succeeded in keeping the League at least officially clear of all politics. But in 1915 at the Annual Congress, Piaras Béaslaí proposed his famous motion that the League stood for a Free and Gaelic Ireland, free from foreign influences, and the motion was carried. This moved the League into the field of Nationalist and revolutionary politics, and Hyde resigned the presidency, being succeeded by Eoin MacNeill.

In 1925 he was appointed to the Senate of the Irish Free State and although he left the Senate the following year, his stature as a scholar and as a man above politics was so great that in 1937 when the new Irish Constitution created the post of President of the Irish Free State, he was the almost unanimous choice of the major political parties. He held office from 1938-45 and did not seek re-election.

Most of his writing was translation. For his translations from Irish into English see Part I. In Irish he collected poems and folk tales and wrote a small number of short plays. The list of titles by themselves seem meagre. But his life was his monument. The best known and loved of his books is *The Love Songs of Connacht*, London and Dublin 1893, which he collected, edited and translated. In Irish, *Leabhar Sceálaíochta*, Dublin 1889 (a collection of folk tales), *Casadh an tSúgáin*, published in *Samhain*, Dublin 1901 (trans. by Lady Gregory as *The Twisting of the Rope*, a one-act play); *An Cleamhnas*, published in the *Gaelic Journal*, 1904 (also a one-act play); *Amhráin Chúige Chonnacht: an leath rann*, Dublin 1922; *Mise agus an Connradh*, Dublin 1937 (an account of his work with the Gaelic League); and *Sgéalta Thomáis Uí Chathasaigh*, Dublin 1939 (stories of Mayo told by Thomas Casey, collected and edited, with translations, by D.H.); *Mo Thurus go hAmerice*, Dublin 1937 (about fund-raising for Gaelic League in 1905).

I

INGLIS, Liam, OSA, b. Co. Limerick 1709, d. Cork 1778. He had already begun to make his name as a poet when he joined the Dominicans in 1740. Refusing to take the vow of poverty, he swiftly left the Order to join the Augustinians. He was in Rome in 1749. He became Prior in Cork in 1769. Although he had taken a vow to write no more poetry as a religious, he either broke the vow or was released from it. His poetry ranges from love to politics, and he made at least one attempt at an *aisling*. See *Cois na Bríde*, ed. Ristéard Ó Foghludha, Dublin 1937. See also *The Poets and Poetry of Munster*, John O'Daly, Dublin 1850, and *Reliques of Irish Jacobite Poetry*, John O'Daly and Edward Walsh, Dublin 1860, 2nd ed. 1866.

K

KEATING, Geoffrey (CÉITINN, Seathrún), b. Co. Tipperary *c.* 1570, d. Co. Tipperary *c.* 1649. The origin of the family name was Norman, Etienne. The family had remained Catholic, and Irish in sympathy. The boy was sent to Bordeaux to study for the priesthood, and also studied in Salamanca, returning to Ireland in 1610 as a Doctor of Theology. As parish priest of Tubrid in his home county he is supposed to have preached a sermon against the mistress of Squire Moclar and for that reason to have been driven out of the parish. Legend describes him as living in a cave at this period, where he wrote his famous *History of Ireland.* He travelled in Ireland for many years, but by 1634 he was again a parish priest, in Cappoquin, Co. Waterford. By 1644 he had returned to Tubrid near Clonmel and was building a chapel there. According to tradition he was murdered in the Church of St Nicholas, Clonmel, by Cromwellian soldiers, having been a partisan of Eoghan Ruadh Ó Néill in the rebellion of 1641 and after that of the Ormondes, writing elegies for members of the Dunboyne and Ormonde families. Some incident must have caused him to change parties because he also wrote a poem against the Ormondes. If the story of his murder is true, his death probably occurred towards the end of 1649.

Keating's poetry suggests that he had been trained in one of the bardic schools but he uses an assonantal metre in much of his work that was considered vulgar by the bardic traditionalists. His long, assonantal elegy *Lá Dá Rabhas ar Maidin go Fánach* contains an early example of the *aisling* or vision theme later to become very common; the vision is of Ireland as a woman, or a goddess, and it contains a political promise of national resurrection.

His principle work is *Foras Feasa ar Éirinn,* written between 1629 and 1631. It has been printed, edited and translated into English several times, first in an unsatisfactory edition by Dermond O'Connor, Dublin 1723; 2nd ed. Westminster 1726, with an appendix collected from the remarks of the learned Dr Anthony Raymond of Trim. William Haliday began an edition of which vol. 1, Dublin 1811, was the only one to appear. Haliday unfortunately dying before he could complete the work. The ITS brought out vol. I translated with notes by David Comyn 1902, and vols II and III translated with notes by the Rev. Patrick S. Dinneen, 1908.

Dánta Amhráin is Caointe Sheathrúin Céitinn, Dochtúr Diadhachta, collected and edited by the Rev. John MacErlean SJ, Dublin 1900; *Trí Bior-ghaoithe an Bháis,* ed. Robert Atkinson (RIA, Irish MS Series, vol. II, Part 1.) Dublin 1890, and *Eochair-Sgiath an Aifrinn,* ed. Patrick O'Brien, Dublin 1898, contain most of Keating's other important works. The first consists of his collected poems, written at different times. The second, *The Three Shafts of Death,* is a spiritual essay written in 1625. The third, an

explanation and defence of the Mass, was probably written ten years earlier.
The earliest MS copy of *Foras Feasa ar Éirinn*, the *History of Ireland*,
was translated in 1636, and is now in the Franciscan Archives, Dublin.
The language is modern Irish and is considered a model of style.
For an early Latin translation see LYNCH, John.

L

LAWS. Early and mediaeval Irish society was regulated by an elaborate
and highly codified system roughly analogous to modern Civil Law. The
law tracts were written down in the 7th and 8th centuries, though in most
cases they enshrine much earlier customs and traditions, originating in
pre-Christian Ireland. They are sometimes referred to as the 'Brehon Laws'
a name derived from the 'Brehons', hereditary legal families who administered them. They were compiled in the Law schools run by these families.
Once written down, the laws were considered immutable, at least in theory.
In practice they were continually changing, as can be seen from the glosses
and commentaries written on them by generations of legal students. They
continued to apply in Gaelic Ireland until the 17th century.

An edition of the most important law tracts was published in the 19th
century: W. N. Hancock, T. O'Mahony, A. Richey and R. Atkinson (eds),
Ancient Laws of Ireland, 6 vols, Dublin and London 1869- 1901. Many
individual tracts have been published over the years. All the surviving tracts
were collected in D. A. Binchy (ed.), *Corpus Iuris Hibernici*, 7 vols, Dublin
1979. V.H.

LEABHAR BREAC, see BOOK OF DUNIRY.

LINÍN, P. D., pseud. of Róisín Bean Mhic Dhonnchadha, has written
several books, of which the best-known is *Maidhc Bleachtaire,* Dublin
1961.

LOCHLANNACH, AN, see Ó LOCHLAINN, Gearóid.

LORGA LIATHBHÁN, see Ó hANNRACHÁIN, Peadar.

LUIBHÉID, Tomás, b. Co. Kerry 1904, d. Dublin 1980. Teacher in Kerry
and Galway, then in Irish School, Dublin, 1928. Became Principal. Wrote
plays for children and school readers, as well as translating many plays for
radio. Published *Cois Cnoic Is Cuain,* short stories; and the first part of
an autobiography, *Ag Tagairt Don Scéal,* 1973, both Dublin.

LÚID, Séan (John Lloyd. See Part I), b. Co. Limerick 1741, d. Co. Clare
1786. Wrote a history of Co. Clare in English, and some poems, mostly
in Irish, but some in English, and at least one, on the death of Mary Bawn
Mac Donnell, is in both languages. It can be found in *A Collection of*

Poems, written on Different Occasions by the Clare Bards, in Honour of the Mac Donnells of Kilkee and Killone, collected and edited by Brian O'Looney, Dublin 1863. He wrote a number of *aislingí,* or vision-poems of the kind increasingly favoured by poets throughout the 18th century. He himself seems to have been a wandering school-teacher.

LYNCH, John, b. Galway *c.* 1599, d. probably in Brittany, *c.* 1673. Supposedly the son of the famous Galway teacher, Alexander Lynch, he himself was put to school with Dubhaltach Mac Firbisigh, and also with the Jesuits. Ordained about 1622 he was on the run as a priest until the Rising of 1641 permitted the re-opening of Catholic churches the following year. He became Archdeacon of Tuam, and for a time kept a school in the neighbourhood. On the surrender of Galway to the Cromwellians in 1652 he fled to France. During the last 20 years of his life he published a number of works in Latin, with the general intention of improving Ireland's reputation as a civilised country. To this end he translated Keating's *Foras Feasa ar Éirinn* into Latin and published it in St Malo about 1660; wrote *Cambrensis Eversus* (under the pen-name Gratianus Lucius), St Malo, 1662. It is intended as a refutation of the 'slanders' of Giraldus Cambrensis about Ireland. He dedicated this book to Charles II. He also wrote answers to Richard Ferral the Capuchin, who had called for enmity between Irish and Anglo-Irish. *Cambrensis Eversus* was translated and published with notes by Matthew Kelly, Dublin 1848.

LYNCH, Richard, b. Galway *c.* 1611, d. Salamanca 1676. Entered Jesuit Order 1630, in Compostella, where he was educated, and became rector of the Irish College of Seville 1637. These last two dates throw doubt on 1611 as the date of his birth, which may well have been ten years earlier. He was a brilliant and subtle theologian. He wrote *Universa Philosophia Scholastica,* 3 vols, Lyons 1654, *Sermones Varios,* Salamanca 1670, and *De Deo Ultimo Fine,* 2 vols, Salamanca 1671. The careers of men such as this, far more than the better-known and more colourful careers of emigré soldiers, demonstrate how much Ireland lost by the English occupation. It was not simply the romantic and inevitable loss of the Gaelic clan culture; it was all opportunity of developing a modern culture that was Irish and not English.

M

MAC AINGIL, Aodh, see MAC CATHMHAOIL, Aodh.

MAC AIRT, Seán, b. Ulster 1918, d. 1959. Ed. QUB, MA 1941. In 1952 established the Ulster Place Names Society and was editor of its Bulletin. Prepared *Leabhar Branach; the Book of the O'Byrnes,* for Dublin Institute for Advanced Studies, 1944, and *Annals of Innisfallen* with translation and indices, also for the Institute, 1951.

MAC AMHLAIGH, Dónall, b. Galway 1926. Ed. Kilkenny. Emigrated to England 1951, to work as navvy, builder's labourer and grave digger. Has written humorous, nostalgic articles in Irish and in English for *Irish Times,* adventure stories for children, in Irish, a television play in Irish, *Saighdiúirí* which won Oireachtas Prize 1964, and was shown on RTE 1965. His books are *Dialann Deoraí,* Dublin 1960, trans. by Valentine Iremonger as *An Irish Navvy,* 1964 (see Part I); *Saol Saighdiúra,* Dublin 1962, being an account of his time as a soldier in an Irish-speaking battalion of the Irish Army; and *Diarmaid Ó Dónaill,* Club Leabhar selection, Dublin 1965, being an autobiographical novel. *Sweeney agus Scéalta eile,* Dublin 1970 (short stories); *Schnitzer Ó Sé,* Dublin 1974; *Beoir Bhaile* 1981.

MAC AN BHAIRD. Bardic family of Ulster, and particularly Donegal, *fl.* 12th to 17th centuries. *The Annals of the Four Masters* notice more than 20 members of the family, all of whom were attached to the O'Donnells of Donegal. At least one member of the family was also a scholar and historian (see MAC AN BHAIRD, Aodh Buidhe). The family was particularly rich in poets between 1570 and 1630, in a last flowering of its relationship with the O'Donnells, and finally with the O'Neills as well. Some of the family are noticed individually in this book. Others are the several poets with the Christian name Gofraidh, all flourishing at this period: Gofraidh (Geoffrey the Rhymer) of Sligo, *fl.* 1600; Gofraidh Fionn, *fl.* 1610; Gofraidh Óg who wrote a poem to Hugh O'Neill's daughter Máire; Gofraidh Mac Briain Mac An Bhaird, *fl.* 1600, who like Eoghan Ruadh his cousin wrote a lament for Niall Garbh on his death in the Tower of London. There is also Laoiseach, *fl.* 1600, whose poetry complains bitterly of the ruin and decay of the old Gaelic order and the servile copying by the Irish of the new English ways. Maolmuire Mac Connladh belongs to the same generation but died earlier than the others, being killed in battle against the English, 1597. His most famous poem is *A Dhúin Thíos atá in Éanar,* dedicated to a ruined O'Donnell fortress, one of the many which Red Hugh destroyed himself, rather than allow them to fall into the hands of the English. For the poems of all these men and others of their period, see *Dioghluim Dána* and *Aithdhioghluim Dána* by L. McKenna SJ., Dublin 1938 and 1939; *Dánta Grádha* collected by Tomás Ó Rathile, English introduction by Robin Flower, Cork 1926; Eleanor Knott, *An Introduction to Irish Syllabic Poetry 1200-1600,* Cork 1928; and a number of issues of *Studies* between 1919 and 1926, in which O. J. Bergin wrote on 16th and 17th-century Irish poets. See also *A Fhir Ghlacas a Ghalldacht,* ed. and trans. O. J. Bergin, *Irish Review II,* 1912, concerning Laoiseach; two of Maolmuire's poems ed. J. MacErlean in *Eoin Ó Cuilleanáin,* Dublin 1912, and *Measgra Dánta,* ed. T. F. O'Rahilly, Cork 1927.

MAC AN BHAIRD, Aodh Buidhe (Hugh Ward, or Hugh MacAnward),

b. probably Co. Donegal c. 1580, d. probably Louvain 1635. Certainly buried in Louvain. One of the great band of 17th-century Gaelic scholars who enriched Louvain. Joined Franciscan Order in Donegal and went to Salamanca and then to Paris. Became Professor of Theology in the Irish College of Louvain, where he worked with Fr Colgan to prepare the *Acta Sanctorum Hiberniae*. See COLGAN, John. Another collaborator in the work was Micheál Ó Cléirigh, who returned from Louvain to Ireland to collect MSS. Ward died before Ó Cléirigh had completed his collection, and Ó Cléirigh remained in Ireland to use the MSS as a basis for the *Annals of the Four Masters*. See Ó CLÉIRIGH, Micheál.

MAC AN BHAIRD, Eoghan Ruadh, b. probably Co. Donegal c. 1570, d. probably Co. Donegal c. 1630. His ancestors were hereditary poets to the O'Donnells for at least four centuries. Eoghan Ruadh became chief poet to Red Hugh O'Donnell about 1600. After Red Hugh's flight to Spain, Eoghan Ruadh remained in Ireland in the service of Rory O'Donnell, Red Hugh's brother. When Rory finally surrendered to the English, Eoghan Ruadh wrote a poem condemning his treachery. Despite this he also wrote a lament for Rory in 1608, after Rory's death in Rome, and another poem, *A Bhean Fuair Faill ar an bhFeart,* addressed to Rory's sister. James Clarence Mangan turned this poem into English, with the title *O Woman of the Piercing Wail*. The sister, Nuala, left her husband Niall Garbh when he too went over to the English, and exiled herself in Rome. Niall Garbh died in the Tower of London in 1626, and Eoghan Ruadh's last datable poem is a lament for him. Obviously the passage of 20 years had softened old enmities.

A Bhean Fuair Faill ar an bhFeart, edited with Mangan's translation by O'Connellan, *Ossianic Society Transactions,* V,294-308, Dublin 1860. For other poems by Eoghan Ruadh, see *Dioghluim Dána,* Dublin 1938, and *Aithdioghluim Dána,* Dublin 1939 (both ed. by L. McKenna SJ). See also *Studies, VIII,* 1919; *Studies, X,* 1921; *Studies, XIV,* 1925 Dublin, in all of which O. J. Bergin deals with unpublished Irish poems of Eoghan Ruadh.

MAC AN BHAIRD, Fearghal Óg, b. probably Donegal c. 1550, d. Louvain c. 1620. Another member of the great bardic family. His chief patron was Turlough Lynagh O'Neill (in Irish Luineach, meaning the foster-son of Ó Luinigh). In an early poem of about 1575 Fearghal urged O'Neill to seize the leadership of Ireland. Later he supported Hugh, 'The Great O'Neill', and in a late poem begged Hugh to return from his exile in Rome. Another of his surviving poems is on the death of Red Hugh O'Donnell in Spain.

Possibly as a result of his political poems Fearghal was exiled to Scotland and wrote of his unhappiness there, a part of it because of the impossibility of hearing Mass. He wrote a lament for the lost religion of the Scots. From Scotland he went to the Continent and ended his life in poverty and even distress in Louvain. While there he appealed to the head of the Irish College for assistance, and is likely to have got it if there is any justice, because there was an old debt of gratitude between the family of Florence Conry,

MAC AODHAGÁIN

founder and first President of the College, and the Mac an Bhaird family.
For Fearghal's surviving poems see *Leabhar Cloinne Aodha Buidhe*, T. O.
Donnchadha, Dublin 1931; *Dioghluim Dána*, Dublin 1938, and
Aithdioghluim Dána, Dublin 1939 (both ed. L. McKenna SJ); *Studies*, VIII,
1919; *Studies*, IX, 1920, O.J. Bergin.

MAC AN BHEATHA, Proinsias, b. Belfast 1910. Ed. Belfast and Dublin.
Employed in Customs and Excise, Dublin. Has written for *Inniu* since the
foundation of the magazine in 1943. He himself was one of the founders
of Glún na Bua which created *Inniu* as its voice and he has told the story
of this campaign and the related splits and quarrels in the Language Revival
movements of the 1940s in his *Téid Focal le Gaoith*, Dublin 1967, a Club
Leabhar selection. Before that he had published a Life of James Connolly,
Tart na Córa, Dublin 1963, also a Club Leabhar selection, and *Irish for
the People*, Dublin 1944, 1945 and 1966. His *Aiste ar Sheosamh Mac
Grianna*, an essay on the work of Seosamh Mac Grianna, was published
Dublin 1967. Novels: *An Faoileán Bán*, Dublin 1975; and *Cnoc na
hUamha*, Dublin 1978. Also *Roth an Mhuilinn*, Dublin 1980; and *Téann
Buille le Cnámh*, 1983.

MAC AN FHIR LÉIGHINN, An tAth. Eoin SJ (Fr John McErlean), b.
Belfast 1870, d. 1940. Joined Jesuit Order 1888 as novice. Collected and
edited the poetry of Seathrún Céitinn in one volume, *Dánta Amhráin is
Caointe Sheathrúin Céitinn*, Dublin 1900. Ordained 1904 and spent a year
in Spain. On his return began collecting the poems of *Dáibhidh Ó Bruadair*
for the ITS: vol. I, 1910, vol. II 1913, vol. III 1917.

MAC AN LEGA, William, *fl.* 1475. A scribe with some medical training
or at least interest. He translated a number of medical and legal texts from
Latin into Irish, and often interpolated scraps of Irish verse or stories into
the body of his MSS. His best known translation is a life of Hercules, *Stair
Ercúil ocus a Bás,* which Gordon Quinn edited with an English translation,
Dublin 1939.

MAC AODHA, Breandan S., b. Belfast 1934. Ed. QUB. Professor of Geography UCG since 1968 and Director of Survey of Galway Gaeltacht. One
of the founders of *Studia Hibernica*. Edited collections of stories and poems
by modern Irish writers: *Cnuasach*, 1966 and *Cnuasach II*, 1968.

MAC AODHAGÁIN, Baothghalach Mór, *fl.* 1550-1600 probably in Co.
Galway, where the family owned Dún Daighre (now Duniry). The family
at this period were the keepers of the *Leabhar Breac*, and for generations
had been poets and brehons. His poem on the Holy Trinity is in
Aithdioghluim Dána, ed. L. McKenna SJ for the ITS, Dublin 1939.

MAC AODHAGÁIN, Flann, *fl.* 1600-50. Of the same family as Baothghalach, but a Tipperary branch, famous for several generations as historians. His authority on Irish historical matters was considered so great
that Micheál Ó Cléirigh submitted the MS of the *Annals of the Four Masters*

297

to him for criticism and approval.

MAC AONGHUSA, Críostóir, b. Co. Offaly 1906. Ed. UCG. *Cladóir agus Scéalta Eile,* Dublin 1952. *Ó Ros Muc go Rostov,* Dublin 1972, a collection of essays. Father of the journalist Proinsias Mac A.

MAC AONGHUSA, Proinsias, b. Galway 1933. See Part 1 for work in English. In Irish has published *Eamon de Valera: na Blianta Reabhloideacha,* 1982, and *Gaillimh agus Aistí Eile,* 1983. Ed. *Aeriris,* 1976.

MAC ARTÚIR, Roibéard (also known as Robert MacArthur and Robert Chamberlain), b. Co. Louth 1571, d. Louvain 1636 or 1638. Ed. Salamanca and returned in 1599 as a Doctor of Divinity and priest to become counsellor to Hugh O'Neill, Earl of Tyrone. In 1601 he returned to Spain as the earl's ambassador, looking for armed assistance for the Irish cause. After the defeat of Kinsale and the later Flight of the Earls MacArthur was in France, and in 1607 was at Douai to receive O'Neill. He seems to have accompanied him to Rome, but in 1610 he was in Louvain where he joined the Franciscan Order and helped set up the Irish language printing press there in 1611. After Mac Cathmhaoil's death in 1626 MacArthur was offered the archbishopric of Armagh but declined it. He also refused the Presidency of the College of Louvain. His literary fame is based on his share in the famous Contention of the Bards, 1617-20, in which the bards of the north and of the south of Ireland boasted their patrons' respective claims to supremacy. The chief poets involved were Lughaidh Ó Cléirigh for the North and Tadhg Mac Dáire Mac Bruaideadha for the South. MacArthur intervened to reproach both sides for the futility of their contest at a time when the whole of Gaelic culture was being destroyed and scattered. This plea for common sense and attention to the real world was roundly condemned by Tadhg, a thing which has happened more than once in connection with Irish culture. See *Iomarbhágh na bhFileadh,* ed. with trans. and notes by L. McKenna SJ, ITS 1918.

MAC BRUAIDEADHA, Maoilín Óg, b. Co. Clare *c.* 1530, d. Co. Clare 1602. Member of the bardic clan which provided poets and chroniclers for several of the great families of Clare: His branch of the clan served the O'Gradys and the O'Gormans. He is highly praised by the Four Masters as both historian and poet. See *Measgra Dánta,* ed. T.F. O'Rahilly, Cork 1927.

MAC BRUAIDEADHA, Tadhg Mac Dáire, b. Co. Clare 1570, d. 1652. Belonged to the family which by hereditary right provided poets and chroniclers to the O'Briens of Thomond. He himself was ollamh to Donogh O'Brien, 4th Earl, and was one of the chief poets of his time. He was the instigator of the famous Contention of the Bards, writing a poem in which he boasted of the superiority of the O'Briens over the O'Neills, and therefore of the south over the north. The debate lasted from 1617-20, Lughaid Ó Cléirigh being the principal poet on the northern side of the controversy.

Tadhg's Inauguration Ode to Donogh O'Brien, *Mor atá air Theagusc Flatha* (Lessons or Advice for a Prince), achieved great fame and has been translated and edited many times. According to tradition, Tadhg was killed in 1652 by a Cromwellian soldier who had been granted Tadhg's estate. Although an old man at the time, Tadhg resisted the usurper and was struck down by him. The same kind of combativeness had led him to hurl poetic abuse at Roibéard Mac Artúir for intervening in the great Contention with a plea for common sense.

For the text and translation of the Advice to a Prince, see *A Grammar of the Iberno-Celtic or Irish Language*, Charles Vallancey, Dublin 1773; *Advice to a Prince*, Theophilus O'Flanagan, *Transactions of the Gaelic Society of Dublin*, 1808, partly reprinted in *Gaelic Journal I*, 1883. See also *Dánfhocail*, T. F. O'Rahilly, Dublin 1921; *Dioghluim Dána* and *Aithdioghluim Dána*, both ed. L. McKenna SJ, Dublin 1938 and 1939; and *Iomarbhágh na bhFileadh – The Contention of the Bards*, edited with translation, notes and glossary by L. McKenna SJ, for ITS, 1918.

Tadhg's brother Domhnall was also a poet of some note, and is mentioned by McKenna and O'Rahilly. In this connection see also O'Rahilly's *Dánta Gradha*, Cork 1926.

MAC CÁBA, Cathaoir (Charles McCabe), b. Co. Cavan, *c.* 1700, d. 1740. Friend and companion of Carolan, and best remembered for his elegy on Carolan's death. See Charlotte Brooke, *Reliques of Irish Poetry*, Dublin 1789; Thaddaeus Connellan, *Selection of Irish Melodies, Poems and Moral Epigrams*, Dublin 1829; James Hardiman, *Irish Minstrelsy*, Dublin 1831, and *Gaelic Journal*, XIV, 1904. Some of Mac Cába's MSS are preserved in the British Museum Library, but most of his work has survived orally. He is an example of the untaught, peasant rhymer, unconsidered by the graduates of the bardic schools which were still in existence in his time; but nevertheless popular with the people.

MAC CAIRTEÁIN, Liam an Dúna (William MacCartain), b. Doon, Co. Cork, *c.* 1670, d. 1724. President of the Blarney Academy following the death of Diarmuid Mac Sheagháin Bhuidhe Mhic Charrthaigh in 1705, an honour due more to his learning than his talents as a poet. See John O'Daly, *The Poets and Poetry of Munster*, 2nd series, Dublin 1860. Many of his MSS are in the British Museum.

MAC CANA, Proinsias. Ed. QUB and Sorbonne. Professor of Early Irish Language and Literature, UCD. Works include *Branwen, daughter of Llyr*, Cardiff 1958; *Celtic Mythology*, 1970, rep. 1983; *The Mabinogi*, Cardiff 1977; *Literature in Irish*, 1981. Editor with Tomás Ó Floinn of *Scéalaíocht na Ríthe*, Dublin 1956. The book is illustrated by Micheál Mac Liammóir.

MAC CARRTHAIGH, Diarmuid Mac Sheagháin Bhuidhe, b. Co. Cork *c.* 1630, d. Co. Cork 1715. His lifetime saw the end of organised Gaelic society, in which the poet had an honoured and understood place in relation to his chief and patron, and in which the principal duty of a poet was to give honour to his chief. He probably studied his poetic craft at the famous Blarney Academy which was under the protection of the MacCarthys of Cork. He learned to write the difficult *dán díreach* metre, the traditional and ancient metre of the Bardic schools. Significantly this fell out of fashion as the century progressed and the fortunes of the Gaelic aristocracy declined. Mac Carrthaigh like other poets of his time went over to the looser and more popular *amhrán* metre which a generation or so earlier would have been despised as beneath the abilities and attentions of a learned poet. By the time he himself became President of the Blarney Academy it had lost most of its traditional authority and meaning, and become simply a Court of Poetry.

The reign of the Catholic James II brought new hope to some Irishmen and Diarmuid wrote a poem in praise of things he saw happening or hoped would happen. It is written in the ordinary language of the people. But James failed and the Wild Geese fled and Mac Carrthaigh, grown old, looked at a world in ruins. In 1697 his horse died, a tragic loss for a poor and ageing man. In a famous poem *An Fhalartha Gharm* (The Black Palfrey), he laments not only the horse's death but the lack of patronage and honour for poets in this new and desolate time. In the old days he would have gone to The MacCarthy, his patron, and obtained a new horse in exchange for a poem of praise. But now he must walk. He asks if any who hear or read his poem, whether layman or poet, will buy him a new horse. A political debate began in which the generations divided. His contemporaries understood perfectly that a poet must be cherished and honoured, and should have a patron. The younger poets scorned him as a parasite, and said a poet must buy his own horse. As much as any one piece of literature can do, this poem and the debate it caused divide the old Gaelic world from the English world preparing itself for the Agricultural and Industrial Revolutions. And yet as soon as one writes this one thinks of Samuel Johnson, 50 years later, hoping for patronage from Lord Chesterfield, and showing as much indignation on failing to receive it as ever Mac Carrthaigh or Ó Rathaille had done. But they were better poets.

See *Amhráin Diarmaid Mac Seáin Bhuidhe Mac Carrthaigh,* ed. Tadhg Ó Donnehadha, Dublin 1916.

MAC CARRTHAIGH, Eoghan an Mhéirín (the Handy), b. Co. Cork 1691, d. Co. Cork 1756. An itinerant builder specialising in mills, he travelled throughout the south of Ireland. He wrote poetry of quality in both English and Irish and was a friend of Liam Ruadh Mac Coitír with whom he composed a well-known poetic dialogue in 1738. He wrote another with Piaras Mac Gearailt of Waterford. He composed a number of vision poems, elegies and love songs and at least one poem praising the Pretender and his family. Most of his work seems to have been written for singers as much as for recitation. Although he was a craftsman by trade he seems to have had a good classical education, possibly in France. See John O'Daly, *The Poets and Poetry of Munster,* Dublin 1850.

MAC CATHMHAOIL, Aodh (also known as Mac Caghwell, Mac Aingil, and Cavellus), b. Co. Down 1571, d. Rome 1626. Spent some years of his early life in the Isle of Man. Hugh O'Neill sent for him to become tutor to his sons. After the defeat of the earls, he went to Spain and entered the Franciscan Order in Salamanca. Not long afterwards he was teaching in Louvain where Colgan and Patrick Fleming were among his pupils. He went to Rome 1623, and in 1626 was made Archbishop of Armagh. He died while still preparing to return to Ireland. He wrote in Irish and in Latin, and is popularly remembered as the foremost composer of Christmas carols in Irish. His more scholarly work was on theology and metaphysics. *Scáthán Sacrameinte na hAithridhe* (or *Tractatus de Poenitentia et Indulgentiis)*, Louvain 1618; *Scoti Commentaria*, Antwerp 1620, and *Quaestiones in Metaphysicam etc.*, Venice 1625, suggest that he was in Antwerp and Venice as well as Louvain and Rome at this period. He was engaged in the Franciscan defence of Duns Scotus against the Dominican-inspired attacks of Bzovius and Jansen, and published two books, *Apologia pro Johanne Duns-Scoto adversus Abr. Bzovium* (in which he unwisely tried to claim Scotus as an Irishman) and *Apologia Apologiae pro Johanne Duns-Scoto*, Paris 1623. See also Paul Walsh, *Gleanings from Irish MSS*, 1930, 2nd ed. 1933.

MAC CIONNAITH, An tAth. Lambert SJ (Rev. Lambert McKenna), b. Dublin 1870, d. 1953. Ed. Royal University of Ireland. Studied Scholastic Philosophy in Europe, returning to teach in Jesuit Colleges. Became interested in Irish literature and began to collect and edit Irish religious poetry. He edited The Contention of the Bards in 2 vols for the ITS, *Iomarbhágh na bhFileadh*, 1918, 1920. Edited many volumes of poetry, including *Aongus Fionn Ó Dálaigh*, Dublin 1919; *Philip Bocht Ó hUiginn*, Dublin 1931; and most important of his works, two anthologies of Irish bardic poetry prepared for the ITS, *Dioghluim Dána*, Dublin 1938, and *Aithdioghluim Dána*, Dublin 1939. He also edited *The Book of Magauran: Leabhar Méig Shamhradháin*, Dublin 1947; and *The Book of O'Hara: Leabhar Eadhra*, Dublin 1951.

MAC CLÚIN, An tAth. Seoirse, b. Co. Clare 1894. One of the many scholars who visited the Blaskets (1919-20) to study particular problems of Irish. Produced a dictionary of rare words and idioms of Kerry Irish, *Réiltíní Óir*, Dublin 1922. Wrote many short stories in Irish, including a volume, *Binn is Blasta*, Dublin 1922. Compiled *Caint an Chláir*, Dublin 1940, 2 vols.

MAC COITIR, Liam Ruadh, b. Co. Cork *c.* 1660, d. Co. Cork 1738. President of the Blarney Academy after the death of Liam an Dúna Mac Cairteáin. Collaborated with Eoghan an Mhéirín Mac Carrthaigh in a dialogue, shortly before he died in 1738. See *Cois na Cora*, ed. Risteárd Ó Foghludha, Dublin 1937.

MAC CONMARA, Donnchadh Ruadh, b. Co. Clare 1715, d. Co. Waterford 1810. Educated in Rome for the priesthood but expelled for wildness, and returned to Ireland, as a schoolmaster in Co. Waterford. He was at the Court of Poetry held by Piaras Mac Gearailt in Cork in 1743 and shortly afterwards decided to emigrate to Newfoundland, which throughout the 18th century was a magnet for Waterford emigrants. His first attempt failed leaving him with empty pockets outside a Waterford tavern. A second attempt succeeded. Some historians have questioned whether he ever reached Newfoundland, but his long and most famous poem, *Eachtra Giolla an Amaráin* (The Adventures of a Luckless Fellow), which describes an emigrant voyage there, is so full of convincing detail that it is impossible to believe that he simply imagined his journey.

He returned to Ireland in 1756, again as a schoolmaster, was dismissed for drunkenness and turned Protestant to get the job of Parish Clerk in Rossmire, an apostasy of as little weight as Aindrias Mac Craith's. He lost this job too, and turned Catholic again. It may have been then that he went travelling in Europe. At some stage of his life he was in Hamburg, where it is said that he wrote *Bán Chnoic Éireann Óigh* (The Fair Hills of Ireland), considered by most critics to be his finest poem, full of nostalgia and homesickness.

Apart from these two poems he wrote satires, humourous verse, and a great Song of Repentance, *Duain na hAithrighe,* that places him high among all Irish poets and very high among the poets of the 18th-century twilight.

The Adventures of a Luckless Fellow, trans. Percy Arland Ussher, 1926 (in one volume with the same translator's version of *The Midnight Court,* see under MERRIMAN, Brian); an earlier translation was made by Standish Hayes O'Grady under the name S. Hayes, *Adventures of Donnchadh Ruadh MacConmara, a Slave of Adversity,* Dublin 1853. His poetry was edited by Ristéard Ó Foghludha, *Donnchadh Ruadh 1715-1810,* Dublin 1908, and again as *Donnchadh Ruadh MacConmara 1715-1810,* Dublin 1933. See also *Eachtra Giolla an Amaráin; or The Adventures of a Luckless Fellow & other poems,* ed. Tomás Ó Flannghaile with a life of the poet by John Fleming, Dublin 1897, rep. 1907.

MAC CONMARA, Séumas. His novel *An Coimhthigheach,* Dublin 1939, rep. 1943, 1950, 1967, has been one of the most successful of all novels in Irish. It concerns a priest wrongly accused of and imprisoned for a crime. Last reprinted in 1970, with the spelling of the title modernised as *An Coimhthíoch.*

MAC CONMIDHE, Flann, *fl.* 1600. His poem to the Blessed Virgin is included in *Aithdioghluim Dána,* L. McKenna SJ, Dublin 1939.

MAC CONMIDHE, Giolla Brighde Albanach, b. Ulster *c.* 1180, d. Ulster *c.* 1260. It is possible that this lengthy name conceals two poets instead of one, both Giolla Brighde, one known as Albanach and the other, Mac Conmidhe, but there are strong arguments against this view. The by-name Albanach means 'The Scotsman' not because he was born there but because he went there on an important occasion, to recover the famous harp of Donough (Donach) Cairbreach O'Brien, King of Thomond. He wrote a dialogue poem on his mission, the dialogue being with the Scotsman who then possessed the harp. Other poems celebrate the kingship of Donough Cairbreach and of Cathal Mór of the Wine-red Hand, King of Connacht.

Giolla Brighde went to Palestine, either as a pilgrim or crusader, from 1218-21 and another of his poems laments the hardships of the journey. Towards the end of his life he came under the patronage of Aodh Mac Felim Ó Conchobhair, King of Connacht, but was also, curiously enough, ranked as the chief poet and chronicler of Ulster, one of the arguments for there being two poets of the same forenames. Some of his personal poetry begs God for the gift of a son. He stands at the beginning of the great bardic revival which commenced with the Norman invasion, perhaps stimulated by it, and continued for 150 years, into the beginning of the 14th century. It is a measure of the antiquity and continuity of Irish poetry that one can speak of a stylistic 'revival' which ended 100 years before recognisable English poetry began.

See E. Knott, *An Introduction to Irish Syllabic Poetry,* Cork 1928; *Measgra Dánta,* Cork, 1927; J. G. O'Keefe, *Poems on the O'Donnells,* Irish Texts II, Dublin 1931; *Dioghluim Dána,* and *Aithdioghluim Dána,* ed. L. McKenna SJ, Dublin 1938 and 1939; P. Walsh, *Gleanings from Irish MSS,* Dublin 1933.

MAC CONSAIDÍN, Séamus, b. Co. Clare *c.* 1745, d. Co. Clare 1782. A friend of Eugene O'Curry's father, and himself a scholar and doctor. His work has no great poetic value, but he is interesting as an example of the continuing tradition of scholarship among Irish speakers and poets throughout the 18th century. See John O'Daly, *The Poets and Poetry of Munster,* Dublin 1850.

MAC CRAITH, Aindrias, b. Co. Limerick 1708, d. probably Co. Limerick *c.* 1795. Known as An Mangaire Súgach, the Merry Pedlar, he was originally a schoolmaster, like his great friend and fellow poet Seán Ó Tuama an Ghrinn. And like Ó Tuama, he found other things more congenial than schoolmastering. He wandered the countryside, drinking, making up poems, reciting them for the price of a few more drinks or for nothing but the pleasure of hearing them, and going to Croom to Seán's 'Dun', meaning Seán Ó Tuama's public house, for some more of the hospitality that was soon to reduce Seán Ó Tuama to the same state of poverty as the Pedlar's own. Aindrias like several of his fellow-poets became a Protestant for a time, to earn the price of a few weeks comfort. But the Protestant Minister threw him out of his congregation, and not much wonder. He was more likely to be singing drinking-songs than hymns. Corkery compares his drinking-songs to Robert Burns at his best.

On another occasion he was driven out of Croom itself by the parish priest, either for a satire he had written against the priest and his people, or because of the apostasy he had just been guilty of. It inspired some of

MAC CRAITH

his best and most tragic poetry. '*Is fánach faon mé is fraochmhar fuar*,' one verse begins, that Corkery translates 'A wanderer and languid am I, furious and cold, weak, prostrate, disease-smitten, wretched on the mountain-top, with none, alas to befriend me – except heather and the north wind.' And these were the last friends that he had, as he grew old, and all his friends died who had once made him welcome. He travelled the roads of the south and the mountains into his old age, and died somewhere unknown, under a hedge, or in a poor man's shed. 'Who is he? Where is he from? Where is he going?' another of his lines says. '*Cá háit, cia hé, cá taobh'n-ar ghluais?*'

Riseárd (sometimes Risteárd) Ó Foghludha has edited his poetry in *Filídhe na Máighe*, and *Éigse na Máighe*, Dublin 1906 and 1952.

MAC CRAITH, An tAth. Micheál SJ, b. Co. Waterford 1872, d. 1951. Best known for his edition of *Cinn-lae Amhlaoibh Uí Shúileabháin* (The Diary of Humphrey O'Sullivan), with trans. and notes, ITS 1936, 4 vols.

MAC CRAITH, Seán Mac Ruadhri, *fl.* 1350, in Co. Clare. His family were hereditary poets to the O'Briens of Thomond and his chief work is a history of Thomond from 1204, when Donough Cairbreach assumed the throne, to 1317, when the O'Briens were victorious in their long struggles against the de Clares. One passage in the book describes the building of Bunratty Castle as a de Clare stronghold. Unlike most Irish chronicles, the book gives vivid and sometimes detailed pen pictures of people, of mediaeval warfare in Ireland, and of events. *Caithréim Thoirdhealbhaigh* (The Triumphs of Turlough) with intro. and index by Robin Flower, S. H. O'Grady, ITS 1929. E. Curtis, 'The Wars of Turlough', Irish Review II & III, 1913. A MS copy of 1509 is preserved in TCD library.

MAC CRIMTHAINN, Aed, *fl.* 1120-1160. The 12th-century scribe who compiled *The Book of Leinster* at Terryglass near Clonmacnoise. It contains several parts: *The Book of Invasions*, the *Táin Bó Fraich*, the *Táin Bó Cúailnge*, the *Dindshenchas*, together with poetry and historical passages.

MAC CRUITÍN, Aindrias, b. Co. Clare *c.* 1650, d. Co. Clare 1738. A school-teacher and poet, member of a family that provided many poets and chroniclers for the O'Briens. He wrote a famous poem addressed to a 'fairy chief' which was recited in Clare long after his death. See John O'Daly and Edward Walsh *Reliques of Irish Jacobite Poetry*, 2nd ed. 1866, and John O'Daly, *The Poets and Poetry of Munster*, 2nd series, 1860, both pub. Dublin.

MAC CRUITÍN, Aodh Buidhe, b. Co. Clare *c.* 1670, d. Co. Clare 1755. He was a cousin of Aindrias Mac C. and was at school under him in Moyglass. He was at the siege of Limerick, and left Ireland with Sarsfield after the surrender of 1691. In 1693 he was serving in the Irish Brigade in Flanders, under Lord Clare. He must have pleased Clare with his learning as well as his courage, because he became tutor to the Clare children in Paris, and remained with the family for seven years. There is also a story that he was for a time a private tutor to the Dauphin.

In 1714 he returned to Ireland, and published *A Brief Discourse in Vindication of the Antiquity of Ireland,* Dublin 1717, an attack on a recent government-inspired publication *Hibernia Anglicana* by a miserable man called Cox. Mac Cruitín was imprisoned for his book and while in goal wrote *The Elements of the Irish Language, Grammatically Explained in English,* a work later published in Louvain 1728. Released from prison, he returned to Paris and there with the Rev. Conor Begley wrote an *English-Irish Dictionary,* Paris 1732. Both these works on Irish contain valuable indications of the way vernacular was developing in the early 18th century.

In 1738 (some reference works say 1749 but this is surely wrong) his cousin Aindrias Mac C. died and Aodh Buidhe Mac Cruitín returned to Ireland to take up his hereditary post of ollamh to the O'Briens. One of his longer poems marks the occasion, and describes his sadness. He opened a small school at Cnoc an Aird, and died there. See John O'Daly, *The Poets and Poetry of Munster,* Dublin 1850, and B. O'Looney, *A Collection of Poems. . . by the Irish Bards,* Dublin 1863. Also John O'Daly and Edward Walsh, *Reliques of Irish Jacobite Poetry,* 2nd ed., Dublin 1866.

MAC CUARTA, Séamus Dall, b. Co. Louth *c.* 1647, d. near Slane 1732. Like Carolan whom he knew (and to whom it has been suggested he wrote his famous poem of welcome, *Fáilte don Éan,* Greetings to the Bird), Séamus Dall was blind from childhood, and perhaps as a result received a more intensive education than he might otherwise have done. He certainly knew a great deal of Irish history and literature. He came to be considered the chief northern poet of his time, north Leinster, the area of his main wanderings, being included in the 'north'. One of his best-known poems consists of a dialogue between himself and a castle that a certain rapacious Pádraic Ó Murchadha was despoiling of its stones to build something humdrum and sordid for his own use.

Legend describes Séamus Dall sitting blind under a sheltering bush to gain his inspiration, and his nature poetry has the sadness and also the beauty of such an image. In his old age he outlived his patrons and fell into helpless poverty. About 3000 lines of his poetry survive. See *Rainníní & Amhráin* by Eamon Ó Tuathail, Dublin 1923, and more particularly *Amhráin Shéamais Mhic Cuarta,* ed. Lorcáin Ua Muireadhaigh, Dundalk 1925. His poetry has more recently been edited by Seán Ó Gallchóir, *Séamus Dall Mac Cuarta: Dánta,* Dublin 1971.

MAC CUBHTHAIGH, Art, b. Co. Armagh 1715, d. probably Armagh 1773. Recognised in the north as second only to Séamus Dall Mac Cuarta among northern poets of the 18th century. He is the type, almost the archetype, of the poet of the Gaelic twilight, described with love and anger by Daniel Corkery in *The Hidden Ireland.* A peasant background, great learning got in a hedge school, and therefore a learning already in descent towards pathos, the kind of learning which time and again astonished the educated foreign traveller when he found it in some ragged man on an Irish road; this kind of learning allied with a poetry that was loosening itself from the hard disciplines of the bardic schools and becoming peasant and popular; this learning and this poetry in the head of an itinerant gardener, a man calling at the houses of the Ascendancy and of the well-got Irish, who had made their peace with the English, to see if they needed a hedge trimmed or a bush pruned. In Armagh once he wrote a satire on the house-keeper of the parish priest of Creagán, calling her down for the miserable skinflint that no doubt she was. The priest banished him from the parish (even by the mid-18th century, and despite those Penal Laws which still remained on the Statute Books, the Catholic parish priest had become not only a tolerated but a locally powerful figure, almost a member of the Establishment, providing he minded his policital manners) and it took a most humble and lavish poem in praise of the same dreadful woman to win permission to return to Armagh.

On another occasion Art fell out with the local authorities and hid in Creagán cemetery. His *aisling* or vision poem arising from this experience. *Úir-chill an Chreagáin,* became a popular song in south Ulster and lived in folk-memory for generations. There is a slanderous story that Art became a Protestant, and remembering his praise of the priest's housekeeper the story is probably true.

He wrote a poem to the same castle that Séamus Dall Mac Cuarta had lamented 50 years before, and he also wrote an elegy to Peadar Ó Doirnín, the northern poet. Much of Art's poetry was for singing, and he was known by the people as 'Art of the Tunes'. See *Abhráin Airt Mhic Chubhthaigh agus Abhráin Eile,* ed. Énri Ó Muirgheasa, Dublin and Dundalk 1916, and 2nd ed. Dundlak 1926; more recently, *Art Mac Cumhaigh: Dánta,* ed. Tomás Ó Fiaich, Dublin 1973.

MAC CUMHAILL, Fionn, see MHAC CUMHAILL, Fionn.

MAC CURTIN, Hugh, see MAC CRUITÍN, Aodh Buidhe.

MAC DOMHNAILL, Seán Clárach, b. Co. Cork 1691, d. Co. Cork 1754. His family had held land and he retained a farm near Ráth Luirc, which became the seat of Courts of Poetry, over which Seán Clárrach presided, being considered chief poet of Munster. His half of the 18th century was less terrible for Munster than the second half, but it was hard enough, and his most famous poem is a savage epitaph for the local villain-landlord, Colonel Dawson of Aherlow. 'Squeeze down his bones, O ye stones,' Seán Clárach begged, the Colonel having been a man who grudged even fallen twigs to the poor who were dying of cold for want of fuel. 'He would whip streams of blood down from their quarters.'

When the poem became known to the authorities Seán Clárach had to leave the district for a time, but he returned and died in peace on his farm. He is remarkable for a number of things, although only the satire on the Colonel has the force of great poetry, the rest of his work being graceful rather than great. He is the first writer who seems to have recognised that not only the way of life, but the Irish language itself was doomed unless people like himself and his fellow-poets defended it. His poetry was edited for the Gaelic League by Pádraig Uí Duinnín, Dublin 1902, and by Risteárd Ó Foghludha, Dublin 1933, rep. 1935, 1944.

MAC DUINNSHLÉIBHE, Cormac, b. Co. Donegal *c.* 1420, d. Co. Donegal 1480. His family were hereditary physicians to the O'Donnells and Cormac himself was trained in the 'Arabian' school of medicine. He translated Isaac's *De Dietis* into Irish and Walter de Burley's *De Dosibus.* See the edition by Shawn Sheaher, Washington, Catholic University of America, 1938.

MAC ÉIL, Eoin, see MACHALE, John.

MACENTEE, Máire, see MHAC AN tSAOI, Máire.

MAC FHEORAIS, Seán, b. Co. Kildare 1915, d. 1984. Poet. School-teacher in Limerick, Leitrim, Kilkenny and Finglas 1955-78. *Gearrcaigh na hOíche,* Nenagh 1954; *Léargas: Dánta Fada,* Drogheda 1964. Won number of poetry prizes at Oireachtas and from Radio Éireann. His best-known work is the long poem *Oícheanta Airnean.*

MAC FHINN, Monsignor Pádraig Eric, b. Co. Galway 1895. Ed. UCD and Rome. Ordained Rome 1919. Researcher in Church History, Vatican Library. Lecturer in Education, UCG, 1931. Member Dept. Education, Chairman Irish Folklore Commission, Chairman Commission of Irish Place Names. Wrote a biography of Fr Michael O'Hickey, *An tAthair Mícheál P. Ó hIceadha,* Dublin 1974.

MAC FHIONNGHAILE, sometimes spelled Mac Fhionnlaoich, Peadar (Cú Uladh), originally Peter MacGinley, b.Co. Donegal 1857, d.1940. Not a native speaker, but had some Irish as a child. Joined British civil service in 1878. Returned to Ireland 1893 and joined the newly-founded Gaelic League, becoming its President 1923-25. Wrote *Handbook of Irish Teaching,* Dublin 1903, a number of plays and edited anthologies of Irish verse. His best-known works are *Eachtra Aodha Ruaidh Uí Dhomhnaill,* Dublin 1911; *Conchubhar Mac Neasa,* Dublin 1914; and *An Cogadh Dearg agus Sgéalta Eile,* Dublin 1918.

MAC FIRBISIGH, Dubhaltach, b. Sligo 1585, d. near Sligo 1670. His family were chroniclers to the O'Dowds of Sligo. He was educated in the old Gaelic style, by the Mac Egans of Ormond and the O'Davorens of Clare. As a student he copied and preserved the *Annals* of Ossory and Leinster. He spent many years teaching in Galway, where he had among his pupils John Lynch and Roderick O'Flaherty. While living in the College of St Nicholas in Galway he compiled his *Genealogies of the Families of Ireland.* When Galway fell to the Cromwellians in 1652, Mac Firbisigh fled for protection to Sir James Ware in Dublin, bringing his MSS with him. In Sir James's house he wrote *A Treatise on Irish Authors, a Martyrology,* in verse; and began compiling a Glossary, now lost. On Sir James's death in 1666 he returned to Sligo, destitute. Four years later he set out for Dublin again on foot, and was murdered on the road by a young man. His principal works are to be found in *Annals of Ireland* (AD 571-913); *Three fragments copied from ancient sources by D. Mac F., ed. with trans. and notes from a manuscript preserved in the Burgundian Library Brussels*, by John O'Donovan, printed for the Irish Archaeological and Celtic Society, Dublin 1860.

Chronicum Scotorum. A Chronicle of Irish Affairs from the Earliest Times to 1135 (by D. Mac F.), with a supplement containing the events from 1141 to 1150, ed. with a trans. by William M. Hennessy, 1866; *The Genealogies, Tribes and Customs of Hy-Fiachrach, commonly called O'Dowd's Country*, trans. and notes by John O'Donovan, Dublin 1844; *On the Fomorians and the Norsemen, by D. Mac F.*, ed. with trans. and notes by Alexander Bugge, Christiania 1905. *The Annals of Ireland* (1443-68) were translated into English by Mac Firbisigh himself for Sir James Ware in 1666, and this MS was edited and published by John O'Donovan, Dublin 1851. The Irish Manuscripts Commission published *Genealogical Tracts I*, ed. J. O'Raithbheartaigh, Dublin 1932. These included Mac F.'s introduction to the *Book of Genealogies, Lecan Miscellany* and *The Ancient Tract on the Distribution of the Aithech-Tuatha.*

MAC FIRBISIGH, Giolla Íosa Mór, b. Sligo *c.* 1360, d. Sligo *c.* 1430. A member of the family that provided chroniclers to the O'Dowds and for generations maintained Gaelic and bardic schools under their protection. Giolla Íosa with some of his relatives compiled *The Yellow Book of Lecan*, completed about 1390. In 1417 Giolla Íosa completed *The Great Book of Lecan*. Both books are compilations of older material, chronicles, poetry and legend and of great value not only as literature but for the historian also. See *The Genealogies, Tribes and Customs of Hy-Fiachrach, commonly called O'Dowd's Country* with trans. and notes by John O'Donovan, Dublin 1844.

Giolla Íosa was an ancestor of Dubhaltach Mac Firbisigh.

MAC GABHANN, Micí, b. Co. Donegal 1865, d. Co. Donegal 1948. Eldest of 12 children of Gaelic-speaking peasant family. Went to work at 9 years of age, as a herder, taken on at a hiring fair. Went to Scotland as a labourer at 15 and at 20 went to America, mining in Montana and the Klondyke. Returned to Ireland 1902 comparatively rich with Klondyke gold, and bought a large house and substantial farm. Towards the end of his life told his life story, in Irish, to Seán Ó hEochaidh. It was published in 1959 in Dublin as *Rotha Mór an tSaoil*, ed. Proinsias Ó Conluain, and won the Club Leabhar award. It was translated into English by Valentin Iremonger as *The Hard Road to Klondyke* (see Part I), 1962.

MAC GEARAILT, Muiris Mac Dháibhí Dhuibh, b. Munster *c.* 1550, d. Munster *c.* 1612. A descendant of the Norman FitzGeralds, his father lost his estate during the Geraldine Rising and was killed in 1581. Muiris remained in Kerry, but possibly spent some time in Spain. One of his best poems is a description of a ship setting out for Spain from Ireland. See Charlotte Brooke, *Reliques of Irish Poetry*, Dublin 1789; John O'Daly, *Self-Instruction in Irish*, Dublin 1846; *Gaelic Journal*, VII, 1897; *Dánta Grádha*, collected by Tomás Ó Rathaille, with English versions by Robin Flower, Cork 1926; *Measgra Dánta*, also ed. T. Ó Rathaille, Cork 1927; *Éigse I*, 1939, where H. R. McAdoo edits a poem by Mac Gearailt.

MAC GEARAILT, Piaras, b. Co. Cork 1709, d. Co. Cork 1791. Like his older contemporary, Seán Clárach Mac Domhnaill, Piaras was born into a family that had held much land and still held some, the farm of Ballykineally. For the times, and for Catholics, the Mac Gearailts were well-off. Three of Piaras's brothers were educated in Spain. Seán Clárach had been left in comparative peace on his farm, but as the century advanced, and the pressure on land grew greater with increasing population and the agricultural revolution, steps were taken to drive Catholics from their holdings. Piaras was faced with either losing his land, the last remnants of his family's once substantial estate, or apostatising. He turned Protestant and regretted it all his life, without, however, turning back to the Catholic Church. It was a common enough thing to have done and few reproached him for it. To one of those who did he answered in a poem full of agony of mind.

He also wrote of Mary in a moving poem, 'Characteristics of the Blessed Virgin', that his great sorrow in the Protestant faith was the absence of any honour done to Christ's mother, *Tuile na nGrás, agus Tonn Chliodna na Trócaire* ('Flood of Graces, and Cleena's Wave of Mercy' in Corkery's translation). Another of his best-known poems is 'The Munster War Song', an *aisling* devoted to that constant delusion of the Munster poets, the coming of the Pretender to save Ireland. The thought of such innocent, simple men devoting their poetry to invocations of that drunken wastrel sets the teeth on edge.

During a long life he held Courts of Poetry on his farm, as Mac Domhnaill had done, and sent out invitations signed Piaras Mac Gearailt, Aird-Shirriam Leatha Mogha, or High Sheriff of Mogh's Half, meaning the south of Ireland or Munster. Most of the southern poets of his time must have come there, making little of their host's official Protestantism. Towards the end of his life he made a manuscript copy of many of his poems for a Miss Creagh, possibly a grandniece or great-grandniece of Miss Creagh who married Micheál Coimín in 1702. The MS is now in Maynooth. In his very old age he either lost his farm at last, or handed it on to one of his children, because he died in Clashmore, in the house of his son-in-law. His poetry is edited by Riseárd Ó Foghludha in *Amhráin Phiarais Mhic Gearailt*, Dublin 1905.

MAC GEOGHEGAN, Conall, *fl.* probably Clonmacnoise 1600-40. Author of the English version of the lost Irish *Annals of Clonmacnoise,* which he

completed in 1627. Entries in the *Annals* range from the 5th to the early
15th century, and there is a mythological introduction.

MAC GINLEY, Peter T., see MAC FHIONNGHAILE, Peadar.

MAC GIOLLA BHRIGHDE, Niall, b. Co. Donegal 1861, d. Co. Donegal
1938. Although he grew up as a native speaker of Irish he was unable to
write in Irish until he was an adult, taught by 'Tomás Bán' (Tomás Ua
Concheanáinn), the Gaelic League enthusiast. He won several Feis prizes
for poetry, and contributed Irish poems to the *Derry People*. His earlier
poetry is collected in *Blátha Fraoich*, Dublin 1905. See also a biography
to Liam Ó Connacháin, *Niall Mac Giolla Bhríde*, Dublin 1974.

MAC GIOLLA CAOIMH, *fl.* 1014. A Munster poet, one of the many who
wrote a lament on the death of Brian at Clontarf, and of the desolation
and sorrow that followed the deaths of so many chieftains. See James
Hardiman, *Irish Minstrelsy*, vol. II, Dublin 1831; E. MacNeill, 'Ráith
Ráithleann, Ráith Chuirch is Chéin', *Gaelic Journal*, VII, 1896.

MAC GIOLLA GUNNA, Cathal Buidhe, b. Co. Cavan *c.* 1690, d. near
Carrickmacross 1756. He claimed to have been educated for the priesthood,
but earned his living, when he did earn it, as a carrier or porter. He spent
much of his time wandering the roads, drinking and womanising. He was
said to have married several times, and probably failed to marry many
more times. He seems to have been banished at one time or another from
every parish in Cavan and finally the outraged priests of the county ordered
that no Catholic should give him shelter even for a night. When he was
dying one disobedient parishioner let him into his hut and went off to fetch
the priest. Before he returned with him the poet was dead and had written
a poem of repentance on the wall of the hut. Tradition claimed that his
dead body was surrounded with a halo of light, a proof of God's forgiveness.
Apart from this legend he is remembered for two famous poems; his poem
of repentance *Aithreachas Chathail Bhuidhe*, and an earlier poem in which
he describes finding a yellow bittern dead on the ice of a lake, and compares
himself to the bird, *AnBonnán Buídhe*. See *Duanaire na Midhe*: collected
by J. H. Lloyd, Gaelic League Series, Dublin 1914. More recently, *Cathal
Bui; Amhráin*, ed. Breandán Ó Buachalla, Dublin 1966.

MAC GIOLLA IASACHTA, Éamonn, see MAC LYSAGHT, Edward.

MAC GIOLLA MEIDHRE, Brian, see MERRIMAN, Brian.

MAC GIOLLA PÁDRAIG, Brian Mac Toirrdhealbhaigh, b. *c.* 1585, d.
Ossory, murdered, 1652. Ordained Louvain 1610 and lived for years in
exile. One of his few surviving poems is a farewell to Ireland. He returned
as Vicar Apostolic of Ossory and was murdered there in the Cromwellian
invasion. For some of his poetry see *Measgra Dánta*, ed. T. F. Ó Rathaille,
Cork 1927. His major claim to remembrance is that he copied out *The
Book of the O'Byrnes*, and by so doing saved for posterity much of the
bardic poetry of Leinster.

MAC GIOLLARNÁTH, Seán, b. Co. Galway 1880, d. 1970. Worked in London as a young man, returning to Dublin as editor of *An Claidheamh Soluis*. Courier for IRA during War of Independence; District Justice West Galway, 1925-50. Wrote several volumes on Irish wild birds, *Saol Eánacha*, Dublin 1925, etc. Collected folk tales, local history and reminiscences in Connacht. *Peadar Chois Fhairrge*, Dublin 1934 (memories of an old man); and *Annála Beaga Ó Iorrus Aithneach*, Dublin 1941 (local history).

MAC GRADAOIGH, Augustine, see MAG RAIDHIN, Augustine.

MAC GRIANNA, Séamus (pseud. MÁIRE), see Ó GRIANNA, Séamus.

MAC GRIANNA, Seosamh (Iolann Fionn), b. Co. Donegal 1900. Brother of Séamus Ó Grianna, the difference of surname being agreed on with his brother either to avoid confusion of them as writers, or for simple difference of taste when they adopted the Irish forms of the English name Green. Like his brother, Seosamh was a school-teacher, and later a political prisoner during the Civil War 1922-24. With Seamus, considered to be among the finest modern Irish writers. He published a short-story collection, *An Grádh agus an Ghruaim*, Dublin 1929; *Eoghan Rua Ó Néill*, Dublin 1931; *Padraic Ó Conaire agus Aistí Eile*, Dublin 1936; *An Bhreatain Bheag*, Dublin 1937; *Na Lochlannaigh*, Dublin 1938; *Mo Bhealach Féin*, Dublin 1940, rep. 1941, 1965, 1968, 1970 and 1984. Club Leabhar selection for 1967. In recent years there has been a strong revival of interest in his work. One of his finest books, witheld from publication by An Gúm for many years, *An Druma Mór*, was pub. Dublin 1972 and rep. 1983; *Dochartach Duibhlionna agus Scéalta Eile*, repub. Belfast 1976, and *Ailt*, Belfast 1977. He has been ill for many years, and unable to continue writing.

MAC HALE, John (Mac Éil, Eoin), b. Co. Mayo 1791, d. Tuam 1881. As a child he was deeply affected by the landing of the French at Killala, and the subsequent hanging of his own parish priest by the victorious English. He grew up with a deep hatred of what the English represented in Ireland, and a determination to preserve Irish culture and the Irish language. Educated in Castlebar and Maynooth, ordained 1814, Professor of Theology, Maynooth, 1820-25, Archbishop of Tuam 1834. Next to Daniel O'Connell he was the greatest popular figure in pre-famine Ireland, called by O'Connell 'the Lion of St Jarlath's', that being his residence in Tuam. He opposed Newman's plans for a Catholic University in Dublin, saying that an Englishman was out of place in such a context.

In literature Mac Éil's major importance is that he bridged, in one sense, the gulf between the last of the Gaelic writers, and the first of the Irish Revivalists; the gulf that is between such men as Eoghan Ruadh Ó Súilleabháin and Douglas Hyde, the one dying seven years before Mac Éil's birth, the other founding the Gaelic League twelve years after his death. These two figures are separated by much more than a long lifetime. One belonged to a still living, if rapidly dying, natural culture, with roots in the Iron Age, an organic creation of which the language and literature were no more and no less than a natural and inevitable expression. The culture formed the language; a culture of clan loyalties and clan hatreds; passionate, beautiful, wild, religious, and aristocratic in a sense incomprehensible to the town-based culture of the English.

The other figure, Douglas Hyde, belonged to the world of the English, and despite their every intention he and his collaborators in the Revival movement did not and could not recreate the old culture; they could only hope to create a new one in the image of the old and even that hope might be in vain.

Mac Éil provided a bridge not only in time between these primary figures, but in style between their opposed styles. While he had a fine knowledge of Irish he had very little knowledge of Irish literature. Or if he had the knowledge he did not allow it to influence him. His Irish is almost a mental translation from English, using English rather than Irish metres and rhythms. He translated Homer into Irish, the Pentateuch, hymns, Tom Moore's songs, and wrote a catechism and a prayer book in Irish among many other works. See his *An Teagasg Criostaighe*, Dublin 1839; *Turas na Croiche*, Dublin 1855 (a translation of St Alfonso Liguori's *Way of the Cross*); *Craobh Urnaighe Crábhaighe*, Dublin 1853.

McKENNA, Lambert see MAC CIONNAITH, An tAth. Lambert SJ.

MAC LIAG, Muirchertach Mac Chonchertaigh, b. Mayo or Sligo *c*. 960, d. after 1015. Began in the service of the O'Kellys on the upper Shannon, and later moved to Kincora and the service of the O'Briens, after the death of Flann Mac Lonáin. He became chief poet and secretary to Brian Bóroimhe and most of his work that survives is about Brian. His poem on the death of Brian at Clontarf was translated by Mangan. What is usually accepted as Mac Liag's masterpiece, *The War of the Gael with the Gall* (written with some help from Erard Mac Coise), describes the wars of Brian against the Norsemen, ending with the Battle of Clontarf, but also contains legendary material of great interest. One legend, of the faery-woman and her lover Dunlaing who returned to his kin to die beside his friend, Brian's son, was used by W. B. Yeats in *The Grey Rock*.

See James Hardiman, *Irish Minstrelsy*, vol. II, Dublin 1831; Kuno Meyer, 'On Brian Borumha', *Eriu IV*, Dublin 1908; Kuno Meyer, *Fianaigecht*, Dublin 1910; 'A Poem by Mac Liag' (text from *Book of Lecan*), trans. Owen Connellan, *Ossianic Society: Transactions*, V, Dublin 1860; *Cogadh Gaedhel re Gallaibh. The War of the Gaedhil with the Gaill, or the invasion of Ireland by the Danes and other Norsemen*, ed. with trans. and introduction by James Henthorn Todd, 1867. In his introduction Todd discredits Mac Liag's authorship, but ascribes the poem to an eye-witness of the Battle of Clontarf, or to some poet who had his information from eyewitnesses.

MAC LIAMMÓIR, Micheál, b. Cork 1899, d. Dublin 1978. Taken to

London 1907 by parents, remaining there until 1914, the last four years as a child actor. He spent some time in Spain at this period, but returned to London to act, and also learned Irish in a Gaelic League class at Ludgate Circus, and studied painting in the Slade School. Returned to Ireland 1916, and within a few years had exhibited paintings in Dublin, London, Sicily, Paris and Berlin. His style was influenced by Aubrey Beardsley. In 1928 formed a partnership with Hilton Edwards, presenting Mac Liammóir's play *Diarmuid agus Gráinne* in the Taibhdhearc Theatre in Galway. Later that year they founded the Gate Theatre. For Mac Liammóir's theatrical and other writing in English, see Part I. He had already written occasional pieces in Irish as well as *Diarmuid agus Gráinne*, pub. Dublin 1935, and continued with plays, essays, poetry and translations from English and Russian. *Lá agus Oidche,* Dublin 1929; *Oidche Bhealtaine* (a play for children), Dublin 1932; *Lúlú* (short play), Dublin 1933; *Ceo Meala Lá Seaca* (essays), Dublin 1952; *Aisteoirí Faoi dhá Sholas* (diary of a tour with the Gate Theatre Company in the Levant and Egypt), Dublin 1956; *Bláth agus Taibhse,* (poetry), Dublin 1964. Translations include *Salomé,* from Wilde; *Gaisge is Gaisgidheach* (Shaw); *Prunella* (Barker); and *Ag Iarraidh Mná* (Tchekov). He received many literary honours, including the 1957 Douglas Hyde Award, the 1960 Lady Gregory Medal for Literature, and a Doctorate of Laws from TCD, 1963.

MAC LYSAGHT, Edward (Éamonn Mac Giolla Iasachta), b. at sea, 1887, of a Clare family named Lysaght, emigrating to Australia. For details of his career and his important work in genealogy and 17th-century Irish history, see Part I. Worked for a number of years in National Library as Chief Genealogical Officer and Keeper of Manuscripts. *Cúrsaí Thomáis,* a novel, Dublin 1927; rep. Dublin 1969; *Toil Dé,* Dublin 1933; *An Aifric Theas,* Dublin 1947 (he was several years in Africa as a journalist).

MAC MAGHNUIS, Proinsias, see MACMANUS, Frank.

MAC MAGHNUSA MHEG UIDHIR, Cathal, b. Ulster 1439, d. Ulster 1498. Became Archdeacon of Clogher. Spent some time on an island in Lough Erne, Co. Fermanagh, where he compiled *The Annals of Ulster,* which begin with the mission of Palladius in the 5th century, and end in 1498. Some versions continue the *Annals* until 1588 and there is additional material carrying other versions into the 17th century. *Annales Ultonienses,* ed. Rev. Charles O'Conor, Buckingham 1826. *Annala Uladh,* ed. with trans. and notes W. M. Hennessy and B. MacCarthy, 4 vols, Dublin 1887, 1893, 1895, 1901. There are MS copies in TCD and Oxford (Rawlinson B 489).

MAC MANUS, Francis (Proinsias Mac Maghnuis), b. Kilkenny 1909, d. Dublin 1965. For his work in English see Part I. Was for many years Head of Talks and Features, Radio Éireann, and a significant influence in Irish cultural life through the radio series of Thomas Davis Lectures. *Seal ag Ródaíocht,* Dublin 1955, was the diary of a journey to America.

MAC MAOLÁIN

MAC MAOLÁIN, Seán, b. Co. Antrim 1886, d. 1973. Won 1st prize for Oireachtas Ode 1912. Large number of plays, stories, and volumes of verse. *Éan Corr*, Dublin 1937; *Finnscéal agus Firinne* (short stories), Dublin 1942; *Algoland*, Dublin 1947; *Lomramh Ghlómair*, Dublin 1952; and autobiography: *Gleann, Airbh go Glasnaíon*, Dublin 1969.

MAC MEANMAIN, Seán, b. Co. Donegal 1891, d. 1962. Teacher of Irish for many years in McDevitt Institute, Glenties. At one time lost his position as teacher for refusing to swear an oath of allegiance to the State. *Scéalta Goiridhe Geimhridh* (stories), Dublin 1915; *Fear Siubhail* (novel), Dublin 1924; *Inné agus Inniú (stories), Dublin 1929*; *Tri Mhion-Dráma*, Dublin 1936; *Ó Chamhaoir go Clapsholas*, Dublin 1940; *Mám as mo Mhála*, Dublin 1940 (stories of the old days); *Mám Eile as an Mhála Chéadna*, Dublin 1954; *Rácáil agus Scuabadh*, Dublin 1955; *Crathadh an Phócáin*, Dublin 1955; *Stair na h-Éireann*, Dublin 1956.

MAC PIARAIS, Pádraig, see PEARSE, Patrick Henry.

MAC RUAIDHRÍ, Micheál (pseud. 'Mearthóg Guill'), b. Co. Mayo 1860, d. 1936. One of the last of the traditional story-tellers. He was never 'educated' in any formal, modern sense, but received the oldest kind of education, from the local story-tellers and men of learning, by word of mouth. Some of what he learned he wrote down years later in stories and collections of wise sayings. *An Fiaclóir*, Dublin 1893; *Beatha Aodha Uí Néill*, for the Oireachtas of 1903; *Bréaga Éireann*; *Éan an Chéoil Bhinn*; *Lúb na Caillighe*, for Connradh na Gaeilge 1910; *Mac Mic Iascaire Bhuidhe Luimnighe*, for Connradh na Gaeilge 1910; *Triúr Clainne na Bárd-Scolóige*, for Connradh na Gaeilge 1914.

MAC SIOMÓIN, Tomás, b. Dublin 1938. Ed. UCD and Cornell. Botanist. Lecturer, Kevin St College of Technology. Poetry includes *Damhna agus Dánta eile*, Dublin 1974 (Arts Council award), *Aogán*, 1981, and *Cré agus Clairseach*, 1983.

MAC SUIBNE, Pádraig, b. Donegal 1942. Ed. Maynooth. Teacher in Donegal and now Drogheda. Collection of short stories being prepared for publication. Poetry: *Taibhsí an Chreagaín*, Dublin 1976; *Spaisteoireacht*, with Fr Pádraig Ó Fiannachta, Maynooth 1980; *Mairtín Ó Direáin: Selected Poems*, trans. with Douglas Sealy, 1985.

MAC TOMÁIS, An tAth. Peadar, b. Co. Roscommon 1893, d. 1948. Ordained Maynooth 1919, taught for a period in Coláiste Muire, Galway. Wrote the Oireachtas Ode for 1944, having in other years won a number of prizes for Irish poetry. See also *Days of Destiny*, Dublin 1919, and *Songs of the Island Queen*, Dublin 1919.

MAC UISTÍN, Liam, b. Dublin 1929. Ed. UCD. Plays include *Cóiriú na Leapa*, Dublin 1967; *Liombó*, Dublin 1969; *Pocléim*, Dublin 1971; all three published Dublin between 1969 and 1973. *Post Mortem*, pub. US

1977; *An Táin,* Dublin 1979; *Mír agus Éadaoin,* Dublin 1979; and *Deirdre,* Dublin 1982. Has won awards in Oireachtas literary competitions and his work was selected for inscription in National Garden of Remembrance, Dublin.

MAEL ÍSU UA BROLCHÁIN (the servant, or the tonsured of Jesus), b. *c.* 970, d. 1038, probably in Derry. Wrote fine religious poetry, some of it preserved in the *Liber Hymnorum,* other pieces in *The Yellow Book of Lecan.* See Kuno Meyer, 'Mael Isu's Hymn to the Archangel Michael', *Gaelic Journal IV,* 1890; Kuno Meyer, 'Neue Mitteilungen aus Irischen Handschriften', *Archiv für Celtische Lexikographie III,* 1906; Kuno Meyer, *Selections from Early Irish Poetry,* Dublin 1909; *Goedilica. . .with Eight Hymns from the Liber Hymnorum,* text and trans. Whitley Stokes, Calcutta 1866, 2nd ed. 1872; *Irish Litanies,* text and trans. C. Plummer, London 1925.

MAEL MAEDÓC UA MORGAIR, see MALACHY.

MAEL MUIRE MAC CÉILECHAIR, b. *c.* 1040, d. 1106, probably at Clonmacnoise. Scribe at Clonmacnoise, and preserver by copying of *The Book of the Dun Cow.* The book contains *The Voyage of Bran, The Voyage of Mael Dúin, Connla's Visit to the Otherworld, Adamnán's Vision of Heaven and Hell,* Dallan Forgaill's poem in praise of Colum Cille, stories from *The Ulster Cycle* including *The Wooing of Emer, Bricriu's Feast, The Wasting Sickness of Cú Chulainn,* and the *Táin Bó Cúailgne* itself.

MAEL MURU (sometimes Maolmuru of Fathan), b. *c.* 820, d. 884 or 886. Called by the Four Masters 'a well taught, skilful poet and intelligent historian', and by the others 'the Irish Nennius.' Most of his work is historical, either on the origins of the Gaels and the genealogies of the ruling families, or on the histories of individual kings from the time of Tuathal the Legitimate in the 2nd century AD to his own generation and Flann Sionna. See *The Irish Version of the Historia Britonum of Nennius,* ed. with trans. and notes, from *The Book of Leinster,* by Rev. James H. Todd, Dublin 1848.

MAG RAIDHIN, Augustine (sometimes Mac Gradoigh), b. Roscommon *c.* 1340, d. Clonmacnoise 1405. Spent many years as a Canon of St Augustine on Saints Island, Lough Ree. As a scribe he kept the *Annals of Clonmacnoise,* and brought them up to date from the year 1088, where his predecessor Tighernach had left off. After his death his own successor wrote of him in the *Annals,* 'the chief professor of good oratory of Western Europe.' Besides his work as a compiler and scribe he wrote other books, including a *Life of St John the Divine.*

MAGUIRE, Nicholas, b. Carlow 1460, d. Leighlin 1512, became Bishop of Leighlin 1490, where he compiled histories of the diocese and the Irish Church.

MAHONY, Cornelius (sometimes called Connor or Constantine Mahony), b. Co. Cork *c.* 1600, d. probably Portugal after 1660. Famous for his

MÁIRE

Disputatio Apologetica, Lisbon 1645. Above any single book, this Latin treatise on the rights and obligations of kings and the rights of their people against them, in an Irish context, illustrates the paradoxes of Irish religion and Irish nationalism. Broadly speaking, Mahony's thesis was that a heretical monarch had no divine right to the allegiance of an orthodox people, and that Ireland belonged to the Irish. No claim of religion or of nationalism obliged them to be subject to Charles II. By 1647 copies of the book were circulating in Ireland and reached the Catholic Confederacy's headquarters at Kilkenny. There, instead of being welcomed, its propositions struck horror into the hearts of men who although they were fighting the English king at intervals, were doing so 'for God, King and Country'. Or so they said. They saw the book as a threat to benefits which they held only because at one time or another the king had granted them to them. Accordingly they had the book burned by the public executioner and declared it a penal offence to possess a copy. Seen from either a Catholic or a nationalist standpoint this was both illogical and outrageous but from the standpoint of men who were already part of the Establishment, and simply wished to become the whole of it, deriving their authority from a king who himself would retain no authority over them, it was entirely logical. Every Irish revolution before and since has contained a similar element, on the one hand rebelling against the English crown's pretensions, and on the other beating down any attempt at a true revolution.

Disputatio Apologetica de Jure Regni Hiberniae pro Catholicis Hibernis Aversus Haereticos Anglos, Lisbon 1645.

MÁIRE, see Ó GRIANNA, Séamus.

MALACHY, St (Mael Meadóc Ua Morgair), b. Armagh 1095, d. Clairvaux 1148. Became a monk at Bangor where he was chosen abbot in 1121 or according to some accounts 1123. He became a leader of the reform party in the Irish Church, intent on developing the diocesan system and the authority of the bishops at the expense of the authority of the great monastic abbots who for centuries had dominated the Celtic Church. He was elected Bishop of Down and Connor in 1124-25 and soon after was nominated for the archbishopric of Armagh, against an usurping incumbent, a member of a family that held the see almost as of hereditary right. He gained possession from 1134-37 and then retired to his original bishopric. Still bent on strengthening the ties between the Irish Church and Rome he travelled to Rome 1139-40, visiting Bernard of Clairvaux on the way. His intention had been to obtain pallia for the Irish archbishops. He failed in this, but was himself appointed Papal Legate. In 1148 he set out for Italy again, this time with support of an Irish synod, but he got no further than Clairvaux where he died in St Bernard's arms. In 1190 he was canonised by Clement III.

His *Life* was written by St Bernard and he achieved a legendary fame during the Middle Ages, a fame which may explain the attribution to him of the *Prophecies of St Malachy.* They consist of 111 versions or mottoes, describing as many popes, reigning from the time of Malachy to the present day and some 15 years on. These prophecies first appeared in 1595, published at Venice by the Benedictine monk Arnold Wion, as *Lignum Vitae*. The prophecies up to 1595 are remarkably or perhaps unremarkably accurate. Those for later popes very often seem strikingly apt, each motto a kind of simple clue or hint at the nature of the papal reign, or at some key characteristic of the pope concerned. If the prophecies are to be trusted, the papacy will come to an end within the next 15 years or so. See Lord Bute, *Dublin Review*, October 1885, J. F. Kenney, *Sources for the Early History of Ireland*, vol. 1., 1929.

MALACHY (of Ireland), *fl.* 1310. A Franciscan, supposedly educated at Oxford and according to Father Luke Wadding said to have rebuked Edward II to his face in a sermon. He is the reputed author of *Libellus Septem Peccatorum Mortalium*, Paris 1518, a denunciation of the government of Ireland, insofar as early 14th-century Ireland could be said to have a government.

MAOLIOSA, see BENEDICT, An tAth.

MARBHÁN, b. Connacht *c.* 570, d. Connacht *c.* 630. Half-brother of Guaire the Hospitable, King of Connacht. Despite his partly royal birth he was a hermit, and one of his finest poems is an answer to his half-brother's astonishment at his preference for the woods, against the joys of a palace. See *King & Hermit: A Colloquy between King Guaire of Aidne and his Brother Marbhán. Being an Irish Poem of the 10th Century*, ed. and trans. Kuno Meyer, Dublin 1901. '10th century' in this title refers to the version of the poem treated by Kuno Meyer. Such a poem, first transmitted orally and then by generations of scribes, changed in details of language and grammatical structure with the centuries.

Marbhán played a part in the story *The Proceedings of the Great Bardic Assembly*, where he aids his half-brother against the poetic attacks of Seanchan Torpéist.

MARBHÁN, see Ó CIARGHUSA, Seán.

MARTYROLOGIES. These are calendars recording the names and commemorating the feast days of the Early Irish saints. There are four principal calendars: the 8th-century *Féilire Œngussa Céli Dé: The Martyrlogy of Œngus the Culdee*, (ed.) Whitley Stokes, 1905; the 8th-century *Martyrology of Tallaght*, (ed.) R. Best and H. Lawlor, 1931; the 12th-century *Féilire Huí Gormáin: The Martyrology of Gorman*, (ed.) Whitley Stokes, 1895; the 17th- century *Martyrology of Donegal*, (ed.) J. O'Donovan, Dublin 1864. V.H.

MAUDE, Caitlín, b. Ros Muc 1941, d. 1981. Ed. UCG. Teacher, actress and singer of traditional songs. She wrote one play, *An Lasair Choille*. Her poetry, highly regarded by critics, appeared in magazines, particularly *Comhar*, and anthologies. A collection of her poems, *Dánta*, Dublin 1984.

MEARTHÓG GHUILL, see MAC RUAIDHRÍ, Micheál.

MERRIMAN, Brian (Brian Mac Giolla Meidhre), b. Co. Clare *c.* 1747, d. Limerick 1805. His father is supposed to have been a small farmer and Brian was educated in a hedge school and by wandering poets. In 1770 he was a teacher in Feakle, in Co. Clare. A few years later he rented 20 acres in the neighbourhood and took up farming. He may have continued teaching at the same time because a tradition tells of his pupils helping to build dry-stone walls round his fields. He married about 1790 when already middle-aged and perhaps at the same time moved to Limerick City to become teacher of mathematics in a town school. His obituary in the *General Advertiser & Limerick Gazette* of 29th July 1805 read in part, 'Died on Saturday morning in Old Clare Street, after a few hours illness, Mr Bryan Merryman, teacher of mathematics, etc.' Nothing in this banal outline suggests that 'Irish literature in the Irish language may be said to have died with him.' Yet that was Frank O'Connor's opinion, who also compared Merriman to Burns, and to Merriman's advantage.

This reputation rests on one long poem, *Cúirt an Mheán Oíche (The Midnight Court).* O'Connor, the greatest translator of Merriman, claims that the poet and poem were much influenced by Burns and the Enlightenment, and although this is not the general opinion, which holds that Merriman came first, O'Connor's 'feel' for the poem demands a respectful hearing for his opinion.

The poem is an *aisling,* but a satirical *aisling,* which makes fun by implication of all the romantic *aislingí* which preceded it. The poem describes the poet falling asleep and being visited in a dream by a fairy woman, who takes him to the Midnight Court of Queen Aoibheal, queen of the fairies of North Munster. There he is made to answer for his failure to marry despite his middle-age, and a number of young women complain of the calculating habits of the local men, who will marry old hags for money, or stay single when beautiful girls are dying for the want of love. A girl also complains of the celibacy of the clergy when above most men they can afford to support a wife. The poet is about to be severely beaten by the assembled women in judgement for his faults when he wakes.

The poem's tone and style is earthy, humorous and colloquial and it would be possible to read it with pleasure and still miss the great poetic skill of the writing. From a folklore point of view (one which has been very little explored) the poem has immensely ancient roots. Socially, the poem is also of great interest and it has been used as evidence for a severely declining marriage rate caused by the general feeling of hopelessness at the economic and political conditions of the country. Certainly, any student of Irish marriage problems in the 19th and 20th centuries will recognise the characters and attitudes in the poem. At the same time it must be born in mind that when Merriman was writing, the population of Ireland was steeply and dangerously increasing; that there had already been famines caused in part by over-population and that 50 years later the population would be touching the ten or eleven million mark.

But none of these elements is the one which has made *The Midnight Court* the most controversial piece of Irish literature. No poem, no single work, has been so often banned, so hypocritically treated by authority, or regarded as so dangerous. The nearest parallels one can find, and they are pallid by comparison, are those attitudes of 19th-century English dons and schoolmasters toward Sappho and Catullus; an agonised wish that the poets had been worse poets (so that they could be ignored), or 'better' characters (so that they could be read without danger by the young). One has the impression, reading some of the anguished controversies over Merriman, that Irish authority could even have forgiven him writing about sex, if only he had not been so funny about it. Anyone who wishes to understand Ireland, the Irish Language Revival and present day Irish culture, could do no better than begin by studying *The Midnight Court* and its publishing history. See *Mediae Noctis Consilium (Cúirt an Mheadhóin Oidche), a heroic comic poem in Irish Gaelic*, Dublin 1897; *The Midnight Court literally translated from the original Gaelic*, by Michael C. O'Shea, Boston, privately printed, 1897; *The Midnight Court tr. from the Gaelic of B. Merriman & The Adventures of a Luckless Fellow tr. from the Gaelic of Denis MacNamara*, by Percy Arland Ussher, with a preface by W. B. Yeats and woodcuts by Frank W. Peers, London 1926; *The Midnight Court* trans. by Frank O'Connor, London and Dublin, 1945 (this edition published by Maurice Fridberg); *The Midnight Court* trans. by Lord Longford, introduction by Padraic Colum, *Poetry Ireland* No. 6, July 1949; *Cúirt an Mheadhón Oidhche* ed. by Riseárd Ó Foghludha, Dublin 1912, 2nd ed. 1949; *Cúirt an Mheadhon Oidhche* trans. by David Marcus, Dublin 1953 (privately printed at Dolmen Press for author); *Cúirt an Mheán Oíche*, ed. David William Greene for Cumann Merriman, Dublin 1968; *The Midnight Court* trans. by Cosslett Ó Cuinn, with drawings by John Verling, Cork 1982; and in Europe, *Cúirt an Mheadhóin Oidhghe: Ein Komisches Epos in Vulgäririschen Sprache. Mit Einleitung etc.*, von Ludw. Chr. Stern, Halle 1904. The Frank O'Connor translation is now most easily available in his anthology of Irish verse, *Kings, Lords, & Commons*, 1961, rep. Dublin 1970.

MEYER, Kuno, b. Hamburg 1858, d. Leipzig 1919. Studied at Edinburgh and Leipzig and in 1884 became lecturer in German at University College of Liverpool. His passionate interest in Celtic languages and literatures led him to found The School of Irish Learning in Dublin 1903, and in the following year the school's journal, *Eriú*. He also founded or helped found a number of Celtic reviews and journals in Germany, and in 1911 he was appointed Professor of Celtic at the University of Berlin. A very long list of his publications on Celtic subjects includes *The Voyage of Bran*, 1895; *Early Relations between Gael and Brython*, 1896; *Stories and Songs from Irish MSS*, I and II, 1899; *Four Old Irish Songs of Summer & Winter*, ed. and trans. 1903; *The Death Tales of the Ulster Heroes*, trans., Dublin

1906; *Fianaigeacht,* trans. Dublin 1910; *Selections from Ancient Irish Poetry,* 1911; rep. 1928. One of the central figures in the Irish Revival and perhaps the greatest of the band of European and English scholars who have devoted their working lives to Celtic Studies.

MHAC AN tSAOI, Máire (Máire MacEntee), b. Dublin 1922. Ed. UCD and Sorbonne. For her writing in English see Part I. Has won many prizes for Irish poetry, including the Oireachtas. Qualified as a barrister and then joined the Dept. of External Affairs, serving in Paris and Madrid. Visited the Congo during the UN intervention in Katanga. Worked on the preparation of the *English-Irish Dictionary.* Married to Conor Cruise O'Brien. Volumes of poetry include *Margadh na Saoire,* Dublin 1956; *A Heart Full of Thought* (translations from Irish), Dublin 1959; *Codladh an Ghaiscígh,* Dublin 1973; *An Galar Dubhach,* Dublin 1980.

MHAC CUMHAILL, Fionn (Magnus Mac Comhgnaill), b. Co. Donegal, brought up a native speaker. Taught Irish, travelled in America and worked as a cowpuncher, returned to work in Dublin as a clerk. Published a school text-book, *An Meadhon-Leabhar,* Dublin 1922; and several novels, *Tusa, a Mhaicín,* Derry 1922; *Sé Dia an Fear is Fearr,* Dublin 1928; *Na Rosa go Bráthach,* Dublin 1939; *Gleann na Coilleadh Uaignighe,* Dublin 1946; *Lascaire na gCiabh-Fholt Fionn,* Dublin 1955; *An Sean-Fhód,* Dublin 1969. He also published an autobiographical story, *Maicín,* Dublin 1946; and a further vol. of autobiography, *Gura Slán le m' Óige,* Dublin 1974.

MYLES NA GOPALEEN, see Ó NUALLÁIN, Brian.

N

NEILSON, William, b. Co. Down 1774, d. Co. Down 1821. Presbyterian minister and schoolmaster of liberal outlook, a friend of Catholics and keeper of a school in Dundalk which was open to pupils of every religion. As a student he had written an English grammar which became a text-book in Ulster schools. His *Greek Exercises in Syntax,* Dundalk 1804, went through 8 editions in 42 years. In 1808 he published *An Introduction to the Irish Language,* Dublin, 2nd ed. 1843. *Greek Idioms,* Dublin 1810; *Elementa Linguae Graecae,* Dublin 1820, followed. He became Professor of Hebrew in Belfast, and in 1821 he was elected to the Chair of Greek, Glasgow University.

NÍ CHÉILEACHAIR, Síle, b. Co. Cork 1926, school-teacher in Limerick until her marriage in 1953. Published *Bullaí Mhártain* (short stories) with her brother Donncha Ó. C., Dublin 1955.

NÍ CHONAILL, Eibhlín Dubh, b. *c.* 1748, d. *c.* 1800, daughter of

Domhnall Mór O'Connaill of Derrynane, grandfather of the Liberator. One of 22 children, she first married an O'Connor, who died within six months of the wedding. She then met Colonel Art O'Leary of the Irish Brigade, newly returned from Austrian service, and eloped with him against the wishes of her family. They lived near Macroom and being subject to the Penal Laws as Catholics, Col. O'Leary could not own a horse worth more than £5. He had a famous mare and a wealthy Protestant neighbour named Morris offered him £5 for it which in law he could not refuse. He challenged Morris to a duel and Morris had him outlawed. The O'Learys were besieged in their house, Eibhlín Dubh loading the guns for her husband. The soldiers were beaten off and the Colonel escaped, only to be betrayed by a peasant. He was ambushed and shot by soldiers in May 1773. His riderless, bloodstained mare came to Eibhlín Dubh at the house and brought her to where the Colonel lay dead, beside a furze bush, an old woman keening over his body. Eibhlín composed a lament for him, *Caoineadh Art Uí Laoghaire*, now considered one of the finest works in 'modern' Irish poetry.

In the lament she tells much of the story, but it has been held that she offers a more favourable version of her own conduct than she might have done. Frank O'Connor in the note to his translation in *Kings, Lords & Commons*, NY 1959, London 1961, Dublin 1970, points out that the lament contains a defensive note from the beginning and draws attention to the curious passage in which Art O'Leary's sister accuses the widow of sleeping while others 'wake' the dead man, an accusation which Eibhlín Dubh rejects with the excuse that it was not sleep but the crying of her children that took her from the wake.

She contrived to have the soldiers responsible for shooting her husband transported and Morris himself was later shot dead in Cork by Art O'Leary's brother. It is curious to think that this story took place in 1773, two years before Eibhlín's nephew, Daniel O'Connell the Liberator, was born, the man who more than any other Irishman was to bring an end to the last vestige of the Penal Laws with Catholic Emancipation.

Besides Frank O'Connor's translation, the poem is included in *The Last Colonel of the Irish Brigade*, by Mrs Morgan John O'Connell. There are editions by Seán Ó Cuív, Dublin 1923, with the spelling *Caoine Airt Uí Laoghaire*, and by Seán Ó Tuama, Dublin 1961, reprinted 1963, 1965 and 1968, with the same spelling.

NÍ DHOMHNAILL, Nuala, b. England 1952, brought up speaking Irish in Nenagh, Co. Tipperary. Lived in Turkey for several years. Now lives in Ireland. Collection of 68 poems, *An Dealg Droighin*, Cork 1981. *Féar Suithinseach*, Má Nuad 1984. Versions in English by Michael Hartnett in *Raven Introductions 3*, Dublin 1984.

NÍ GHRÁDA, Máiréad, b. Co. Clare 1899, d. Dublin 1971. Ed. UCD. School-teacher for some years, and later chief announcer for Radio Éireann. Became a publisher's editor in Dublin. Friend of Peig Sayers, and author of a number of text-books. Best known for the play *An Triail*, Dublin Theatre Festival 1964, English translation performed Dublin 1965. When first submitted to the Irish Life play competition, one of the adjudicators was so filled with horror at the brothel-scene that he 'hoped it would never be performed,' a small instance of one of the problems facing the writer in Irish. An earlier play *Giolla an tSolais*, 1954, won an Abbey Theatre award. *An Triail*, Dublin 1978.

NÍ LAOGHAIRE, Máire Buidhe, b. *c.* 1770, d. 1830. Her poetry is included in a number of anthologies. See *Filíocht Mháire Bhuidhe Ní Laoghaire* ed. An tAth. Donncha Ó Donnchú, Dublin 1931.

NÍ MHAOILEÓIN, Úna, sister of Bríd Bean Uí hEigeartaigh. Lives in London. *Le Grá Ó Úna*, Dublin 1958; *An Maith Leat Spaigiti*, Dublin 1965 (the account of travels in Italy). A journey to Tunis is described in *Turas go Túinis*, Dublin 1969. Works as illustrator and translator.

NÍ MHUIRÍOSA, (sometimes Mhuirgheasa), Máirín, b. Dublin 1906, d. Dublin 1983. Ed. UCD. Critic and scholar, best known for *Réamh Chonraitheoiri*, Dublin 1968, repub. 1978, biographical and historical notes on workers for the Language Revival in the early days of the movement, between 1876 and 1893. *Gaeil agus Breathaigh Anallód*, Dublin 1974, deals with links between Ireland and Wales. Oireachtas Prize. *Traidisiún Liteartha na nGael*, Dublin 1980 (with D. E. Williams).

O

Ó BEACHAIN, Breandán, see BEHAN, Brendan.

Ó BRIAIN, An tAth. Ceallach OFM, b. Limerick 1915. Ed. Limerick, Galway, Rome, where he received his DD. Provincial of Irish Franciscans 1960-66, reappointed for period 1966-72. Has travelled widely in Africa and N. and S. America. *Eitic*, Dublin 1953 (philosophy).

Ó BRIAIN, An tAth. Conn or Conchubhar, b. Ireland 1650, d. Caisleán Ó Liatháin 1720. Ed. Toulouse, received DD, returned to Ireland 1677, becoming parish priest of the village in which he died. He may have been born there, also. His poetry is to be found in *Fiche Duain*, ed. Shán Ó Cuiv, Dublin 1917; and more extensively in *Carn Tighearnaigh*, ed. Risteárd Ó Foghludha, Dublin 1938.

Ó BRIAIN, Liam, b. Dublin 1888, d. Dublin 1974. Ed. UCD and Germany. Joined Volunteers 1914; fought in Stephen's Green area in Easter Week Rising of 1916. Imprisoned later for two years. In 1917 named as Professor of Romance Languages, UCG. Stood for Mid-Armagh in 1918 election and was defeated by Unionist. Imprisoned in Belfast for organising Republican loan in Armagh. Released February 1920, and became 'a judge without a wig' on Galway Connemara circuit, i.e. an 'unofficial' judge recognised by Sinn Féin and the people, but not by the still sovereign British authorities. Rearrested and interned in November, released on signing of Treaty, December 1921. During this time he retained his professorship, holding it until 1958. In 1928 named Director and trustee of the Galway Gaelic theatre, the Taibhdhearc, becoming its president in 1931. His share in forming the cultural life of the Free State and of the later Irish Republic is difficult to overestimate. A member of the Censorship Appeal board for 15 years, 1953-68, member of original advisory committee of Radio Éireann, Chairman of Club Leabhar for 18 years, etc. His books include translations of La Rochefoucauld and of La Bruyère; of Elinor Butler's *Geography*, as *Geográif a don Ghaedheal Óg*, Dublin 1929, rep. and revised 1933 and 1935; and his recollections of 1916, *Cuimhní Cinn*, Dublin 1951, repub. Dublin 1974.

Other works are a large number of plays translated from French and English, for the Gaelic Theatre in Galway; Henri Ghéon's *La Parade du Pont au Diable* as *Geamaireacht Dhroichid an Diabhail*, 1932; Synge's *Deirdre of the Sorrows* as *Déirdre an Bhróin*, 1932; *The Singer* by Patrick Pearse (see Part I) as *An t-Amhránaidhe*, 1936, six years before its first professional production in English, at the Abbey; Ghéon's *Le Chat Botté* as *Cat na mBróg*, 1936; Molière's *Le Dépit Amoureux* as *Grádh Cásmhar*, 1937; *Coriolanus*, 1938 (an adaptation rather than a translation); *Nationale Six* by Jean-Jaques Bernard, as *Ar an mBóthar Mór*, 1943; *The Golden Apple* by Lady Gregory as *An tUbhall Óir;* and Diego Fabbri's *Procés à Jésu* as *An Chúis i naghaidh Íosa,* being a selection of them. The importance of this kind of work lies in its opening of windows onto European and English literature for the once-closed world of Gaelic. It is hard for the English-reading public, familiar with half a dozen literatures through innumerable translations, to realise the mental starvation of the Irish reader. This starvation as much as economic factors urges the monolingual Gaelic speaker to acquire English, and having done so to despise Irish.

O'BRIEN, Flann, see Ó NUALLÁIN, Brian.

O'BRIEN, Frank, b. New York 1935. Professor of English Literature, Hollins College, Virginia. Frequent visitor to Ireland. Has written *Filíocht Ghaeilge na Linne Seo*, Dublin 1968; *Duanaire Nua Fhilíochta*, Dublin 1969; and *An Piarsach Óg agus Conradh na Gaeilge*, Dublin 1975.

O'BRIEN, Paul (An tAth. Pol Ó Briain), b. Co. Meath *c*. 1750, d. Maynooth 1820. Great-nephew of Turlough Carolan, the harper, and great-grandson of another, lesser-known poet, William O'Brien of Clare. Paul's father was a well-to-do farmer in Co. Meath and Paul was entered for the priesthood about 1770. In 1802 he became Professor of Irish at Maynooth. He was active in the Gaelic Society of Dublin and wrote the introduction to the first volume of its proceedings, in Irish verse, Dublin 1808. The following year he published *A Practical Grammar of the Irish Language,* for his students at Maynooth. It is interesting for its illustration of the Meath dialect.

Ó BROIN, Leon, b. Dublin 1902. Secretary, Dept. of Posts and Telegraphs 1948-67. Member of Folklore Commission. Has written plays, short stories, biography and history. *Árus na nGábhadh agus Scéalta Eile,* Dublin 1923 (short stories); *Ag Strachadh leis an Saol agus Scéalta Eile,* Dublin 1929 (short stories); *An Rún agus Scéalta Eile,* Dublin 1933 (short stories); *Parnell,* Dublin 1937 (biography); *Emmet,* Dublin 1954 (biography); *Miss Crookshank agus Coirp Eile,* Dublin 1951 (on the bodies preserved in St Michan's church); *Comhcheilg sa Chaisleán,* Dublin 1963 (biography); *Na Sasanaigh agus Éirí Amach na Cásca,* Dublin 1967 (Easter Rising), are among his main publications. His plays include *Slán le Muirisg,* Dublin 1944; *An Boisgín Ceoil,* Dublin 1945, and *An Oíche úd i mBeithil,* Dublin 1949. He has also translated a number of books into Irish. *An Maidíneach,* Dublin 1971. For work in English see Part I.

Ó BRUADAIR, Dáibhidh, b.probably East Cork *c.* 1625, d.somewhere in Munster 1698. Born of well-to-do family, and well-educated in Irish, Latin and English, with a good knowledge of history, much of it drawn from his admired contemporary, Geoffrey Keating. His poetry and genealogical learning won him a reputation, but the wars, and the advancing destruction of the Gaelic nobility and culture, left little room for poets and genealogists to prosper, and by middle age he was reduced to earning his living as an itinerant farm labourer. He still received patronage and protection from Sir John FitzGerald, a Kerry landowner of the older stamp, and a Catholic, but in 1680 Sir John himself was brought to England as a prisoner on suspicion of a share in the infamous Titus Oates's so-called plot. Ó Bruadair wrote a poem assuring Sir John that King Charles II would be convinced of his loyalty when he saw him. A more perceptive, or less neccessitous, poet might have asked 'loyalty to what?' The poem, and the incident, help to illustrate the contorted situation of Ireland, in which a Gaelic poet could write of the 'loyalty' of an Irish-Norman, Catholic nobleman to an English Protestant king, and no one thought this to be strange praise. After the surrender of Limerick in 1691, Sir John, with thousands of others, followed an English Catholic king to France, leaving Ó Bruadair, and everyone else who had been foolish enough to believe in them, to the mercies of the Dutchman, William of Orange. Government agents watched and hounded Ó Bruadair, as they did every poet and learned man of the old culture, recognising that the true enemy was not the weakling James, or the featherless Wild Geese, but the men who kept the Gaelic world alive in their minds and hearts, and told the people that there was another, older, better world than that of Dublin and London; a world worth preserving even at the cost of a man's life. If the Williamites could kill the poets they could control the nation, and they knew it.

Even in these last years of misery Ó Bruadair had some protectors, John

Bourke of Cahirmoyle in Co. Limerick, and MacDonogh MacCarthy of Duhallow, Co. Cork among them. One hopes that when his time came he died in shelter in one of their houses. For his poetry see ITS's edition *Duanaire Dháibhidh Uí Bhruadair*, ed. and trans. by John C. MacErlean, 3 vols, 1910, 1913, 1917.

Ó BUACHALLA, Breandán, b.Cork 1936. MA Celtic Studies, QUB. Studied in Germany and America. Professor of Modern Irish UCD. Published catalogue of Irish MSS in Belfast Public Libraries 1962; *I mBéal Feirste Cois Cuain*, Dublin 1968 (on Irish Revival movements in Belfast 1760-1860. Won Butler Family Award); edited *Peadar Ó Doirnín: Amhráin*, Dublin 1969, including some controversial poems omitted from another edition of the poet's work. Co. editor of *Nua-Dhuanaire Cuid 1 and 2*, Dublin 1975; and ed. *Cathal Buí: Amhráin*, Dublin 1975.

Ó CADHAIN, Máirtín, b. Co. Galway 1907, d. Dublin 1970. Born and brought up in an Irish-speaking district, he became a school-teacher, and also a member of the IRA in the 1930s. His Republican activities cost him his teaching post and he spent a period as a labourer and freelance teacher, while continuing his work for the IRA. At the end of the '30s he was IRA recruiting officer and responsible for enrolling Brendan Behan among others. During the Second World War he spent five years in the Curragh internment camp, and used the time to teach Irish and other subjects to his fellow prisoners. In 1949 he became official translator on the Oireachtas staff and in 1956 became a lecturer in Modern Irish at TCD. He was elected Professor 1969 and Fellow 1970. He was also Guest Lecturer at QUB. From the beginning of his teaching career he collected material of folklore and language interest in the Irish-speaking districts of Galway and compiled a major vocabulary of the Galway dialect of Irish.

He was an authority on Irish literature and culture and contributed to the German Encyclopaedia of World Literature. He learned Scottish Gaelic, Welsh and Breton, and translated from all three into Irish. He also translated from English and French. He had a wide knowledge of European literature and read Russian, German, and Italian among his other languages.

Bás nó Beatha?, translated from the Welsh of Saunders Lewis, is an account of the Welsh language. This, with his genius as a teacher of Irish and his many other translations and services to the language, would make him a considerable figure in the history of the Irish Revival even if he had never written a creative work in Irish. But it is as a novelist and short-story writer that Ó Cadhain most deserves consideration. He is recognised not only as the greatest writer in Irish of his generation, and perhaps of the century, but also as a writer who deserves a place in the highest rank of contemporary European Literature. UNESCO chose his novel *Cré na Cille*, Dublin 1949, for translation into several major European languages, along with other masterpieces written in the world's lesser-known languages.

Unhappily this kind of critical acclaim, even when it is international, cannot be an entire substitute for a wide and deeply-rooted native reader-ship. Added to the problem that in Ireland readers of Irish are a minority in the population – a popular book in the Irish will number its sales in hundreds against thousands of an equivalently popular book in English published in Ireland – Ó Cadhain wrote a learned and idiosyncratic Irish which many readers even from his own district found taxing. Not all those who bought his books were capable of or willing to make the effort neces-sary to enjoy them. In Ó Cadhain's case the poignancy attached to all attempts to write for a very restricted readership reached the level of tragedy. And no one was better aware of this than Ó Cadhain himself. Where for example Pádraic Ó Conaire may well have hoped that the newly-established Free State would spread the use of Irish throughout the popu-lation, Ó Cadhain, 40 years later, knew that not only had this not happened, but that there was no rational prospect that it ever would happen. In 1962 he said, 'The truth is that Irish is no longer a living language. . . It is difficult to give of one's best in a medium that is likely to be dead before the writer.' Yet he did give of his best. His books include *Idir Shúgradh agus Dáiríre* (short stories), Dublin 1939; *An Braon Broghach*, Dublin 1948 (Club Leabhar selection|); *Cré na Cille*, 1949, the novel mentioned above, praised by many critics as the best book in Irish published since the Revival began; *Cois Caoláire* (short stories), Dublin 1953; *An tSraith ar Lár* (short stories with a novella), Dublin 1967, awarded the £2000 Butler Family Prize; and *An tSraith Dá Tógáil*, Dublin 1970, published a few weeks before his death.

Recent editions and reprints include, *An Braon Broghach*, 1968; *Cré na Cille*, 1970 and 1979; *Cois Caoláire*, 1971; *As an nGéibheann*, 1973 (letters to Tomás Bairéad from internment); *Idir Shúgradh agus Dáiríre*, 1975; *An tSraith Tógtha*, 1977; all Dublin. *Selected Poems*, Kildare 1984. He also wrote an invaluable essay on Irish literature, *Páipéir Bhána agus Páipéir Bhreaca*, Dublin 1969; and a novel *Athnuachan*, highly praised by critics who read it in MS, but which he refused to allow to be published, regarding it as unsatisfactory.

Ó CAITHNIA, Liam P., b. Co. Cork 1925. Ed. Cork and Dublin. Christian Brother and teacher; now a full-time writer. *Scéal na hIomána*, 1980; with Cardinal Tomás Ó Fiaich, *Art Mac Bionaid: Dánta*, 1980; *Micheál Ciosóg*, 1982; *Báirí Cos in Éirinn*, 1984; *Apalóga na bhFilí 1200-1650*, 1984; all pub. Dublin.

Ó CAOIMH, Eoghan, b. Co. Cork 1656, d. probably Doneraile 1726. His family were hereditary bards in the Cork area, and were also landowners of substance. He was well educated and wrote for a time in the old, formal *dán díreach* metre, later changing to the newer *amhrán* measure. He married in 1680, but after his wife's death in 1707, he took Holy Orders and became parish priest of Doneraile. His reputation stands more on his learning that his poetry. See *The Gael*, vol. XIX, 45, 1900, and *Catalogue of Irish MSS in the British Museum* prepared by S. H. O'Grady, completed by Robin Flower, pp. 527-8. Also 'An tAthair Eoghan Ó Caoimh; a Bheatha agus a

Shaothar,' *Gadelica I,* pp 1-9 and 101-11, 1912.

Ó CAOMHANAIGH, Seán (later added Mac Murchadha as middle name; pseud. Seán an Chóta or Seán a'Chóta, Sean the Coat), b. Co. Kerry 1885, d. Dublin 1946. Ed. Kerry and Dublin, emigrated to America for several years, returning to become a teacher in St Andrew's College, Dublin. Later employed by Dept of Education to collect words and phrases of the Kerry dialect of Irish, as part of a larger scheme to preserve all possible dialect variants from each Gaeltacht. Like many aspects of the government language policy this got no further than its beginnings, and Seán the Coat's manuscript volumes, up to a dozen of them, lie mouldering in the National Library. He also worked for some years on de Bhaldraithe's *Irish-English Dictionary.* His best-known published work is *Fánaí,* Dept of Education, Dublin 1927. He translated Aesop, as *Fabhail Sgéalta ó Aesop* in 3 vols, and also the stories of Maurice Le Blanc as *Sgéalta na hAráibe.* It is a thin legacy for a man who was a true original as well as a scholar. Many remember him with his wide-brimmed hat and the coat of his nickname, either travelling the valleys of Dingle with his donkey, or sitting outrageously improbable in a Dublin bar, and it is still possible that one of the organisations supposedly interested in Irish culture will find the money to print what he spent the best of his life collecting.

Ó CAROLAN, Turlough, see CAROLAN, Turlough.

Ó CASAIDE, Tomás, *fl.* 1750, b. probably in Roscommon, but possibly in Ulster in the first quarter of the century. Entered the Augustinian novitiate but was expelled, probably because of a love affair with a girl, Máire, to whom his love poem, 'Béal Átha hAmhnais', was written. He got himself to Europe and enlisted in the French Army, deserting shortly after. He travelled north to Hamburg, was taken prisoner by bandits, escaped again, and returned to Ireland as a travelling story-teller. *Eachtra an Bhráthair Ultaigh* (sometimes titled *Eachtra agus Imeacht an Athar Tomás a Caissidí)* is a prose and verse account of his adventures, unusual for being mainly in prose (see Micheál Coimín's entry), as well as interesting for its description of the life of an Irish adventurer in Europe. The MS was copied twice at least towards the end of Ó Casaide's life, one copy of 1773 being in the RIA, the other, of 1782, being in the British Museum. It was edited by Mairghréad Nic Philbín in *Na Caisidigh agus a gCuid Filidheachta* (with some of his poetry), Dublin 1938. She considers that he was the author of the still well-known song 'An Caisdeach Bán.'

Included in the book is some poetry by a kinsman of Tomás, Eamonn (or Eadhmon) Ó Caiside.

Ó CATHÁIN, Diarmaid, b. New Ross 1951. Ed. Dublin, Rome, as clerical student; subsequently UCC and Tübingen. *Eachtra sa Bhlascaod* (a children's story written first when the author was 14), Dublin 1975. *Caoimhín Abú* (school stories) won Oireachtas Prize in MS, 1973, pub. Dublin 1975.

Ó CATHÁIN, Liam, b. Co. Tipperary 1896, d. Co. Tipperary 1969.

School-teacher in Manchester for many years. President of Cumann na Múinteorí in 1959. Best known for a very successful trilogy of historical novels: *Ceart na Sua*, Dublin 1964; *Ceart na Bua*, Dublin 1968; and a third volume still to be published. The first two volumes were both Club Leabhar selections. Another novel is *Eibhlín a' Ghleanna*, Dublin 1954, and he has also written a play, *U.N.O. i bPollachliste*, Dublin 1962.

Ó CEALLAIGH, Seán (b.1872), see UA CEALLAIGH, Seán.

Ó CEALLAIGH, Seán, b. Co. Clare 1934; now a farmer, as well as a contributer to various Irish language magazines. Best known for his biography of Fr O'Growney, *Eoghan Ó Gramhnaigh*, Dublin 1968.

Ó CEALLAIGH, Seán T., b. Dublin 1882, d. Dublin 1966. Early and deeply involved in the struggle for independence, close associate of De Valera. President of Ireland 1945-59. Autobiography, *Seán T.*, vol. 1, ed. Proinsias Ó Conluain, Dublin 1963, dealing with life until 1916. Vol. 2, ed. Pádraig Ó Fiannachta, Dublin 1972, goes up to 1923.

Ó CEALLAIGH, An tAth. Tomás (Íbh Maine), b. Co. Sligo 1879, d. France 1924. Professor of Education, UCG. Translated and wrote several plays in the early 1900s. His best-known translation was *Caitlín Ní Uallacháin*, Dublin 1905, from the Yeats' play *Cathleen ni Houlihan*.

Ó CEARBHALLÁIN, Toirdhealbhac, see CAROLAN.

Ó CÉILEACHAIR, Donncha, b. Co. Cork 1918, d. 1960. School-teacher for 12 years and then engaged on preparation of *English-Irish Dictionary*. Has written a biography of Father Dinneen, the great Irish lexicographer, with Proinsias Ó Conluain, *An Duinníneach*, Dublin 1958. With his sister Síle, wrote *Bullaí Mhártain*, Dublin 1955. Other works include *Iognáid Loyola*, Dublin 1962; *Dialann Oilithrigh*, 1972.

His father, Domhnall Bán, published *Scéal mo Bheatha*, Dublin 1940 (an autobiography).

Ó CEILEACHAIR, Séamas, see Ó CÉILLEACHAIR, Séamas.

Ó CÉILLEACHAIR, Séamas, sometimes Ó Ceileachair, b. Co. Cork 1916. School-teacher in Co. Clare; highly praised as a poet. Has written nursery rhymes, *Hup Hup*, Dublin 1952; *Bláth an Bhaile*, Dublin 1952 (poetry); *Coillte an Cheoil*, Dublin 1955 (poetry); *An Graiméar Nua*, Dublin 1962, 8 subsequent editions, all sold out, (a text-book for schools), and has edited anthologies of poetry, *Nua-Fhilí (1942-52)*, Dublin 1956, rep. 1962, new ed. 1965, now a standard work on university courses; *Nua-Fhilí (1953-63)*, Dublin 1968; *Nua-Fhilí 3*, Dublin 1979.

Ó CÉIRIN, Cyril, b. 1934. Worked as navvy in England for 10 years, and as hard-rock miner in S. Africa. Freelance journalist in Irish and English in Ireland, taking BA in UCD. Now teaching in Limerick. Oireachtas prize winner 1977, for poetry. Trans. An tAth. Peadar Ó Laoire's *Mo Scéal Féin* as *My Story*, Cork 1970; has pub. criticism, *An tOilithreach Gaelach*, Cork

1973; and ed. anthology of Limerick poets (including own work) as *Breith*, Limerick 1974. In English, *Wild & Free*, Dublin 1978, with wife Kit, a guide to folklore recipes, etc.

Ó CIANÁIN, Tadhg, b. Co. Fermanagh *c.* 1575, d. possibly Rome, *c.* 1625. The family were hereditary chroniclers to the Maguires of Fermanagh and in something like this capacity Tadhg took part in the Flight of the Earls in 1607, when Hugh O'Neill, and his kinsman O'Donnell with 90 of their chief followers and allies, took ship from Ulster for the Continent and exile. Tadhg kept a detailed acount of the flight from Ulster and the journey to Rome, not on a high level of political reasons and plans, but a plain man's view of what actually happened each day, what they ate and did, how they felt, what the various towns they passed through were like, culminating with their arrival in Rome and the subsequent arrival there of the King of France. The book is unique and might repay reprinting. An edition with translation into English and notes was made from the original MS for the Record Society of Maynooth by P. Walsh, *The Flight of the Earls*, Dublin 1916.

Ó CIARGHUSA, Seán (Cloch Labhrais and Marbhán), b. Co. Waterford 1873, d.Dublin 1961. Editor of *An Sguab*, 1924-26. Has published plays, short stories, essays and novels, including *Onncail Seárlaí*, Dublin 1930; *Bun an Dá Abhann*, Dublin 1933 (both novels); *Cloch Labhrais*, Dublin 1943 (reminiscences); and *Gearrscoil*, Dublin 1960.

Ó CLÉIRIGH, Cúchoigríche, b. Co. Donegal *c.* 1590, d. Co. Mayo 1664. Son of the poet and biographer Lughaidh Ó C., and cousin of Micheál Ó Cléirigh, chief of the Four Masters. When Micheál returned to Ireland from Louvain about 1625 he asked Cúchoigríche to help him in his researches, gathering material for the *Acta Sanctorum Hiberniae* then being written at Louvain by Colgan and Ward. These researches turned up so much secular material, and this material was obviously so valuable and so in danger of being lost, that the Ó Cléirighs and their other helpers began assembling a factual chronicle that became the *Annals of the Kingdom of Ireland*, the *Annála Ríoghachta Éireann* (see Ó CLÉIRIGH, Micheál). In popular description these became known as the *Annals of the Four Masters* after the four chief historians engaged in the compilation. Cúchoigríche was one of them.

During the period of the work which stretched over the years 1625-36, he lost his landholding in Donegal and was forced to remove to Mayo, where he died, in the village of Ballycroy.

Ó CLÉIRIGH, Lughaidh, b. Donegal *c.* 1570, d. probably Donegal *c.* 1620. One of the participants in the Contention of the Bards of 1617-20. He wrote a life of Red Hugh O'Donnell in Irish prose which was edited by P. Walsh in *Archivium Hibernicum* VII, Dublin 1922. He was an uncle of Micheál Ó Cléirigh, chief of the Four Masters, and father of Cúchoigríche, another of the Masters. Other editions by Denis Murphy, Dublin 1893;

Ó CLÉIRIGH

and Paul Walsh, ITS 1940.

Ó CLÉIRIGH, Micheál, b. Co. Donegal 1575, d. Louvain *c.* 1645. As a young man was known as Tadhg, presumably his baptismal name, and as Tadhg an tSléibhe, or Tadhg of the Mountain. He became a Franciscan lay brother at Louvain, taking the name in religion of Michael, and gaining the by-name of Poor Brother Michael. He also gained a reputation as a scholar, particularly of Irish history, and when Ward and Colgan were preparing the *Acta Sanctorum Hiberniae* they chose Brother Michael to return to Ireland and gather MS materials. At least part of the reason for this choice, besides his own scholarship, was that he belonged by birth to a family of historians that had served the O'Donnells for more than 300 years. Accordingly he had many relatives and connections in the north with access to materials not easily available to a stranger.

Micheál returned to Ireland about 1627 and stayed there until 1642. During this time he and his assistants went far beyond the terms of their original mission. It might be said that at a moment when it was in danger of being lost for ever, Micheál Ó Cléirigh rescued the past of Ireland. He certainly collected the deeds of the saints he had been sent to find, but he also collected the materials for a factual history, which became *Annála Ríoghachta Éireann* (Annals of the Kingdom of Ireland), edited and translated many times. The most famous edition is that of John O'Donovan, *The Annals of the Four Masters,* 6 vols, Dublin 1848-57 (see Part 1). The title comes from the fact that Ó Cléirigh had three principal helpers, each like himself regarded as a master historian; his cousin Cúchoigcríche Ó Cléirigh, Fearfeasa Ó Maolchonaire and Cúchoigcríche Ó Duibhgeannain. These four were further assisted by members of their families, particularly the Ó Cléirigh and Ó Maolchonaire families, and in particular instances by many other scholars.

During their work they were supported by the Franciscans in Donegal and protected by Feargal Ó Gadhra (or Ferral O'Gara), Lord of Moy Gara and Coolavin, who in turn had strong connections with the ruling authorities, being himself a Member of Parliament. When the *Annals* were finished in 1636 the Four Masters dedicated their work to Feargal.

The *Annals* are mostly exactly that: a plain chronicle of facts and dates, of battles, coronations and deaths of kings, raids of pirates, foundations and destructions of abbeys and castles, marriages, treaties and quarrels of the great. But dry as this chronicle may be, it provided what never previously existed for the whole past of Ireland – a framework against which other, richer facts could be placed and seen in perspective, and against which the wealth of Irish legend could be measured, with a fair chance of discovering how much of the legend was based on fact, and what the real facts must have been like. And here and there in the work it comes alive with sudden startling flashes of anecdote and quotation. If this work of rescue had not been carried out in the brief lull between Kinsale and the Civil War and Cromwell, it could never have been done. MSS would have been burned, historians scattered, knowledge lost. All this happened, but the Four Masters had made their record and preserved it.

Micheál also prepared a descriptive king-list of all the kings of Ireland, *Réim Ríoghraidhe;* edited and copied the definitive version of the *Book of Invasions,* the *Leabhar Gabhála;* and a lexicon of difficult Gaelic words, the *Sanasán* or *Foclóir,* printed Louvain 1643, as one part of the Irish Franciscan attempt to establish a definitive Irish grammar, vocabulary and prosody. All this work was achieved during about 15 years and almost as a by-product of his original task which resulted in the *Martyrologium Sanctorum Hiberniae.* John O'Donovan translated this work for the Irish Archaeological and Celtic Society as *The Martyrology of Donegal,* ed. J. Henthorn Todd and William Reeves, Dublin 1864.

Ó COBHTHAIGH. A bardic family settled in Westmeath during the 15th and 16th centuries. Among the best-known members were Dermot, *fl.* 1550-70. His best work is a long lament of 150 verses for his wife and his kinsman Uaithne who were murdered together at Ballinlig in Westmeath in 1556. He also wrote some theological verse. MSS preserved in RIA.

Domhnall, son of An Clasach Ó C. He was a soldier as well as a poet and was killed in 1446 in battle together with both his sons on Croinis Island in Lough Ennell. His only surviving work is a poem of 168 verses, *Aire Riot A Mhic Mhurchadha,* urging the Leinstermen to resist the English.

Muircheartach, *fl.* 1580, a dependent of the Nugent family for whose members he wrote a number of laments. MSS in the RIA.

Tadhg, *fl.* 1550, best known for the praise poem to Manus O'Donnell, who gave the author a mare for each of its 20 verses. See *Dánta Grádha,* anthology of Irish love poetry of 16th and 17th centuries, collected and ed. by T. F. O'Rahilly, Dublin 1916, 2nd ed. enlarged and revised, Cork 1926.

Uaithne, murdered 1556 with the wife of his kinsman Dermot (see above), wrote a poem on the justice of God and another in praise of James Earl of Desmond.

Ó COILEÁIN, Seán, b. Co. Cork 1754, d. Co. Cork 1817. Except for Raftery, the last of the poets of the old tradition. Born in the year that Seán Clárach Mac Domhnaill died, he lived on until three years after Eoin Mac Éil was ordained in Maynooth, and Mac Éil is a man of the Revival. It was in the year of Ó Coileáin's death that William Carleton must have left Tyrone to find his fortune in the south, and although Carleton's parents spoke Irish, Carleton would write in English. It would never cross his mind that he might write in his father's language. It never crossed Ó Coileáin's mind that he should do anything else. But the tragedy of his dying world is in his life. Like many of his contemporaries he drank to drown himself, but whereas Aindrias Mac Craith was known as 'merry,' and Seán Ó Tuama was nick-named 'of the merriment,' Ó Coileáin seems to have found only bitterness at the bottom of his cups. He was a schoolmaster, which can be a bitter occupation for a man who has no liking for it, and first his habits drove his wife away from him, and then when he had taken up with her sister, he drove this second 'wife' into such a state of mind that she burned down the house.

Yet this man, who must have been very difficult to like, was known as the Silver Tongue of Munster. And he wrote at least two poems which are as good an epitaph as most men could wish. In a way one of them could be taken as an epitaph to the whole 1500 year tradition of Irish poetry, if we regard that tradition as ending with Ó Coileáin and Merriman and Raftery, and a new tradition beginning with the Gaelic League and the Revival.

The first of the two poems is *An Buachail Bán*, The Fair-haired Boy, and it is no more than another, though fine, Jacobite *aisling*, another vision of Ireland saved by the Prince across the water. The other poem is so great and so strange that it has been suggested that Ó Coileáin could not have written it: *Machtnamh an Duine Dhoilghíosaigh,*' the Meditation of the Sorrowful One. The poet is wandering by the sea-shore, full of the sorrow of life and its harsh destinies and changes, when he finds himself beside the ruins of an abbey and thinks of all the changes of fortune that its walls have seen. He wonders about its history and who built it. And here too critics have found reason to doubt that the poem is Ó Coileáin's. He would not have had to ask such questions. He knew the answers, being full of the history and culture of the district, and a schoolmaster as well. And Corkery points out that the metre of the poem is not all that a Gaelic scholar-poet would have made it. There are mistakes that one cannot imagine Ó Coileáin making.

Yet if he did not write it, who did? It is written in a metre that was already long obsolete. It is just conceivable that it was written a generation or two earlier and that Ó Coileáin merely found it and copied it. The poem is frequently compared to Gray's *Elegy in a Country Churchyard,* published in 1750, and it is possible that the Irish poem was deliberately modelled on the English one. There is a tradition of a priest reading Gray's poem to Ó Coileáin and challenging him to write a similar poem. Did this tradition apply originally to some earlier poet than Ó Coileáin, writing at a time when Gray's *Elegy* was first making a stir? It is possible. But the questions still remain – who was that earlier poet: how did his name become forgotten and why was his work attributed to Ó Coileáin?

All in all, it seems easier to believe that Ó Coileáin did in fact write the poem as an old man in 1815, who could say 'If death come to me, with relief a true welcome I'd give it.' It fits the man and the time. And could speak for all Gaelic poetry, that had begun with unknown poets in the dawn of the language, as the carts and the chariots rolled across the plains of Europe, and then with such men as Torna the Learned, fosterer of King Niall of the Hostages; and with Columba and King Aldfrith who wrote in Irish as Flann Fionn, and Flann who was 'the Virgil of the race of Scotia'; and that continued through the centuries. 'Woe, within your shelter now

Ó CONAILL

I find only heaps of earth and bones.' *'Och, ni fhionnaim anois fád'iadh/ Ach carnán criadhta cnámh!'*

Both language and people were tired from persecution, and the terrible shadow of the Famine might already be felt creeping towards them, only a generation away. *'Dá bhfóirfeadh orm an bás/ Badh dhearbh m'fháilte fá n-a chómhair!'*

The Irish text of the elegy is in *Irish Minstrelsy*, vol II, James Hardiman, Dublin 1831, English paraphrases were made by Thomas Furlong and by Samuel Ferguson.

O'COINEEN, Enda Padraig, b. Galway 1955. Ed. UCG. Travelled in US, Canada and the West Indies. Returned to Ireland across North Atlantic in 17-foot inflatable boat. Journalist. Travel book,*Kilcullen*, Dublin and Cork 1978.

Ó COISDEALBHA, Tomás Láidir, *fl.* 1660. Lived in Co. Roscommon. Remembered as the writer of the famous poem *Úna Bhán*, about the wife of Aodh Ó Ruairc. She was the poet's mistress according to another, anonymous poem *Féuch Féin an Obair-si a Aodh,* and a traditional story centred on Lough Cé tells of her death at her father's hand after she had proposed a toast to the poet. This story belongs to a far earlier period and Úna Bhán was substituted for the original heroine because of her local fame. See Marcus MacEnery's essay in *Eigse*, IV, Part II, RIA 1943.

Ó COISTEALBHA, Seán, b. Inverin 1930. Number of Oireachtas Prizes for poetry, and also gold medal as actor. Several plays published, including *Ortha na Seirce, An Tincéara Búi,* both 1967, and *Pionta Amháin Uisce,* 1978, also Dublin. Has translated many children's books into Irish.

Ó COLGAIN, Seán, see COLGAN, John.

Ó CONAILL, Feardorcha (Conall Cearnach), b. Connemara 1876, d. 1929. Worked on RIA *Dictionary,* and was lecturer in QUB. *A Grammar of Old Irish,* Belfast 1912. Ed. works of An tAth. Peadar Ó Laoghaire.

Ó CONAILL, Peadar, b. Co. Clare 1775, d. Co. Clare 1826, a schoolmaster and a tragic instance of the neglect of Gaelic learning at the beginning of the 19th century. He spent much of his life (some accounts say 40 years which would require an earlier birth date than the accepted one) gathering materials for a comprehensive Irish dictionary. He is said to have visited Wales, the Scottish Highlands and the Hebrides searching for rare words and variations.

When he died, his manuscript still unpublished, his nephew Anthony took it to Daniel O'Connell for patronage. The Liberator told him that his uncle had been a fool to spend his life on such useless labour. The MS was later sold in Tralee for a few shillings. Fortune preserved it from lighting fires or stuffing cracks in walls, and it is now in the British Museum. Thomas O'Rahilly (see Part 1) called Ó Conaill the finest Irish scholar of his time.

Ó CONAILL, Seán, b. Kerry *c.* 1675, d. *c.* 1725, perhaps as bishop. The Liberator O'Connell was descended from a brother or a cousin of Seán Ó C's. His *Tuireadh na hÉireann* (Dirge of Ireland) is a verse-history, and was edited by Douglas Hyde in *Lia Fáil II*, 1932.

Ó CONAIRE, Colm, see PEARSE, Patrick Henry.

Ó CONAIRE, Pádraic, b. Galway 1883, d. Dublin 1928. Ed. Rosmuc, and briefly in Blackrock College, before going to sea. He spent several years in the British civil service, where he began writing in Irish, winning Oireachtas Prize in 1904, with a short story *Páidín Mháire.* By the time he left the civil service in 1914 he already had a reputation as an important new figure in Irish writing. He had won another Oireachtas Prize in 1909 with his story *Neil* and had a number of stories and a play published.

From 1914 to his death he remained in Ireland, writing only in Irish against many temptations to make more money by writing in English. He loved children and wrote many stories for them, which at first glance seems curious in a writer whose adult stories contain the hard cruelty of reality. But children love reality and are willing to accept cruelty as part of life, which is why Grimm's Tales are better for children than Enid Blyton's.

Ó Conaire's style had been accused of a certain poverty in comparison to the richness of Ó Laoghaire, but a better word would be spareness. He wastes no adjectives and goes into no long descriptions. He carries the stamp of his period, naturally, but has worn much better than for example his highly praised English contemporary Thomas Burke, whose stories have the same hard centre but a much thicker sugar-coating. Burke felt that he needed to apologise to his readers for shocking them. Ó Conaire knew that he did not need to.

In English Ó Conaire reads with an entirely undeserved effect of false-simplicity that diminishes his chance of wide acceptance. This may be because English readers have been trained up on the long, heavy-textured novel, Austen and Dickens and Eliot and Trollope, and accept such a texture as the normality of literature. The story in which nothing inessential is included is foreign to them, which may explain why such writers as T. F. Powys, another contemporary of Ó Conaire and not unlike him in some respects, have been more admired than read in England. *Padraic Ó Conaire,* Swords 1982, is a translation of 15 of his best-known stories.

In Irish editions Ó Conaire's chief works are *Bairbre Ruadh* (a play), Dublin 1908, rep. 1929; *Deoraidheacht,* Dublin 1910 and 1916; *An Sgoláire Bocht,* a story written in 1904 but pub. Dublin 1913; *Tír na nIongantas,* Dublin 1913 and 1917; *An Cheád Chloch,* Dublin 1914; *An Crann Géagach* (essays), Dublin 1919; *Béal an Uaignis,* Dublin 1921; Síol Éabha, Dublin 1922; *Brian Óg* (a novel), Dublin 1926; *Beagnach Fíor,* Dublin 1927; *Fearfeasa Mac Feasa,* Dublin 1930; *M'Asal Beag Dubh,* Dublin 1944 (rep. several times). His *Seacht mBuaidh an Éiríghe Amach* (first pub. 1918) was a Club Leabhar selection for 1967. Recent editions and reprints include, *Beagnach Fíor,* 1954; *Scothscéalta,* 1956 and often since (a collection of stories); *Seacht nBua an Éirí Amach* (revised spelling), 1970; *Deoraíocht* (revised spelling), 1973; all pub. Dublin.

Ó CONAIRE, Pádraig Óg, b. Co. Galway 1893, d. 1971. One of Patrick Pearse's first pupils in Scoil Éanna. Joined IRB 1913. On Dáil Éireann translation staff 1931-58. News reader in Irish on Radio Éireann for many years. Stories, poems, translations and a successful novel, *Ceol na nGiolcach,* Dublin 1939 (Oireachtas Prize for 1938), rep. 1940, repub. Dublin 1960, rep. 1976. Other books include *Anam Páiste,* Dublin 1924; *Eán Cuideáin,* Dublin 1936, rep. Dublin 1970; *Fuine Gréine,* Dublin 1967 (Club Leabhar selection); *Déirc an Díomhaointis,* Dublin 1972.

Ó CONCHUGHAIR, Seán, b. Roscommon *c.* 1330, d. 1405. A Franciscan. Translated St Bernard's *Book of the Passion of Christ* into Irish.

Ó CONCHÚIR, Doncha, b. 1918. Ed. UCC. Teacher. Now Principal in Ballyferriter National School. Publications *Corca Dhuibhne,* Dublin 1973, an examination of life in the Dingle peninsula from the Neolithic Age to the 16th century; *Corca Dhuibhne,* its peoples, their buildings, a bilingual illustrated guide to the peninsula, Ballyferriter, 1977; and *An Saol Beo,* trans. of Part I-IV of *The Living Past* by Tim McGillicuddy. Active in local co-operative movement. Founder member and Vice-President of Kerry Archaeological and Historical Society.

Ó CONGHAILE, Caoimhín, b. Dublin 1912, d. 1979. His father was killed on Easter Monday 1916 in the assault on Dublin Castle. Spent his childhood holidays in Spiddal and West Cork, in Irish-speaking homes. Was a Schools Inspector. Won Oireachtas Prizes for music and poetry. *Dánta,* 1964; and *Báidíní Páipéir,* Dublin 1971.

Ó CONLUAIN, Proinsias, b. Benburb 1919. Civil servant, and on editorial staff of An Gúm, the government publishing house. Joined staff of Radio Éireann 1947, as scriptwriter. Has written on the Irish film industry, particularly *Scéal na Scannán,* Dublin 1953, a history of the film as art and as industry, with particular reference to Ireland. Ed. *Rotha Mór an tSaoil,* the life story of Micí Mac Gabhann, Dublin 1959; and edited *Seán T.,* vol. 1 of the life story of Seán T. Ó Ceallaigh up to his release from Reading Gaol after the 1916 Rising. This was published in Dublin 1963, and like all Ó Conluain's other books was a Club Leabhar selection. Has written, with Donncha Ó Céileachair, *An Duinníneach,* the life and times of An tAth. Pádraig Ó Duinnín, the lexiographer, Dublin 1976. Founder member of Cumann Cheol Tíre Éireann, the Folk Music Society of Ireland; frequent contributor to its publications.

O'CONNELL, Frederick (Conall Cearnach), b. Connemara 1876, d. Dublin 1925. Ed. TCD. Ordained Church of Ireland 1902. Rector of Achonry 1907, and later lecturer in Celtic Languages and Literature QUB. Had learned Irish in Connemara Gaeltacht as a child, and was much involved in Gaelic journalism. After the death of his wife he turned completely to journalism and writing, becoming Assistant Director of the newly formed Radio Éireann shortly before his death in a street accident in 1925. A linguist and scholar with immensely varied interests he published *A Grammar of Old Irish*, Belfast 1912; *An Irish Corpus Astronomiae*, London and Belfast 1915 (with R. M. Henry); translations of Keating's *Three Shafts of Death* and of *The Midnight Court; Guaire* (2 vols with notes and vocabularies); *Don Cíochoté* (ditto); and *Bricrim* (notes and vocabularies), all Dublin. He also published work in English and translations from Arabic and Persian.

O'CONNOR, Frank, pen-name of Michael O'Donovan, b. Cork 1903, d. Dublin 1966. For his life work in English see Part I. An Irish scholar, O'Connor's main contribution to Irish literature was in translating Irish poetry into English. Any reader without Irish who wishes to find the flavour of Irish verse, Old, Middle and Modern, can do no better than read O'Connor's *Kings, Lords, & Commons*, NY 1959, London 1961, Dublin 1970. Other translations include *The Wild Bird's Nest*, Dublin 1932; *Lords and Commons*, Dublin 1938; *The Little Monasteries*, Dublin 1963, rep. 1976. With Professor David Greene edited and translated *A Golden Treasury of Irish Poetry, A.D. 600–1200*, 1967.

Ó CORCORA, Donncha, see FIACHRA, An tAth.

Ó CORCRÁIN, Brian, *fl.* 1600, remembered for the romance *Eachtra Mhacadimh an Iolair* (The Adventures of Eagle-Boy), in which a king's son is stolen by an eagle as a small baby, and suffers innumerable adventures before regaining his heritage. Ó Corcráin was a bard, but the romance is in prose, with bardic verses inserted as lays spoken by the different characters at critical moments in the story. This type of mixed prose and verse story was popular at the time, and finds parallels in Scandinavian literature of a much earlier period. Ó Corcráin says in a preface to his work that his source was French. See *Dioghluim Dána*, L. McKenna SJ, Dublin 1938. Editions by R. A. S. MacAlister, *ITS* X, 1908; and E. W. Digby and J. H. Lloyd, *Adventures of Eagle-Boy*, Dublin 1912.

Ó CORRBUÍ, Máirtín, b. Co. Tipperary 1912. Has written 18 books in Irish, including *Cois Sionna*, 1957; *Ar Scáth a Chéile*, 1959; *Cé Mharaigh an Cúnta*, 1965; *Greim na Talún*, 1974; and *Saol na mBeach* (on bees), 1974. *Leacht na Laige*, 1983 (for children). Also, *An tÉan Cluanna*, 1985. All pub. Dublin. Winner of numerous Oireachtas Prizes. Has also written in English a history of the barony of Kerry.

Ó CREAG, Séamus, b. Co. Donegal 1861, d. 1934. Wrote *Modern Irish Grammar*, 1900, but is best remembered for two popular collections of Irish songs, *An Craoibhín Úr*, Derry 1920, rep. Dublin 1928; and *An Craoibhín Ceoil*, Dublin 1929. He himself arranged the music for many of the songs, as also in *An Ceoltóir*, Dublin 1903, Derry 1925.

Ó CRIOMHTHAIN, Tomás, b. Great Blasket 1856, d. Great Blasket 1937. Lived and reared 10 children on a stony small-holding inherited from his father, living a life of archaic simplicity that contrasted strongly and beautifully with a rich and complex language and culture. As foreign and mainland-Irish interest in the Irish language increased with the Revival movement of the late 19th century, scholars and students of Irish sought in the remotest corners of Ireland for the purest sources of the language, undefiled by English influence and if possible even by knowledge of English on the part of the Gaelic-speaking peasants. The purest district of all was discovered in the Blasket Islands off the Atlantic coast of Kerry. Robin Flower, the English scholar and translator of Irish, spent his summers there for years. Brian Ó Ceallaigh of Killarney spent a year there during the First World War, and among his peasant-teachers was the farmer-fisherman Ó Criomhthain. After Ó Ceallaigh left the island Ó Criomhthain sent him whenever possible a daily account of the island's doings. These journal-notes struck Ó Ceallaigh's literary fancy and he had them edited by An Seabhach and published as *Allagar na hInise*, Dublin 1928. He also urged Ó Criomhthain to write his own life story. This appeared in 1929 as *An tOileánach*, Dublin, and was swiftly recognised as a major event in modern Irish literature. Edited by An Seabhach, like the Island Diary, it reached its fourth edition in 1967, and the poet and critic Maire Mhac an tSaoi has called it 'one of the solid achievements of Irish literature.' In 1934 an English translation by Robin Flower was published in London as *The Islandman*, and sadly the translation has had little of the success of the original. This is in part the fault of the translator whose knowledge of Irish was better than his ability to render it in suitable English. The beauty of Ó Criomhthain's Irish is its spare and sinewy hardness, like the life it described. Robin Flower's English has little of this quality and the book has been neglected by English critics in favour of the much lusher, and in Irish inferior, *Twenty Years A-Growing* of O'Sullivan. But this kind of failure can be paralleled in the history of translations from every language. Towards the end of his life Ó Criomhthain dictated stories to Robin Flower, who wrote them down in Irish as *Seanchas ón Oileán Thiar*. They were published in Dublin in 1956, edited by Séamus Ó Duilearga. *An tOileánach*, new ed. 1973, and 1980; *Allagar na hInise*, new ed. 1977; both pub. Dublin.

Ó CUINN, Cosslett, b. Co. Antrim 1907. Ed. TCD. Gold Medal in Classics. Ordained Church of Ireland 1931. Canon of St Patrick's. Professor of Biblical Greek TCD. Retired 1971. Has translated from French and German into English, and made an abridged English version of *The Midnight Court* for recitation by actors (recorded by Mercier Press, Cork). Poetry in Irish: *Slánú an tSalachair*, Dublin 1978 (satiric poem in praise of dirt); and trans. the New Testament, *An Tiomna Nua*, Dublin 1970.

Ó CUÍV, Shán, b. Macroom 1875, d. 1955. Journalist on many Irish language papers. Editor of the *Freeman's Journal* and the *Evening Telegraph*,

1901-24. Wrote a large number of school text-books in Irish, plays, and stories, such as *Domhnall Donn agus Sgéilíní Eile*, Dublin 1929. Other works include his edition of *Caoine Airt Uí Laoghaire*, the Lament for Art O'Leary, Dublin 1908, rep. 1923.

Ó CURRAOIN, Seán, b. Connemara. Legal translator in Dáil. Poetry: *Soilse ar na Dumhchanna*, Dublin 1985. Short stories: *Tinte Sionnaigh*, Connemara 1985.

Ó DÁLAIGH. The greatest poetic family of Ireland, with branches in many parts of the country, particularly in Meath, Clare, Kerry and Cork, but also in Offaly and other places. Their fame extends over many centuries, from the 6th-century poet Dálach, pupil of St Colman, with notable members in each generation. The most famous are described separately under their own heading. Other members of the family deserving individual mention here are:

Aonghus Ruadh Mac Chearbhaill Buidhe, of Meath, *fl.* 1300-50. He served Rory O'Mulloy of Offaly.

Cearbhall, of Ossory, *fl.* 1590-1630, who wrote *Eibhlín a Rúin* in honour of Eibhlín Caomhánach, daughter of a nearby chief. They fell in love and eloped to the anger of her father. He is also remembered for the romance *Tochmarc Fhearbhlaidhe*, ed. Eoghan Ó Neachtain, Dublin 1911.

Diarmuid Mac Taidhg Mhic Diarmuda Óig, of Kerry, *fl.* 1620-80.

Gofraidh Fionn, of Cork, *b.c.* 1320, d. 1387. Attended the great feast of Uí Maine given by William O'Kelly for the bards and brehons and harpers of Ireland in 1351. One purpose of the feast was to celebrate the great recovery of Gaelic Ireland against the Normans, in retreat for much of the 14th century. Gofraidh Fionn listened to the boasting with an obviously cynical ear, writing afterwards that the poets of Ireland earn their bread by telling the Gaelic chiefs that they will defeat the foreigners, and prophesying to the foreigners that they will destroy the Gaelic chiefs. Nevertheless, in another poem he defended the art of poetry, and was himself one of the major Irish poets of the Norman-Irish period. Some of his poetry is still part of the oral tradition. See Eleanor Knott, *Filidh Eirionn go haointeach*, William Ó Ceallaig's Christmas Feast to the Poets of Ireland, A.D. 1351, *Eriu* V, Dublin 1911.

Lochlainn Óg, of Munster, *b.c.* 1550, *d.c.* 1616, famous for his poem lamenting the flight of the Gaelic chieftains and the out-lawry of the Catholic gentry, *Cáit ar Ghabhadar Gaoidhil* (Whither Have Gone the Gaels?).

Many poems by various Ó Dálaigh poets can be found in Fr McKenna's anthologies, *Dioghluim Dána*, Dublin 1938, and *Aithdioghluim Dána*, Dublin 1939. See also *Dánta Grádha* (Love Poems, 1350-1750), Tomás Ó Rathile, with English versions by Robin Flower, Cork 1926.

Ó DÁLAIGH, Aongus Fionn, also known as Aongus na Diadhachta, b. probably Meath *c.* 1520, d. 1570. Famous for his poem to the Blessed

Virgin, *Grian na Maighdean Máthair Dé* (The Sun of All Maidens is the Mother of God). His poetry occurs in many collections: Tadhg Gaedhealach Ó Suilleabháin, *Pious Miscellany,* ed. John O'Daly, Dublin 1858; *Fáilte Romhat a Rí na n-Aingeal,* ed. C. Ward, Dublin 1911; L. McKenna SJ, *Dioghluim Dána,* Dublin 1938, among others.

Ó DÁLAIGH, Aonghus Mac Daighre, b. probably Wicklow or Meath *c.* 1540, d. *c.* 1600. Poet to the O'Byrnes of Wicklow, and author of the great Irish war poem, *Dia Libh a Laochradh Ghaoidheal,* which Samuel Ferguson translated or paraphrased closely in his poem 'God be with the Irish Host.' The Irish text is in the *Leabhar Branach* (the Book of the O'Byrnes). See also *Songs of the Irish Rebels,* P. H. Pearse, Dublin 1918, for verses by Ó Dálaigh. The war poem has been edited several times: in James Hardiman *Irish Minstrelsy,* vol. II, Dublin 1831; by J. H. Lloyd, *Gaelic Journal IX,* 1889; and by T. Flannery in *Seacht Sárdhánta Gaedhilge,* Dublin 1908.

Ó DÁLAIGH, Aonghus Ruadh known also as Aonghus na nAor, or Angus of the Satires; b. perhaps Meath, *c.* 1550, d. Tipperary, murdered, 1617. Offers a most curious footnote to Irish poetry, having been a hired poetic agent for the English invaders, Carew and Mountjoy. They bribed him to travel about Ireland composing and reciting satires on the Gaelic chieftains who gave him hospitality; the purpose of the satires being to arouse enmity between chiefs and clans and so make the English conquest easier. This seems to be the first instance of the hallowed English technique of dividing by libel, of which later Irish history offers many examples and variants, notably Parnell and Casement. *The Tribes of Ireland: a Satire,* by Aenghus O'Daly, with poetical translation by the late James Clarence Mangan, together with an historical account of the family of O'Daly and an introduction to the history of satire in Ireland, by John O'Donovan, Dublin 1852.

Ó DÁLAIGH, Donnchadh Mór, b. probably Meath *c.* 1175, d. Co. Roscommon 1244. Brother of Muireadach Albanach, and the greatest Irish religious poet of the late Middle Ages which in *literary* terms in Ireland may be called the Early Modern period. By tradition he was Abbot of Boyle, where he died, but this may be a respectful legend arising from the vast esteem in which his poetry was held. He founded the branch of the family that settled in Clare so that apparently he married, even if he did indeed take orders later. His poetry passed swiftly into the popular repertoire, and some of it is still recited in the Gaeltacht, having been passed down by oral tradition through more than 20 generations.

Because of his great reputation many poems composed by later poets in his style were at one time ascribed to him. See Kuno Meyer, 'Anecdota from Irish MSS' XI, *Gaelic Journal V,* Dublin 1894; C. Ward, *Mil na mBeach,* Dublin 1911; L. McKenna SJ, *Dán Dé, the Poems of Donnchadh Mór O Dálaigh and the Religious Poems in the Dunaire of the Yellow Book of Lecan,* Dublin 1922.

Ó DÁLAIGH, Muireadach Albanach, b. Co. Meath *c.* 1180, d. Ireland, *c.*

ÓDÁLAIGH

1250. He became chief poet to the O'Donnells, but incurred the bitter enmity of Donal O'Donnell by killing one of his servants. He fled for protection to the Burkes of Clanricard, a Norman family then settled in Connacht for 30 years and already adopting Irish manners. O'Donnell ravaged their territory in pursuit of Muireadach and the Burkes passed him on to the O'Briens. He fled from that family to Limerick, and still pursued by the hatred of the O'Donnells escaped to Dublin. The O'Donnells pursued him even there and the Dubliners sent him to Scotland. The Clan Mac Muircadhaigh there is supposed to be descended from him.

From Scotland he appears to have gone on a pilgrimage to the Holy Land, perhaps in expiation of the murder that had begun his troubles. On his return he offered a praise-poem to his old enemy who accepted it and rewarded him with land and cattle. In his last years he entered a monastery, as his brother Donnchadh Mór may also have done.

His poetry must be looked for in a number of places, since it has not yet been collected in one volume. *Studies,* XIII, 1924, contains an article by O. G. Bergin which includes Muireadach's lament for his dead wife, one of his best pieces that occurs in the *Book of the Dean of Lismore,* and is noticed by the Four Masters. *Studies,* IX, 1920, and XIV, 1925, contain other materials discussed by O. G. Bergin. The praise-poem to Donal Mór O'Donnell and a companion piece are discussed by E. C. Quiggin, 'Prolegomena to the study of the later Irish Bards, 1200-1500', *Proceedings of the British Academy,* vol. V, Appendix A, 1913.

Measgra Dánta, ed. T. F. Ó Rathaille, Cork 1927, and L. McKenna SJ, *Aithdioghluim Dána,* Dublin 1939, deal with other of his poems.

Ó DÁLAIGH, Tadhg Camchosach ('Crooked Legs'), *fl.* 1375. Trained in a bardic school, he joined the Franciscans, and the account of his friends' efforts to dissuade him from leaving the school, and Ireland, and his own feelings about this, are in one of his best poems. Another poem celebrates the building of a hostel for learned men at Emania, by Niall Mór Ó Néill. See *Measgra Dánta,* ed. T. F. Ó Rathaille, Cork 1927.

O'DALY, Dominic (sometimes Daniel Daly), b. Co. Kerry 1595, d.Lisbon 1662. Almost certainly a member of the Kerry branch of the famous poetic family of Ó Dálaigh, and cousin to Diarmuid Mac Taidhg Mhic Diarmuda Óig. Whether by parental influence or personal choice, he turned from his Gaelic, bardic heritage (a choice symbolised by the now accepted spelling of his surname) and entered the Dominican Order in Galicia, taking the name in religion of Dominic de Rosario. He studied in Bordeaux, and returned briefly to Kerry before going to the new University of Louvain as a professor. Went on a mission for his Order to Philip IV in Madrid, and was instructed to create an Irish College of Dominicans in Lisbon, being appointed Rector of it in 1634. He established a convent of Irish Dominican nuns there in 1639, and when Portugal recovered its sovereignty in 1640 he became adviser to the Queen of Portugal.

During the previous two or three years he must have visited Ireland at

Ó DOIRNÍN

least once, because part of the bargain with Philip IV over the establishment of the convent was that O'Daly should recruit Irish troops in Limerick to serve in the Netherlands against the Dutch.

After 1642 O'Daly was sent by the King of Portugal on a mission to Charles I, who urged him to visit Ireland and help bring about a coalition of royalist factions against the parliamentarians. In turn O'Daly urged the king to grant civil and religious liberties to the Catholic Irish. He failed to extract guarantees and was diplomatically unable to visit Ireland on the king's behalf.

In 1656 he was Portuguese envoy to Louis XIV where again he was involved in negotiations with the English royalists, now exiled. The subject was once more the employment of Irish troops, and obtaining support for Prince Charles.

Returning to Portugal he was made Bishop-Elect of Coimbra, and President of the Privy Council of Portugal.

His history of the Geraldine family, *Initium, incrementa, et exitus familiae Geraldinorum Desmoniae Cornitum. . .* Lisbon 1655, was translated into French, Dunkirk 1697, by the Abbé Joubert, and into English as *The Geraldines, Earls of Desmond,* Dublin 1847, new ed. 1878, by the Rev. C. P. Meehan.

Ó DIREÁIN, Máirtín, b. Aran Islands 1910. Native Irish speaker, joined postal service in 1928. Also acted, 1928-37, in Gaelic Theatre in Galway, until transferring to Dublin. Employed in Postal Censorship 1939-45. Considered one of the best and most powerful of modern Irish poets. Two early volumes followed by *Rogha Dánta,* Dublin 1949; *O Mórna agus Dánta Eile,* Dublin 1957; *Ár Ré Dhearóil,* Dublin 1962 (winning the Arts Council triennial prize for the years 1962-64); *Cloch Choirnéil,* Dublin 1967 (sharing one of the Butler Family Prizes for 1967 with Eoghan Ó Tuairisc); as well as these collections of poetry, *Feamainn Bhealtaine,* Dublin 1961, a collection of autobiographical essays; *Crainn is Cairde,* Dublin 1970; *Ceacht an Éin,* Dublin 1980, *Dánta, 1939-79,* Dublin 1980; *Béasa an Túir,* Dublin 1984; and *Tacar Dánta/Selected Poems,* Newbridge 1984. Awarded Hon. D.Litt.NUI, 1977; and Ossian Prize for Poetry by FVS Foundation of Hamburg 1977. Selected same year by Irish Dept of Foreign Affairs to represent Ireland at Warsaw Autumn Poetry Festival. His brother Tomás is also a poet.

Ó DOIBHLIN, Breandán, b. Co. Tyrone 1931. Ed. Derry, Maynooth, Rome; DD. Professor of Modern Languages, Maynooth, 1958. Critic, novelist and poet. *Néal Maidne agus Tine Oíche,* Dublin 1964 (Oireachtas Prize and Club Leabhar selection). *Amhráin Dóchais,* Dublin 1970 (poetry); *Litríocht agus Léitheoireacht,* Dublin 1973 (literary criticism); *Íseáia,* Dublin 1975 (translation of *Isaiah);* and a novel, *An Branar gan Cur,* Dublin 1979.

Ó DOIRNÍN, Peadar, b. Co. Louth, *c.* 1704, d. Co. Louth 1768 (possibly

1769). A schoolmaster, he spent most of his time teaching in Louth and Armagh, although a tradition suggests that for a period he was in exile, for having taught Irish. A notorious local 'Tory-hunter' known as Johnston of the Fews, was his long-time enemy, and may have succeeded in driving him out of the district for a time. But he certainly returned, and died sitting at his desk in the schoolroom, the children thinking for a time that he had simply fallen asleep. A considerable body of his poetry survives; nature poems, political verses and humorous verses, some of them full-blooded in the 18th-century manner. This full-bloodedness still has the power to shock some Irish tastes, and when a bi-centenary volume was published in 1969 in Dublin, some of his poems were omitted. *Peadar Ó Doirnín*, ed. Seán de Rís, Dublin 1969; and *Peadar Ó Doirnín, Amhráin*, ed. Breandán Ó Buachalla, Dublin 1969. The latter volume includes the three poems omitted from the bi-centenary volume.

Ó DOMHNAILL, Maghnus, b. Donegal *c*. 1500, d. Donegal 1563. Became chief of the O'Donnells and married as his second wife Lady Eleanor FitzGerald, sister of the lately-executed 'Silken Thomas' FitzGerald. On her side the marriage seems to have been merely a means of gaining temporary protection for her nephew, the last of the Kildare FitzGeralds. When the boy was safe on the Continent she left Maghnus, and he, either in anger, or to protect himself against English suspicions, took the oath of fealty to the English crown. His own son then rebelled against him and Maghnus was imprisoned.

Like many of the Gaelic chieftains of his generation and the immediately succeeding one, Maghnus was as much Renaissance prince as clan chief. He wrote love poetry and satiric verse of considerable merit, and a *Life of St Colmcille* (Columba) which is much more than a devotional work. He dictated it to scribes in 1532, having caused his scholars to translate the Latin and Irish sources, principally Adamnan's *Vita Sancti Columbae*, into contemporary Irish. To these he added local oral traditions, still rich in Donegal and still richer then, it being St Colmcille's home territory, and the O'Donnells descended from the saint's close kindred.

The book's style is racy and full of humour and gives some indication of what Irish literature might have become it it had been allowed to develop naturally, and if the aristocratic influence had survived. One can imagine a 20th-century Maghnus writing an Irish *Gattopardo*.

See *Laoithe Cumainn*, Cork 1925; *Dánta Grádha*, collected by Tomás Ó Rathile and trans. by Robin Flower, for some of Maghnus's poetry, and *Beatha Colaim Chille*, ed. and trans. A. O. Kelleher and Gertrude Schoepperle, Chicago 1918.

Ó DOMHNAILL, Niall, b. Donegal 1908. Ed. UCD, civil servant, employed in An Gúm, and ed. *Fóclóir Gaeilge-Béarla*, 1978, consultant ed. Tomás de Bhaldraithe; *Ghearr-Fhoclóir Gaeilge-Béarla*, 1981. Director of Club Leabhar. *Bruighean Feille*, Dublin 1934; *Seanchas na Feínne*, 3 parts, Dublin 1942-43; *Forbairt na Gaeilge*, Dublin 1951 (an essay putting forward the argument that the attempt to revive Gaelic through the Gaeltacht, Irish-speaking areas has failed and that if the Revival is to come it must come from Dublin); *Na Glúnta Rosannacha,* Dublin 1952. Shortly afterwards the author changed the spelling of his name to Ó Donaill. Has translated Padraic Colum, Scott, Stevenson and other writers into Irish.

Ó DOMHNALLÁIN, Pádhraic, b. Co. Galway 1884, d. 1960. Translated Chekov and Mérimée into Irish. His best-known work is *Dréachta,* Dublin 1935, rep. 1956.

Ó DONAILL, Niall, see Ó DOMHNAILL, Niall.

Ó DONNCHADHA, Éamon, b. Co. Cork 1876, d. Cork 1953. Schoolteacher in Cork, in 1916 joined staff of UCC, lecturing in Modern Irish. Became a magistrate in the Sinn Féin courts during the War of Independence. Returned to UCC as Professor of Modern Irish. Wrote and translated a number of text-books in Irish grammar, elementary science and geometry.

Ó DONNCHADHA AN GHLEANNA, Séafradh, b. Co. Kerry 1620, d. Co. Kerry *c.* 1685. After the Cromwellian wars when poets and other hunted men flocked into the remaining Gaelic strongholds for protection Séafradh took many of them under his wing at Glenflesk. He himself wrote a courtly, traditional poetry in the old *dán díreach* metre, mostly on the usual themes of such poetry, laments, elegies, and formal verses in praise of his home valley, but he was capable of lighter and suppler verse, for instance a charming poem about one of his spaniels, killed while chasing a mouse. *Dánta Shéafraidh Uí Dhonnchadha an Ghleanna,* ed. Pádraig Ua Duinnín, Dublin 1902.

Ó DROIGHNEÁIN, Muiris, b. Co. Cork 1906, d. 1979. Ed. UCC, teacher in Belfast. As book reviewer and journalist in Irish on Irish language questions, argued forcefully for allowing and encouraging a natural development of Irish in line with English, and for the adoption of standard spelling and grammar based on usage. *Taighde i gComhair Stair Litridheachta na nua Ghaeidhilge ó 1882 Anuas,* Dublin 1936, rep. 1937. *An Sloinnteoir Gaeilge agus an tAinmneoir,* Belfast 1966. *Nua Gach Bia,* a dictionary of cookery, Dublin 1973.

Ó DROMA, Solomon, *fl.* 1400, transcribed, but perhaps did not translate, the Irish version of the *Aeneid* to be found in the *Book of Ballymote.* He was a pupil of the Mac Egans, the poetic family responsible for compiling the book. *The Irish Aeneid,* ed. and trans. George Calder, for ITS, 1907.

Ó DUÁIN, Odhrán, OFM, b. Co. Limerick 1927. Ed. UCG, Rome; ordained 1953. Teacher in Gormanston and Agricultural College, Multyfarnham. Writes as critic for *Inniu.* Books: *Froinsias, 1965,* a life of St Francis; *Meas na Filíochta, 1968; Rógaire Easpaig, 1975; Páis an Tiarna, 1976; Duilsé na Soiscéil, 1980;* and *An Eaglais Óg, 1980.* All pub. Dublin.

Ó DUBHAGÁIN, Seán Mór, *fl.* 1350, d. probably 1372. Chief poet to the

O'Kellys, and author of a vast topographical poem on the distribution of the clans and septs at the time of the Norman invasion. He completed the work for Ulster and Connacht and Meath. It was fully completed by Giolla-na-Naomh Ó Huidhrin in 1420.

John O'Daly, *The Kings of the Race of Eibhear*, Dublin 1847; *The Topographical Poems of John O'Dubhagain* and *Giolla-na-Naomh O'Huidhrin*, ed. from RIA MSS with trans. and notes etc. by John O'Donovan, Dublin 1862.

Ó DUBHDA, Peadar, b. Dundalk 1881, d. Dundalk 1971. Ed. Dundalk, leaving the National School at 12 to become messenger boy. Taught himself Irish and in 1899 helped form branch of Gaelic League in Dundalk. Improved his spoken Irish during Gaeltacht holidays, and collected songs and traditional stories. Wrote music for Oireachtas competition and won awards. Applying for a certificate to teach Irish, he was examined by Patrick Pearse, who gave him a temporary certificate of competence in 1914. Active in politics before and during the Rising he spent much of the latter half of his life translating the Douai Bible into Irish. He also spent much effort in arguments with the hierarchy about the use of Irish in churches, most particularly in Gaeltacht parishes. He believed that the Church's indifference was the most powerful influence against the Revival.

His illuminated MS of the Irish Bible was completed in 1953 and its 3000 pages are in the National Library.

Ó DUBHGHAILL, Séamas (Beirt Fhear), b. Co. Kerry 1855, d. 1929. Spent over 40 years in excise service in England, Ireland and Scotland. He was a life-long friend of David Comyn and published extracts from their correspondence about the development of the Language Movement. *Beirt Fhear ó'n dTuaith* (Two Men from the Country), pub. in Irish and English with notes, for Gaelic League, Dublin 1903. His *Tadhg Gabha* was a prize winning story at the Oireachtas, 1900; *Cainnt na Cathrach* won First Prize at the 1910 Oireachtas. *Beartín Luachra*, Dublin 1927.

Ó DUIBHGEANNÁIN, Maghnus, b. *c.* 1350, d. *c.* 1425, chief compiler of the *Book of Ballymote*. The MS is in the RIA and was published by it with an introduction and notes by Robert Atkinson, Dublin 1887.

Ó DUIBHGINN, Seosamh, b. Co. Armagh 1914. Imprisoned in Belfast 1934 for Republican activities. Irish journalist. Has published an autobiography about the struggle for existence in Belfast during the war years of the 1940s, *Ag Scaoileadh Sceoil*, Dublin 1962, Club Leabhar selection. *Séamas Mac Giolla Choille* (on the poet), Dublin 1972. Edited *An Muircheartach*, Dublin 1970, an unusually luxurious publication for Irish language books, containing large selection of photographs taken in Gaeltacht areas by Tomás Ó Muircheartaigh, a former Uachtarán of Conradh na Gaeilge. More recently, *Tuairisc*, 1982.

Ó DUIBHIR, An tAth. Antoine, parish priest of Cobh, d. 1946. Wrote a biography of O'Connell that became a Club Leabhar selection when published after his death. *Dómhnall Ó Conaill,* Dublin 1949.

Ó DUILEARGA, Séamas, see DELARGY, James Hamilton.

Ó DUINNÍN, An tAth. Pádraig, b. Co. Kerry 1860, d. Dublin 1934. One of the greatest names in the Language Movement and one of the great characters of Dublin. Every user of the National Library in the '20s and early '30s remembers the gentle, shabby old man chewing apples and raw carrots with a pile of books around him like a rampart.

The National School he went to was built of bricks taken from the demolished walls of Eoghan Ruadh Ó Suilleabháin's house, and as a young Jesuit novice he was taught by Gerard Manley Hopkins. After several years teaching in Jesuit colleges in Limerick and Dublin and a year in retreat in Belgium, he decided in 1900 to leave the Order. He joined the Gaelic League where he became friends with the Secretary, Patrick Pearse, and devoted much of his time to editing Irish MSS. This work, with plays, poems, stories and above all his *Irish-English Dictionary,* occupied the rest of his life. He collapsed on the steps of the National Library on his way home one day, dying a few days later.

Cormac Ó Conaill (an historical novel), Dublin 1901, 2nd ed. with glossary and English synopsis, Dublin 1902, new ed. Dublin 1952. His plays include *Creideamh agus Gorta* (an historical play about the Famine), Dublin 1901; *An Tobar Draíochta,* Dublin 1902, 2nd ed. 1904; *Gírle Guairle,* Dublin 1904; *Comhairle Fithil,* Dublin 1909, translated into English as *Fitheal's Counsels,* Dublin 1909; *Teactaire Ó Dhia* (or a Messenger from God, another play about the Famine), Dublin 1922.

His editions of Irish poets include *Aogáin Ó Rathaille; Eoghan Rua Ó Súilleabháin; Seán Clárach Mac Domhnaill; Séafraidh Ó Donnchadha an Ghleanna; Tadhg Gaelach Ó Súilleabháin;* and *Piaras Feiritéir;* he also edited MS of Keating's *Foras Feasa at Éirinn,* among many other works.

His great monument however is the *Irish-English Dictionary,* pub. for ITS, Dublin 1904; revised and enlarged edition 1927, 3rd edition still further enlarged 1934. He had brought out a schools edition, 1910, and *A Concise English-Irish Dictionary,* Dublin 1912, also for schools.

Ó DUNAIGHE, Seán, b. 1882. *Plúr na Gaeilge,* Dublin 1923; *Inghean an Ghearaltaigh,* Dublin 1926; *An Crann Cuilinn,* Dublin 1933.

Ó DÚNN (sometimes UA DUIND), Giolla-na-Naomh, b. Dooregan 1102, d. Lough Ree 1160. Chief poet of Leinster. Some of his poetry appears in the *Book of Ballymote.* His chief extant works concern the descent of certain tribes from Milesius, the tombs of the Kings of Leinster, and the King-list of Connacht.

ŒNGUS THE CULDEE, *fl.* 800-50, author of the *Féilire,* a calendar of saints and festivals, with a verse for every day in the year. These verses provide the most extensive collection of Old Irish poetry that survives. The

Saltair na Rann, a collection of poems about incidents in biblical history, once ascribed to Œngus, is no longer considered to be his.

Œngus's after-name 'the Culdee', properly Céile Dé, means 'Vassal of God' and was applied both to hermits and to scribes, it being clear that most hermits were assumed to act as scribes in their solitude. Most Culdees were learned men and formed a loose association that in later centuries assumed the characteristics of an Order under the rule of abbots. By Œngus's time religious reforms in Ireland were drawing the Culdees into actual monasteries.

Culdees spread from Ireland to Northumbria, Scotland and traditionally as far as Iceland, where they were exterminated by the first Norse settlers.

Ó FAOLÁIN, Éamon. Assistant Editor of Debates, Dáil Éireann, until 1977. Translated President Kennedy's speech to the Oireachtas into Irish. Has written plays, short stories, and other works. *An Bráithreachas Dubh,* Dublin 1952; *Sirriam Phecos,* Dublin 1952; and *An Lann Tolédo,* Dublin 1957; all praised by critics.

Ó FARACHÁIN, Roibeárd (orig: Riobárd; in English Farren, Robert), b. Dublin 1909. d. Dublin 1984. Controller of programmes Radio Éireann 1947-74. Poet and short-story writer. Short stories in Irish, *Fíon gan Mhoirt,* Dublin 1938. For writing in English see Part I under Ó FARACHÁIN.

Ó FIAICH, An tAth. Tomás, b. Co. Armagh 1923. Ed. Maynooth, UCD. Ordained 1948. Postgraduate studies in Louvain. Became Professor of History Maynooth. Leading figure in Language Revival movement. Consecrated Archbishop of Armagh and Primate of All Ireland, 1977. Created Cardinal 1979. *Gaelscrinte i gCéin* (Irish missionary saints in Europe), Dublin 1961; *Má Nuad,* Maynooth 1972; *Art Mac Cumhaigh: Dánta,* Dublin 1973; *Oliver Plunkett: Ireland's New Saint,* Dublin 1975; *Oilibhéar Pluincéid,* Dublin 1976; *Ard MacBionaid: Dánta,* Dublin 1980 (with Liam Ó Caithnia); *Saint Oliver of Armagh,* Dublin 1981. Irish American Cultural Institute Award 1980, for his work on translating Bible into Irish.

Ó FIANNACHTA, An tAth. Pádraig, b. Co. Kerry 1927. Ordained 1953, curate in Wales until 1959. Now Professor of Welsh and Old Irish in Maynooth. *An Chomharsa Choimhthíoch,* Dublin 1957. *De Valera,* vol. I, with T. P. Ó Néill, Dublin 1968. Vol. II, 1970. Trans. Bible into Irish, Dublin 1966-78, and the Missal, Dublin 1973. Travel: *Ó Chorr na Móna go Bangalore,* Dublin 1976, etc. Poetry: *Rúin,* Maynooth 1972, *Donn Bó,* Maynooth 1976. *Spaisteoireacht,* Maynooth, 1980, with Pádraig Mac Suibhne. Joint ed. RIA *Dictionary of the Irish Language,* Dublin completed 1979; ed. *Táin Bó Cuailnge,* Dublin 1966, and *Léachtaí Cholm Cille XI, – an Dúlra sa Litríocht,* Dublin 1980. *Ón bhFuacht go dté an Teas,* Maynooth 1982; *Ag Siúl na Teorann,* Má Nuad 1984.

O'FLAHERTY, Liam, b. Aran Islands 1897, d. Dublin 1984. For his work in English see Part I. His short stories in Irish, *Dúil*, Dublin 1953, are partly translations from stories already published in English, but with some differences. Repub. Dublin 1979.

O'FLAHERTY, Roderick, b. Co. Galway 1629, d. Co. Galway 1718. His father died when he was two, and he inherited Moycullen Castle and estate. He lost these by confiscation during the Cromwellian invasion and spent much of his life in attempts to recover them by law suits, without success. What he did recover was almost valueless and he spent his old age in deepening poverty.

As a boy he had studied under Dubhaltach Mac Firbisigh, author of the great *Genealogies of the Families of Ireland,* and other historical works, and he could thus draw directly on Irish tradition when he prepared his own Latin history of Ireland, the *Ogygia; or, a Chronological Account of Irish Events collected from Very Ancient Documents faithfully compared with each other & supported by the Genealogical & Chronological Aid of the Sacred and Profane Writings of the Globe.* This was published in Latin, in London, 1685, and was the first history of Ireland to reach the English public, or that section of it that could read Latin. The origins of the book appear to lie in a correspondence between O'Flaherty and John Lynch, Archdeacon of Tuam and son of one of O'Flaherty's tutors. The *Ogygia* was translated into English by the Rev. James Hely, Dublin 1793, in 2 vols.

O'Flaherty also wrote a description of West Connacht, edited for the Irish Archaeological Society by James Hardiman, Dublin 1846.

Ó FLOINN, Críostóir, b. Limerick 1927. Teacher and journalist in Ireland, and worked in England at a variety of jobs. Has written a number of historical and adventure novels for young people and many children's books. Plays include: *Cóta Bán Chríost* (Taibhdhearc Award 1966), 1967; *Is é Dúirt Polonius,* 1967; *Aggiornamento,* 1969; *Mise Raifteirí an File,* 1974; *Solas an tSaoil,* and *Mair, a Chapaill,* 1980. Novel: *Oineachlann,* 1968. Poetry: *Éirí Amach na Cásca 1916,* 1967; *Aisling Dhá Abhann,* 1977; all pub. Dublin. For work in English see Part 1.

Ó FLOINN, Tomás, b. Co. Waterford 1910. Teacher. Entered Department of Education and became Assistant Secretary. Has translated Old Irish poetry and stories into modern Irish versions. *AthBheo,* 1955; *Scéalaíocht na Ríthe,* with Proinsias Mac Cana, 1956; *AthDhánta,* 1969; *Toghail na Téibe,* 1984; all pub. Dublin.

Ó FOGHLUDHA, Risteárd (sometimes Riseárd; pseud. Fiachra Éilgeach), b. Youghal 1873, d. 1957. Teacher, and later journalist in England. Returned to Ireland, and became editor of An Gúm, the government publishing house. First Director of Place Names Commission set up in 1946. A native Irish speaker, and a devoted scholar and editor of Irish poetry, and of Irish place names. His published work spans a period of almost 50 years, including editions of Merriman. *Cúirt an Mheadhan Oidche,* Dublin

Ó GADHRA

1912, rep. 1949; *Eoghan Rua Ó Súilleabháin*, Dublin 1937; Éamonn de Bhfál, Dublin 1946; Éigse na Máighe, Dublin 1952; and the great Dictionary of Irish Place Names containing 7000 entries, *Log-Ainmneacha*, Dublin 1935. Besides these he wrote biographies, translated from French and from Russian, in particular Tolstoy and Chekov.

Ó GADHRA, Nollaig, b. Co. Limerick 1943. Ed. UCC, Harvard and Salzburg. Journalist and broadcaster. *Gandhi,* Dublin 1969; *John Boyle O'Reilly agus an Glór Gael-Mheiriceánach,* Dublin 1976, a study of the IRB conspirator who escaped from Australian penal settlement and became editor of the *Boston Pilot.* Oireachtas Prize 1975. *Éamann Iognáid Rís,* Dublin 1977, a life of the founder of Irish Christian Brothers. *Richard J. Daley – Méara Chicago,* Dublin 1979; won Oireachtas Prize in MS, 1977. *Guth an Phobail,* Dublin 1984.

Ó GADHRA, Seán Óg, b. *c.* 1680, d. 1720. One of the last of the 'Learned poets,' writing in the *dán díreach* metre at a period when this was already archaic. *Dánta is Amhráin Sheáin Uí Ghadhra,* ed. An tAth. Mac Domhnaill, Dublin 1955.

Ó GALLAGHER, James, see Ó GALLCHOBHAIR, Séamus.

Ó GALLCHOBHAIR, Séamus (James O'Gallagher), b. Ulster 1681, d. Kilkenny 1751, Catholic Bishop of Raphoe 1725-37, and of Ossory 1737-51. For a part of his life as bishop he was on the run from the authorities, hiding on islands in Lough Erne. There, and in his dioceses, he composed and preached sermons in rich and distinguished Irish, on subjects that appealed to his peasant listeners. The sermons were immensely popular and were first printed in Dublin in 1737. A large number of editions and translations into English followed. Principal editions are *Sermons in Irish-Gaelic,* with literal idiomatic translations on opposite pages, and Irish-Gaelic vocabulary, Dublin 1877; *The Sermons of the Right Reverend Dr. Gallagher, trans. from the original Irish by James Byrne, revised and corrected by a Catholic Priest,* Dublin 1807, 1819, 1835; *Seacht Seanmóir Déag* (17 sermons), Dublin 1911.

Ó GALLCHOBHAIR, An tAth. Tomás, b. Co. Cork, 1894. Ed. Maynooth; Professor at Fermoy College 1920-34, parish priest of Ballymacoda near Youghal. Translator of T.C. Murray's plays and *Schuster's Bible History.*

Ó GAOITHÍN, Micheál (An File), b. Blasket Islands 1904, d. 1974. Poet, son of Peig Sayers. *Is Truagh ná Fanann an Óige,* Dublin 1953; *Coinnle Corra* (poems), Dublin 1968, and *Beatha Pheig Sayers,* Dublin 1970.

Ó GAORA, Colm (An Gruadach Bán), b. Galway, 1887, d. 1954. Teacher, political prisoner. Collected Irish folk songs in Connacht: *Sídheog na Rann,* Dublin 1911. *Obair is Luadhainn nó Saoghal sa nGaedhealtacht,* Dublin 1937; and *Mise,* Dublin 1943, new ed. 1969, books of reminiscence.

Ó GEALACHÁIN, Peadar, b. Co. Meath *c.* 1800, d. *c.* 1860. A hedge

348

Ó GORMÁIN

schoolmaster, he agreed to work as an Irish teacher for the Irish Bible Society, one of the many Catholics seduced into apostasy about this period by the promise of employment (Carleton was another). He was denounced for his apostasy by his parish priest, but his easier circumstances allowed him to copy a number of manuscripts that might otherwise have been lost. He preserved the poetry of Seamus Dall Mac Cuarta in this way, see Joseph H. Lloyd, *Duanaire na Mídhe,* Dublin 1914.

Ó GLACAN, Niall, b. Donegal *c.* 1590, d. Bologna 1655. Trained in medicine in the old Gaelic tradition, which combined the disciplines of surgeon, apothecary and physician in the style of Galen. Was in France in 1628, treating cases of the plague in the area Clermont-Toulouse. He wrote a *Tractatus de Peste,* Toulouse 1629, which is simply a formal medical description of the plague without literary interest. He became physician to the King of France and Professor of Medicine in Toulouse University. In 1646 removed to Bologna, also as Professor, and there published *Cursus Medicus* 1646-55, a study of the system of Galen unvitiated by later medical practice.

Ó GLAISNE, Risteárd, b. Cork 1927. Ed. TCD. Secondary school-teacher. Biographies: *Ian Paisley agus Tuaisceart Éireann,* Dublin 1971; *Conor Cruise O'Brien agus an Liobrálachas,* Dublin 1974. Travel: *Raon mo shiúil,* Dublin 1972; *Cuairt Ghearr,* Dublin 1975; *Cad a deir tú leis na hAlbanaigh,* Galway 1978. Also, *Bun-Ghaeilge; a concise guide to Irish,* Dublin 1962; *Saoirse na mBan,* Dublin 1973; and *Ceannródaithe,* Dublin 1974 (first of a series of essays on modern Irish writers) and *Raidio na Gael tachta,* 1982.

Ó GNÍMH, Fearflatha, b. Ulster *c.* 1540, d. Ulster 1640. He was bard to the O'Neills of Clandeboye, and as a young man or possibly as a boy, he accompanied Shane the Proud on his journey to treat with Elizabeth in London in 1562. He is credited with rousing the O'Neills by his poetry to a sense of their role as leaders of the North against the English. His two most famous poems are *Mo Thruaigh Mar Táid Gaoidhil* and *Beannacht ar Anmain Éireann.* The former was printed in the *Irish Magazine & Monthly Asylum for Neglected Biography,* III, Dublin 1810, and in James Hardiman, *Irish Minstrelsy,* vol. 11, Dublin 1831; see also *Measgra Dánta,* Cork 1927, and issues of *Studies,* VIII, IX, XIV, XV, between 1919-26, containing articles on early Irish poetry by O. J. Bergin; and L. McKenna SJ, *Dioghluim Dána,* Dublin 1938.

Ó GÓILIDHE, Caoimhghín, b. Dublin 1913. Teacher and journalist; has written text-books in Irish and edited several anthologies. *Dánta,* Macroom 1938; *De Bharr na gCnoc,* Dublin 1954.

Ó GORMÁIN, Mael Muire, b. probably Louth *c.* 1110, d. Louth 1181. Abbot of Cnoc na nApstol near Louth; author of a Martyrology in verse, edited by Whitley Stokes as the *Félire Húi Gormáin – the Martyrology of Gorman,* 1895.

Ó GORMÁIN, Muiris (originally Mac Gormáin), b. Ulster *c.* 1700, d. 1794. Schoolmaster, scribe and poet, poetic rival and enemy of Peadar Ó Doirnín. See *Clogher Record* I for his poetry, an article by Professor S. P. Ó Mórdha. Best remembered for his manuscript copies, which are to be found in most of the great Irish collections and in the British Museum; see *Clogher Record* II. Helped Charlotte Brooke gather the materials for her *Reliques of Irish Poetry,* 1789 (see Part 1).

Ó GRÁDAIGH, Eoghan, b. London 1902, of Irish parents. Joined Connradh na Gaeilge as a boy, and was fighting between 1919 and 1922. Served in the Labour Court of Dublin. *Gunnaí Bagair,* Dublin 1944; *An Spiorad Do-Chloíte,* Dublin 1954; *An Fear Fada Caol,* Dublin 1959, rep. 1963; *Ruathar Anall,* Dublin 1962.

Ó GRAMHNA, Eoghan, see O'GROWNEY, Eugene.

Ó GRIANNA, Séamus (pseud. 'Máire'), b. Co. Donegal 1891, d. 1969. Brother of Seosamh Mac Grianna. Has also used prefix Mac on occasion. Became a school-teacher in Tyrone, Dublin and Donegal, from 1912-20. In the period of the first Dáil became an organiser under the Ministry of Education. Was on the Republican side during the Civil War 1922-24, spent two years in prison. After 1932 entered the civil service, helped by the new Fianna Fáil government. Much of his work was translating English boys' books into Irish, which appeared both to him and others a dire waste of great talent. Is considered one of the major Irish writers of the century, although his style has been attacked both as 'too difficult' and 'too homely.' Books include novels: *Mo Dhá Róisín,* 1921; *Caisleáin Óir,* 1924; *Cioth agus Dealán* (considered by many his best book), 1926; *Feara Fáil,* Dundalk 1933; *Thiar i dTír Chonaill,* 1940; *Nuair a bhí mé Óg,* 1942; *Saoghal Corrach* (autobiography) 1945; *An Teach nár Tógadh agus Scéalta Eile,* 1948; *Tarngaireacht, Mhiseoige,* 1958, rep. Dublin 1984; *An Bhratach,* 1959; *An Draoidín,* 1959; *Ó Mhuir go Sliabh,* 1961; *Suipín an Iolair,* 1962; *Uná Bhán agus Scéalta Eile,* 1962; *Cúl le Muir agus Scéalta Eile,* 1961; *Bean Ruadh de Dhálach,* 1966; *Le Clap-Sholus,* 1967; *An Sean Teach,* 1968; *Oidhche Shamhraidh agus Scéalta Eile,* 1968; all pub. Dublin where not Dundalk. New editions since Ó G.'s death include *Caisleáin Óir, Cith is Dealán,* both Cork 1976, and *Nuair a bhí Mé Óg,* Cork 1979.

One of his short stories *Grást ó dhia ar Mhici,* trans. by Séamas Ó Neill for *Irish Writing,* appeared later in the anthology, *The Irish Genius,* NY 1959, and gives an idea of the earthy humour of his writing, a long way removed from the civil service puritanism of much of the Revival. There has been a constant tension and conflict between the genuine Irish writers, born to the oral Gaeltacht tradition, and the civil servants who have controlled a large part of the means of publication. It has often seemed that the more Gaelic the writer, the more difficulties he would find in getting his work printed. This has affected even the dead. See for example Peadar Ó Doirnín.

Ó GRÍOFA, Muiris, b. *c.* 1710, d. 1778. Schoolmaster and poet, remembered for his lament on the death of Eoghan Ruadh Súilleabháin, printed many times, for example, *Fáinne an Lae,* April 1918; and for the famous Jacobite poem *An Seabhac Siubhail,* the wandering hawk of the title being the Pretender. See John O'Daly, *Poets and Poetry of Munster,* Dublin 1849 and subsequent editions; John O'Daly, *Reliques of Irish Jacobite Poetry,* Dublin 1844, etc.

O'GROWNEY, Fr Eugene (An tAth. Eoghan Ó Gramhna), b. Co. Meath 1863, d. Los Angeles 1899. Ed. Maynooth. His interest in Irish was aroused by a chance meeting with an Irish-speaking labourer who replied in Irish to the boy's English greeting. O'Growney determined to learn the language and spent the rest of his life, apart from his religious duties, studying and teaching the language, becoming Professor of Irish in Maynooth, 1891. He became a friend of Douglas Hyde, helped found the Gaelic League, and edited the *Gaelic Journal* in succession to John Fleming. A serious illness in 1894 drove him to California, but he continued to contribute Irish lessons to the *Weekly Freeman* by post, and began to write Nationalist articles and Language Revival propaganda in American papers. A final illness came after an operation. He himself dated his ill-health from a ghostly apparition in his childhood, in a bedroom in a house into which his family had just moved. Local tradition held it to be haunted and said that the previous owners never used that room.

Fr O'Growney was buried in Los Angeles, but Irish-Americans raised a subscription to return his body with due honour to Ireland, and it was reburied in Maynooth 1901. He is remembered for his *Simple Lessons in Irish,* first published serially and later as a book. For his works see Agnes O'Farrelly, *Leabhar an Athar Eoghan – The O'Growney Memorial Volume,* Dublin 1904.

Ó hAIMHIRGÍN, Osborn Joseph, see BERGIN, Osborn Joseph.

Ó HÁINLE, Cathal, b. Co. Westmeath 1940. Ed. Maynooth, UCD and Munich. Lecturer TCD. Critic; *Éigse Lár na hÉireann 1500-1750,* Maynooth 1975; *Promhadh Pinn,* Maynooth 1978 (on aspects of Irish literature from 16th century to the present); *Rosamh: Gearrscéalta an Phiarsaigh,* Dublin 1979.

Ó hAIRTNÉIDE, Mícheál, b. Limerick 1941. Lecturer in creative writing, Thomond College Limerick. *Adharca Broic* and *Daoine,* 1978, and *Do Nuala: Foidhne Chrainn,* 1984; *An Lia Nocht,* 1985; all pub. Dublin.

Ó hANNRACHÁIN, Peadar (Lorga Liathbhán), b. Co. Cork, 1877, d. 1965. The child of native speakers, but did not learn Irish until late in his school days. Joined the Gaelic League and became a travelling teacher of Irish 1901-18. In the same years edited various Gaelic journals, and became involved in politics. Fought in the War of Independence and was interned in Ireland and England. Much of his work is buried in newspaper files. An

'Itinerarium' of Ireland, based on his Gaelic League adventures, is in *Claidheamh Soluis*, 1908, and another 'Itinerarium' appeared the following year in issues of the *Irish Nation*. His best short story, *Tar Éis na Fearthainne*, was printed in *Fáinne an Lae*, 1918. *Nuala de Barra* which appeared in 1914 in *Claidheamh Soluis*, was reprinted 30 years later in a volume of the same title. Other volumes include *Mar Mhaireas É* (reminiscences of the time spent as a travelling teacher), Dublin 1953, followed by a second volume dealing with the period 1917-19, Dublin 1955. The best-known and perhaps best of all his books is *Fé Bhrat an Chonnartha*, Dublin 1944.

Ó hAODHA, Micheál, b. Clare 1918. As a boy paid 2/6d a week to learn Latin and Greek from the last of the hedge schoolmasters, Matt Tuohy of Killaloe. Radio Éireann producer of plays for many years, appointed 1965 to board of directors of Abbey Theatre. Plays include *Ordóg an Bháis*, Dublin 1943; *Dlí na Feirme*, Dublin 1965; and the first Abbey pantomime in Irish, *Muireann agus an Prionnsa*, 1945.

Ó hAODHA, Séamas, b. Cork 1886. Ed. UCC. In Department of Education for many years. Criticism: *Padraig Mac Piarais, Sgéalaidhe*, 1922; *Aodhagán Ó Rathaille*, 1925. Poetry: *Uaigneas*, 1928; *Caoineadh na Mná agus Dánta Eile*, 1939; *Ceann an Bhóthair*, 1966. All pub. Dublin. Also wrote a number of plays.

Ó hAODHA, Tomás, b. Co. Clare 1866, d. 1935. Native Irish speaker, became a teacher in Dublin. Wrote a novel, *An Gioblachán*, Dublin 1903; a number of plays, including *Mainchín*, 1912; and several volumes of short stories, among them *Giolla na Leisge agus Sgéalta Eile*, Dublin 1924.

Ó hARTAGÁIN, Cionaith, b. probably Meath, *c.* 910, d. 975. Wrote historical and chronicle poems, from one of which it appears that the Lia Fáil, the Stone of Destiny, was still in place on the Hill of Tara in the 10th century. See Edward J. Gwynn, *Poems from the Dindshencas* (text, translation and vocabulary), Dublin 1900; George Petrie, 'History and Antiquities of Tara Hill,' *RIA Transactions*, XVIII, 1837; Eugene O'Curry *Lectures on the MSS Materials of Ancient Irish History*, 1861 (text from the *Book of Ballymote* with trans.); Whitley Stokes, 'On the Deaths of Some Irish Heroes,' *Revue Celtique*, XXIII, 1902.

Ó hÉIGEARTAIGH, Diarmuid, b. Co. Cork 1856, d. 1934. School-teacher for most of his working life. *Tadhg Ciallmhar*, Dublin 1934 (a story); *Is Uasal Ceird*, Dublin 1968, edited from Ó hÉigeartaigh's notes by Stiofán Ó hAnnracháin (an account of the author's life, and the traditions and people of his neighbourhood).

Ó hÉIGEARTAIGH, Pádraig, b. Co. Kerry 1871, d. Massachusetts 1936. Was taken to America as a boy of 12 and went to work in a cotton mill. In 1891 moved to Springfield, Mass., and found a book in Irish, *Filidheacht Chúige Mumhan*, in a second-hand bookshop. He learned to read and write Irish from this and became a teacher of Irish in the newly formed

Springfield Irish Society, of which he was co-founder. He also began to write poetry in Irish, and on the tragic death by drowning of his small son wrote his masterpiece, *Ochón, a Dhonnchadh,* which first appeared in *Claidheamh Soluis,* 7th April 1906, and in many anthologies since. One of the very few modern instances of an emigrant writing in Irish.

Ó hÉIGEARTAIGH, Seán, b. Cobh 1931. Schools Inspector in Dublin. Poet. *Cama-Shiúlta,* Dublin 1964.

Ó hEITHIR, Breandán, b. Aran Islands 1930. Ed. UCG. Newspaper editor and broadcaster, columnist in Irish. *Thar Ghealchathair Soir,* Dublin 1973; *Lig Sinn i gCathú,* Dublin 1976, rep. 1984. *Willie the Plain Pint agus an Pápa,* Dublin 1977; and a translation *Lead Us into Temptation,* Dublin 1978 (from the Irish). In English, *Over the Bar,* Swords 1984, about the GAA, told from an intensely personal viewpoint.

Ó hEOGHUSA, Eochaidh (O'Hussey), b. Enniskillen *c.* 1570, d. *c.* 1617. Chief poet or ollamh to the Maguire chiefs of his day, in the old style of ollamh whose privileges ranked him with bishops and kings. He had the right to share the chief's bed. He was one of the two foremost poets of his day, his rival being Tadhg Dall Ó hUiginn. His brother, or possibly cousin, Gille-Brighde, also a fine poet, went to Louvain as a priest.

His most famous poem describes the winter campaign of 1599-1600 when Hugh Maguire was in the south with O'Neill. He laments the fierce cold the chiefs are suffering: 'Where is my Chief, my Master, this black night? Movrone' (in Mangan's free translation). When Hugh was killed in battle Eochaidh compares him to the pelican who gives her blood to her own children to save them. Another famous poem praises the beauty of Rose O'Byrne, who was taken by the English and burned alive in the yard of Dublin Castle.

He was the last of the traditional ollamhs. After Kinsale and the Flight of the Earls some of the structure of Gaelic society survived in the west and the south-west but the spirit was gone from it, and with it the possibility of any poet occupying the almost mystical and ritualistic position of ollamh in the sense that Eochaidh and his predecessors did. Eochaidh himself received a grant of land in the plantation of Ulster and to that extent began to make his peace with the new order. His last poem translates the recent war into classical terms, Red Hugh O'Donnell appearing as Caesar, the English leader as Pompey and Hugh Maguire as Crassus.

See Tomás Ó Rathile, *Dánta Grádha,* Cork 1926; Eleanor Knott, *An Introduction to Irish Syllabic Poetry of the period 1200-1600,* Cork 1928; *Dioghluim Dána* and *Aithdioghluim Dána,* both by L. McKenna SJ, Dublin 1938 and 1939; also articles by O. J. Bergin in *Studies,* VII, 1918; X, 1921; XI, 1922 and XII, 1923; and S. H. O'Grady *Catalogue of Irish MSS in the British Museum* (pp. 448-81).

Ó hEOGHUSA, Gille-Brighde (also sometimes Bonaventure, Giolla-Bhrighde and Maelbhrighid), b. Enniskillen *c.* 1575, d. Louvain 1614.

Probably a brother of Eochaidh and like him educated in the poetic schools. Entered Louvain as a Franciscan 1607, and the following year published a book of Christian doctrine in Irish, *Teagasc Críostaidhe*, at Louvain, rep. Antwerp 1611. A long poem by Gille-Bríghde under the same title was published at Paris 1642. See T. Ó Rathile, *Measgra Dánta*, Cork 1927; L. McKenna SJ, *Dioghluim Dána*, Dublin 1938; O. J. Bergin, 'Unpublished Irish Poems' in *Studies*, VII, 1918 and *Ériu*, VIII, 1916-17; and *Irish Ecclesiastical Record*, XXXI, 1928, and *Irish Book Lover*, XVIII, 1930, both containing articles by Paul Walsh.

Ó hIARNÁIN, Colm, b. Aran Islands 1914. Farmer and fisherman. Short-story writer: *Gleann an Chuain*, Dublin 1978.

Ó hICÉADHA, An tAth. Micheál (Fr Michael P. O'Hickey), b. Co. Waterford 1861, d. 1917. Paradoxically, this great figure in the Language Revival published nothing in Irish and appears here in defiance of logic. Professor of Irish in Maynooth from 1896, he was sent to Rome in 1906 to discuss the future development of the college. He was at the same time deeply involved in a quarrel with the Irish hierarchy over the question of 'compulsory Irish' in the educational system and particularly for the matriculation certificate. The quarrel grew so heated that the bishops dismissed him from his chair. In Rome he pleaded not his own cause, but that of the Irish language. He returned to Ireland in 1917, the case still unsettled, and died shortly after. Máirtin Ó Cadhain has described him as one of the only two men of whom it could be truly said that they died for the language, it being generally thought that Father O'Hickey died of a broken heart at the rejection of his ideal.

O'HICKEY, Michael P, see Ó hICÉADHA, An tAth. Micheál.

O hIFEARNÁIN, Liam Dall, b. Tipperary 1720, d. Tipperary 1760. Blind from birth he became, like Carolan and perhaps under the same stimulus of a physical handicap, a scholar of repute and a poet deserving remembrance. He studied poetry at the bardic school in Co. Limerick and often returned there. He spent his life in great poverty. See *Ar Bruach na Coille Muaire*, ed. Ristéard Ó Foghludha, Dublin 1939.

Ó hIFEARNÁIN, Mathghamhain, b. *c.* 1580, d. *c.* 1640. Many of his poems complain of the sad decline of the true art of poetry in his time and the equal ruin of the old, pastoral way of life by the new agriculture. He advised his son not to follow his footsteps as a poet because if would only bring him misery: *A Mhic ná Meabhraigh Éigse*. Again he wrote *Ceist Cia Chinneochadh Dán?* (Who Would Desire a Poem?). During the Contention of the Bards, when the poets of Ulster and of the South hurled boastful verses at one another, claiming the supremacy of Ireland for their own princes, Mathghamhain, like some of the Louvain poets, castigated them for an absurd and blind vanity, 'What are Tadhg and Lughaid about... They possess, alas, only a little part of the land, the Princes about whom they dispute,' the second 'they' being Tadhg Mac Dáire Mac Bruaideadha and Lughaidh ó Cléirigh.

See O. J. Bergin, *Irish Review*, III, 1913; L. McKenna, *Iomarbhágh na Bhfileadh*, 1918; and S. H. O'Grady, *Catalogue of Irish MSS in the British Museum* (pp. 392-93).

Ó hÓDHRAIN, Micheál, b. Co. Mayo 1932. Has written short stories, *Sléibhté Mhaigh Eó*, Dublin 1964, Club Leabhar selection. Has also written many plays in Irish and English, for broadcasting. Other works include *Ar Son na Treibhe* (For the Sake of the Tribe), Dublin 1964; *An Tine Bheo*, etc.

Ó hÓGÁIN, Dáithí, b. Co. Limerick 1949. Ed. UCD. Lecturer in Irish folklore UCD. Short stories: *Breacadh*, Cork 1973. On An Club Leabhar list 1973. Ed. *Munster Folksongs*, 1980. *Duanaire Osraíoch*, 1980; *Duanaire Thiobraid Árann*, 1981; *Cois Camhaoireach*, 1982; *An File*, 1982; Cóngar na gCrosán, 1985; all pub. Dublin. *The Hero in Irish Folk History*, NY 1985.

Ó HUALLACHÁIN, An tAth. Colmán OFM, b. Dublin 1922, d. Co. Meath 1979. Entered Franciscan Order 1940. Ph.D. Louvain, studied applied linguistics in US. Professor of Ethics Maynooth, became Director of Language Institute of Ireland, Dublin. Senior Lecturer and Head of Irish Studies, New University of Ulster, from 1974 until his death. One of the key figures in modern teaching of Irish, laying emphasis on simplicity and scientific method. *Ridire Mhuire gan Smál*, Dublin 1951 (biography of Fr Max Kolbe); *Foclóir Fealsaimh*, Dublin 1958 (philosopher's dictionary); *Bunchúrsa Foghraíochta*, with Sister Mary Annuntiata, Dublin 1966 (a first course in phonetics); *Irish Grammar*, with Micheál Ó Murchú, Coleraine 1976.

Ó hUANACHÁIN, Micheál, b. Dublin 1944. Ed. Dublin. Journalist in RTE, and poet. Poetry: *Go dTaga Léas*, 1971; *Crann Tógála*, 1979; *Aibítir Mheiriceá*, 1982; all pub. Dublin.

Ó hUID, Tarlach, b. London 1917. Parents of Northern Unionist and Orange sympathies, but Ó hUid became a Nationalist with a republican outlook. Interned by Stormont authorities 1940-45 for IRA activities. Has written short stories and novels. *An Bealach chun a'Bhearnais*, Dublin 1949 (a novel, Club Leabhar selection); *Taobh Thall den Teorainn*, Dublin 1950 (short stories, Club Leabhar selection); *An Dá Thrá*, Dublin 1952 (novel, Club Leabhar selection); *Ar Thóir mo Shealbha*, Dublin 1960 (memoirs, 1917-40); *Eachtra Nollag*, Dublin 1960 (a detective story for teenagers); and *Éalú*, Dublin 1961 (historical adventure). *Adios*, Dublin 1975 (novel); *Rachtanna*, Dublin 1975 (poems). Now editor of *Inniu*.

Ó hUIDRIN, Giolla-na-Naomh, *fl. c.*1420. See Ó DUBHAGÁIN, Seán Mór.

Ó hUIGINN. A family of hereditary poets living in Sligo and famous for many generations, from the 13th to the 17th centuries at least. Their principal patrons were the O'Connor-Sligos. Best known of the family were:

Ó hUIGHINN

Domhnall, b. *c.* 1440, d. 1502 on returning from a pilgrimage to Compostella. He wrote a long praise poem to Ian Mac Donald, *Misde Nach Édmar Éire,* see J. Frazer and J. G. O'Keefe, *Poems on the O'Donnells 1200-1600,* 1931.

Maolmuire, d. Antwerp 1591 (?), brother of Tadhg Dall (see separate entry), joined the Franciscan Order and studied and taught at Louvain, and later in Rome. In 1538 in Rome was appointed Archbishop of Tuam and wrote his best-known poem, *A Fhir Théid Go Fiadh bhFuinidh,* describing the conflict in his mind between a longing for the contemplative life and his love for Ireland. He died at Antwerp on the journey to his archdiocese, where he had expected to find martyrdom. His poetry is rougher than his brother's, but more human and sympathetic. See S. H. O'Grady, *A Fhir Threbus in Tulaig, A Catalogue of Irish MSS in British Museum* (pp. 392-93), and L. McKenna SJ, *Aithdioghluim Dána,* Dublin 1939.

Maolsheachlainn na n-Uirsgéal (Malachy of the Fables), *fl.* 1430. Granted land by O'Connor-Sligo on which he conducted a school of poetry. Some of his people, perhaps students rather than servants, stole cattle from his patron and he was expelled, winning his way back into favour and possession with a poem. L. McKenna SJ, *Dioghluim Dána,* Dublin 1938; Eleanor Knott, *An Introduction to Irish Syllabic Poetry of the Period 1200-1600,* Cork 1928; and *Uasal Ferontas Fergail,* ed. P. Walsh, *Irish Book Lover XXVI* (pp. 86-87), Dublin 1939.

Mathghamhain, b. Sligo, *c.* 1520, d. Sligo 1585. Father of Tadhg Dall and Maolmuire. He himself was court bard of the O'Byrnes of Wicklow, but appears to have returned to Sligo before he died. For some of his poetry see L. McKenna SJ, *Aithdioghluim Dána,* Dublin 1939.

Tadhg Mór, *fl.* 1400, tutor and poet to Manus O'Connor, brother of the King of Connacht, and his supporter in his civil war against his brother. See L. McKenna SJ, *Dioghluim Dána,* Dublin 1938, and the same author's edition and trans. in *Studies,* XXIX, 1940, of Tadhg Mór's *A Fir táinig ré tásg mBriain.*

Tadhg Óg, d. Co. Galway 1448, son of Tadhg Mór, and the most eminent bard of his time, and even the century. Like his namesake and descendant Tadhg Dall 150 years later, Tadhg Óg addressed his court poetry not to one great family alone but to a number of them, and indeed almost the same group of north-western families that Tadhg Dall wrote for: the O'Connor-Sligos, the O'Neills, the MacWilliam Burkes, the O'Kellys. One interest to be found in his poetry is the detailed description it gives among other matters of the life of a court bard himself. See J. Frazer and J. G. O'Keefe, *Poems on the O'Donnells, 1200-1600* (Irish Texts II, i-iii), 1931; and L. McKenna SJ, *Dioghluim Dána,* Dublin 1938.

Tuathal, d. 1450, brother of Tadhg Óg and his successor. See L. McKenna SJ, *Dioghluim Dána* and *Aithdioghluim Dána,* Dublin 1938 and 1939.

Ó hUIGINN, Tadhg Dall, b. Ulster *c.* 1550, d. Co. Sligo before 1617, by murder. Blind, and a court bard but seemingly a freelance, addressing his poems of praise to Maguires and O'Neills, O'Rourkes and O'Connor-Sligos with apparent independence. He was one of the great poets of his day, writing a clear, easy and at the same time brilliantly polished verse that is almost Augustan in its perfection. He remained indifferent to the violent social changes of the time, at least in his poetry, and neither lamented the decadence of the times, like Mathghamhain Ó hIfearnáin, nor the cruelty of the English and the death of Irish chieftains like Eochaidh Ó hEoghusa. In his poetry that itself seems to belong to the English 18th century in its limpid style, the Gaelic world of the 15th century still lives. Nor did he commonly write satires as most of his contemporaries did, and yet a satire cost him his life. He possessed property and a substantial house in Co. Sligo and 'six men of the O'Haras' as the later trial described them came there and emptied it of food and drink. Tadhg wrote a satire on them that so stung their feelings that they returned and murdered his wife and child, cut out Tadhg's tongue and beat him to death. They were brought to trial in 1617 and found guilty. See S. H. O'Grady, *Sluag Seisir Táinic dom Thig*, ed. and trans. pp. 439-42 of *Catalogue of Irish MSS in British Museum*; Rev. A. MacDonald, *Daoin Saor Siol Cholla* in *The MacDonald Collection of Gaelic Poetry* (pp. 1-5), Inverness 1911; and Eleanor Knott's *An Introduction to Irish Syllabic Poetry of the period 1200-1600*, Cork 1928, and her *A bhFuil Againn dar chuir Tadhg Dall Ó Huiginn (1550-91)*, ed. with trans. for ITS, 1922.

Tadhg Dall's brother became Archbishop of Tuam, and was also a poet, see MAOLMUIRE in the entry on the Ó hUIGINN family.

O'HUSSEY, Eochaid, see Ó hEOGHUSA, Eochaidh.

Ó LABHRA, Colm, see COLMCILLE, An tAth.

Ó LAOGHAIRE, Donnchadh, b. Co. Cork 1877, d. Co. Cork 1944. Ed. France, Germany and Belgium; teacher; became Professor of Gaelic and French at St Peter's College, Wexford. A musician and translator of Swift, the Grimm Brothers, and Hans Anderson, a group of volumes of his translations appearing in Dublin in 1939, among them *Eachtra an Ghiolla Mhóir, Feoil agus Ceoil* and *Lios na Sídhe*. Also published *An Péarla Dubh*, Dublin 1952 (trans. of *La Perle Noire* by Sardou).

Ó LAOGHAIRE, Pádraig, b. Co. Cork 1871, d. Cork 1896. Native speaker. Taught Patrick Pearse Irish in a room in Dame St. Worked on the *Irish Dictionary* for Fr Dinneen. Wrote poetry and stories. Remembered for *Sgéalaidheacht Chúige Mumhan* published in 7 parts, Dublin 1895, rep. Dublin 1904-09 (old Munster folk tales); and *Cainnt na nDaoine*, Dublin 1920 (the conversation of the people). His health broke down in Dublin and he returned to Cork to die of tuberculosis.

Ó LAOGHAIRE, An tAth. Peadar, b. Co. Cork 1839, d. 1920. Bi-lingual from the cradle, his parents being fluent in Irish, but also well-educated in English. He gained a scholarship to Maynooth and was ordained 1867.

He took an interest in politics and more than an interest in the Land War, but his acquaintance with Archbishop Mac Hale (see MAC HALE, John) aroused his interest in the language as a political instrument, although it was many years before he began to write in Irish and to devote himself to the Language Revival. Fortunately, he did not allow the archbishop to influence his style, nor did he follow the other disastrous course of his contemporaries, a deliberate archaism, a copying of the most elaborate 18th-century conceits. The problem he had to face was that while there were still native-speakers there were no longer any native-writers; there were no living rivals or standards against which to measure and sharpen his own style. There were only Mac Hale's examples, which were almost English, translated into Irish; and the antiquarians, many of whom seemed to admire a phrase the more, the less intelligible it was to the ordinary reader.

In this vacuum, Fr Ó Laoghaire wrote Irish as he had heard it spoken: short, crisp and simple sentences with the pungency and intelligence that spoken Gaelic still possessed, and still possesses where the pressure of English is not slowly strangling it.

Fr Ó Laoghaire wrote short stories, novels, memoirs, religious essays; retold old stories and classics, translated the Gospels and the *Imitation of Christ,* and established a style that has been called 'the perfection of sophistication,' chosen by such scholars as Bergin as the model for all modern Irish prose.

His most famous work is the folk-novel *Séadna,* the adventures of a country cobbler in conflict with the Devil. First published as a serial it was printed in book form in Dublin 1904. *Niamh,* Dublin 1907; *Sliabh na mBan Bhfionn,* Dublin 1914; *Mo Sgéal Féin* (autobiography), Dublin 1915; *Ag Séideadh agus ag ithe,* Dublin 1918; *Críost Mac Dé,* Dublin 1925.

In *An Craos Deamhan* he retold in modern Irish the famous Middle Irish legend *Aislinge Mhic Conglinne,* and this is held to be one of his masterpieces. He also wrote a number of plays.

Fr Ó Laoghaire's contribution to the style of modern Irish writing is uncontested. Some critics are less happy about his influence on the content of Irish novels. Patrick Power in *A Literary History of Ireland* holds him responsible for Irish writing's 'narrow and confined view of life'. He both bowdlerised and distorted, turning his back on towns and writing almost exclusively of peasant life, as if this was the only worthwhile life, and the only truly 'Irish' life. At the same time he excluded even from peasant life all the robust and bawdy side of it that until the 19th century had been one of the hallmarks of Gaelic writing.

Ó LEOCHÁIN, Seán, b. Athlone 1943. Ed. UCG. Teacher in Athlone. Poetry published includes *Bláth an Fhéir,* 1968; *An Dara Cloch,* 1969; *Saol na bhFuíoll,* 1973; *Idir Ord agus Inneoin,* 1977, Arts Council prize for best book of poetry in Irish, 1971/2/3; *In Absentia,* 1980; all pub. Dublin.

Ó LIATHÁIN, Annraoi, b. Co. Galway 1917, d. Dublin 1981. Civil servant. Worked on *Irish-English Dictionary* for Dept. of Education. President of Connradh na Gaeilge 1950-52. Published a number of novels, some with an historical background. *Oscar*, 1954; *Laochra na Machairí*, 1958 (about American Red Indians); *Claíomh an Díoltais*, 1961; *Dún na Cinniúna*, 1966 (historical novel set in 1644); *Pící Loch Garman*, 1964 (on 1798); *Cois Móire*, 1964, etc. More recently *Luaithreach an Bhua*, 1969; *Buíon Éireannach in Albain*, 1975; *Nead na gCreabhar*, 1977; all novels; and *Gleann an Leasa*, 1973, short stories. Also *Cois Siúire*, 1982. All pub. Dublin.

Between 1946 and 1948 was out of the civil service, having been dismissed for taking part in the agitation arising from Seán Mac Eochaidh's hunger strike. During a part of this period of intellectual exile he earned his living by hunting rabbits.

Ó LOCHAIN, Cuan (sometimes Ó Lothcain), b. Co. Meath *c.* 970, d. 1024. For two years before his death in battle one of the joint Regents of Ireland, following the death of the High King Malachy II in 1022. This gives added authority to some of his writings, particularly on the privileges and taboos of the kingship, a copy of which appears in the *Book of Lecan*. He also wrote on the topography and names connected with the River Shannon; the Hill of Tara; the Hill of Druim Criaich (Drumcree in Westmeath); and the Hill of Taillte (Teltown in Meath) and the traditional assemblies and sports connected with it. His writings on Tara appear in the *Book of Ballymote*.

Ó LOCHLAINN, Gearóid, b. Liverpool 1884, d. 1970. Brought to Ireland as a child. Studied at University of Copenhagen, travelled widely in Europe, taught elocution by Frank Fay. Acted with Hilton Edwards and Micheál Mac Liammóir. Wrote many plays and translations. His book *Ealáin na h-Amharclainne* was a Club Leabhar selection for 1967, rep. 1984. Plays include *Na Fearachoin*, Dublin 1946.

Ó LONGÁIN, Micheál Óg, b. Co. Cork 1766, d. 1837, probably in Cork. Son of an Irish scholar and scribe who was trained in the Bardic School of Co. Limerick. Joined the United Irishmen in 1797 and acted as their courier in the south. While travelling took any opportunity to copy old MSS. Fought in '98 and was on the run after the Rising. In 1800 was married and working as a farm labourer, perhaps still in bad odour with the authorities and in semi-hiding. Later became a school-teacher in Cork and in his spare time a scribe-copyist for the Bishop of Cork, Dr Murphy, a patron of Gaelic literature. For the bishop he made facsimiles of the *Leabhar Breac,* the *Book of Leinster* and the *Book of the Dun Cow,* these facsimile MSS being destined for the RIA.

As a poet he is distinguished for breaking with the Jacobite tradition of the Munster poets and writing as a Republican. His most famous poem is *Buachaillí Loch Garmain* (The Boys of Wexford), in which a ghost tells the story of the Battle of Vinegar Hill and blames Munster for sitting idly by while Leinster fought.

Ó LÚING, Seán, b. Co. Kerry 1917. On translation staff of Dáil Éireann since 1943. *Art Ó Griofa* (life of Arthur Griffiths), 1953; *John Devoy,* 1961; *Ó Donnabháin Rosa I,* 1967, II, 1979 (life of O'Donovan Rossa); *In Ard-Chathair na hEorpa,* 1976 (about Brussels); and poetry, *Bánta Dhún Úrlann,* 1975, and *Déithe Teaghlaigh,* 1984, all pub. Dublin. See also Part I.

Ó MAELCHONAIRE, Flaithrí, b. Co. Roscommon 1561, d. Madrid 1629. Belonged to a bardic family but went to Spain as a boy, studying for the priesthood in Salamanca. Entered Franciscan Order 1584, and gained a great reputation as a scholar. Accompanied the Spanish expedition to Kinsale in 1601 and after the defeat returned to Spain with Red Hugh O'Donnell. He interested both the King of Spain and the Pope in the idea of founding an Irish College where Irish students could be trained for the Church and Irish books and learning could be propagated. Louvain was chosen as its home and the College was founded in 1607. In 1609 he was made Archbishop of Tuam but was unable to return to Ireland. He was one of the Louvain scholars who condemned the futile and notorious Contention of the Bards, and besides such occasional Irish writing, wrote in Latin, and translated a Spanish treatise on the spiritual life into Irish. His own book of Christian Doctrine, *Sgáthán an Chrábhaidh,* was published at Louvain 1616. This is in large part a translation of *El Desseoso,* published in Barcelona 1515, in Catalan, and accordingly the Irish book is often referred to as the *Desiderius.*

See *Desiderius; otherwise Sgáthán and Chrábhaidh,* ed. T. F. O'Rahilly, Dublin 1941.

Ó MÁILLE, Micheál, b. Connemara 1880, d. 1911. Brother of Tomás. A school-teacher and journalist. Many of his essays are in *An Claidheamh Soluis,* 1901-05; rep. as *Diarmaid Donn,* Dublin 1936. Volumes of stories include *Eochaidh Mac Ríogh 'n Éirinn,* Dublin 1904; rep. as *Eochaidh Mac Ríogh agus an Giolla Dubh,* Dublin 1945, rep. 1950.

Ó MÁILLE, Tomás, b. Connemara 1883, d. 1938. Brother of Micheál. Ed. Manchester, Freiburg, Baden and Berlin. Professor of Irish UCG 1909. With Micheál Breathnach wrote *Irish in 30 Lessons,* for the Linguaphone Series, 1927. *An Béal Beo,* 1936, rep. 1937, is one of his best-known works. He edited the poems of Carolan, *Amhráin Cearbhalláin,* 1916; co-editor with his brother Micheál of *Amhráin Chlainne Gaedheal (An chéad chuid),* 1925; and wrote *Micheál Mac Suibhne agus Filí an tSléibhe,* 1934. All pub. Dublin.

Ó MÁILLE, Tomás S. Professor of Modern Irish UCG. Published Irish translation of *A Desecration,* Dublin 1937. *Sean-Fhocla Chonnact,* 2 vols, Dublin 1948, 1952; and poetry, *Breacadh,* 1973, and *Liosta Focal as Ros*

Muc, 1974, both pub. Shannon.

Ó MAOILEOIN, Séamas. Intelligence Officer with Michael Collins during War of Independence. *B'fhiú an Braon Fola,* Dublin 1958.

Ó MAOLCHATHAIGH, Séamas, b. Co. Tipperary 1898. Spent 44 years as a teacher in his native district. Published an account of the district and its people. *An Gleann agus a Raibh Ann,* Dublin 1963, rep. 1964, 1974. Club Leabhar selection.

Ó MAOLFHABHAIL, Art, b. Limerick 1932. Ed. Dublin, now works for Place Names Commission. Has published a volume of poems, *Aistí Dána.*

Ó MAOLMHUAIDH, Proinsias, b. Co. Meath *c.* 1605, d. Rome 1677. Professor of Theology at San Isidore; famous as the writer of the first Irish grammar to be printed, *Grammatica Latino-Hibernica,* Rome 1677. He was also a poet and the grammar contains one of his poems in Irish. He wrote in Latin on theology and philosophy; and on the refutation of heresy. *Lucerna Fidelium,* Rome 1676; and ed. Pádraig Ó Súilleabháin, OFM, Dublin 1962.

Ó MATHGHAMHNA, Donnchadh Caoch, b. Cork 1700, d. Cork 1740. A native speaker, he spent his life among English-speaking neighbours, and some of the small amount of his poetry that survives laments his loneliness among what he regards as foreigners. His poetry is considered particularly fine. See *Dál na h-Éigse: Saothar Suadha,* 2 parts, Dublin 1908 and 1912. Also *An Claidheamh Soluis,* April 1908, and *The Irish Rosary,* February 1918, April 1919.

Ó MATHGHAMHNA, Fínghin, b. Co. Cork *c.* 1430, d. 1496. Translated *Mandeville's Travels,* the fabulous account of a journey to the Holy Land and the Near East and India, written originally in French about 1375. It makes an interesting comment on the literary and cultural contacts between Gaelic Ireland and the Continent that such a book was translated into Irish in 1475, at the height of the Gaelic political revival. The MS is in the British Museum.

Ó MATHÚNA, Seán P., b. New York 1930. Ed. UCD. Teacher. Now lecturer in Education UCD. Has written on linguistics, particularly regarding the learning of a second language. *Múineadh an Dara Teanga,* Dublin 1975; and *An tAthair William Bathe, C. Í.* (his life and contribution to linguistics), Dublin 1979.

Ó MILÉADHA, Pádraig, b. Waterford 1877, d. Dungarvan 1947. Grandfather a native speaker with little English. Worked in Welsh mines. Married Eilín Ní Chuilleanáin 1911. Taught night classes for Conradh na Gaeilge. Founded branch of Volunteers in Welsh mining village of Clydach 1914. Sacked from mine because of prolonged strike 1922. Taught for Conradh na Gaeilge again, and became a teacher in Dungarvan Tech. Wrote poetry in style of 18th-century Munster poets. Publications include *Duanta Aneas,*

Dublin 1934 (see DENVIR); *An Fiannaidhe Fáin,* Dublin 1934; and *Trí Glúine Gaedheal,* Dublin 1953.

Ó MÍODHCHÁIN, Tomás, b. Co. Clare 1754, d. Co. Clare 1806. Wrote political poetry which shows an intellectual grasp of events beyond that of most of his contemporaries; see Brian O'Looney, *A Collection of Poems... by the Clare Bards,* Dublin 1863.

Ó MUIMHNEACHÁIN, Aindrias, b. Co. Cork 1905, active all his adult life in teaching and in the Language Movement. Member of An Coiste Gnó, the Gaelic League executive, for 40 years. *An Claidheamh Solais – Tríocha Bliain de Chonradh na Gaeilge,* Dublin 1955; *Na Múinteoirí Taistil,* Dublin 1962; *Dóchas agus Duainéis,* Dublin and Cork 1975; *Seanchas an Táilliúra,* Dublin and Cork 1978.

Ó MUIREADHAIGH, An tAth. Réamonn, b. Co. Armagh 1938. Ordained 1962. Poet. *Athphreabadh na h-Óige,* Dublin 1964; *Arán ar an Tábla,* Dublin 1970.

Ó MUIRGHEASA, Énrí (Feargus Mac Roigh), b. Co. Monaghan 1874, d. Dublin 1945. Parents Irish-speaking, but as often happened at that period they did not speak it to the children or encourage them to learn it, and it was only the foundation and rise of the Gaelic League that gave some of this deprived generation the stimulus to learn their parents' language. Became an inspector of primary schools and a tireless worker for the language. Spent much of his leisure collecting folklore material and encouraging local archaeological societies in whatever district he was stationed. Collected and edited 100 Irish poems in *Céad de Cheoltaibh Uladh,* Dublin 1915; published *Amhráin Airt Mhic Chubhthaigh,* Dublin 1916 (the poetry of Art McC.); *Amhráin na Midhe,* part 1, 1934; *Dánta Diadha Uladh,* Dublin 1936, rep. 1969; *Dhá chéad de Cheoltaibh Uladh,* Dublin 1934, repub. Dublin 1974.

Ó MULCHRÉIBE, Risteárd (see Part I under CREAGH, Richard, for his writings in English), b. Limerick 1525, d. London 1585. Ed. Louvain, made Archbishop of Armagh 1564, arrested and imprisoned twice by the English and finally poisoned (?) in the Tower 1585. He wrote *De Lingua Hibernica* and *Topographia Hiberniae,* the MSS being preserved in TCD.

Ó MULCONAIRE, Tanaidhe, *fl.* 1100. Poems occur in *Leabhar Gabála,* on wars of Firbolg and Tuatha Dé Danann. See G. Lehmacher SJ, *Tuatha Dé Danann fo Diamair,* in *Zeitschrift für Celtische Philologie,* XIII, 1921.

Ó MULCONAIRE, Torna, b. Roscommon *c.* 1250, d. 1310. Chief poet to the O'Connors of Roscommon. Some of his poems, together with those of his 5th-century namesake, Torna the Learned, suggested to the 17th-century poets Tadhg Mac Dáire Mac Bruaideadha and Lughaidh Ó Cléirigh the idea of a poetical contest between North and South, that became known as the Contention of the Bards.

Ó MULLÁIN, Seán, b. Co. Cork 1920. Native Irish speaker. Ed. St Patrick's

Training College, Dublin. Teacher. Headmaster Killea Boys' National School, Dunmore East, since 1949. Novelist: *An Dubhchrónach*, Dublin 1953; and many short adventure novels for teenagers, between 1960 and 1976. Among them *Cosaint an Ghleanna*, Dublin 1972, and *Fir Chláimh*, Dublin 1976.

Ó MURCHADHA, Diarmuid, b. Co. Cork 1928. School-teacher in Crosshaven. *Buacháillí Baíre*, Dublin 1959, a novel for young people, Club Leabhar na nÓg choice; *Liam de Róiste*, Dublin 1976. Historian of Crosshaven.

Ó MURCHADHA (na Ráithíneach), Seán, b. Co. Cork 1700, d. Co. Cork 1762. Last head of the famous Blarney Academy of Poets, although by his time as head it had moved to Whitechurch in the same county. He wrote pleasant verses rather than important ones and had little interest in politics, which drew rebukes on his head from Pádraig Ó Súilleabháin, to which he replied in one of his best poems. Another good poem was an elegy for Máire Ní Chruadhlaoich. His poetry was edited by Tadhg Ó Donnchadha, *Dánta Sheáin Uí Mhurchadha na Ráithíneach*, Dublin 1907.

Ó MURCHADHA, Tadhg (Seandún), b. Co. Cork 1843, d. Cork 1919. A semi-literate tailor in Cork City and a great character in the first days of the Gaelic League in Cork. With the help of two 'scribes,' Donnchadh Pléimionn and Diarmuid Ó Murchadha, he supplied a column in Irish to the *Cork Weekly Examiner* and wrote a number of works, some of which are collected and edited in *Sgéal Sheandúin*, ed. Toirdhealbhach Mac Suibhne, Dublin 1920.

Ó MURCHÚ, Liam, b. Cork 1929. Ed. Cork. Assistant Controller of programmes RTE. Plays: *Spéir Thóirní*, 1963, Oireachtas Prize; *In Iothlainn Dé*, 1965, Irish Life Theatre Award; *Na Connerys*, 1974. Autobiographical work: *Cosmhuintir*, 1975. All pub. Dublin. He became famous for his chat-show on RTE, *Trom agus Éadrom*.

Ó NEACHTAIN, Seán, b. Co. Roscommon 1655, d. Co. Meath 1728. The son of well-to-do parents who owned a substantial amount of land. Either from a quarrel or some other cause he left home to become a day-labourer in Meath, where he married his master's daughter. He wrote comic stories in prose, and poetry ranging from imitations of the old models in the *dán díreach* metre (which he did not truly understand) and of Latin and Greek epic material, to dramatic poems which are really recited plays, each character speaking in verse. When he wrote in simple metres he could be excellent, and his work enjoyed a great reputation. Part cause was that he wrote in an Irish almost free from local dialect forms, so that it was acceptable over a wide area. See James Hardiman, *Irish Minstrelsy*, Dublin 1831 and *Filidheacht*, ed. Una Ní Fhaircheallaigh, Dublin 1911.

His son Tadhg lived in Dublin and wrote an *Irish-English Dictionary* between 1734 and 1739, unpublished, of which the MS is in TCD. He also wrote some poetry, uninteresting for quality, but fascinating for glimpses of the existence of a Gaelic sub-world in 18th-century Dublin.

Ó NÉILL, Séamas, b. Co. Down 1910, d. Dublin 1981. Ed. Belfast and Innsbruck. Taught Irish history. Short stories, *An Sean Saighdiúr agus Scéalta Eile,* 1945, new ed. 1979; and novels, *Tonn Tuile,* Dublin 1947, a best-seller, repub. Dublin 1974; *Ag Baint Fraochán,* Dublin 1955; also poetry and plays, including *Iníon Rí Dhún Sobhairce,* produced in Taibhdhearc Gaelic Theatre 1953, and pub. Dublin 1960, repub. Dublin 1975. Other plays: *Faill ar an bhFeart,* 1967; *Iníon Rí na Spáinne,* 1978, both Dublin. *Lámh Dhearg Abu!* (essays), Dublin 1982.

Ó NÉILL, Tomás P., b. Co. Carlow 1921. Ed. Carlow and UCD. Appointed Assistant Keeper of Printed Books, National Library, 1947. Left to work on Irish and English biography of Éamon de Valera, published in both languages as separate volumes, Dublin 1968. Also wrote biography of Fintan Lalor, *Fiontán Ó Leathlobhair,* Dublin 1962. Acted as historical adviser on films *Mise Éire* and *Saoirse.* Teaches in UCG.

Ó NUALLÁIN, Brian (Flann O'Brien, and Myles na Gopaleen), b. Strabane 1912, d. Dublin 1966. A brilliant student at UCD, contributing comic essays in Old Irish to the university magazine. For his work in English see Part 1. He began writing a column in Irish for the *Irish Times* under the title *Cruiskeen Lawn,* but changed to English after a brief period. However he continued to insert remarks and anecdotes in Old, Middle and Modern Irish as the spirit moved him, together with tags of Latin, Greek, German and French. Devotees who were and are legion, may remember other languages, all used with scholarship and point. His one book in Irish, *An Béal Bocht,* Dublin 1941 (The Poor Mouth), is regarded as a classic of modern Irish humour. Reprinted Dublin 1975; English trans. by Patrick C. Power pub. 1973 with illustrations by Ralph Steadman.

Ó NUALLÁIN, Ciarán, b. Strabane 1910, d. Dublin 1983, older brother of Brian. Ciarán founded the Irish literary magazine *Inniu* under the title *Indiú* in 1943, and had published several books: *Oiche i nGleann na nGealt,* Dublin 1939; *Eachtraí Pharthaláin Mhic Mhórna,* Dublin 1944; *Amaidí,* Dublin 1951; *Óige an Deartháir,* Dublin 1973, is a memoir of his brother. *Amaidí,* 1983.

Ó NUALLÁIN, An tAth. Gearóid, b. Omagh 1874, d. 1942. Ed. Dublin and Germany. Professor of Irish Maynooth 1909-40. Wrote textbooks, *The New Era Grammar of Modern Irish,* Dublin 1934, etc. Also short stories, *Dia Diabhail agus Daoine,* Dublin 1922; *Seán agus Mia,* Dublin 1923, which also appeared in an English trans. the same year, as *Intrusions.* President of the Society for the Preservation of the Irish Language.

O'RAHILLY, Egan, see Ó RATHAILLE, Aodhagán.

O'RAHILLY, Thomas Francis (Tomás Ó Rathaille, but often Ó Rathile), b. Kerry 1883, d. 1953. Ed. Dublin and Aberdeen. Professor of Irish TCD

1919-29; Research Professor Gaelic Languages, NUI, 1929-40. Founder and Editor of *Gadelica,* a periodical devoted to modern and early modern Irish literature. Director School of Celtic Studies in Dublin Inst. for Adv. Studies 1941-47. Contributed to *Gadelica, Eriú, Celtica,* etc. For his major works in English see Part I. His principal work in Irish was as an editor of *Dánta Grádha,* Cork 1926, and *Measgra Dánta,* Cork 1927, both collections of Irish verse, and of Flaithrí Ó Maelchonaire's *Desiderius: otherwise Sgáthán an Chrabhaidh,* Dublin 1941.

Ó RATHAILLE, Aodhagán (Egan O'Rahilly), sometimes spelled Ó Rathile, b. Co. Kerry 1670, d. Co. Kerry *c.* 1728. Studied at Killarney which at the end of the 17th century played the part of a Catholic University, half-Classical, half-Gaelic. His father died while Aodhagán was a boy, leaving his widow well provided for. She owned most of their home townland of Scrahanaveal, but the family was in some sense tenant to Eoghan MacCarthy, and the poet regarded the MacCarthy's as his chiefs, and himself as properly their poet. Like his older contemporary Ó Bruadair, he saw the old world that he admired and loved falling into ruin, and the class of Gaelic chieftains whom he longed to serve being destroyed and replaced by planters and upstarts and apostates.

He is famous for his laments and satires on the new, planter class of landowners, who had no conception of the worth of a poet or of poetry or of the true nature of hospitality. It is easy to feel sympathy for Ó Rathaille, who like Ó Bruadair fell into destitution towards the end of his life, and easy to fall into the error of believing that in his poetry speaks the true voice of Ireland; a savage cry of anguish and betrayal and hatred of the foreigner. It is necessary to remember that Ó Rathaille was speaking for a comparatively small class, the well-to-do tenants and clients of the great families, men left behind to face total ruin when their chiefs fled after Limerick in 1691. Forty years earlier the landless men who must have formed the majority of the population had welcomed Cromwell as a liberator from the oppressions of the Gaelic aristocracy, and they can have been little worse off under the planters of the new order, than they had been under the Gaelic chiefs of the old.

It was only with the slow grind of the 18th century and repeated famines that it was borne in on the poorest Irish that they were treated even worse than the poorest English. Ó Rathaille is a wounded snob rather than an outraged patriot; nevertheless, as Frank O'Connor said, he was 'one of the great snobs of literature' and his poetry is in the front rank of Irish literature. It was edited for the ITS by Pádraig Ua Duinnín, 1900. Revised edition 1911. Translations of individual poems occur in almost any anthology of Irish poetry.

Ó RATHILE, Tomás, see O'RAHILLY, Thomas Francis.

Ó REACHTABHRA, Antoine (Anthony Raftery), b. Co. Mayo *c.* 1784, d. Mayo *c.* 1835. Blind from a childhood illness like Carolan, but less educated and nothing like as fine a musician. He played the violin after a fashion, and wandered the Mayo countryside more as a beggar than as a wandering poet of the old kind. He composed for people almost as poor as himself and although his verses lived in the memory of the people, almost all the facts of his life were forgotten. Thus ended, in a gentle trudge of feet and verse, 1500 years of living poetic tradition, stretching from a time before St Patrick, into the smoky dawn of the 19th century.

Among the stories told of Raferty was that his praise-poems brought ill-fortune to the subject. The girl Máire Ní Eidhin whom he praised in a famous poem is supposed to have died shortly afterwards.

His poetry is a pleasant but pedestrian affair, suitable for reciting at fairs and in public houses, and easy to memorise, as folk-poetry needs to be. But here and there flashes of true poetry dart out from his songs and doggerel like lightning from clouds.

Raftery himself formed part of that great throng of poverty that filled the roads of Ireland at the beginning of the 19th century; the same crowds that the young William Carleton saw on his slow travels south in 1818 and 1819; vagabonds, Whiteboys and Ribbonmen on the run, landless peasants like Carleton himself, beggars, loose women, evicted tenants, old soldiers returned from the French wars and the Peninsula, rogues and horse-dealers, tinsmiths and packmen, widows and children; gathering in any shelter to rest for a night, and glad to hear a story or a song, or a poem that would make the cold less piercing, and blunt the hunger. Such gatherings listened to Blind Raftery, and carried his verses with them the next day.

Douglas Hyde edited his poems, *Abhráin atá Leagtha ar an Reachtúire,* Dublin 1903, rep. with additional material 1933 and 1969. Individual poems occur in many anthologies; for example his ballad on the hanging of Anthony O'Daly, the Whiteboy captain, in 1820.

O'REGAN, Maurice (sometimes Regan), b. Leinster *c.* 1125, d. Leinster *c.* 1200. Poet and chronicler to Dermot Mac Murrough, the King of Leinster largely responsible for bringing the Normans into Ireland. He seems to have been sent by Dermot to Wales in 1168 to renew and seal the bargain Dermot had already made the year before with Strongbow, and to urge its fulfilment. Maurice witnessed the whole of the Norman invasion and is supposed to have written an account of it and a life of Dermot. This work was translated into French (Carew MSS, Lambeth Palace, No. 596) and from French into English in a number of versions, one by Sir G. Carew, *Hibernica,* I, 1747-50, who claims to have translated the Irish MS into French in the first instance; and a better English version by G. H. Orpen as *The Song of Dermot and the Earl,* Oxford 1893. Some doubt exists about O'Regan's authorship and it had been suggested that the work was simply taken down at his dictation or written up from his remembrances when he was an old man. If this was done by one of Raymond le Gros' retainers it would explain the fact that the earliest MS is in French, and that it was in the possession of the Carews, descendants of Raymond.

Ó RIAIN, Flann, b. 1929. Cartoonist, both political and for children. Creator of famous Irish TV cartoon programme, *Dáithí Lacha*. Collected cartoons: *I gComhar le Doll,* and *Euphoria is a lovely word,* both Dublin. Children's books: *Dáithí Lacha; Dáithí Lacha,* 1967, and *Suas agus Síos.*

Ó RIAIN, Liam P. (William Patrick Ryan), b. Templemore 1867, d. London 1942. Journalist in Dublin and London, where he became Assistant Editor of the *Daily Herald.* For work in English see Part I. Wrote stories, plays and poetry in Irish; *Seanchas Filíochta,* Dublin 1940, etc. Also a work on European contributions to Gaelic scholarship and literature, *Gaedhealachas i Gcéin,* Dublin 1933. Remembered as author of one of the early Irish novels, *Caoimhghin Ó Cearnaigh,* Dublin 1913.

Ó RÍORDÁIN, Seán, b. Co. Cork 1917, d. Cork 1977. Considered one of the best of the modern Irish poets. In *Rí na nUile,* Dublin 1964, rep. 1966, 1971, he translated Irish religious poetry of 9th-12th centuries into modern Irish. His own poetry is collected in *Eireaball Spideoige,* Dublin 1952, and *Brosna,* Dublin 1964, Club Leabhar selection for 1967. Both rep. 1976.

Also, *Línte Liombó,* Dublin 1976, and *Tar Éis Mo Bháis,* Dublin 1978. *Scáthán Véarsai,* 1980 (collected poems ed. Cian Ó hÉigeartaigh). A biography and critique, *Seán Ó Ríordáin – Beatha agus Saothar,* by Seán Ó Coileáin, 1982.

Ó RODAIGHE, Tadhg, b. Co. Leitrim *c.* 1660, d. Leitrim 1710. One of the dwindling number of poets of his time who wrote in the *dán díreach* metre, and for that reason little regarded by the audience available to him, mostly peasant, who appreciated simpler styles. See T. Ó Donnchadha, *Leabhar Cloinne Aodha Buidhe,* Dublin 1931.

Ó RUADHÁIN, Seán, b. Co. Mayo 1883, d. Dublin 1966. Pioneer in the Language Revival movement, becoming a friend of Douglas Hyde and travelling the west at the beginning of the century as an Irish teacher. Became Professor of Irish at Carysfort Training College, Blackrock. His best-known book is the novel *Pádraic Máire Bán,* Dublin 1932, repub. 1934, 1935, 1937, 1938. Translated Dickens and Stevenson into Irish and also wrote short stories, *Grinn-Sgéalta,* Dublin 1929; *An Mothallsin Ort,* Dublin 1967.

Ó RUAIRC, Conchubhar, b. Co. Cork 1913. School-teacher. During a long period of unemployment in the 1930s collected folklore materials and local remembrances, *An Stáca ar an gCarraigín,* Dublin 1962, and *Gort na Gréine,* Dublin 1966. Many of these stories had appeared previously in Irish journals and magazines such as *Comhar* and *Feasta.* His intention has been to correct the sentimental, Kiltartan view of Irish country people as innocent figures of gentle fun and touching simplicity and to present them as they really are, peasants as tough and earthy as peasants have to be anywhere to survive at all, and above all in the rock and bog landscape of West Cork. He has also cried out against the policies of a 'native government' 'which never moved to help until it was too late. . . and deserted homesteads dot the countryside.'

Collected poems, *Feartlaoi;* short stories, *Seandaoine,* both Dublin 1973.

Ó SÁNDAIR, Cathal, b. England 1922, his father being English and his mother Irish from Dublin. Ed. Dublin and worked in civil service, at the same time writing schoolboy's stories in Irish. These had an enormous, and for publications in Irish, an unheard-of success. For the first time Irish children were being offered something to read that they wanted to read, in Irish, and they devoured the adventures of Reics Carlo and Reamonn Óg, Captaen Toirneach and Captaen Speirling as eagerly as their English contemporaries devoured Sexton Blake or the Saint. Between 1943, when the first Reics Carlo book, *Na Mairbh a d'Fhill,* was published, and 1958 when Ó Sandair emigrated to Canada, over 100,000 copies of his books had been sold. This must be seen in the context of Irish publishing where sales are numbered in the hundreds, and an edition of 2000 copies may take years to sell. Ó Sandair returned from Canada and the flow of books has continued, including *Mo Cahra, mo Namhaid,* Dublin 1967; *An glór glé glinn fadó* (a collection of short stories), Dublin 1981 ; *Fáilte ar ais, a Reics* (detective story), 1982.

Ó SÉAGHDHA, Pádraig (Conán Maol), b. Co. Kerry 1855, d. Ireland 1928. From an Irish speaking family but only learned to read Irish as an adult, when he was already a customs officer stationed in Cardiff. Wrote for local Welsh paper, the *Western Mail,* under the pseud. 'John Desmond,' and on being transferred to Belfast began to write in Irish, taking the pseud. 'Conán Maol' from one of the heroes of the Fianna. Meaning Conan the Bald, it had point in his case because he too was prematurely bald. His main interest was in Irish history and legend. *Éire,* Dublin 1907, rep. 1921, and *Seághan An Díomais* (Shane the Proud), written in Irish and English, Dublin 1901. Also wrote a play *Aodh Ó Néill,* Dublin 1902.

Ó SÉAGHDHA, Pádraig (Gruagach an Tobair), b. Glengariff 1864, d. Glengariff after 1926. Became a school monitor or pupil-teacher at 14, and at 18 was in charge of a school in Kenmare. For two years, 1889-90, he taught in Dublin, spending the rest of his life in West Cork. He was one of the pioneers of Irish teaching in schools, several years before the founding of the Gaelic League in 1893. His books include *Ánnala na Tuatha,* 3 parts, Dublin 1905-07; *An Sgoraidheacht,* Dublin (a play); *Déanamh an Cleamhnais,* Cork 1926 (a play); and *Fastuím,* Cork 1926, containing translations of Sheridan's *School for Scandal* and *St Patrick's Day or the Scheming Lieutenant,* with Goldsmith's *She Stoops to Conquer.*

Ó SEARCAIGH, Seámas, b. Co. Donegal 1887, d. Dún Laoghaire 1965. Ed. QUB, became lecturer in Dept. of Celtic Studies UCD and at Maynooth. Ended his career as President of the Irish College, Cloghaneely, Co. Donegal. Books include *Faire Phaidi Mhóir,* Dublin 1914; *Ceol na n-Éan agus Sgéalta Eile,* Dundalk 1919 (stories); *Foghraidheacht Ghaeilge an*

Tuaiscirt, Belfast 1925 (on Ulster dialect); *Pádraig Mac Piarais,* Dublin 1928 (a life of Pearse); *Sgéalta ar an tSean-Litridheacht,* Dublin 1945; *Beatha Cholm Cille,* Dublin 1967; and many others.

Ó SIADHAIL, Mícheál, b. Dublin 1947. Ed. TCD and Oslo University. Now researcher in Dublin Inst. for Adv. Studies. Poetry: *An Bhliain Bhisigh,* 1978; *Runga,* 1980; and two collections in English, *Springnight,* 1983; *The Image Wheel,* 1985, Co-author with Arndt Wigger *Cumann,* 1982; *Córas Fuaimeanna na Gaeilge,* 1975; all pub. Dublin.

Ó SIOCHFHRADHA, Micheál, b. Co. Kerry 1901. Schools Inspector in Co. Clare. Has translated plays by T. C. Murray and Sheridan into Irish, and written short stories, *Soineain 's Doineann,* Dublin 1953.

Ó SIOCHFHRADHA, Pádraig (An Seabhac), b. Dingle 1883, d. Dublin 1964. Ed. Dingle. Teacher and organiser for the Gaelic League in Munster 1903-22 and also for the first Irish government 1920-22. Became Editor for Gaelic League 1922, remaining a civil servant for Free State government also, until 1932, when he was appointed Senator and took a commercial post as editor for Educational Co. of Ireland. Wrote text-books, short stories, plays, new versions of old Irish tales. Is best remembered by generations of school children for *Jimín Mháire Thaidhg,* Dublin 1921, repub. Dublin 1984, a novel for young people about the adventures of a small boy. It first appeared as a serial in *An Lóchrann,* 1919-20. *Seáinín,* Dublin 1922; *Máirín; An Baile Seo 'Gainne,* Dublin 1913 (a collection of his short stories), helped to make him one of the best-loved Irish writers of the century. Among other works he produced an edition of *Tomás Ó Criomhthain: An tOileánach. Jimín* and *An Baile Seo 'Gainne* were reprinted together as *Seoda an tSeabhaic,* Dublin 1974. Trans. diaries of Wolfe Tone as *Beatha Theobald Wolfe Tone,* Dublin 1937.

Ó SÍOTHCHÁIN, An tAth. Micheál, b. Waterford 1871, d. Sydney, Australia 1948. When he was ten years old his family moved to Dungarvan in Co. Waterford, where Gaelic was still spoken by the older people. He tried to learn the language from them but met the suspicious hostility that characterised many Irish speakers before the founding of the Gaelic League. Irish was still the badge of inferiority and to a lesser extent of political untrustworthiness (seen from the dominant British viewpoint). Anyone, even a child, seeking to learn the language, was at best misguided and at worst dangerous. There was a vague feeling that someone might blame the 'teacher' for filling the child's head with 'wrong ideas.' The enormous achievement of the Gaelic League was to change this situation and make the language a badge of pride. That this achievement did not survive political independence is another and tragic matter.

Ó Síothcháin was ordained at Maynooth 1895, received an MA (Hons) Oxon 1897, was made Professor of Classics at Maynooth, and also travelled and studied in Germany, receiving his Ph.D. at Bonn 1900. In 1906 with several others he founded Ring College in Co. Waterford, with the idea of restoring a Waterford Gaeltacht, and of teaching spoken living Irish to students who would visit Ring for a summer course or a short period that would not interfere with their normal schooling. In 1919 became President of Maynooth. In 1922 was made Assistant Archbishop of Sydney.

His books include *Seanchainnt na nDéise,* Dublin 1906 (on the Irish dialect of Waterford); *Cnuasacht Trágha,* Dublin 1908; *Gile na mBláth,* Dublin 1912; *Ladhar den Lus Mór,* Dublin 1919.

Ó SNODAIGH, Pádraig, b. Carlow 1935. On staff of National Museum. Critic, poet and researcher. President Conradh na Gaeilge 1974-79. *Comhghuaillithe na Reabhlóide 1913-1916,* Dublin 1966, deals with Irish history immediately prior to the Rising of 1916. Won a Butler Family Book Award 1967. *Hidden Ulster,* Dublin 1973, revised and expanded ed. 1977. *Rex,* 1981, won special award in the Oireachtas 1979. *Veinéiseach Eigin,* 1983 (trans. from Italian of Giuseppe Sarto). *Cumha agus Cumann,* 1985; with Rose Angela Barone, *Caitlín Maude, File-poet-poeta,* 1985; co-ed. with Arthur Mitchell, *Irish Political Documents 1916-49,* 1985; all pub. Dublin. Runs own publishing company, Coiscéim.

Ó SÚILEABHÁIN, Amhlaoibh, see O'SULLIVAN, Humphrey.

Ó SÚILEABHÁIN, Muiris, b. Great Blasket 1904, d. Connemara 1950, by drowning. His mother died before he was a year old and he was brought up on the mainland until he was 7, speaking only English. His father bringing him back to the island, he went to school there and learned Irish, remaining until 1927, when he left to join the Civic Guards in Dublin. He was stationed in Connemara and there wrote his now famous autobiography, *Fiche Blian ag Fás,* Dublin 1933, translated the same year by Moya Llewelyn Davies and George Thomson as *Twenty Years A-Growing,* 1933. It has been translated into many languages and reprinted many times, most recently, Dublin 1976; and has come to be regarded outside of Ireland as the classic Irish book of this century. It is a gentle, loving, homesick remembrance of his childhood, and the life of the islands, and deserves its success, but Irish critics prefer the harsher style of Ó Criomhthain in *Allagar na hInise,* and *An tOileánach.*

After the successful publication of his book, which he had written with nothing more in mind that the amusement of the old women still living on the Blaskets, the few that then remained, Ó Súileabháin left the Guards but remained in Connemara. He was drowned bathing.

Ó SÚILLEABHÁIN,Diarmuid, b.Béarra 1932, d. Dublin 1985. Taught in Gorey, Co. Wexford. MIAL. Contributed to *An Phoblacht.* First made a name with the novel, *Súil le Muir,* Dublin 1959. *Dianmhuilte Dé,* Dublin 1964, and *Caoin Tú Féin,* Dublin 1967 (won the Oireachtas Prize for 1966) had brought him high praise from critics, one of whom, Pádraig Ó Croiligh in *Irisleabhar Muighe Nuadhat,* Dublin 1966, compared him to Zola. He also wrote plays: *Bior,* 1965; *Macalla,* 1966; and *Lens,* 1966. His novel *An Uain Bheo,* 1968, won the Oireachtas Prize for 1967. *Trá agus Tuil-*

leach, 1967; *Múintir,* 1971; *Maeldún,* 1972; *Gealach Reatha,* 1982; and two novels, *Ciontach* and *Aistear,* both 1983.

Ó SÚILLEABHÁIN, Eoghan Ruadh, b. Co. Kerry, 1748, d. Co. Kerry 1784. An Irish Robert Burns, with a more tragic and pathetic life story as befitted the country he lived in. His part of the country had escaped the worst of the oppressions of the 18th century because the Mac Carthys still had power there, and in some senses it was a surviving fragment of the old Gaelic world. The Mac Carthy Mór could still protect his people from the local representatives of English authority. Ships came and went between France and Kerry and paid their respects to the Mac Carthys rather than the Revenue.

Eoghan Ruadh went to school near Killarney, and already as a boy gained a reputation as a poet. He learned English, and a good deal of Irish history, and as soon as he left school opened a school of his own. But bad times and his own preference for girls and drink closed the school almost as soon as he opened it, and he found himself reduced to hiring himself out as a *spailpín,* or itinerant farm labourer. He wrote a poem to a blacksmith named FitzGerald, asking him to make a fine spade for him 'Because the spade is the only thing keeping me now' and with it he can earn 6d a day and his keep.

After one of his *spailpín* journeys he returned to his home parish of Faha to find a great argument going on between the married and single men of the parish, following a hurling match between the two camps which the married men had won. He wrote a satire on the married men that crushed them and ended the controversy. It must have been within a year or so of this that Brian Merriman began to write *The Midnight Court,* which also turns on a controversy over marriage and bachelorhood and the duties of a bachelor.

Not long after this his fortunes looked up. He became tutor to the Nagle family near Fermoy. But again he betrayed himself, seducing Mrs Nagle instead of teaching her children, and he was driven away from the house at gun-point, lucky not to have been shot. He joined the British Navy in desperation, sailing under Rodney for the West Indies. Despite the traffic between Kerry and France, it was already more natural for an Irishman down on his luck to join the British forces than the French or Spanish or Austrian services.

After Rodney's defeat of the French admiral de Grasse off Dominica in 1782 he wrote a panegyric in English, 'Rodney's Glory', which won him an interview with the admiral, and a reward. (The English government was less enthusiastic about the victory, retiring Rodney on a pension). Sad to say, the panegyric is very poor poetry, no more than doggerel, and it is hard to imagine successfully explaining to the magnificent Rodney that the tarry oaf in front of him who had written that amusing rubbish in halting English was one of the great Irish lyric poets of the century. It would simply have confirmed his prejudice that Catholic Irishmen were ruffians in any language, and that their own language must be a barbaric dialect. (Although curiously enough the officer who brought Ó Súilleabháin to Rodney was himself a Kerryman and an Irish speaker.) Even 60 years later George Borrow almost apologised to his English readers for having himself learned Irish as a child in a garrison town in Ireland in the early 1800s, calling it a poor, barbarous dialect. That the language contained great wealth of culture was as hidden from Borrow as from Rodney, and that the poor labourer in naval uniform was one of its glories, was an inconceivable joke.

Eoghan Ruadh returned to England, left the navy and joined the army, and it was during his unpromising year of military service that he wrote some of his famous *aislingí*, such as *Ceo Draoidheachta*. Determined to get out of the army he created evil-smelling sores on his legs with spear-wort, which mystified the English doctor and horrified his fellow soldiers. He won his discharge, and wrote home to the parish priest that he was returning to open another school. This lasted for one brilliant year, but possibly again the poet was better at entertaining his scholars than teaching them, and the school broke up in the summer of 1784.

He hoped to get some kind of help from a local notability, Colonel Cronin, and wrote him a praise-poem which the Colonel ignored. He then wrote a satire on him, and whether or not the Colonel understood it, the Colonel's servants revenged it on Eoghan Ruadh in a Killarney ale-house, one of them knocking him senseless with a pair or iron fire-tongs. It is much the same thing that happened to Behan in Dublin 180 years later.

He recovered his senses and made his way up the mountains to Knockna-gree and a hut that sheltered fever patients. The fever he had may have been more from a disease than a broken head and when he reached the hut he was clearly dying. He was put to bed and nursed, but even then he is supposed to have grabbed the young girl who was tending him and seduced her there in his sick-bed. The story goes that this last act of over-indulgence killed him when otherwise he might have recovered. But he was not a man to recover. He died writing a poem. *Sin é an file go fann/ Nuair thuiteann an peann as a láimh* (Weak indeed is the poet/ when the pen fails from his hand).

Corkery describes how, 130 and more years after Eoghan Ruadh's death, he himself heard stories upon stories of Eoghan Ruadh by Munster firesides, and in the back lanes of Cork, and how old men and old women who would not have known Shakespeare from Douglas Hyde could recite long poems by Eoghan Ruadh and loved him as Eoghan of the Sweet Mouth.

His songs and poems were collected by An tAth. Pádraig Ua Duinnín for the Gaelic League, Dublin 1901, rep. 1902, 1923. A long biographical and critical essay is included in Daniel Corkery, *The Hidden Ireland*, Dublin 1924, paperback ed. Dublin 1967, continuously reprinted.

• **Ó SÚILLEABHÁIN**, Muiris, see **Ó SÚILEABHÁIN**, Muiris.

Ó SÚILLEABHÁIN, Seán, b. Co. Kerry 1903. School-teacher for 12 years.

Registrar and archivist for Irish Folklore Commission 1935-75. Has done research in Sweden. For his work in English see under O'SULLIVAN, Sean in Part I. *Saoghal na bPáistí,* Dublin 1935; *Láimh-Leabhar Béaloideasa,* Dublin 1938; *Diarmuid na Bolgaighe agus a Chóimhursain,* Dublin 1937; and *Caitheamh Aimsire ar Thorraimh,* Dublin 1961, trans. as *Irish Wake Amusements,* Cork 1967, rep. 1980.

Ó SÚILLIOBHÁIN, Tadhg Gaedhealach, b. Co. Limerick 1715, d. Waterford 1795. As a young man wandered about Cork and Waterford writing verse of no great interest, except for the fact that one of his political poems earned him a term of imprisonment in Cork City. Like many of the Munster poets of the 18th century he was a sentimentally fierce Jacobite. In middle-age he settled in Dungarvan and became deeply religious, turning his poetry to spiritual themes, but still using the simple language and metres of his secular verses. There is nothing very original or deep in his thinking, but the simplicity and sincerity of his poems pleased a wide audience and in 1802 the Bishop of Raphoe, or possibly one of his parish clergy, collected Tadhg's poetry in *Timothy O'Sullivan's Irish Pious Miscellany; to which is added a poem on the Passion of Our Saviour, by the Rev. Dr. Coyle, Roman Catholic Bishop of Raphoe,* Clonmel 1802. The book was swiftly and immensely popular. Reprinted about 40 times in Clonmel, Cork and Dublin, some of the poems were set to music and sung like hymns, rather than songs, the music often being popular folktunes of the district. The book was republished with additional matter, by John O'Daly, Dublin 1858, and in a scholarly edition with notes as *Amhráin Thaidhg Gaedhealaigh Uí Súilleabháin iar n-a gcruinniughadh is a gcur i n-eagar leis an Athair Pádraig Ua Duinnín,* Dublin 1903. *The Gaelic American* published the Miscellany serially in NY, October 1910–February 1911, ed. Richard Foley under the pen-name 'Fiachra Éilgeach.'

Ó SÚILLIOBHÁIN, Tomás Ruadh, b. Co. Kerry 1785, d. Co. Kerry 1848. A hedge schoolmaster, he was one of the first poets to recognise and write of Daniel O'Connell's greatness, whom he salutes in terms that an earlier generation of poets might have used of Prince Charlie. He seems to have seen O'Connell as in a sense a continuer of the Jacobite cause.

He is also remembered for his poem *Amhrán na Leabhar, Song of the Books.* Crossing by boat from Caherdaniel to Portmagee, there was an accident and all his books were lost. It was a tragedy for a poor itinerant teacher, and he wrote a lament for his precious volumes: Cato, Euclid, Keating's History, the Psalter of Cashel, manuscript copies of nationalist tracts, the New Testament, and Bishop Ó Gallchobhair's Sermons. The poem gives an insight into the equipment of a hedge schoolmaster. His poetry was collected and printed by Séamus Dubh as *Amhráin Thomáis Ruaidh; The Songs of Tomás Ruadh O'Sullivan the Iveragh Poet,* Dublin 1914.

O'SULLIVAN, Humphrey (Ó Súileabháin, Amhlaoibh), b. Co. Kerry *c.*

1780, d. Co. Kilkenny 1837. The son of a school-teacher and himself a teacher until his Kilkenny-born wife Mary Delahunty brought him a draper's shop in Callan, Co. Kilkenny, as her dowry, in 1812. He spent the rest of his life as an active burgess and councillor, and his fame rests on the diary he kept of his activities for the years 1827-35. In these volumes he talks of everything from his work, to the weather, to the building of Dun Laoghaire harbour and the Liffey walls. He has been called the Samuel Pepys of Ireland, and the diary is certainly unique in Irish literature. The MS is in the RIA, and presents difficulties to the untrained reader. Part of the diary for 1827 was printed in *Gadelica*, 1912-13, edited by Seamus Ó Casaide. Rev. Michael McGrath SJ edited the entire text and published it with a translation into English as *Cinn-lae Amhlaoibh Uí Shúilleabháin*, 4 vols, ITS, 1936. Paperback ed., trans. Tomás de Bhaldraithe, Cork 1979.

O'SULLIVAN BEARE, (sometimes O'Sullevan Beare, in Irish Ó Súilleabháin Béarra), Philip, b. Dunboy *c.* 1590, d. Spain *c.* 1660. Nephew of Donell O'Sullivan Beare, Lord of Dunboy. Sent to Spain in 1602 where he later entered the Spanish army. After the defeat of the chiefs and the fall of Dunboy his family joined him in exile. His history of Ireland, which is chiefly a detailed history of the Elizabethan wars, is based on much first-hand information. He adapts Virgil's description of ruined Troy to Ireland after Kinsale. *Historiae Catholicae Iverniae Compendium*, Lisbon 1621; repub. Dublin 1850, ed. Matthew Kelly. O'Sullivan also wrote a life of St Patrick, *Patriciana Decas*, Lisbon 1629, and later on became involved in controversy with Archbishop Ussher.

Ó TIOMÁNAIDHE, Micheál, b. Co. Mayo 1853, d. 1953. Collected a large number of folk tales from the West, most of them still unprinted. *Abhráin Ghaedhilge an Iarthair*, Dublin 1906 (for the Gaelic League. A collection of Irish songs from the West). *Targaireacht Bhriain Ruaidh Uí Chearbháin agus Stair-Sheanchus le n-a Choir*, Dublin 1906 (also for Gaelic League. Red Brian's Prophecy and other historical matter); *Sgéalta Gearra an Iarthair*, Dublin 1910 (stories from the West); *An Lampa Draoidheachta agus Naoi Sgéalta Eile*, Dublin 1935 (more stories).

Ó TREASAIGH, Lorcan, b. Dún Laoghaire 1927. Actor, singer and writer. Compère on CIE's Radio Train 1957-77. Assistant ed. *Nuacht* (CIE's house magazine) 1981-85. Poetry: *Seamair*, 1972. Thirteen radio plays, including *Tairseach Neimhe* (verse play), 1972, won RE prize. Short stories: *Uisce Bás agus Beatha*, Dublin 1975, won Oireachtas Prize. Novel: *An Doras Grianlasta*, Dublin 1984.

Ó TUAIRISC, Eoghan (Eugene Watters), b. Co. Galway 1919, d. Wexford 1982. School-teacher and soldier, travelled Ireland in a horse-drawn caravan; married to a painter. Wrote in English and Irish. Irish novel *L'Attaque*, Dublin 1962 (Hyde Memorial Award), new ed. 1980; Irish poetry, *Lux Aeterna* (including *Hiroshima Mass)*, Dublin 1964 (again won Hyde Award); *Dé Luain*, Dublin 1966 (American Cultural Award); and a play,

Ó TUAMA

Lá Fhéile Michíl, Dublin 1967 (Oireachtas Prize). *Murder in Three Moves,* Dublin 1960, an English novel. *Focus,* with Desmond Egan, Dublin 1972 (essays on English poetry); *New Passages,* Dublin 1973 (poems); *Rogha an Fhile,* Dublin 1974 (anthology of Irish poetry with trans.); *An Hairyfella in Ifreann,* a play first produced Galway 1974; *The Hedgeschoolmaster,* Cork and Dublin 1975 (novel); *Infinite Variety,* Dublin and London 1976 (theatre history); *Aisling Mhic Artáin,* a play (Oireachtas Prize), first produced Dublin 1977, pub. Dublin 1978. *An Lomnochtán,* Cork and Dublin 1978 (novel); *Fornocht do Chonac,* 1981; and *Dialann sa Díseart,* 1981 (which includes poems by his wife Rita E. Kelly). First of the Aosdána members to die.

Ó TUAMA, Seán ('an Ghrinn'), b. Co. Limerick 1706, d. Co. Limerick 1775. Briefly a school-teacher and then an inn-keeper, who welcomed any Gaelic poet, and was himself a poet. When he heard of the death in 1754 of Seán Clarach Mac Domhnaill, his friend, and until then chief poet of the south, he called together his fellow poets for a commemoration, and not only that, but for a council as to how both Irish poetry and the Irish language were to be kept alive against the encroachment of English. His own Irish betrays the fact that in his time his district was losing the language, but both he and his poetry were looked up to as leader and example of the old culture, and he deserves respect.

Tragically, his poetry ruined him. He paid more attention to it than to his inn-keeping, or else he never charged his poet guests, and towards the end of his life his inn was lost to him and he was some kind of servant to a Mrs Quinn, keeping her hens for her and receiving little respect. He called her in some bitterly unhappy verses the Dame of the Slender Wattle, and bewailed the time that his pockets were full of money and his head empty of cares except for his friends. These friends included Seán Clarach and Aindrias Mac Craith, who formed with several others a school known as *Filí na Máighe,* the poets of the Maigue valley. Riseárd Ó Foghludha edited their poetry twice, in *Filidhe na Máighe,* Dublin 1906, and in *Éigse na Máighe,* Dublin 1952.

Ó TUAMA, Seán, b. Cork 1926, native speaker. Ed. UCC. Professor of Irish UCC since 1967. Won Arts Council Scholarship for Irish writers under 35, spending a year in France 1955-56 studying modern drama. Ph.D. thesis on relationships between Irish folksong and mediaeval French poetry, published as *An Grá in Amhráin na nDaoine,* Dublin 1960. Has written plays and poetry as well as critical essays, *Caoineadh Airt Uí Laoghaire,* edited with long introductory essay, Dublin 1961, repub. Dublin 1979; *Faoileán na Beatha* (his own poetry), Dublin 1962 (Club Leabhar selection); *Moloney agus Drámaí Eile* (three short plays), Dublin 1967; *Gunna Cam agus Slabhra Óir* (a play) 1967, rep. 1974; collected poems, *Saol fó Thoinn,* 1978; *Filí faoi Sceimhle,* 1978, a study of Seán Ó Ríordáin and Aogán Ó Rathaille. And ed. *Nuabhéarsaíocht 1939-49,* latest reprint 1974. Co-ed. with Thomas Kinsella, *An Dunaire,* Dublin 1981.

P

PATRICK, Bishop, b. *c.* 1025 in Ireland, d. 1084. Educated in England, made Bishop of Dublin 1074, drowned in Irish Sea on a journey to England 1084. Wrote in Latin and Irish mostly on religious subjects and visions of the type popular in mediaeval verse, but also translated an Irish MS on the Wonders of Ireland. See *The Writings of Bishop Patrick*, ed. Aubrey Gwynn, Dublin 1955, in the series *Scriptores Latini Hiberniae,* vol. 1.

PATRICK, Saint, properly Succat, son of Calpurnius, grandson of the priest Potitus, b. *c.* 385, possibly in South Wales, d. near Armagh, *c.* 461. Captured as a boy of 16 by Irish pirates and brought to Ireland as a slave, probably in the Antrim area; escaped about 407 on a ship carrying 'race hounds' to Bordeaux. Seems to have returned to his family in Wales, felt a vocation to convert the Irish and became a cleric in Gaul, possibly under St Germanus of Auxerre. Legend made St Patrick not only a personal friend of St Martin of Tours, but his blood-kin. There seems no foundation for either claim and St Martin was dead several years before the earliest possible date for Patrick's arrival in Gaul, but it is possible that he was deeply influenced by him at second hand, and that he brought Sulpicius Severus's *Corpus Martinianum* with him on his eventual return to Ireland. In the meantime he spent a period in the monastic settlements of Lérins off the coast of Provence, where he adopted the Eastern view of the monastic life. His wish to return to Ireland met opposition, but possibly his project led to the mission of Palladius in 431 to the 'Christians already in Ireland.' It seems clear that ordinary traffic had brought both Christian ideas and Christian individuals to Ireland, and Irish travellers may have been converted abroad and returned, without there yet being any organisation for the converts. After Palladius's early death Patrick was consecrated bishop and at last permitted to go on his mission, by tradition in 432.

He is held to have converted Ulster, Connacht and Munster, the assumption being that Leinster was already partly Christianised. His *Confessio* describes his mission, in a Latin not quite of continental quality. By his own account some of his rivals held him to be ill-educated. He set up a diocesan system that was to be submerged in the monastic movement of the following century. It is possible that he visited Rome in 441. Almost nothing else can be said of him with even so much certainty.

His *Epistola ad Milites Corotici* protesting about the ill-treatment of a group of his converts by soldiers from Cardigan reflects the kind of life he and his converts led as Christians in a still largely pagan country; in constant danger of violence and persecution. Other fragments of his writings, the *Dicta Patricii,* preserved in the *Book of Armagh,* are probably genuine, with the exception of the last piece. Aside from these writings, Patrick is traditionally held to have influenced the codification of the Brehon Laws and their adaptation to the requirements of Christianity.

The controversies surrounding every detail of Patrick's life are legion. The Irish *Annals* give two dates for his death, the later being *c.* 490. This with other factors has led to the suggestion that there were two missionaries of the same name, and Zimmer and T. F. O'Rahilly identify the earlier with Palladius. There seems little reason to accept this.

Despite the lack of certainty regarding details, there can be no doubt that an actual Patrick was the principal missionary in Christianising Ireland, and that as such he was the principal instrument in founding Irish literacy and literature. While manuscripts must have circulated in pre-Christian Ireland, and been read and even written, there was no Irish literature; simply orally recited stories and poems which changed from generation to generation as their reciters altered or added to them or subtracted from them, or simply forgot them. Patrick, besides introducing an organised religion, introduced as a side-effect an organised literature. Approaching the kings and chiefs first as potential converts and their immediate followers next, he drew into the Church exactly the class that had been the guardians and transmitters of oral tradition, and taught them the value of committing such traditions to writing. Apart from the Church's need of numerous copies of the Gospels, the Psalms, and the Epistles, Patrick set his followers an example by writing his own *Confessio*. And perhaps most important of all, Patrick himself was trained in a world still impregnated with literary traditions. When Patrick was born, Britain and Wales were a province of the Roman Empire. Literature was still a part of civilised life. The same was true of Gaul when he came there to enter the Church.

Prudentius and Sidonius Apollinaris were his older and younger contemporaries. Boethius was not born until 20 years after Patrick's death. Even though he himself claimed little education, he belonged to an educated world and brought its traditions with him into Ireland. When Augustine came to England in 597, none of this remained true. When Germany and Northern Europe were Christianised it was still less true. Alone of the countries of Northern Europe Ireland received its Christianity from a Southern Europe not yet turned entirely against the old culture, and this must go some way towards explaining why and how Ireland preserved so much of its own pagan traditions and created from them so rich, and at the same time so pagan an early literature. Pagan-cultured ollamh became Christian-cultured abbot with far less inner conflict, far less of a chasm between his two lives, than could ever have been the case in Germany or Saxon England or Scandinavia. Only in Iceland, where Christianity also came gently, and did not come at all until culture was reviving in the West, was there any comparable handing on and melting of one tradition into the other. If St Patrick's coming had been delayed by 200 years, as it might well have been, early Irish literature would be as poverty stricken as early English, with its borrowed Beowulf and handful of late poems.

There are many scholarly lives of St Patrick and a vast literature, much of it dealing with St Patrick's own writings: L. Bieler *Codices Patriciani Latini*, 1942; J. Gwynn, *Introduction to Liber Ardmachanus*, 1913; J. H. Todd, *St Patrick, Apostle of Ireland*, 1863; and the same title, E. MacNeill, 1934; T. F. O'Rahilly, *The Two Patricks*, 1942, among many others.

PEARSE, Patrick Henry (Pádraig Mac Piarais, pseud. 'Colm Ó Conaire'), b. Dublin 1879, d. Kilmainham Gaol, Dublin, executed, 1916. For his writings in English see Part I. Ed. CBS Westland Row, Dublin, and in the Royal University Dublin. Became Secretary of the Publications Committee of the Gaelic League. In 1903 became editor of *Claidheamh Soluis*. In 1912 became editor of *An Macaomh* and also of *Bárr Buadh*. In 1908 he had founded Scoil Eanna and in the next few years he spent much time on the Continent studying European methods of education, particularly in Belgium where a bi-lingual system was in operation. His ideal was to create a system which would liberate a child's mind rather than constrict it, and encourage it to develop in whatever direction suited its talents, rather than force it in some predetermined direction that suited the teacher or the 'system.' Recent reforms in Irish education promise to fulfil this ideal. Added to this general purpose was a desire to make the child Irish rather than colonial English; a desire which led him finally to Easter Week and Kilmainham. All his plays, stories and poetry are intended to serve the dream of an Ireland both free and Irish, and he could not conceive of its being the one without the other; nor of any 'freedom' that left Ireland for all practical purposes an English-speaking state. His Irish writings are collected in *Scríbhinní*, Dublin and London 1919. *Selected short stories of Pádraic Pearse*, Cork 1976; and a story for children, *Poll an Phíobaire*, Dublin 1977.

PEMBRIDGE, Christopher, probably of Dublin, *fl.* 1370, author of *Annales Hiberniae*, covering the years 1162-1370. The MS is in the Bodleian, and was printed in London in William Camden's *Britannia*, the 6th ed. of 1607, translated into English by Philemon Holland, 1610, reprinted many times, the best-known edition being Gough and Nichols, in 4 vols, 1806.

PLÉIMION, Seagan, see FLEMING, John.

PONCE, John, b. Co. Cork 1603, d. Paris 1670. As a boy was sent to Louvain and entered Franciscan Order. Associated there with Fr Colgan and Fr Hugh Ward. Called to Rome by Luke Wadding, 1625, and there taught philosophy and theology at St Isidore's. Became Wadding's assistant in the work of editing Duns Scotus. Much of his writing, all in Latin, was concerned with Scotus's philosophy, such as *Integer Cursus Theologiae*, Paris 1652, or Scotus's life, such as *Scotus Hiberniae Restitutes*, in which he claims Scotus as an Irishman against two fathers who claimed him as an Englishman. Apparently no Scottish Franciscan was present to point out that Scotus was born in Roxburgh. But Ponce also wrote about Irish affairs: *Vindiciae Eversae*, Paris 1652; and more important *Deplorabilis*

Populi Hibernici Pro Religione, Rege et Libertate Status, Paris 1651.

POWER, Richard, b. Dublin 1928, d. Bray 1970. Civil servant. For work in English see Part 1. Wrote plays in Irish: *Saoirse,* 1955, *Oidhreacht,* 1957; and an account of life on the Aran Islands, and with Irish-speaking labourers on an English building site, *Úll i mBarr an Ghéagáin,* Dublin 1959 (Club Leabhar Prize).

POWER, Victor, b. Co. Kildare 1930, brother of Richard. Ordained 1954. Deeply interested in Gaelic amateur drama movement; has written a number of one-act and longer plays in Irish. *Umar na h-Aimleise,* 1961. Won the Oireachtas Prize twice – in 1959 for *Aisling 'sna Comaraigh,* and *Umar na h-Amleise,* 1961. Other plays include *Ní Togtha ar an Óige,* 1962, and in English *Young Men in a Hurry,* 1964, which won main drama award, Athlone, 1964. *Blood Brothers* (about 1916 Rising), won All Ireland Drama Award 1966.

PRÚT, Liam (also Liam F.), b. Nenagh 1940. Ed. Nenagh and Dublin. Dáil translator. Poetry: *Fíon as Seithí Óir,* 1972; *Asail,* 1982; *An Dá Scór,* 1984. Short stories: *Seán-Dair,* 1985. All pub. Dublin. *Mairtín Ó Direáin: File Tréadúil,* Maynooth 1982.

R

RAFTERY, Anthony, see Ó REACHTABHRA, Antoine.

RIGGS, Pádraigín, b. Co. Tipperary 1949. Ed. UCC. Lecturer in Irish language and literature UCC. Essays, *Donncha Ó Céileachair,* Dublin 1978; ed. *An Chéad Chloch,* 1978 (Sean Phádraic Ó Conaire's short stories, first pub. in 1914).

ROSENSTOCK, Gabriel, b. Co. Limerick 1949, German father, Irish mother. Ed. UCC. Assistant editor of *An Gúm* until 1981. Freelance broadcaster in Irish. Collected poems, *Susanne Sa Seomra Folctha,* Dublin 1973; *Méaram,* Dublin 1978; *Mignars,* 1985. With Cathal Ó Searcaigh and Bill Doyle, *Tuirlingt,* Dublin 1978. *Smionagar,* Dublin 1978, collected plays and stories. Trans. *Ri na Catóire,* Dublin 1979, from novel by Jan Terlouw. Verse for children, *An tOchtapas,* 1977; *An Béar Bán,* 1978; *An Chrosóg Mhara,* 1979; *Méaram,* 1981; *Om,* 1983; *Nihil Obstat,* 1984; *Níl aon Tinteán, An tSine Beo* (cartoons), 1984; all pub. Dublin.

RYAN, William Patrick, see Ó RIAIN, Liam P.

S

SALINGER, William (sometimes Saint Leger), b. Kilkenny 1600, d. Compostella 1665. Studied in Sicily, entered Jesuits, returned to Ireland about 1636, and was made Superior of Irish Province 1641 and rector of Kilkenny College. When Kilkenny was taken by Cromwell he escaped to Galway and at the end of the Cromwellian war fled to Spain where he became rector of the Residence of Compostella. There he wrote a life of Archbishop Walsh, of Cashel, *De Vita et Morta Illustrissimi Domini Thomae Valesii, Archiepiscopi Casiliensis in Hibernia,* Antwerp 1655.

SAYERS, Peig, b. Dunquin, Co. Kerry 1873, d. 1958. Spent much of her life on the Great Blasket, where she was known as the Queen of the Storytellers. Robin Flower wrote of her story-telling: 'her words could be written down as they leave her lips, and they would have the effect of literature with no savour of the artificiality of composition.' Her autobiography and her 'reflections' have become Irish classics, to set alongside the books of her fellow-islanders Muiris Ó Súileabháin and Tomás Ó Criomhthain. *Peig,* ed. M. Ní Chinnéide, Dublin 1936; *Machtnamh Sean-Mhná,* the same editor, Dublin 1939, new ed. 1980, and *An Old Woman's Reflections,* trans. from the Irish by S. Ennis, 1962. *Beatha Pheig Sayers,* Dublin 1969, is her life story told by her son Maidhc. See Ó Gaoithín, Micheál.

SEABHAC, AN, see Ó SÍOCHFHRADHA, Pádraig.

SEANCHÁN TORPÉIST, b. Connacht *c.* 570, d. 647. Successor to Dallan Forgaill as chief of the poets of Ireland, and one of the leaders in the Great Bardic Assembly, during which he avenged Dallan against King Guaire. He is reputed to have saved the *Táin Bó Cúailnge* from oblivion. If this is in any way based on truth it gives a possible date for the compilation of the first MS copy of the story in the first half of the 7th century. This would explain the survival of the apparently 6th-century verses known as *rosc* in the otherwise 8th-century version preserved in the *Book of the Dun Cow,* itself a late 12th-century MS. Seanchán wrote a *Lament for Dallan,* and a poem on the *Battles of Fergus.* See James Hardiman, *Irish Minstrelsy,* Dublin 1831; *Ossianic Scoiety Transactions,* V, 1860, article by Owen Connellan on one of Seanchán's poems in the *Book of Lecan;* and Whitley Stokes, *Three Irish Glossaries,* London 1862. Also *Sanas Chormaic,* ed. W. Stokes, trans. John O'Donovan, Calcutta 1868.

SEANDÚN, see Ó MURCHADHA, Tadhg.

SEDULIUS, Coelius, *fl.* 5th century. Poet, author of a number of hymns and secular verses; *A Solis Ortus Cardine* and *Hostis Herodes Impie,* with *Carmen Seculare* among others. His poetry was edited by Huemer, Vienna 1885.

SEDULIUS SCOTUS or **SCOTTUS**, sometimes called 'of Liége', b. probably Kildare, *c.* 820, d. probably Liége *c.* 880. He has been confused with another Sedulius, more properly Siadhal, son of Feradach, abbot of Kildare, who died in 828, and it is possible that Sedulius grew up in the Kildare monastery under Siadhal, and adopted his name. In 848 a mission was sent from Ireland to tell Charles the Bald of the victory over the Northmen at Sciath Nechtain, and Sedulius may have been attached to the mission. Soon afterwards he arrived with two companions in Liége, asking hospitality from Bishop Hartgar. Sedulius remained in Liége for at least ten years, gathered a group of Irish clerics and scribes round him, and copied a number of important Classical MSS, both Latin and Greek; the Greek Gospels with Latin version inter-lined; the Pauline Epistles in Greek and Latin, Priscian, Horace, Servius on Virgil, St Augustine and others. Many of these MSS came to St Gall later. From an Irish viewpoint the greatest interest in the MSS lies in the marginal jottings by the scribes in Irish; poetry, comments, invocations to Irish saints, etc.

Sedulius's own poetry, mostly in Latin, is of considerable merit and reveals a happy and festive nature. He writes a flattering poem to Count Robert, 'the golden hope of our Muse,' and receives 25 dozen bottles of wine in reward. He writes of his contempt and loathing for beer 'like a beast of prey clawing at a man's guts.' He writes odes of welcome to visiting notables, including the Empress Ermengard, who embroidered his verses in a tapestry. He grumbles about the weather and the state of the cell he lives in with its leaky roof and draughts. His voice comes across the centuries as intensely human as Brendan Behan's and offers a corrective to the view that Ireland's contribution to the Faith was entirely puritanical.

See Hellmann, *Sedulius Scottus,* Munich 1906; Helen Waddell, *Mediaeval Latin Lyrics,* 1929, latest reprint 1952.

SEITHFÍN MÓR, *fl.* Offaly *c.* 1440. His praise-poem to O'Connor of Offaly and his wife Margaret O'Carroll describes one of the great bardic festivals that were a feature of the Gaelic political and cultural revival of the 15th century. *Bríathra Cogaidh Con Chath Laigneach,* article by O. J. Bergin in *Studies,* IX, 1920.

SENCHUS MÁR. The earliest surviving Irish code of laws, as revised shortly after the establishment of Christianity in Ireland. By tradition this revision was carried out by three kings, three saints, and three historian-lawyers, under the personal supervision of St Patrick, and for centuries it was known as *Cáin Patraic* or *Patrick's Laws.* Only fragments have survived, the oldest now being in TCD. A facsimile edition of these MSS fragments were published by the Irish MSS Commission, introduced and described by R. I. Best and Rudolf Thurneysen, Dublin 1931. See also *Senchus Mór,* 6 vols, Dublin 1865, 1869, 1873, 1879, 1901 (vol. 5 and Glossary, vol. 6).

SEOIGHE, Seán Mainchín, b. Co. Limerick 1920. Travel writer in English and Irish, and on staff of Limerick County Council. *Maraíodh Seán Sabhat Aréir,* Dublin 1964, a life of the Limerick republican activist Seán Sabhat, killed in 1957 in a raid on a northern police barracks. *Cois Máighe na gCaor,* Dublin 1965, was a Club Leabhar choice.

SGEILG, see UA CEALLAIGH, Seán.

STAPLETON, Theobald, b. Kilkenny *c.* 1585, d. Flanders *c.* 1650. A priest in Flanders, he published at Brussels in 1639 one of the first books in which Irish is printed in Roman typeface, *Cathechismus seu Doctrina Christiana Latino-Hibernica.* The book has a long appendix giving directions for reading Irish.

STERNE, John (sometimes Stearne), b. Meath 1624, d. Dublin 1669. Grand-nephew of Archbishop Ussher. Studied Medicine at Cambridge, returning to Dublin and TCD to become Professor of Law. Also practised medicine in Dublin and founded Irish College of Physicians 1660, becoming Professor of Medicine TCD 1662. *Animi Medela,* Dublin 1653; *Aphorismi de Felicitate,* Dublin 1664; *De Destinatione,* Dublin 1672.

STOKES, Whitley, b. Dublin 1830, d. London 1909. Ed. St Columba's and English Bar, 1855; in the Indian legal service 1861-82, where he became interested in philology and Indo-European dialects in relation to Sanskrit and Vedic. His first work, *Irish Glosses,* 1860, was the first treatment of an Irish text as a contribution to this branch of philology. He published *Three Irish Glossaries,* London and Edinburgh 1862, and thereafter a great number of critical editions of Irish texts, such as the *Saltair na Rann: A Collection of Middle-Irish poems,* Oxford 1883; and the *Dinnshenchas,* 1892-3; *Lives of Saints from the Book of Lismore,* ed. with trans., Oxford 1890.

SYMON SEMEONIS or **FITZSIMON,** b. probably Dublin *c.* 1300. Joined the Franciscan Order in Dublin, and in 1323 set out with a companion, Hugo the Illuminator, on a pilgrimage to the Holy Land. They reached Cairo, where Hugo died, and Symon obtained permission from the Sultan to continue to Jerusalem. Symon wrote a detailed *Itinerarium* of his journey, which is interesting for many things, including the first reference in European literature to the Gypsies. He also saw a polo match, which he describes as 'hurling on horseback.' The *Itinerarium* makes a number of comparisons between western and eastern customs and ways of life. It ends abruptly as Symon comes in sight of Jerusalem, and it was long assumed that he had died there. It now seems possible that he may have returned to Ireland, via Norwich, and the unfinished state of the MS may be due to any of several causes. An imperfect edition was brought out at Cambridge in 1778 by Nasmith, the MS being in Corpus Christi College, Cambridge. the Dublin Inst. for Adv. Studies published an edition, ed. and trans. by Mario Esposito in *Scriptores Latini Hiberniae,* vol. IV, Dublin 1960.

T

TIGHERNACH, b. Munster *c.* 1020, d. Clonmacnoise 1088. Abbot of Clonmacnoise and Roscommon and author of the earliest Irish chronicle that survives, *The Annals of Clonmacnoise,* sometimes known as *The Annals of Tigernach,* as in the edition of Whitley Stokes, with trans., *Revue Celtique,* XVI-XVIII, 1895-97. The *Annals,* which carry the story of Ireland from the earliest times to 1088, attempt to correlate Irish events with events in Europe. They were continued to the year 1405 by Augustine Mag Raidhin.

TITLEY, Alan, b. Cork 1947. Ed. UCD. Travelled in East Europe and Africa. Lecturer in Irish language and literature, St Patrick's College, Drumcondra. Novelist. *Méirscrí na Treibhe,* a novel set in a newly independent African state, (major award for fiction in Oireachtas 1977) pub. Dublin 1978, and a Club Leabhar selection. *Stiall Fial Feola,* Dublin 1979, a Gothic novel set in contemporary Dublin dealing with cannibalism and human sacrifice. Compiled bibliography of Máirtín Ó Cadhain's published works: *Máirtín Ó Cadhain: Clár Saothair,* Dublin 1975.

TÓCHAR MÁIRTÍN, see BREATHNACH, Micheál.

TÓIBÍN, Nioclás, b. Ring 1890, d. 1966, teacher and broadcaster. His novel *Róisin Bán an tSléibhe,* Carlow 1922, was an Irish bestseller. Also wrote *An Rábaire Bán,* 1928, an Irish grammar, short stories, and many translations into Irish, including *Notes of an Irish Exile. Duanaire Déiseach,* Dublin 1978.

TÓIBÍN, Seán, b. Co. Waterford 1887, d. 1971. Was a school-teacher in Cork for many years. Collected folk stories and songs, and wrote a grammar, *Irish for All,* Dublin 1922; a prayerbook for children, *Ursa an Anama,* Cork 1923; *Tíreóluidhe Tosaigh* (first steps in geography), Dublin 1930; *Blátha an Bhóithrín* (on wild flowers), Dublin 1955, rep. 1965. *Troscán na mBánta,* Dublin, rep. 1973.

TÓIBÍN, Tomás, b. Cork 1920. Teacher and civil servant. Poet. *Súil le Cuan,* Dublin 1967; *Collected Poems,* Dublin 1969; *Fuinneoga,* Dublin 1980; *Duilliúr,* 1983. Has translated a number of French, German and Spanish plays into Irish, and Gogol's *Inspector General* from the Russian.

TOMÁS BÁN, see UA CONCHEANÁINN, Tomás.

TORNA, see UA DONNCHADHA, Tadhg.

TORNA EIGEAS (the Learned), *fl.* 400. The fosterer of Niall of the Nine Hostages who died 423, and his chief poet. Three poems are ascribed to him by tradition, mediating between Niall and the Prince of Cashel. These are considered a foreshadowing of the 17th-century Contention of the

Bards and form a preface to the MSS copies of the Contention. One of Torna's poems occurs in the *Book of the Dun Cow,* and is translated by Eugene O'Curry in *Manners & Customs of the Ancient Irish,* vol. II, Dublin 1873. See also *Revue Celtique,* XVII, 1896, an article by Arbois de Jubainville; Kuno Meyer's *Ueber die Alteste Irische Dichtung,* II, 1914; and John O'Donovan, *The Genealogies, Tribes and Customs of Hy-Fiachrach,* Dublin 1844.

U

UA CEALLAIGH, Seán (pseud. SGEILG), b.Valentia Island 1872, d.1957. Grew up in a largely native-speaking area without himself learning much Irish as a child. As a young man in Dublin he perfected his Irish and was encouraged to write by Tadhg Ua Donnchadha. He became President of the Gaelic League 1919-23. His many works include *Amugha i mBaiblean* (comic essays about a journey to London) which appeared during 1900 in *Claidheamh Soluis; Saothar ár Sean i gCéin,* Dublin 1904 ('the work of our ancestors abroad'); *Beatha Lorcáin Naomhtha Uí Thuathail,* Dublin 1905 (a life of St Lawrence O'Toole); *Feithe Fodhla,* Dublin 1905 (several editions in following years); *Brian Bóroimhe,* Dublin for Gaelic League, 1906; *Scéaluidhe Éireann,* Dublin 1908 (several editions); *Leabhar na Laoitheadh* and *Eachtra an Amadáin Mhóir,* both pub. Dublin 1912, and both running into many editions; *Beatha Bhreandáin,* Dublin 1915. After 1916 Ua Ceallaigh became deeply involved in politics and published little. He was elected in 1918 to the British parliament when Sinn Féin swept away the Irish parliamentary party, not, of course, taking his seat. In the elections for the first Dáil he was elected for Louth-Meath and became Chairman of the Dáil 1919-1921. He was Speaker 1925-30; and President of Sinn Féin 1926-30. In 1936 he published *Liúdaidhe Óg na Leargadh Móire.*

UA CONCHEANÁINN, Tomás (Tomás Bán), b. Aran Islands 1870, d. 1960. Learned Irish as a child, but emigrated to America in 1885 with some of his family and continued his schooling in California and New York. Became accountant and set up practice in Mexico. Returned to Ireland on a visit in 1898 and was asked by the Gaelic League to become their first organiser, in effect an itinerant language teacher. He did this until 1911. In 1912 he became an insurance inspector in Galway, having six years earlier married Helena Walsh, later to become Senator Helena Concannon and an author, see Part I.

He wrote a number of text-books, some of them with his wife, plays, translations and stories. *Gormfhlaith,* Dublin 1905 (an historical sketch); *Inis Fáil,* Dublin 1926, and *Eamhain Macha,* Dublin 1926 (both jointly with his wife), are his best-known books.

UA DONNCHADHA, Tadhg (pseud. Tórna), b.Co. Cork 1874, d.Cork 1949. Editor of *Gaelic Journal*, 1902-09. Professor of Irish UCC 1916-44. Also Dean of Faculty of Celtic Studies. Wrote many text-books on Irish grammar. Edited important collections of Irish MS, including poetry of *Diarmuid Mac Sheáin Bhuidhe Mac Carrthaigh*, Dublin 1916. He translated some of the works of Pádraic Colum, Lady Gregory, George Moore and Jules Verne into Irish and published a handbook for students on the art of writing Irish poetry, *Bhéarsaidheacht Gaeilge*, Dublin 1936. His last work was *Sean Fhocail na Mumhan*, Dublin 1962. In addition to the above, his principal books were editions of the poetry of Séan Ó Murchadha na Ráithíneach for the Gaelic League, Dublin 1907; the poetry of Aodhagán Ó Rathaille (with P. Ó Duinnín) for the ITS, 1911; the poetry of An tAth. Pádraigín Haicéad, Dublin, 1916; and the *Leabhar Cloinne Aodha Buidhe* I, for the MSS Commission, Dublin 1931.

UA DUINNÍN, An tAth. Pádraig, see Ó DUINNÍN, An tAth. Pádraig.

UA MAOILEOIN, Pádraig, b. Co. Kerry 1913. Spent 30 years in Garda Síochána, now temporary civil servant engaged on new Irish-English Dictionary. *Na h-Aird Ó Thuaidh*, Dublin 1960, reminiscences of life in Dunquin as a child. *Bríde Bhán*, Dublin 1968, novel of Gaeltacht life, rep. 1983. Has also translated P. A. O'Siochain's *Criminal Law of Ireland* and *Law of Evidence* into Irish. *De Réir Uimhreacha*, Dublin 1969. *Ár Leitheidí Arís*, Dublin 1978 (essays); and *Fonn a Níos Fiach*, Dublin 1978 (historical novel), a Club Leabhar choice. More recently, a novel, *Ó Thuaidh*, 1985.

UISÉIR, Pádraig (pseud. of Pádraig Mac Caomhánaigh), b.Co. Antrim 1922. Ed. QUB. Ordained Maynooth 1947. *Seans Eile*, Dublin 1963, novel of priest's life; and *Kao er Wen*, Dublin 1965, biography of Bishop Galvin, co-founder of the Maynooth Mission to China. Both books Club Leabhar selections.

UÍ THALLAMHAIN, Caitlín Bean, b. Dublin. Won Club Leabhar competition 1966 with biography of Countess Markievicz written for young people. Published as *Rós Fiáin Lios an Daill*, Dublin 1967. *An Pictiúr ar an mBalla*, a biography of Joseph Mary Plunkett, Dublin 1973; *Iníon an Tincéara Rua*, Dublin 1976; *Sinéad: Scéal Shinéad Bean de Valera*, Dublin 1979.

USSHER, Percy Arland, b. London 1897, d. Dublin 1980. For work in English see Part I. *Cainnt an tSean-Shaoghail*, Dublin 1948, an account of farming life in the Déise, taken down from the conversation of Tomás Uí Mhuirthe. Trans. *Cuírt an Mheán-Oiche*, 1926. See MERRIMAN, Brian.

W

WADDING, Luke, b. Co. Waterford 1588, d. Rome 1657. His mother was related to Peter Lombard, Bishop of Armagh, and his father was a well-to-do citizen. He was one of 14 children, and received a good classical education. Left an orphan at 14, he was sent to Lisbon where he entered the Jesuit seminary. He left after half a year and going to Oporto entered the Franciscan Order, taking his vows in 1613., He studied Hebrew at Salamanca and also travelled through Spain and Portugal preaching. In 1618 he was attached to the Spanish mission sent to Rome to promote the doctrine of the Immaculate Conception. The following year in Rome he was appointed head of a commission to write the history of his Order. For the remainder of his life he was engaged on this work, published in 8 vols, as *Annales Ordinis Minorum,* Rome 1625-54. But his fame rests on his editing of the works and philosophy of Duns Scotus, his great predecessor in the Order, in 16 vols, Rome 1639. He also published a bibliography of Franciscan authors, *Scriptores Ord. Minorum,* Rome 1650, but these and other writings give little idea of the role that Father Wadding played in Rome and the Franciscan Order. He is said to have been considered worthy of consideration for the Papacy. He founded the Irish Franciscan College of St Isidore in Rome 1625, and the Ludovisian College there for secular priests. As a member of the Commission for the Reform of the Roman Breviary he inserted the Feast of St Patrick, March 17th, as a Feast of the Universal Church. Politically he attempted to secure European intervention in the Irish wars of the 1640s and was responsible for Innocent X sending Archbishop Rinuccini to Ireland. Because of his influence, the Vatican was sympathetic during these years to the Irish cause and a solemn *Te Deum* was sung in the Basilica of St Mary Major after the news arrived of Eoghan Ruadh O'Neill's victory at Benburb in 1646. The Pope sent O'Neill his blessing via Fr Wadding.

Despite his influence, Fr Wadding refused all honours and died a simple priest.

WADDING, Michael (Godinez), b. Waterford 1591, d. Mexico 1644. Cousin to Luke Wadding, and possibly his companion briefly at Salamanca about 1613, where he was in the Irish seminary. He had entered the Jesuit novitiate 1609, and after taking his final vows went as a missionary to Mexico, where he adopted the name Godinez. His *Pratica de la Teologia Mistica,* 1681, has gone into many editions.

WALSH, Dick, b. Limerick 1937. Ed. Clare. Political correspondent *Irish Times.* Has written *Géarchéim in Éirinn,* Dublin 1971.

WALSH, Nicholas, b. Waterford *c.* 1530, d. Ossory 1585. Son of the Protestant Bishop of Waterford and himself Bishop of Ossory. Studied in

France and England and with others translated the New Testament into Irish. A man, James Dalland, whom he had accused of adultery, stabbed him to death.

WARD, Hugh, see MAC AN BHAIRD, Aodh Buidhe.

WARE, James, b. Dublin 1594, d. Dublin 1666. His father was Auditor-General of Ireland and he succeeded him in this post 1632. In the Civil War he was twice imprisoned by the Parliamentarians as a Royalist, and in 1649 expelled from Ireland. In London and France he continued collecting materials for his histories and on the Restoration returned to Dublin and his post. He gathered a large collection of Irish MSS, employing Dubhaltach Mac Firbisigh to make copies and translations. He himself wrote in Latin. His main works are *Archiepiscoporum Casseliensium et Tuamensium,* Dublin 1626; *De Scriptores Hiberniae,* Dublin 1639, this being dedicated to Strafford; *De Hibernia et Antiquitatibus eius Disquisitiones,* 1654; *Rerum Hibernicarum Annales, 1484-1558,* Dublin 1665; with many other books, such as editions of Campion, Hanmer, Marlborough; Spenser's *View of the State of Ireland* and Bede's *Epistolae,* 1664. *De Praesulibus Hiberniae,* Dublin 1665, an account of Irish bishops from the earliest times, includes the earlier *Archiepiscoporum Casseliensium et Tuamensium.* Like his near contemporary Micheál Ó Cléirigh, he helped both to preserve invaluable materials that would otherwise have been lost for ever and to bring Irish history from the world of mediaeval tradition into that of critical enquiry. *The Whole Works of Sir James Ware,* 3 vols, Dublin 1739-64, edited by Walter Harris, husband of Sir James's grand-daughter.

WATTERS, Eugene, see Ó TUAIRISC, Eoghan.

WHITE, Stephen, b. Clonmel 1575, d. abroad 1647. A Jesuit and Professor of Scholastic Philosophy in Ingoldstadt. Returned to Ireland 1638-40. Both in Ireland and on the Continent spent much of his time searching for Irish MSS. Found a copy of Adamnan's *Vita Sancti Columbae* in a chest in the town library of Schaffhausen. He was in correspondence with both Fr John Colgan at Louvain and Archbishop Ussher in Dublin, supplying both of them with MS material. He wrote a number of religious works and one propagandist book, *Apologia pro Hibernia adversus Cambri Calumnicis,* 1615.

WILMOT, Séamus, see DE BHILMOT, Séamus.

THE AUTHORS

Anne M. Brady, née Cannon, was born in Dublin in 1926, graduated in English from UCD, and worked as a library assistant at Carleton University, Ottowa, for a time. She now lives in Dalkey, Co. Dublin. Her Irish historical novel, *The Winds of God,* was published in 1985, and another is in preparation.

Brian Talbot Cleeve was born in England of Irish parents in 1921. A graduate of the University of South Africa, with a Ph.D. from the National University of Ireland, he is an internationally known writer and broadcaster. He has published some 30 novels as well as works on religious philosophy, Irish coinage and Hamlet. His recent books include *1938: A World Vanished,* 1983, and *A View of the Irish,* 1984. He lives in Dublin.

Remember that no human production under the sun
is without mistakes, and that frequently good workmanship
is unjustly blamed through envy and hatred of enemies,
and also through their ignorance.

JOHN O'DONOVAN (1809-61)